COMPUTER SCIENCE

COMPUTER SCIENCE

EDITED BY

ALFONSO F. CARDENAS, Ph.D.

Computer Science Department
University of California, Los Angeles

LEON PRESSER, Ph.D.

Department of Electrical Engineering
University of California, Santa Barbara

MIGUEL A. MARIN, Ph.D.

Department of Electrical Engineering
McGill University, Montreal

WILEY-INTERSCIENCE, a Division of John Wiley & Sons, Inc.
New York • London • Sydney • Toronto

Library of Congress Catalog Card Number: 71–169162

ISBN 0–471–13468–6

Printed in the United States of America.

10 9 8 7 6 5 4 3 2 1

To

Alfonso and Elvira Cardenas Mora
Blanca and Liza Presser
Thérèse Marin

Preface

The computer is the most sophisticated tool ever developed by man, and it will remain as his most powerful instrument for decades to come. Our lives are constantly affected by the ever-growing applications of computers. In the future the computer utility will be as common as are the telephone or electric power utilities today. As a consequence of the continuing research and development devoted to this formidable tool and its applications, an extensive and impressive body of knowledge has emerged. The new discipline has been called "information science" by some and "computer science" by others. We have chosen Computer Science as the title of our book, which is an introduction to this fascinating subject.

Our choice of topics is the result of our biases and of practical considerations. The material included here is not intended as a definition of what is or what is not computer science; instead, it is an aggregate of important topics that span a major portion of computer science.

This book is intended as (1) a source for self-study of computer science, (2) a reference volume for computer specialists to familiarize themselves with the topics covered, (3) required reading of a serious student of computer science, and (4) a textbook for various courses and seminars (for example, computer systems, formal and programming languages).

The background required for an understanding of this book is (with few exceptions) the maturity of an advanced undergraduate student in engineering or the physical sciences and a basic understanding of a computer system. An introductory level is maintained throughout the volume, and each chapter is essentially self-contained. However, the relationship among chapters is clearly delineated. Sufficient references are included to allow the interested reader to pursue a topic further.

This volume is divided into two parts.

Part I, "Systems Technology," consists of nine chapters that cover a major portion of the core area of knowledge required to understand the constituents of (digital) computers and how they may be organized into an integrated system. Chapters 1 and 2 discuss the types of basic circuitry (*hardware*), their fabrication techniques, and the methods employed to form more complex functional units from the basic circuitry. These chapters also discuss the impact of advanced microelectronics technology on the design of digital systems. Chapter 3 deals with the topic of arithmetic in digital computers. It includes most of the important schemes known as well as problems and limitations in computer arithmetic. Chapters 4 and 5 are concerned with the architecture of computer systems. Chapter 4 presents an overview of the factors that must be considered in the implementation and configuration of an integrated computer system. It also comments on the future evolution of computer systems. Chapter 5 starts with a description of a simple computer and clearly justifies the development of the many architectural features of present-day computers. It then discusses large-scale computer systems. Chapter 6 is devoted to operating systems, that is, the set of programs (*software*) and hardware facilities responsible for the automatic supervision and coherent operation of a computer system. This is a complex topic and Chapter 6 offers a unified discussion of the subject. Chapters 7 and 8 discuss the modes of operation of computer systems. Chapter 7 examines and classifies, in a brief and qualitative manner, on-line computing graphic display—a device external to the computer system and the computer itself alternately act upon each other. Graphical display systems are becoming important components in on-line operation; thus, particular attention is given, in Chapter 7, to this type of interactive device. Chapter 8 analyzes a recent development in the operation of computers: computer networks. The basic idea of networks is to centralize programming systems, data, and applications programs at the most appropriate computer center of the net and allow a user access to the computing capability of any of the interconnected centers. This chapter also discusses the modeling and analysis of these networks as well as of time-sharing operation—a computer system shared by many (remote) users who each appear to have sole possession of the system. Chapter 9 explores analog and hybrid computer systems rather than digital systems. Analog computers are important and will continue to predominate in some significant applications, for example, the solution of differential equations. Furthermore, in some instances a better approach to problem solution is to combine analog and digital techniques into a hybrid system.

Part II, "Languages, Translators, and Applications," consists of five chapters. Chapters 10 and 11 deal with the ubiquitous programming languages—a critical component in man-computer communication. Chapter 10 classifies, extracts, and outlines the characteristics of a number of programming languages. Chapter 11 considers the implementation of processors (for instance, compilers), which transform programs written in a programming language into an equivalent form understandable to the computer. Chapter 12 studies formal languages and their related automata. This chapter develops the mathematical preliminaries necessary to study the subject and provides a sound introduction to many aspects of this sophisticated area of knowledge. Chapters 13 and 14 discuss computer applications. The possible range of computer applications is limited only by the imagination of the humans who apply them. In these chapters we attempt to convey the flavor of the utilization of computers in business applications. Chapter 13 presents a qualitative overview of the ever-growing business applications of computers. It stresses the great impact of computers in business organizations. Chapter 14, "Management Information Systems," deals with the much-discussed use of computers as a base upon which information systems are set up to help managers in their decision-making task. This chapter reviews the characteristics and evolution of successful management information systems.

We express our gratitude to the many people whose criticisms and cooperation made this volume possible. Particularly, we thank all of the contributors who worked so sedulously on this project. Also we thank Lowell Amdahl, Robert Balzer, Pete England, Gerald Estrin, Abraham Glatzer, Adolfo Guzmán, James Howard, Leon Levine, Shan Liu, Lawrence McNamee, John Milsum, Frederic Mowle, Theodore Nieh, John Rettenmayer, Harry Schrage, Cesar Toscano, Robert Uzgalis, Willis Ware, and Roger Wood.

Alfonso F. Cardenas
Leon Presser
Miguel A. Marin

Los Angeles, California
Santa Barbara, California
Montreal, Quebec
May 1971

Contents

COMPUTER SCIENCE

PART I

Systems Technology

Hardware Technology

Donald F. Calhoun

Hughes Aircraft Company
Culver City, California

1. THE DEVELOPMENT OF DIGITAL SEMICONDUCTOR ELECTRONICS

The first generation of digital computers utilized vacuum tubes as the basic electronic components in the design of the required logic networks. As a

1

result, the cost, volume, power consumption, logic delay, and failure rates of these networks were quite high compared to the equivalent semiconductor networks of today. As an example, some of the first computer systems built had an expected mean time between failures of only a few minutes and assembled circuit costs of $100 per vacuum tube. Since the vacuum tube generation, two generations of semiconductor electronics have succeeded and have contributed great advances toward systems with low cost and power, small volume, high speed, and very high reliability. Figure 1 illustrates the dramatic changes that have occurred through the first three generations of digital computers and that is now continuing in the fourth generation. The changes are basically the result of the very high efficiency of the "batch fabrication" semiconductor techniques which allow highly controlled material processing steps to be automatically applied to very large numbers of circuits at the same time.

The second generation of computer electronics was the first to make use of the transistor and diode semiconductor components. These were wired together with the necessary resistors and capacitors on "printed circuit" (PC) boards. The one-by-one assembly of these components into the required circuits was the prime limiting factor in their size, cost, and reliability. The effort to integrate beyond simple transistor electronics was inspired by the potential cost and performance gains realized by effective utilization of batch semiconductor processes. The natural means of utilizing the batch processes at that time (1958) was to fabricate on a single semiconductor "chip" all of a circuit's components and the necessary interconnect between these components. For some time these circuits were limited by processing capabilities to simple "gates" (i.e., memoryless logic circuits discussed in Chapter 2 by Miguel A. Marin and George J. Klir) and "flip-flops" (i.e., binary memory circuits). But by "integrating" what used to be many separate components and interconnect wires into a single, small portion (termed a "die" or a "cell") of a semiconductor wafer, significant advantage was taken of the batch fabrication processes.

As the techniques, equipment, and control over these processes have been refined, the percentage of processed circuits that are operable (i.e., the yield) has significantly improved. As a result, the economical integration has been possible of more and more complex circuit functions on a single semiconductor chip. The level accomplished for the second computer generation was the single transistor or diode chip while the third generation has been characterized by integrated circuit (IC) chips. Figure 2 is a picture of a two-inch diameter wafer of about 1000 cells, each cell containing three 3-input NAND gate logic circuits. At the present time, further levels of complex function integration are current and forthcoming and are described by the broad labels of medium scale integration (MSI) and

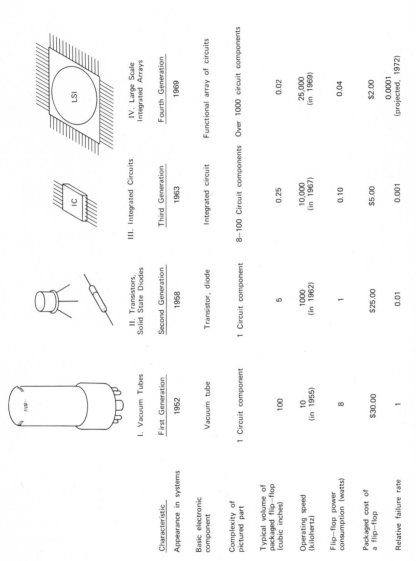

Characteristic	I. Vacuum Tubes First Generation	II. Transistors, Solid State Diodes Second Generation	III. Integrated Circuits Third Generation	IV. Large Scale Integrated Arrays Fourth Generation
Appearance in systems	1952	1958	1963	1969
Basic electronic component	Vacuum tube	Transistor, diode	Integrated circuit	Functional array of circuits
Complexity of pictured part	1 Circuit component	1 Circuit component	8–100 Circuit components	Over 1000 circuit components
Typical volume of packaged flip–flop (cubic inches)	100	5	0.25	0.02
Operating speed (kilohertz)	10 (in 1955)	1000 (in 1962)	10,000 (in 1967)	25,000 (in 1969)
Flip–flop power consumption (watts)	8	1	0.10	0.04
Packaged cost of a flip–flop	$30.00	$25.00	$5.00	$2.00
Relative failure rate	1	0.01	0.001	0.0001 (projected, 1972)

Figure 1. The characteristics of four generations of electronic components.

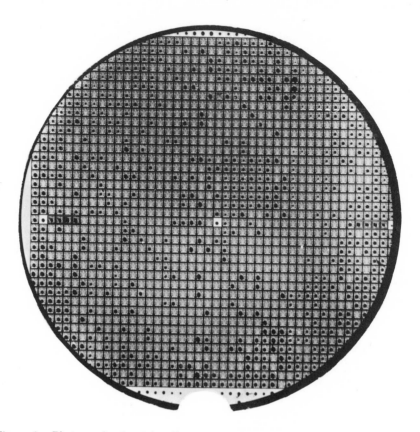

Figure 2.   Photograph of a 2-in. diameter integrated circuit wafer of three-input NAND gates (inked cells indicate those cells are nonfunctional).

large scale integration (LSI). This fourth generation of electronics aims at the fabrication of complex logic and memory functions within a single MSI chip or LSI array. This chapter is directed primarily at the fabrication, design considerations, and comparison of semiconductor logic and memory circuits with a conclusion that discusses the future design and fabrication challenges to the implementation of advanced LSI logic arrays.

2. DESIGN CONSIDERATIONS IN USING
SEMICONDUCTOR COMPONENTS

Various design capabilities are required in completely specifying a digital computer. The broad categories are those of the system, functional, logic, and circuit design tasks. The system design (also termed "system architecture" and discussed in depth by Earl C. Joseph in Chapter 4) specifies the system organization that will meet the intended system capabilities such as its software requirements, speed, word length, input-output interface, maintenance, compatibility to other systems, size of memory, possibly its size and power dissipation, and also its cost. These requirements will limit the choices of processor-memory organization as well as the types of hardware units that can be used in the various computer subsystems. Classically, a computer system is composed of software plus three basic hardware types of subsystems. These are the input-output units, memory, and a central processing unit (CPU), which includes the arithmetic and control sections. The input-output units include such standard units as teletypewriters, punched card or tape readers, line printers, and cathode-ray tube displays. Today many of these units are being designed with their own small semiconductor CPU's and buffer memories to improve communication between the computer and users in on-line, time-sharing modes. It is classically in the memory and CPU subsystems that semiconductor electronics have application, as will be discussed in this chapter.

Having narrowed our consideration to the electronic hardware used in computer CPU's and memories, we can be somewhat more specific in design requirements. Herein, the system designer must specify the basic processor-memory organization that will meet the overall system requirements. In order to do this, he will have to complete a block-diagram design of the processor and be confident that each of the functional blocks used can be designed within his assumptions of cost, time, speed, and power, as described in Chapter 2. The means of organizing the processor-memory are discussed by Earl C. Joseph in Chapter 4. The functional blocks that are specified include, as examples a 36-bit one-microsecond adder, a 64-word 16-bit 200-nanosecond read-only memory (ROM), a two-microsecond 4096 word random-access memory (RAM) of 36 bits, a 10-MHz 8-bit up-down counter, and other units such as shift registers, decoders, multiplexers, and the like. Although a system designer may not know the design intricacies of these functional blocks, he must have assurance that they can meet the requirements placed on them by the rest of the processor-memory design and that those requirements are sufficient and necessary.

Often the specifications made by a system designer are more general than an organizational description of the functional blocks to be used. That is, an instruction repertoire with required execution times could be given with the problem then being that of designing the processor and memory so as to meet most economically these requirements. And thus, trade-offs are made between machine performance requirements, machine organization, and cost. The systems designer must determine from the persons responsible for the detailed processor and memory design the characteristics of the various possible design approaches. Intimately involved in determining these characteristics are the semiconductor logic and memory circuits that are selected for the design.

Trade-offs are made in the functional organization of the specific subsystem designs by weighing the performance and cost measures that would result from the possible alternative designs. But in order to determine the performance and cost measures of different designs, specific electronic components must be chosen from those currently available. At this point, semiconductor electronics have had profound effects on the design choices of digital computer systems built since the early 1950s. The development of more and more complex semiconductor parts within a single, low-cost package has greatly influenced the design of computer processors and memories. As a result of the semiconductor circuit developments, digital processing systems (for instance, computers) have offered far improved and more reliable capabilities.

2.1. Second-Generation (Discrete Component) Design Considerations

During the second computer generation, designs were predicated on the use of "discrete" components (i.e., individual diodes and transistors) as the basic semiconductor parts. In order to minimize parts and assembly costs, the design rules required that the number of diodes and transistors be minimized, since they were more expensive than resistors and capacitors. With this criteria, functional designers and logic designers would compare estimates of the cost and performance measures of various subsytem organizations. That is, designs using various arithmetic and control processing algorithms would be compared to see which ones provided the highest performance per dollar. The performance has often been measured in so-called computer "throughput rate," as determined by the typical number of instructions (or operations) per second that the machine can perform. The decision of processor-memory organization was then based on comparing the performance per dollar of each design after each design had been minimized in estimated component count.

After the basic processing approach and functional organization were selected, two detailed design efforts remained for second-generation computers. These were the detailed logic design (outlined in Chapter 2) and the circuit design. The task of logic design has been to specify the types of circuits and the logical interconnections between these circuits that would implement each of the required functional blocks, using circuits built efficiently with available electronic components. The functional blocks of adders, registers, counters, decoders, multiplexers, and the like were implemented basically from logic gates (AND, OR, and INVERT, for instance), flip-flops, and certain special circuits. The logic circuits, in turn, were electrically designed by circuit designers who must see that the right transistors, diodes, resistors, and capacitors were selected for efficient design in terms of cost, speed, noise immunity, stability, compatibility with other circuits, and system reliability. Many transistor types were available and the technology was advancing so rapidly that difficulty existed in "freezing" designs before they had been somewhat antiquated by better components for the price. As a result, evaluation of the component performance parameters (e.g., transistor betas, leakage currents, saturation voltages, breakdown voltages, and switching times) led to many novel circuit designs which increased the number of available designs for each type of logic circuit. Thus, a great emphasis and burden during the second generation was placed on circuit designers to efficiently use the available (but rapidly changing) electronic components in the design of the basic circuits. In contrast, the logic designer was working from a smaller base of logic circuit types (gates and flip-flops) and one of less fluctuation. Thus his design could be novel only in the means by which he minimized the number of circuits and logic delays while realizing the required functions.

2.2. Third-Generation (Integrated Circuit) Design Considerations

The circuit-logic design emphasis changed markedly in the third-generation computer systems which made wide use of integrated circuits as the basic semiconductor part. No longer were there individual components to select, to design into circuits, and to assemble. This was all accomplished within the integrated circuit package. The circuit designs were most commonly accomplished by the component supplier and not by the system manufacturer as before. A typical IC gate was soon packaged in about the same volume and for the same or lower prices than single transistors had been. Later we shall study in detail the batch fabrication processes that so greatly improved the semiconductor chip yield that this became technically and economically feasible. The effect of IC's on computer design was that of an extended breadth in the choices of available circuits from which a logic designer could configure his required functional units. Each of these circuits was efficiently designed circuit-wise as well as for electrical compatibility with a wide range of other IC's. Although many circuit concerns remained, the detailed circuit designs were no longer the responsibility of computer designers. Instead, a circuit "understanding" was needed so that the chosen IC's could be configured into the required functional units.

With the advent of integrated circuitry, a new burden in design optimization has been placed on the logic designer. Component minimization (i.e., of the number of resistors, transistors, and so on) is no longer the most meaningful goal. Instead, the speed, power, and cost have to be weighed first in the selection of a "logic family." Logic families have included circuit designs based on resistor-transistor logic (RTL), diode-transistor logic (DTL), transistor-transistor logic (TTL), emitter-coupled logic (ECL), current-mode logic (CML), various metal-oxide semiconductor (MOS) technologies, and others. Within each of these families there are a significant number of compatible types of gates (AND, OR, NAND, NOR, Exclusive-OR, AND-OR-INVERT, for instance), various types of flip-flops (J-K, R-S, D), and other necessary circuits such as line drivers and receivers. These circuits provide a full complement from which the logic designer can choose, basing his decision on their performance per dollar in his system and not just on the component count, which is no longer a visible quantity. That is, the cost of a design is now based on how efficiently these circuits (and not necessarily the components within them) are used.

As an example, J-K flip-flops with multiple J and K inputs as well as preset and preclear lines are available as common low-cost IC's. Many times a design calls for a simpler J-K flip-flop than this, and thus actually requires fewer components. But the cost, size, and delay of the IC flip-flop usually are significantly less than the minimum flip-flop designed with separate discrete components. As another example, the exclusive-OR of two inputs could be implemented with either many separate components, five two-input NAND gates, or one exclusive-OR gate. Except in certain situations, the best choice is the single exclusive-OR gate, since it is optimally designed for that function and is enclosed in one small, low-cost package. But this brings up another new parameter to IC design: minimization of part types. In general, if only slight inefficiencies result from designing as many identical assemblies of circuits as possible and/or which use only a small set of the available circuit types, then significant circuit procurement, assembly, and maintenance cost savings can result. Thus, if that "efficient" selection of an exclusive-OR circuit is the only time it is used or causes that assemblage of circuits to be different from others, then it should not be used. Such "minimization of part types" is simply the selection of as few circuit types as can be used to efficiently meet the design requirements.

In addition to the selection of a logic family based on speed-power-cost trade-offs and the minimization of circuit types used, it is also important to standardize the modules or boards that the IC's are mounted and interconnected on. As an example of module standardization, consider the design of a 64-bit binary adder with carry look-ahead. Such an adder can quite efficiently be designed as eight 8-bit adder groups with identical carry look-ahead logic between the eight groups. If integrated circuits with three 3-input gates per package were used, then each adder group would probably require about 40–50 IC packages which could be mounted and interconnected on a single PC board. As a result, the 64-bit adder would be built from 8 identical assembly boards. Many other possible designs exist for this one function, but such a high module standardization will save much in the fabrication and assembly costs as well as in the design of interconnections and board testing. A strong competitor to such a design would be to use full adder IC's (rather than simple gate IC's), which would require many fewer IC's since each full adder has three or four times as many equivalent logic gates and would thus require perhaps only two or three boards. The design techniques that allow standardization are based on the "functional organization and partitioning" of systems so that efficient duplication of certain logic arrays (or functions) are obtained. Efficient array duplication should match well the arrays and assembly boards to the available technologies and should not be wasteful of parts or speed in order to obtain the standardization.

There is one last important design consideration that was first brought about by the use of integrated circuits. That is, the need to obtain a high "gate-to-pin ratio" at each "packaging level" of a logic design. Gate-to-pin ratio means the ratio between the amount of logic that is implemented in a package or on an assembly board and the number of input and output lines (or "pins") that are used for that package. The first- and second-level packages for IC designs are generally accepted to be the integrated circuit itself and the printed circuit (PC) assembly board on which some number (usually 10–80) of these IC's are mounted. Both the IC package and the PC board have connectors with some fixed number of leads. This number is often the limitation in the amount of logic that can be incorporated in a certain packaging level. For example, consider a 14-lead IC "flat-pack" used as the first level package for 3-input NAND gates. Since two lines must be used for power and ground and each gate requires four lines (one output, three inputs) then the flat-pack is pin-limited to accommodating only

(14-2) = 12 signal lines per pack. Since there are 4 signal lines per gate, the maximum number of gates is 3 for that package. Whereas, significantly more logic function would be realized in the same package if those lines were used for two full adder circuits (each having three inputs and two outputs). Such commonly used circuits would require only $(2 + 2 \times 5) =$ 12 lines and would accomplish the equivalent logical function of 20 NAND gates. Thus, in comparison, the simple NAND gate first level package would realize a gate-to-pin ratio of only $3/14 = 0.214$ gates per pin, whereas the first level full adder package would obtain $20/12 = 1.667$ gates per pin. Gate-to-pin ratios near 1.0 are quite good at first-level packaging. It should be evident that higher first-level gate-to-pin ratios indicate that better usage was made of the semiconductor batch processes, and that the same logic complexity can thus be built with fewer packages and fewer interpackage connections, which are significant cost and reliability factors. In the example considered above, seven triple 3-input NAND gate packages would have to be mounted and interconnected to accomplish the same logical function of a single dual full adder package.

The importance of obtaining high gate-to-pin ratios is present in second (and higher) levels of packaging as well. For example, there are usually 80 connection pins on many PC boards and thus no more logic than (80 × gate-to-pin ratio) gates can be assigned to any card. Thus, a design that realizes a gate-to-pin ratio of 1.0 (typical of conventional centralized control designs) could use only 80 gates per card, whereas a gate-to-pin ratio of 3.5 (as realized by the partitioned and distributed control described in reference 1) could use 280 gates per card. Assuming that the 280 gates could be interconnected as required on the single PC board, a decrease of 71.4% in the number of required PC boards could be obtained. In general, system cost is largely a function of the total number of parts used, and minimizing the part count is achieved by partitioning as large a quantity of logic as possible onto each part. The primary limitation to the amount of logic in a given level of packaging is the number of pins that interface with the "outside world." Also, of course, the power dissipation and package wireability must be considered as absolute limits. There are more detailed discussions of the logic design techniques in Chapter 2.

2.3. Fourth-Generation (LSI Functional Array) Design Considerations

The wide usage of integrated circuits in third-generation computers reduced the circuit design tasks to those of guaranteeing electrical compatibility between circuits and calculating their delays, noise margins, junction temperatures, and the like. Thus, the large task of selecting, testing, and interconnecting discrete components into circuits was replaced by the fully integrated and batch-fabricated circuit packages. A further level of integration (termed LSI for large scale integration) is now taking place which offers fully interconnected "arrays" of circuits as the basic semiconductor part. The impact of LSI on the design of digital systems involves both the tasks of system architecture and logic design.

A single definition of LSI has not been offered, basically because the definition is still dependent on the approach taken in the fabrication and interconnection of the LSI arrays. However, the result of each of the approaches is the development of significantly more complex logic functions upon single semiconductor cells or arrays of cells than has been available from integrated circuits. The definitions that have been made of LSI specify certain conditions: (1) the interconnection of at least 100 equivalent gates of logic in a single first level package, (2) the fabrication of complex circuit arrays on a monolithic (i.e., single) semiconductor chip, (3) the fabrication of circuit arrays so complex as to require multilevel interconnect on monolithic chips, and (4) the interconnection of many good circuits on a full semiconductor slice which is so complex as to have defective circuits (which, therefore, must be avoided in the interconnection). The result of most definitions is that the semiconductor part placed in the first-level package has sufficient complexity to consider it as an entire functional unit.

The complex functional logic arrays being built on single chips are meeting two very different objectives (and necessarily so at this time). First, many complex array designs are taking the form of "standard" logic arrays (such as a long shift register, an 8-bit adder, an 8-bit up-down counter, and a 64-bit random-access memory). These have general application to many digital system designs and can thus be made available to all designers economically as fully designed and tested parts, just as integrated circuits have been during the third generation. The other objective being met by the current LSI arrays is that of the more "custom" array designs. Custom arrays are required because each system organization has many nonstandard logic arrays (especially those used in the conventional control units). These arrays must be individually designed to meet somewhat unique requirements. As a result, certain LSI approaches (especially the Texas Instruments Discretionary Wiring, Fairchild Micromatrix, and Motorola Polycell) aim at providing a large array of simple logic gates for which a designer can specify his particular logic requirements and then have the necessary custom interconnection of these gates generated to provide those requirements. The use of custom LSI has significant potential advantage over integrated circuits in cost, reliability, weight, and even speed and power. However, it does not have the significant impact on logic design that the availability of completed and low-cost standard function arrays has. Custom arrays introduce new cost trade-offs and efficiencies to the system designer and new design guidelines to the logic designer, but they have less effect on the introduction of new system design choices or a reduction in the logic design burden itself.

Standard LSI functional arrays can offer the system designer new design alternatives of higher processing capability at equal cost, or equivalent capability at reduced costs. For example, a 64-bit adder could be built from integrated circuits by using the simple ripple-carry technique or, at about the same cost, from 8-bit complex adder chips that have a built-in carry look-ahead feature. The complex adder chips would provide considerably higher-speed additions and thus more processing capability while requiring fewer parts and smaller volume than the IC assembly. The logic design for the adder would also be reduced to the simple task of correctly interfacing the eight necessary 8-bit adder chips.

The above example of using complex functional parts as building blocks to implement designs that otherwise may not have been economically justified is a reality today. The same is true with certain other semi-conductor arrays such as "scratch-pad" and "read-only" memories, long shift registers, multiplexers, and up-down counters. But it is yet unknown how profound the impact of LSI arrays will be in allowing significant changes in the basic computer architecture. Efforts to organize particular digital systems around LSI array technology have been reported in the literature [1–3]. Whether significant standardization can be made for all required areas of digital logic (and not just the somewhat special parts listed above) is not yet known. If complex arrays of a few hundred gates can be defined that either have wide application or have high usage in their particular application, it can then be expected that the batch semicon-ductor processing technologies can provide these arrays at much less cost than an equivalent number of assembled integrated circuit gates. Such reductions in the logic costs will allow designers to use more sophisticated processing algorithms and obtain processing capabilities greater than before at the same cost. Also a lower cost per gate will allow designers to use the arrays differently with less cost concern for unused circuitry. For example, an LSI up-down counter may, in a particular design, never require counting down. If no up-counter, by itself, were available in LSI, it would be most efficient to use the LSI up-down counter rather than a more efficient counter (in number of gates) built with intergrated circuits.

Thus far, it has been pointed out that certain complex functions are already available as economical MSI and LSI parts and that a designer can even afford to use them somewhat inefficiently. Such an opportunity to have an economical design without using all of the circuits will also allow redundant circuits for fault detection, fault masking, certain partitioning techniques, and as a means of enhancing the applications for each function.

If large scale integrated circuit arrays can be defined that have general application in most processor logic and memory areas (except perhaps the large main memory), then the processor-memory design tasks will be reduced to the selection and interconnection of the necessary functional parts. There can then be a one-to-one correspondence between functional blocks in the processor-memory block diagram and the semiconductor parts used to build the system. The classical logic design will have been completed in order to fabricate the LSI units initially. When the logic design is done for each unit, the intended system application often will not be known. For some time, however, the LSI fabrication technologies will be exchanging ideas and attempting to find efficient functional units that can have wide application to different processor-memory organizations. There has been increasing discussion in the literature of new system organizations that can most effectively utilize the potential complex, very reliable, and low-cost LSI functional arrays (Chapter 4 of this volume) [4–6].

Thus far I have pointed out many of the considerations involved in the design and effective use of the semiconductor technology most prominent in each computer generation. Now I shall describe the semiconductor fabrication processes and survey today's technologies in bipolar and MOS circuits. Since the technology and design considerations are so strongly related, the reader without sufficient technology background may need to cover the preceding survey material again after completing the chapter.

3. FABRICATION PROCESSES OF MONOLITHIC SEMICONDUCTOR CIRCUITS

The flow diagram in Figure 3a shows the basic processing steps involved in the fabrication of bipolar integrated circuits. The fabrication of single transistor chips would not require the steps shown for transistor isolation (since they would later be physically separated) nor the metalization necessary to interconnect components. The interconnection of many individual circuits using further metalization levels above a wafer (i.e., LSI) requires the same semiconductor processing steps as IC's plus the additional processes such as shown in Figure 3b to generate array interconnection masks and to fabricate the multilevel metalization required for array interconnection. The purpose of this section is to cover the basic techniques used in fabricating integrated circuits as a means of understanding the

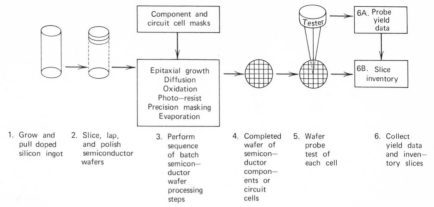

Figure 3a. The wafer processing steps common to transistors, integrated circuits, MSI chips, and LSI arrays.

capabilities and limitations of semiconductor circuit arrays. These techniques are covered extensively in References 7–9.

3.1.   Semiconductor Wafer Fabrication

As first steps in the fabrication of semiconductor arrays it is necessary to grow single crystals of semiconductor material (expecially silicon), to saw these into thin slices (also termed "wafers"), and then to lap and polish the individual slices as described in Figure 3a. The basic starting material is very pure silicon in a polycrystalline form. This silicon, along with any "doping impurity" that is to be added, is placed in a very pure quartz crucible and set inside a graphite susceptor. The susceptor and crucible are placed in a controlled, inert atmosphere of a quartz cylinder. Outside the cylinder, RF induction coils surround the susceptor and are used to heat the silicon until it is completely molten and the temperature is stabilized just above the silicon's melting temperature. At this time, a small, highly perfect, and oriented "seed" crystal is dipped into the melt for a short time, then rotated, and slowly withdrawn. As a result, a single, oriented crystal is pulled from the melt. The "pulled" crystal is typically $1\frac{1}{2}$ or 2 inches in diameter and 10 inches long, depending on the initial size of the melted silicon, pull rate, and the melt's surface temperature during the growth. The silicon melt can be doped with a suitable n- or p-type impurity to any desired conductivity, limited only by the impurity's solubility in silicon. If a Group V element from the Periodic Table (e.g., phosphorus) is used as the impurity dopant, the number of electrons within the melt will be

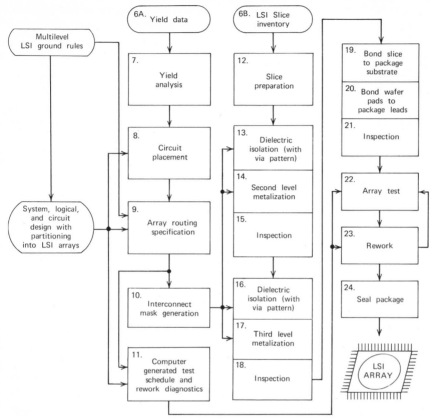

Figure 3b. LSI array fabrication steps required beyond the wafer processing steps in Figure 3a.

enhanced over that of pure silicon since the atoms of these elements are "donors" of an essentially free electron after they form a covalent bond with the silicon atoms. Such donor-doped silicon is termed "n-type" silicon because the dominant carriers are negative electrons. If a Group III element (e.g., boron) is used as the dopant, electron vacancies ("holes") exist in the bond with silicon causing such elements to be termed "acceptor" impurities, since they can accept free electrons. Such acceptor-doped silicon is termed "p-type," since the dominant carriers are the positive "holes." Typical impurity concentrations are one part per ten million, and thus about 10^{16} impurity atoms per cubic centimeter are added to the silicon.

After the single crystal has been grown, it is often ground to a uniform diameter using a "centerless" grinding technique. X-ray diffraction is then used to determine the crystallographic orientation of the structure so that a small "flat" area (later used in the scribing process for reference) can be ground along the length of the crystal. The crystal is then sawed into wafers by using a diamond saw. The wafers are next "lapped" with a suitable abrasive to the required thickness (0.006 to 0.010 inches), after which they are polished to a mirror finish and etched to remove surface imperfections. The preliminary processing steps are, at this point, finished and the processes that will impart to each wafer the desired array of semi-conductor junctions and connections can be undertaken.

3.2.   Semiconductor Circuit Fabrication

The processes of epitaxial growth, impurity diffusion, oxidation, photo masking, and vacuum evaporation are performed on the wafers to fabricate the required semiconductor junctions, passive circuit components, and component interconnections. The diffusion, oxidation, and masking steps are each used more than once in fabricating integrated circuits. The means by which certain wafer areas can be selectively processed (or masked) is based on the photoresist technique in which patterns are actually photo-graphed on a photosensitive emulsion covering the wafer. The basic steps described in this section are shown in Figure 4.

The fabrication of n-p-n and p-n-p junction transistors is the basis for manufacturing monolithic integrated circuits (as well as MSI and LSI circuits). The boundary between a p-type region and an n-type region within a single crystal is called a p-n junction. A structure with a single such p-n junction can act as a diode, since it has the ability to rectify alternating current or to function as a switch. The transistor is a two-junction device in which the junctions separate three regions that can be either n-p-n or p-n-p. An electrical contact can be affixed to the three regions, which are called the emitter, the base, and the collector. If individual transistors are being fabricated, the wafer substrate acts as the collector for all transistors and as the parent material into which the individual transistor base and emitter regions are fabricated by consecutive masked etching and diffusion steps. For integrated circuits, however, a common collector is not allowed, since transistors in the same integrated circuit must be electrically isolated from one another. This isolation can be accomplished by using an addi-tional diffusion step to build another semiconductor layer which will form a p-n diode junction from the substrate to each transistor collector. Alterna-tively, a silicon dioxide isolation can be used which diminishes the parasitic capacitance, raises the isolation breakdown voltage, and reduces isolation

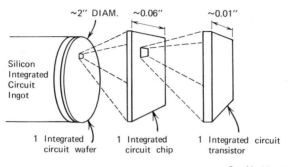

~2" DIAM.   ~0.06"   ~0.01"

Silicon
Integrated
Circuit
Ingot

1 Integrated   1 Integrated   1 Integrated circuit
circuit wafer   circuit chip   transistor

1a. Growth of N–type   1b. Oxidation   2a. Masking and etching
epitaxial film

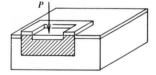

2b. First diffusion

3. Oxidation; masking and etching;
and second diffusion

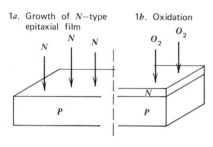

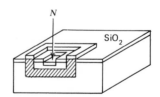

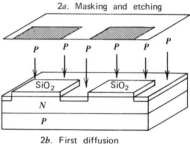

4. Oxidation; masking and etching;
and third diffusion

5. Masking and etching to establish
emitter, base, and collector contacts

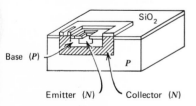

Base (P)

Emitter (N)   Collector (N)

Figure 4. Semiconductor processing steps in fabricating an integrated circuit transistor

17

leakage current. The transistor for monolithic IC's thus differs from the conventional single transistors in that it requires an additional isolation layer as well as processes to interconnect the individual components into circuits.

Of the basic semiconductor circuit fabrication techniques available, the "epitaxial-diffused" technique is most widely used and has a number of inherent advantages. Fabrication of an epitaxial-diffused integrated circuit begins with the thermal growth of an epitaxial film of n-type silicon upon a p-type silicon wafer. This film will become the collector region of transistors or an element of the diodes and diffused capacitors associated with a circuit. Subsequent diffusion processes form the remaining elements of the transistors, diodes, capacitors, and resistors. The epitaxial film grows on the wafer as an exact extension to the silicon crystal structure. Such an epitaxial film growth provides an excellent starting material for the fabrication of monolithic IC's. The impurity concentrations in the "epi" layer can be controlled within wide limits, and complex impurity densities can be grown without the need of impurity compensation which is required in diffused layers. The diffusion process, rather than growing a doped film *upon* the wafer surface, diffuses impurity atoms *into* the silicon substrate by applying a high concentration of such atoms to the wafer surface at elevated temperatures.

An integrated circuit wafer of $1\frac{1}{2}$- or 2-inch diameter will contain several hundred circuit "dice" or "cells" arranged in a monolithic, rectangular array on the wafer. Each good semiconductor die is packaged as an integrated circuit. Usually only one type of circuit die (such as a flip-flop, three logic gates, or a full adder) is processed repetitively in this array, but often a pattern of various circuit types is processed. Certain approaches to large scale integration, for example, process as many as three or four different logic cells on a wafer to allow higher logic efficiency. In either case, the processing steps that are used in the fabrication processes are performed on each wafer as a whole without requiring any special attention to the individual die or the various components and interconnect within the die. This is because the processing selectivity necessary to define specific components and interconnect on the wafer is obtained by the use of precision masked etching techniques. These techniques are dependent on light-sensitive organic compounds, known as "photoresists," which when exposed by ultraviolet (UV) light through a photographic mask delineate over the entire wafer the various patterns prescribed by the mask. The surface on which these patterns are produced can be either the semiconductor wafer, or an oxide or metal film covering the wafer. In most applications several hundred (often identical) images of transistor junctions or IC connections are placed within a single photo mask. The use of a "step-and-repeat" exposure of a basic image across the mask forms an array of such images of required dimensions and spacings. Now we shall examine in more detail the basic semiconductor processes that use this selective masking technique to fabricate integrated electronic circuits.

After the p-type silicon wafer has been sliced and polished and an n-type layer is grown epitaxially on the wafer, a thin film of silicon dioxide is then thermally grown over the "epi" layer. This film serves both as the vehicle for the photolithographic masking process and acts as a passivation for the junctions formed. The wafer is then covered with a uniform film of photo-resist which, unless polymerized, is quite soluble in certain liquids. By exposing it to the UV light through the appropriate mask, the polymeriza-tion (i.e., hardening) takes place only in the desired areas. The unpoly-merized film is readily removed, exposing the portions of the SiO_2 layer that can then be "etched" away, leaving untouched the SiO_2 in the areas covered by the polymerized emulsion. Since the commonly used dopants diffuse much more slowly in SiO_2 than in silicon, the remaining silicon dioxide can serve as a mask for preventing exposure in the areas under the SiO_2.

The first masked diffusion is made so that p-type impurities diffuse through the epitaxial layer to the p-type substrate. The areas covered with SiO_2 are now isolated islands of n-type silicon surrounded by p-type so that there is always a back-biased isolation diode between any two of these n-type regions. During the diffusion cycle, a new layer of SiO_2 is grown over the diffused p-type region, and the oxide over the n-regions grows thicker.

A second diffusion pattern is used to form the transistor base regions, resistors, and anode elements of diodes and junction capacitors. It is etched in the silicon dioxide layer, using the photolithographic process previously described. P-type impurities are diffused through the openings, stopping in the islands of n-type epitaxial silicon. A layer of silicon dioxide is then grown over the diffused p-type regions. This oxide coating is selectively etched to open windows in the base regions to permit a final n-type (phos-phorous) diffusion to form transistor emitters and the cathode regions of diodes and capacitors. After a silicon dioxide layer is grown, the semi-conductor junction formation in the monolithic circuits is complete.

In order to permit interconnection between the various circuit com-ponents, another set of windows is etched in the silicon dioxide layer at the points where contact is to be made to each of the various components of the integrated circuits. After a thin, even coating of aluminum is vacuum-deposited over the entire surface of the wafer, the one-level interconnection pattern between components in the monolithic circuit is selectively formed with photoresist techniques. The undesired aluminum areas are etched away leaving the required interconnection pattern between transistors, resistors, diodes, and capacitors. The cross-section of a completed resistor, transistor, and capacitor network is shown in Figure 5 with its equivalent circuit. An electrical "wafer probe test" is next made of each individual wafer die to determine and mark (as in Figure 2) all nonfunctioning cells. That is, very thin probes are brought in contact with the connection points (termed "pads") of each of the processed dice. An electrical test is made and each defective die receives a drop of magnetically sensitive ink which facilitates the removal of the bad dice after the wafer is separated into the individual circuit chips.

The wafers are "scribed" with a diamond-tipped scribing tool and separated into individual circuit dice. After removal of the defective dice, the good chips are individually mounted on ceramic package substrates and wires only 0.001 inch in diameter are bonded from the circuit connection pads to the proper package leads. The package is then sealed and final tests

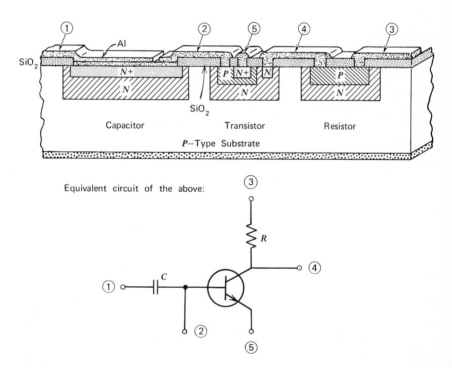

Figure 5. Cross-section of a completed integrated circuit wafer and its equivalent circuit.

are made to verify both the electrical and environmental performance of the packaged IC. This completes the fabrication of monolithic epitaxial-diffused integrated circuits. The fabrication of the circuits used in MSI and LSI arrays is essentially the same. MSI and LSI circuits must be probe-tested more thoroughly, however, to insure that no marginal or defective circuits are included in the array. In addition, the size of the packaged "die" will be much larger and more complex for MSI and LSI arrays. The package for the Discretionary Wiring [10] and the Pad Relocation [11] LSI approaches encloses, in fact, an entire semiconductor wafer of over 1000 processed gates.

4. COMPARISON OF BIPOLAR INTEGRATED CIRCUITS

A significant number of circuit design approaches have been used in fabricating bipolar integrated circuits. The first classification of approaches relates to whether the design allows the transistors to enter what is called "saturation." Basically, a transistor enters saturation when it has ample base-emitter drive and comparitively little collector current. As a result, forward conduction of the base-collector junction occurs, and a significant delay is required to remove the stored charge in the base when the transistor is later turned off. However, means of preventing saturation have required increases in power dissipation and circuit complexity. In addition, lower processing yields and reduced circuit noise margins are characteristic of nonsaturating logic. The advantage, of course, is an important reduction in circuit delays. A lower bound gate delay for saturating circuits is about 4–6 nsec (1 nsec $= 10^{-9}$ sec), but emitter-coupled logic (ECL) nonsaturating gate delays have been obtained under 1 nsec.

The prime "logic family" types of saturating circuit designs include RTL (resistor-transistor logic), DTL (diode-transistor logic), and TTL (transistor-transistor logic). RTL has also been known as DCTL (direct-coupled transistor logic). These names are derived from the particular way that components are used within the circuits. Each family is manufactured by a number of the large semiconductor companies and an entire line of various logic gates, flip-flops, adders, registers, counters, decoders, and the like are typically available as integrated circuits. Since TTL is most ideally suited for integrated circuit fabrication, it is apparently becoming the most widely used. Both TTL (by Texas Instruments and Motorola et al) and DTL (by Fairchild et al) are being used in MSI and LSI array designs. Detailed descriptions of these circuit designs and their application to MSI and LSI arrays are in the literature [7, 10, 13–15].

The performance comparison of various digital integrated circuits usually must consider: (1) speed, (2) power dissipation, (3) cost, (4) availability of various circuit types, (5) noise immunity, (6) compatibility with other circuits, (7) "fan-in" and "fan-out" capability, and (8) the possibility of "wired-or" operation (i.e., the ability to tie outputs directly together to perform a second level of logic). The cost, availability, noise immunity, compatibility restrictions, and the fan-in/fan-out can best be determined by consulting the appropriate manufacturer's catalog [13]. The range of speed and power dissipation for RTL, DTL, and TTL gates can be given here. The typical gate propagation delay for RTL is 15–30 nsec, for DTL 10–20 nsec, and 8–15 nsec for TTL. The corresponding power requirements are about 20 mw (i.e., 20 mw or 20×10^{-3} watt) for RTL, 20–30 mw for DTL, and 10–15 mw for TTL. DTL and certain TTL can use wired-or operation, but RTL cannot. Both TTL and DTL perform the NAND logic function for positive logic, whereas RTL performs the NOR function.

Transistor-transistor logic embodies one of the first really new circuit ideas of the integrated circuit era. With discrete components, designers tended to use relatively inexpensive resistors, capacitors, and diodes wherever possible and to minimize the transistor count within a gate. IC fabrication techniques, however, make the transistor the smallest, most inexpensive, and highest performance component. This fact is best taken advantage of by TTL designs which replace with a "multi-emitter" transistor the input resistor-transistor pairs of RTL or the input and voltage translation diodes of DTL. Figure 6 presents a simple circuit design of an RTL, a DTL, and two TTL NAND gates. The use of low-level TTL has significant advantages in cost and speed when large capacitive loads do not have to be driven.

Certain practical approaches are currently being pursued to minimize the delay in removing stored base charge in saturated transistors. These include antisaturation feedback diodes, substrate-controlled saturation transistors to limit saturation, and gold doping to reduce the lifetime of stored carriers. The prime means around the saturation problem, however, has been the use of nonsaturating circuit designs which have included the families of ECL (emitter coupled logic) and CML (current mode logic). Although the third generation of Motorola's ECL circuits (i.e., MECL III) obtain gate delays of about 1 nsec, the corresponding power requirement is 80–100 mw. Other nonsaturating gates have obtained 2 nsec delays with about 50 mw power dissipation. As a result, nonsaturating circuit power requirements are significant, but may be justified when very high logic speeds are required.

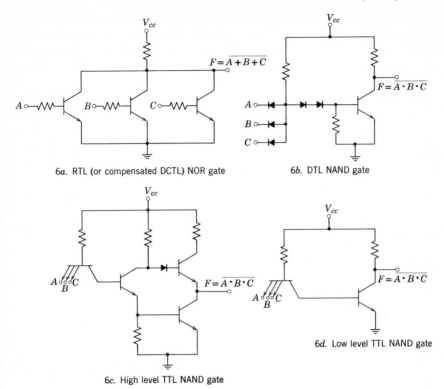

6a. RTL (or compensated DCTL) NOR gate   6b. DTL NAND gate

6c. High level TTL NAND gate

6d. Low level TTL NAND gate

Figure 6.   Bipolar circuit design of common logic gates.

5.   SEMICONDUCTOR FIELD EFFECT TRANSISTORS (FET's)

The previous sections have described the well-accepted conventional "bipolar" transistor semiconductor technology. Although the two technologies are frequently competitors in the same application and use quite similar fabrication techniques, bipolar and field effect transistors (FET's) differ markedly in their mode of operation and performance. Both devices have three terminals, but the FET is a voltage-controlled, majority carrier device, whereas the bipolar transistor is a current-controlled, minority carrier device. Actually the FET has many characteristics similar to triode and pentode vacuum tubes, such as device impedance. The FET has both high input and high output impedance levels. The bipolar transistor has low input impedance and high output impedance.

The bipolar transistor is a device in which current flow depends on the bias applied to the base-emitter and collector-base junctions. The current flow can be that of either holes or electrons, depending on whether the transistor is *p-n-p* or *n-p-n*, respectively. The FET, in contrast, is a device in which the current flow from the source contact to the drain contact is dependent on the drain to source voltage which induces a "field effect" in the "channel" between the source and drain. This field effect acts to vary the channel conductance, and can be of an "enhancement" or a "depletion" mode, depending on the design and the voltage applied to the gate contact. The enhancement mode occurs if the source-to-drain conductance (and therefore its current) increases as the gate voltage is varied from zero volts. Similarly, the depletion mode refers to a decreasing source-to-drain conductance (and therefore decreasing current) as the gate voltage is applied. It is this modulation of channel conductance that makes possible the FET operation.

There have been two basic approaches to the design and fabrication of FET devices. These are the junction FET and the insulated gate FET (or IGFET) of which the latter has now received widespread acceptance for its inherent advantages. The junction FET (JFET) makes use of a reverse-biased *pn* junction (between the gate and channel), around which a depletion layer forms naturally. As the reverse voltage is increased, the depletion layer spreads further into the channel material, thus modulating the source-to-drain current flow. When the depletion layer has spread across the entire channel, the channel resistance is so high that essentially no current (except a very small "leakage" current) can flow. The gate voltage for which this condition first occurs is termed the "pinch-off" voltage. The basic shortcoming of the JFET is that only depletion mode channel operation is possible. In addition, the JFET is more vulnerable to surface field effect phenomena.

After extensive work at RCA Laboratories, a metal oxide semiconductor (MOS) FET with an insulated gate was announced in 1962. Such a device permits both depletion and enhancement mode channel operation. The MOSFET is now also commonly referred to as the IGFET. The design and operation of the MOSFET can perhaps be best explained by Figure 7. Notice that the oxide dielectric covers the entire channel region. A metallic film overlays this dielectric and also covers the entire channel region. The gate contact is made to this metallic overlay. The metallic film and the semiconductor channel region thus act as the plates of a capacitor with the oxide layer acting as the dielectric. A positive voltage applied to the gate contact induces corresponding negative charges on the other side of the dielectric, that is, into the semiconductor channel region. Higher positive gate voltages increase the negative induced charge in the channel, thus inducing an *n*-type channel between the source and drain. Such a channel increases the channel conductance between source and drain, thus en-

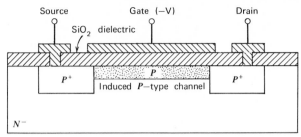

Figure 7. *P*-channel MOS transistor cross-section.

hancing the channel current flow. As a result, the current from source to drain can be modulated by controlling the gate voltage, since it directly determines the channels conductance. A depletion mode MOSFET is basically similar to the above enhancement mode design except an *n*-type channel is fabricated with moderate conductance and the application of a negative gate voltage then introduces a depletion layer which retards the current flow. Although *n*-type channels were referred to above, both depletion and enhancement mode MOSFET's are fabricated more commonly with *p*-type channels. Certain operational and fabrication trade-offs exist with the choice of mode and channel type.

6. COMPARISON OF BIPOLAR AND FET DEVICES

In comparing the circuits of bipolar and FET technologies, it is most important to consider, for each, the potential yield and process complexity, the potential component density, speed/power performance, and the ability to drive capacitive loads. Each of these will now be considered in turn.

The processing yield of cells is very dependent on the wafer area required for the fabricated circuits and also on the number, type, and control of the necessary processing steps. The diffusion steps are especially important, since they involve masking, photoresist, and oxidation operations involving high temperature steps. Integrated bipolar transistors require three diffusion processes (one each for the emitter, base, and collector), whereas single induced-channel type MOSFET's require only one diffusion. Other diffused channel MOSFET's require two diffusions. The bipolar transistor requires ten high temperature operations and MOS transistors as few as two. According to Warner [9], the bipolar integrated circuit fabrication is about 45% more difficult than the MOSFET, since 32 major bipolar process steps are required and only 22 MOSFET major steps. Control of the semiconductor surface and the oxide interface has been a significant MOS problem that now seems to be under control. In general, the processing yields of MOSFET circuits have been such as to allow the fabrication of 100 gate arrays at the same yields realized for 20–30 gate bipolar arrays. Part of this advantage comes from the simpler MOS processes which provide higher yields and a significant part is because a greater MOS component packing density is allowed as will be discussed. From the simpler processing standpoint alone, MOS chips of dimension 0.08 inch square should have roughly the same yields as bipolar chips 0.06 inch square. These area-yield comparisons are quite difficult to make and should only be taken as generalizations. When comparison of bipolar is made to the more recent complementary MOS (i.e., both n- and p-type channels processed on the same wafer), the complexity of processing and the yield-area MOS advantages are nearly lost. However, complementary MOS offers extremely low power dissipation at operating speeds between the single channel MOS and the bipolar. The low power dissipation is allowed by designing the circuits so that, except for the short switching period, there is always one of a complementary pair of MOS transistors which acts as an open circuit between the power supply and ground.

Three factors determine the maximum component packing density of a semiconductor technology. These are the device area, device spacing, and interconnect area requirements. The device area is determined by the fabrication technology as well as the circuit requirements. Device spacing is affected by the device isolation required as well as interconnect ground rules. Since MOS circuits can be operated at lower current levels than bipolar, both the device and interconnect areas can be correspondingly smaller (within the resolution limits of processing). Bipolar circuits require a reasonably large isolation junction around each device. MOS devices are naturally isolated, however, by a low conductance material with each terminal isolated by a reverse-biased p-n junction. A certain additional area efficiency of MOS results from the fact that the gate can be biased with a fixed voltage to provide a resistive characteristic in a rather small area. These advantages add up to the ability to fabricate usually 3 to 5 times as many MOS components in a reasonably large size chip (e.g., 0.10 to 0.20 inch square) as can be done with bipolar devices. In addition, MOS, in some cases, has a more efficient device utilization which allows perhaps 20% more circuit function from the same number of components. The MOS advantages do not exist, however, for low to moderate complexity circuit arrays. This is because MOS circuits which have inputs or outputs that are not on the same chip require about the same large area as bipolar devices in order to produce sufficient current to drive the remote circuit. In addition, small chip arrays are largely taken up with input and output connections and device interconnections. Thus, bipolar and MOS have no significant area differences for circuit arrays less complex than about 60–80 gates (or about 7000 square mils), and for complexities in excess of this MOS has an advantage of being able to pack 3 to 6 times as many components in the same chip area.

It is in the speed/power performance that the bipolar technology has the very significant advantage. According to H. C. Josephs [12], bipolar TTL logic circuits have a speed/power factor of advantage of 15 over MOSFET's Since in many applications performance cannot be sacrificed, bipolar circuits have this as a significant edge over MOS circuits. Whereas, MOS circuits with gate delays of 75–100 nsec can be fabricated, emitter-coupled logic (ECL) bipolar gates with delays of only 0.9–1.5 nsec are being fabricated. MOS has the inherent advantage of lower power dissipation in arrays of at least medium complexity, but the speed/power efficiency is significantly in favor of bipolar logic when speed is important.

A perhaps somewhat underrated factor in comparing MOS and bipolar characteristics is the inherently lower MOS transconductance (a measure of the ability to charge capacitances, and therefore "drive" other circuits). For the same level of technology, a bipolar transistor has about an order of magnitude higher transconductance. As a result, bipolar circuits can more readily drive a number of other circuits along lengthy connections, whereas larger area MOS devices would be required in such situations. Thus, not only is it desirable to have the higher drive capability for typical circuit applications but, without it, MOS loses its important area and component density advantages for all chips in the size range of integrated circuits. For large chips the advantages are not lost, since most devices will then be used internal to the chip only. As a result, MOS may never have much usage as simple IC's, but possesses the inherent cost and complexity advantages in MSI and LSI arrays. In summary, MOSFET technology can best be used in the applications for which high speed and current handling capability are not the prime objectives.

Approaches to improving the speed of MOS devices have centered on both structural and device innovations. The structural innovations have included complementary symmetry, smaller devices, thicker oxides, ion implantation, and other materials research. Recent circuit work toward increasing MOS logic speeds has concentrated on eliminating the need for charging interstage capacitances through high resistance transistors. The approach usually involves the use of special clocking and gating circuits (e.g., "two-phase" and "four-phase") to both precharge the capacitances and provide the necessary low resistance paths. The alternatives for higher speed MOS are typically complementary or clocked single channel MOS.

Advocates are strong on both sides; complementary MOS loses the processing simplicity and area advantages of single channel MOS, whereas clocked single channel circuits require more devices, have certain usage restrictions, and complicate routing. Further investigation is left to the reader [7, 9, 10, 13–15].

7. SEMICONDUCTOR MEMORIES

Semiconductor memories (except simple flip-flops) have been impractical because of high cost prior to the advent of the MSI and LSI technologies. Now, however, there is wide speculation [16–19] on the use of semiconductor memories in all but the very large bulk memories such as magnetic drum and disc systems in excess of one million words. The advantage to semiconductor memories is the very significant speed increase over other memories of the same cost. Very small ferrite-core, flat-film magnetic, and plated-wire magnetic memories are considered either too slow inherently or too expensive to allow implementations of 200 nsec cycle times for low to medium size buffer and main memories. For memories slower than 500 nsec cycle time, it may be some time before the batch fabrication efficiencies of either bipolar or MOS memories allow them to be cost competitive with the accepted magnetic memories. [References 7, 10, and 15 offer good general treatment of semiconductor memories in addition to what will be discussed here.]

The attractiveness of semiconductor memories is based on a combination of speed, size, cost, compatibility with logic circuits, and the possible provision of logic within the memory. The disadvantages are the "volatility" of either bipolar or MOS memories and the higher power dissipation. Both of these factors are because semiconductor memories employ active (i.e., "powered") circuits which lose their stored contents if power is turned off (i.e., they are volatile). In addition, the speed domain over which semiconductor memories can be cost effective is limited from 20 nsec to perhaps 400–500 nsec. Only bipolar could be used for cycle times below 150 nsec, whereas single channel MOS could be used in the slower applications. Complementary MOS or single channel MOS with bipolar addressing and decoding circuits would apply to the medium speed applications in the above domain. The MOS technology offers significant power savings where applicable.

In current and forthcoming large computer designs, there is often a memory hierarchy including each of the following types: main and buffer storage, conventional CPU registers, sequential, scratch pad, read only, and associative (or content addressable) memories. It is in medium to large main and buffer memories that the application of semiconductor arrays is most questioned on the basis of cost, power, an volatility. However, if, semiconductor main frame memories become justifiable on these accounts an avenue will be opened for very significant speed improvements (by a factor of 5–10) in central processors, since there will then be a compatibility in logic and memory speeds. Already, 256-bit bipolar general purpose memory chips are being made available and are being incorporated into low complexity buffer memories such as required for I/O terminals and peripheral computer equipment. The basic bipolar storage cell using four components is shown in Figure 8a. Cycle times under 100 nsec with 2 mw power dissipation are reported. Figure 8b shows the counterpart MOS storage bit.

The use of semiconductor circuits in conventional CPU registers has long been required to allow reasonable processing rates. In these cases, bipolar (or MOS) flip-flops have been employed in the accumulator, program counter, and the several other CPU data registers. As a result, these registers are a part of the logic delays within the CPU. Semiconductor sequential registers (commonly termed shift registers) have also been incorporated in CPU designs for some time. They are commonly used as data delay devices, counters, and serial computer registers. Both MOS and bipolar LSI shift registers of length over 1000 bits are now available. Extensive applications exist for these in small, slower digital computers, electronic calculators, and certain peripheral computer units.

Scratch-pad memories fill the requirements of very high speed memory for short-term storage. Generally interim calculation results or data about

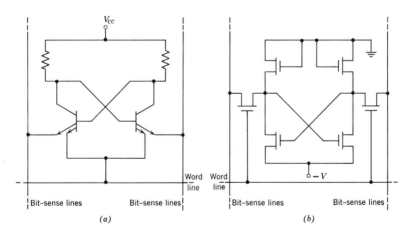

Figure 8.   Example designs of a bipolar and MOS storage bit. (a) Multi-emitter bipolar storage bit; (b) P-channel enchancement mode MOS storage bit.

to be used are stored in a high speed scratch-pad to improve overall calculation rates. The speed of a scratch pad should thus be comparable to that of the logic operations (say 5–100 nsec). The speed requirements dictate bipolar nonsaturating or low level TTL circuits at this time. A 16-bit 50 nsec ECL compatible chip (the MC1036) was made available by Motorola in 1968, with a 256-bit scratch pad in preparation.

Read-only memories (ROM) are special-purpose memories for control applications and the translation of code and other data. Frequently, ROM's are used as a low cost alternative to an equivalent logic array for the determination of a fixed set of information (such as in a multiplication table). That is, the multiplier and multiplicand could be used exactly as the address in an ROM multiplication table for which the contents of each word is the product of the respective operands.

ROM's are more commonly used to provide the control signals necessary in a CPU. Classically, these have been generated from extensive amounts of gates and flip-flops to decode and transform instruction and timing information into usable control signals. Such code translation is easily accomplished by an ROM which contains in each word the control signals for one computer instruction. Another significant ROM application is for the pattern generation signals for characters on a CRT (cathode-ray tube) display. Already, 1024-bit ROM's have been made available with cycle times under 50 nsec. Economical arrays of up to 16,384 bits are being projected for the near future.

Associative memories have been discussed in the literature for many years, but have had very limited use because of the amount of logic required within the memory. An associative or content addressable memory (CAM) retrieves information not by accepting the data in a specified physical location, but by searching the data by its content to determine if and where specific information exists. For example, an alphabetical list of students and class grades might be stored in memory. If the memory is associative, all (if any) of the names of students who recieved a "D" could be readily obtained, and far more efficiently than if each students record had to be brought from a conventional memory one-by-one and processed in the CPU to determine this. There are significant applications potentials and machines with certain "creative" abilities are the possible result as well as extremely powerful computing systems. Because of the cost, power, and lack of standardization, however, the use of associative memories will likely be limited to certain important special processors and applications such as memory paging tables.

A very important factor to remember about the development of each of the memories described (except possibly the associative) is that such memories offer a significant degree of standardization and regularity in their LSI design. These characteristics allow a very high volume production potential from simpler design and fabrication procedures than required of general logic arrays. As a result, LSI memories possess significant advantages and backing compared to the less regular and custom LSI logic requirements.

8. THE CHALLENGES OF LSI AND FUTURE DIGITAL ELECTRONICS

A discussion of the challenges of large scale integrated logic arrays offers an important insight into the future of digital electronics. The prime challenges fall into the areas of (1) the refinement of advanced semiconductor circuit technologies, (2) the definition of widely used logic arrays of high complexity, (3) the extensive use of computer-aided design techniques to allow low cost, and (4) the reliable testing and packaging of large arrays. The preceding sections of this chapter described the technologies used in the fabrication of integrated circuit wafers. The same semiconductor processing technologies are employed in fabricating MSI and LSI arrays. As was pointed out, MSI circuits use significantly larger portions of the wafer than do IC's to allow the implementation of arrays as complex as processing yields allow. As a result, perhaps 100–200 MSI circuit chips can be processed on a 2-inch diameter wafer, compared to 800–1000 IC circuit chips. In contrast, certain LSI approaches make use of an entire semiconductor wafer (interconnecting good circuits only, of course) for the fabrication of each LSI array. As a result, integrated circuits contain 1–20 equivalent gates of logic and require only one level of interconnect metalization; MSI chips contain 20–200 equivalent gates of logic and typically use two planes of interconnect metalization; while LSI is characterized by array complexities in excess of 100 equivalent gates of logic requiring usually three levels of metalization. From these generalizations, let us consider the implications to the design and application of high complexity (especially the LSI) logic arrays.

A prime characteristic of LSI is the attempt to integrate into each package a maximum amount of logic function. By so doing, the fullest advantage is taken of the batch processing techniques and large potential improvements are possible in the cost, reliability, performance, and volume of dlgital processing systems. But if any one of the four above-listed challenges are not sufficiently met, such improvements may not be possible. Important accomplishments have already been made in MSI/LSI, especially in semiconductor memories (as discussed in the preceding section) and in standard MSI functions (such as adders, decoders, shift registers, and counters). Less significant has been the application of LSI arrays to more general arithmetic and control unit designs. But this must wait for further development of the efforts in design and fabrication. Such efforts at Texas Instruments allowed the delivery, in early 1969, of a terrain-following radar computer implemented with thirty-four discretionary wired 1½-inch diameter general logic arrays, averaging nearly 200 gates per array.

Although the semiconductor processing steps are essentially an extension of integrated circuit technology (by the addition of two more interconnect levels), important advantages seem to be forthcoming for LSI from refinements in the fabrication of certain current and advanced circuit designs. The current technology must be refined to allow cost-effective yields of entire wafer arrays. The more advanced designs include low-level TTL, Schottky-barrier diodes for saturation limiting, complementary MOS, ion-implanted MOS, and the like, as well as smaller geometry components and innovations in materials research. Each of these techniques attempts improvement in the speed-power-size figure of merit attainable from the circuits. The accomplishment of such refinements will be responsible for much of the higher complexity, lower power, and maximum performance possible with batch fabricated LSI arrays.

But whatever the capabilities of the semiconductor processing technologies, the logic design of arrays that can make reasonably efficient use of the technology is required. A commonly experienced paradox is that designs which are widely usable in various systems (i.e., "universal") are seldom very efficient in specific applications. There are certainly exceptions to this, but it is true for most computer designs. For previous circuit technologies, there was little concern over this. With the fabrication of entire LSI wafers, however, there are certain high costs (for array layout, logic simulation, mask generation, and test sequence generation) associated with the proliferation of array designs. And if there are not high quantity requirements, these costs may therefore make the LSI array approach uneconomical. It is thus desired to design array functions that have a high utilization so that the associated "nonrecurring" design costs can be written off over a large quantity of parts. With such important advantages to be realized, it is expected that future designs will make use of new system architecture, universal cells, uniform cellular logic, redundancy, and other techniques to promote design standardization.

A certain alternative to design standardization is the efficient use of computer-aided design (CAD) to make possible low initial array design costs. Figure 9 shows the CAD tasks required in designing and fabricating LSI hardware from the initial system design specification. Important CAD work has been done in providing circuit design and simulation capabilities [20–28], but the areas of logic design (Chapter 2), partitioning, logic routing, and test sequence generation leave much to be accomplished. A

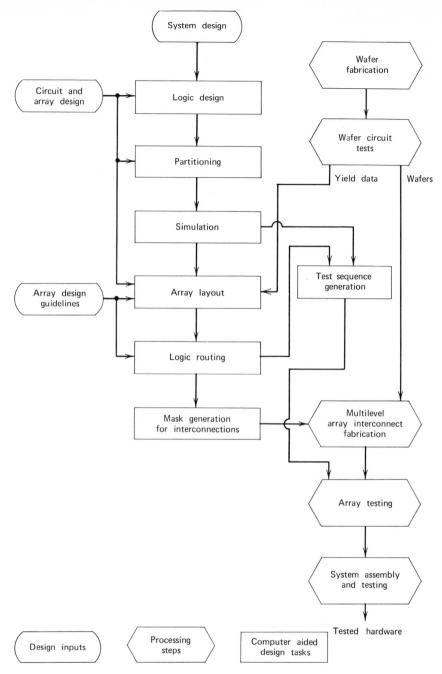

Figure 9. LSI design and fabrication tasks.

large part of the applicable LSI CAD work in routing and testing is held proprietary and furthermore is limited in application to certain array designs and complexities. Certain semiconductor companies have almost entirely based their MSI and LSI general logic approaches on low cost CAD techniques for the implementation of nonuniversal designs. These include the Texas Instruments "Discretionary Wiring" LSI, the Motorola "Polycell" MSI, and the Fairchild "Micromatrix." By extending these approaches to the more complex and general logic arrays anticipated in the future, low-cost and fast turn-around designs will be possible both for the widely used array functions as well as the functions that are required in low to medium quantity. Many believe that effective computer-aided design techniques are the key to eliminating the high initial design cost as a deterrent to the large-scale semiconductor processing capabilities.

The above challenges have related to the design and fabrication of LSI arrays. It cannot be forgotten, however, that reliable means of testing and packaging these arrays must be provided. The testing is complicated by a large amount of logic of which only a small number of the interconnect lines can be monitored to test the array. Computer programs are required to generate a sufficient set of tests, and high speed automatic testers are required to execute these tests. Testing may be aided by redundancy employed for fault detection, but may be significantly complicated if employed for logic efficiency, yield enhancement, or improved reliability. The packaging challenge is essentially that of reliably containing and integrating into a system a large array having as many as 100 connection points and a considerable power dissipation (perhaps 2–10 watts). The design and fabrication challenges discussed above are not entirely new to semiconductor electronics, but they can be expected to be most instrumental in the degree of application of LSI digital arrays.

9. REFERENCES

1. Beelitz, H. R., Muller, H. S., Linhardt, R. J., and Sidman, R. D., "Partitioning for Large Scale Integration," *International Solid-State Circuits Conference Digest* February 1967, pp. 50–57.

2. Calhoun, D. F., "High Speed Modular Multiplier and Digital Filter for LSI Development," *AFIPS Conference Proceedings* (FJCC), Vol. 33, San Francisco, December 1968, pp. 847–855.

3. Erwin, F. D., and McKevitt, J. F., "Characters—Universal Architecture for LSI," *AFIPS Conference Proceedings* (FJCC), Vol. 35, Las Vagas, November 1969, pp. 69–76.

4. Hudson, D. M., "The Applications and Implications of Large-Scale Integration," *Computer Design*, June 1968, p. 38.

5. Notz, W. A., Schischa, E., Smith, J. L., and Smith, M. G., "Large Scale Integration," three papers, *Electronics*, February 20, 1967, pp. 130–139.

6. Walter, C. J., Walter, A. A., and Bohl, M. J., "Setting Characterisics for Fourth Generation Computer Systems," *Computer Design*, October 1968, pp. 48–55.

7. Khambata, A. J., *Introduction to Large-Scale Integration*, Wiley, New York, 1969.

8. Warner, R. M., Jr., and Fordemwalt, J. N. (Eds.), *Integrated Circuits—Design Principles and Fabrication*, McGraw-Hill, San Francisco, 1965.

9. Warner, R. M., Jr., "Comparing MOS and Bipolar Integrated Circuits," *IEEE Spectrum*, Vol. 4, No. 6, June 1967, pp. 50–58.

10. Petritz, R. L., "Current Status of Large Scale Integration Technology," *IEEE Journal of Solid-State Circuits*, Vol. SC-2, No. 4, December 1967, pp. 130–147.

11. Calhoun, D. F., "The Pad Relocation Technique for Interconnecting LSI Arrays of Imperfect Yield," *AFIPS Conference Proceedings* (FJCC), Vol. 35, Las Vegas, November 1969, pp. 99–109.

12. Josephs, H. C., "A Figure of Merit for Digital Systems," *Microelectronics and Reliability*, Vol. 4, 1965, pp. 345–350.

13. Manufacturers' Circuit Catalogs; for example, *Integrated Circuit Catalog*, Texas Instruments, Inc., Dallas, Texas, published biennially, and *The Semiconductor Data Book*, Motorola, Inc., Phoenix, Airz., Fifth Edition, 1970.

14. Lynn, D. K., Meyer, C. S., and Hamilton, D. J. (Eds.), *Analysis and Design of Integrated Circuits*, McGraw-Hill, New York, 1967.

15. Spandorfer, L., "Large Scale Integration: an Appraisal," in *Advances in Computers*, Vol. 9, 1968, pp. 179–238.

16. Hodges, D. A., "Large Capacity Semiconductor Memory," *Proceedings of the IEEE*, July 1968, pp. 1148–1162.

17. Iwersen, J. E., Wourinen, J. H., Jr., Murphy, B. T., and D'Stefan, D. J., "Beam-Lead Sealed-Junction Semiconductor Memory with Minimal Cell Complexity," *IEEE Journal of Solid-State Circuits*, December 1967, pp. 196–201.

18. Potter, G. B., Mendelson, J., and Sirkin, S., "IC Scratchpads Sire a New Generation of Computers," *Electronics*, April 4, 1966, pp. 118–126.

19. Raisanen, W., "LSI Memories," *Electronic Design*, Vol. 24, November 21, 1968.

20. Freitag, H., "Design Automation for Large Scale Integration," presented at WESCON Convention, August 23–26, 1966, Session 10.

21. Hanne, J., "Computer Aids Speeds Discretionary Wiring," *Electronic Design*, Vol. 24, November 21, 1968, pp. C10–C16.

22. Hazlett, L. H., Lynn, D. K., Meyer, C. S., and Narud, J. A., "Computer-Aided Design," *Motorola Monitor*, Vol. 6, No. 3, 1968, pp. 34–39.

23. Lathrop, J. W., Clark, R. S., Hull, J. E., and Jennings, R. M., "A Discretionary Wiring System as the Interface Between Design Automation and Semiconductor Array Manufacturer," *Proceedings of the IEEE*, Vol. 55, November 1967.

24. Mays, C. H., "Computer-Aided Design for Large Scale Integration," *International Solid-State Circuits Conference, Digest of Technical Papers*. Vol. 10, February 16, 1967, pp. 46–47.

25. Taxin, H. M., "Interactive Graphics and the Computer-Aided Design of Digital Systems," Ph.D. Dissertation, University of California, Los Angeles, 1970.

26. Calhoun, D. F., "Computer-Aided Design Requirements of Complex Digital Integrated Circuit Arrays," *Proceedings IEEE International Conference on Systems, Networks, and Computers,* Oaxtepec, Mexico, January 1971, pp. 529–537.

27. Bennetts, R. G., and Lewin, D. W., "Fault Diagnosis of Digital Systems—A Review," *Computer,* IEEE Computer Society, Northridge, Calif., July/August 1971, pp. 12–20.

28. Calhoun, D. F., Corrigan, L. I., and Fox, G., "A Philosophy for and Experience with Automated Test Generation for Digital Modules," paper 4A-2, *Conference Record,* Region Six IEEE Conference, Sacramento, Calif., May 1971.

Logic Design

Miguel A. Marin

McGill University
Montreal, Quebec

George J. Klir

State University of New York
Binghamton, New York

1. INTRODUCTION

In Chapter 1 the basis electronic components of a digital computer system are studied from the viewpoints of the historical, technological, electronic structure and overall computer design implications. Although all of these aspects and their close relationship must be considered in the architectural development stage of a digital computer system (Chapter 4), it is convenient to determine the structure of interconnections of the basic system components by using a convenient abstract model for each component. This modeling process is generally known as *logic design*. Depending on how detailed the structure of interconnections is specified as a result of a consideration of the system's architecture, one is either concerned with *macro-* or *micro-*logic design. Thus, the determination of the major building blocks of various complexities, such as memory units, arithmetic processors, input-output units, registers, decoders, their specifications and interconnections, may be considered as the result of applying *macro-logic design techniques* at various levels to the specific computer system architecture. On the other hand, the determination of the structure of interconnections of the entire system or a subsystem, in terms of basic logic elements, such as gates and flip-flops, and considering them as "black boxes" with a given behavior, is known as *micro-logic design*. The relation between the micro-logic and macro-logic levels is not the same under all circumstances. It depends on the selection of the basic logic building blocks.

With the advent of LSI (Large Scale Integration) technology, it may be possible to choose "off the shelf" subsystems of considerable complexity, such as arithmetic processors, registers, counters and adders, but the problem of interfacing (connecting) these subsystems with proper logic elements and controlling devices to obtain an overall adequate systems performance will still remain. Hence, depending on the technology used, the micro-logic design of the entire computer system may lead either to a single LSI integrated package, or may result in a discrete electronic component realization (i.e., a realization containing transistors diodes, resistors, and the like). As discussed in Chapter 1, the latter result was customary before technology made possible the development of integrated circuits. At the present time, some parts of the system are already available as LSI packages and therefore it is customary to consider as micro-logic design that part of logic design that deals with the set of techniques used to asssemble these building blocks with basic logic elements.

Although micro-logic design techniques (which were initiated, for example, in the 1930s by Nakashima [50], Shannon [63], and others for contact networks) were considerably advanced in the 1950s and the early 1960s, little can be said in favor of the macro-logic design. The techniques of macro-logic design presently still depend to a considerable extent on the intuition and experience of the designer (see Chapter 4). The rapid advancement of solid-state electronic technology (Chapter 1) has opened many new challenging problems not existing in the early switching techniques of the 1950s and early 1960s, which were primarily oriented toward realizations of switching circuits with discrete electronic components.

In this chapter we direct our attention almost exclusively to micro-logic design; the reason being that we believe it still constitutes the foundation upon which digital systems designers rely either to interface existing subsystems or to design entirely their logic structure. The emphasis, however, is not on the historical development but rather on the principles and techniques that have survived or seem capable of surviving in the future.

The descriptive presentation of this chapter intends to give the reader an overall view of the state of the art in logic design including computer-aided techniques.

2. FORMULATION OF THE LOGIC DESIGN PROBLEM

The general procedure followed in any design task starts by defining a behavior and other specifications or characteristics of the system to be designed. The latter are given as a set of limiting values for the parameters defining the system's performance. For example, if the task is to design a binary adder (binary addition represents the behavior in this case), the limiting factors could be: speed less than 100 nanoseconds, operand length 32 bits, cost less than X dollars. With this information the designer proposes an *organization* of the system consistent with the given specifications. He may, for example, propose in this case of an adder design (discussed in detail in Chapter 3), a serial version composed of a 32 bit register, a full-adder, and a carry flip-flop.

It is well known that if the set of given basic element types is not adequate then the synthesis of the system generally cannot be completed [40–42, 74, 75]; if it is adequate, the system structure may not be unique. The possible solutions should then be analyzed to find which of them best matches the given specifications such as cost and reliability. Because of the variety of meaningful design constraints, it is almost impossible to envisage the existence of a general procedure which could take into consideration every possible set of constraints. The existing synthesis methods are usually elaborated for some kind of objective function which, in many cases, is not the one pertinent to the specified design problem. In these cases, an adequate objective function is stated (for example, cost, as a number of elements, external connections) and a synthesis method is applied in such a way as to minimize (or maximize) the objective function. Because of their complexity, it is found for most design problems that either it is difficult to state the objective function mathematically or the known synthesis methods are applicable to different objective functions which sometimes may be in conflict with the one in question. This is the case, for example, in the synthesis of logic circuits where redundancy of elements is needed for reasons of reliability. Therefore the standard minimization techniques of logic circuits with two levels of logic elements may not suffice, although they are quite adequate when cost requirements dominate.

The problem of designing a given logic circuit involves essentially the following five steps.

1. The proposal of an organization from a word description of the circuit.

2. The determination of a suitable code for the input and output values and a description of the circuit's behavior.

3. The determination of the set of basic element types (repertoire) sufficient to realize any logic circuit.

4. The application of a synthesis method to determine a structure of the circuit compatible with the design constraints.

5. The selection of an optimal structure among those satisfying the given design constraints.

Let us comment briefly on each of the above steps.

The word description of the logic circuit to be designed is usually ambiguous since it is given in terms of a natural language. This means that the design problem so defined may have different interpretations depending upon the reader. Supposing that the problem is precisely defined, it is then convenient to construct a model which depicts the desired behavior. Usually this model is a block diagram of the proposed organization. Different block diagrams may be derived, each one pertaining to a particular aspect of the behavior of the circuit. For example, a model for a serial adder consists of a block diagram of its major components or a diagram describing waveforms of inputs and outputs as a function of time.

Logic circuits are classified into two main categories: those whose outputs do not depend upon the past input values, and those whose outputs do depend on the past input values. The former class is known as *memoryless* (combinational) logic circuits and the latter as *sequential* logic circuits.

In the synthesis of both classes of logic circuits, the transformation of the word description into a mathematical model is needed. In memoryless logic circuits, the propositional calculus is used for this purpose. In essence the procedure consists of associating with each proposition of the word description a (Boolean) variable which assumes either the value 0 or 1 depending on its nonvalidity or validity (or vice versa), respectively. A set of Boolean equations is the final product of this transformation, and therefore the theorems applicable to Boolean algebra produce useful algorithms for analysis and synthesis. In sequential circuits, sequences of input and output values must be included in the mathematical description of the logic circuits.

A logic circuit is generally designed either to interact with other circuits or with a human through transducers. Therefore, the problem of *coding of information* must be considered when formulating the problem mathematically. If a Boolean variable ought to represent a certain proposition related to the circuit and at the same time a physical representation of its validity or nonvalidity, an agreement should be made regarding what physical quantity should correspond to each abstract set of values of the Boolean variables, and what meaning (validity or nonvalidity of propositions) is attributed to them. This problem is known as the *coding problem* and it is present in both categories of logic circuits. In both cases, depending on how the designer chooses the information code, different structural complexities may arise when applying synthesis procedures. This problem has not yet been solved satisfactorily. In Section 4 further comments on this problem are given.

The problem of selecting a set of basic elements that suffice to synthesize any given memoryless logic circuit is similar to the problem of determining whether the set of Boolean functions that they represent is complete, meaning that it can generate any given Boolean function. This problem has been theoretically solved, and theorems exist to verify whether a set of building blocks satisfies the requirement of completeness [41, 42, 55, 74, 75]. An adequate repertoire of basic elements must be complete. Obviously, an immense variety of catalogues of basic building blocks can be produced. The selection of an adequately sized catalogue is a compromise between many factors as outlined in Chapter 1.

Synthesis methods applicable to any logic circuit, any given repertoire of basic logic elements, and capable of handling any set of given constraints are yet to be found. However, promising methods do exist which accept a variety of design constraints. These may be handled by using either optimization techniques such as linear or nonlinear programming or by reformulating into a set of simultaneous Boolean or pseudo-Boolean relations.

Finally, the *selection of optimal structures* to realize a desired logic circuit implies the satisfaction of a given objective function (generally cost). In some synthesis methods, the objective function is checked as the synthesis algorithm progresses; in others, a synthesis is completed and then checked for acceptance as to whether the objective functions is satisfied.

In the following sections we shall discuss these problems in detail as they relate to memoryless logic circuits (Section 3) and sequential circuits (Section 4).

3. MEMORYLESS LOGIC CIRCUITS

As defined in the previous section, a memoryless logic circuit is an interconnection of logic elements whose output values at a particular time are solely dependent on the values of the inputs. This type of circuit is basic to the design of digital systems and the main objective is to obtain a realization satisfying a given set of requirements, ultimately related to the cost and performance of the circuit.

A general procedure for designing these circuits involves the following steps:

1. Transformation of the given specifications into a table or maps representing certain logic functions.

2. Composition of these functions using available logic elements.

3. Optimization of this composition to satisfy the requirements imposed upon the circuit.

Step 1 requires the selection of a code to represent input and output states. Although this selection is done *arbitrarily* in many cases, it may have a strong influence on the overall cost of the circuit [14, 51]. An assignment between values of physical quantities and the logic values 0 and 1 represents another effect of Step 1. This assignment is normally known as positive (for example, $+5$ volts represents 1, -8 volts represents 0), negative (-8 volts for 1 and $+5$ volts for 0), or mixed logic (parts of the circuit use positive and negative logic). Once an input code, an output code, and a type of logic (i.e., either positive or negative logic) are selected, maps are usually used to list the values of the logic function(s). The assignment of 2^n possible values of n inputs to squares of a rectangular map is not unique. There are $2^{(2^n)}$ such different maps. The map most widely used is the Karnaugh map [34], although the Marquand map introduced in 1881 [44] has been adopted by others [40, 42, 49, 64, 66], especially for the implementation of computer programs for logic design. In the Marquand map the decimal equivalent of the binary values of the inputs are assigned row-wise to squares of the map in an ascending natural order. This makes the construction of maps for a large number of variables (larger than 5) simple (Section 5). Step 2 consists of composing the functions by functions representing logic elements of the repertoire. The selection of a sufficient repertoire has been theoretically solved, completely [55, 74, 75]. However, it is not clear from a practical point of view whether one complete set of functions is more economical than another one for a particular problem. The technological reasons explained in Chapter 1, together with the proper cost evaluation function, should determine the size and variety of the repertoire. This cost function is not the same in all design circumstances. For example, a selection of NAND (*not-and*) logic elements may prove to be uneconomical when compared with a repertoire containing NAND and EXCLUSIVE-OR elements. If the cost associated with NAND elements and EXCLUSIVE-OR elements is the same, a full-adder, for example, may be implemented with the second repertoire more economically than with only NAND elements. This demonstrates an important point, namely that the economical circuit realization depends on:

1. The types of elements available in the repertoire.
2. The costs of the elements in the repertoire.
3. The efficiency of the synthesis technique usually measured by the engineering hours required for the completion of design.

Diodes and transistors were used in early switching circuit design techniques to produce a repertoire of AND, OR, and NOT logic elements which constitutes a complete set of functions. Minimum number of these logic elements was the objective of the synthesis. Methods based on a normal (nonfactored) Boolean form were elaborated to solve fully the minimization problems so formulated; all of these methods were originally based on the one-to-one correspondence between the AND, OR, NOT relations of Boolean algebra and the AND, OR, NOT logic elements. This minimization problem was first formulated and solved by Quine [56, 57], in terms of normal Boolean forms leading to two-level circuits. Later other minimizations of two-level AND, OR, NOT logic circuits were elaborated [48, 59, 66, 72].

Various generalizations of the classical problem of the minimization of the normal Boolean form have been offered, for example, the minimization of groups of normal Boolean forms [6, 40, 53] and multiple level and absolute minimization [1, 43].

The economical realization of complex repertoires; the physical limitation of the logic elements, such as *fan-in* (number of inputs to a logic element); *fan-out* (number of elements that can be connected to a given element output, and *time-delay* (delay of a signal traveling through a logic element); and the requirements imposed on the overall circuit, such as the number of interconnections and external pins, have imposed new conditions on the well-known synthesis methods mentioned above. As yet we are not aware of a synthesis method that solves the entire problem. Both heuristic and algorithmic methods exist to solve one or another aspect of the synthesis problem, and all methods are practically restricted to a small number of input variables (less than 20) [7]. The combinatorial nature of memoryless logic circuits makes it impossible to obtain a manual solution to problems involving large number of variables (see Section 5). Heuristic methods proposed by Breuer [8], together with the linear programming techniques for cost function optimization are possible approaches to the problem.

A second approach is the one based on the theory of decomposition, first proposed by Ashenhurst [5] and further developed by Curtis [12] and by Marin [47]. This method formulates the synthesis problem as an iterative decomposition of the function(s) in terms of the elements of the repertoire.

The decomposition procedure, which is invariant for any given repertoire of logic elements, consists of solving a set SB of Boolean equations. This invariance makes the synthesis algorithm independent of the development of technology. The large number of computations involved in the decomposition procedure suggests the utilization of computer methods and the use of an interactive graphic system for the rapid selection and processing of adequate constraint equations which are formulated as Boolean or pseudo-Boolean relations [26, 42] and are added to the original set SB.

Finally a third approach to the problem is often used: the logic net (interconnections of logic elements in the repertoire) is designed by using the designer's intuition and experience. Once the logic diagram is produced, partitioning techniques (usually trial-and-error methods) are applied to determine how the elements may be arranged into individual packages to minimize the overall cost and number of interconnections. A final drawing of the partitioned blocks is then produced for automatic checking through computer simulation methods.

From the above discussion, we may conclude that the synthesis of memoryless circuits is governed by many factors (such as reliability, easy diagnosis, and economics) that greatly depend on the advancements of technology. However, synthesis techniques exist that do not fully solve the complete problem, but they are independent from the trends of technology and still allow the insertion of technological constraints. From the theoretical point of view the synthesis problem of memoryless circuits is a well-studied subject and offers no major difficulties.

4. SEQUENTIAL LOGIC CIRCUITS

As defined in Section 2, a switching circuit whose output signals depend on the instantaneous values of the input signals and on some or all past values of the latter is called sequential. When such circuits are treated through an abstract model, they are called sequential logic nets. Their study can then be carried out rigorously and independently of specific switching elements.

Sequential circuits are widely used in computer systems. The control unit (discussed in Chapter 5), for example, is a sequential circuit whose adequate design and performance influences every subsystem of the computer.

When treating sequential logic nets, many of the comments for memoryless circuits apply equally. The large scale integration of today's electronic technology imposes optimization criteria not existing in classical methods. In applying LSI techniques, standardization is highly desirable in order to decrease the initialization cost. By standardization we understand the ability to produce a repertoire of building blocks (in this case, sequential building blocks) to obtain any given sequential logic net. The main problem in standardization is that sequential circuits are designed for specific "sequencing" tasks which vary widely from one computer to another, and the theory of decomposition based on a given repertoire is not fully developed. Moreover, the requirements of this repertoire are not yet known.

In the synthesis of sequential logic nets, it is customary to use a block diagram in which two parts are explicitly distinguished (Figure 1). The part called "memoryless" reacts instantaneously to input values with no delays in signal propagation. The part called "memory" is responsible for memorizing the essential features of the past history of the circuit. The memoryless part contains two classes of inputs: *internal* (coming from the memory) and *external* (coming from the circuit environment). The outputs of the memoryless part are external signals going to the environment of the circuit and internal output signals entering the memory part.

Memory elements may be classified into two categories:

1. Pure memory elements or those that reproduce at their output the incoming signals t seconds later (delay elements).

2. Other memory elements whose structure can be composed of a memoryless part and delay elements.

The well known SR, T, JK flip-flops [28] are examples of these memory elements.

The block diagram (Figure 1) that models a sequential switching circuit is classically of two types:

1. Finite-state model (S-model) (Figure 2).
2. Finite-memory model (M-model) (Figure 3).

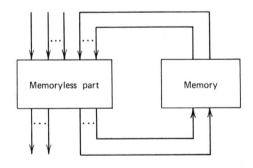

Figure 1. Block diagram of a sequential logic net.

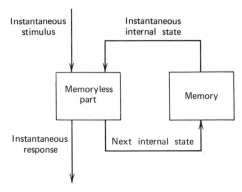

Figure 2.   Basic finite-state model [37, 39].

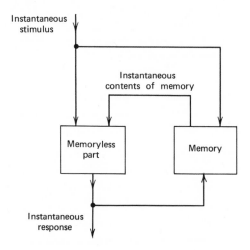

Figure 3.   Finite-memory model [37, 39].

In the S-model values of external variables are not stored. In the M-model only values of external variables are stored. From the standpoint of the class of realizable behaviors, the S-model is more general than the M-model and has been extensively used to synthesize any given sequential circuit. For this reason it is known as a universal model. The M-model, however, is not universal. There are some behaviors that cannot be synthesized in terms of this model. However, when applicable, it may produce better realizations depending on the optimization criteria used.

From the engineering point of view, it has proved to be convenient to combine the two previous models into a universal one called the *combined*

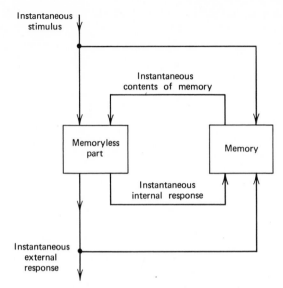

Figure 4. Combined model.

model or C-model (Figure 4) [37, 39, 42]. The latter can degenerate into either an S-model or an M-model depending on what type of inputs enter the memory part of the circuit. The C-model is the most general paradigm of this kind (split into memory and memoryless parts) that can be proposed.

The behavior of an sequential logic net is, by definition, a mapping from sequences of external input signals to external output signals. The internal signals stored in the memory part represent the *internal state*. Since a non-pure memory element consists of a memoryless part and delay elements, we shall agree in that the memory part of a sequential circuit under the C-model contains only delay memory elements.

Under the previous assumptions the synthesis task is divided in the following steps.

1. The word description of the problem is transformed into a symbolic mathematical representation (tables, matrices, graphs) of the so-called *state-transition structure* depicting a set of internal states and a set of transitions between these states. Each transition is labeled by the stimulus and the response associated with it. This procedure is called *abstract synthesis*. Clearly it is independent of the type of model used in the synthesis. Although abstract synthesis has been extensively studied, the present results are not satisfactory [10, 22, 24, 54]. The only general method that really solves all aspects of this problem was developed by Tal [25, 68,

69]. The method is systematic yet too tedious for manual application to practical problems. The computer implementation of Tal's method (see Section 6) with on-line interaction could be an answer to this limitation.

2. Once the state-transition structure is obtained, it may be convenient to *decompose* it into smaller parts in order to reduce the synthesis to a workable size. Although some aspects of decomposition of sequential circuits have been studied [4, 10, 30] the problem of decomposition, subject to constraints or to a fixed repertoire with the aim of optimizing the cost, speed, and interconnections, is still unsolved. The dependency of the decomposition on these parameters is not clear and, therefore, the general practice is to follow intuition and experience to produce practical circuits which are either readily obtainable (counters and shift registers, for example) or easily synthesized. The question of a complete repertoire of sequential modules that will suffice for any synthesis is still open. Its successful answer, we believe, could produce a general method of decomposition and synthesis suitable for LSI technology.

3. Each decomposed part of the state-transition diagram is synthesized separately. At this stage it is possible to introduce certain design criteria such as the number of delays and the number of memoryless building blocks. Three levels of synthesis are important here:

(*a*) *The selection of a model.* We have seen above that the C-model is the most general of its kind which may produce more economical realizations than the M-model or S-model. A procedure has been developed to compare roughly various models for a particular design problem [39]. The selection is made following certain evaluation formulas that are based on the number of inputs and outputs of the memoryless part, and the number of memory elements. These numbers indicate to the designer the type of circuits he may choose from. The formulas used in the model evaluation are independent of the selection procedure proper. This is of great advantage, since different evaluation formulas could be developed as technology advances.

(*b*) When a model is chosen, the internal states must be somehow coded by values of some internal variables. A solution of this problem, usually called the *state assignment problem*, may affect considerably the ultimate complexity of the memoryless part of the circuit measured in terms of the number of basic logic building blocks. Although this problem has been studied extensively [13, 16, 27], no general method producing the *best* internal code for given design constraints has been developed thus far.

(*c*) Having selected an adequate state assignment, the task remains to complete the *synthesis of the memoryless part of the circuit.* The general method discussed in Section 3 can be applied here.

We may conclude from the above discussion that the problem of the synthesis of sequential circuits is far from solved. While LSI technology is concerned with standardization and little importance is given to the actual count of logic elements used, the theoretical tools and synthesis methods available are more concerned with the count of the logic elements than with decomposition based on a certain repertoire. This unfortunate situation discourages, in many cases, logic designers from using theoretical methods for synthesis. Many designers rely on their intuition and experience more and more. We believe, however, that it is feasible to develop methods that are theoretically sound and, at the same time, sufficiently flexible to be applied under different design circumstances and technologies.

Finally, let us comment briefly regarding the synchronization of sequential circuits. Thus far we have only considered the general synthesis procedure and the problems that exist in any kind of sequential circuit. In practice, sequential circuits are classified into two classes: *synchronous* and *asynchronous*. The former class is characterized by the fact that each transition in the circuit is controlled by an external pulse source called a clock and, therefore, no ambiguities exist in the internal transitions provided that the clock period T is larger than the maximum propagation delay within the circuit. This timing precaution will assure that the circuit is in the steady state before the next stimulus is accepted into the circuit. In asynchronous circuits, this external synchronizing source is not available and each transition of the circuit as a reaction to a certain stimulus should bring the circuit to a steady state before the next stimulus can be accepted into the circuit. In order to avoid uncertainties of this kind, proper coding of the internal states is required allowing only one internal variable (input to the memory part) to change value at each transition of the circuit. Thus two or more internal changes can not occur simultaneously, since this simultaneity is physically not realizable without an external clock. This problem has been extensively dealt with in the literature [20, 38, 70, 73] and adds a further constraint to the solution of the state assignment problem.

5. COMPUTER-AIDED LOGIC DESIGN

In the two previous sections we have discussed some general aspects of the synthesis of logic circuits. All of the procedures used for synthesis require an extensive amount of computation in order to arrive at optimal solutions. The reason for this is twofold:

1. The problems are of combinatorial nature which makes them manually intractable even when they are of reasonable size.
2. The searching techniques for optimal solutions are in many cases "trial-and-error" investigations of all existing solutions.

For these reasons computers are very important as an aid in the synthesis of logic circuits.

Although we are far from having a fully automated and flexible logic design system, which could accept both the system's specifications and produce ready-to-assemble logic drawings, some interesting and promising results have been obtained in this direction [7].

A computer-aided logic design procedure may be envisaged as decomposed into blocks or parts as shown in the flowchart of Figure 5 and may be considered as a part of a complex computer design automation program. The branches A and B in the flowchart correspond, respectively, to the sequential and memoryless circuit synthesis. We shall consider each branch separately.

With respect to automated methods (algorithms) for sequential circuits design (branch A in Figure 5), no general procedure exists today insofar as we know, although aspects of it are being presently studied and programmed for computers. The abstract synthesis, which constitutes the first step in the procedure, has not been programmed for a computer. The algorithms offered by Gill [22], Gray and Harrison [24], or based on various applications of regular expressions [28, 9] (see Chapter 12) do not solve the problem of abstract synthesis satisfactorily or generally. The Tal algorithm [25, 68, 69] solves the problem completely and generally but its generality produces large decision tables which must be handled to generate a state transition structure of the desired sequential circuit. The manipulation of large decision tables and the realization of a special question-answer game, on which the Tal method is based, offers no major difficulty beyond the semantics problem but they are difficult to implement on present computers.

The problem of decomposition of sequential circuits, which seems quite attractive for LSI techniques, was studied by Hartmanis and Stearns [30] and others [2, 4, 19, 36, 70]. It may be adapted to obtain decompositions contained in a given catalogue of already available off-the-shelf sequential circuits. To our knowledge, this aspect of decomposition has not been programmed for a computer.

As with the decomposition problem, no general computer programs exist which, starting from the state transition structure, will produce a sequential circuit diagram in terms of memoryless building blocks and their interconnections. However, Elsey [17] has reported an algorithm for the complete synthesis of large asynchronous sequential circuits.

Another attempt in this direction, in which several types of sequential circuits are considered, is the approach proposed by Klir and Marin [39, 42]. Its flexibility to accept various objective functions and evaluation formulas makes it attractive as a general methodology. Some parts of this methodology have been programmed for a computer: the evaluation

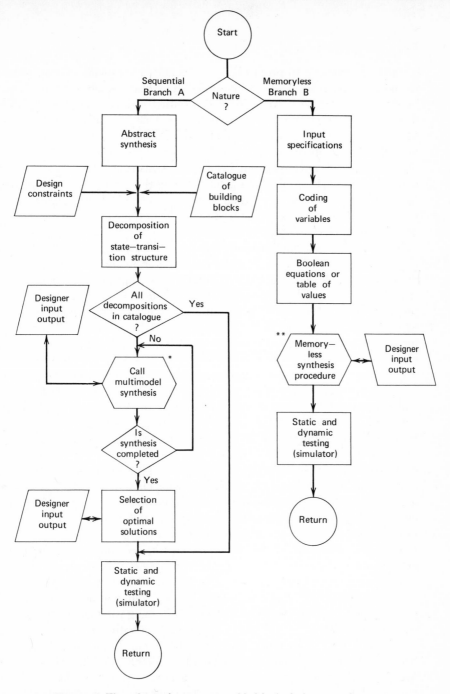

Figure 5. Flow chart of a computer-aided logic design procedure.

* See Reference 39 for detailed flow charts.

** See Reference 47 for detailed flow charts.

of models according to proposed formulas and the implementation of the memoryless part for a given inventory. The state assignment problem, however, remains to be programmed awaiting a development of general algorithms. A great amount of research effort has gone into the solution of this problem for the last decade and many authors are still active in this field. Yet the problem has not been satisfactorily solved. A computerized algorithm for this purpose was developed by Armstrong [3] in 1962. Dolotta and McCluskey [16] proposed a good study on the subject two years later. For the choice of assignments their method uses weight factors, which may be altered depending on specific design constraints or based on design experience.

In the multimodel methodology mentioned above and shown schematically in branch A of Figure 5, an important step following the generation of the acceptable models is the selection of the optimal ones under the specific design considerations. Although various formulas similar to that proposed by Kellerman [35] may simplify the selection of models, it is not expected that the former factor will be completely eliminated. The reason for this man-machine interaction is mainly that it is undesirable in many cases, even impossible, to program a machine to cope with every possible decision alternative. The design constraints of a particular circuit may be so different from one synthesis problem to another that it would be more realistic to let the designer ultimately choose from some reasonable number of acceptable solutions. Also we should mention here that because of the trend of mass production of integrated circuits (IC) and LSI circuits, the economy of a logic circuit in general will not reside in the count of logic elements, for example, but rather on how fast an acceptable solution can be found. The present large disproportion between the cost of engineering hours and the cost of individual electronic components suggests that we optimize the synthesis time at the expense of a minimum hardware realization which is generally a time-consuming process.

To take advantage of this economic factor, computer manufacturers extensively use *logic simulators* to generate the logic of their new computers.

Logic simulators have been developed by almost every major computer manufacturer for internal use. Generally, logic simulators are computer programs that accept Boolean equations describing the machine to be designed and that make an evaluation and produce both static and dynamic simulations of the logic diagrams that realize them. Logic simulators have been studied by Gorman and Anderson [23], Proctor [54], and Estrin and Mandell [18]. An automated logic design generator called ALERT [21] was developed by IBM. The ALERT system accepts the architecture of a machine written in Iverson's language [32] and transforms it into Boolean equations. These equations are transformed into logic diagrams by using the IBM Logic Automation [11] and Design Automation Programs [23]. The advantage of ALERT, as stated by Friedman and Young [21], is that it "allows faster development of new computers, immediate documentation and improvement of quality since the designer may investigate rapidly different design alternatives without waiting for logic generation." The limitations of such design tools seem to be:

1. The large computer required for such programs.
2. The utilization of specific set of building blocks (the one used by the manufacturer) in the generation of logic diagrams.

Now let us consider the automated design of memoryless switching circuits. This involves (Figure 5, branch B) the development of computer programs to generate Boolean equations. Programs like ALERT [21] and LOTIS [62], for example, may well produce the desired input to logic synthesizers using a catalogue of building blocks and designers constraints. The simplified version of this synthesis problem involves Boolean logic minimization, and programs have been developed for two-level single (or multiple) output AND-OR logic circuits [6, 67]. Using NAND, NOR (*not-or*) elements, Dietmeyer and Schneider [15] and recently Su [67] have developed programs for synthesis of memoryless circuits. Su takes into account design or logic-element constraints such as the number of logic levels, fan-in and fan-out, etc. Programs based on Roth's simplification procedure for Boolean trees were developed by IBM [60]. The method used is based on the successive decomposition of the desired switching circuit considering it as a Boolean graph. At each decomposition stage a table of combination is generated and a survey of the logic elements available in the catalogue is carried out to determine whether a logic element exists that realizes the desired decomposition. In general it is required to investigate all possible decompositions in order to find an optimal one under the design specifications. Another approach to this problem, also based on the theory of decomposition, uses the resolution of systems of simultaneous Boolean equations.

The main drawback in the computer implementation of the above logic design algorithms is the long computer time required to arrive at an optimal solution. This fact, together with the existence of logic simulators, overshadows the economy of those types of programs in actual design practice.

An attempt to develop a common foundation for the automation of logic design problems started with Svoboda [65] and his Boolean Analyzer which was developed at UCLA and applied to some logic problems by Marin [46, 47]. The philosophy used is summarized as follows: Design automation is just another problem where a large set of statements is presented, some with known, some with unknown validity. Therefore, if a design automation problem can be stated in terms of Boolean relations (implications between Boolean expressions, equalities) the solutions of these will give the unknown validities. The number of Boolean variables in such equations is usually very large, thus making uneconomical their computerized solution via standard programming techniques. However, parallel hardware processors, such as the Boolean or pseudo-Boolean Analyzers [65, 45] which may operate as a part of an automatic computer, may be the answer to the problem of processing large numbers of Boolean terms in reasonable time.

Some applications of the above philosophy to logic design problems such as the synthesis of three-level NAND memoryless logic nets [46] have been investigated [47] and solved by using a Boolean Analyzer simulator [47, 58].

6. CONCLUSIONS

1. The classification of logic design into macro- and micro-design is continuously changing. The fast development of technology makes the difference between the two levels of logic design gradually less and less significant mainly because of the development of off-the-shelf IC and LSI packages. There is an intensive search for new methods and tools for solution of logic design problems under new circumstances.

2. Boolean and pseudo-Boolean relations of various kinds represent an important tool for solutions of many problems in logic design. Methodologically, this tool is considerably independent of the technology. On the other hand, its application requires new hardware consideration in contemporary computers. Boolean and pseudo-Boolean analyzers represent initial steps in this direction.

3. Although there are many specific topics concerning the design of combinational circuits that have not been solved satisfactorily (for instance, a possibility of feedbacks in combinational circuits, diagnostics, synthesis based on some reliability requirements, coding of input and output states, threshold logic, and cellular structures), there are no major gaps in the theory of combinational circuits.

4. As far as the design of sequential circuits is concerned, some stages of the design have not been solved satisfactorily, namely, the abstract synthesis, the model selection, and the state assignment problem. The abstract synthesis, although solved theoretically, produces serious difficulties when practically implemented. Lack of sophisticated formulas for model evaluation makes the model selection very difficult in many cases. The variety of objective functions produces difficulties in the solution of both the model selection and the state assignment.

5. The application of computers in logic design is intensively studied with the ultimate goal to completely automate the whole procedure of logic design. Although large portions of logic design have been programmed for computers, a real success in this area will probably depend on new considerations in computer hardware.

6. Some areas of logic design, which may be expected to be very important in the future, have not been sufficiently investigated yet. An example is the logic design of probabilistic circuits which are needed for adaptive or self-organizing systems.

7. REFERENCES

1. Abhyankar, S., "Absolute Minimal Expressions of Boolean Functions," *IRE Trans.*, Vol. EC-8, No. 1, pp. 3–8, 1959.

2. Ablow, C. M., and Yoeli, M., "Synthesis of Automata by Decomposition Techniques," Stanford Res. Inst., Contract AF 19(628) 5092, September 1966.

3. Armstrong, D. B., "A programmed algorithm for assigning internal codes to sequential machines," *IRE Trans.*, Vol. EC-11, pp. 466–472, 1962.

4. Arbib, M. A. (Editor), *The Algebraic Theory of Machines, Languages and Semigroups*, Academic Press, New York, 1968.

5. Ashenhurst, R. L., "The Decomposition of Switching Functions," *Proc. of an Intern. Symp. on the Theory of Switching. Part I*, pp. 74–116, Harvard University Press, Cambridge, Mass., 1959.

6. Bartee, T. C., "Computer Design of Multiple Output Logical Network," *IRE Trans.*, Vol. EC-10, No. 1, pp. 21–30, 1961.

7. Breuer, M. A., "Design Automation of Digital Computers," *Proceedings of IEEE*, Vol. 54, No. 12, December 1966, pp. 1708–1721.

8. Breuer, M. A., "The Use of Mathematical Programming in the Implementation of Boolean Switching Functions," Ph.D. dissertation, University of California, Berkeley, 1964.

9. Brzozowski, J. A., "A Survey of Regular Expressions and Their Applications," *IRE Trans.*, Vol. EC-11, No. 3, pp. 324–335, 1962.

10. Booth, T. L., *Sequential Machines and Automata Theory*, Wiley, New York, 1967.

11. Case, P. W., Graff, H. H., Griffith, LeClercq, A. R., Murley, W. B., and Spence, T. M., "Solid Logic Design Automation for IBM System/360," *IBM J. Res. Develop.*, Vol. 8, pp. 127–140, April 1964.

12. Curtis, H. A., *A New Approach to the Design of Switching Circuits*, D. Van Nostrand, Princeton, N. J., 1962.

13. Curtis, H. A., "Systematic Procedure for Realizing Synchronous Sequential Machines Using Flip-Flop Memory," Parts I and II, *IEEE Trans. on Computers*, Vol. C-18, No. 12, Vol. C-19, No. 1, 1970.

14. Davis, W. A., "An Approach to the assignment of Input Codes," *IEEE Trans.*, Vol. EC-16, No. 4, pp. 435–442; 1967.

15. Dietmeyer, D. L., and Schneider, P. R., "A computer oriented factoring algorithm for NOR logic design," *IEEE Trans.*, Vol. EC-14, pp. 868–874, 1965.

16. Dolotta, T. A., and McCluskey, E. J., "The Coding of Internal States of Sequential Circuits," *IEEE Trans.*, Vol. EC-13, No. 5, pp. 549–562, 1964.

17. Elsey, J., "An Algorithm for the Synthesis of Large Sequential Switching Circuits," Coordinated Science Lab., University of Illinois, Report No. R-169, May 1963.

18. Estrin, G., and Mandell, R., "Metacompiler as a Design Automation Tool," 1966 Proc. Share Design Automation Conference.

19. Ferrari, D., and Grasselli, F., "A Cellular Structure of Sequential Networks," *IEEE Trans. on Computers*, Vol. C-18, No. 10, October 1969.

20. Friedman, A. D., and Menon, P. R., "Synthesis of Asynchronous Sequential Circuits with Multiple Input Changes," *IEEE Trans.*, Vol. C-17, No. 6, pp. 559–566, 1968.

21. Friedman, T. D., and Yang, S. C., "Methods Used in an Automatic Logic Design Generator (ALERT)," *IEEE Trans. on Computers*, Vol. C-18, No. 7, pp. 593–614, July 1969.

22. Gill, A., "Realization of Input-Output Relations by Sequential Machines," *ACM Journal*, Vol. 13, No. 1, pp. 33–42, 1966.

23. Gorman, D. F., and Anderson, J. P., "A logic design translator," *Proc. FJCC*, pp. 86–96, 1962.

24. Gray, J. N., and Harrison, M. A., "The Theory of Sequential Relations," *Information and Control*, Vol. IX, pp. 435–468, 1966.

25. Gusev, L. A., and Tale, A. A., "The Possibilities of Constructing Algorithms for the Abstract Synthesis of Sequential Machines Using the Questionnaire Language," *Automation and Remote Control*, Vol. 26, No. 3, pp. 510–520, 1965.

26. Hammer, P. L., and Rudeanu, S., *Boolean Methods in Operations Research*, Springer-Verlag, New York, 1968.

27. Harring, D. R., *Sequential Circuit Synthesis: State Assignment Aspects*, The M.I.T. Press, Cambridge, Mass., 1962.

28. Harrison, M., *Introduction to Switching Theory*, McGraw-Hill, 1966.

29. Hartmanis, J., "Loop-free structure of sequential machines," *Inf. Control*, Vol. 5, pp. 25–43, 1962.

30. Hartmanis, J., and Stearns, R. E., *Algebraic Structure Theory of Sequential Machines*, Prentice-Hall, Englewood Cliffs, N.J., 1966.

31. Holst, P. A., "Bibliography on Switching Circuits and Logical Algebra," *IEEE Trans.*, Vol. EC-10, No. 4, pp. 638–661, 1961.

32. Iverson, K. E., *A Programming Language*, Wiley, New York, 1962.

33. Johnson, M. D., and Lackey, R. B., "Sequential Machine Synthesis Using Regular Expressions," *Computer Design*, pp. 44–47, September 1968.

34. Karnaugh, M., "The Map Method for Synthesis of Combinational Logic Circuits," *Trans. AIEE, Part I, Comm. and Electronics*, Vol. 72, pp. 593–599, 1953.

35. Kellerman, E., "A Formula for Logical Network Cost," *IEEE Trans.*, Vol. C-17, No. 9, pp. 881–884, 1968.

36. Kohavi, Z., and Smith, E. J., "Decomposition of Sequential Machines," Proc. 6th Ann. Symp. on Switching Circuit Theory and Logical Design, Ann Arbor, Mich., pp. 52–61, October 1965.

37. Klir, G. J., "A Note on the Basic Block Diagram of Finite Automata from the Engineering Point of View," *Trans. IEEE*, Vol. EC-16, No. 2, pp. 223–224, 1967.

38. Klir, G. J., and Hlavicka, J., "Logical Design of Sequential Asynchronous Circuits," *Information Processing Machines*, Vol. 11, pp. 135–165, Csechoslovak Academy of Sciences Press, Prague, 1965.

39. Klir, G. J., and Marin, M. A., "A Multimodel and Computer Oriented Methodology for Synthesis of Sequential Discrete Systems," *IEEE Trans.*, Vol. SSC-6, No. 1, pp. 40–48, 1970.

40. Klir, G. J., and Seidl, L. K., "Synthesis of Switching Circuits," *ILIFFE*, London, 1968.

41. Klir, G. J., *An Approach to General Systems Theory*, Van Nostrand Reinhold, New York, 1969.

42. Klir, G. J., *Introduction to Methodology of Logic and Switching Circuits*, Van Nostrand Reinhold, New York, 1971.

43. Lawler, E. L., "An Approach to Multi-Level Boolean Minimization," *J. Assoc. Comp. Mach.*, Vol. 11, No. 3, pp. 283–295, 1964.

44. Marquand, A., "On Logical Diagrams for n Terms," *Philosophical Magazine*, Vol. XII, pp. 266–270, 1881.

45. Marin, M. A., and Klir, G. J., "On Computer Aspects of Pseudo-Boolean Integer Programming," Engineering Report, Department of Electrical Engineering, McGill University, Montreal, Canada.

46. Marin, M. A., "Synthesis of TANT Networks Using a Boolean Analyzer," *The Computer Journal*, August 1969.

47. Marin, M. A., "Investigation of the Field of Problems for the Boolean Analyzer," Ph.D. dissertation, Department of Engineering, UCLA, June 1968.

48. McCluskey, E. J., "Minimization of Boolean Functions," *Bell System Techn. Jnl.*, Vol. 35, No. 6, pp. 1417–1444, 1956.

49. Nadler, M., *Topics in Engineering Logic*, New York, McMillan, 1962.

50. Nakashima, A., "Theory of Relay Circuit Composition," *Nippon El. Com. Eng.*, No. 3, pp. 197–206, 1936.

51. Nichols, A. J., and T. H. Mott, Jr., "State Assignment in Combinational Networks," *IEEE Trans.*, Vol. EC-14, No. 3, pp. 343–349, 1965.

52. Patt, Y. N., "Synthesis of Switching Functions Using a Minimum Number of Integrated-Circuit Modules," Stanford Electronics Laboratory, Technical Report No. AFAL-TR-67-142, December 1966.

53. Polansky, R. B., "Minimization of Multiple-Output Switching Circuits," *AIEE Trans.*, Part I, Comm. and Elect., Vo. 80, pp. 67–73, 1961.

54. Proctor, R., "A Logic Translator Experiment Demonstrating Relationship of Language to Systems and Logic Design," *IEEE Trans. on Computers*, Vol. EC-13, pp. 422–443, August 1964.

55. Post, E. L., "Two-Valued Iterative Systems of Mathematical Logic," *Annals of Mathematics Studies*, Vol. 5, Princeton University Press, Princeton, N.J., 1941.

56. Quine, W. V., "The Problem of Simplifying Truth Functions," *American Mathematical Monthly*, Vol. 59, No. 8, pp. 521–531, 1952.

57. Quine, W. V., "A Way to Simplify Truth Functions," *American Mathematical Monthly*, Vol. 62, No. 9, pp. 627–631, 1955.

58. Raz, N., "Synthesis of Cellular Logic Using A Boolean Analyzer Simulator,"

Department of Electrical Engineering, McGill University, Montreal, Canada, Technical Report.

59. Roth, J. P., "Algebraic Topological Methods for the Synthesis of Switching Systems," *Trans. of the Amer. Math. Soc.*, Vol. 88, No. 2, pp. 301–326, 1958.

60. Roth, J., "Minimization over Boolean Trees," *IBM J. Res. and Develop.*, Vol. 5, pp. 543–558, November 1960.

61. Roth, J. P., "Systematic Design of Automata," 1965 Fall Joint Computer Conf., AFIPS Proc., Vol. 27, Part I, Washington, D.C., Spartan Books, 1965, pp. 1093–1100.

62. Schlaeppi, H. P., "A Journal Language for Describing Modern Logic Timing and Sequencing (LOTIS)," *IEEE Trans. on Computers*, Vol. EC-13, pp. 439–448, August 1964.

63. Shannon, C. E., "A Symbolic Analysis of Relay and Switching Circuits," *Trans. AIEE*, Vol. 57, pp. 713–723, 1938.

64. Svoboda, A., "An Algorithm for Solving Boolean Equations," *Trans. IEEE*, Vol. EC-12, No. 5, pp. 557–558, 1963.

65. Svoboda, A., "Boolean Analyzer," *Proc. of the IFIP Congress* in Edinburgh, Scotland, August 1968. Booklet D, pp. 97–102, North Holland Publ. Co., Amsterdam, 1968.

66. Svoboda, A., "Some Applications of Contact Grids," Proc. of an Intern. Symp. on The Theory of Switching, Part I, pp. 293–305, Harvard Univ. Press, Cambridge, Mass., 1959.

67. Su, Y. H., "Computer Oriented Algorithms for Synthesizing Multiple-Output Combinational and Finite Memory Sequential Circuits," Ph.D. Dissertation, Department of Electrical Engineering, University of Wisconsin, Madison, 1967.

68. Tal, A. A., "The Abstract Synthesis of Sequential Machines from the Answers to Questions of the First Kind in the Questionnaire Language," *Automation and Remote Control*, Vol. 26, No. 4, pp. 676–682, 1965.

69. Tal, A. A., "Questionnaire Language and the Abstract Synthesis of Minimal Sequential Machines," *Automation and Remote Control*, Vol. 25, No. 6, pp. 946–962, 1964.

70. Tan, C. J., Menon, P. R., and Friedman, A. D., "Structural Simplification and Decomposition of Asynchronous Sequential Circuits," *IEEE Trans. on Computers*, September 1969, Vol. C-18, No. 9, pp. 830–838.

71. Tracey, J. H., "Internal State Assignment for Asynchronous Sequential Machines," *IEEE Trans.*, Vol. EC-15, No. 4, pp. 551–560, 1966.

72. Urbano, R. H., and Mueller, R. K., "A Topological Method for the Determination of the Minimal Forms of a Boolean Function," *IRE Trans.*, Vol. EC-5, No. 3, pp. 126–132, 1956.

73. Unger, S. H., *Asynchronous Sequential Switching Circuits*, Wiley-Interscience, New York, 1969.

74. Wernick, W., "Complete Sets of Logical Functions," *Trans. Amer. Math. Soc.*, Vol. 51, pp. 117–132, 1941.

75. Yablonskii, S. V., "Constructions of Functions in k-Valued Logic," (In Russian), Trudy Matem. Inst. V. A. Steklova, No. 51, Ird. Akademii Nank USSR, Moscow, pp. 6–142, 1958.

Arithmetic

Chin Tung

IBM Research Division
San Jose, California

1. INTRODUCTION

This chapter deals with number representations and arithmetic in digital computers. Even though the discussion refers principally to binary number systems, the results are generally applicable to higher-radix systems as well. Because of space limitations, we must omit some important topics (such as error analysis) and some details of the topics discussed. The bibliography at the end of the chapter lists some of the relevant literature in the field.

In Section 2, various number representations are discussed. Representation of negative numbers, binary and other radix representations, conversion of representations from one radix to another, and floating-point and fixed-point representations are of particular interest.

The process of addition can be viewed as composed of two phases: the formulation of sum and of carry. The possibility that a carry may propagate the full length of an adder has been a severe factor limiting the speed of an addition. Section 3 considers various techniques for reducing the length of carry propagation.

Basic product formulation and multiplier coding are the main topics of Section 4 on "Multiplication." Division, usually regarded as the inverse process of multiplication, is discussed in Section 5.

Section 6 introduces unconventional number systems. Residue and signed-digit number systems are discussed. Finally, we comment briefly on the computational time and complexity of basic arithmetic functions made in Section 7.

2. NUMBER REPRESENTATIONS

A number may assume various symbolic representations. In natural languages, the English "three" is definitely different from the French *trois*, even though both represent the same quantity. Mathematically, the same quantity can be expressed as "3" in decimal notation, as "11" in binary notation, and so on. In machine design we are primarily concerned with the expense of implementing a given number representation and with how well arithmetic can be performed with that representation. In particular, our interest is restricted to a number system with finite representation because of the physical limitations of machines. As a result, underflows, overflows, scaling, complementation, precision, significance, and round-off error characterize the machine number system and, consequently, its arithmetic. The following notation is used throughout this chapter:

$+$: Arithmetic addition
$-$: Arithmetic subtraction
or adjacency: Arithmetic multiplication
$/$: Arithmetic division
$^{-}$ (overbar): Additive inverse
$\vee$: Logical OR
$\wedge$: Logical AND
$\veebar$: Logical EXCLUSIVE-OR
$\ulcorner$: Logical NOT (at left or above)

2.1. Symbolic Representations

The relation between the abstract notion of a number and its physical representation can be described briefly as follows: Given a finite set of symbols A, called *digit values*, we can generate by certain rules another finite set B. Usually the members of B assume the form of a finite *n-tuple* $(b_1, b_2, \ldots, b_n)$, called here a *word* where b_i's are members of A. The size, r_i, of a subset of digit values that b_i can assume is defined as the *radix* (or *base*) at position i. If $r_i = r_j$ for all i and j, then B is called a *fixed-radix* number system; otherwise, B is said to be *mixed-radix*. The conventional decimal system is fixed-radix and the British monetary system is mixed-radix. Next we have to associate the members of B with the members of a finite collection of numbers, C. If every member of C has a unique associated image in B, then B is said to be a *nonredundant* and *complete* number system. B is called *redundant* if the members of C have more than one associated image in B. If any member of C has no image in B then B is called an *incomplete* system. The fact that each member of B is an *n*-tuple indicates that a number system is usually *positional*, that is, a given symbol or digit value has different significance when it is placed at different positions [19].

The conventional decimal system is a nonredundant, complete, and positional, number system. For example, "1969" is the only representation for the number "one thousand nine hundred and sixty-nine." Because the system is positional, the digit "1," for example, cannot be positioned at any other place without altering the association between "1969" and "one thousand nine hundred and sixty-nine." In addition, the left "9" has the significance of representing "nine hundred" and the right "9" representing "nine." The set of digit values of the decimal system has ten values: $(0, 1, \ldots, 9)$. If $\bar{1}$ (minus one; $\bar{i}$ means minus i or the additive inverse of i) is allowed to be included in this set, then the system is changed from nonredundant to redundant. A simple example will illustrate this change— "197$\bar{1}$" represents the same number as "1969". That is: $1 \times 10^3 + 9 \times 10^2 + 7 \times 10^1 + \bar{1} \times 10^0 = 1 \times 10^3 + 9 \times 10^2 + 6 \times 10^1 + 9 \times 10^0$.

2.2. Radix

Even though human beings have been used to the decimal system, nearly all computers are internally binary-coded. The popular choice of internal binary coding of digital computers is based on such factors as efficiency of representation and reliability of operation, among others.

An array of n r-state registers has r^n different configurations which, in turn, can represent r^n different numbers (in a nonredundant number system). Physically, what is required for such a representation is $n \cdot r$ entities. As a result, $n \cdot r$ can be defined as a measure of efficiency of this physical representation. From another viewpoint, $n \cdot r$ is also proportional to the cost of implementing this representation. It can be shown that $r = e = 2.71828 \ldots$ is the most efficient radix [83]. For integral values of r, $r = 3$ results in minimum cost. The costs for $r = 2$ and $r = 4$ are slightly greater than the minimum cost for $r = e$ and are equal.

In addition to the fact that the binary radix is the second best candidate, reliability of operation is another important consideration. The ambiguity or fuzziness in detecting a binary element is less than that of a ternary or decimal element; hence, the chance of misinterpreting the states of computing elements during a computation in a binary machine should be lower than that in a nonbinary machine.

Internal binary coding by no means excludes the possibility of using other radixes in computers. To users, some computers may appear octal, decimal, hexadecimal, or other radices. Conversion between radices, is, therefore, the next topic in order.

Assume that a number x with radix r is represented as

$$x_{-m}x_{-m+1} \ldots x_{-1}x_0. \quad x_1 x_2 \ldots x_n$$

with its algebraic value equal to

$$\sum_{i=-m}^{n} x_i r^{-i}$$

denoted by X. The conversion processes for the integer and the fraction parts of a number from radix r_a in the form of X to radix r_b in the form of Y are different; hence, for the integer part:

$$X = \ldots + x_{-3}r_a^3 + x_{-2}r_a^2 + x_{-1}r_a + x_0 \big| r_a$$
$$Y = \ldots + y_{-3}r_b^3 + y_{-2}r_b^2 + y_{-1}r_b + y_0 \big| r_b \tag{2.1}$$

Since the algebraic value, denoted by Z, remains invariant during conversion,

$$X = Y = Z. \tag{2.2}$$

Dividing Z by r_b will yield

$$\frac{Z}{r_b} = \ldots + y_{-3}r_b^2 + y_{-2}r_b + y_{-1} + \frac{y_0}{r_b} \tag{2.3}$$

that is, the remainder after the first division is the least significant digit of Y, y_0. Successive divisions of the integer part of the quotient by r_b will, therefore, generate y_{-1}, y_{-2} .... Each y_i certainly has its value bounded (inclusively) by 0 and $r_b - 1$.

As an example, convert 37 in radix 10 to radix 2 and then to radix 16. Conversion from radix 10 to radix 2.

		Remainder	*New Digit*
2	37	1	y_0
2	18	0	y_{-1}
2	9	1	y_{-2}
2	4	0	y_{-3}
2	2	0	y_{-4}
2	1	1	y_{-5}
	0		

Thus, 37 (radix 10) = 100101 (radix 2).

2. Conversion from radix 10 to radix 16.

		Remainder	*New Digit*
16	37	5	y_0
16	2	2	y_{-1}
	0		

Thus, 37 (radix 10) = 25 (radix 16).

Next for the fraction part:

$$X = x_1 r_a^{-1} + x_2 r_a^{-2} + \ldots$$
$$Y = y_1 r_b^{-1} + y_2 r_b^{-2} + \ldots \tag{2.4}$$
$$X = Y = Z$$

Multiplying Z by r_b will give

$$Z r_b = y_1 + y_2 r_b^{-1} + \ldots \tag{2.5}$$

This says that the integer part of $Z r_b$ is the desired digit y_1. As a result, successive multiplications of the fraction part of the product by r_b will generate y_2, y_3, ...

As an example, convert 0.625 in radix 10 to radix 2 and then to radix 16.

1. Conversion from radix 10 to radix 2:

	Integer Part	New Digit
0.625		
2		
1.250	1	y_1
0.250		
2		
0.500	0	y_2
0.500		
2		
1.000	1	y_3

Thus, 0.625 (radix 10) = 0.101 (radix 2).

2. Conversion from radix 10 to radix 16:

	Integer Part	New Digit
0.625		
16		
A.000	A	y_1

Thus, 0.625 (radix 10) = 0.A (radix 16). (Note that A, B, C, D, E, and F are used to represent 10, 11, 12, 13, 14, and 15 in radix 16 system.) Since the integer conversion process consists of successive divisions of the remaining integer part of the quotient, eventually there will be a zero quotient and the process will terminate. The integer conversion is thus exact. On the other hand, because of successive multiplications of the remaining fraction parts of products which may never be zero, the fraction conversion process may not terminate naturally. As a result, the conversion may not be exact. For instance, 0.5 (radix 10) = 0.11 . . . (radix 3) [83].

2.3. Representation of Negative Numbers

Thus far, we have been dealing implicitly with positive numbers in our discussion. Negative numbers may be represented in either the sign and magnitude form or complement form. The basic idea in *sign and magnitude* representation is as follows: Assume that n bits (2^n different configurations) are enough for representing all the positive numbers to be covered. Then the addition of one bit to the original n bits will double the capacity for representing numbers. As a consequence, the newly acquired capacity can be assigned to represent negative numbers.

With pencil and paper we append a plus or minus sign in front of an un-signed number, that is, the magnitude of the signed number, to make it into a signed number. The default condition (omission of the sign) implies that the number is nonnegative. Within the computer, the sign and mag-nitude convention usually (not necessarily) interprets the leftmost bit as the sign and the remaining bits as the magnitude. Traditionally, 0 is desig-nated as plus and 1 as minus. With this representation, sign and magnitude computations are separate. For instance, $x + (\bar{y})$ where $x < y$, we have to detect signs, evaluate $(y - x)$, and finally append minus sign to the mag-nitude difference.

Alternatively, negative numbers can be represented in *complement* forms. There are two types of complement representation: radix complement and diminished radix complement. The complement representation enjoys the advantage that no sign computation is necessary. For if $\bar{y}$ can be represented by $R - y$ conveniently where R is greater than the largest number y can represent, then

$$x - y = x + \bar{y} = x + (R - y) \text{ Mod } R \tag{2.6}$$

As a result, subtraction can be replaced by a modulo addition.

There are two major factors in choosing R. First, R must be so chosen that modulo R addition can be done easily. Second, given y, finding $(R - y)$ should be simpler than a subtraction. With $(n + 1)$ digits at hand, we can assign the first r^n configurations from $(00 \ldots 00)$ to $[0(r - 1) \ldots (r - 1)]$ to represent numbers from 0 to $r^n - 1$. The last r^n configurations, from $[(r - 1)0 \ldots 0]$ to $[(r - 1) \ldots (r - 1)]$, are available for representing nega-tive numbers. If R is chosen to be $r^{n+1} - 1 = (r - 1)(r - 1) \ldots (r - 1)$, then $R - y$ can be formed by complementing each digit of y with respect to $(r - 1)$, that is, $y_i + (R - y)_i = (r - 1)$. This complementing process is especially simple in the binary system. One simply changes every 1 to 0 and every 0 to 1 in y in order to obtain $R - y$. For modulo $(r^{n+1} - 1)$ addi-tion, the carry out of the most significant digit (leftmost) position assumes a value of r^{n+1}. Thus, whenever there is a carry out of the leftmost digit position, unity should be added to the rightmost digit position to account for the difference between r^{n+1} and $(r^{n+1} - 1)$. With such a choice of R, the representation of numbers is called the *diminished radix complement* repre-sentation. In the binary system it is known as the *1's complement* repre-sentation. Another choice of R is $R = r^{n+1}$. Obviously modulo r^{n+1} addition is simpler, since we can just ignore the carry out of the leftmost digit posi-tion. To find $R - y$ is slightly more complicated than before. To find $R - y$ when $R = r^{n+1}$, first replace y_i with $(r - 1) - y_i$, then add (modulo r^{n+1}) unity to the rightmost digit position. The choice of representing $\bar{y}$ with

$(r^{n+1} - y)$ is called *radix complement* representation in general and is called *2's complement* representation in the binary system.

With $(n + 1)$ bits in the binary system, we can represent numbers ranging from $-(2^{n+1} - 1)$ to $(2^{n+1} - 1)$, inclusively, with representations for plus zero and minus zero in sign and magnitude form and in diminished radix complement form. In radix complement form there is a unique representation of zero; hence, the range extends to $(-2^{n+1}, 2^{n+1} - 1)$, inclusively. As an example, for $n + 1 = 4$, we have the various representations shown in Table 1.

Table 1

Decimal Equivalents	Binary Sign and Magnitude	Binary Radix Complement (2's)	Binary Diminished Radix Complement (1's)
7	0111	0111	0111
6	0110	0110	0110
5	0101	0101	0101
4	0100	0100	0100
3	0011	0011	0011
2	0010	0010	0010
1	0001	0001	0001
0	0000	0000	0000
−0	1000	0000	1111
−1	1001	1111	1110
−2	1010	1110	1101
−3	1011	1101	1100
−4	1100	1100	1011
−5	1101	1011	1010
−6	1110	1010	1001
−7	1111	1001	1000
−8	—	1000	—

One way of finding the algebraic value of a given binary number in complement representation is as follows: Assign to the leftmost bit a weight (-2^n) for 2's complement representation and a weight $(-2^n + 1)$ for 1's complement representation. The remaining bits assume the normal weights. As an example, with $(n + 1) = 4$, 1011 represents -5 in 2's complement form since $(-1 \times 2^3 + 1 \times 2 + 1) = -5$. On the other hand, 1011 represents -4 in 1's complement form, since $(-1 \times 2^3 + 1 + 1 \times 2 + 1) = -4$.

2.4. Fixed-Point and Floating-Point Representations

Number representations are sometimes classified as fixed-point or floating-point. For the *fixed-point* representation, as the name implies, a fictitious radix point is placed at a fixed location, usually either to the left of the most significant digit or to the right of the least significant digit. With such an arrangement the number is always either a fraction or an integer. The main difficulty of fixed-point arithmetic is the limited range implied by such a representation and, hence, the need to scale all the numbers to satisfy this limited range. To overcome this difficulty, floating-point representation is employed.

A *floating-point* number N, defined by the triplet (m, r, e), has the value

$$N = m \times r^e \qquad (2.7)$$

where m, the *mantissa*, may be a signed fraction or integer, r is the radix, and e, the *exponent*, is a signed integer. Notice that the exponent may have a radix different from r. By adjusting r and e, the range of numbers covered is considerably enlarged.

Floating-point representation has some interesting characteristics. *Exponent overflow* is said to occur if the exponent of the result is positive and exceeds the allowable exponent range. Depending on the sign of the mantissa the result may be regarded as a positive or negative infinity. The fact that the exponent is smaller than the allowable range constitutes an *exponent underflow*. In such a case the result may be interpreted as infinitesimal positive or negative, again depending on the sign of the mantissa. The difference of two floating-point numbers with equal mantissas and exponents will produce a result of the form (o, r, e). This is an indeterminate quantity with unknown sign and the significance of the original numbers is lost all at once. The exponent e and the $(n + 1)$ zeros of the mantissa only indicate the order of magnitude; hence, the term "order-of-magnitude zero" is used to designate this singularity.

Precision refers to the number of digits needed during the calculation to retain the desired number of significant digits in the result. To simplify, we have a precision of n digits (bits) plus a sign digit as in the previous examples. In a pencil-and-paper calculation, precision can vary as the situation demands. For the mechanized calculation in a digital computer, such a flexibility does not exist. The designer must, in advance, make a decision on precision which is at best a compromise among the requirements of numerous problems with which the computer is expected to deal. Once a digital computer is designed, the number of digits representing a number is usually fixed. To maximize precision is to maintain as many significant digits as possible. In this respect, floating-point representation is better than fixed-point representation.

Leading zero digits (in radix r) in a floating-point number may be removed by shifting the mantissa to the left and decreasing the exponent accordingly. This process is called *normalization*. Numbers without leading zero digits are called normalized; otherwise, unnormalized. Normalization could also be used to correct overflow after addition by shifting the resultant mantissa to the right until the most significant digit is again in the high-order position and then appropriately increasing the exponent [10].

As an example, one of the IBM System/360 data formats is shown below.

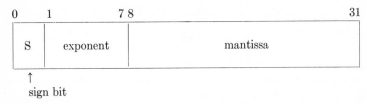

The mantissa is a true fraction expressed in radix 16 digits with the radix point assumed to be immediately to the left of the high-order fraction digit. To provide the proper magnitude for the floating-point number, the fraction is considered to be multiplied by a power of 16. The exponent portion, bits 1–7, indicates this power. The bits within the exponent field can represent numbers from 0 through 127. To accommodate large and small magnitudes, the characteristic is formed by adding 64 to the actual exponent. The range of the exponent is thus -64 through $+63$. This technique produces an exponent in excess 64 notation. Both positive and negative quanties have a true fraction, the difference in sign being indicated by the sign bit. The number is positive or negative accordingly as the sign bit is zero or one.

The range covered by the magnitude (M) of a normalized floating-point number is in short precision $16^{-65} \leq M \leq (1 - 16^{-6}) \times 16^{63}$.

3. ADDITION

3.1. Basic Concepts

The adder is the basic organ in an arithmetic processor. As will be seen later, all other arithmetic operations can be obtained with additions, complementations, and shifts. Therefore, a fast adder is essential to a fast arithmetic processor. In general, a faster adder requires more complicated logical circuitry. As a result, engineering decisions must be made to determine the proper balance between addition time (speed) and circuit complexity (cost). In this section, starting with a description of the basic characteristics of addition, we shall investigate how addition speed can be improved. Let

$$x \equiv \text{operand 1}$$

$$y \equiv \text{operand 2}$$

$$z \equiv \text{incoming carry}$$

$$s \equiv \text{sum}$$

$$c \equiv \text{outgoing carry}$$

The arithmetic relationship characterizing binary addition at digit position (stage) i is given by

$$2c_i + s_i = x_i + y_i + z_i \tag{3.1}$$

The corresponding logical relationship can be expressed as:

$$
\begin{aligned}
c_i &= (x_i \wedge y_i) \vee [z_i \wedge (x_i \veebar y_i)] \\
&= (x_i \wedge y_i) \vee (z_i \wedge x_i \wedge \overline{y_i}) \vee (z_i \wedge \overline{x_i} \wedge y_i) \\
s_i &= z_i \veebar (x_i \veebar y_i) \\
&= (x_i \wedge y_i \wedge z_i) \vee (x_i \wedge \overline{y_i} \wedge \overline{z_i}) \vee (\overline{x_i} \wedge y_i \wedge \overline{z_i}) \\
&\quad \vee (\overline{x_i} \wedge \overline{y_i} \wedge z_i) \\
z_{i-1} &= c_i
\end{aligned} \tag{3.2}
$$

Similarly, binary subtraction can be defined for digit position i. Let

$$x, y \;:\; \text{same as before}$$

$$z \equiv \text{incoming borrow}$$

$$d \equiv \text{difference}$$

$$b \equiv \text{outgoing borrow}$$

then, arithmetically,

$$-2b_i + d_i = x_i - y_i - b_i \tag{3.3}$$

and, logically,

$$
\begin{aligned}
b_i &= (\overline{x_i} \wedge y_i) \vee [z_i \wedge \overline{(x_i \veebar y_i)}] \\
&= (\overline{x_i} \wedge y_i) \vee (z_i \wedge x_i \wedge y_i) \vee (z_i \wedge \overline{x_i} \wedge \overline{y_i}) \\
d_i &= z_i \veebar (x_i \veebar y_i) \\
&= (x_i \wedge y_i \wedge z_i) \vee (x_i \wedge \overline{y_i} \wedge \overline{z_i}) \vee (\overline{x_i} \wedge y_i \wedge \overline{z_i}) \\
&\quad \vee (\overline{x_i} \wedge \overline{y_i} \wedge z_i) \\
z_{i-1} &= b_i
\end{aligned} \tag{3.4}
$$

Although human beings are accustomed to performing addition and subtraction in sign and magnitude form, a mechanized implementation of binary addition/subtraction in complement representations is simpler. Since negative numbers can always be coded in complement forms, subtraction of y from x can always be treated as addition of $(-y)$ to x. We shall, therefore, confine our discussion to addition.

For convenience, let a,b be the magnitudes of x,y. Then

$$x = a \qquad \text{if} \qquad x \text{ is positive}$$

$$x = R - a \qquad \text{if} \qquad x \text{ is negative}$$

Therefore

1. $x = a$ and $y = b$ (3.5)
   $x + y = a + b$ according to (3.2)

2. $x = a$ and $y = R - b$ (or $x = R - a$ and $y = b$)
   Arithmetically $(x + y)$ should yield the same result as $(a - b)$; hence
   $$\begin{aligned} x + y &\equiv R - (b - a) \bmod R \text{ if } a \le b \\ &\equiv \qquad (a - b) \bmod R \text{ if } a > b \end{aligned}$$ (3.6)

3. $x = R - a$ and $y = R - b$
   Arithmetically $(x + y)$ should yield the same result as $(-a - b) = -(a + b)$; hence
   $$x + y \equiv R - (a + b) \bmod R$$ (3.7)

The above analysis insures us that the proper modulo R addition with digit-wise operations defined by (3.2) will yield correct results. Modulo R binary addition in the diminished radix complement is slightly more complicated. Since $R = 2^n - 1$, if there is an outgoing carry from the most significant stage, then the carry should be discarded and unity should be added to the least significant stage. Conventionally, the carry from the most significant stage could be used, in logic design, to trigger the addition of unity at the least significant digit position. Thus, the term "end-around carry" has been used. Radix complement binary addition enjoys the advantage of possessing no end-around carry, yet the formation of $\bar{y}$ from y is more complex than in the diminished radix complement form (as noted previously in Section 2). The formation of $\bar{y}$ from y is necessary in subtraction since $x - y \equiv x + (-y)$.

What has been described thus far in this section applies to fixed-point addition/subtraction. For floating-point addition/subtraction the following procedure is taken: First, the exponents of the two operands are adjusted to equality; usually the smaller exponent is increased while shifting its mantissa to the right. Second, the fixed-point addition/subtraction is performed on the adjusted mantissas. For example: Suppose $N_1 = +0.5749 \times 10^2$, $N_2 = +0.2930 \times 10^1$, then

$$N_1 + N_2 = (0.5749 \times 10^2) + (0.2930 \times 10^1)$$
$$= (0.5749 + 0.0293) \times 10^2$$
$$= 0.6042 \times 10^2$$

The word size (or register size) is usually fixed; hence, overflow is said to occur when the range of the result of an arithmetic operation is inconsistent with the range of numbers assigned in advance by the designer. For example, with the assignment

$$x = x_0 \cdot x_1 \ldots x_n$$
$$y = y_0 \cdot y_1 \ldots y_n$$

in radix complement form

$$-1 \leq x < 1$$
$$-1 \leq y < 1$$

Thus, the sum

$$-2 \leq x + y < 2$$

may lie outside the assigned range.

Overflow occurs during addition only when both operands are of the same sign (and during subtraction only when both operands are of different signs). In sign and magnitude form the carry from the most significant bit position into the sign bit position signals the occurrence of overflow. In either complement form the occurrence of overflow is indicated by the fact that the sign of the sum is different from the sign of the input operands. For floating-point operations the overflow is usually corrected by shifting the result to the right and increasing the exponent accordingly.

3.2.   Schemes for Fast Addition

A review of our previous discussion would suggest that the carry propagation is the bottleneck insofar as addition is concerned. Equation 3.2 indicates that, at any stage, the sum and carry are not only a function of the input digits at that stage but are also a function of input digits to the right of the given stage. In diminished radix complement form, because of the end-around carry, addition can be envisioned as being performed on a circle. Therefore, the input carry to stage i may have been generated at stage $i - 1$. As a simple example, suppose that the inputs are $(0,0)$ at stage i, are $(1,1)$ at stage $i - 1$, and are $(1,0)$ or $(0,1)$ at the remaining stages. The carry generated at stage $i - 1$, according to (3–2), has to propagate left all the way to the most significant stage, then enter at the least significant stage in the form of end-around carry, and finally is absorbed at stage i. A carry generated at stage i and absorbed at stage $i - k$ is said to produce a carry-propagation chain of length k. The length of the carry-propagation chain in the above example is equal to the word length. The carry-propagation situation in sign and magnitude and radix complement additions may seem to be better than in the diminished radix complement addition since there exists no end-around carry. The worst case (i.e., carry generated at the least significant stage and absorbed at the most significant stage), however, still remains the same. During an actual addition, many carry-propagation chains of different lengths arise. Various existing schemes for faster addition have been devised with a common goal of reducing carry-propagation chains. In the remainder of this section we shall describe only the schemes designed for conventional, primarily binary, number systems. Addition schemes for unconventional number systems will be discussed in Section 6.

3.2.1.   *Carry Completion Recognition Carry Logic*

Let the adder length (or word length) be n. If one constructs an adder strictly according to (3.2), he has to allow ample time to accommodate the worst case—a carry propagating through n stages. Most of the time, however, there are a number of carry-propagation chains arising during an addition with lengths less than n. The actual addition time is therefore the time needed for the longest carry-propagation chain plus the time needed for forming the final sum. The time overhead of fixed-time adder designed according to (3.2) is therefore undesirable. Potential saving of addition time, as suggested by the fact that the longest carry-propagation chain is usually much less than n, is very attractive if some means of recognizing carry completion can be provided [24].

If both inputs (x_i, y_i) at stage i are detected to be $(1,1)$, then certainly there will be a carry from stage i to stage $i - 1$. Consequently, the sum and carry of stage $(i - 1)$ can be formed according to (3.2) without further delay, since all inputs are certain and available now. Similarly, if both (x_i, y_i) are $(0,0)$, then certainly there will be no carry from stage i to stage $i - 1$, regardless of what may happen to the right of stage i. For convenience of discussion, let the carry be called 1-carry and no-carry be called 0-carry; hence, $z_i^1(z_i^0)$ will be the incoming 1-carry (0-carry) and $c_i^1(c_i^0)$ the outgoing 1-carry (0-carry). At the time the addition starts, 1- and 0-carries are generated and then they propagate left through those stages whose inputs are either $(0,1)$ or $(1,0)$. Finally, they end up at stages where inputs are either $(0,0)$ or $(1,1)$. The longest propagation-chain determines the addition time. The sum and carry logic equations are defined as:

$$s_i = (x_i \wedge y_i \wedge z_i{}^1) \vee (\overline{x_i} \wedge \overline{y_i} \wedge z_i{}^1)$$
$$\vee (x_i \wedge \overline{y_i} \wedge z_i{}^0) \vee (\overline{x_i} \wedge y_i \wedge z_i{}^0) \qquad (3.8)$$

$$c_i{}^1 = (x_i \wedge y_i) \vee (x_i \wedge \overline{y_i} \wedge z_i{}^1) \vee (\overline{x_i} \wedge y_i \wedge z_i{}^1) \qquad (3.9)$$

$$c_i{}^0 = (\overline{x_i} \wedge \overline{y_i}) \vee (x_i \wedge \overline{y_i} \wedge z_i{}^0) \vee (\overline{x_i} \wedge y_i \wedge z_i{}^0) \qquad (3.10)$$

The carry completion recognition logic is given by

$$cc_i = (z_i{}^1 \wedge \overline{z_i{}^0}) \vee (\overline{z_i{}^1} \wedge z_i{}^0) \qquad (3.11)$$

where cc_i is the carry completion recognition signal of the ith stage. Notice that the carry to stage i can be either 1-carry or 0-carry but not both. The condition that $cc_i = 1$ for all i indicates the end of carry propagation. It has been found that the average length of the longest carry-propagation chain is approximately

$$\log_2 (5n/4) \qquad (3.12)$$

where n is the number of stages in the adder [28, 55]. One of the main characteristics of this adder scheme is that it is self-timing and thus the addition time is variable.

3.2.2. Exclusive-OR Carry Logic

The equations characterizing this logic are the same as in the basic formulation. The difference is in the hardware implementation. Three switches are required per digit position (Figure 1). The first switch is closed if and only if $(x_i \veebar y_i) = 1$. The second switch clamps c_i to the "1" voltage level and is closed if and only if $x_i \wedge y_i = 1$. The third switch clamps c_i to the "0" voltage level and is closed if and only if $\overline{x_i} \wedge \overline{y_i} = 1$. During the quiescent state the first two switches are open and the last one closed. After the application of the input operands, x and y, only one of the three switches will remain closed and the carry will travel along the path of consecutive closed switches where $(x_i \veebar y_i) = 1$. The speed gained in this design results from the fact that the carry propagation chain has only one logical element per stage [31, 32, 59].

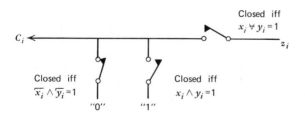

Figure 1.   Exclusive-OR carry logic.

3.2.3.   Simultaneous Carry Logic

In an adder with ripple carry logic, adder delay must be allowed for the worst case, that is, the carry-propagation chain is equal to the adder in length. In a simplified way it could be said that the carry completion recognition scheme allows the adder delay to be whatever the addition actually takes by detecting the end of the longest propagation chain. Simultaneous (look-ahead) carry logic takes a different approach. Equation 3.2 can be rewritten as

$$
\begin{aligned}
c_i &= (x_i \wedge y_i) \vee [z_i \wedge (x_i \veebar y_i)] \\
&= (x_i \wedge y_i) \\
&\quad \vee (x_i \veebar y_i) \wedge (x_{i+1} \wedge y_{i+1}) \\
&\quad \vee (x_i \veebar y_i) \wedge (x_{i+1} \veebar y_{i+1}) \wedge (x_{i+2} \wedge y_{i+2}) \\
&\qquad \vdots \\
&\quad \vee (x_i \veebar y_i) \wedge \ldots \wedge (x_{i+1} \veebar y_{i+1}) \wedge (x_n \wedge y_n) \\
&\quad \vee (x_i \veebar y_i) \wedge \ldots \wedge (x_{n-1} \veebar y_{n-1}) \wedge (x_n \veebar y_n) \wedge z_n
\end{aligned}
\tag{3.13}
$$

Without regard to the *fan-in* and *fan-out* (number of input and output leads, respectively) limitations imposed by the physical switching circuitry, the time required to generate the outgoing carry at any stage i is equal to the time for generating $x_j \veebar y_j$ plus the time for one AND and one OR levels delay. However, this fast scheme may not be feasible in practice. To overcome the fan-in and fan-out limitations, auxiliary functions are defined. With $g_i = (x_i \wedge y_i)$, $p_i = (x_i \veebar y_i)$, and $n = i + 8$, Equation 3.13 is rewritten as

$$
\begin{aligned}
c_i &= g_i \\
&\quad \vee (p_i \wedge g_{i+1}) \\
&\quad \vee (p_i \wedge p_{i+1} \wedge g_{i+2}) \\
&\quad \vee (p_i \wedge p_{i+1} \wedge p_{i+2} \wedge g_{i+3}) \\
&\quad \vee (p_i \wedge p_{i+1} \wedge p_{i+2} \wedge p_{i+3} \wedge g_{i+4}) \\
&\quad \vee (p_i \wedge p_{i+1} \wedge p_{i+2} \wedge p_{i+3} \wedge p_{i+4} \wedge g_{i+5}) \\
&\quad \vee (p_i \wedge p_{i+1} \wedge p_{i+2} \wedge p_{i+3} \wedge p_{i+4} \wedge p_{i+5} \wedge g_{i+6}) \\
&\quad \vee (p_i \wedge p_{i+1} \wedge p_{i+2} \wedge p_{i+3} \wedge p_{i+4} \wedge p_{i+5} \wedge p_{i+6} \wedge g_{i+7}) \\
&\quad \vee (p_i \wedge p_{i+1} \wedge p_{i+2} \wedge p_{i+3} \wedge p_{i+4} \wedge p_{i+5} \wedge p_{i+6} \wedge p_{i+7} \wedge g_{i+8}) \\
&\quad \vee (p_i \wedge p_{i+1} \wedge p_{i+2} \wedge p_{i+3} \wedge p_{i+4} \wedge p_{i+5} \wedge p_{i+6} \wedge p_{i+7} \wedge p_{i+8} \\
&\qquad\qquad \wedge z_{i+8})
\end{aligned}
\tag{3.14}
$$

Equation 3.14 can, in turn, be written as Equation 3.16 with the substitution of

$$P_j = p_j \wedge p_{j+1} \wedge p_{j+2}$$

$$G_j = g_j \vee (p_j \wedge g_{j+1}) \vee (p_j \wedge p_{j+1} \wedge g_{j+2}) \qquad (3.15)$$

$$c_i = G_i$$
$$\vee (P_i \wedge G_{i+3})$$
$$\vee (P_i \wedge P_{i+3} \wedge G_{i+6})$$
$$\vee (P_i \wedge P_{i+3} \wedge P_{i+6} \wedge z_{i+8}) \qquad (3.16)$$

For example, to implement a carry generation function as shown in Equation 3.14, a fan-in of ten is required. Suppose such a requirement cannot be met and a fan-in of four, instead , is provided. Auxiliary functions, P_j and G_j, as defined in (3.15), and c_i in (3.16) apparently do not violate the fan-in condition. Auxiliary functions are used to alleviate the fan-in and fan-out limitations by increasing the logical depth. For larger words more than one level of auxiliary function may have to be developed (in the same manner as the one above) in order to meet the given fan-in and fan-out requirements [43, 76].

3.2.4. Carry Skip Logic

Carry skip logic is also known as *anticipated carry logic*. It is roughly speaking a relaxed form of simultaneous carry logic with ripple carry logic permitted. It is best illustrated with a simple example. As shown in Figure 2 the adder is divided into fixed groups, each of four bits. The incoming carry appearing at the input of the group in which $x_j \vee y_j = 1$ for every stage is transmitted to the next group through a special skip gate. At the same time the carry is also permitted to ripple within the group to allow determination of the various sum bits. The optimal size of equal groups has also been studied. Assume a worst case in which a carry is initiated in the least significant digit and is propagated, but not beyond (as in 2's complement form), the most significant digit. Under this assumption the optimal group size is $\sqrt{n/2}$ where n is the adder length [40]. In general the carry propagation situation is not as bad as the worst case. This fact implies redundancy in the equal group size logic, since the final carry distribution is completed before it may be used. This redundancy may be reduced by increasing the relative size of inner groups in relation to those groups at the extremes. The optimum configuration can be obtained by increasing the group size by one for each group from the two extremes up to the middle. The maximum propagation time ratio of a 60-bit adder composed of 6-bit groups to a 60-bit adder composed of groups with sizes (4, 5, 6, 7, 8, 8, 7, 6, 5, 4) is

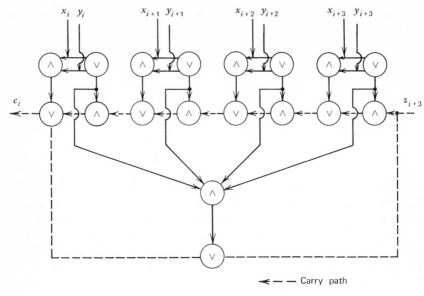

Figure 2.   Carry skip logic.

about 19/15. A further development of the carry skip logic is to provide intra-group and inter-group skip gates [29, 40, 41].

3.2.5.   Carry Storage Logic

Let x and y be the input augend and addend. At each digit position only one half-adder is used. The outputs from the half-adder are the first partial sum s^1 and the first partial carry c^1; they are stored separately in two registers without letting the carry propagate. The first partial sum is equal to the digit-wise exclusive-OR of x and y and the first partial carry is equal to the digit-wise conjunction of x and y, shifted one place to the left. Let s^i and c^i be the ith partial sum and carry. The above process is repeated.

$$s^{i+1} = (s^i \veebar c^i)$$
$$c^{i+1} = 2(s^i \wedge c^i)$$

(3.17)

The recursive process stops when the partial carry is identically zero. In the worst case, n steps may be required for adding two n-digit numbers [11].

A variation of the carry storage concept gives rise to a scheme known as *carry-save adder* (CSA). A CSA, employing full adders at all digit positions, adds two or more operands. A simple example is used to illustrate this scheme. Suppose we want to obtain the sum of u, v, x, and y with four bits

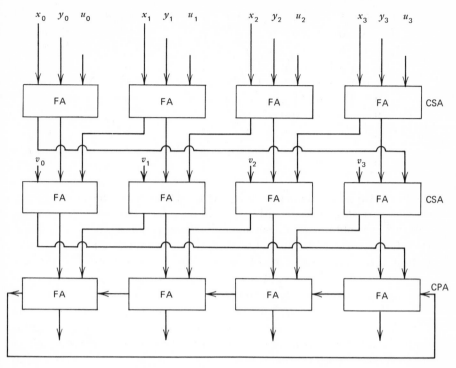

Figure 3. Carry-save adder. FA, full adder.

each, 1's complement form being used for representing negative numbers. A CSA structure for this purpose is shown in Figure 3. In the first two levels, designated by CSA, each FA accepts three inputs and generates two outputs, partial sum, and carry. The partial carry is not allowed to propagate but is fed to the stage at its left as an input. The partial carry from the leftmost stage is fed into the least significant stage. The last level of CSA has two outputs and there are no more new operands to be summed; then these two operands can be added together with any scheme. Shown in Figure 3 is a CPA (carry-ripple-adder) for summing the last partial sum and carry [43, 75]. The application of CSA will be further demonstrated in Section 4.

3.2.6. Conditional Sum Logic

The conditional sum scheme is somewhat different in concept from the previous approaches. Its design is based on the computation of "conditional" sums and carries that result from the assumption of all possible carry distributions. The basic rationale is illustrated with a simple example.

i	0	1	2	3	4	5	6	7	Assumed Incoming Carry	Time Interval
x_i	0	0	1	0	0	0	1	0		
y_i	1	0	1	1	0	0	0	1		

	stages 0–7	Assumed Incoming Carry	Time Interval
	0 1 0 0 1 0 0 1 0 0 0 0 0 1 0 1	0	1
	1 0 0 1 1 1 1 0 0 1 0 1 1 0 1 0	1	
	0 1 0 1 0 1 0 0 0 0 1 1	0	2
	0 1 1 1 1 0 0 0 1	1	
	0 1 1 0 1 0 0 0 1 1	0	3
	0 1 1 1 0 1	1	
	0 1 1 0 1 0 0 1 1	0	4

We have two 8-bit numbers x and y. At level one we assume the incoming carry at any stage may be either 0 or 1. Therefore, two sets of the carries and sums are obtained for each stage. For example, at stage 6, $x_6 = 1$ and $y_6 = 0$; the carry and sum will be (0,1) if the incoming carry is 0 and will be (1,0) if the incoming carry is 1. Since the incoming carry to the rightmost stage should be known in advance, the second row at stage 7 in level 1 is actually redundant. At the second level, we examine the carries between a pair of digits. For example, between the pair of stage 2 and stage 3, the carry (into stage 2) is still not determined; hence, the carry-sum configuration of stage 2 at this level may be either (1,0) or (1,1). For the pair of stages 6 and 7, the situation is different. Since stage 7 has a zero incoming carry, stages 6 and 7 will yield sum bits (1,1) with a carry 0 into stage 5. The carry into stage 4 is 0 in both cases; hence, stage 4 will give rise to a single carry-sum configuration (0,0). This process of carry selection continues for quartets, octets, and the like. The number of levels, that is, the number of steps of this process, are no greater than

$$1 + \overline{\log_2 n} \tag{3.18}$$

where n is the adder length and $\overline{x}$ is the smallest integer greater than x.

3.3. Summary

Each scheme discussed above has its own merits and drawbacks. It is likely that an optimum design will employ certain combinations of more than one of the schemes described. In general, it is rather difficult to make a fair comparison among all the schemes because there is no set of evaluation criteria commonly agreed upon. However, some interesting comparisons, valid under certain conditions, have been made; they are contained in the literature [17, 37, 40, 62].

4. MULTIPLICATION

4.1. Basic Concepts

Given the multiplicand, $x = x_0 \cdot x_1 \ldots x_n$, the multiplier, $y = y_0 \cdot y_1 \ldots y_n$, and their algebraic values X and Y, respectively, the fundamental scheme of multiplication in a digital computer is described by the following recursive relation:

$$P^{(j+1)} = (1/r)(P^{(j)} + y_{n-j}X) \tag{4.1}$$

where $P^{(j)}$ is the jth partial product, $P^{(0)} = 0$, $j = 0, 1, \ldots, n - 1$ for a positive multiplier, and r the radix. Repeated use of (4.1) results in

$$P^{(n)} = (\sum_{i=1}^{n} r^{-i}y_i)X \tag{4.2}$$

where $P^{(n)}$ is the desired product $P = XY$ if Y is positive (with $y_0 = 0$). Terminal corrections are needed if Y may be of either sign:

1. *Sign and magnitude.* $P^{(n)}$ is equal to the absolute value of the desired product P, that is, $P^{(n)} = |P|$. The rule for determining the sign of the final product is the same as the usual rule governing the multiplication with pencil and paper. That is, the sign of the final product is positive if the signs of X and Y agree; negative, otherwise.

2. *Radix complement.* As previously shown in Section 2.3, the algebraic value of y in radix complement form is

$$Y = -y_0 + \sum_{i=1}^{n} y_i r^{-i} \tag{4.3}$$

Consequently

$$P^{(n)} = X(\sum_{i=1}^{n} y_i r^{-i}) = (Y + y_0)X = P + y_0 X$$

$$P = P^{(n)} - y_0 X \tag{4.4}$$

A terminal subtraction, as indicated by (4.4), is necessary to obtain the desired product.

3. *Diminished radix complement.* In diminished radix complement form the algebraic value of y is

$$Y = -y_0 + \sum_{i=1}^{n} y_i r^{-i} + y_0 r^{-n} \tag{4.5}$$

Consequently

$$P^{(n)} = X(\sum_{i=1}^{n} y_i r^{-i}) = (Y + y_0 - y_0 r^{-n})X$$

$$= P + Xy_0 - y_0 r^{-n}X$$

$$P = P^{(n)} - Xy_0 + y_0 r^{-n}X \qquad (4.6)$$

The terminal correction in (4.6) can be carried out by setting $P^{(0)} = y_0 X$ at the beginning of the recursive process and subtracting $y_0 X$ at the end.

An example of the radix complement multiplication is:

$$X = \frac{9}{16}, \qquad x = 0.1001$$

$$Y = -\frac{7}{16}, \qquad y = 1.1001$$

$$P = XY = \frac{-63}{256}$$

$P^{(0)} =$ 00.00000000	$y_4 = 1$
$+) \; y_4 X =$ 00.10010000	
00.10010000	
$P^{(1)} =$ 00.01001000	$y_3 = 0$
$P^{(2)} =$ 00.00100100	$y_2 = 0$
$P^{(3)} =$ 00.00010010	$y_1 = 1$
$+) \; y_1 X =$ 00.10010000	
00.10100010	
$P^{(4)} =$ 00.01010001	$y_0 = 1$
$+) -y_0 X =$ 11.01110000	
$P =$ 11.11000001	

4.2. Multiplier Coding

Equation 4.1 exhibits multiplication as a repetitive addition. With an adder of given speed there exists, in general, two ways of improving the speed of multiplication: coding the multiplier to reduce the number of additions required, or saving the carry temporarily. These two approaches are not exclusive, but rather complement each other.

According to Equation 4.1 multiplication consists of n additions and n one-digit right shifts. Recognizing the fact that when y_{n-j} is 0 only a shift is required would reduce the number of additions to $n/2$ in the average. In other words, there are on the average two shifts between two consecutive additions. A technique of coding the multiplier into a signed digit form such that the average number of additions is smaller than $n/2$ has been developed [19, 43]. The basic rationale is

$$2^{k+n+1} - 2^k = 2^{k+n} + 2^{k+n-1} + \ldots + 2^k$$

$$\underbrace{100 \ldots 0\bar{1}}_{n+2} = \underbrace{0111 \ldots 1}_{n+2} \tag{4.6}$$

This identity indicates the possibility of replacing a sequence of add and shift operations in a multiplication by subtraction, multiple shifts, and addition. Coding may be performed sequentially starting from either the low-order or the high-order digit positions. The following table defines the rules of coding a conventional binary multiplier (y) into a canonical signed digit multiplier (y') starting from the low-order end. Again, z_i is the incoming carry and c_i the outgoing carry of stage i.

y_{i-1}	y_i	z_i	y_i'	c_i	
0	0	0	0	0	
1	0	0	0	0	
0	1	0	1	0	
1	1	0	$\bar{1}$	1	with $z_n = 0$
0	0	1	1	0	
1	0	1	$\bar{1}$	1	
0	1	1	0	1	
1	1	1	0	1	

These rules can also be stated in the following manner:

$$
\begin{aligned}
z_n &= 0 \\
c_i &= 1 \quad \text{if} \quad (z_i + y_i + y_{i-1}) \geq 2 \\
&= 0 \quad \text{if} \quad (z_i + y_i + y_{i-1}) < 2 \\
y_i' &= y_i + z_i - 2c_i
\end{aligned} \tag{4.7}
$$

For example,

Conventional	0.001010111
Coded Canonical	$0.010\bar{1}0\bar{1}00\bar{1}$

The rules given above produce a canonical signed digit coding with the property that every pair of nonzero digits is separated by at least one zero. Therefore, the average number of zeros in between two consecutive nonzero digits, is, assuming the probability of a zero digit is one-half,

$$\sum_{i=1}^{\infty} i \cdot \left(\frac{1}{2}\right)^{i} = 2 \tag{4.8}$$

where i is the length of a string of zeros in between two nonzero digits and $(1/2)^{i}$ is the associated probability. Thus, the average number of shifts between two add/subtract operations is three and the average number of add/subtracts is $n/3$ if all possible shifts are provided. If only single and double shifts are available the average number of shifts is reduced to $1\frac{3}{4}$. Suppose all shifts are two digits in length; this is essentially radix four arithmetic. The multiplicand and two times multiplicand must be available. The average number of add/subtracts is still $n/3$ and the average number of shifts is, of course, $n/2$. Other variations are possible. Some schemes are summarized on page 166 of Reference 19.

There is another well-known multiplier coding scheme in conjunction with uniform shifts. Let us take uniform shift of 2, for example. The general rules are defined below [43]:

Multiplier	Operation	Multiplier	Operation
0 − 00	+0	1 − 00	−4 + 0 = −4
0 − 01	+2	1 − 01	−4 + 2 = −2
0 − 10	+2	1 − 10	−4 + 2 = −2
0 − 11	+4	1 − 11	−4 + 4 = 0

From the above it is seen that both two times and four times the multiplicand are needed. Coding can start from either the high- or the low-order end. When the least-significant bit is a one, special handling is required. Usually, the complement of the multiplicand is added either at the beginning or at the end of the normal operation, depending on whether coding is done from the low or high order end.

4.3.   Multiplication Employing Carry-Save Adders

Multiplier coding aims at reducing the number of add/subtract operations and consequently increasing the number of shifts in between two consecutive add/subtract operations. The next problem in improving the speed of multiplication is how to perform the summation of multiple operands efficiently. Equation 4.2

$$P^{(n)} = (\sum_{i=1}^{n} y_{i}r^{i})X \tag{4.2}$$

shows that multiplication is essentially a summation of many multiples of multiplicands which are uniquely determined by the bit pattern of the multiplier. In light of this observation, an interesting multiplication scheme employing a coded multiplier and carry-save adders (CSA) operating in conjunction with the pipelining concept has been developed.

Assume that

$$n = mk \quad \text{and} \quad k = 2h \tag{4.9}$$

where n is the word length and m, k, h are all positive integers. Equation 4.2 is rewritten as

$$P^{(n)} = \sum_{i=1}^{k} y_i X r^i + \sum_{i=k+1}^{2k} y_i X r^i + \ldots + \sum_{i=n-k+1}^{n} y_i X r^i \tag{4.10}$$

Furthermore, define

$$PP^{(0)} = 0$$

$$PP^{(1)} = \sum_{i=1}^{k} y_i X r^i$$

$$PP^{(2)} = PP^{(1)} + \sum_{i=k+1}^{2k} y_i X r^i$$

$$\vdots$$

$$PP^{(j)} = PP^{(j-1)} + \sum_{i=(j-1)k+1}^{jk} y_i X r^i \tag{4.11}$$

$$\vdots$$

$$PP^{(n)} = PP^{(m-1)} + \sum_{n-k+1}^{n} y_i X r^i = P^{(n)}$$

where $PP^{(j)}$ stands for the jth partial product. The above equation defines a process with two phases. Phase one is the evaluation of

$$\sum_{i=(j-1)k+1}^{jk} y_i X r^i$$

and phase two is the recursive operation of accumulating what has been newly obtained with the partial product $PP^{(j-1)}$. In phase one, coding the $k(=2h)$ multiplier bits will yield h multiples of the multiplicands $(0, \pm 2X, \pm 4X)$. These multiples can be summed into two operands with a CSA net like the one shown in Figure 3 (without the CPA). These two operands can then be added to the previous partial product to obtain a new partial product. Since there is no feedback loop involved in the above CSA net,

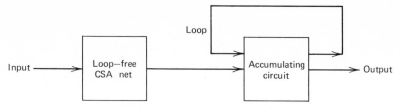

Figure 4.   Abstract diagram of pipelined multiplication.

two consecutive groups of h multiples of the multiplicand need to be separated by only one logical level, thus constituting a *pipeline*. The only requirement is that when the two operands representing the sum of the jth group of h multiples come out of the CSA net, the previous partial product should be already available for accumulation. If this ideal state cannot be attained, an artificial delay may have to be inserted. The above scheme is diagrammed in Figure 4. The accumulating circuit usually also uses CSA's. If so, after m interations the product XY is in the form of two operands which can then be fed into a conventional adder. The above discussion reveals only the basic rationale of this scheme; the actual implementation may require considerable modifications [2, 43, 75].

5.   DIVISION

5.1.   Basic Concepts

Without loss of generality it will be assumed that both the dividend and the divisor are positive fractions with the divisor normalized in order to simplify the discussion. Division is an inverse process of multiplication; hence, it consists essentially of a sequence of subtractions and shifts. The recursive relationship is described by

$$x^{(j+1)} = rx^{(j)} - q_{j+1}d \qquad (5.1)$$

where

j = the recursive index ($j = 0,1, \ldots , n - 1$)

r = the radix

$x^{(0)}$ = dividend

$rx^{(j)}$ = partial dividend at the jth step

$x^{(j+1)}$ = partial remainder after the jth step

$x^{(n)}$ = the final remainder

d = the divisor

q_j = the jth quotient digit

It is necessary that q_j be so selected that $d > x^{(j+1)} \geq 0$. It follows that $q_{j+1} = 0,1, \ldots, r - 1$ if $x^{(0)} < d$. Implicitly, the condition, $x^{(0)} < d$, is assumed, since the given dividend and divisor can be shifted appropriately to satisfy the condition. Examination of the recursive relationship reveals that it consists of the selection of q_{j+1}, the formation of $q_{j+1}d$, the shift of $x^{(j)}$ to form $rx^{(j)}$, and then the subtraction. The selection of q_{j+1} is clearly the most difficult step in division. Efforts to improve division speed are essentially efforts to find the appropriate values of q_{j+1} in a fast and convenient way.

5.2. Restoring Division

The scheme conventionally known as restoring division will now be described briefly for the case $r = 2$. Since $q_{j+1} = 0,1$, we always choose the quotient digit equal to one and perform

$$x'^{(j+1)} = 2x^{(j)} - d \tag{5.2}$$

to obtain the tentative partial remainder $x'^{(j+1)}$. If $x'^{(j+1)}$ is nonnegative, then our choice $q_{j+1} = 1$ was correct. Otherwise, the restoration step is initiated,

$$x^{(j+1)} = x'^{(j+1)} + d \tag{5.3}$$

and the correct q_{j+1} is 0. Thus, binary restoring division, to obtain n-digit quotient, requires n subtractions, n left shifts (by 1 bit), and $n/2$ (on the average) additions. The above description is diagrammed in Figure 5. Even though this method is straightforward and easy to understand, it is evident that we pay a heavy penalty in restoration steps because of our brute-force choice of $q_{j+1} = 1$ at the beginning of each iteration [17, 19].

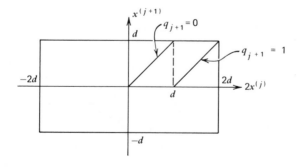

Figure 5.   Restoring division.

5.3. Nonrestoring Division

Intuition suggests that one might improve the restoring division by removing the restoration process. This implies that, at every recursive step, the quotient digit chosen must be legal in the sense that, even though it is not the "best" choice, the error incurred is remediable and the remedy does not consume extra add/subtracts. To achieve this we have to relax the restriction $x^{(i+1)} < d$, to $\left| x^{(i+1)} \right| < d$, and then, in the binary case, q_{j+1} is either $+1$ or -1. Therefore, at each step, the divisor is either added to or subtracted from the partial dividend. The divisor is subtracted when $2x^{(i)} > 0$ and added when $2x^{(i)} < 0$. The process may be terminated if $2x^{(i)} = 0$. The resultant quotient is expressed in a signed-digit form and conversion to conventional form is needed if the environment demands it. Thus, nonrestoring binary division requires n additions/subtractions, n single-digit left shifts, and precise sign determination. Consider the division of $d/3$ by d, for example (Figure 6). If $x^{(0)} = (1/3)d$ then $2x^{(0)} = (2/3)d$, $q_1 = 1$ and $x^{(1)} = (-1/3)d$. For the second step, $2x^{(1)} = (-2/3)d$, $q_2 = -1$, and $x^{(2)} = (1/3)d$. This continues for $j = 3, \ldots, n - 1$ [19].

Both schemes, restoring and nonrestoring, can easily be generalized for fixed radix number systems with $r > 2$. For restoring division

$$x^{(i+1)} = rx^{(i)} - q_{j+1}d \qquad j = 0,1, \ldots, n-1 \qquad (5.4)$$

where

$$0 \leq x^{(i+1)} < d, \, x^{(0)} < d \qquad \text{and} \qquad q_{j+1} = 0,1, \ldots, r - 1$$

For nonrestoring division

$$x^{(i+1)} = rx^{(i)} - q_{j+1}d \qquad j = 0,1, \ldots, n - 1 \qquad (5.5)$$

where

$$\left| x^{i+1} \right| < d, \, x^{(0)} < d \qquad \text{and} \qquad q_{j+1} = -r + 1, \ldots, -1, +1, \ldots, r - 1$$

Figure 7 depicts nonrestoring division for $r = 4$.

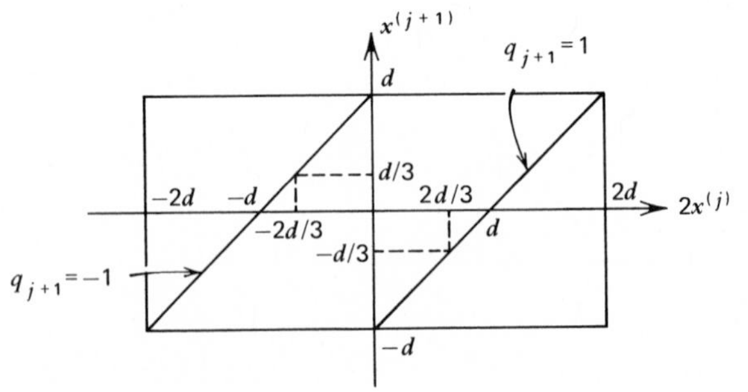

Figure 6.   Binary non-restoring division.

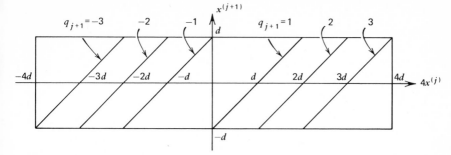

Figure 7. Radix 4 nonrestoring division.

5.4. S-R-T Division

In nonrestoring division 0 is not a legal quotient. A quotient digit equal to 0 means that, for this particular step, no subtraction or addition is involved, only a shift is needed. In actual implementation, addition/subtraction is a more time-consuming operation than shifting. The failure to utilize this potential advantage in nonrestoring division due to the exclusion of 0 from the legal quotient digit set is undesirable. Again, let us restrict ourselves to the binary case. Figure 8 shows, in contrast to Figure 6, the recursive relationship in a nonrestoring division scheme where 0 is a legal member of the quotient digit set. The rules for selecting q_{j+1} are:

$$\text{If } d \leq 2x^{(i)} \qquad \text{then} \qquad q_{j+1} = 1$$
$$\text{If } -d \leq 2x^{(i)} < d \qquad \text{then} \qquad q_{j+1} = 0 \qquad (5.6)$$
$$\text{If } 2x^{(i)} < -d \qquad \text{then} \qquad q_{j+1} = -1$$

where $\frac{1}{2} \leq d < 1$ as assumed before. The difficulty with this set of rules is that we need full comparison of $2x^{(i)}$ with d or $-d$. Consider then the following alternate set of rules. If

$$\frac{1}{2} \leq 2x^{(i)} \qquad \text{then} \qquad q_{j+1} = 1$$
$$-\frac{1}{2} \leq 2x^{(i)} < \frac{1}{2} \qquad \text{then} \qquad q_{j+1} = 0 \qquad (5.7)$$
$$2x^{(i)} < -\frac{1}{2} \qquad \text{then} \qquad q_{j+1} = -1$$

This set of rules defines the S-R-T division (see Figure 9). (The S-R-T-method was proposed independently by *S*weeney, *R*obertson, and *T*ocher [43, 58, 72].) Here the comparison is made against a constant $\frac{1}{2}$; this process is very simple in the binary case. It has the effect of normalizing the partial remainder by shifting over leading zeros if the partial remainder is positive and leading ones if the partial remainder is negative. The quotient digits of

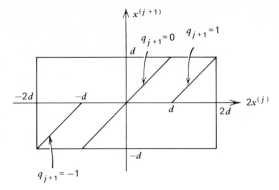

Figure 8. Binary nonrestoring division with 0 as a legal quotient digit.

the S-R-T method will be in a signed digit form. An example [19] is given in Table 2. Since d has a range to vary, the efficiency of the S-R-T method will depend on the magnitude of the normalized divisor. For example, if $d = \frac{1}{2}$ the shift average is 2. The overall shift length is about 2.60 [18, 19].

Table 2

<table>
<tr><td colspan="4" align="center">d = 0.1101
At step α, $2x^{(j)}$ = 0.000110</td></tr>
<tr><td>j</td><td>$2x^{(j)}$</td><td>q_{j+1}</td><td>Operation</td></tr>
<tr><td></td><td>0.000110</td><td>0</td><td>Shift</td></tr>
<tr><td>$\alpha + 1$</td><td>0.001100</td><td>0</td><td>Shift</td></tr>
<tr><td>$\alpha + 2$</td><td>0.011000</td><td>0</td><td>Shift</td></tr>
<tr><td>$\alpha + 3$</td><td>0.110000</td><td>1</td><td>Shift, subtract d</td></tr>
<tr><td>$\alpha + 4$</td><td>1.111000</td><td>0</td><td>Shift</td></tr>
<tr><td>$\alpha + 5$</td><td>1.110000</td><td>0</td><td>Shift</td></tr>
<tr><td>$\alpha + 6$</td><td>1.100000</td><td>0</td><td>Shift</td></tr>
<tr><td>$\alpha + 7$</td><td>1.000000</td><td>−1</td><td>Shift, add d</td></tr>
<tr><td>$\alpha + 7$</td><td>1.101000</td><td>0</td><td>Shift</td></tr>
<tr><td>$\alpha + 8$</td><td>1.010000</td><td>−1</td><td>Shift, add d</td></tr>
<tr><td>$\alpha + 9$</td><td>0.001000</td><td>0</td><td>Shift</td></tr>
</table>

5.5. Higher-Radix Division

With respect to division, higher radix number systems have the potential advantage that the number of iterations of operation (5.1) and consequently the execution time are decreased as the radix is increased. However,

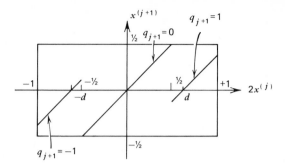

Figure 9. Binary S-R-T division.

more difficulties are encountered in forming the multiples of the divisors and in selecting an appropriate quotient digit than in the binary system. For example, obtaining $3d$ is more awkward than obtaining d or $2d$. The comparison process will not be as simple as it is with the binary S-R-T method. As a rule of thumb, in a higher-radix number system the number of multiples of divisor should be kept small and full length comparison of the partial dividend needed in selecting quotient digits should be avoided. Excellent treatment of this topic can be found in References 5 and 57.

5.6. Division by Convergence

The divisor and dividend can be considered the denominator and numerator of a fraction. On each iteration both numerator and denominator are multiplied by a factor, R_k, so that the resultant denominator converges quadratically toward unity and the resultant numerator converges quadratically toward the desired quotient.

$$\frac{N_0}{D_0} \cdot \frac{R_0}{R_0} \cdot \frac{R_1}{R_1} \cdots \cdot \frac{R_n}{R_n} \text{ and } N_0 R_0 R_1 \ldots R_n \Rightarrow \text{Quotient}$$

when

$$D_0 R_0 R_1 \ldots R_n \Rightarrow 1 \tag{5.7}$$

where N_0 is the dividend and D_0 the divisor (assumed positive and normalized).

The selection of R_i is the crucial part of this method. The divisor can be expressed as

$$D = 1 - \delta \tag{5.8}$$

with $0 < \delta \leq (r - 1)/r$ since D is normalized. If we select

$$R_0 = 1 + \delta \tag{5.9}$$

then

$$D_1 = DR_0 = (1 - \delta)(1 + \delta) = 1 - \delta^2 \tag{5.10}$$

Clearly, $1 - \delta^2$ is closer to unity than $1 - \delta$. Furthermore, we select

$$R_1 = 1 + \delta^2 \tag{5.11}$$

$$D_2 = D_1 R_1 = (1 - \delta^2)(1 + \delta^2) = 1 - \delta^4 \tag{5.12}$$

In general

$$R_i = 1 + \delta^{2^i}, \qquad D_i = D_{i-1} R_{i-1} = 1 - \delta^{2^i}$$

and

$$D_i < D_{i+1} \qquad \text{since} \qquad \delta^{2^i} > \delta^{2^{(i+1)}}$$

Notice that R_i is formed by taking the radix complement (2's complement) of D_i, since

$$D_i + R_i = 1 + \delta^{2^i} + 1 - \delta^{2^i} = 2 \tag{5.13}$$

The simplicity of obtaining R_i from D_i is a key merit of the method. This process will converge and the division iteration terminates when D_{i+1} is no longer greater than D_i because of the given precision of a machine.

The faster the convergence (hence the smaller the δ) the better this method will be. Consequently, this method will be more appreciated in a binary number system. However, the advantages of the method can be retained in a higher-radix system if we allow the divisor to be normalized with respect to bits. A fast multiplication scheme is very important to the success of this method, since this method essentially consists of a series of multiplications [2].

5.7. Deterministic Generation of Quotient Digits

There also exists another class of division processes characterized by the deterministic generation of quotient digits. The principle of this approach to division is to bring the divisor into a specified range so that the quotient digit at each iteration is always the most significant digit, plus a constant, of the partial remainder in consideration [34, 35, 52, 67, 73].

Assume that the divisor is a positive number. At each iteration

$$x^{(j+1)} = rx^{(j)} - q_{j+1}d \tag{5.1}$$

where $\left| x^{(j+1)} \right| < d$ if q_{j+1} is a correct choice. This constraint can be put in a different form

$$(rx^{(j)} - q_{j+1}d) < d \tag{5.14}$$

or

$$(q_{j+1}d - rx^{(i)}) < d$$

That is

$$\left(\frac{rx^{(i)}}{q_{j+1} + 1}\right) < d < \left(\frac{rx^{(i)}}{q_{j+1} - 1}\right) \qquad (5.15)$$

If it is desired that $q_{j+1} = x^{(j)}_{j+1}$ then

$$\left(\frac{rx^{(i)}}{x^{(j)}_{j+1} + 1}\right)_{\max} < d < \left(\frac{rx^{(i)}}{x^{(j)}_{j+1} - 1}\right)_{\min} \qquad (5.16)$$

which states that d must therefore lie in the range bounded by the maximum value of $rx^{(i)}/(q_{j+1} + 1)$ at one end and the minimum value of $rx^{(i)}/(q_{j+1} - 1)$ at the other. Furthermore

$$\left(\frac{rx^{(i)}}{x^{(j)}_{j+1} + 1}\right)_{\max} = 1 \text{ approximately} \qquad (5.17)$$

and

$$\left(\frac{rx^{(i)}}{x^{(j)}_{j+1} - 1}\right)_{\min} = \frac{r - 1}{r - 2}, \qquad (5.18)$$

hence

$$1 \le d < (r - 1)/(r - 2) \qquad (5.19)$$

or

$$d = 1 + e \qquad \text{where} \qquad 0 \le e < 1/(r - 2) \qquad (5.20)$$

As a result, once the divisor is brought into the range specified by Equation 5.20, there is no need for comparison in selecting a correct quotient digit. We shall illustrate this characteristic by presenting an algorithm based on Reference 67. Assume that d is in the range; then the rest of the division algorithm is described as follows.

1. $j = 0$.
2. $x^{(i+1)} = x^{(i)} - r^{-(i+1)} \cdot x_{j+1}^{(i)} \cdot e$.
3. If $x_{j+1}^{(i+1)} = x_{j+1}^{(i)}$ go to (5); otherwise go to (4).
4. $x^{(i+1)} = \text{sgn}(x_{j+1}^{(i)}) \cdot r^{-(i+1)} \cdot e + x^{(i+1)}$.
5. If $j = n - 1$ go to (7); otherwise go to (6).
6. $j = j + 1$; go to (2).
7. Stop.

r: the radix; $x^{(j)}$: the jth partial remainder; $\text{sgn}(x_j) = x_j/|x_j|$.

Notice that the recursive step 2 is different from Equation 5.1 but they are arithmetically equivalent.

At the end of n iterations, the left n digits of $x^{(n)}$ are those that have been used as if they were quotient digits, denoted as q, and the rest of $x^{(n)}$, denoted as y, may be considered the remainder. The arithmetic relation characterizing the above algorithm is

$$x^{(n)} = x^{(0)} - qe = q + y$$

or

$$x^{(0)} = q(1 + e) + y = qd + y \qquad (5.21)$$

Thus the above computation is verified to be a division. An example with $r = 10$ is given in Table 3. Observe that the above example shows that the division is done in a "restoring" manner as steps 2 and 3 reveal. In fact, it can be done in a "nonrestoring" manner [67] by employing complement forms for subtraction and by detecting carry (borrow) which changes the value of $x_{j+1}^{(j)}$. The "restoring" manner description is used here solely for the sake of easier understanding.

Table 3

Radix 10
Dividend: 0.6542
Divisor: 1.0400

0.6 5 4 2 0 0 0 0	
$-$) 0.0 2 4 0 0 0 0 0	$6 \times e \times 10^{-1} \ldots 6$
0.6 3 0 2 0 0 0 0	
$-$) 0.0 0 1 2 0 0 0 0	$3 \times e \times 10^{-2}$
0.6 2*9 0 0 0 0 0	$3 - 1 = 2$
$+$) 0.0 0 0 0 4 0 0 0 0	$1 \times e \times 10^{-2}$
0.6 2 9 4 0 0 0 0	
$-$) 0.0 0 0 0 3 6 0 0 0	$9 \times e \times 10^{-3} \ldots 9$
0.6 2 9 0 4 0 0 0	
$-$) 0.0 0 0 0 0 0 0 0 0	$0 \times e \times 10^{-4} \ldots 0$
0.6 2 9 0 4 0 0 0	

$$0.6542/1.0400 = 0.6290 + 0.4000 \times 10^{-4}$$

* 3 is changed to 2.

6.   UNCONVENTIONAL NUMBER SYSTEMS AND ARITHMETICS

6.1.   Residue Number System

In this section, we consider two unconventional number systems: the residue number system and the signed-digit (S-D) number system. The residue number system is most easily understood in terms of linear congruencies.

The *congruence* relationship is given by

$$A \equiv a \text{ Mod } m \tag{6.1}$$

which reads, A is congruent to a modulo m. The congruence implies

$$A = a + mt \tag{6.2}$$

where A, a, t, and m are integers; a is called the *residue* and m the *modulus* or *base* of the number A. Of particular importance is the *least positive residue*, that is, $0 \leq a < m$. For convenience the term residue will refer to the least positive residue unless otherwise specified and a shorthand notation will be used for designating residues.

$$\left| A \right|_m = a \tag{6.3}$$

For example, $10 \equiv 1 \text{ Mod } 3$, or $\left| 10 \right|_3 = 1$. Given

$$\left| A_1 \right|_m = a_1, \ \ldots, \ \left| A_n \right|_m = a_m$$

then

$$\left| \sum_{i=1}^{n} A_i \right|_m = \left| \sum_{i=1}^{n} a_i \right|_m \tag{6.4}$$

and

$$\left| \prod_{i=1}^{n} A_i \right|_m = \left| \prod_{i=1}^{n} a_i \right|_m \tag{6.5}$$

A residue number representation associated with a natural number is formed from the residues of this given number with respect to a set of moduli. With n moduli, $(m_1, \ \ldots, \ m_n)$, relatively prime to each other, we have $\prod_{i=0}^{n} m_i$ unique n-tuples for presenting $\prod_{i=0}^{n} m_i$ unique numbers. One possible rule of representing a given natural number A in the residue form $a = (a_1, \ \ldots, \ a_n)$ with a set of moduli, $m = (m_1, \ \ldots, \ m_n)$ is

$$a_i = \left| A \right|_{m_i}$$

For example, with $m = (m_1, m_2) = (2,3)$ we have six doublets for representing numbers from 0 to 5. Since

$$\left| 4 \right|_2 = 0 \qquad \text{and} \qquad \left| 4 \right|_3 = 1$$

$$4 \leftrightarrow (0,1)$$

Employing the basic properties outlined by (6.4) and (6.5), we briefly state the rules of residue addition and multiplication as follows: Given two natural numbers, A and B, we designate its sum with S and product with P. $m = (m_1, \ldots, m_n)$ is the set of moduli to be used and it is assumed that $M = \prod_{i=1}^{n} m_i$ is no less than P, that is, overflow is assumed not to occur. The residue representation of A, B, S, and P are $a = (a_1, \ldots, a_n)$, $b = (b_1, \ldots, b_n)$, $s = (s_1, \ldots, s_n)$, and $p = (p_1, \ldots, p_n)$ respectively; $\oplus$ and $\odot$ indicate residue addition and multiplication. Therefore, we state that

$$S = A \oplus B, \text{ i.e., } s_i = \left| a_i + b_i \right|_{m_i} \tag{6.6}$$

and

$$P = A \odot B, \text{ i.e., } p_i = \left| a_i \cdot b_i \right|_{m_i} \tag{6.7}$$

For example

$$(m_1, m_2, m_3) = (2,3,5), \quad \prod_{i=1}^{3} m_i = 30$$

$$A = 7, a = (a_1, a_2, a_3) = (1,1,2)$$

$$B = 4, b = (b_1, b_2, b_3) = (0,1,4)$$

$$S = 11, s_1 = \left| 1 + 0 \right|_2 = 1 = \left| 11 \right|_2$$
$$s_2 = \left| 1 + 1 \right|_3 = 2 = \left| 11 \right|_3$$
$$s_3 = \left| 2 + 4 \right|_5 = 1 = \left| 11 \right|_5$$

$$s = (s_1, s_2, s_3) = (1,2,1)$$

$$P = 28, p_1 = \left| 1 \cdot 0 \right|_2 = 0 = \left| 28 \right|_2$$
$$p_2 = \left| 1 \cdot 1 \right|_3 = 1 = \left| 28 \right|_3$$
$$p_3 = \left| 2 \cdot 4 \right|_5 = 3 = \left| 28 \right|_5$$

$$p = (p_1, p_2, p_3) = (0,1,3)$$

Subtraction is obtainable in the residue number system by employing a complement representation consisting of the additive inverses of the positive residue representations and by partitioning the residue number range into two approximately equal parts. The additive inverse of a residue number is defined by

$$\left| a_i + a_i' \right|_{m_i} = 0$$

Consequently

$$\left| A + A' \right|_M = 0$$

The partition of the residue number range can be illustrated with a simple example. Consider $m = (2,3,5)$. The residue representations corresponding to natural number 0 to 14 are considered positive; the rest, corresponding to 15 to 29, are considered inverse representations and are associated with negative integers from -15 to -1. Residue subtraction, $\ominus$, can now be defined by

$$A \ominus B = A \oplus B' \tag{6.8}$$

The above discussion reveals that the residue number system is very attractive in terms of multiplication and addition. Its main disadvantage is associated with the determination of magnitudes. It has also been pointed out that overflow detection, sign detection, and division [19] involve considerable complexity. Nevertheless, for classes of problems characterized by the absence of the need for division, the existence of a well-defined range for the variables, and by the fact that the signs of variables are known, the application of the residue number system would result in a reduction of the overall computation time. There is excellent literature concerning residue number systems [17, 19, 21, 23, 66, 68].

6.2. Signed-Digit Number Systems

Signed-digit (S-D) number systems [6, 7] employ redundant, positional representations with a constant integer radix $r \geq 3$, in which the allowed digit values are a sequence of $2a + 1$ integers:

$$\{\bar{a}, \ldots, \bar{1}, 0, 1, \ldots, a\} \tag{6.9}$$

The value of a, the maximum digit magnitude, is chosen from the following range:

$$\tfrac{1}{2}(r_0 + 1) \leq a \leq r_0 - 1 \qquad \text{for odd radices } r_0 \geq 3 \tag{6.10}$$

$$\tfrac{1}{2}r_e + 1 \leq a \leq r_e - 1 \qquad \text{for even radices } r_e \geq 4$$

Some of the important characteristic properties of S-D representations are:

1. The algebraic value Z of the number z

$$Z = (z_{-m}z_{-m+1} \ldots z_0 \cdot z_1 z_2 \ldots z_n)$$

is given by

$$Z = \sum_{i=-m}^{n} z_i r^{-i} \tag{6.11}$$

2. Algebraic value $Z = 0$ if and only if $z_i = 0$ for all i.

3. The sign of the algebraic value Z is given by the sign of the most significant (leftmost) nonzero digit.

4. The additive inverse $-Z$ is formed by changing the sign of every nonzero digit individually.

5. The addition and subtraction of two S-D operands x and y satisfies

$$s_i = f(x_i, y_i, x_{i+1}, y_{i+1})$$

for all positions i, where s_i are digits in the representations of the sum or difference

$$s = x \pm y$$

There are no carry-propagation chains in S-D addition (or subtraction), that is, any digit of the sum is a function of only two adjacent digits of the operands. The logical time of one addition is independent of the length of the operands and is equal to the time required by two digital positions. The two-digit addition algorithm consists of two steps. In the first step, an *interim sum* w_i and a *transfer digit* t_{i-1} are computed from the sum of the input digits x_i and y_i.

$$w_i = x_i + y_i - rt_{i-1} \tag{6.12}$$

where

$$
\begin{array}{lll}
t_{i-1} = 0 & \text{if} & |x_i + y_i| < a \\
t_{i-1} = 1 & \text{if} & x_i + y_i \geq a \\
t_{i-1} = \bar{1} & \text{if} & x_i + y_i \leq \bar{a}
\end{array}
$$

In the second step, the sum digit s_i is obtained by the addition:

$$s_i = w_i + t_i \tag{6.13}$$

The conversion of a conventional number to the S-D form can be performed in the following manner. The incoming conventional digit m_i replaces the sum $x_i + y_i$ in (6.12); the digits w_i and t_{i-1} are generated for every m_i and then the addition (6.13) yields the S-D form. An example of the system with $r = 10$ and $a = 6$ (minimal redundancy) is:

Position i	0 1 2 3 4 5
Conventional digits m_i	0 2 6 9 5 7
Interim sums w_i	2 $\bar{4}$ $\bar{1}$ 5 $\bar{3}$
Transfer digits t_i	0 1 1 0 1
S-D digits s_i	0.3 $\bar{3}$ $\bar{1}$ 6 $\bar{3}$

For reconversion to conventional decimal form, the S-D number is considered to be the sum of a positive and a negative conventional number, and a conventional subtraction is performed:

$$0.3\ \bar{3}\ \bar{1}\ 6\ \bar{3} = 0.3\ 0\ 0\ 6\ 0$$
$$+\ (-0.0\ 3\ 1\ 0\ 3)$$
$$=\ 0.2\ 6\ 9\ 5\ 7$$

S-D multiplication is carried out in a straightforward way. S-D division may be done either by the S-R-T method or by the technique characterized by deterministic generation of quotients digits [73].

7. CONCLUDING REMARKS

Arthmetic is performed by switching elements in a computer. Switching elements cannot respond instantaneously; there is one intrinsic delay between the instant that incoming signals appear on the input leads and the instant that an outgoing signal appears on the output leads. Obviously this intrinsic delay, denoted by Δt, is an important factor in determining computational speed. Another factor is the fan-in capability of the switching element, denoted by q. Fan-in is the physical limit on the number of input leads a switching element can have. With given switching elements, that is, with fixed q and Δt, the minimum times required for addition and multiplication have been carefully studied [78–80]. In a simplified manner, the result is briefly summarized below.

For an n-digit adder, provided that numbers are represented with unique (nonredundant) combinations of 0's and 1's, the minimum time required for performing addition is $\overline{\log_q 2n} \cdot \Delta t$ (where $\overline{x}$ means the smallest integer greater than x), irrespective of the hardware or algorithm invloved. Addition of conventional numbers is performed in a modulo-N manner where N may be eigher 2^n or $2^n - 1$. If a residue number system is used, we shall find the largest constituent modulus to be the bottleneck, since the addition is performed at each modulus simultaneously (without carry). If we denote the largest power of a single prime that divides N as N', then the number of bits required in this modulus addition, is $\overline{\log_2(N')}$, denoted as N''. The minimum addition time is therefore

$$\overline{\log_q 2N''} \cdot \Delta t$$

Similarly, for n-bit multiplication the minimum multiplication time is found to be $\overline{\log_q 2(n - 2)} \cdot \Delta t$. This formula indicates that the multiplication process is not necessarily slower than addition and may even be faster.

The rationale behind this apparent contradiction of intuition lies in how numbers are represented. A modulo multiplication scheme can be devised to verify this point [79].

We shall discuss a few implications of the minimum time formulas, the details and derivations of which can be found in the original literature. First, the results hold true for nonredundant number systems only. In redundant number systems, computational speed can be increased; the price paid is the increase of the complexity of the switching element and hence, its intrinsic delay. Second, the absolute bounds on speed serve as one of the guidelines for evaluating various designs. The formulas do not and cannot completely decide which approach the designer should take; what they do provide is a quantitative measure of the effect on the speed of arithmetic operations that any imaginable change in hardware can produce. Thus, although residue arithmetic seems to offer higher addition and multiplication speeds, it has not been used generally because the determination of magnitude, and hence sign detection and overflow detection, is rather difficult in residue representations. This example suggests that the interpretation of the results of arithmetic operations is equally or even more important than computational speed. The last and probably the most important implication is that the absolute bounds on speed do not pose as an insurmountable hindrance to the improvement of the overall computational speed of a computer. Evaluation of the performance of a computer involves two important factors—thruput and response. Generally, *thruput* refers to the output rate and *response* concerns with the delay between input and output. As to response, the absolute limits on the speeds of addition and multiplication may act like the "speed of light." Where thruput is concerned, they do not. This point can be illustrated with a simple argument. If one can present a new pair of numbers to a pipelined adder before it finishes adding the previous pair, then the rate at which sums are obtained is increased. Furthermore, if new pairs of numbers are fed at an interval of Δt, then the rate of output will be one sum per Δt, even though the addition speed for each pair still has not exceeded the limit. The possibility of "pipelining" in this way suggests that the addition time has no vital effect on the computer insofar as thruput is concerned. Today, there are two important approaches to the improvement of arithmetic processor performance. The first is a classic one—reducing the switching element delay, Δt. The second is a new challenge—analyzing the suitability of a given problem to "pipelining." In either approach, the impacts of large-scale integration should be carefully investigated.

8. REFERENCES

1. Aiken, H., and Semon, W., "Advanced Digital Computer Logical Design," Wright Air Develop. Center Tech. Rept. No. WADC-TR-59-472, Harvard Univ., Cambridge, Massachusetts (1959).

2. Anderson, S. F., Earle, J. G., Goldschmidt, R. E., and Powers, D. M., "The IBM System/360 Model 91; Floating-Point Execution Unit," *IBM J. of Research and Development*, **11**, 34–53 (1967).

3. Ashenhurst, R. L., "The MANIAC III Arithmetic System," *APIPS Conference Proceedings*, **21**, (1962 SJCC), 195–202.

4. Ashenhurst, R. L., and Metropolis, N., "Unnormalized Floating-Point Arithmetic." *J. Assoc. Computing Machinery*, **6**, 415–429 (1959).

5. Atkins, D. E., "Higher Radix Division Using Estimates of the Divisor and Partial Remainder," *IEEE Trans. on Computers*, **17**, 825–934 (1968).

6. Avizienis, A., "Signed-Digit Number Representations for Fast Parallel Arithmetic," *IRE Trans. Electron. Computers*, **10**, 389–400 (1961).

7. Avizienis, A., "Binary-Compatible Signed-Digit Arithmetic," *AFIPS Conference Proceedings*, **26**, Part 1, (1964 FJCC), 663–672.

8. Avizienis, A., "On the Computational Time and Complexity of Arithmetic Functions," Assoc. Computing Machinery Symposium on Theory of Computing, Los Angeles, Calif., May 5–7, 1969.

9. Bedrij, O. J., "Carry-Select Adder," *IRE Trans. Electron. Computers*, **11**, 340–346 (1962).

10. Buchholz, W., Editor, *Planning a Computer System*, McGraw-Hill, 1962.

11. Burks, A. W., Goldstine, H. H., and von Neumann, J., "Preliminary Discussion of the Logical Design of an Electronic Computing Instrument," Part 1, Vol. 1, Inst. Advanced Study, Princeton, New Jersey (1946).

12. Cheney, P. W., "A Digital Correlator Based on the Residue Number System," *IRE Trans. Electron. Computers*, **10**, 63–70 (1961).

13. de Regt. M. P., "Negative Radix Arithmetic," *Computer Design*, May, June, July, August, September, October, 1967.

14. Driese, E. C., Glen, G. E., and Young, R. E., Jr., (Scope, Inc., Falls Church, Va.), "Computer Applications of Residue Class Notations," *ASD TR* **61-189**, September 1961. (Aeronautical Systems Division, AF Systems Command, USAF.) ASIIA Document No. AD-269 123.

15. Ehrman, J. R., "Logical Arithmetic on Computers with Two's Complement Binary Arithmetic," *Comm. of Assoc. Computing Machine*, **11**, 517–520 (1968).

16. Estrin, G., Gilchrist, B., and Pomerene, J., "A Note on High-speed Digital Multiplication," *IRE Trans. Electron. Computers*, **5**, 140 (1956).

17. Flores, I., *The Logic of Computer Arithmetic*, Prentice-Hall, 1963.

18. Freiman, C. V., "Statistical Analysis of Certain Binary Division Algorithms," *Proc. IRE*, **49**, 91–103 (1961).

19. Garner, H. L., "Number Systems and Arithmetic," *Advances in Computers*, **6**, 131–194 (1965).

20. Garner, H. L., "Finite Non-Redundant Number System Weights," Tech. Note No. 04879-6-T, Univ. of Michigan, Ann Arbor, Michigan (1962).

21. Garner, H. L., "The Residue Number System," *IRE Trans. Electron. Computers,* **8**, 140–147 (1959).

22. Garner, H. L., "A Ring Model for the Study of Multiplication for Complement Codes," *IRE Trans. Electron. Computers,* **8**, 25–30 (1959).

23. Garner, H. L., Arnold, R. F., Benson, B. C., Brockus, C. G., Gonzalez, K., and Rosenburg, D. P., "Residue Number Systems for Computers," A. F. Systems Command. Aeron. Systems Div. Tech. Rept. No. ASD-TR-61-483, Univ. of Michigan, Ann Arbor, Michigan (1961).

24. Gilchrist, B., Pomerene, J., and Wong, S. Y., "Fast Carry Logic for Digital Computers," *IRE Trans. Electron. Computers,* **4**, 133–136 (1955).

25. Goldstein, M., "Significance Arithmetic on a Digital Computer," *Comm. of Assoc. Computing Machinery,* **6**, 111–117 (1963).

26. Gray, H. L., and Harrison, C., Jr., "Normalized Floating-Point Arithmetic With an Index of Significance," Proc. 1959 Eastern Joint Computer Conference (Dec. 1–3, 1959, Boston), 244–248.

27. Guffin, R. M., "A Computer for Solving Simultaneous Equations Using the Residue Number System," *IRE Trans. Electron. Computers,* **11**, 164–173 (1962).

28. Hendrickson, H. C., "Fast High-Accuracy Binary Parallel Addition," *IRE Trans. Electronic Computers.* **4**, 465–469 (1960).

29. Jarvis, D. B., Morgan, L. P., and Weaver, J. A., "Transistor Current Switching and Routing Techniques," *IRE Trans. Electronic Computers,* **3**, 302–308 (1960).

30. Keir, Y. A., Cheney, P. W., and Tannenbaum, M., "Division and Overflow Detection in Residue Number Systems," *IRE Trans. Electron. Computers,* **11**, 501–507 (1962).

31. Kilburn, T., Edwards, D. B. G., and Aspinall, D., "Parallel Addition in Digital Computers, A New Fast Carry Circuit," *Proc. IEE* **106**, *Pt. B,* 464–466 (1959).

32. Kilburn, T., Edwards, D. B. G., and Aspinall, D., "A Parallel Arithmetic Unit Using a Saturated-Transistor Fast-Carry Circuit," *Proc. IEE* **107**, *Pt. B,* 573–584 (1960).

33. Klir, J., "A Note on Svoboda's Algorithm for Division," *Information Processing Machines,* **9**, 35–38 (1963, Prague, Czech.).

34. Krishnamurthy, E. V., "On a Divide-and-Correct Method for Variable Precision Division," *Comm. of Assoc. Computing Machinery,* **8**, 179–181, (1965).

35. Krishnamurthy, E. V., and Nandi, S. K., "On the Normalization Requirement of Divisor in Divide-and-Correct Methods," *Comm. of Assoc. Computing Machinery,* **10**, 809–813 (1967).

36. Lehman, M., "Short-Cut Multiplication and Division in Automatic Binary Digital Computers," *Proc. IEE,* **105**, *Part B,* 496–504 (1958).

37. Lehman, M., "A Comparative Study of Propagation Speed-Up Circuit in Binary Arithmetic Units," Intern. Federation Inform. Process. Socs. Conf., Munich, 671–676 (1962).

38. Lehman, M., "High Speed Digital Multiplication," *IEEE Trans. Electron. Computers,* **6**, 204–205 (1957).

39. Lehman, M., "The Minimization of Assimilations in Binary Carry-Storage Arithmetic Units," *IEEE Trans. Electron. Computers,* **12**, 409–410 (1963).

40. Lehman, M., and Burla, N., "Skip Techniques for High-Speed Carry-Propagation in Binary Arithmetic Units." *IRE Trans. Electron. Computers*, **10**, 691–698 (1961).

41. Lehman, M., and Burla, N., "A Note on the Simultaneous Carry Generation System for High-Speed Adders," *IRE Trans. Electron. Computers*, **9**, 510 (1960).

42. MacLean, M. A., and Aspinall, D., "Decimal Adder Using a Stored Addition Table," *Proc. IEE (London)*, **105B**, 129–135 and 144–136 (1958).

43. MacSorley, O. L., "High-Speed Arithmetic in Binary Computers," *Proc. IRE*, **49**, 67–91 (1961).

44. Meggit, J. E., "Pseudo-Division and Pseudo-Multiplication Processes" *IBM J. Res. Develop.*, **6**, 210–226 (1962).

45. Merrill, R. D., Jr., "Improving Digital Computer Performance Using Residue Number Theory," *IEEE Trans. Electron. Computers*, **13**, 93–101 (1964).

46. Metropolis, N., and Ashenhurst, R. L., "Significant Digit Computer Arithmetic," *IRE Trans. Electronic Computers*, **7**, 265–267 (1958).

47. Metropolis, N., and Ashenhurst, R. L., "Basic Operations in an Unnormalized Arithmetic System," *IEEE Trans. Electron. Computers*, **12**, 896–904 (1963).

48. Metze, G., "A Class of Binary Divisions Yielding Minimally Represented Quotients," *IRE Trans. Electronic Computers*, **11**, 761–764 (1962).

49. Metze, G., and Robertson, J. E., "Elimination of Carry Propagation in Digital Computers," Proc. Intern. Conf. Inform. Processing, Paris, 1959 UNESCO/NS/ICIP/G.2.10, pp. 389–396 (1959).

50. Mitchell, J. H., Jr., "Computer Multiplication and Division Using Binary Logarithms," *IRE Trans. Electron. Computers*, **11**, 512–517 (1962).

51. Nadler, M., "A High Speed Electronic Arithmetic Unit for Automatic Computing Machines," *Acta Technica (Czech. Acad. Sci.)*, **6**, 464–478 (1958).

52. Nandi, S. K., and Krishnamurthy, E. V., "A Simple technique for Digital Division," *Comm. of Assoc. Computing Machinery*, **10**, 299–301 (1967).

53. Rao, T. R. N., *The General Properties of Finite Weighted Number Systems*, Ph.D. Thesis, Univ. of Michigan, Ann Arbor, Michigan (1964).

54. Reitwiesner, G. W., "Binary Arithmetic," *Advances in Computers*, **1**, 232–308 (1960).

55. Reitwiesner, G. W., "The Determination of Carry Propagation Length for Binary Addition," *IRE Trans. Electron. Computers*, **9**, 35–38 (1960).

56. Richards, R. K., *Arithmetic Operations in Digital Computers*, D. Van Nostrand Co., 1955.

57. Robertson, J. E., "A New Class of Digital Division Methods," *IRE Trans. Electron. Computers*, **7**, 218–222 (1958).

58. Robertson, J. E., "Two's Complement Multiplication in Binary Parallel Digital Computers," *IRE Trans. Electron. Computers*, **4**, 118–119 (1955).

59. Salter, F., "High-speed Transistorized Adder for a Digital Computer," *IRE Trans. Electron. Computers*, **9**, 461–464 (1960).

60. Salter, F., "Reducing Computing Time for Synchronous Binary Division," *IRE Trans. Electronic Computers*, **10**, 169–174 (1961).

61. Sasaki, A., "Addition and Subtraction in the Residue Number System," *IEEE Trans. Electronic Computers*, **16**, 157–164, (1967).

62. Sklansky, J., "An Evaluation of Several Two-Summan Binary Adders," *IRE Trans. Electron. Computers*, **9**, 213–226 (1960).

63. Sklansky, J., "Conditional Sum Addition Logic," *IRE Trans. Electron. Computers*, **9**, 226–231 (1960).

64. Stein, M. L., "Divide-and-Correct Methods for Multiple Precision Division," *Comm. of Assoc. Computing Machinery*, **7**, 472–474 (1964).

65. Stein, M. L., and Pope, D. A., "Multiple-Precision Arithmetic," *Comm. of Assoc. Computing Machinery*, **3**, 652 (1960).

66. Svoboda, A., "The Numerical System of Residual Classes," *Digital Information Processors*, Hoffmann, W., Editor; Interscience Publishers, New York, 1962; 543–574.

67. Svoboda, A., "An Algorithm for Division," *Information Processing Machines*, **9**, 25–32 (Prague, Czech., 1963).

68. Svoboda, A., and Valach, M., "Rational Numerical System of Residual Classes." In *Stroje na Zpracovani Informaci*, Sbornik V, pp. 9–37., *Nakl. CSAV*, Praha, 1957 (in English).

69. Sweeney, D. W., "An Analysis of Floating-Point Addition," *IBM Systems Journal*, **4**, 31–42 (1965).

70. Szabo, N. S., "Sign Detection in Nonredundant Residue Systems," *IRE Trans. Electron. Computers*, **11**, 494–500 (1962).

71. Taub, A. H., Gillies, D. B., Meager, R. E., Muller, D. E., McKay, R. W., Nash, J. P., and Robertson, J. E., "On the Design of a Very High-Speed Computer," Rept. No. 80, Digital Computer Lab., Univ. of Illinois, Urbana, Illinois (1957).

72. Tocher, K. D., "Techniques of Multiplication and Division for Automatic Binary Computers," *Quart. J. Mech. Appl. Math.*, **11**, 364–348 (1958).

73. Tung, C., "A Division Algorithm for Signed-Digit Arithmetic," *IEEE Trans. on Computers*, **17**, 887–889 (1968).

74. Wadey, W. G., "Floating-Point Arithmetics," *J. of Assoc. Computing Machinery*, **7**, 129–139 (1960).

75. Wallace, C. S., "A Suggestion for a Fast Multiplier," *IEEE Trans. Electron. Computers*, **13**, 14–17 (1964).

76. Weinberger, A., and Smith, J. L., "A One Microsecond Adder Using Megacycle Circuitry," *IRE Trans. Electron. Computers*, **5**, 67–73 (1956).

77. Wilson, J. B., and Ledley, R. S., "An Algorithm for Rapid Binary Division," *IRE Trans. Electron. Computers*, **10**, 662–670 (1961).

78. Winograd, S., "On the Time Required to Perform Addition," *J. of Assoc. Computing Machinery*, **12**, 277–285 (1965).

79. Winograd, S., "How Fast Can Computers Add " *Scientific American*, **219**, 93–100 (October 1968).

80. Winograd, S., "On the Time Required to Perform Multiplication," *J. of Assoc. Computing Machinery*, **14**, 793–802 (1967).

81. Knuth, D., *The Art of Computer Programming, Vol. 2—Seminumerical Algorithms*, Addison Wesley, 1969, pp. 161–451.

82. Chu, Y., *Digital Computer Design Fundamentals*, McGraw-Hill, 1962, pp. 1–88.

83. Ware, W., *Digital Computer Technology and Design*, Wiley, 1963.

System Architecture

Earl C. Joseph

UNIVAC Defense Systems
Division Sperry Rand Corporation

1. INTRODUCTION TO COMPUTER SYSTEM ARCHITECTURE

The topic of computer system architecture has grown to be large and complex. This chapter is not a reiteration of past computer system architectures—such a historical survey is outlined in Chapter 5. Instead, I shall offer some thoughts and questions about what will be witnessed in the future with the hope that they will fire the reader's imagination to pursue the task of solving the problems. Also I shall interpret the technological signs of the times and the computer's impact by briefly mentioning just the major trends.

First, what is meant by architecture when referring to it in the context of computer system architecture? *Computer architecture*, like the trend in the architecture in modern buildings, is functionally oriented. I shall define the architecture of computer systems as the orderly style, structure, and process of the system that is necessary for it to achieve its purpose. The computer system's purpose is (1) to solve (compute) problems, (2) to control processes or systems, and (3) to provide information. Furthermore, recognizing that computers do nothing without proper programs, such a definition must include the hardware, the software, and the humanware (computer application by humans) as the three basic components. To date, little has been written on the software aspects of computer system architecture. This chapter attempts to partially fill this gap (see also Chapter 6).

At the outset, let me establish a hierarchy in order to distinguish the various levels within the architecture of a computer system [27]. The highest level or most inclusive level will be referred to as the system; the computer system will be all inclusive. Other types of systems or subsystems within the computer system are the processor system, the memory system, the input/output (I/O) system, the peripheral system, and the communications system. The next level below the subsystems will be the specific functional units themselves, for example, processor, central processor (CPU), remote processor, memory, I/O control, multiplexer, tape unit, and disk storage. Sometimes this description will include even lower levels in the hierarchy by referring to the arithmetic section and even lower when discussing components, the fabric of computers, such as integrated circuits (IC), and logic gates. Because of the increased importance and usage of the remote terminal, I shall generally distinguish them from other types of peripherals.

1.1. Architectural Forms

What are the architectural forms [4, 58] in computer systems? Originally the computer was functionally quite similar to a mechanical calculator except that it was electronic. The next step was to add some memory to feed the calculator with data and hold a simple stored instruction sequence in order to control the computer automatically. This latter storage of instructions allowed them to be called an automatic computer when a conditional transfer of control (decision) type instruction was included. The sequence of instructions soon became known as the program. Such simple devices as console lights, switches, and a typewriter were added to get data in and out of the calculator. This, then, is how the calculator evolved into the electronic digital computer. These early computers were not systems in the sense that we use the term today, nor were they referred to as computer systems. The electronic calculator was developed into a system only when enough subsystems had been added so that it could be used to solve complete problems rather than just performing a few calculations. Most of the early computers were special-purpose, primarily scientific, and were not intended for nor applied to general problem solving.

The next major step in the evolutionary process toward today's typical (but varied) architecture was the addition of features that allowed for much more data handling. This ushered in the era of data processing. Such systems were considerably more general-purpose in their applicability. The data processing functions that were added consisted of more decision and data manipulative instructions rather than primarily arithmetic operations. There were other additions, including: more memory for data; a multitude of peripherals for both "on-line" and "off-line" data input and output handling; and "I/O buffering" to allow concurrent I/O data transfers operations to occur with the arithmetic processing. By giving the ability to transfer data from or to slow devices like the typewriter off-line from the computer, usually through the use of magnetic tape, the on-line operations of the computer were greatly enhanced through faster operation. The addition of input/output memory buffers further speeded computer operations by allowing I/O communications to be performed at memory speeds.

With the advent of mass storage and, more recently, the remote terminal the computer's power is now becoming easily available for handling information. It is now capable of transforming data facts into true information that can be used directly by humans without the further manual manipulation required of past systems. Each evolutionary step has produced an increasing number of architectures.

What makes a new architecture emerge, grow, and evolve [27]? There are five factors. The first is, obviously, need. Another certainly is technical innovation. The third factor comprises special features that solve a current knotty problem (such as programming) or a feature that enhances a specific application. The fourth is the general-purpose applicability of the change—whether it allows the new architecture to serve multifaceted market areas.

The fifth factor involves a change that simply offers a better way to use the huge investment in existing software or hardware. In addition, the ever-increasing complexity of civilization (with a corresponding increase in the complexities of industry, economics, technology, and society) has caused an urgent need for putting the computer on-line to assist us [22].

With nearly 100,000 computers in use throughout the world [12] it comes as no surprise to find a multitude of different computer system architectures. (There are about 70,000 computers in use in the United States, approximately 10,000 computers in use in other countries, and an additional uncountable number of computers in use by the military in various nations.) Forecasters are predicting an even greater variety of architectures for the future. We are rapidly approaching the era, in the next few years, when system logic designers will have relatively large and complete functions on somewhat standardized large scale integrated circuit (LSI) chips/wafers for use as building blocks (see Chapters 1 and 2). Because such *modular functions* as memory, processing, and control will become low priced due to LSI, drastic changes in computer system architecture are emerging. In the past, without this modularity and economic freedom, the architecture of a computer system was "cast into concrete" once the system was installed. But this is not true for the coming decade. We see designs that not only allow the programs to be changed but that will also allow the hardware architecture to be changed. Dynamic architecture variations will occur both under program control and through evolutionary developments that will drastically extend the life of a computer system. In the past with few exceptions, the life of a computer system has been about five years and very seldom extended beyond. The average user today can look forward to at least a decade of system use. This will come about simply because the modularity of the systems of the next decades will allow them to be updated *piecemeal*—an evolutionary process allowing advances on a functional basis to be added as they occur.

1.2. Architectural Trends [2–4, 9, 28, 35, 41]

The avalanche of present attention in the field is for architectures to be more responsive to the user's application needs. To meet this challenge, one of the newest architectural changes that will have a far-reaching impact on future systems will be building parts of programs into the hardware [29] again on a modular basis. Computers will be "tailorable" to special system and application needs. This feature alone could mean that each computer system architecture will be individually different from all others. Yet, it is expected that such tailored computer systems will remain program compatible with one another. This rebirth of special-purpose systems will come about while the evils of past incompatibilities will be corrected. From all this, future computer system architecture will be more general-purpose and at the same time more special-purpose through the use of program adjuncts cast in hardware. Also, these adjuncts will extend the language of their host systems as well as system life. Thus the user will be the one who ultimately benefits from the resulting architectures.

During the past decade the computer field, faced with burgeoning computer applications, was also faced with some technical trends that brought about major architectural changes. In many cases, an order of magnitude or more change has occurred. Such large technical changes opened new application areas which, in turn, are forcing new technical innovations to the surface in order to meet the new challenges. These trends, which will continue to have an impact on future computer system architecture, include:

- Decreasing cost of hardware logic, memory, and CPU.
- Increasing processor capability and memory capacity.
- Increasing numbers of programs, both system and application, available to many users.
- Increasing *time-sharing* (multiple users sharing available computer time usually via remote terminals—see also Chapter 7) and *multiprogramming* [39] (concurrent operation of more than one program or loosely, parallel processing—see also Chapter 5).
- Increasing variety in man-interfaceable terminals.
- Increasing use of terminals, remote computing, and communications.
- Increasing complexity of system software—automatization of computer control and operation.
- Increasing programming costs relative to hardware costs over the life of a computer system. This comes along with longer system life and is desirable, since it means more of the dollar costs are being spent on the application rather than acquiring the tools.
- Increasing use of larger common files (a *file* is a collection of related information in computer readable form).
- Increasing use of the computer to assist man rather than just record keeping and scientific calculations.
- Increasing use of information.
- Increasing numbers and variety in high-level computer languages.
- Increasing systems reliability [27, 28, 50].

Furthermore, as we move further into the seventies, we can expect substantial increases in the use of automation.

Order of magnitude changes in technology have a tendency to generate revolutionary environmental changes when they occur over a short period of time as they have been recently in the computer field. It is not surprising, amidst these rapid technical improvements, that we find ourselves in a surfeit of technology without the capability of absorbing it and are faced with many problems. The major deficiencies or problem areas are in the development of programs, the inefficient operation of computer systems, and management. Many of these problems are primarily of a nontechnical nature. Yet they foretell major technical computer system innovations in architecture and changes yet to come; for many innovations and changes will be required to solve these problems. In the computer field the short-term future tends to be invented from a knowledge of existing problems by transferring present research to the development of next-generation equipment and software to obtain the desired solutions. This process has a three- to ten-year lead time.

Architecture styles called *multiprocessors* (more than one CPU), *overlapped/pipelined* (parallel execution of computer subcommands), *arrays* (an arrangement of processors and memories in an array form), *serial/parallel*, and *minicomputer* (a very small scale computer) are all terms that refer more to their design structure than their intended use. True, they do suggest how the computer system architecture will perform its task, from the designer's viewpoint ans sometimes from the programmer's/user's viewpoint, but not in the functional application sense. Whereas terms like scientific, business, command and control, real-time (actual time of a physical process), and time-shared do give an application connotation. But these terms, except for the latter, are falling into disuse. Perhaps all this results from the former era when computer system architecture design was only practiced by a few designers at computer manufacturing plants, and those people named the architectures. Perhaps in the coming decade, as computer system modules become available separately by each constituent computer function for the user to piece together an individual computer system architecture, this practice will change.

The casting of parts of programs into logic hardware (which we are on the threshold of) seems to be the wave of the future. In the early days, we went from performing the multiply as a subroutine sequence of a multitude of programmed add and shift instructions to a single instruction. This marriage of hardware and software techniques speeded the multiply function by nearly 50-fold and greatly eased its programming. This prototype of today's design trend toward a richer and higher level language has taken a long time to be expanded upon. This is mainly because of the high cost of past logic hardware which has and is being drastically changed with the advent of the higher levels circuit integration, medium scale integrated circuits (MSI) and LSI, bringing about very low-cost logic.

Today, the implications of our domestic revolutions are just beginning to be understood. Even so, they are starting to have an impact on computer system architecture design by bringing about the distribution of the computer's power to points where needed via remote computer terminals. Thus, such architectures allow the computer to be applied to the real problems of society by amplifying and extending the human mind's power much like the machines in the industrial revolution extended man's muscles.

Unlike Wright's buildings, computers are no so much being built to match the surroundings of their location but to match the needs of their intended applications. As this trend matures in the 1970s, man can expect to gain back much of his lost individualism as computer systems are built more and more to fit the individual's need. This is coming about by innovations that circumvent the constraining problem of designs that serve the needs of mass production. One such innovation consists of mass-produced standard modules which can be pieced together to form a variety of individualized special-purpose computer system architectures. Such an innovation is demanded by the necessity of production economics and the demand for more functionally tailored systems. Some computer architects are unprepared for this type of construction because their old products were not modular. Application demands have primarily pushed the frontiers of computer system architecture. The intended use of the computer has the sobering effect of adding the realism needed to produce functional architecture. It adds an impetus to bring about a complete system over and above the incentives produced by technical innovation. The rapid developments in civilization today in the large cities, which many characterize it as the development toward dehumanization, have caused acute social unrest. These pressures are creating a new need for the application of computers for solving the growing social problems in the inner cities. This, in turn, is spawning new computer system architectures which adapt to people, are on-line in real-time, and are available to a multitude of users.

Some have said that art culture in America has not kept pace with science and technology. Yet, computer system architecture is a practical art meeting a genuine need for the individual and society. Is not this simply another example of how we have culturally matured? The science-based technology of computer system architecture is certainly one of the great creative art forms of our time.

2. HARDWARE ARCHITECTURE

The hardware architecture consists of such functional units as processors, memories, I/O controllers, and peripherals as well as consideration of its logic and memory components.

Architecture designers must look to new nontraditional solutions to existing problems, but their first and perhaps their most difficult task is to locate the problems. In our present era of a maturing computer field no longer in its infancy, much inertia is building up. This keeps new ideas from surfacing and being developed into products. Today's problems will tend to be with us a lot longer than desired and longer than they were in the past. Considerable user sensitivity and dissatisfaction will have to build up to bring about more rapid changes. In the meantime, designers will continue to look for solutions that they can hold in abeyance until they can be implemented. The computer system architect works within many other constraints. One hardware constraint is the speed of electrical pulse transmission. As with all other obstacles, the designer becomes innovative in bypassing and overcoming the constraints by a variety of methods. To overcome the speed limitation problem, the design circumvention innovations in use consist of:

- Applying large-scale integration of components allowing shorter wires and higher densities, giving rise to increased speed.
- Using smaller elements that require the switching of less material requiring less power and dissipating less heat.
- Using more complex hardware (systems and instructions) to increase the systems *throughput* (a measure of system efficiency; the rate at which work can be handled by a computer system—sometimes measured in terms of instructions executed per second) by reducing the number of operations performed. Thus, requiring less memory and fewer references to memory as well as requiring fewer instructions.
- Anticipating and performing more operations ahead of their usage time and performing more operations in parallel.
- Restating problem solutions into shorter machine computable sequences.
- Performing more operations locally by distributing control.
- Building physically smaller systems.
- Reducing heat problem by cooling, using leads to conduct and dissipate heat, and making electrical components from materials that are also good heat conductors as well as good electrical conductors or insulators.

Thus, the circumvention of a constraint has great impact on the physical properties and economics of the computer system architecture and requires new trade-offs.

Although the technology is available to build even more sophisticated computer system architectures than I will suggest, solutions to users problems such as programming are the pacing incentives for new systems. at present, this preoccupation demands considerable compatibility with past systems so that past software can be used. Computer user's management are especially interested in capitalizing on past software investments. Thus, next-generation architectures tend to be imitations of their predecessors with simple evolutionary improvements. This will continue until the problems created grow in magnitude to the point where revolutionary changes are required. In going from second-generation to third-generation computers, a revolutionary change occurred which resulted in systems that generally were not compatible with the past generation. The resulting traumatic experience for the user probably will prevent the occurrence of such a computer revolution in the future.

To overcome this constraint, designers are leaning toward architectures that allow the revolutionary new features to coexist with the old. Some architecture configurations and features allowing this coexistence are:

• Extendible or enhanceable language systems.

• *Microprogram* (programming with the micro or sub-commands) structures overlayed (really underlayed from the user's and designer's vewpoints but overlayed from the historical viewpoint) on the traditional macro structure which allows application tailoring. Further, this microprogramming feature allows the computers logic to be used both for the old and new features by allowing logic restructuring under program control.

• Read only memories for holding microprograms to structure machine for application or compatibility desired.

• Variable word length—especially in the data area.

• Expanded and tailorable I/O sections.

• Standard logic modules containing relatively large subfunctions which can be pieced together to form tailored architectures.

Each architecture's performance is *application sensitive;* it performs better on one task than another. The ideal performance range is so different for the varied applications of computers that it is now difficult to visualize a single computer system architecture that meets the needs of more than a few applications. Furthermore, even in the same application area, it is difficult to imagine a single architecture that meets the varied desires of users—especially with the large number of architectural features available in the designer's tool kit. Thus, the ever-present question in new computer system design is: What should be included for the flexibility and capability of the system versus what should be left out for efficiency and economic considerations? In reality this choice leads to compromise. There results a proliferation of variety that fluctuates in accordance with the current biases and pressures of both the application needs and the designer's wishes.

Two early and current trends in computer design foretell major future transformations in the architecture of computer systems. The first is the ever-increasing importance placed on concurrency of operation. That is, the method used to alter the architecture to achieve greater capability has been toward performing more functions in parallel. This trend is accelerating; larger and larger functions are being paralleled. Such parallelism generally improves system utilization. The other trend is the long-sought achievement of computer independent programming. There is considerable evidence that the next-generation system architectures will achieve this goal. Architectures that allow algorithmic language description to be independent of the computer environment are almost a certainty in the near future. Such programming generality—giving the ability to move a program between computers, from old to new computers, from one manufacturer's to another's, and the ability to evolve and maintain a program within a changing computer hardware environment without in any way altering the program description—is the goal of many contemporary designers. As each new generation of computers emerges, it is usually faster and more complex than its predecessors. Also it was and still is common practice of each new computer system designed to push the state of the art—especially the components of the new architecture.

Many applications spawn new architectures, and when they do a definite need usually exists. Thus, few question the need for such a great variety of architectures. That is, few except those interested in the cost of being different and those interested in compatibility and standardization. This group includes many computer users. Yet, unquestionably, certain applications require different architectures. It is certainly not true nor clear, however, that each different application requires a different incompaticle architecture. Furthermore, it is equally true that there is not necessarily one single optimum architecture that best satisfies the needs of a specific application.

The economics surrounding programming now dictates that computer systems remain in use much longer than in the past—as much as five years or longer.

This problem of programming dictates that the software investment on the current or old system must be salvable or capitalizable. This means that new architectures tend to be similar to the old ones even though hardware components change radically. With this emphasis on making new systems compatible with old or current ones, systems architectures that are innovatively new are difficult to sell to management and customers. In the face of these squelching problems, we still are seeing a formidable number of new architectures.

The distinguishing feature that sets one architecture apart from all others is the arrangement of the basic building blocks. Yet the subtleties of evolved change, the hardware differences, where the intra- or intercomputer communication interfaces are sliced, and a host of other considerations can also be the distinguishing factor or factors.

What are the basic building blocks of the architecture of a computer system? For first-generation computers, of the Von Neumann type, the functional building blocks were inter-mixed physically and were only distinguishable on paper. These early functional building blocks were Control (C), Memory (M), Arithmetic (A), and Input/Output (I/O).

The early designers of computer architectures in the 1940s and the early 1950s were primarily concerned with computers rather than the computer system. Therefore, they did not include the simple peripherals: paper tape, console, typewriter, magnetic tape, and card units as part of the architecture, since they were usually separate from the so-called computer. All computer architectures to date make use of these same four functional building blocks and the different architectures come about by virtue of:

- Fragmentation of the classical functions into subfunctions or multiple modules.
- Special added features.
- How and which building blocks are combined.
- Additional interface matching and control units.
- Which building blocks are multiple functions.
- Design sophistication of specific building blocks.
- Synchronous or asynchronous function operation.

Computer architectures can be broken down into four basic types:

- Unit computers—Von Neumann type.
- Parallel computers—multiprocessors.
- Array computers.
- Netted systems—distributed processing—coupled systems.

Each of these classes has many variations on the theme. Many considerations spawn different architectures or architecture variations; examples are:

- Purpose/application/function.
- Size/capacity/speed.
- Arithmetic/control/housekeeping operations.
- Memory/hierarchy/type/speed.
- Logic/memory/components.

- Reliability/availability/maintainability.
- Program/language/instruction repertoire.
- Input-output system/peripherals/control.
- Special-purpose adjuncts.

To further stretch the capability of computer systems, functions are paralleled for concurrent operation, and multiple functions are added to gain higher speed, to gain greater storage capacity, to gain higher data I/O transferability. Parallel architectures come in many forms.

Fewer than 100 instruction types were included in the repertoires of first-generation computers. The instructions were simple and their format contained two basic parts: an instruction function code and an address field. The address field contained one, two, or three addresses. In the early days of computer design a great controversy raged over which architecture was best—primarily the argument centered around whether to choose single or two address machines. Today, computer repertoires consist of 100 to 200 different instructions with many function modifiers. In these more sophisticated second- and third-generation types of computers, each instruction has many variations, which makes them very complex. This complexity leads to many user problems, especially for the systems programmer. There is an indication that the next evolutionary step in instruction repertoires is toward an extensible language type. Such systems would consist of a standard or basic repertoire and would allow, through processes like emulation (imitation) or microprogramming, additional instructions to be defined.

Usually the additional instructions are more complex than the basic set, like subroutines which are made up of combinations of the basic instructions. The added complexity is in the logic design; it is not added complexity for the programmer. In fact, by building some high usage subroutines into the logic, programming is simplified. Still other systems will allow modules of subroutines cast in hardware to be plugged in to extend the computer language. The direction in which these systems are moving is toward an instruction repertoire language that is adaptable to man for the semantic jargon required for tailoring to various and specific applications.

Architectures that make extensive use of small high-speed local memories for arithmetic stacks, scratch pad, index registers, and the like can effectively and efficiently use a combined half- and full-word instruction repertoire. These systems, if the repertoire is well chosen, can reduce the amount of storage required to hold the instruction portion (not the data) of programs to almost one-half in terms of the number of bits required. This significant savings is important for two reasons: (1) memory is the most costly hardware item in the central system (excluding remore peripherals), and (2) memory reduction is an important weight saving consideration—especially in aerospace systems.

Buried in the complex details of the hardware of today's systems is a major trend toward putting the computer on-line with humans. What future architectures will evolve as we go to more and more on-line usage of computers?

The advent of the multiuser time-shared system, with man on-line remotely, has come into widespread use through the advent of remote terminals such as cathode ray tube (CRT), typewriter, touch-tone telephone, and teletype. These terminal oriented systems, which allow the computer's power to be relatively easily and economically available, have in themselves spawned or spread the use of special architectures.

When each new system springs upon the market place, its components exhibit a higher level of complexity. For as the designer is forced to consider larger high performance systems the number of circuit constraints and their complexity increases sharply over the smaller system of yesteryear. Such a burgeoning complexity toward larger systems is making it mandatory for the computer to come to the aid of the designer. The resulting computer-aided design technology that is evolving finds applications for both the large and small systems as well as for systems optimized for high performance or for the category of system in which low cost is the primary constraint. But, with the computer helping in the design process, the designer finds greater flexibility and new freedoms, which allows still more complex system architectures to evolve.

A question that is often asked is, "Why are computers practical for so many and varied on-line applications today?" Some answers are:

- Computers are now large enough, general-purpose enough, fast enough, and economical enough.
- Memories have sufficient capacity and are economical enough.
- The advent of time-sharing of the computer allowing multiple access computing allows many users to use the computer at the same time.
- Much more than a basic set of computer programs to support specific applications are now available.
- Real-time control for automatic control of other equipment is now a reality.

What about the future [16]? What lies around the corner that is going to make it even easier to use the computer? Are we going to have total operating systems to support the computer system operation? Already operating system parts are being partially built out of the logic hardware. One of the more important types of programs we are going to have is the packaged program—modules of application programs and modules of systems programs packaged so that the user can piece together a system in the real time of need. We cannot do that very easily today, because today's computers do not adapt language-wise to the way you and I communicate —the way we want to use computers. Next-generation computers will adapt to man. They will allow the language of the computer to be extended to the language that we use, dynamically as we need that language.

In addition, the cost of the graphic terminal will be reduced drastically in the near future. In fact, in the 1970 decade we can expect to be able to afford the graphic terminal on just about every manager's and technical specialist's desk. We can also expect some breakthroughs in the mass memory area during the 1972 to 1975 era. Subsequently, we can expect extremely large and fast memories in the order of magnitude of 100 million bits or more. Also, these future mass data storages will be very low-cost. They will be *random access* (access time independent of location) and high speed. We will be able to get at masses of data in microseconds.

As you can see, there are many changes coming in future computer system architecture but, even so, we find that our computers are going to stay in the field a lot longer!

There are still many areas that need to be researched, developed, evolved, optimized, and implemented in computer system architecture design. Some of the questions that arise are:

- What architectures are needed for terminal oriented systems?
- What are human performance principles?
- What human operations can or cannot be aided?
- What kind of language will be used: symbolic, image symbols, or a total graphic language?
- What is information, rather than just data? How can useful information be separated from irrelevant data?
- What is the desirable user procedural environment for various applications?
- What applications are enhanced and by how much? What is a measure of worth? What is a measure of performance? What is a measure of efficiency?
- What type of input is needed or is optimum for a particular application?
- What is the value to man (scientist, engineer, politician, and housewife, for instance) in having a "live" terminal available? What would its impact be on society?

- What new features are required? What new problems can be anticipated through the use of the added new features?
- How or what should be designed into a system to satisfy individual variations or preferences? What should be varied?
- When is hard copy needed? Will hard copy be needed in the future?
- Should we culturally and aesthetically evolve the system rather than simply allowing it to evolve functionally and physically?
- How can we move the man-machine interface closer to man? How do we build the system (machines) to adapt to man rather than requiring man to adapt it? Should we always do this?
- Should we design for the user, system effectiveness, cost effectiveness, or to sell more products?
- Is there a real impact on software? If so how will this impact be felt?
- Can we define man-machine evaluation methods and measures?
- What system trade-offs should we make? What are the parameters to put into trade-off equations? What are the trade-off equations?

2.1. Logic Technology [8]

It now seems that the incentive for reducing the cost of a computer through the use of LSI will not materialize. Instead, more functions will be added. This comes about mainly because the CPU only represents 5 to 10% of the total system cost and by adding functions other higher cost areas, like programming, can be significantly reduced. The factors to be considered are:

- By building more functions, especially subroutines (parts of programs), from LSI logic the programming effort can be greatly reduced. Since today programming represents considerably more than 50% of the total spent by users for computers, this trade-off becomes overwhelmingly more important than trading-off one hardware technique for another hardware technique.
- To reap low cost benefits from LSI it will be necessary to design and build standard functions that can be replicated in vast numbers for use in systems. Such is the case when LSI is applied to the memory area and since the cost of the memory in computer systems represents more than the cost of the logic in the CPU, typically twice as much or more, this area of application for LSI is becoming quite important.
- From the replication of standard module viewpoint, the largest area of application seems to be in the peripherals and terminal subsystems. For these devices it is not uncommon to have thousands, ten of thou-

sands, and hundred thousands of identical devices whereas the replication for the processor area is in terms of hundreds or thousands. Thus, the use of LSI for logic in peripherals for extending their capability—for making them more "intelligent"— is most promising and the expected trend.

The use of LSI requires that the designer apply new and different thinking to the architecture of his system. Is a bit slice or a register slice or a function slice of the system optimum for LSI? Probably all three are optimum, depending on the complexity of the system and the LSI component. In the design of an arithmetic section, for example, a consideration arises on how to perform the multiply. Should it be performed one bit at a time or by two or more bits. In the past, since it takes fewer logic gates to implement the multiple use an algorithm for one bit at a time, the one bit system was usually employed. But, for those systems requiring the fastest speed possible, implementing the multiply by performing the steps two bits (or four bits or more) at a time becomes important. The cost consideration usually ruled it out of contention; however, with the advent of MSI and LSI this is no longer true. Thus, designs that were previously prohibitively expensive or logically difficult now have become simpler and economically feasible. Studies of computer system architectures designed by using MSI indicate that it will be less costly, faster, more reliable, and smaller. LSI will prove still more efficient. Thus, we must conclude that the incentives to use MSI and LSI are great and will have drastic impact on the architecture of computers during both the immediate and more distant future.

The speed of logic is usually in the low nanosecond range and is starting to enter the subnanosecond range. The evolution of circuitry from *integrated circuits* (IC)—a few logic gates per chip, to *medium-scale integration* (MSI)—thirty to a hundred gates per chip, and finally to *large-scale integration* (LSI)—more than a hundred logic gates per chip, is now well established. LSI with many hundreds of gates available to designers and wafers with tens of thousands of gates can be expected in the mid-1970 decade.

2.2.   Memory System Architecture

The current *memory hierarchy* in the architecture of computer systems consists of as many as five separate levels in the larger systems:

- *Control Memory.*   The purpose of control memory is for holding data and instruction controls currently being executed for fast access. It stores data from intermediate calculations, address indexing information, and certain other control information. In some processors it also holds instructions. It is very high-speed, ranging from subnanoseconds to microseconds. It has a capacity from a few registers to thousands of words. In smaller systems the main memory is sometimes used. It is found in most processors and in some I/O controllers, peripherals, and terminals.

- *Main Frame Memory.* The main frame memory stores the resident programs of instruction sequences and the data operands for instructions which are constants and variables for application and system support programs. It is usually random access and high speed, in the range of hundreds of nanoseconds to a few microseconds in the larger systems. Medium-scale systems speeds vary from a few microseconds to tens of microseconds. Small-scale system speeds can be as slow as milliseconds. The memories storage capacity ranges from a few thousand words to as much as a half million words. For the modern system using a high level language, it typically ranges in capacity from tens of thousands to approximately a hundred thousand words in size. It is usually modular and normally uses modules of modest size.

- *Extended Main Memory.* Extended main memory is an extension of the main frame memory. A few architectures are beginning to emerge which extend the capacity of the main frame memory through the use of bulk storage. *Bulk Storage* is usually a large module but with speed characteristics similar to the main frame memory. Its capacity varies but usually approaches the high end of the main frame memory range.

- *Direct Access Secondary Memory.* The direct access secondary is a hierarchy of memory which usually is not random access but rather is serially addressed since it is commonly a rotating type memory. Its purpose is to hold programs and data that will be called into later use. These memories have a higher capacity that the main memories but are slower. They usually operate in the millisecond range.

- *Mass Memory.* The mass memory's main purpose is to hold files— massive amounts of data. These memories are primarily of the rotating type with access speeds in the millisecond range. Their capacity varies widely with millions to many billions of bytes. (A *byte* is a group of bits used as a unit, e.g., a character, of usually six or eight bits. The eight-bit byte has become a standard unit.)

What is the state of the art and trend in computer memories? Will magnetic core memories continue to be the main memory element in use by 1975? Many of the phenomenal achievements, both in computer applications and their technical achievements, can be attributed to the continuing advances occurring in the memory areas. The current and projected near term memory technologies for high-speed control memories are semi-conductors, ferrite cores, and delay lines with semiconductors predominating. For the main frame memories, ferrite cores will be the most used element although plated wires and planar magnetic films will be used in some applications. The extended main frame memories (bulk storage) will remain almost exclusively ferrite core. In the direct access secondary memory areas for intermediate capacity mass memory the competing technologies will be the removable disc file, stationary discs, and drums. Wire, film, and optical memories are also being considered for these applications. In fact, the removable disc file may take over the magnetic tape market for mass storage by 1975. Other important mass storage devices for the future, in addition to magnetic tape, are metalized mylar tapes and photodigital stores.

Many special-purpose memories will also be used [30]. The cost per bit is the main inhibiting factor when one considers the exotic and hearalded memory breakthroughs. In 1975, one can expect core memories to still dominate; low-cost million bit or more semiconductor memories will be in use; high speed, low cost, random access 100 million byte memories will be in use; and the cost of the main frame memory will be considerably less than a penny a bit. Today, the typical cost per bit of main frame memory is about five cents. When these projected events occur, computer system architecture will again be altered drastically so that we can capitalize on these improvements.

Similarly the logic cost per gate (logic functions of "and" or "or") will become considerably less than a penny. Typically logic costs about ten cents per gate today. In fact, its cost is dropping faster than the cost per bit of main memory and it is expected to drop much lower. Certainly the impact of these technical advances on computer system architecture cannot be ignored.

In the hardware architecture area, as well as all other areas in the computer field, the key is system evolution rather than revolution. It is seldom that the old system is so cumbersome and obsolete that total reform is required when designing its replacement. Such a revolution does occur from time to time in the hardware component area without causing an attendant revolution in the systems architecture and usage areas. This kind of situation is necessary in order to reduce the programming task for the next generation system.

When we cross the threshold toward mass application of large-scale integration for the logic of our computers, it is time to reassess system architecture. One determination to be made concerns the advantages of non-conventional memory hierarchical structures. There are many compelling reasons and mandatory trade-offs to be considered for breaking existing traditional memory levels into additional hierarchical levels. LSI with its promise of low cost logic, will make it feasible to replace costly programmed subroutines with skeletonized, general-purpose, subroutines which are cast in hardware logic. These subroutines are sometimes referred to as "primitives" or "macros." One way of implementing these primitives in a next-generation system is to build a large Read-Only Memory (ROM) capable of holding many primitives. The primitives would most likely be microprogrammed and therefore, to gain speed of operation, it would be necessary for the ROM to have higher speed than the main store—usually it would be about 5 times faster and it might be as much as 20 times faster. Furthermore, to hold all the primitives that will be needed by the many different programs, the ROM would have to be very large—typically tens of thousands of words would be required, while some applications would require as many as a hundred thousand words.

Another method of storing the primitives would be to use a conventional high-speed memory capable of both reading and writing operations. Through the use of such a conventional memory, the primitives could flow dynamically from the main store to this memory as required for their execution. The memory required for this application need not be large (it requires only a few hundred to a few thousand words, depending on its speed, the rate at which it can be loaded, and its rate of use). The smaller size memory required in this case means that higher operating speeds can be obtained than are possible using a very large ROM. Although ROM memory organizations generally offer higher speed operation because of fewer electronics circuits, this advantage is lost because of the very large memory size required to store the primitives. The trade-offs to be considered when deciding which path to follow is not a simple one. Many parameters must be considered including the economic parameters in each case.

2.3. I/O System Architecture

The concept of channel and device controllers (*communication subsystems*) has evolved (see Chapter 5) from the I/O functional section of the early computers and has been extended. In fact, the I/O section has spawned perhaps the greatest variety of changes in computer system architectures to date.

Their purpose, of course, is to get data in and out of the computer faster. Also the trend today for future systems is toward making systems more easy to communicate with and easier to operate. The biggest bottleneck in the past has been and is the input problem. Since it is still the biggest bottleneck, "direct input" systems are again coming into vogue but these new systems do not require central processor attention, *Direct input* systems allow the user to key data directly into the computer's buffer memory without additional error prone intervening steps. This has spurred the growth of peripheral processing systems. Many of these systems are of a man-machine interactive conversational nature.

In early systems the arithmetic (main) processor was called on to perform these I/O tasks. The trend is now toward more separation of these I/O tasks from the computer's main task with the addition of I/O processors. The processor functions for controlling and performing these I/O operations are of both the stored program type and the wired logic type. In some systems strategic and critical function programs tend to be either wired in or stored in hard to alter read-only memories. Some are microprogrammed.

Peripherals and terminals come in a vast variety—both on-line and off-line devices. Some types are:

- Maintenance consoles (switches and lights).
- Typewriter (attached I/O).
- Paper tape (readers and punches).
- Card (readers and punches).
- Auxiliary storage—magnetic tape, bulk core, drum, and disc memory.
- Special-purpose sensors and control devices.
- Multiplexers.
- Modems.
- Remote terminals (typewriter, card, teletype, telephone, graphic, CRT).
- Clocks.
- Line Printers, plotters, displays.
- Microfilm.
- Optical character readers.

The small inexpensive easily transportable tape cassette is rapidly springing onto the scene as are many other *point-of-entry* (collecting inputs where they occur and entering them from the remote point directly onto a computer readable medium) systems.

2.4. Minicomputer Architecture

The biggest impact on the computer system architecture is yet ot come. Industry is just beginning to use extremely simple computers in automobiles, appliances, homes, and for industrial control. Today we stand on the threshold of these application areas; however, such applications will snowball rapidly during the next decade. Their proliferation will greatly outstrip the application computers found in these last decades. Because their design and manufacture is simple, compared to larger computers in general use, and because there is a huge market area, many competitive companies are and will continue to enter the field. Each will find an application-area niche, primarily because of the particular innovative approach employed. For this reason considerable variety can be expected.

The minicomputer is ushering in this era. Only a few years old, it already has as many or more producers than other architectures that have been around for a long time. Contrast this situation with the large complex highly parallel systems whose architecture is about a dozen years old with only a few manufacturers producing systems.

In the supercomputer area (see Chapter 5), few architectures and few systems exist because of the extremely high risk and high development costs involved.

Looking ten years ahead the futurist (planner, manager, designer, and user) is prone to ask, "What will be some of the fastest growing applications? What future architecture will be used, or which one will find the most application"? Some believe it will be the minicomputer. Before the mid-1960 decade there were few minicomputers. By 1968 the second generation minicomputer was being proliferated into many thousands of applications. In 1969, a few years after the introduction of second-generation systems, third-generation minicomputer architectures were rapidly emerging. First generation minicomputers were of two types. Special-purpose minicomputers were being used by the military before the 1960 decade for control applications. In the commercial business area, first-generation minicomputers were primarily card devices. The minicomputer's phenomenal acceptance comes about from its replacement, enhancement, and use for:

- Desk calculator—more capability.
- Card system—the minicomputer provides more functions than the typical punched card calculator.
- Small stand alone computer for individual or small groups.
- Terminal and peripheral controllers.
- A general-purpose computer for performing special-purpose applications especially in control systems.

Each of these application areas spans a somewhat different minicomputer architecture. In most cases, they are miniature versions of large architectures. In order to make them extremely low cost, however, major differences exist. They have far fewer features and instructions. In general, they are slower. Memory is used considerably more for registers, control information, and the like. Few have the sophistication of floating point arithmetic common in larger systems. Newer minicomputers tend to use microprogramming and read only memory to hold macro overlay instruction control programmed into the micro structure. Most tailor their I/O section to the application area and to special interface requirements. In larger computer systems the architecture contains a multitude of features. In the minicomputer each architecture stresses and contains only very few features; this leads to considerable variety in the number of different architectures. Furthermore, some minicomputers are characterized (beyond being just simpler by serial by bit or character operation) by use of wired logic operations, nonstored program control, or plugboard control. Thus, the minicomputer is not always a smaller version emulating its larger cousins. Since they are quite inexpensive to obtain and use they tend to be used very inefficiently. That is, they are allowed to remain idle for long periods of time like any other tool; for example, the slide rule or mechanical desk calculator. Thus, they tend to be a slave to man rather than man being a slave to them as is all too often the case with the larger system, from the viewpoint of keeping them busy.

3. SOFTWARE ARCHITECTURE

The software architecture structure is far more complex than the hardware architecture. First, the number of logic gages in the central hardware system seldom goes much beyond 100,000 in number even in the super scale computers. Typically the number of gates range from 3000 for small-scale computers to 30,000 for large-scale computer systems. The system software (usually a little larger and considerably more complex than the complete complement of application programs of a given system!) typically consists of more than a million words (instructions). Thus, in most instances, it is over an order of magnitude more complex than the hardware logic of computer systems.

Furthermore, the various software architecture functions far outnumber the few hardware architecture subsystems of processor, memory, I/O, arithmetics, peripherals, and terminals.

The basic components of the software architecture consist of the systems programs and the application programs. The system program structure consists of the support programs for system and program control, basic standard subroutines (math type, for example), program and hardware testing, maintenance programs, and the various language systems. System software relieves the programmer from having to write common large segments of programs over and over again almost identically for each program.

Moreover, through the use of system softwear it is possible to control the overlapped running of a number of programs. In addition, system software automates computer operation. The application or operational programs consist of a variety of programs, each somewhat unique, for performing the desired application task. But perhaps the main benefit of the system software is to ensure the integrity of the total computer system [47].

3.1. Application Programs

The list of application architecture functions varies considerably depending on user needs and the application area—military, business, scientific, real-time, aerospace, or government (government applications are usually much larger than commercial applications). One could enumerate thousands of applications [12]. The general architectural structure includes the special control of the operations to be performed and the control of data. Much of this control is for special subroutine call up and use which sets parameters and initializes the operation. Many applications are the continuous repetition of simple tasks. Others are *recursive*—a repetitive task where each repetition is based on the previous result. Still others are *sampled data systems* (sampling of physical events at regular time intervals), which cause cycles to be repeated over and over again as each new real-time input event occurs. Some work with tremendous amounts of data (files) which primarily transfer data from one form to another with little or no computation on the data being performed—the typical data processing task. Yet others, the scientific calculations, require complex calculations to be performed on relatively small amounts of data. Some tasks are simple record keeping with some coupled with lots of outputs from the files. A huge problem area arises for those systems requiring massive files to be searched for information—foretelling of future advances in both hardware and software.

The scope and complexity of software architecture is far bigger than I can cover in this survey.

Application program architecture breaks down into two basic subsystems: the data design and the process design. Each is unique for its particular application but is influenced by the language, the operating system, and the computer system available to the user. Of course, the trend is to make them as system independent as possible, rather than just machine independent.

3.2. System Programs [20–23, 26, 33, 37, 42, 47, 49, 59]

The *system program* has a variety of names such as *firmware* (includes both hardware and software supplied by the computer manufacturer), *operating system,* or simply the *software.* The control portion of the operating system consists of many parts (see also Chapter 6):

- *Interrupt control.* Control system responsiveness to the external environment.
- *Scheduler and allocator.* Schedules which programs are to be run (and when) and allocates memory for their execution.
- *Dispatcher.* Implements the schedule.
- *I/O control (handlers and symbionts).* Controls data transfers/communications to and from the computer.
- *Error control and error processing.* Controls and handles errors so that error-free operation is obtained and the integrity of the system is maintained.
- *Supervisor and monitor.* Oversees and monitors the operation of programs.
- *Priority control.* Determines and controls the order in which programs will be executed.
- *General housekeeping.* Takes the burden off the of programmer by performing many routine tasks.
- *Task control.* Controls the internal operation of tasks when required —to get data, to call subroutines, and the like.
- *Real-time control.* In real-time systems, controls task execution such that operations are performed meeting external timing requirements.

Task control has the primary end job in the operating system for controlling the execution of all tasks (programs). Even though it is the main task, it turns out to be the smallest part of the program but the most talked-about portion. The above structural components are for the general-purpose systems now in vogue on the third-generation systems. The pendulum is swinging away from such general-purpose operating systems toward more modular and special-purpose systems. The trend is also to add language processors to the operating system architecture.

The evolutionary trend of the executive operating system programs started with controls being built into each application program and the common set of library subroutines, utility routines, and a constant pool. The early systems were controlled primarily from the console and shortly thereafter via control cards. Today the punched card is still used for control in many systems. The next evolutionary development in the operating system broke out the control portions from each application program into a separate program. In the early days this was called the supervisory program. The early military command and control applications and real-time military control applications added interrupt control for initiating executive operations. In these early real-time systems it was primarily the synchronous external interrupt that provided the control function. A number of I/O handlers and control programs were also part of these early systems. In these synchronous systems the workload was usually dedicated to one specific task and the workload was well established during the design stage. In a sense, these were very special-purpose executives. The next development added batch control (control of many jobs—a batch of jobs). Then came multiprogramming in a limited sense. I/O tasks and application processing were performed concurrently. This was closely followed by time-sharing. As the executive became more complex by taking over a variety of common operator and program functions. it soon became necessary to control its operation through control commands. Simple control commands were first inserted via punched card and have evolved into job control languages to give user control over the system operation. In all of these control situations except for the very first, some sort of priority control was either programmed in or set in via the control cards. With the advent of time-sharing the priority control varied with the jobs being run and the workload. All this further complicated the multiprocessing capabilities of these operating systems. Then came demand real-time, remote batch operations, and multiprocessing systems, which further complicated the operating systems. This growth is proliferated at an increased rate of complexity of approximately a factor of 10 each 5 years. This leads to the present general-purpose executive which now is quite inefficient in terms of the amount of overhead required in its use. The Department of Defense and the Bureau of Standards of the United States feel that this overhead is as high as 75% of the computer system operation. Because of this high overhead there is a trend away from the general-purpose type system. New hardware features are being added to facilitate executive programs. In fact, many designers are discovering that software is just another form of logic as they build parts of these system programs into the hardware.

There are four basic language levels associated with the use of computers (see also Chapters 7, 10, and 11):

- Natural

    English (or other language natural to humans).

    Conversational or on-line interactive—allowing the user/programmer real-time control and intervention.

    Graphic.

- High-level programming

    Problem oriented—oriented semantically toward the application rather than oriented to the programmer.

Procedure or programmer oriented (FORTRAN, COBOL, PL/I)—the most commonly used language level for computers.

- Macro

    Assembler.

    Machine peculiar instructions.

- Micro

    Micro programmed.

    Logic subcommands (nonprogrammable wired-in logic).

The overwhelming trend is toward a great variety of higher-level languages. Yet, the trend in software languages is toward the standardization of a few base codes like COBOL, FORTRAN, and PL/I which are extended/enhanced in a variety of ways. But the development of quick and easy special codes, each fitting the semantic desires of a specific application area, primarily as extensions to the base programming languages, continues and will proliferate in both the number of different languages and their use. The trend is also toward codes for extending the base languages to the more English-like semantics that the human can understand. All language programs are becoming more modular and are being developed through the use of meta systems (languages for describing languages). The efficiency of these higher level languages, in practice, now surpasses that which is possible through the use of machine language programming. As a result, even the programmers of real-time control for military systems are switching away from their traditional machine language coding and using higher level languages.

The business of selling software separately from the hardware, although still in its infancy, is becoming big business. With the advent of the package program and separate pricing of software, programs are becoming both less costly and more useful. The latter comes about because of the huge proliferation of the great variety of application programs that the user can select from to piece together solutions to this problems. Programs are emerging that exploit the hardware more fully.

Managers, designers, and users alike need to know the options and alternatives open to them both in their daily work and for the future [26]. The decisions made by the software systems architect must be based on what the users want and need. This is the direction that systems programming is turning to now that success has been achieved in meeting the basic operating system needs. System programs for each computer generation, however, lag hardware introduction by about three to five years with the present trend indicating that this lag will increase. The third-generation hardware did not initially bring along with it third-generation programs, nor will the fourth generation. Operating systems programs must employ their hardware much more efficiently than the application programs in order to satisfy user demands. This comes about since they are a required part of the overhead the user pays in the use of a computer system on all jobs.

The user continues to demand for the ability to use more of the capability of the equipment. In the past, the user had to find the means to do so. With the advent of third-generation operating systems this burden on the part of the user has been greatly reduced. It very largely has been taken over by these systems programs. Fortunately, this is the case in the multi-programming environment, since it is far too complex for individual users to control system efficiency. Improved communications facilities have greatly helped to solve this problem by putting the computers power where the remote batch operations and time-sharing can be most easily performed. Future operating systems for time-sharing will provide for multiple terminal support. Such system software will support a multitude of different types and numbers of remote terminals.

We are approaching the period when half of the computer's population will be on-line in the time-sharing mode and causing new languages to emerge. They will be compatible and have the capability to do syntax checking, eliminating errors, and automatic debugging in the English language. In remote batch work job-to-job handling capability and file handling will be upgraded. Some dedicated files will also be remoted. The overwhelming trend is the acceleration of the present shift from batch processing toward on-line, in real-time, remote, and conversational computing. All programs will become more modular and will compatibly adapt to individual user special requirements.

Software is dictating many changes in system architecture for the future. The remote user will have easy access to common files, library files, all languages, control over system priority, and considerably increased automation of his total task. From all of this in both software and hardware areas, it becomes increasingly clear that we are quietly evolving into the fourth computer generation. There are significant changes to come in the characteristics of the fourth-generation system, however, as it pursues this evolutionary course. From the design viewpoint there will be better cost performance; more modularity and further movement into subsystems; more hardware embodiment of control functions and parts of programs; complete specialization of input/output functions for processing both in the central and remote system; improved and increased automation of diagnostic capabilities which will yield higher reliability, availability and maintainability; and manufacturing improvements that will improve the economic factor for both hardware and software. There will be an expanded use of the multiprocessing and multiprogramming functions spurred on by the development of more powerful language extensions and better and more efficient operating systems. There is a strong trend toward netted systems (communications connected computers—see Chapter 8) consisting of one or more large central computers feeding hundreds and thousands of remotely located terminals through a multitude of smaller remotely located computers connected via communications systems. At these terminals there will be many new functions and capabilities added including some data processing functions and an English language capability. One of the main tools for the user will be computer graphics (see Chapter 7). The active computer graphic display terminal greatly assists in the automation of programming and program debugging. To a large extent, it will replace the huge volume of printed computer output produced today. It will also replace drafting boards and drafting instruments. It is becoming one of the most important working tools for the manager, designer, engineer or programmer.

On many graphic terminals there are light pens that allow the user to point the item shown on the CRT face to cause selections and changes to be made. Also, usually included are function keys that allow the user to control what is displayed and, in many cases, call up programs to provide the desired display. With these connected man-controlled devices and associated keyboards, the input problem through such terminals is drastically changing and easing the way we communicate with the computer. Computer graphics is having a revolutionary impact on computer operations and its full impact is yet to come. It is resulting in the trend toward developing more interactive management and engineering information systems. This in turn rapidly increases the use of computers through time-sharing services. One of the main benefits of time-sharing is that it provides faster interaction and feedback of the computer system and its programs. Time-sharing is already significantly reducing the man-hours required to develop programs. Meanwhile, to support such efforts the number of new problem-oriented languages is booming over what was available in the past decade. The result is a significant increase in the communications level and an increase in the ability of users and computers to communicate with each other. This man-computer communications advance has resulted in a growing number of computer system architecture changes, especially toward netted systems.

Another pending architecture change is one that splits out some of the processors capability for *dedicated I/O processing*. This development is causing the processor function to be split into a number of parts in the central system. This will result in transferring some of the functions to the remote areas. In particular, the I/O processing breakout greatly facilitites time-sharing. In such a system the communications from the remote terminals are fed to an I/O processor which then communicates with the common or shared memory between the central processor and the central I/O processor. A private memory, direct paths to the CPU memory, and an I/O interface with the CPU are also associated with the I/O processors. The I/O processor is usually somewhat less capable than the central processor. It seldom has such frills as floating point operations and an extensive repertoire. Because it has its own memory for processing I/O and files, the CPU's role and control functions are greatly reduced allowing it to service a multitude of remote users.

The coming era is bringing with it many new trends in programs. Compatible program modules represent one such trend. With these modules, the user can piece together the parts he needs for his operation. Thus, the user creates a complete computer system architecture tailored to individualistic needs and one which he can update in a piecemeal fashion. In such an era, when a new breakthrough comes, the old system isn't hauled away, when the new is brought in, as was the case in the past. In such new systems the user will simply remove an old module and replace it with a new compatible one. In this fashion it will be feasible to add breakthroughs as they occur rather than waiting for a complete new system to be designed and built. Furthermore, the user will be able to piece together the desired hardware and software system from a variety of sources: from different manufacturers and from old systems. Such user and application tailored systems can be considerably more efficient than a typical general-purpose system.

With the expanded use of the remote terminal, *conversational programming systems* are rapidly springing up. They allow the system and application programmer at a remote console to build, modify, and debug on-line. Conversational programming gives the user the ability to perform these operations while the program is at any level of construction or operational use within the computing system. The ability to alter and display specific variables and portions of the program during execution of an object program is a great boon to on-line debugging. The architecture of the conversational systems emphasizes larger memories, remote terminals, languages, and a time-sharing operating system.

The only way to beat the problems of the old system, when designing its next generation replacement, is for the designer to understand its problems, its niceties, and its intended application areas. Only in this way can the designer correct the problems, carry over the desirable features, and add required new features. For all our past rhetoric about problems with programming, since we don't completely understand it, programming continues to loom as a huge major problem yet to be solved. Is this because of the way we approach programming as a craft? To many, especially computer designers, programming is neither an art nor a science. To them it is truly a craft, since it exhibits all the traits of the crafts; that is, the programmer cannot tell you what he does or needs nor can he tell you what the program does. The latter partially results from the complex nature of most programs (their rapid development due to ever shorter schedules) and partially from the fact that a complex program never is completely debugged. For most programs, it is impossible to check all possible paths or data input combinations that would be necessary to completely test out a program and all its parts.

3.3.   Software Impact on Hardware [27, 29, 53]

Most computer users have been up-tight in software for so long that their managers just assume that many of the problems have been solved, when in reality, they have not been. In many instances, the incentive to achieve lowest cost by both management and government actually results in high cost programming. This is brought about by a continuing demand for a number of items that experience through the years has proved to raise the cost of software. For example, always buy the minimum equipment required to do the job. This results in a programming requirement to over-optimizing the programs in order to make them fit the system. Since jobs always grow, the minimum system needs to be constantly upgraded, which in the past normally meant reprogramming of old programs. Another method is to use programmer trainees or programmers unfamiliar with the application area. This causes an exponential increase in the number of people required and thus compounds the problems, especially the interface problems. Programming costs are predominately labor costs, which today is the most costly item. Furthermore, the critical bottleneck is in obtaining experienced programmers. There simply are not enough competent programmers to go around nor do we have the facilities to train enough of them fast enough.

Managers in many industries are getting hard-nosed over the stratospheric cost of making the computer pay off. When mulling over the problem of reducing costs, programming always crops up as the major cost item. This heightened attention is causing many demands for reform and much research is going on to reduce programming costs and problems. One thing that is occurring is that the computer function is moving under control of higher level management. We are no longer in the era when there was general lack of knowledge of the computer in upper management. Management now usually knows what computers are and what they can and cannot do; however, there are still many managers who lack a knowledge of programming and who expect too much too fast from new programs. Nor do these managers understand the vast number of problems normally encountered in the implementation of a new program. Also these problems are strengthened by much overselling of the capability of programs. Even though programming has been performed for several decades, programmers and managers alike still do not know how to estimate the effort and scheduling necessary to complete debugged programs. The user is often trapped into making unrealistic plans for using software, which will rarely be ready when promised. Part of the problem in programming today is that the programmer must know:

- The application.
- The programming language—how to select the proper one and how to use it.
- How to program.
- The operating system.
- The hardware system.

Moreover, since many programs number many tens of thousands and hundreds of thousands of words, they are generally difficult to understand and debug by one person. This huge complexity brings about the need for a cooperative team effort to complete programs. Because programmers use a symbolic language and since programming enters into areas not traversed before, much semantic jargon builds up on the spot making the communication problem difficult at best. In addition, whether the computer is used to assist management or the programmer, it requires that each learn the individual jargon and rules of usage of many different programs. In many cases, this is such a difficult task that many individuals shy away from using the computer. To solve this problem, programs for supporting remote terminal usage are beginning to tell the user the rules on how to use each individual program dynamically during use.

Another often overlooked problem in the use of third-generation computers results from their use of operating systems. That is, in the past, it was sufficient to have expert operators, expert maintenance personnel, and expert programmers available to assist users and programmers. For the third-generation system, in addition, operating system experts are needed in order to keep the system operating.

The solution of these programming problems will require a considerable number of technological innovations. We are entering the 1970s with the technology to meet this challenge but with the past decade's inertia to impede its application. We can expect programming problems to be with us for some time to come. It may, as many people predict, even get worse before it gets better. Certainly, if the present trend continues, it will get worse before new solutions are implemented.

Some of the solutions waiting to be implemented are:

- Compatible hardware and software modules.
- Building parts of programs in the hardware—subroutines cast into hardware.
- Building in higher level languages which are extendible.
- Allowing system programmers to have program control over structure of system and intrinsic control over the logic.
- Program instrumentation features for system and program optimization.
- Building terminals which contain more functions allowing easier man-machine interaction.
- Automatic handling of I/O and automated data management.
- Adding specific features to ease the programming task.
- A multitude of program products—packaged programs.
- Adding features to automate debugging and the operating system.
- Technical and management information systems.
- Application tailored systems.
- Computer aided training and instruction for programmers.

Such a sample list of things that could be done to computer systems to ease the programming task indicates that the pressure is already building up to get away from the traditional architecture.

The gap between the user and the computer system, which needs to be filled as we face this decade with its increasing programming problems, is managerial as well as technological. Any solution will require revolutionary changes to be implemented in an evolutionary fashion in both of these fields. Although it is primarily true that we have been too successful with our technical innovations far outstripping our ability to manage their use, it seems that still more technological innovation will be required to make our computer systems easier to use and manage.

We can better visualize the present state of affairs with computer systems by looking at efficiency. In third-generation systems new applications and changes to old applications blossom faster than it is possible to take the time to optimize them, and thus, they tend to be less efficient than desired. Also, the system program's burgeoning complexity for meeting all the needs of all anticipated system use has made the operating system in general quite inefficient for specific tasks. Both problems add up to the user paying a considerable amount of *overhead* (nonproductive computer time for the application). In fact, the average efficiency of today's computer systems according to Dr. Herbert Grosch, Director of the Center for Computer Science and Technology, United States National Bureau of Standards, is less than 25%. Thus, the real big payoff today, in computer system design, is not by engineers making a circuit a little faster or running a memory a little faster causing a percentage increase in performance, but by making the computer system more efficient. Design work going on today in both the hardware and software areas (by building in some of the subprograms into hardware) should bring the computer system efficiency level close to 75%. That is, a factor of three times greater than today rather than just a small percentage increase.

From the above, one can see the need for making more than hardware versus hardware trade-offs. The necessity for making system trade-offs of hardware versus program, hardware versus use, and program versus use becomes clear.

4. ARCHITECTURE BY COMPUTER GENERATIONS

Being currently in the third generation of computers with a rapid evolution toward the fourth puts us at a decision point for the future with considerable anticipation for tomorrow's systems. In order to place future architectures in a better perspective it is constructive to view the past generations of computers from the decades of the 1950s and 1960s as prologue for the systems of the 1970s. In general, the many innovations experienced in these last decades will continue to accelerate with more and more of them coming from the software areas in the next decade. Software and hardware products will experience a greater planned performance evolution away from the seemingly haphazard progress of the past and reactive (to problem fires) engineered systems.

If there is one feature that can be singled out as characterizing system architecture through four generations of computers, it is *change*. Therefore, to glimpse future architectures there certainly is nothing more vital and fascinating than the understanding, the anticipation of, and the direction of change.

The *third generation computer system* is characterized by:

- IC components
- Communications oriented.
- Remote terminals.
- Direct access to files—emphasis on mass storage.
- Large fast internal memories—a hierarchy of memories.

- Common peripheral interface—multitude of peripherals.
- Operating systems—program compatibility.
- Multiprogramming.
- High level programming languages.
- Compatible (program-wise) line of computers encompassing small-, medium-, and large-scale systems available from individual manufacturers.

The most often asked question today about future computer system architecture is, "What is the next (fourth) generation?" This question is followed by:

- What new features will be added?
- What type of components will be used?
- What does it consist of?
- When will be come about?
- Will it evolve from the last generation—or will it be revolutionarily different?
- What will characterize it?
- What new problems will it bring about?
- What old problems will it solve?
- Will it have built-in aids for easing or solving problems with programming, debugging, executive programs, system software, and languages?
- Will new languages be required?

Past generations of computers were primarily characterized by their hardware components, since as each generation was ushered in it was accompanied with revolutionary new hardware, whereas actually there were many other changed architectural features of much greater importance to the user. As we move from the third to the fourth generation on into the fifth generation, these other features are taking on more significance. Thus, the answer to the question "What is the *fourth generation?*" is a complex one.

4.1. Past, Present, and Future Generations

In order to present more clearly the answers to these questions, this section outlines some of the hardware and software characterizations that typified each of the past generations [45] together with some obvious ones for the future.

- Hardware/logic component type (by generations):
  1st—Tubes
    - 1947—Government
    - 1951—Industry/commercial
  2nd—Transistors
    - 1958–60
  3rd—Integrated circuit packages
    - 1963–66
  4th—MSI/Hybrid/LSI
    - 1969–71
- Main memory:
  1st—Delay lines/drums/CRT/magnetic cores.
  2nd—Magnetic cores.
  3rd—Magnetic cores.
  4th—Magnetic cores/semiconductor/multiple hierarchy.
- Speed—processor average instruction and memory cycle time:
  1st—Milliseconds and microseconds (100's).
  2nd—Microseconds (10's).
  3rd—Microsecond or less.
  4th—Nanoseconds (100's to 10's).
- Computer system architecture type:
  1st—Computer—not a system in today's terms.
  2nd—Unit computer.
  3rd—Unit computer/multiprocessor/netted systems/arrays (few)/compatible product line.
  4th—System modules—allowing all types.
- Software:
  1st—Machine language/subroutines/utility routines/symbolic assemblers.
  2nd—Higher level languages (COBOL and FORTRAN)/monitors/macro assemblers.
  3rd—Multitude of program languages/operating systems/multiprogramming/data management/time sharing/package programs.
  4th—Extendible languages/meta compilers/meta system programs/programs in hardware/multitude of application programs/modular programs.

- Instruction and data stream:

  1st—Single instruction and single data stream over same channel as input/output stream.

  2nd—Single but separate instruction, data, and input/output streams/ overlapped instruction streams/input/output buffering/interruptable input/output.

  3rd—2nd plus separate and multiple instruction, data, and input/ output streams/remote batch/time-sharing (100's of users).

  4th—3rd plus time-sharing (1000's to 10,000's of users)/separate streams for instruction and data in processor, memory, and input/ output processors.

- Personal (users)—level and where trained:

  1st—A few specialists.

  2nd—University awareness.

  3rd—Some computer science degrees.

  4th—High school and college graduates trained in computers.

- Instruction repertoire—number of instructions:

  1st—less than 100 simple types.

  2nd—About 100, each with variations (modifiers).

  3rd—About 200 complex types, each with many variations/micro-programmed/emulation.

  4th—Rich extendible language/macro-micro coupled/instruction control of architecture structure (reconfigurable architecture).

- Computer media:

  1st—Typewriter/paper tape/computer console switches and buttons/ cards/all usually on-line.

  2nd—Magnetic tape/off-line input/output/memory as peripherals/ interrupt.

  3rd—Mass memory/disc/multicomputers (computer-to-computer communications)/data phone.

  4th—Remote terminals/time-sharing/graphics/telephone system connected.

- User interface and usability:

  1st—User transforms himself to use system/user worked in machine language.

  2nd—Special and limited higher level symbolic programming languages/real-time application with man out of loop entrusting computer to do some process control.

3rd—Complex and more general high level languages/operation aids and control/less human adaption required but still considerable/ systems which respond more directly to user/time-sharing.

4th—Networks of computers/global data banks and libraries/tremendous variety in languages meeting special needs of most users/ extendible languages/remote computer power to user/computer language adapts to man.

- Input/output systems:

1st—Character by character/central processor instruction direct control/synchronous stuttering operation/slave of processors individual operations.

2nd—Interrupt initiated input/output/asynchronous control of transfers/buffered/real-time interface and control to machines/external function control over peripherals/muitiple channels, and multiple paths to storage/scatter-gather (non-contiguous operation of transfers)/separate control of input/output from processor/slave of processor's initiation/stream control/continuous operation of transfers/ modular/overhead functions performed by processor.

3rd—Simple separate processors or processor functions to handle input/outputs/independent operation/central processor can also be slaved to external world/computer controlled and connected communications/computer controlled switching/input/output control over job/simple handling of remotes.

4th—Independent and private memory for input/output processing/ complex separate input/output processors/remoting of input/output tasks to data source at data collection and dissemination points/ capability for handling thousands of remotes.

- Input/output channels:

1st—No channels—computer waited for manual operations to feed cards, mount tapes, and the like.

2nd to 4th—Multiple external channels/multiple internals paths or spigots to and from outside and memory/direct and indirect paths to and from memory/register control per channel/multiplexing/peripheral communication controllers/program controlled/wired logic controlled/batching/message handling.

In the first two generations, computer systems were built which spasmodically and incompatibly covered the total performance range and computer applications, with many gaps. With the third generation came families of program compatible computers which filled the gaps covering a large range of capabilities. In the fourth generation it is expected that standard and *compatible modules* will be built from which compatible families of systems can be built. Soon, however, the computer that a typical user will buy, rent, use, or sees will be a computer terminal remotely connected to a utility system. Future *computer utilities* will be much like the power and telephone services of today. Thus, with such a utility system the computer will be more and more thought of as a true aid to man dispelling much of the past worry that computers would replace man.

The architecture of information processing systems, in the past, came about not so much from reacting with culture and society but as a reaction to some specific applications of the day. As more remote terminals go into use this trend is rapidly changing, and as such, aesthetic and social concerns are becoming more important. First-generation architectures resulted to fill the need of classical calculations for scientific uses. The second generation added the business applications for simple record keeping and the handling of large quantities of data. In the third and further generations a multitude of applications—complex problem solving, on-line man assistant, solving society's problems, and a host of others—are molding architectures.

4.2. The Next Generation

Further architectures need to have a pleasing and easy interactibility for the user and it is this type of architecture that will pass the test of time and remain in use. Alien systems, nonman language compatible systems for example, are not apt to fall into this category of aesthetically pleasing systems. There are many features that the *fourth generation* of computers will emphasize. These features include:

- Many programs.
- Communications and control systems.
- Optimal use of available communications interfaces.
- Widely diversified applications.
- Use of new built-in hardware for application subroutines, system programs, control, and communications.
- Most processing will be real-time that will meet the recipient's re-response time requirement.
- Modular readily expandible hardware and software systems.
- Design will allow piecemeal updating—permit parts (functions, system components) to be updated; thus, the fourth generation system need not become obsolete.
- Efficient operation.

- Source data collection—cards and attendent keypunching will be a secondary source of input.
- Design will emphasize reduction of total system cost.
- Simpler new software—simplified in terms of user convenience rather than in terms of function.
- System designed to operate/function without device-specific software.
- On-line diagnostics—automatic and simultaneously performed with normal system operations—compatible with I/O routines.
- LSI will be phased in—MSI will be used.
- Family systems and families of modules.
- More microprogramming.
- Reduced maintenance costs—less down time—more systems relaability.

There are many ways to characterize computer generations, as can be seen from the foregoing. Each characterization or feature can be shown to be evolving as each generation's advances indicate. Each characterization, however, may or may not follow in the expected time span. That is, the time scales for the above generations are not all the same and generally are quite different. For example, software generations lagged behind hardware innovations. This obviously occurs, since a computer system needs to be in use for quite some time before a full complement of software becomes available for it. In the main, next generation systems are not characterized by their hardware components alone, as many were in the past, but by a multitudinous mixture of hardware and software features. Since the Government has funded the developments of many of the features that went into the making of each computer generation, the dates of their occurrence are to a marked degree clouded in military secrecy and have been omitted. Furthermore, from the many features out-lined, that have been added to each generation, over the last two decades, the rapid pace of computer technology is vividly protrayed. In contrast, however, the slow chronology of technical advances leading to the early computers in the 1950s gives a perspective of today's snowballing innovative advances as can dramatically be seen from the following:

- Cave art paintings—50,000 years old.
- Abacus—3500 B.C.
- Written language—Sumerian—3300 B.C.
- Printing—Non-movable type—1200 A.D.
- Printing press—Gutenberg—1440.

- Mechanical adder (digital)—Pascal—1642.
- Mechanical multiplier—Morland—1666.
- Mechanical adder and multiplier—Leibnitz—1671.
- Telecommunications—Telegraph—Lesage—1774.
- Automatic Loom (weaving machine)—punched card control—Jacquard—1801.
- Difference engine—Babbage—1822.
- Telegraph—Morse—1844.
- Boolean algebra—Boole—1850.
- Telecommunications—Telephone—Bell—1876.
- Punched card—Hollerith—1885-1891.
- Commercial adding machine—Burroughs—1888.
- Tape recorder (telegraphone)—Poulsen—1898.
- Vacuum tube—Edison—1884, Fleming—1904, DeForest—1906.
- Theoretical possibilities of computer logic and information theory formulated—Turing and Shannon—1936.
- Automatic calculator—Analytical engine—Aiken—1937.
- Automatic sequenced controlled calculator—Harvard—1944.
- Stored program computer concept—John Von Neumann—1946.
- ENIAC—Electronic Numerical Integrator and Calculator—Eckert and Mauchley—1946.
- Transistor—Shockley/Bardeen/Brattain—1948.
- UNIVAC I—Universal Automatic Computer--first commercially available computer—1951.
- Subroutine Concept—Wilkes—1951.

5. APPLICATION IMPACT ON ARCHITECTURE [34, 36, 38, 54, 60, 61]

There are many trade-offs being made involving applications that will have a future drastic impact on the architecture of computer systems. This section discusses only a few to give an idea of the trend.

For example, probably the most used computer terminal for the 1970 decade will be the *telephone* as we go to more on-line usage of computers. The telephone companies in the United States are gearing to reach the 1980 decade when it is expected that more than half of the telephone lines will be used for computer communications. Numerous reasons can be cited for this trend:

- Low cost of the terminal.

- Easy availability—already in every business and on most individual's desks and at their homes.
- Ease of connectability to the computer system.
- Computer dial up and call up technology is available.
- Voice output by computer technology is available.
- Pushbutton—touch tone input.
- Needed in information systems to implement the *current awareness function* (to allow the computer to call individuals to make them currently aware of an event or new information).
- Already connected to a world wide communication net and data buses.
- Many phone attachments available for activating and using a variety of I/O devices and media systems via the telephone.
- Advent of the picture for the future as a computer graphic terminal.

A quiet revolution is occrring that is changing our society, especially in the management and technical areas. Its effects are becoming widespread. It is the spread of the on-line ubiquitous computer penetrating all levels of management, engineering, and manufacturing. The results are many concrete benefits. Management, design, manufacturing, and marketing is being assisted and automated by the computer. Such automation of these tasks serves as a catalyst in applying them to solving the real problems in society. This progress is making the proliferation of computers and automation a welcome revolution—especially since the 1960 decade dispelled the myth of the 1950 decade that they would bring about mass unemployment. Instead, the many new jobs they create, for both their application and their implementation, cause the opposite concern for thw 1970 decade—a drastic shortage of people in the technical and management areas to man all the new jobs made possible. As a result, the feedback solution loop is causing more automation, and new architectures for this automation are thus being spawned.

Although the completely automated manufacturing plant is still an extremely rare reality, the trend is definitely toward more automated production. The complex technology of the hardware logic and the programmed computer-based control systems found in the military are rapidly being transferred to industry for its automation. The architecture for these systems adds remote controllers, sensors, and actuators and their control to the typical real-time system architecture. Here the time scale is that of machines and secondarily of humans. But the missing link of automatic materials-handling subsystems must be filled in the 1970s before much further progress is possible.

Today we are in the midst of a revolution where information is assuming greater importance and timely dissemination has become a necessity in modern business and Government. Its use is on an explosive increase in a period when so much of it is on paper that it is inundating us all. It has become one of the most important energy sources feeding the decisions we make—constantly altering the way we manage and perform our work. It is exploding around us in many forms and from a multitude of medias. It has already created a new utility—the information utility. There are many tools for handling information, but the computer is rapidly becoming the principal one for the future, since it allows the profusion of information to be effectively disseminated automatically. I expect the computer, the communications, and the publishing industries to become more closely related and interwoven.

Will much of future technical communications and discussions be a dialogue between one or more users of information and a remote computer? Will one of the roles of the computer be to piece together retrieved information to hold up its end of the two-way conversation? If the amount of information we now use and need to retrieve is a problem—what about the future? The information growth rate is quickening, both in the amount produced and the amount used. Can we cope with the 10 to 1 increase in the technical literature expected in the next few decades with present day methods—or even with projected near future systems? Can we provide a means of searching the ocean of literature made available in the last five years for use in molding what we do in the next five years? In the future, will the best way to send an idea or decision around a company be to wrap it in the computer communications system—electronically and automatically?

Will the remote graphic terminal represent a new media for business in the 1970s? Will its impact on industry be as great as TV has been on society? If so, what new hardware features and software features for application and system programs are required? Will this new computer media system creep along the road leading to the age of the "paperless society"—the age of electronic information dissemination?

The trend for *on-line computer systems* is toward architectures that have properties of:

- Real time.
- Time-shared utility type system.
- On-line multiple remote connection to managers, technicians, equipments, and users through the computer terminal or through other sensors and effectors.
- Profile files on each individual's interests and needs which are dynamically updated with use.
- Current awareness operations—the system makes the user aware of

items of specific interest, rather than either flooding the user with all information or requiring him to query the system.

- Integration of total operations—including administration, planning, management, technical, design, manufacture, sales, and customer aids.
- Centralized common data banks and information distribution systems.
- Information retrieval—the availability of low cost mass memories is making information retrieval economically feasible.

All this projected aid by the computer and its application leads to the not so obvious fact that computer programs must be open-ended systems that dynamically evolve with usage. All areas will grow by evolving. These areas include hardware, system architecture, the large data banks as well as the programs themselves.

It is easy to point an accusing finger at systems programs as the main culprit for the problems facing the computer industry today—for the hardware maintenance types, this is a welcome relief. Thus, researchers of next-generation systems architectures are investigating high cost softwear areas with the idea of replacing some of this expensive software with inexpensive hardware. This will, of course, increase the cost of the hardware. Since hardware logic represents consideraly less than 15% of the total system cost, an increase in the cost of hardware will not materially increase the total cost of the system. In fact, if the research and development work which is being conducted is successful, the total cost of the system should decrease by a considerable amount since the cost of programming and operation will be greatly reduced. The types of program functions that are being studied for inclusion in the logic to solve today's problems in future systems are:

- Primitives—commonly used subroutines which are required for the programming of a variety of applications.
- High level language—built into the hardware—languages that are more adaptable to man and that are extendible to application, user needs, and semantics.
- Memory management aids.
- Features to enhance and reduce the operating system programs.
- Debugging aids.

5.1. Design Trade-Offs [27, 51, 56, 62]

Today the program designer and future computer system designer are "instrumenting" [7, 28, 44] programs, much like using an oscilloscope on hardware, while the programs are run dynamically. The program-instrumenting process gathers statistical data on the use of such system resources as subroutines, registers, memory, peripherals, and time. From this analysis, the program designer obtains the information needed to optimize a program —increase the speed of its operation and make it more efficient. The system designer obtains the information needed to build next-generation systems by using hardware for parts of the program in order to ease the programming problem and make the system more efficient. Design studies indicate that by building in these features, which often require little additional hardware, operation of such a computer system will be greatly enhanced. Tomorrow's solutions for the executive control program will reduce its size and overhead by more than 50% and yet double its capability by using built-in logic.

One approach to making computers capable of being programmed more easily by the user is to build in higher level language capabilities. Since language changes dynamically with use and varying applications, it will be necessary for future computer architectures to be capable of being both: (1) conditioned to a desired language, and (2) adapted to the special language requirements of each user. This is the direction that computer designs for future systems are taking—toward language enhanceable (extendible) processor systems.

The computer's role in changing the direction and complexion of the future is perhaps the greatest technological factor in existence today. This alone is (or should be) a considerable and overwhelming motivating incentive for the designer to be innovative in producing new architecture designs to meet the needs of society for the future. And this is exactly what is happening in the computer field, since designers allow the predicted applications of the future to pace their efforts. The successful designs and designers are the ones who anticipate the shape of the future. To this end, partially because of the high cost of programming, the trend is to design architectures and build computer systems that are more capable than we need now so that we can use them longer. One method that can be viewed as a trend to achieve this end is an architecture that is evolvable through modular and piecemeal updating. In such a system the user then acquires only the capacity and capability needed at any point in time. This trend has been in existence in the hardware area for a number of years and is just beginning to pervade the programming field.

What features are required for modular systems which are piecemeal updatable? The minimum requirements are: (1) asynchronous operation at the interface between functionals and between modules—requires a better definition of computer architecture functions than we have today, and (2) compatible modules—at the interface.

No matter how much a system designer has dealt with the design of a new computer architecture, he really begins to learn about the problems that a user encounters only when the designer becomes a user himself. The first thing that he learns is how many areas there are that need improving. This comes about quite simply because: (1) computers are a complex architectural structure with a multitude of functions, and (2) the trade-off of one logic function against another is extremely simple compared to the trade-off of hardware against such use parameters as programs, programming, system operation, system control, and applications. Past computers have made only small intrusions into this trade-off area leaving much to be accomplished by future designers in order to make computer systems easier to use. An easier method of communicating with the computer system, both from the language and I/O standpoints, is especially needed. We need to remove the middle man—the applications programmer who stands between the user and the system.

The design of a computer system and its hardware in terms of its programming interface, the concomitant operating system and compilers, is a complex trade-off [32, 55] problem that cannot be performed without the aid of a computer in the design process. Until relatively recently, trade-offs of one hardware function versus another hardware function were only performed in the design process.

Today, and in the future, total system effectiveness must be considered. To do this requires considerable analysis and simulation. Technology is sufficient to meet this challenge. It is necessary to apply the computer's power to computer system architecture design to assist the human designer. The key to meaningful computer system architecture comparisions of worth is through application benchmarks [31]. The *application benchmark* is a program made of a user's typical "bread and butter" operations and some problem operations that are then programmed or simulated for each architecture under consideration. The benchmarks then give his analysis a firm ground for comparing the various performance parameters of interest. Some performance parameters considered are:

- System costs—hardware and software.
- Operation time, cost per job, and cost per specified mix of jobs.
- Ease of programming.
- Control features and overhead.
- Reliability—when benchmark program is run on object machine.
- Ease of debugging.

5.2.   Societal Impact on Design [5, 6, 10, 16, 19, 35, 48, 52]

Of course, the most exciting and happily one of the most rapidly expanding application areas of computers is the attack on society's problems. This event, spurred on by the larger forces and directions of this moment in history, is allowing the computer to be of benefit to many people.

This frontal attack on society's problems of urban decay, civil rights, upgrading ghettos and their dwellers, environmental pollution, world wide starvation, transportation, civil disobedience, and the like brings satisfaction for those involved unlike any before—this is also true for those who apply computers in these areas and for the computer architecture designers. The difficulty at this moment in history is that there is a feeling that computers designed for waging wars by the industrial-military consortium are good enough for helping in these social areas—and they are. But, the computer architect also realizes that better suited systems could be designed.

In the United States there is a trend away from the applications of computers in the hard science areas, in the federal government, toward the application of computers in the soft social areas for Health Education and Welfare (HEW), Housing and Urban Development (HUD), the Department of Transportation (DOT), and other Governmental agencies. This trend is expected to have an impact on future computers bringing with it many changes. Such application areas require computer systems and features designed for:

- Large data base systems.
- On-line information dissemination systems.
- Global libraries with on-line remote retrieval.
- Computer utility systems.
- Interactive systems capable of meeting the requirements and semantics of nontechnically oriented people.
- Automated on-line teaching—computer aided upgrading of the underprivileged.
- On-line computer assistance for the under-learned and under-learnable.
- Current awareness systems—computer systems which call up individuals.

6. CONCLUSION

In brief, future trends have been cited as the vehicle for describing computer system architectures in order to show the task and role of prediction that the architectural designer must do to plan the next generation computer system. Predicting the future [16,41] is the most important thing that the computer architect performs. Furthermore, the impact of the designs of computer architects and computer usage must be studied to aid design decision making.

There are many computer system architectures [2, 3, 4, 27, 40]. This chapter discusses only the automatic digital computer conceptual frameworks which are instruction controlled through the acquisition of data and instructions from memory. Other types, not covered, are:

- Analog (see Chapter 9).
- Hybrid—analog/digital (see Chapter 9).
- Simple control devices.
- Preconditioned learning systems—self-adaptive, self-organizing, and artifically intelligent.
- Biological computer systems—the brain, DNA/RNA, and the like.

Moreover, in the area covered, only the surface has been scratched; for many specific architectures were not spelled out by delineating exhaustively hardware, software, and systems for:

- Special-purpose—application tailored systems.
- General-purpose by scale— minicomputers, small, medium, and large computers, and supercomputers.
- Category types—unit, parallel, and array.
- System and application programs.

For the reader desiring more detail, the numerous computer conference proceedings [1, 43] and computer journals [11–15, 17, 18, 24, 25] offer a rich source of material and bibliographic information.

Architectures can be combined so that the resulting computer is more capable than its separate components. For example, the multiprocessor (with its multiple resources of memories, processors, and I/O sections) can give a system with ability (reliability) to perform a task which is considerably greater through its redundancy than the capability of its individual functional units. Thus, the study of the purpose of each architectural form becomes a necessity for both the designer and the user of computers. Also the lack of aesthetic consideration in architectural design (the lack of consideration of computer design as an art) causes a "mismatch" of interconnected units leaving much to be desired functionally.

The architects' weird new temples are not the buildings of old nor the smokestacks of industry but, rather, the new practical art of the architicture of computer systems. This architecture is not caged by fences, but caged it is, indeed, by the problem of programming. Living in the shadow of past generation's system problems, the designer is rapidly researching new architectures that will solve this problem area. Thus, new architectures are coming about to fill not only new functions but also to meet demands for solving today's problems. In doing so, they use and consult the materials available—such as LSI, semiconductors, information flow, operating systems, and magnetics.

Computer system architecture can no longer be disengaged from society's values. The avant garde movement in computer design is toward easing the user's problem and is receiving instant recognition through the rapid proliferation of the computers power via its remote terminals. As a result, the computer is finding wider application in the social areas for solving man's real problems.

Until recently in the United States, the government supported most of the research and development that allowed so much innovative progress in the computer field. This is no longer the era that we are in nor can we expect to grow back into it during the coming decade. Industry is slow to pick up the research and development expenses previously supported by the government and thus is allowing the conservative tendency of management to emerge. This tendency, typical of mature industries no longer in their infancy, tends to prevent innovations from surfacing as quickly and developing into new products. This situation will continue until it reaches a point that the user can no longer tolerate. Only then will research and development incentives and funds become available. In the meantime, innovations are still being created rapidly but these innovations seldom find their way into new products. Nonetheless, we can expect considerable advances in the coming decade. The growth in the number of computers for the coming decade (although it varies depending on who is predicting) is expected to continue at its rapid growth rate of about 20% per year. In Europe this growth rate is somewhat higher at the present time. For some computer architectures the short-term growth rate will be considerably greater. For example, the minicomputer market is expected to double each year as is the market for computer remote terminals for a number of years to come.

Generally, today we are still extremely reluctant to entrust much of what we do to computers. For example, there is the fear by the general public that computerized national data banks will invade individual privacy. Perhaps this will be the most significant change that is likely to occur in the 1970s; for the more we use these advanced systems the more our confidence in them increases. As we perfect our systems and their reliability, more and more of our work will be entrusted to them.

This chapter certainly is not the sum total of the what and how of computer system architecture, but it indicates the trend. Furthermore, the trends point out the momentous thinking that is occurring to bring about needed reforms. Although the information revolution started about two decades ago with the advent of the computers, its real impact is now just being felt with a considerably greater impact expected. Also, there are many alternatives and counter trends to be considered in computer technology and their impact—many more than were touched upon here.

One of the things I hope this chapter points out to the student of computers is the vast area of things yet to be done in the computer field. There are opportunities galore, in the future, for the individual to be innovative both in the application and design of computers—in fact, today, we are only at the threshold of what can and needs to be accomplished.

There is perhaps no technological development in modern history which today offers more potential for beneficial changes that will aid mankind than the computer coupled with newly evolved systems for handling information. New doors, other than the "Gutenberg rut," have been opened for the user of information so that he need no longer wait for information nor be deluged with paper. To understand the potential impact on society requires an understanding of computers and their importance to modern man. Furthermore, we need to understand the direction in which they will evolve. The main purpose of this chapter has been to describe computer system architecture, show the direction in which they may evolve, and to touch upon the expected impact. For, in the predictable future, the widening use of the digital computer in society in a certainty. There is no doubt that computers and communications together, in a beneficial and innovative integration, can lead to profoundly effective systems for easing some of the problems facing mankind today. The greatly expanding use of computers in the social areas tends to make one optimistic about future society. Such trends, coupled with architectures designed to better fit society's needs, are ushering in a new era for man.

It has been implied, here and by others, that computer system architecture is presently passing through a moment of tremendous change in history. Such change, bringing about the time when the computer can aid us in almost everything we do, will certainly cause major and significant improvements for science, engineering, and management accompanied by a major impact on society. Will it thus cause much social change and upheaval? If we are, in fact, on the eve of such a fundamental remaking for the future, we must think about the impact of our activities. Will such a reformation, with the computer on-line helping us, be able to assume a new role for linking the ever deepening social crisis of our time with solutions?

In the past decade, computer system design and use were characterized by the simplicity of the existence of a few different architectures. But this is not the case today and for the future there will be considerably more plurality in architectures.

As new computer system architectures are put into use a new future in the areas of their application is created. At the onset of their application they solve many of the old problems encountered with the old systems and methods. As time passes, however, new problems emerge and some old ones persist. These problems require new solutions. The architecture designer is then called upon to solve these new problems through a new architecture. In the process, he creates a new future for the society by the application of his system. This in turn creates the requirement for the designer to foster a new professionalism for studying the future consequences of his innovations. The designers of today are just becoming aware of this responsibility to society. Since this is an area that needs strengthening in the future, the pressure for many alternative computer system architectures will continue.

In concluding this survey of trends in the art and science of computer system architecture, it remains for the student to extend its boundaries to further horizons. There is no question that computers will raise man's abilities and push his horizons, both for good and evil, but the real question is: Which direction will man pick to apply the computer to amplify? The architecture designer can facilitate this choice through the features and programs designed and supplied for their application.

7.   REFERENCES

1. *AFIPS Conference Proceedings*, all volumes of the Fall and Spring Joint Computer Conferences.

2. Alt, F., and Rubinoff, M., *Advances in Computers*, Vols. I–IX, New York Academic Press, 1960–1967.

3. Amdahl, G. M., "Architecture for On-Line Systems," *Computers and Communications—Toward A Computer Utility*, Prentice-Hall, 1968, pp. 109–118.

4. Anderson, James P., "New Directions for Information Systems Through Advances in Machine Organization," *Information System Science and Technology*, Thompson Book Co., 1967.

5. Armer, Paul, *Computer Aspects of Technological Change, Automation, and Economic Progress*, The Rand Corporation, 1966, p. 3478.

6. Armer, Paul, "Social Implications of the Computer Utility," *Computers and Communications—Toward a Computer Utility*, Prentice-Hall, 1968, pp. 191–198.

7. Bemer, R. W., and Ellison, A. L., "Software Instrumentation Systems for Optimum Performance," *Proceedings IFIP Congress 68*, August 1968, pp. C39–C42.

8. Bloch, E., and Henle, R. A., "Advances in Circuit Technology and Their Impact on Computing Systems," *Proceedings IFIP Congress 68*, August 1968, Invited paper section, pp. 24–39.

9. Bucholtz, W., *Planning a Computer System*, MCGraw-Hill, 1962.

10. *Communications, Computers and People*, The RAND Corporation, 1965, (AD 624 431).

11. *Communications of the ACM*, all issues.

12. *Computers and Automation*, all issues.

13. *Computer Design—The Magazine of Digital Electronics*, all issues.

14. *Computer Journal*, all issues.

15. *Computing Surveys, ACM*, all issues.

16. *Daedaulus*, Journal of the American Academy of Arts and Science, Special Issue: "Towards the Year 2000: Work In Progress," Summer 1967.

17. *Data Processing Magazine*, all issues.

18. *Datamation*, all issues.

19. Dechert, Charles, Ed., *The Social Impact of Cybernetics*, Simon and Schuster, 1967.

20. Flores, Ivan, "Basic Research in Software," *Computers and Automation*, February 1966.

21. Flores, Ivan, "Computer Software," *Science and Technology*, May 1969, pp. 16–25.

22. Gruenberger, Fred, ed., *Computers and Communications—Toward a Computer Utility*, Prentice-Hall, 1968.

23. Hammer, Carl, "Critical Evaluation of Software Packages," *Computers and Automation*, August 1966.

24. *IBM Systems Journal*, all issues.

25. *IEEE Transactions on Computers*, all issues.

26. Joseph, E. C., "Cybernetics and the Management of Large Systems," *Cyberntics and the Management of Large Systems*, edited by E. M. Dewan, Spartan Books, 1969.

27. Joseph, E. C., "Evolving Digital Computer System Architectures," *IEEE Computer Group News*, Vol. 2, No. 8, March 1969, pp. 2–8.

28. Joseph, E. C., "Computers: Trends Toward the Future," *Proceedings of IFIP Congress 68*, Edinburgh, Scotland, August 1968, Invited paper section, pp. 145–157; and *Automation*, Vol. 16, No. 6, June 1969, pp. 70–76.

29. Joseph, E. C., "Subroutines Cast Into LSI Hardware," *Proceedings of IEEE Second Annual Computer Conference*, June 1968.

30. Joseph, E. C., "Target Track Correlation with a Search Memory," *Proceedings of the Sixth Annual Mil-E-Con*, Wasinghton, D. C., 1962.

31. Joslin, E. O., "Application Benchmarks: The Key to Meaningful Computer Evaluations," *Proceedings ACM 20th National Conference*, August 1965, pp. 27–37.

32. Knight, K. E., "Changes in Computer Performance," *Datamation*, Vol. 12, No. 9, September 1966, pp. 40–54; "Evolving Computer Performance 1963–1967," *Datamation*, Vol. 14, No. 6, January 1968, pp. 31–35; and *Datamation*, Vol. 14, No. 5, May 1968, p. 11.

33. Knuth, Donald E., *The Art of Computer Programming*, Vols. 1–2, Addison-Wesley, 1968–1969.

34. Licklider, J. C. R., *Libraries of the Future*, MIT Press, 1965.

35. Maron, M. E., *Computers and Our Future*, The RAND Corporation, 1966.

36. Martin, James, *Design of Real-Time Computer Systems*, Prentice-Hall, 1967.

37. Maurer, W. D., *Programming: Introduction to Computer Languages and Techniques*, Holden-Day, 1968.

38. McLeod, John, ed., *Simulation: The Dynamic Modeling of Ideas and Systems with Computers*, McGraw-Hill, 1968.

39. Mensh, Michael, "Multiprogramming: What It is . . . When To Use It . . . What to Look For . . .," *Computers and Automation*, February 1968.

40. Minsky, Marvin, *Computation: Finite and Infinite Machines*, London: Prentice-Hall International, 1967.

41. Naval Supply Systems Command, *A Fifteen-Year Forecast of Information-Processing Technology*, Final Report, January 20, 1969.

42. Opler, Ascher, "Fourth-Generation Software," *Datamation*, January 1967.

43. *Proccedings of the ACM Meetings*, all issues.

44. Presser, L., and Melkanoff, M. A., "Software Measurements and Their Influence Upon Machine Language Design," *Proceedings of the SJCC 1969*, AFIPS Press, pp. 733–737.

45. Rosen, Saul, "Electronic Computers: A Historical Survey," *Computing Surveys, ACM*, Vol. 1, No. 1, March 1969.

46. Rosen, Saul, *Programming Systems and Languages*, McGraw-Hill, 1967.

47. Rosin, Robert, F., "Supervisory and Monitor Systems," *Computing Surveys, ACM*, Vol. 1, No. 1, March 1969.

48. Sackman, Harold, *Computers, System Science and Evolving Society*, Wiley, 1967.

49. Sammet, Jean E., *Programming Languages: History and Fundamentals*, Prentice-Hall, 1969.

50. Sellers, Frederick F., Jr., Hsiao, MuYue, and Bearnson, Leroy, W., *Error Detecting Logic for Digital Computers*, McGraw-Hill, 1968.

51. Singh, Jagjit, *Great Ideas on Information Theory, Language and Cyberneics*, Dover Publications, 1966.

52. *Social Implications of the Computer Utility*, The RAND Corporation, August 1967.

53. Stein, D. L., and Glasier, J. L., "The Impact of Third-Generation Computers on System Design," *Proceedings of Wescon 1967*, Session 16/1.

54. Stimler, Saul, *Real-Time Data-Processing Systems*, McGraw-Hill, 1969.

55. Stimler, Saul, and Brons, K. A., "A Methodology for Calculating and Optimizing Real-Time System Performance," *Communications of ACM*, Vol. 11, No. 7, July 1968, pp. 509–516.

56. Tou, Julius T., ed., *Advances in Information Systems Science*, Vol. I Plenum Press, 1969.

57. Tucker, S. G., "Microprogram Control for System/360," *IBM Systems Journal*, 1967, pp. 222–241.

58. Von Neumann, J., Barks, A. W., and Goldstine, H. H., "Preliminary Discussion of the Logical Design of an Electronic Computing Instrument," Princeton, N. J., Institute of Advanced Study, 1947.

59. Wegner, Peter, *Programming Languages, Information Structures, and Machine Organization*, McGraw-Hill, 1968.

60. Wilkes, M. V., *Time-Sharing Computer Systems*, Elsevier, 1968.

61. Wilkes, M. V., and Needham, R. M., "The Design of Multiple-Access Computer Systems: Part 2," *Computer Journal*, Vol. 10, February 1968.

62. Zadeh, L. A., and Polak, E., *System Theory*, McGraw-Hill, 1969.

Chapter 5

Large Scale Systems

Jean-Loup Baer

University of Washington
Seattle

1. INTRODUCTION

This chapter introduces some extensions to the concept of the Von Neumann machine and reviews the architecture of large computer systems that already have been built or designed.

1.1. The Von Neumann Machine

It is customary to represent a digital computer as a Von Neumann machine—or stored program computer—that is, a system composed of five basic units (Figure 1).

The functions of these units can be summarized as follows.

- The input transmits data and instructions from the outside world to the memory.
- The memory stores instructions and data, intermediate and final results.
- The arithmetic-logical unit performs arithmetic and logical operations.
- The control interprets the instructions and causes them to be executed.
- The output transmits final results and messages to the outside world.

For the execution of a particular instruction, the following sequence of actions is undertaken:

1. The control requests and fetches from the memory the next instruction to be executed.

2. The control decodes the instruction.

3. Depending on the results of Step 2, either:

(a) An operand is fetched from the memory, stored in a register of the arithmetic-logical unit and control is given to the latter in order to perform an operation; or

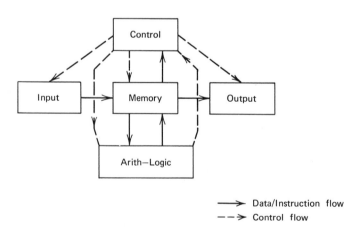

Figure 1. A Von Neumann machine.

(b) An operand is stored, from a register of the arithmetic-logical unit, in the memory; or

(c) A request is made to the input to accept a word from the outside world; or

(d) A request is made to the output to transmit a word to the outside world.

4. Upon termination of the above step, go to Step 1.

Today, many of the small computers are of this architectural type. However, in larger systems where speed is a dominant factor, improvement is obtained—aside from faster components—by doing more in parallel [1]. Three main areas in which this parallelism is present can be singled out:

- Overlapping of operations.
- Input–output concurrency.
- Parallel processing.

1.2. Operations Overlap

In the above description of a Von Neumann machine, the execution of an instruction was considered as a sequence of events. However, it can readily be seen that some of the steps can be done concurrently on successive instructions. For example, while the control unit decodes an instruction and generates the address of an operand, the next instruction could be fetched. That is Step 1, on one hand; Step 2 and part of Step 3, on the other hand, could be overlapped. Furthermore, if the memory is *interleaved* (that is, split into independent modules so that cells corresponding to consecutive addresses are in different modules and can be accessed simultaneously) then the fetching and storing of data/instructions can be performed in parallel. For example, we reproduce in Figure 2 the idealized timing chart of the concurrency among successive instructions in the IBM 360/91 [2].

As can be seen, during the accessing of one instruction the generation of the addresses of consecutive instructions is performed as well as the beginning of the accessing of these instructions. This latter part implies the interleaving of the memory modules. The same process is repeated for the fetching of the operands. Notice that the timing is idealized, since it may well happen that two operands are in the same memory module and cannot be accessed simultaneously. The chart also shows concurrency during execution of the instructions. As will be seen later, this can be accomplished either through multiple arithmetic units, pipelined functional units, or a combination of both.

The chart of Figure 2 enhances the need for a temporary storage unit for

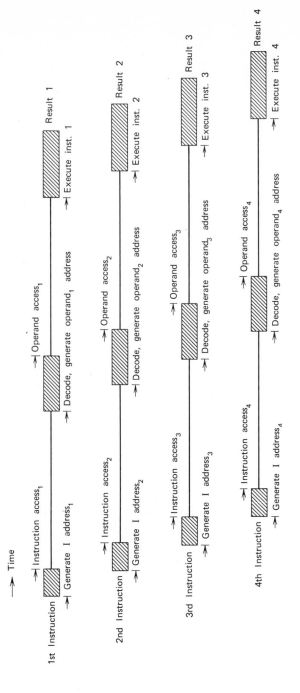

Figure 2. Instruction concurrency in the IBM 360–91. (Reproduced from D. W. Anderson, F. J. Sparacio, and R. M. Tamaluso, "Machine Philosophy and Instruction Handling," *IBM Journal of Research and Development,* Vol. 11, No. 1, page 9, January 1967).

158

the operands and for the instructions. This device, called *look-ahead*, can be defined [3] as a "virtual memory for the arithmetic unit." Now the arithmetic unit does not have to communicate with the memory but only with the look-ahead from which it receives instructions and operands and to which it returns its results. However, the look-ahead is not always 100% efficient, since there can be a break in the sequencing of instructions because of branching or interrupts. An *interrupt* can be seen as a subroutine call invoked automatically by hardware [56]. The elaborate recovery procedures are outside the scope of this chapter and descriptions can be found in the literature [2, 3]. In cases where there is a sequence of instructions to be repeated iteratively, and the number of these instructions is small enough so that they can all be contained in the look-ahead, then there is no need to access these instructions from the memory and the time for the memory fetches is saved. We say, then, that we are operating in the *loop mode*.

1.3. Input/Output Concurrency

In the Von Neumann machine discussed previously, communication with the outside world through the input and output units was done one word and one instruction at a time. Although this was the way it was implemented in the early computers, this method was soon discarded—first, because of the difficulties involved in programming such as the synchronization with the peripheral devices and second (and mainly), because of the time wasted in waiting, since the external devices were (and still are) much slower than the other units. In the next generation of computers, *buffering* and *independently controlled I/O units* were added.

An *I/O buffer* is a storage device for a number of words. Instead of transmitting to (or from) the outside world a word at a time, the existence of a buffer allows transmission of several words at the rate dictated by the speed of the external device. The main advantages are [4]: fewer interactions between input/output operations and the computation, that is, fewer interrupts; waiting periods for individual I/O operations are eliminated; and there is no programming difficulty of timing.

But these last advantages are not sufficient, and improvement can be obtained by allowing the I/O units to communicate directly with the memory under minimum supervision by the control unit. This latter concept of "compute-independent" I/O units or *channels* is now present in most computer systems of significant size. A *channel* [5] is a special-purpose computer whose instruction set is specialized for control of transmission between memory and peripheral devices. Now the central processor controls initiation of the channel processing, and the channel reports completion of its task via interrupts. Moreover, the control unit can ask for the status of the channel.

In the system, more than one channel can be active simultaneously and although a channel can control only one device at a time, many devices may be physically connected to a channel. If the channel is a *multiplexor*, the devices can time-share it. *Selector* channels (i.e. high-speed channels), on the other hand, are dedicated to a single device and are said to operate in the *burst mode*. The concept of channel can be emphasized even more, so that the special-purpose computer gets more general as in the peripheral processors of the CDC 6600 [6].

Although a great deal of concurrency can be obtained via buffering and channel independence, generally, programs will have to wait for completion of some I/O action since the external devices are several orders of magnitude slower than the central processor. This leads to the concept of multi-programming which is defined below.

1.4. Parallel Processing

As stated above, programs are generally I/O bound. It is then advantageous to have more than one program resident in the memory in such a way that while some programs are waiting for completion of their I/O requests, another may use the resources of the central processor. This technique is called *multiprogramming*—that is, the time and resource sharing of a computer system by two or more programs resident simultaneously in main memory.

In some applications (e.g., daily weather forecasting) involving a large amount of computations and with stringent deadlines, it may be necessary to have more computing power. The ameliorations previously described, which can be applied to systems with a single processing unit, are not sufficient and the next step is to link several computers or duplicate some processing units in order to perform simultaneously different parts of the program. This technique is called *multiprocessing*—that is, the simultaneous processing of two or more portions of the same program by two or more processing units. Among the latter, the I/O processors are excluded—that is, overlapping of I/O operations with arithmetic operations is not considered as multiprocessing.

Now, one can combine multiprocessing and multiprogramming, and by *parallel processing* we will mean either technique or a combination of the two.

Notice that multiprogramming involves sharing of the hardware in order to minimize the idleness of the different parts of the system. In what is generally called *time-sharing* [7] (see Chapters 7 and 8), the additional burden of keeping busy the users of interactive devices exists. Therefore, fast responses must be provided to some of the messages sent from these units.

The main goal of batch multiprocessing is fast throughput of jobs, that is, full completion of a job as soon as possible. In contrast, the main goal of multiprogramming—most often in a time-sharing environment—is fast response time to a variety of random messages. In a complete parallel processing environment, both of the above goals should be obtained. Since they are often contradictory, one has to perform a trade-off between objectives. However, these objectives share common characteristics such as:

Increased efficiency. Depending on the individual (user, system programmer, accountant), efficiency may have different meanings. For a multiprocessor system, seen from the point of view of the user with large production programs, efficiency will be a synonym for fast computation, while for the system designer it may be occupancy of the different processors.

Increased reliability. Reliability is as important and necessary in parallel processing as in standard systems but may be somewhat easier because of the sharing of some equivalent facilities.

Increased capability. With more effort (hardware and software), one should gain speed and be able to treat more complex problems.

Now let us state some of the important questions that arise in the design of large scale systems.

- Is the system going to be homogeneous or nonhomogeneous?
- Is the system going to be general- or special-purpose?
- How will the interconnections between processors, on one hand, and between processors and memory (or memories), on the other hand, be realized?

The answers to these questions will help us to classify the multiprocessor systems of today.

2. EXTENSIONS TO THE VON NEUMANN CONCEPT

Historically, the development of multiprocessors has followed two routes. Either the multiplication of processors is such that any of them can be replaced by another, or each processor has a special function. We call the former type *homogeneous multiprocessors* and the latter *nonhomogeneous*.

2.1. Homogeneous Multiprocessors

The ideal machine, called IT by Murtha [8], would consist of n processors (n being as large as one wishes), each of them having a full instruction set and capabilities of performing asynchronously. Furthermore, each processor could route its result to any other without loss of time. There would be no storage problems, nor indexing, fetching, and storing time penalties. Therefore, IT is only a means of representing the parallelism inherent in a program.

Now, let us examine the more realistic systems, such as the linkage of two or more general-purpose and identical computers (called also multi- or multiple computers [9, 10]). We suppose that all processors share a common set of peripherals and that they operate asynchronously under the direction of an executive program. In order to respect the homogeneity (as well as the reliability), any of the processors must be able to execute this supervisory program. The main problem is then the intercommunication scheme between processors and memories (we will speak of main memory with interleaved features as "memories"). Three main implementations have been proposed [11] and realized.

2.1.1. Crossbar Switch System

With this system, n identical processors can have access via multiple-wire paths to m identical memory modules (Figure 3). For example, in the Burroughs D825 [12] a switching interlock allowed access to any memory by any processor and sharing of a memory by several processors. The switching interlock was composed of a crosspoint switch matrix and of a bus allocator resolving conflicts according to priorities by a set of logical matrices. The design was intended for 4 processors and 16 memories. Along with the stack memory mechanism [13, 14], this scheme is particular of the Burroughs line, and in the latest design for the B8500 there is a provision for interconnection of 15 processors and 16 memories.* Because of the very large number of switches and the need for a large amount of circuitry for selection, control and queueing of conflicting requests, this system can quickly become very costly. Also, full reliability requires duplication of the crossbar matrix. Yet, it is also advocated by other workers [15]. In the cited reference, mention is made of a switch complex designed for a configuration of 24 processors, 32 memories, 32 data + 4 parity bit words and 16 + 2 parity bit addresses. The number of circuits required would be between two and three times the number required for the central processor unit of an IBM 360/75!

---

* A crossbar switch matrix is also used in the CDC-6600[6] for communication between the peripheral processors and the I/O channels.

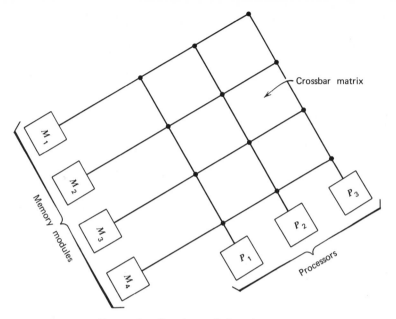

Figure 3.   Crossbar switch system.

Schwartz [16] proposed a modification of this scheme, which he calls a "conveyor belt." To fetch an instruction or data word, the processors place their request in the section of the conveyor facing them. During the "rotation," each memory module is asked to take possible action upon the requests. In a second revolution, the conveyor picks up and distributes the fetched results to the processors. According to Murtha [8], this approach is even more costly and slightly more time consuming. However, it is more modular.

2.1.2. Multiple-Bus Connected System

Each processor has access to any of the M memory modules by its own buses (Figure 4). This system is less costly than the previous one because of the reduction of the cross-points. Also, modularity involves only hardware attachments at the memory access paths (called *ports*), and is therefore easier to implement. Again, control must resolve queueing and conflicting requests.

This system was first implemented on the CDC-3600 [17]. In the XDS Sigma-7 [18], a maximum of six ports provide connection of six independent buses to any memory module. In this latter system, the ports have a fixed priority relationship with respect to each other so that access requests

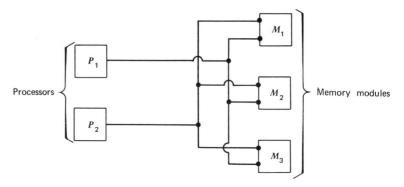

Figure 4.   Multiple-bus connected system.

conflicts are automatically resolved. In the Univac 1108 [19], associated with each of the 4 possible memory modules is a pair of multiple module access units which resolve priority between the 5 possible paths (2 from I/O controllers with highest priority, 3 from processors with lower priority) leading to each module.

This distributed implementation was also preconized for the multi-system IBM/360 [20]—a system composed of n identical CPU's plus the normal amount of peripherals—and in particular the Model 67 [22]; and the General Electric 645 for the MULTICS System [23].

2.1.3.   Time-Shared Bus System

All memory circuitry is shared by all processors yielding a lower cost (Figure 5). Connections between processors and memories need not be continuous, and time-shared techniques can be employed.

This last implementation is less costly, is more flexible for modularity, and control is achieved by using standard time-sharing techniques. Of course, delays may be greater than in the preceding systems. It has been used in the IBM Stretch computer [3], the UNIVAC LARC [10], and is used now in the IBM 360 series for uniprocessors [21] and for communication between the main memory and the peripheral processors of CDC-6600 [6].

2.2.   Nonhomogeneous Multiprocessor Systems

In nonhomogeneous systems, some processing units have special-purpose roles. As a reduction in generality of homogeneous systems, some multiprocessors can be the linkage of general-purpose and special-purpose computers operating concurrently. One of the first systems of this kind was

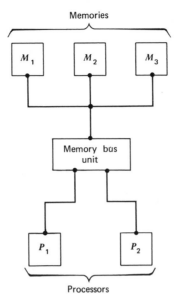

Figure 5.   Time-shared bus system.

PILOT [10], which was composed of 3 processors, the first one handling mainly arithmetic computations, the second housekeeping, and the third I/O operations. This philosophy was generalized and led to the concept of satellite or master computer controlling slave processors. The most general design could be one [24] in which several control computers (the masters) are connected to computing processors (the slaves) and I/O computers through a control multiplexor. Each computer has its private store and shares via the control multiplexor a large common storage complex.

Another approach to the extension of multiple computers is Estrin's fixed plus variable structure computer [25]. The multiprocessor consists of three parts: a fixed part that is basically a standard uniprocessor—originally an IBM 7094, now an XDS Sigma-7—but there is no restriction and it very well could be a multiprocessor; a variable part that is composed of several special-purpose units; and a supervisory system that links the fixed and variable structure computers. The variable computer is original in that it is composed of several units which can be altered and/or connected in order to perform specific functions at a rate greater than general-purpose computers. These alterations and/or connections can be performed either electronically under control of the supervisory system, electro-mechanically by means of switches, or mechanically by changing modules in the variable structure itself. Thus "an inventory of high-speed sub-structures and rules for interconnecting them such that the entire system may be temporarily distorted into a problem oriented special purpose computer" [25] is provided, and this inventory may be updated as "a function of past experience and new technological advances."

Two of the largest very high-speed general-purpose computers, the IBM 360/91 and the CDC 6600, can be classified as nonhomogeneous multiprocessors (as we have seen, two others—the UNIVAC 1108 and the Burroughs B8500—are homogeneous systems). This is because their main computing units consist of special-purpose functional units. This was first applied in the BULL Gamma 60 [10] where special elements were performing, respectively, arithmetic, logical functions, comparisons, and conversions from and to different codes. in the IBM 360/91 [2], parallel execution of different instructions is made possible in the following way: First, the conventional look-ahead procedures are applied in order to allow concurrency of decoding and instruction and operand access, as well as execution of different instructions by means of storage interleaving, buffering, and arithmetic instruction concurrency. As a result of this latter factor, the IBM 360/91 can be considered as a multiprocessor, since its computing unit consists of a fixed-point unit, a floating point adder, and a floating point multiplier-divider which can operate concurrently and independently. In the CDC 6600 [6], the ten peripheral processors having limited arithmetic capabilities share not only a large core memory and 24 operating registers but also an arithmetic-logical unit (CPU) which is itself a multiprocessing unit composed of a set of 10 special purpose functional units, performing respectively addition, multiplication (two), division, long add, shift, boolean operations, increment (two), and branching—which can all function independently.

A variant to these nonhomogeneous machines has been proposed by Aschenbrenner et al. [26]. In this design (called Intrinsic Multiprocessing), several sequence control units (SCU), comparable to the CPU's of conventional general purpose computers minus the arithmetic capabilities, share a set of functional units as adders, multipliers, and the like. All nonarithmetic execution as well as indexing and control is made in the SCU's. A performance degradation of the system can be studied, depending on the number of SCU's and particular functional units, and some of the latter can be added if necessary.

2.3. A New Conception in Memory Organization

Although the IBM 360/85 is not a multiprocessor, it should not be bypassed in a discussion of large computer systems. Its originality resides mainly in its memory organization. Within the central processing unit there exists a high speed storage called *cache* (of cycle time equal to the cycle time of the CPU—80 ns—that is, 10 times faster than the cycle time of the main core memory), which is used as a buffer between CPU and main memory. Main memory is partitioned into sectors (of 1024 bytes), which in turn are divided in blocks (of 64 bytes).

The cache has a capacity of 16 sectors. Tags are associated with the sectors so that one knows the last 16 of them which have been referenced and transferred into the cache. When an instruction or an operand is referenced for fetching, a check is made to see if the sector to which it belongs is active in the cache. If not, a cache sector is assigned to this main memory sector and only the block containing the desired datum is transferred into the cache with a validity bit turned on meaning that a "fresh" block is in the cache. Concurrently with this process the fetched datum is delivered to the CPU. Tagging is updated by letting the new sector replace the one that has not been referenced for the longest time. On the other hand, if the sector is already active, a check is made on the validity bit of the block. If it is off, then the "fresh" block is brought in as above, but without updating of the active sector list; finally, if the validity bit is on, then the fetch is made directly from the cache.

When reference is made for storing, updating is always performed in main memory and in the cache only if the validity bit is on in order to keep "fresh" blocks.

The basic gain here is in reducing the number of main memory fetches by keeping the last referenced blocks in the fast memory. Therefore, there is not as much need for fast access time of the main memory, which may lead to larger but not necessarily more expensive memories.

IBM has announced a new model, the IBM 360/195 [57], which uses both the cache concept and the multiple arithmetic unit of the IBM 360/91. The IBM 370 line also employs the cache concept. This feature could be extended to homogenous multiprocessors [28] with each CPU having its own cache.

2.4.   The Additional Software Problem for Multiprocessor Systems

It is widely recognized that designing a system presently involves at least as much cost in writing programs as in building hardware. In addition to the equivalent of the operating system (Chapter 6) included in the software of a uniprocessor, some more routines which handle not only scheduling of tasks and allocation of resources but also detection of possible parallelism and sharing of the different CPU's must be present in a multiprocessor. For example, when operating in batch mode a choice can be made between making all scheduling and allocation dynamic or allowing some options to be taken "a priori," for example, at compilation time. Also, one may ask if finding the parallelism in an algorithm must be left out of the programmer's work or if changes in high-level languages are necessary, of if a complete "rethinking" may have to be done in order to produce parallel algorithms.

Let us first examine the language problem.

2.4.1. Extensions to Programming Languages

Some extensions to existent programming languages have been proposed for specific use with parallel processing systems. In the Gamma-60 [10], specific instructions were included in the instruction set (e.g., SIMU) to allow the programmer to initiate the different processors in parallel. A complete treatment of how this process should be performed at the machine language level can be found [29] where the concepts of FORK and JOIN are thoroughly analyzed. For example, the FORKS have one of the following forms:

$$\text{L1} \qquad \text{FORK L2, J, N}$$

meaning: begin to process in parallel N streams of instructions which are defined as starting respectively at L1 + 1, L2 and if N > 2, at locations following either L1 or L2. These N parallel processes must join at location J. If N is omitted, only 2 flows are implied (those at L1 and L2), and if N and J are omitted, then the end of the program is the implied junction. In the same manner a JOIN instruction can be defined.

There is an area in programs in which one can generally find a good source of parallelism, namely in loops. For example, in a matrix addition all corresponding elements can be added, pairwise, in parallel. In business applications, the main loop in a payroll program is the same for each man. Therefore, a first extension to conventional programming language should be some type of PARALLEL FOR (or PARALLEL DO) statement (see, for example, Reference 30, which also gives an extensive bibliography on the topic). However, in the only widely used high level programming language which deals with concurrent processes, that is PL/I, only asynchronous events can be specified. This is done in using a TASK attribute when calling a procedure (i.e., a two-way FORK) and JOIN are performed by means of WAIT instructions. The main reason for the lack of PARALLEL FOR in PL/I is that they cannot be used efficiently in a multiprogramming environment with only a single processor while the TASK option can be used thanks to the overlap of I/O and arithmetic operations.

2.4.2. Automatic Recognition of Parallelism

But for the TASK option of PL/I, which is good only for specifying long and few parallel paths, there is no software—or rather programmer defined

—ability to request parallelism in a source program in current programming languages. Hence, several workers have investigated the problem of automatically detecting the parallelism present in a given algorithm programmed for a sequential machine. Two main approaches can be found, depending on the basic unit of computation:

Parallelism at the statement level. This has been done for FORTRAN [31, 32] and restricted ALGOL [33]. The detection of parallelism is performed in two steps. First, a flow chart of the program is drawn automatically to represent the structure of the program. Then unnecessary sequential connections are removed by considering the input/output variables at each statement. These variables can be classified in four categories:

(a) W_i = locations that are only fetched during computation.
(b) X_i = locations that are only stored during computation.
(c) Y_i = locations that are first fetched and then stored.
(d) Z_i = locations that are first stored and then fetched.

Data dependency can be logically described in function of these sets and a resultant essential order can therefore be derived.

Parallelism at the operation level. Several algorithms have been proposed to draw a binary tree from an arithmetic expression. In Reference 34, after a review of previous attempts, an algorithm is given that yields a minimum number of levels in the tree, where a "level" is a set of operations that can be performed in parallel.

To my knowledge, only this second type of automatic detection of parallelism has been attempted on existing systems. Some studies of a FORTRAN compiler for a CDC-6600, which optimized using this approach [35, 36], have been reported. On the other hand, the sequencing of operations ready to be initiated on the functional units of the IBM 360/91 is done dynamically, that is, at run-time through hardware [37].

As early as 1961, foreseeing the advent and generalization of multiprocessors, Brown [38] proposed a method "which is free, at least above a certain minimal level, from the kind of overspecification of sequence constraints that characterizes present programming." This idea has been recently reconsidered [39] where a new programming language is designed in such a way that no variable is assigned values by more than one statement so that all program sequence and concurrence can be determined during compilation without explicit indication.

2.4.3.   Static Versus Dynamic Scheduling

Once the tasks that can be performed concurrently have been determined, they must be scheduled on some resources, that is, assigned to particular processors in a given sequence. The assignment may be simple if only one processor of a kind is in the system, but if there is more than one task waiting, the sequencing depends on the priority policy chosen. If there is more than one processor, then both assignment and sequencing must be performed.

Two main directions can be taken: *a priori* scheduling, where all allocation is performed at compilation time, and *dynamic* scheduling, where it is only at execution time that the decisions are made.

The first method has been mostly investigated at the University of California at Los Angeles [40–42]. The conclusion of the study is that in order for the *a priori* scheduling to compare favorably with a dynamic scheduling, priorities must be defined that take into account both the structure—that is, the degree of parallelism—of the program and the amount of time required for each individual task. Some *a priori* memory allocation algorithms have also been investigated in using this model [40, 43] as well as some *a priori* decision processes for segmentation [44].

Dynamic scheduling is used nowadays in uniprocessor computers under multiprogramming systems. Extensions to multiprocessors have been defined [45] in the following way: When a processor is executing instructions, there exists a collection of information—its state vector—which is sufficient to completely define its state at any moment. This vector has for components the program counter, central registers, and *map* (i.e., a device associating with every program-defined address a physical address) of the running program. In a very simplistic way, one can say that scheduling consists, then, in procedures to determine which task is to be run next when a processor becomes available and to swap vector states between terminating and initiated tasks.

An example of the difference between static and dynamic scheduling can be found in the following memory allocation schemes: In large applications, it may happen that the total amount of memory required by the program and its data is larger than the main memory capacity. In a static solution, the programmer (or a sophisticated compiler) will have to *overlay* its main memory core, that is, decide which parts of his program and/or data are mutually exclusive and can share the same memory locations. For example, if subroutines A and B will never call each other, then they can occupy the same positions in main memory. If, at run-time, B is called while A is present, an overlay will be performed replacing A by B, and vice versa. On the other hand, in a dynamic solution, such as the *virtual memory* concept, there is no practical restriction on the address space—that is, the amount of memory—available to the programmer (and compiler). This address space may in fact be larger than the main memory size. At run-time, when reference is made to an instruction/operand which is not presently in main memory, an interrupt occurs and the monitor takes over in order to fetch the appropriate subroutine/data from secondary memory. An excellent review of dynamic memory allocation schemes can be found in Reference 58.

In this section we have surveyed current and proposed large computer systems which have a structure descending directly from the Von Neumann concept. More of this class of computers will be seen in the future and, as can be gathered from our survey, we are faced with many unsolved hardware and software problems.

3. VECTOR PROCESSORS

A number of applications require manipulations of large sets of ordered data, such as vectors, matrices, and multidimensional arrays. Most often, operations on the member of the set are similar and can be performed concurrently, for example, multiplication of all elements of a vector by a scalar, the first part of a dot product, and so on. Two different approaches have been taken for the realization of fast computing techniques for such processing: the array processors and the pipeline computers.

3.1. Array Processors

The first array processor SOLOMON I [8] led the way to its improved successors, first the SOLOMON II [8] and now the very powerful ILLIAC IV [46]. The latter is an array of 256 processing elements, PE's, which have the capabilities of a standard CPU with a memory of 2000 64-bit words. These PE's are divided in 4 quadrants of 64 PE's each. A quadrant can be visualized as an 8×8 matrix of PE's. Each quadrant is controlled by a control unit, CU, with provision for the CU's to operate independently. Under control of the CU, all PE's of a quadrant execute synchronously the same instructions. Thus the cost of decoding and timing circuits is shared by 64 PE's. Of course, some PE's can be left inoperative, if necessary, by means of a status bit triggered by the CU. This status bit is part of a test result register, present in each PE, which holds the results of conditional tests. Therefore, conditional branches are accomplished by PE tests. As can be seen, a first advantage of array processing is that one CU allows parallel operations of 64 PE's. However, this is not sufficient, since a lot of applications, where synchronous operations of the above type are possible, require processing on a grid (e.g., solution of partial differential equations). Consequently, computing on one point of the grid requires knowledge of the values computed at neighboring points. To effect this, ILLIAC IV provides a direct data path from each PE to its orthogonally neighboring PE's. That is, processor i is directly connected to processors $i + 1$, $i - 1$, $i + 8$, and $i - 8$ (where these numbers are taken modulo 64). To go from processor i to processor j where j is different from the 4 numbers above, a sequence of one step routings is mandatory (the maximum number of routing steps necessary is 7). In fact, simulations have shown that routings of 1 step are most common and routings over 2 steps are very rare. The CU broadcasts instructions and common constants/operands to all PE's therefore reducing memory needs for the PE's and allowing overlapping of common operand fetches with other operations. Input/output, as well as executive programs such as compiling and loading are processed by a standard uniprocessor (a Burroughs B6500). However, reading and writing on and from the PE memories is performed in parallel.

One of the weaknesses of such a design is that the synchronous operations of the PE's plus the fact that each PE has its own memory constrains the addressing of the variables. In order to avoid some of these difficulties, several schemes of skewed storage have been investigated [47]. For example, a straight storage of an $(n + 1) \times (n + 1)$ matrix in a quadrant of $(n + 1)$ PE's is shown in Figure 6. The address a_i for PE_i is the common address

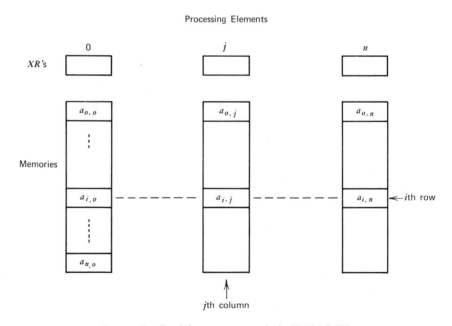

Figure 6.   Straight storage matrix in ILLIAC IV.

determined by the CU for all PE's plus the contents of index register XR_i. Access to one row of the matrix is easily done by setting all index registers to the same value. However, any column is entirely contained in one PE memory. Thus, operation on a single column will make the machine work at only $1/(n+1)$th of its capacity. However, in the skewed storage of Figure 7, rows and columns can be accessed equally well in parallel. For example, accessing ith row demands the loading of PE's register with i for all of them, while for accessing the ith column, the jth index register is loaded with $(j-i) \bmod (n+1)$.

It is interesting to compare the number of arithmetic operations and the occupancy of each processor when one performs some matrix manipulation on an IT machine (cf., Section 2 in this chapter) [8], a uniprocessor and an ILLIAC IV. The following results are obtained [42]: Let t_a be the time spent in an addition, t_m the time spent in a multiplication. Then for the multiplication of the 2 matrices $A(p,n)$ by $B(n,q)$ giving $C(p,q)$, we have for a single processor:

$$T_1 = pnq(t_a + t_m) \qquad \text{where} \qquad T_1 \text{ is the time spent for computation}$$

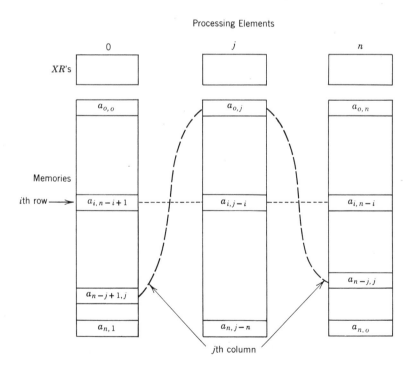

Figure 7. Skewed matrix storage in ILLIAC IV.

This result is evident, since to obtain one element, one needs to compute $\sum_{k=1}^{n} a_{ik}b_{kj}$, which involves n multiplications and additions, and there are pq elements in the resultant matrix.

Since there is only one machine, its occupancy factor $R_1 = 1$. Let us now consider an IT machine. All multiplications of the form $a_{ik}b_{kj}$ can be performed in parallel; therefore, one multiplication time is sufficient. In order to add these products, one needs M additions with $M = [\log_2 n]$ (where $[x]$ is the smallest integer greater than or equal to x). This can be seen easily with the following example: if one wants to add as fast as possible with the constraint that one can add only two numbers on a single adder, $n = 8$ numbers, say $a_0, a_1, \ldots a_7$, one begins to form $b_0 = a_0 + a_1$, $b_1 = a_2 + a_3$, $b_2 = a_4 + a_5$, $b_3 = a_6 + a_7$; in a second phase $c_0 = b_0 + b_1$, $c_1 = b_2 + b_3$ are obtained and finally in a third phase ($\log_2 8 = 3$), the result $d = c_0 + c_1$ is computed. Therefore

$$T_{1T} = t_m + Mt_a$$

During the multiplications, all npq processors will be active, but only half of these will be necessary for the first addition, then half of those for the next one so that the occupancy factor

$$R_{IT} = \frac{t_m + t_a(1 - 2^{-M})}{t_m + Mt_a}$$

For an ILLIAC IV type of machine with straight storage and N processors, if we suppose p, q, and n to be multiples of N, all operations performed by a single processor can be now performed in N parallel paths. If the above assumptions do not hold, in letting

$$^\delta N_B = 0 \text{ if } q \bmod N = 0 \text{ and } ^\delta N_B = 1 \text{ otherwise,}$$

$$M_A = p \bmod N, \, r_A = \left[\frac{n}{N}\right], \, r_B = \left[\frac{q}{N}\right]$$

where $[x]$ is the greatest integer smaller than or equal to x. Then

$$T_N = (t_a + t_m)[p(r_B + {}^\delta N_B)(Nr_A + M_A)]$$

and the occupancy factor is

$$R_N = \frac{q}{N(r_B + {}^\delta N_B)}$$

(See Reference 42 for details.)

Let me comment briefly on this example.

- For a uniprocessor, all three dimensions are equally important for the execution time.

- For an IT machine, timing and efficiency depend only on the common dimension of the matrices for performing the sum process. However, the number of processors required depends equally on the three dimensions.
- For an array computer, the timing depends almost equally on the three dimensions, since when n and q become large with respect to N,

$$T_N \rightarrow \frac{pnq}{N} = \frac{T_1}{N}.$$

The occupancy for this method depends only on q and $R_N \rightarrow 1$ when q becomes large with respect to N.

Notice the comparatively increased effectiveness of array computers if the parallelism consists of doing the same algorithm, for example, matrix multiplication, on independent sets of data or data derived from neighbors.

There is no plan for an official ILLIAC IV language but rather a translator—named TRANQUIL—was considered. It was a collection of data declaration statements, arithmetic operations and control statements, very ALGOL-like but with additional capabilities reflecting the array processor hardware. For example, the arrays could be skewed or straight; there were two types of FOR statements, illustrated by the following two examples:

Example 1.   FOR I   SEQ $\mathfrak{I}$ **DO**

$\qquad$ A[I] ←B [I + 1]; where $\mathfrak{I}$ is the set $\{1, 2, 3, \ldots 10\}$

meaning evaluate first A [1] ←B [2]
$\qquad\qquad\qquad$ then A [2] ←B [3] etc.
$\qquad\qquad\qquad$ until A [10] ←B [11] and all the necessary

routing and indexing is handled by the software.

Example 2.   FOR I   SIM $\mathfrak{I}$ **DO**

$\qquad\qquad$ A [I] ←B [I + 1],

which means perform simultaneously the operations described above, which may involve routing and indexing. Note that

$\qquad\qquad$ **FOR I SIM** $\mathfrak{I}$ **DO**$\qquad$ A[I] ←B [I]

can also be written A [$\mathfrak{I}$] ←B [$\mathfrak{I}$] a la PL/I. For conditional branching, new tests are devised such as

$\qquad\qquad$ **IF ANY X $<$ Y THEN . . . . . ELSE . . .**

or

$\qquad\qquad$ **IF ALL X $<$ Y THEN . . . . . ELSE . . .**

More examples can be found in Reference 47.

Another implementation of array processing, more flexible and less powerful, has been proposed [48]. This machine, VAMP (Vector Arithmetic Multiprocessor Computer), consists of a linear array of n processors which perform synchronously under control of a screen register. By means of a logical accumulator, compress and expand instructions facilitate the storage and handling of sparse arrays. The main originality of VAMP is that the memory accessing can be done in two modes. The first one is similar to ILLIAC IV's. The second one, extension of the classical indirect addressing, consists of fetching n words from the memory (and there may be repeats of the same word) into the registers of the arithmetic unit and then feeding back these words to the memory address registers. Thus, words belonging to the same module can be accessed and sent to the processor's registers. While this scheme is more costly and more time-consuming than the previous one, it lends itself more easily to standard automatic programming.

3.2. Pipe-Line Computers

The concept of pipe-line computing is best explained by the following example: Consider the addition of two vectors A and B of the same dimension n giving a vector C. There are n additions $a_i + b_i$ to be performed. If an addition could be decomposed into p consecutive steps of approximately the same time length so that each step depends only on the outcome of the previous one, then the addition of the two vectors could be done as follows:

	Step 1	*Step 2* ...	*Step p*
Time t	$a_1 + b_1$		
2t	$a_2 + b_2$	$a_1 + b_1$	
⋮			
pt	$a_p + b_p$	$a_{p-1} + b_{p-1}$	$a_1 + b_1$
$(p + 1)t$	$a_{p+1} + b_{p+1}$	$a_p + b_p$	$a_2 + b_2$
nt	$a_n + b_n$	$a_{n-1} + b_{n-1}$	$a_{n-p+1} + b_{n-p+1}$
⋮			
$(n + p - 1)t$			$a_n + b_n$

where t corresponds to the worst case of the longest step. After pt, at the end of each incremental time t, one addition will be performed. Then the addition of the two vectors will take $(n + p)t$ time units instead of n add times required in a conventional computer (note that n add times will be less than npt).

No complete pipe-line computer has been announced on the market. However, the feasibility of such units has been shown [49]. Moreover, in the nonhomogeneous systems where each functional unit performs specific functions, pipe-lining is more readily acceptable. Both floating point units of the IBM 360/91 [2] utilize this technique with $p = 2$. In the CDC-7600 [52], an outgrowth of the 6600, all nine functional units are pipe-lined with different p's. In the I.M.P. design [26] (see Section 2 in this chapter), the functional units common to the sequence control units must be such that they all have the same latency, that is, the same execution time. This can be done by splitting the operations in different states and synchronizing the timing. For example, a floating-point adder could be designed with four stages, respectively:

Stage 1.   Comparison of exponents.
Stage 2.   Shifting of number with smaller magnitude.
Stage 3.   Addition of characteristics.
Stage 4.   Normalization.

However, for a general-purpose arithmetic unit of the pipe-line type, one has to answer the following questions:

- Can two different operations, for example, addition and multiplications, be pipe-lined?
- Can one pipe-line the same operation on different data bases, for example, short and long floating-point operations?
- Can one pipe-line two operations of same type and same data base but the operands not related in any way by indexing? That is, can the two operations $A = B + C$ and $D = B + C$ be pipe-lined? (Note that $A = B + C$ and $D = A + E$ will never be pipe-lined.)

Also, one may think of pipe-lining complete arithmetic units. For example, Bussell [50] investigated, by means of queueing theory and mostly simulation, the use of a variable structure computer as a generalized pipe-line computer composed of two units and appropriate buffers for the solution of partial differential equations. He reported that this method presented some advantages over other parallel configurations.

In Reference 51 a hybrid configuration of a pipe-line computer and a push-down stack computer is investigated as well as the compilation process necessary to use effectively such an organization.

If one wants to consider the pipe-line as a vector processor, all the questions stated above have to be answered negatively, then the analogy between pipe-line and synchronous operations becomes striking. However, look-ahead techniques should resolve the last question as it could be resolved in VAMP.

In comparing very briefly these two types of processors, one can see that the array technique is more global, modular and, on problems with large amounts of "synchronous parallelism," more efficient. On the other hand, pipe-lining would not require as much programming effort, since the parallelism is almost local, and will not have as many difficulties in memory addressing.

4. CONCLUSION

In this chapter we have seen how large computer systems have evolved from the Von Neumann machines concept to the very powerful and sophisticated systems of today. It is customary to record this evolution in terms of "computer generations."

The first generation was characterized by vacuum tubes on the hardware side and by programming in machine language—and later in assembly language—on the software side. Two determinant factors in the transition from the first to the second computer generation were transistors and lower memory costs. Because of increased speed in the circuits, it was realized that some operations should be made in parallel in order to minimize the idleness of parts of the system. This led to the concept of overlapping, memory interleaving, and independent I/O channels. By having more memory at his disposal the system programmer was able to develop more sophisticated software such as compilers (Chapter 11) for a variety of higher-level languages, monitors, and macro-assemblers (Chapter 6) [56].

It is more difficult to find a clear boundary between the second and third computer generations and the distinction is often based on subjective motivations [59]. To me, it appears that the third generation is mostly characterized by the large increase in power of the operating systems, by a better handling of interrupt routines easing the way to on-line (Chapter 7) and real-time systems and the generalization of multiprogramming.

At the same time, some less classical types of organization are sought for. Taking into account the speed and reliability of the circuitry, pipe-line arithmetic units (Chapter 3) are developed. Because of cheaper manufacturing, some systems allow redundancy or decreased efficiency per unit of the system (e.g., in array processing) in order to improve overall throughput.

Now, one already thinks in terms of a fourth generation of computers. But the experts in the field are sharply divided regarding the architecture of the future large systems (see, for example, the position papers [53, 54, 59]). Large scale integration (LSI) could facilitate the replacement of some software functions by hardware elements (e.g., self allocation of I/O channels and auxiliary memories; use of large switching arrays for scheduling and protection of parallel processors). But in no way will LSI be a universal panacea.

Certainly some basic options on the architecture of the future system have to be taken, among which one can list:

- Should we have large centralized facilities with access by remote terminals or a network of small computers?
- Should multiprocessors be homogeneous systems, with their increased reliability, or nonhomogeneous with more efficient special-purpose modules?
- Should one develop large limited-purpose computers such as the ILLIAC IV for the nonsophisticated user with the appropriate software supporting efficiently the hardware?

Some manufacturers may have already partially answered these questions. But whatever alternatives have been chosen, the main difficulty that will confront the *designers* and users of future large computer systems will be (as is already true) to use intelligently and efficiently the abundant resources offered to them.

5. REFERENCES

1. Joseph, E. C., "Evolving Digital Computer System Architectures," *Computer Group News*, **2**, (8), 2–8 (March 1969).
2. Anderson, D. W., F. J. Sparacio, and R. M. Tomaluso, "Machine Philosophy and Instruction Handling," *IBM J. Res. Dev.*, **11**, 8–24 (January 1967).
3. Buchholz, W., et al., *Planning a Computer System*, McGraw-Hill, New York, 1962.
4. Gschwind, H. W., *Design of Digital Computers*, Springer-Verlag, New York, 1967.
5. Hellerman, H., *Digital Computer System Principles*, McGraw-Hill, New York, 1967.
6. Thornton, J. E., "Parallel Operation in the Control Data 6600," *Fall Joint Computer Conference Proceedings*, **24** (Part 11), 33–40 (1963).
7. Arden, B. W., B. A. Galler, T. C. O'Brien, and F. H. Westervelt, "Program and Addressing Structure in a Time-Sharing Environment," *J.A.C.M.*, **13**, (1), 1–16 (January 1966).
8. Murtha, J. C., "Highly Parallel Information Processing Systems," *Advances in Computers*, **7**, 2–116 (1966).
9. Bauer, W. F., "Why Multi-Computers," *Datamation*, **6** (9), 51–55 (September 1962).
10. Curtin, W. A., "Multiple Computer Systems," *Advances in Computers*, **4**, 245–303 (1963).
11. Critchlow, A. J., "Generalized Multiprocessing and Multiprogramming Systems," *Fall Joint Computer Conference, Proceedings*, **24**, 107–126 (1963).
12. Anderson, J. C., S. A. Hoffman, J. Shifman, and R. J. Williams, "D825-A Multiple Computer System for Command and Control," *Fall Joint Computer Conference, Proceedings*, **22**, 86–96 (1962).

13. Gluck, S. E., "Impact of Scratchpads in Design: Multi-functional Scratchpad Memories in the Burroughs B8500," *Fall Joint Computer Conference, Proceedings,* **27** (Part 1), 661–666 (1965).

14. Hauck, C. A., and B. A. Dent, "Burroughs' B6500/B7500 Stack Mechanism," *Spring Joint Computer Conference, Proceedings,* **32**, 245–251 (1968).

15. Lehman, M., "A Survey of Problems and Preliminary Results Concerning Parallel Processing and Parallel Processors," *Proceedings I.E.E.E.,* **54,** 1889–1901 (December 1966).

16. Schwartz, J., "Large Parallel Computers," *J.A.C.M.,* **13,** 25–32 (January 1966).

17. Casale, C. T., "Planning the 3600," *Fall Joint Computer Conference, Proceedings,* **22,** 73–85 (1962).

18. Mendelson, M. J., and A. W. England, "The SDS Sigma-7: A Real-Time, Time-Sharing Computer," *Fall Joint Computer Conference, Proceedings,* **29,** 51–64 (1966).

19. Stauga, D. C., "Univac 1108 Multiprocessor System," *Spring Joint Computer Conference, Proceedings,* **30,** 67–74 (1967).

20. Blaauw, G. A., "The Structure of System/360, Part V-Multisystem Organization," *IBM Systems Journal,* **3,** 181–195 (1964).

21. Blaauw, G. A., and F. P. Brooks, Jr., "The Structure of System-360, Part I. Outline of the Logical Structure," *IBM Systems Journal,* **3,** 119–135 (1964).

22. Gibson, C. T., "Time-Sharing with IBM System 360: Model 67," *Spring Joint Computer Conference, Proceedings,* **27,** 61–78 (1966).

23. Corbato, F. J., and V. A. Vissotsky, "Introduction and Overview of the Multics System," *Fall Joint Computer Conference, Proceedings,* **27** (Part I), 185–196 (1965).

24. Parkhill, D. F., *The Challenge of the Computer Utility,* Addison-Wesley, Reading, Mass., 1966.

25. Estrin, G., "Organization of Computer Systems—The Fixed Plus Variable Structure Computer," *Western Joint Computer Conference, Proceedings,* 33–40 (1960).

26. Aschenbrenner, R. A., M. J. Flynn, and G. A. Robinson, "Intrinsic Multi-Processing," *Spring Joint Computer Conference, Proceedings,* **30,** 81–86 (1967).

27. Conti, C. J., D. W. Gibson, and S. H. Pitkowsky, "Structural Aspects of the System/360 Model 85. I. General Organization," *IBM Systems Journal,* **7,** 2–14 (January 1968).

28. Conti, C. J., "Concepts for Buffer Storage," *Computer Group News,* **2** (8), 9–13 (March 1969).

29. Conway, M., "A Multiprocessor System Design," *Fall Joint Computer Conference, Proceedings,* **24,** 139–146 (1963).

30. Gosden, J. A., "Explicit Parallel Processing Description and Control in Programs for Multi- and Uni-Processor Computers," *Fall Joint Computer Conference, Proceedings,* **29,** 651–660 (1966).

31. Bernstein, A. J., "Analysis of Programs for Parallel Processing," *IEEE Transactions,* **EC-15,** 757–762 (October 1966).

32. Russell, E. C., Jr., "Automatic Program Analysis," Ph.D. Dissertation Department of Engineering, University of California, Los Angeles, 1969.

33. Bingham, H. W., D. A. Fisher, and W. L. Semons, "Detection of Implicit Computational Parallelism from Input-Output Sets," *Burroughs Corp.,* TR-66-4 (December 1966).

34. Baer, J. L., and D. P. Bovet, "Compilation of Arthmetic Expressions for Parallel Computations," *IFIP Congress 1968, Proceedings*, Booklet B, 4–10 (1968).

35. Allard, R. W., K. A. Wolf, and R. A. Zemlin, "Some Effects of the 6600 Computer on Language Structure," *Comm. A.C.M.*, 7 (2), 112–119 (February 1964).

36. Thorlin, J. F., "Code Generation for PIE (parallel instruction execution) Computer," *Spring Joint Computer Conference, Proceedings*, 30, 642–644 (1967).

37. Tomaluso, R. M., "An Efficient Algorithm for Exploiting Multiple Arithmetic Units," *IBM J. Res. Dev.*, 11, 25–33 (January 1967).

38. Brown, G. W., "A New Concept in Programming," in *Computers and the World of the Future*, M. Greenberger, Ed., 250: 289, MIT Press, 1962.

39. Tesler, L. G., and H. J. Enea, "A Language Design for Concurrent Processes," *Spring Joint Computer Conference, Proceedings*, 32, 403–408 (1968).

40. Turn, R., "Assignment of Inventory in a Variable Structure Computer," Ph.D. dissertation, Department of Engineering, U.C.L.A., 1963.

41. Martin, D. F., "The Automatic Assignment and Sequencing of Computations on Parallel Processor Systems," Ph.D. dissertation, Department of Engineering, U.C.L.A., 1966.

42. Baer, J. L., "Graph Models of Computations in Computer Systems," Ph.D. dissertation, Department of Engineering, U.C.L.A., 1968.

43. Bovet, D. P., "Memory Allocation in Computer Systems," Ph.D. dissertation, Department of Engineering, U.C.L.A., 1968.

44. Ramamoorthy, C. V., "The Analytic Design of a Dynamic Look-Ahead and Program Segmenting System for Multiprogrammed Computers," *Proceedings of 21st National A.C.M. Conference*, 229–240 (1966).

45. Lampson, B. W., "A Scheduling Philosophy for Multiprocessing Systems," *Comm., A.C.M.*, 11, 347–360 (May 1968).

46. Barnes, G., R. Brown, M. Kato, D. Kuck, D. Slotnick, and R. Stokes, "The Illiac IV Computer," *I.E.E.E. Transactions*, C-17, 746–757 (August 1968).

47. Kuck, D. J., "Illiac IV Software and Application Programming," *I.E.E.E. Transactions*, C-17, 758–770 (August 1968).

48. Senzig, D. N., and R. V. Smith, "Computer Organization for Array Processing," *Fall Joint Computer Conference, Proceedings*, 27 (Part I), 117–128 (1965).

49. Cotton, L. W., "Circuit Implementation of Fast Pipeline Systems," *Fall Joint Computer Conference, Proceedings*, 27, 489–504 (1965).

50. Bussell, B., "Properties of a Variable Structure Computer System in the Solution of Parabolic Partial Differential Equations," Ph.D. dissertation, Department of Engineering, U.C.L.A., 1962.

51. Stone, H. S., "A Pipeline Push Down Stack Computer," Symposium on Parallel Processors, Monterey, 1970.

52. Bonseigneur, P., "Description of the 7600 Computer System," *Computer Group News*, 2 (9), 11, 15 (May 1969).

53. Slotnick, D. L., "Achieving Large Computing Capabilities Through an Array Computer," *Spring Joint Computer Conference, Proceedings*, 30, 477–482 (1967).

54. Amdahl, G. M., "Achieving Large Computing Capabilities Through the Single-Processor Appraoch," *Spring Joint Computer Conference, Proceedings*, 30, 483–487 (1967).

55. Walter, C. J., M. J. Bohl, and A. B. Walter, "Fourth Generation Computer Systems," *Spring Joint Computer Conference, Proceedings*, **32**, 423–434 (1968).

56. Rosin, R. F., "Supervisory and Monitor System," *Computer Surveys*, **1** (1), 37–54 (March 1969).

57. McLaughlin, R. A., "The IBM 360/195," *Datamation*, **15** (10), 119–122 (October 1969).

58. Randell, B., and C. J. Kuehner, "Dynamic Storage Allocation Systems," *C.A.C.M.*, **11** (5), 297–306 (May 1968).

59. Amdahl, L. D., "Architectural Questions of the Seventies," *Datamation*, **16** (1), 66–68 (January 1970).

SYSTEMS TECHNOLOGY · Chapter **6**

Operating Systems

Robert T. Braden

University of California
Los Angeles

183

1. INTRODUCTION

On most contemporary computers, an application program (the ultimate consumer of computational power) executes in a manner determined both by the computer hardware and by a collection of control, administrative, and service programs called the *operating system*. The earliest operating systems, batch monitors (see Section 4) and floating point interpretive systems (see Section 5), were developed during the 1950's for first- and second-generation machines. Since that time, operating systems have increased greatly in scope and complexity, and now create or control all aspects of the environment within which application programs operate [22].

The meaning of the term "operating system" is sometimes expanded to include the entire set of generalized or system software which is available to a programmer using a particular machine; for example, higher-level-language compilers are included [3]. Although this is perhaps too sweeping a definition, the boundaries of the subject of operating systems are difficult to define. Indeed, as will be discussed in the next section, some (system) aspects of the design of compilers are properly part of the operating system. Compilers, as well as some parts of the operating system—for example, I/O (input/output) control routines (see Section 3)—are executed as if they were application programs. All routines that run as application programs, including compilers and system routines, are referred to as *problem programs*. Problem programs execute under control of a part of the operating system called the *control program*.

Operating systems are having an increasing impact on hardware design. Third-generation hardware was strongly influenced by the requirements of the operating system for concurrent execution of several programs (see Section 4); in the fourth generation the hardware and operating system design will be inseparable, as Earl C. Joseph discusses in Chapter 4.

The central core of the control program, the *supervisor*, is closest to the hardware of the machine (see Sections 5–7). Supervisor functions include allocation of processing time on the CPU (*central processing unit*) and of storage space in HSM (*high speed memory*); see Section 8.

A systematic discussion of operating systems is hampered by the lack of a single well-established set of terminology. Since most important concepts already have two or more terms assigned by different authors, or, more frequently, by different manufacturers, I have tried to avoid inventing any new terms. Instead, I shall use the terms that are most widely recognized.

It is impossible to discuss adequately all aspects of modern operating systems within one chapter or even one book. There is a great variety of different systems for different machines which provide different kinds of computing service—for example, batch-processing, time-sharing, and real-time service (see Section 4 for definitions). This chapter summarizes the elements of operating system design that are *common* to these diverse systems, introduces some of the nomenclature, and mentions the most important conceptual models.

Several important areas had to be omitted. One is the question of efficiency within the operating system: good algorithms, and techniques of trading time against memory space. Other omissions are the practical problems of debugging, installing, and maintaining an operating system, including system integration and system generation; and the design of the system to be stable and reliable in the presence of software or hardware malfunctions.

The bibliography in Section 11 makes no pretense at completeness. Instead, I have included only published papers that are particularly important and informative. Many of the referenced papers contain useful bibliographies that lead further into the literature on operating systems. In addition to the published literature, of course, there are numerous manufacturers' instruction manuals.

2. PROGRAMMING SYSTEMS

2.1. Introduction

Modern operating systems include large packages of system software to aid the preparation, modification, and debugging of complex application programs. Such packages, sometimes referred to as *programming systems*, may include a plethora of higher-level-language compilers, a linkage editor or linking loader, run-time facilities, I/O control routines, text editors, and debugging tools. Compilers are the subject of Chapter 11. That chapter also discusses linkage editors and linking loaders, which are briefly described in the following. I/O control is covered in Section 3. Text editors and debugging aids cannot be discussed here; see References 8, 16, and 37.

Since the software components of programming systems operate at the level of problem programs, their organization and function are largely independent of the control program, which will be discussed in later sections. On the other hand, programming systems depend upon the standards and conventions imposed by the operating system on the structure of user programs. For example, the operating system generally defines standard forms for program modules in punched cards, in HSM, and in peripheral storage; there are also conventions for subroutine linkages and parameter-passing. Such standardization allows modular construction of programs, with easy replacement and combination of program modules written by different people at different installations, perhaps in different programming languages. It would be difficult to overstate the economic importance of this aspect of operating system design.

2.2. Preparation of Program Modules

The conversion of a symbolic *source program* into absolute machine language code in HSM ready to execute is often a complex many-step process. Typically, the following stages may occur.

1. *Macro expansion.* The complete text of the source program is created by substitution of strings of program text in place of text-valued symbols or *macro calls* [36].

2. *Compilation.* The symbolic source text is translated into *object module(s)* of machine language code. This process is called *assembly* if the source text is in symbolic machine language (*assembly language*) [9, 14].

3. *Linkage editing.* A number of separately compiled object modules, and any required library routines, are merged together to form a single program or *load module* [3, 28].

4. *Loading.* The load module is brought into HSM as absolute machine code.

The first compilers and assemblers created object program modules containing only absolute memory addresses, requiring complete recompilation to allow a program to operate in a different region of memory. To relieve this burden, later compilers were designed to create *relocatable object modules*, which contain (1) the object code assembled relative to location zero, and (2) a table often called the *relocation dictionary*. This table indicates which instruction fields contain HSM addresses and therefore need adjustment (*relocation*) for operation in a particular region of HSM. A *relocating loader* adds the program origin address to each address field as the program is loaded into HSM.

To avoid costly recompilation of an entire program to make minor changes in a few routines, a utility called a *linking loader* (LL) was introduced [17]. An LL accepts a number of separately compiled object modules, "links" them together into a single module, and loads the result into HSM for execution. An object module to be input to an LL will generally contain [28]:

1. *Public symbols*, which are defined in this module and may be referenced by other object modules.

2. *External references*, symbolic address fields which are still undefined (*unresolved* or *unbound*) because their value depends upon public symbols defined in separately compiled object modules.

Linking requires a two-pass process analogous to assembly. The first pass allocates storage and defines address values for all public symbols (relative to a common origin), while the second pass uses these values to resolve external references. The LL also searches the system library for modules whose names match any unresolved external references and links these library modules with the program. The second pass of the LL finally relocates all internal addresses and leaves the completed absolute program in memory ready for execution. The LL may also provide some means for equating an unresolved external reference symbol to a different public symbol; the original LL developed by Corbato and McCarthy included a block-structured name-changing mechanism for this purpose [17].

The linking process itself may be too expensive to be performed every time a program is loaded into memory; thus, more recently, the linking and loading functions have been separated. A *linkage editor* [3] links object modules to form a single relocatable *load module* which can be saved in secondary storage and repeatedly loaded with a simple relocating loader. See also Reference 1 for a clever (but extinct) alternative to the linking process.

2.3. Binding Time

An important and useful concept in both hardware and software design is that of *binding time*, the time at which each symbol is bound, that is, replaced by its equivalent text, address, or pure number [27]. For example, a symbol may be bound at macro-expansion, assembly, linkage editing, loading, or execution time. The choice of an appropriate binding time for a symbol is a trade-off between efficiency and programming ease. Program development, debugging, and modification are easiest if binding is deferred as long as possible; however, earlier binding generally leads to greater efficiency of translation and/or execution. The facilities discussed earlier bind all addresses at linkage edit or load time, fixing the structure and HSM allocation of a program before execution. However, some operating systems allow address binding to be deferred to execution time. For example, a problem program may be able to perform a *dynamic call* on a subroutine by passing the name of the desired subroutine to the operating system [3]. The latter allocates HSM dynamically, loads and relocates the subroutine (unless it is already in HSM), and itself enters the subroutine. When the subroutine exits, the operating system returns to the original problem program. Since the dynamically called subroutine may itself perform a dynamic call, the operating system must keep a push-down stack (list) of return addresses. It is also possible for linking to be deferred to execution time; that is, dynamic calls may resolve external references as well as relocate the module [15].

3. INPUT/OUTPUT CONTROL SYSTEMS

Most problem programs require input/output operations to move data between HSM and peripheral storage media such as punched cards, magnetic tapes, magnetic disks, and printed output. Information recorded in peripheral storage is organized into aggregates of related data called *files* (or *data sets*, by IBM [3]). A file is composed of a series of similar data units called *records*.

Most operating systems include a set of routines, usually called the *input/output control system* (iocs) or *data management system*, to handle I/O for problem programs. Typical services that an iocs may perform are the following.

1. *File open and close.* Before an application program can perform I/O operations on a particular file, it asks the iocs to open that file. Opening a file establishes a logical path to it by building necessary tables (*control blocks*) in HSM and performing all necessary initialization for the first input or output request from the problem program. At the completion of I/O on the file, it is *closed*: the associated control blocks are freed, any necessary cleanup is performed, and the file is returned to its unopened state.

2. *Blocking, deblocking, and spanning.* The iocs handles the bookkeeping to allow an application program to deal directly with *logical records*

without concern for the *physical records* (*blocks*) in which the data is actually recorded in the file. There may be multiple logical records per block, while a single logical record may be allowed to *span* two or more blocks. Logical records and blocks may have fixed or variable lengths.

3. *Buffering.* A *buffer* is the area of HSM into which a single block will be read or from which a block will be written by the iocs; also, a buffer may be a data communication region used to pass logical or physical records between the application program and the iocs. The iocs may perform *buffering*, that is, reading ahead on an input file and filling multiple buffers to anticipate the input requirements of the application program, or allowing the latter to fill multiple output buffers before the iocs can write them into the file. This requires (1) *priming* (filling) buffers when a file is opened for input; (2) *draining* (emptying) buffers when an output file is closed or changed to input; and (3) *flushing* buffers (abandoning full buffers) when an input file is closed, changed to output, or backspaced [20].

4. *Direct access space management.* Iocs routines allocate and free space and maintain available space lists on *direct access* devices—disks and drums, for instance. Space allocation may occur automatically as the result of write operations, or it may be explicitly requested by the problem program.

5. *File directory management.* There may be a centralized *file directory* or *catalog* of all permanent files stored on direct access devices and, perhaps, on tape. Batch-oriented systems generally have a single file directory [3], while time-sharing systems (Chapter 8) provide a private file directory to each user and a master directory to locate the user directories [5, 33].

6. *Multilevel storage management.* Many applications require on-line file storage, that is, files that are directly accessible by the machine without human intervention or long delays. Since I/O devices that provide this capability are expensive, a large-scale computer system may include a hierarchy of secondary storage media ranging from low-capacity, fast-access devices like drums, over successively larger-capacity, lower-cost devices such as disks, to libraries of tapes. The iocs may manage this *storage hierarchy* so as to be transparent to the users; unused files "trickle" onto slower-access devices, while files are returned to the highest level automatically on demand. An essential part of such a file system is complete provision for recovery in case of hardware or software failure.

7. *Tape services.* The iocs may provide a variety of services relating to magnetic tape files: creating and verifying tape labels, automatic positioning to the desired file on a multifile tape, and automatically switching to the next reel of a multitape file.

A modern operating system performs the vital function of allowing a problem program to be independent of particular I/O device names, file names, and even device types. Thus, an iocs allows a problem program to make I/O requests by using *symbolic names* for the *devices* [20], and substitutes the appropriate physical addresses of the particular devices which the installation and operating system have chosen. Symbolic device addressing allows the same job to be run at different installations or at the same installation after a hardware change. Furthermore, if a multiprogramming system (see Section 6) is to efficiently share devices like tape drives among jobs executing concurrently, it must be free to assign to a program the particular physical devices which are available.

The system may also allow *symbolic* and parametrized *file naming* [3]; that is, problem programs are written using *dummy file names* in all of their calls upon iocs facilities. When program execution is initiated or when a file is first opened by a program, a binding or connection of file names occurs: an *actual file name* is connected to the dummy name. The actual name is used to locate the file in the directory or on a specified I/O device.

Finally, the system may provide *device-type independence*; that is, I/O operations in a problem program may be independent of the type of device on which the actual file resides [3]. For example, a problem program may specify I/O operations on a direct access device in a manner that is independent of the physical parameters of the device. The program will then function correctly (although not optimally) with its files on disks or drums whose physical parameters fall anywhere in a wide range. Furthermore, if the file is to be read or written in a simple sequential manner, the I/O programming may be independent of whether the file is on a direct access device, on tape, or even on a card reader or printer. The actual file names and device types on which the files reside during a particular run are determined either from the user's system control cards (see Section 4.2) or from the file directory.

4. BATCH-PROCESSING, TIME-SHARING, AND REAL-TIME SERVICE

4.1. Batch Monitors

Before the development of operating systems, all computer jobs were run individually in preassigned time periods under manual control of human operators. Particularly during program debugging, the skill and knowledge of the operator were so important that programmers often had to operate the machine themselves. To increase the efficiency of computer operation, simple operating systems called *batch monitors* were introduced to perform automatic job-to-job transition in a stack, or *batch*, of jobs. See Reference 22 for a historical account of the development of batch monitors.

Today the operation of a large-scale computer is highly automated, with the operating system calling upon the operator only to handle exceptional conditions.

4.2. Batch Job Control

Batch monitors introduced *system control cards*, cards in the user's deck which are instructions to the operating system itself. As the facilities offered by operating systems expanded, the variety and complexity of control cards increased, while their *ad hoc* flavor lingered. Later it was realized that these control cards should be considered statements in a complete language of system control, a *job control language* [3]. Statements in job control language, or *jcl*, are instructions to the job control routines of the operating system. The programmer who is using a batch-processing mode of computer service must supply instructions in jcl for handling any exceptional conditions that may arise during execution of his job; in effect, the jcl statements must substitute for the programmer at the computer console. Therefore, a jcl needs to be a general-purpose programming language, including conditional statements, jump statements, and a macro facility. Macros are particularly important in jcl because they allow an installation to provide a library of job control sequences for common types of jobs, simplifying the work of application programmers. The many jcl's in use today differ widely in complexity and capability, and at present there is little standardization of syntax or function in this important class of computer languages.

By definition, a *job* is a unit of computational work which is independent of all other jobs in the system concurrently. A single job may consist of a number of smaller work units or *steps*. For example, a three-step job might: (1) compile a source program, (2) linkage edit the object module with the library routines it requires, and (3) load and execute the resulting load module. Steps of a job may communicate with each other via peripheral storage; the interdependencies of the steps are defined and controlled by jcl cards. Some batch systems force the steps of a job to run sequentially [3], while others allow steps of the same job to run concurrently where possible [38]. The basic functions of a typical batch operating system are as follows [3, 18, 22].

"Spooling" of system input/output. Concurrent with batch execution, the system transcribes the users' input decks from card readers onto disk storage, and job output from disk to printers; when a job executes, it takes input from, and returns output to, the disk. *"Spool"* is an acronym for *simultaneous peripheral operation on-line.*

Compilation of jcl. The jcl statements are compiled into tables.

Job scheduling. The operating system maintains a table of the batch jobs which have been spooled onto disk awaiting execution, and selects new jobs for execution according to some priority rule.

Resource allocation. For batch system efficiency and to avoid deadlocks (see Section 8.4) certain resources—for example, HSM, tape drives, and disk storage space—may be allocated for the duration of a step and or even the entire job, under control of the tables built from the user's jcl statements.

Executing a step. For each job step, the job control routines locate, load into HSM, and execute the program specified in jcl. Parameters may also be passed to the program from the jcl. The program may be located in a system library or in a user's private library of application programs.

Resource limitation. In order to protect itself against problem programs which enter infinite loops, the operating system imposes limits on the amount of CPU time, storage space, and I/O which a step may consume before it is terminated forcibly. The user generally specifies these limits in his jcl.

Cleanup after execution. A step may terminate *normally* or *abnormally*; in the latter case the system provides the user with program diagnostic information. The operating system must quiesce any incomplete I/O operations for the job, close any files that are still open, and release all resources allocated to the step (see Section 8).

Accounting. The system gathers and records data necessary for charging and verifies the account number supplied in the jcl.

Operator communication and control. The computer operator has a typewriter or display console to receive messages from the operating system, exercise control over system functions, and monitor system activity.

System initialization and recovery. Startup of a large-scale operating system is a complex software function. If the startup follows a system failure or other unscheduled interruption, the operator will normally *warm-start* the system, saving the previously spooled input and output; however, in unfavorable circumstances he will have to *cold-start*, losing all spooled jobs.

4.3. Time-Sharing Service

The difficulty of foreseeing all possible exceptional conditions for a particular job, and the complexity of programming a suitable response for each of these condition in jcl, were two of the original motivations for the development of the *time-sharing mode* of computer service as an alternative to batch processing. Under time-sharing, a number of programmers may have individual remote consoles, typically typewriters or character-displays.

Using the techniques of multiprogramming to be discussed in later sections, the operating system shares the machine among these users so that each has the illusion of "operating" a (pseudo-) computer dedicated to his job. The programmer is then "on-line" again, so he can directly respond to exceptional conditions when they arise. There are other (probably more significant) advantages to time-shared access to a computer. As is well known, the possibility for direct man-machine interaction provided by time-sharing may lead to a qualitative rather than just quantitative improvement in human problem-solving capability [32].

Although a job is a batch-processing concept, it is analogous to a single session at a time-shared console, during which the programmer invokes a number of different processing programs—for example, a text editor, a compiler, a linking loader, and his program—like batch job steps. The programmer exerts control over his pseudo-computer by entering statements in a *time-sharing command language*. For more information on time-sharing, see Chapters 7 and 8 in this book and References 15, 16, 26, 32, 33, and 37. A typical command language is described in Reference 33.

4.4. Real-Time Systems [19]

A computer providing *real-time service* is normally dedicated to a particular mission, calculating "immediate" responses to input signals from an environment and returning information or control signals to that environment. Some real-time systems perform primarily a control function, such as controlling an industrial process or city traffic lights. Others provide retrieval and immediate updating of a particular centralized bank of data, like an airline reservations list or a set of bank accounts. Still others are used primarily to capture and analyze data as it is generated. See Reference 19 for a complete discussion of the basic principles of real-time systems.

4.5. System Management

The operating system that is used to control the flow of batch jobs or time-sharing services embodies and enforces management policies of each computer center. For example, the job-scheduling function of a batch operating system will often enforce a policy of job priorities in selecting the next job for execution. On the other hand, the computer system itself has many attributes of a business organization and some of the same management requirements. Thus, operating systems involve two interrelated management problems: the computer system and the computer center.

A common job-scheduling policy is to give higher priority to shorter jobs, a rule that decreases *average* job completion time from its value with first-come-first-served scheduling. A more subtle advantage of short-job-first scheduling is that it encourages users to set realistically low resource limits on their jobs [4]. Thus, short-job-first scheduling is a management tool designed to reduce the waste of computer resources caused by looping programs and to provide more reliable predictive information for automatic optimization of resource utilization. In many organizations the computer time is a scarce resource that must be allocated among the users. Computer centers have experimented with a wide variety of allocation mechanisms, ranging from strict quotas to free-market models complete with competitive bidding for fast turn-around. Some of these schemes are very elaborate, and their administration is feasible only because it is performed by the operating system itself.

Before multiprogramming was introduced, centers could charge for batch jobs on the basis of simple elapsed time at a fixed rate per hour. Many centers now use a resource-based charging scheme, with separate charges for different computer resources such as CPU time, HSM, I/O device usage. Ideally, the individual resource charges should be interrelated in such a way that if each user writes his program so as to minimize his total cost, the result will be to maximize overall system throughput. Another goal is to create consistent charges: the identical job should result in the same charges each time it is run, regardless of other jobs in the system. Concepts and techniques for charging for computer service are currently undergoing active development.

Development of a charging scheme suited to a particular installation depends on economic, managerial, and political considerations peculiar to that center. It also depends on being able to gather data on resource utilization from the operating system without introducing serious overhead. This in turn may impose (difficult) requirements on the design of the operating system and hardware. The next generation of machines and operating systems will no doubt be designed with careful attention to efficient collection of a wide variety of resource utilization data. Such data are also important for "tuning" a system for optimum performance on a particular workload.

5. HARDWARE CONTROL AND EXTENSION

An important function of many operating systems is to control, modify, and/or extend the hardware. As Earl C. Joseph discusses in Chapter 4, today's computer designer must decide where to draw the line between hardware and software functions; the decision is basically an economic question. The operating system may extend the hardware in a manner which is transparent to an applications program, or even to the rest of the operating system, thereby creating *virtual hardware*. The apparent extension and modification of the machine hardware by the operating system has been termed the *extensible machine* concept [38].

5.1.   Interpretive Pseudocomputers

The floating-point interpretive systems, which were widely used on first-generation machines, were the earliest examples of software-simulated hardware and, in fact, of operating systems. These interpretive systems created complete *pseudocomputers* containing important features that were not available in the real hardware, including floating point arithmetic, index registers, and loop instructions [29]. Many persons were introduced to computers by these interpretive systems, which offered great convenience to their users.

Although the introduction of floating point hardware ended the reign of the early interpretive systems, the technique of pseudomachine creation is still in wide use. Many list and string-processing systems have been implemented as interpreters which effectively create rather exotic pseudo-machines. A number of time-sharing systems include interactive compiler-interpreters which create pseudomachines whose "machine languages" are higher-level languages.

5.2.   Operation Simulation and Microprogramming

Some computers use software to simulate the hardware execution of particular operation codes. When the next instruction fetched for execution contains an operation code which is to be software-simulated, the hardware triggers an appropriate program interrupt (defined in Section 5.3) to cause the simulation subroutine to be executed; afterward, the machine returns to normal hardware decoding of the instruction stream.

It is a natural step from operation code simulation by software subroutines to the use of hardware subroutines written in a more elementary "machine language" and executed by a primitive "inner computer," unknown to the programmer. This technique, called *microprogramming*, is widely used in computers today, and is discussed by both Leon Presser (Chapter 11) and Earl C. Joseph (Chapter 4); see Reference 24 for a survey of the subject. The next major step in the evolution of computer architecture will probably include implementation of parts of the operating system in microprogrammed code.

5.3.   Interrupt Service Routines

Most computers today include *interrupt hardware* which automatically diverts the attention of the central processor to an alternate execution path when necessary to respond to an external or exceptional condition.

A typical machine may recognize any of the following types of interrupt requests: *I/O completion, attention* (unsolicited request for service from external device), *timer expiration, program fault interrupt* (for example, arithmetic overflow, illegal operation code, or illegal operand address), *supervisor call* (see Section 7.3), *page fault* (see Section 5.5), or *machine error*. Within each interrupt type, there may be a number of causes or sources for request signals. I/O completion, attention, and timer expiration are examples of *asynchronous* or *processor-independent* interrupts, since they occur at times that cannot be precisely predicted by the program in execution. On the other hand, program faults, supervisor calls, and page faults are called *synchronous* or *processor-independent* interrupts, or *traps*, since they are the direct result of instruction execution.

The segment of the operating system that acts on or *services* interrupts is closely associated with the machine hardware; indeed, without an *interrupt service routine* (ISR) the I/O hardware of many machines would not function. The result of taking, or *firing*, an interrupt request is typically that the machine simulates a subroutine call operation to enter the ISR at a particular (wired-in) HSM address. The previous CPU state—the contents of registers, the next-instruction address, and other indicators—must be saved so that when service is complete the ISR can restore the previous machine state, and the interrupted computation can continue. Machine architectures differ on the extent to which the interrupt hardware saves the machine state before entering the ISR [30, 31].

Each interrupt source is wired to trigger one of a number of parallel interrupt request paths or *levels*. Each level, when fired, generally causes entry to the ISR at a different address, and the ISR contains a logically separate *Interrupt Handler* (IH) routine for each interrupt level (see Figure 1). The operating system may *disarm* a level, causing interrupt requests to that level to be ignored. Alternatively, the level may be armed but *disabled*, in which case the request is held in a one-bit memory until the level is (re-)enabled by the hardware and the operating system. When a level fires, the interrupt hardware normally disables that level (and perhaps other levels) so that the level can remember another interrupt but cannot fire again while the previous interrupt is being serviced.

Interrupts on different levels are asynchronous and may come simultaneously; each may have a different maximum permissible service time imposed by the external hardware; and service times may vary greatly.

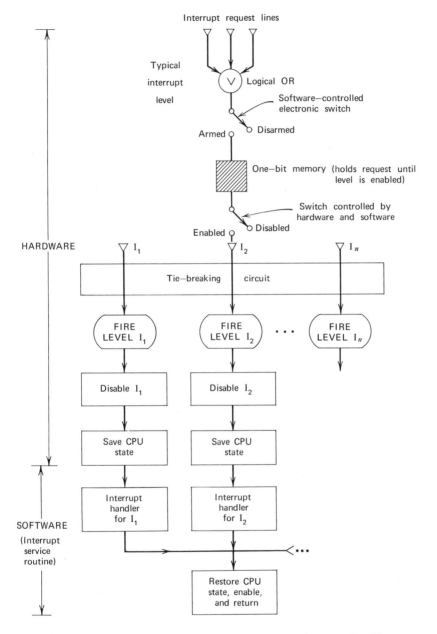

Figure 1. Typical hardware/software organization for interrupt handling.

Thus it is necessary in effect to schedule asynchronous interrupt servicing while incurring little overhead. Additional complications are that an IH routine which is servicing an interrupt may require a function like input/output which itself generates interrupts, and that reentrance of an IH routine due to successive interrupts of the same type may be disastrous. The scheduling of service may be performed entirely by the interrupt hardware or partly by software in the ISR. Usually there is a built-in priority among interrupt levels (the "tie-breaking circuit" of Figure 1). Some machines disable all levels during the servicing of any interrupt; the result is purely sequential service [31]. Others disable only lower-priority levels, and let higher-priority levels interrupt the service of a given level. The ISR software may effectively juggle these hardware priorities by enabling and disabling levels [30].

5.4. I/O Supervision and Pseudodevices

In many machines the control of input/output is shared between the I/O hardware itself and an operating system routine, which we shall call the *input/output supervisor* (ios). An ios is the lowest level in a multilayer structure of I/O control routines. One may think of the ios interface as the effective I/O hardware, since all I/O performed by problem programs and the control program (except the ios itself) must be requested from the ios. Since interrupts are essential to I/O control, the I/O interrupt handler forms part of the ios.

A typical problem program request to the ios for input from disk might be "read the physical block with logical block number B from file F into a buffer of N words starting at memory address A." The ios converts the symbolic file name F to an actual unit address and maps block number B into a (perhaps very complicated) physical address on that unit. If an I/O request cannot be initiated immediately because the required hardware is busy, it is entered into a queue of deferred requests. Whenever an I/O completion interrupt signals a free I/O path, the ios attempts to initiate a deferred request for that path. The ios generally contains hardware-dependent routines to initiate and terminate the operations properly on each type of device, to handle all abnormal situations which arise, and to provide error recovery when possible.

The ios centralizes all I/O control in a single software routine; this is an organizational fact with important consequences. For example, it is a logical place for enforcing file access restrictions and protection against accidental destruction [35]. Furthermore, the ios can mask complexities and irregularities in the I/O hardware, and can generally modify, reorganize, or extend the I/O hardware in a manner which is transparent to the operating system as well as an application program.

In particular, the ios can create virtual I/O devices or *pseudodevices*. A pseudodevice is treated in all respects like a real device by all program levels (including the iocs), down to the ios; the latter, however, detects and simulates all operations requested for a pseudodevice. There are a number of important examples of the use of pseudodevices, both for problem programs and for operating systems [10]. For example, *pseudocard readers* and *pseudoprinters*, actually buffered files on disk, are frequently used to handle the system input and output streams in a batch system. Another example is the use of *pseudodisks* to buffer large segments of normally transient operating system routines in low-speed core memory.

5.5.   Address–Mapping and Virtual Memory [21, 43]

Many machines provide some form of address-mapping hardware that transforms the HSM addresses (*logical addresses*), used by the program being executed by the CPU, into actual (*physical*) addresses in HSM. The set of possible logical addresses available to a program is called its *logical name space*, while the physical addresses 0, 1, 2, . . ., M-1 of a HSM of M cells forms a *physical name space*. Physical name spaces are one-dimensional and contiguous, or *linear*. Address-mapping hardware, under control of the operating system, may create a separate logical name space for each problem program in the system. Futhermore, these logical spaces may differ markedly in size and/or structure from the physical name space of the HSM.

The simplest and most common address-mapping mechanism (Figure 2a) is a *base* or *relocation register* in conjunction with a *limit* register; these

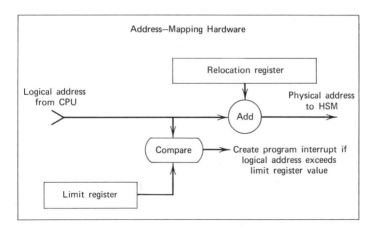

Figure 2a.   Dynamic relocation hardware.

registers are loaded (only) by the operating system. As shown schematically in Figure 2b, the result is to create a linear logical name space that may begin at any address in HSM; therefore, this means of address-mapping is frequently called *dynamic relocation*.

The Atlas computer introduced the concept of a *paged* address-mapping. As shown schematically in Figure 2c, the logical space is divided into *pages* of a convenient length (usually around 1000 words), while the physical space is divided into *page frames* of the same length. A *page table* (set by the operating system) is used by the hardware to map a given page into any page frame. On the other hand, a page can be marked in the page table as *not-present*, and reside in secondary storage rather than in HSM. When the mapping hardware finds the not-present bit on for a requested page, it fires the page fault interrupt. The corresponding interrupt handler then:

(a) Locates the missing page in secondary storage.

(b) Finds space for the page in HSM (which may require that another page be written into secondary storage).

(c) Reads the page into HSM, and enters its address in the page table with the not-present bit off.

(d) Returns to the interrupted program to reexecute the instruction which attempted to access the page.

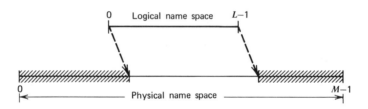

Figure 2b.   Name space mapping performed by hardware of Figure 2a.

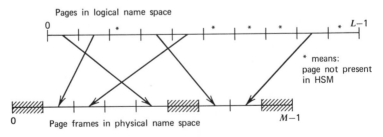

Figure 2c.   Name space mapping performed by paging hardware.

With paged mapping, or *paging*, the logical space can be much larger than the physical address space, creating a *virtual memory* [43] much larger than the HSM hardware of the machine. A virtual memory is a multilevel storage hierarchy (see Section 3), which is transparent to the application programmer.

The Burroughs B5000 [2] introduced a form of memory mapping called *segmentation*, which creates a logical name space that may be considered "two-dimensional" [34]. Segmentation provides a set of separate one-dimensional (linear) name spaces, each defined by different base and limit registers and therefore independently allocatable. Unlike paging, which is (meant to be) transparent to the problem program, segmentation provides an important new facility to programmers. For example, a program can explicitly use different segments for data and program entities which may grow (or shrink) unpredictably and independently. Segmentation also has important advantages for sharing and protection in a multiprogramming environment (see Section 9.2). Several large-scale machines designed specifically for time-sharing use address-mapping hardware which combines segmentation and paging [15, 32].

6. MULTIPROGRAMMING AND MULTIPROCESSING

It is convenient to define a *central processor* (*CP*) as the arithmetic and control elements of a Von Neumann machine—conventional computer architecture discussed in detail in Chapter 5—exclusive of the HSM. A *multiprocessor* is a machine with two or more (normally identical) CP's sharing a common HSM. The traditional term *CPU* will be reserved for a single-CP machine, a *uniprocessor*. We define *multiprogramming* as the *concurrent execution of two or more programs* (where the term "program" is deliberately vague) *on a single CP*. Multiprogramming is widely used for batch processing and is obviously essential if time-sharing or real-time service is to be provided by a single CPU. As we shall see in Section 7, multiprogramming and *multiprocessing* are instances of the same conceptual model, and it is therefore common today to use the single term multiprogramming to include multiprocessing.

6.1. Multiprogramming Systems

Multiprogramming was originally developed (Chapter 5) to allow a single CPU to perform a number of I/O utility operations (for example, tape-to-print), simultaneously with the processing of a stream of batch jobs [18]. The most common application of such utility operations is to *spool* (or transcribe) card input and printer output in support of batch processing on the same machine. Multiprogrammed utility operations led to the simple-priority model for central processor allocation (see Section 8.2) under which highly I/O-bound utility programs are allowed to preempt the CP from more compute-bound batch jobs on the basis of a preassigned priority. The same simple-priority model is widely used to support more complex I/O-bound functions like remote-job-entry, on-line inquiry, and restricted time-sharing, within batch-oriented multiprogramming systems.

As computer configurations grow in size and speed, idle hardware poses an increasing economic problem. The electronic speeds of the CP nearly always exceed the capability of the I/O equipment, and therefore most jobs running on a large-scale computer are I/O bound. Even heavy computational ("number cruncher") programs generally perform bursts of I/O during which the CP is idle. Idle CP time can be reduced but not eliminated by complex I/O buffering schemes; the price is increased programming complexity. Furthermore, even I/O-bound jobs generally use only a fraction of the available I/O equipment and capacity.

For reasons of hardware economics, therefore, most large-scale computers are operated in a multiprogramming mode, sharing the machine's hardware resources—CP time, HSM, and I/O equipment—among a group of concurrently executing jobs which forms the *multiprogramming mix*. On the average, the resource requirements of the jobs in the mix should interleave; therefore, the mix utilizes the machine's resources more efficiently than any single job would. Success of this strategy for improving hardware utilization generally requires that the machine's HSM must be large enough to hold all the programs to which the CP might switch its attention.

There are also secondary benefits from multiprogramming batch jobs: flexible scheduling of job execution (without the complication of *"rolling out"* partially completed jobs, that is, moving them to secondary storage), and reduction of applications programming cost by simplification of I/O buffering. Because of resource-sharing among jobs, multiprogramming may allow an individual batch job to run economically even though it does not contain elaborate buffering schemes or other programming techniques to increase its own utilization of machine resources.

6.2. Multiprocessing

The primary purposes of *multiprocessing* are:

(a) To increase reliability and availability of computational power.

(b) To reduce overhead and simplify the operating system by devoting individual processors to special tasks.

(c) To increase processing speed beyond that obtainable with a single processor of a given type or to push speeds beyond the present limit of hardware technology.

For example, a multiprocessor consisting of several CP's sharing a common HSM is sometimes used to correct an imbalance between memory size and CP speed. If HSM is too large for a single multiprogrammed CP, then much of HSM may be devoted to jobs that are waiting for the CP rather than for I/O. A multiprocessor can correct this imbalance and increase the utilization of the memory resource.

Another form of multiprocessing system uses distinct CPU's coupled via I/O channels (*direct-coupled-system*) [41] or via shared secondary storage units (*indirectly coupled-system*). One CPU may perform all the spooling while the other(s) do only batch processing, sharing the workload in units of complete jobs. Alternatively, all the CPU's may be doing batch processing, while some or all do spooling concurrently; this is called *load leveling*.

There is growing interest in forming networks of geographically separated computers to level loads and make specialized software facilities available remotely (see Chapter 8).

7. THE PROCESS MODEL OF MULTIPROGRAMMING AND MULTIPROCESSING

The previous section discussed the external characteristics of multiprogramming systems for differing modes of service. We consider now the basic system software, or *supervisor*, which provides the underlying multiprogramming control mechanism. An elegant and important model of concurrent program execution, the *process model*, has been developed to cover both multiprogramming and multiprocessing control [5]. Before describing the process model, we introduce the concept of *thread*.

7.1. Threads

Although we have discussed multiprogramming only among separate jobs, actually a single job may (and often does) contain a number of logically independent and asynchronous sequences of execution that we shall call *threads*. Consider, for example, a conversational remote-job-entry subsystem that allows a number of users at remote consoles to type in jobs for batch execution. Such a subsystem is often incorporated into a multiprogramming system as a single never-ending job; however, the processing of each remote console constitutes a logically independent sequence or thread. An input/output buffering system employs, at least implicitly, multiple execution threads, one for each file being buffered and one for the problem program itself. Programs such as these are often simpler to organize if the multithread structure can be made explicit by using the facilities of a multiprogramming supervisor.

We may conceive of each execution thread as a single unbroken sequence although, in fact, the execution of a particular thread may be suspended (interrupted) at any time to let another thread use the CP. Eventually the original thread will resume execution, and the interruption is assumed to have no effect on the result of the execution.

This abstract model of execution sequences makes no distinction between multiprogramming and multiprocessing; instead of being interleaved on a single CPU, each of the execution threads could be executed without interruption on a different CP of a multiprocessor. More generally, the machine may be a multiprocessor with a pool of N processors to be allocated to the execution of T execution threads. If $T > N$, *both* multiprogramming *and* multiprocessing are taking place. The techniques of control, allocation, and synchronization of concurrent execution threads apply as well to multiprogramming on a single CPU as to multiprocessing [25]. Notice that a multi-programming supervisor which is interleaving threads on a single processor may be thought of as creating *virtual central processors*.

7.2. Processes

An execution thread which is known to the supervisor is called a *process* [5] (or *task* [3]). A process is an *instance of execution* of some piece of code, that is, of a program. A process is represented by a *state vector*, which includes the next-instruction location and all other accessible CP registers. Each process may be in one of three states:

Run state.   The process has control of a CP and is executing.

Wait (or blocked) state.   The process is voluntarily waiting for some external event such as an I/O or timer interrupt or for a synchronization signal from another process.

Ready state.   The process is involuntarily waiting and can execute as soon as a CP is allocated to it.

7.3. Multiprogramming Supervisor

Figure 3 shows the overall organization of a multiprogramming supervisor. Each hardware interrupt passes control to the appropriate interrupt handler in the supervisor after the state vector of the interrupted process has been saved and the interrupted process has been placed in ready state.

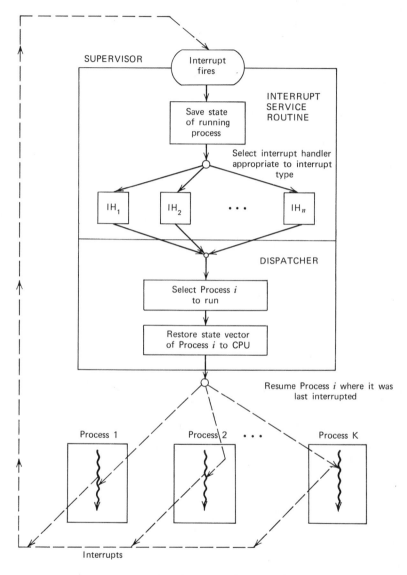

Figure 3. Multiprogramming supervisor.

A process wishing to make a request of the supervisor executes a Supervisor Call instruction, which creates a corresponding interrupt; therefore, all entries to the supervisor are the result of interrupts [25].

In a multiprogramming supervisor, the interrupt handlers do not themselves restore machine status and return to the interrupted program; instead, they exit to a routine called the *Dispatcher*, whose function is to choose a ready process and to put it into run state. The new process may be the same as, or different from, the process that was interrupted. A process is placed in wait state when it executes a Supervisor Call (1) to request a resource that is currently in use by another process, or (2) to relinquish control until some specified event has taken place, like the completion of an I/O operation. When the unavailable resource becomes available or the event occurs, the supervisor marks the process ready again.

If the Dispatcher finds no process in ready state, the supervisor places the CP in a hardware wait condition until an interrupt makes one of the waiting processes ready. On the other hand, if there is more than one process in ready state, then the Dispatcher's selection of a process to run amounts to allocating the central processor resource. Section 8.2 discusses algorithms for this allocation.

If the machine is a multiprocessor, the flow shown in Figure 3 can hold for each CP individually. Each CP may be interrupted by synchronous (processor-dependent) interrupt conditions created within itself, as well as by some subset of the asynchronous interrupts. After servicing an interrupt, a CP may select a different process and execute it, while the original process may be taken up by another processor. There must be an *interlock* in the Dispatcher code to prevent several CP's from entering it simultaneously and, for example, selecting the same process for execution; interlocks are discussed in Section 9.4.

Notice that while every process is a thread, a single process may contain multiple threads which are not distinct processes, since they are not known to the supervisor. For example, the conversational remote-job-entry subsystem mentioned in Section 7.1 might be a single process containing an explicit multithread structure, including its own subdispatcher for (sub-) allocating CP time among its threads.

Every process in the system (except one) is created as the offspring of a parent process; the parent executes a Supervisor Call operation, which is variously named *fork, create,* or *attach* [3, 5]. The result is a *tree* of process dependency; the single process at the top of the tree is created when the operating system is loaded.

By its definition, a process is the entity to which CP time is allocated by the Dispatcher. In addition, the process (or a group of related processes, called a *computation* [5] or *job step* [3]) is generally the internal execution unit to which other machine resources, such as HSM or I/O devices, are allocated.

The parent process passes *resources* and *privileges* to its subprocess, with the important restriction that the subprocess may not have resources or privileges greater than those of its parent. The parent may either give the subprocess *ownership* of a resource or only *share* it with the subprocess. A process may terminate, in which case its parent is signaled in some manner, and all resources it owns are freed.

7.4. Application of Process Model

Consider the process tree in an operating system providing both batch and time-sharing service. Each batch job will be executed by a batch-processing subtree of the complete process tree, under control of a job control process created by the operating system. Individual jobs may create their own subprocess trees for asynchronous I/O functions, for example. Other processes will be created by the operating system to control I/O utility functions, spooling, operator communication, and remote-job-entry [3]. Similarly, a time-sharing control process will create a subprocess for each user logging onto a remote console [26].

A large-scale real-time system is typically organized with many specialized processes working cooperatively [19]. There may be particular processes devoted to handling communication lines, driving displays, reading/writing secondary storage, or performing particular computational tasks. A real-time system such as an airline reservation system or a production control system will usually handle a stream of *transactions* with an assembly-line-like organization of processes. Such a transaction, essentially a packet of data, is sometimes called a thread in real-time work; this usage refers to a *thread of data* rather than *thread of execution*, as the term has been used in this chapter.

8. RESOURCE ALLOCATION

8.1. Shared Resources

A basic concept in multiprogramming is that the computer hardware, extended by the operating system, is composed of a set of *resources* to be shared among the jobs in execution. The operating system, and in particular the supervisor, must control the allocation of these system resources. This section discusses qualitatively some of the basic algorithms used for allocation of CP time and HSM space.

Other shared resources controlled by the supervisor include I/O devices, program segments, and the interval timer. On most machines there is a single hardware interval timer which must be shared among all the processes that wish to use it; the supervisor itself may also use the same hardware timer to determine the time of day.

A single copy of a particular program segment in memory may be a resource to be shared among several processes. The shared code may be *serially reusable,* in which case only one process may execute it at once; or it may be *reentrant,* meaning that several processes can execute it concurrently. Generally a reentrant code segment is a *pure procedure,* never modified by execution.

8.2. Allocation of the Central Processor

The Dispatcher (see Figure 3) is responsible for allocation of the CP resource to the active processes. The diversity of dispatching algorithms in use today is a result of variations among system objectives. In a pure batch system, the objectives are to maximize system utilization while satisfying some management policy on the desirable order of job completion. In a dedicated time-sharing system, the objective is normally to minimize *response time* (the delay in system response to commands entered by users on remote consoles). In a real-time system, the objective is to ensure the timely completion of each of a number of competing computational threads of varying urgency. Most Dispatchers use algorithms that are based on one or more of the following elementary rules.

Rule 1. Simple priority chain. Each process is assigned a unique priority, establishing an ordering among the processes. The dispatcher always selects the highest-priority process that is *ready* (i.e., not in wait state).

Rule 2. Commutator. The processes are ordered in a circular list which the Dispatcher always scans in the same direction. When the current process (the one that was last selected) has voluntarily entered wait state, the commutator advances around the circle and selects the first ready process it finds.

Rule 3. Time-slicing Dispatcher. The time-slicing Dispatcher operates like a commutator which lingers at each process for a fixed time T, called the *time-slice.* Only the process that is currently receiving a time-slice may be in run state, and it runs whenever it is not waiting. At the end of the time-slice, the Dispatcher advances to the next process around the ring, regardless of whether it is ready or waiting.

The "classical" batch multiprogramming algorithm uses a *simple priority chain* (Rule 1) with the most I/O-bound processes having the highest dispatching priorities [3, 18]. The operating system may determine dispatching priorities automatically, or "adaptively," to satisfy the classical model by monitoring the degree of I/O-boundedness of each process and periodically rearranging the chain accordingly. This period is generally chosen long compared to the characteristic interrupt frequency in the system, to minimize Dispatcher overhead.

Rule 3 is mainly of theoretical interest. In the limit of the time-slice T being very small, each of the N tasks under Rule 3 appears to be running at $1/N$th the speed of the real CP. This observation leads to a simple and useful analytical model, the *processor-shared model* [13].

The simplest algorithm commonly used for time-sharing systems is the time-sliced commutator, a combination of Rules 2 and 3 (see Figure 4a). The time-sliced commutator advances to the next ready process when either: (a) the current process enters wait state, or (b) the current process has been in run state for more than a time-slice T.

Operating systems that provide both batch and time-sharing service often use a combination of the earlier algorithms. For example, the *rotating simple priority dispatching chain* combines Rules 1 and 3; processes are normally dispatched according to Rule 1, but every T seconds the highest-priority process in the chain is moved to the bottom. Each process may have its own characteristic time-slice interval, and the time-slices may be chosen to guarantee a minimum fraction of CP time to a particular process (see Figure 4b). Another approach is to build a *priority chain* of *time-sliced commutators* rather than of single processes. The Dispatcher selects the first (or next) ready process in the highest-priority commutator in the chain containing any ready processes (see Figure 4c). This same algorithm (usually without time-slicing) is called a *multilevel queue* and is extensively used in large-scale real-time systems [19].

Some time-sharing systems use the multilevel queue algorithm,

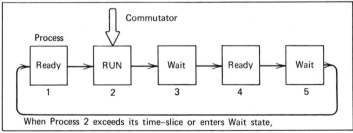

Figure 4a.   Time-sliced commutator.

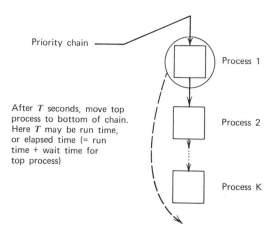

Priority chain

After T seconds, move top
process to bottom of chain.
Here T may be run time,
or elapsed time (= run
time + wait time for
top process)

Process 1

Process 2

Process K

Figure 4b. Rotating simple priority chain.

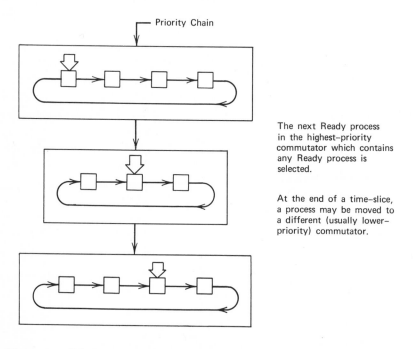

Priority Chain

The next Ready process
in the highest−priority
commutator which contains
any Ready process is
selected.

At the end of a time−slice,
a process may be moved to
a different (usually lower−
priority) commutator.

Figure 4c. Priority chain of time-sliced commutators (multilevel queue algorithm).

moving processes serving user consoles among queue levels in order to optimize (minimize) terminal response time for trivial requests, when there is no way to predict which requests will be trivial and which will require substantial computation. When the time-slice expires on a running process, it is moved to the end of the next-lower-priority queue; it is moved to the top queue when the user sends input from the console. Thus, a short request for CP time gets high priority, while a longer request gradually filters down to the lowest priorities [33].

8.3. Allocation of High Speed Memory

The parts of the operating system that must be permanently resident in HSM generally occupy a preassigned contiguous area called the *nucleus*. The remaining memory, which we call the *dynamic area*, may be used by problem programs, transient operating system routines, and tables created dynamically by the supervisor. Most multiprogramming supervisors provide a *dynamic HSM allocation* function to assign chunks of the dynamic area on demand.

In general, the dynamic allocation function must satisfy requests for variable-sized *chunks*, where *chunk* means a single contiguous area of HSM. The central problem is the tendency for the available memory to become *fragmented* into many small chunks so a request for allocation of a large chunk cannot be satisfied even though it is smaller than the total memory available.

The simplest picture of memory allocation assumes a *homogeneous* dynamic area: the supervisor makes no distinction among the requestors but, instead, satisfies all requests out of a single pool of available chunks. There are two common algorithms for allocation in a homogeneous area: *first-fit*, which chooses the first (i.e., lowest address) available chunk that is large enough, and *best-fit*, which chooses the smallest available area that is large enough. See Reference 14 for an excellent discussion of homogeneous allocation. Unfortunately, fragmentation problems cause allocation in a homogeneous dynamic area to be generally unusable for a multiprogramming supervisor.

We shall now consider four important strategies for reducing fragmentation.

Noncontiguous areas.   Even in the presence of fragmentation, any space request that is not larger than the total available could be satisfied if a set of smaller noncontiguous chunks were allowed. However, the program requesting memory usually wants a single continuously addressable chunk so that simple indexing can be used for access. Software conventions could be imposed to handle arbitrary noncontiguity of memory areas, but this would be exceedingly inefficient.

Quantization. A plausible approach is to allocate only integral multiples of a fixed quantum Q of area size. The larger that Q is, the more this strategy reduces fragmentation by increasing the chance that there will be an available chunk containing just the right multiple of Q. Unfortunately, this strategy generally *reduces* the utilization of memory, because the loss due to partially filled chunks more than offsets the gain due to reduced fragmentation [39].

Compaction. This strategy may be used on machines whose dynamic relocation hardware (see Section 5.5) allows a problem program to operate in any contiguous area of memory with approriate setting of the relocation register(s). When HSM becomes fragmented, the entire memory is compacted by moving all job areas toward one end until there is only one chunk of available space.

Zoning. Under the zoning strategy, HSM is initially allocated in relatively large chunks or *zones* (also called *subpools* by IBM [3]), which are then suballocated into smaller chunks. This reduces fragmentation significantly if each zone can be freed as a whole, releasing large chunks of available space rather than many small chunks. This is accomplished by associating zones with execution entities like jobs or processes which will have a finite lifetime and then terminate, freeing all their HSM. The allocation within a zone may involve subzones, and so on. An elegant and general model of allocation zones has been developed by D. T. Ross [23].

8.4. Deadlocks [11, 40]

When a number of processes are cooperating or sharing common resources, there is a danger that a *deadlock* can develop. In a deadlock, it is logically impossible for two or more processes to proceed ever again because of mutual interlocks. The classical example is of two processes, say A and B, where A has been allocated resource p and is awaiting q, while B has been allocated resource q and is awaiting p. This is a deadly trap that lurks in many guises in a multiprogramming system and, as a result, the resource allocation rules must be carefully defined and somewhat restrictive. The basic solutions currently known for this problem are as follows:

1. Allocate resources always in the same order. Thus, if resource p is *always* allocated before q then the deadlock situation mentioned earlier cannot occur.

2. Request all resources *collectively* and proceed only when all those re-

quested can be simultaneously granted. This rules out dynamic allocation of deadlock-prone resources.

3. If a process already owns resource q and wants to request a new resource p which could cause deadlock (for example, because the established order is allocation of p before q, as above), first *release* q and then allocate p and q collectively, or in the standard order.

9. PROTECTION AND COOPERATION

9.1. Supervisor Mode

The supervisor is the central authority that manages and controls access to shared system resources. Problem programs must be denied the use of certain machine instructions, called *privileged*, to ensure that they cannot usurp the supervisor's authority by accident or by malicious design. In particular, the instructions that

(1) set HSM protection boundaries,
(2) enable/disable interrupt levels,
(3) start and stop I/O channels (discussed in Chapter 5) and devices, and
(4) set the interval timer.

must be privileged, since they control access to the HSM, CP, I/O and interval timer hardware, respectively. The CP hardware contains a binary choice of operating modes, *master* or *supervisor mode* in which privileged instructions can be executed, and *slave* or *problem mode* in which a privileged instruction causes a program fault interrupt. Any interrupt switches the CP to supervisor mode before the ISR is entered. The only way a process in problem mode can enter the supervisor (without causing a program fault interrupt) is by executing a Supervisor Call hardware instruction.

9.2. Storage Protection

Protection of all levels of storage, both HSM and peripheral storage devices, must be a primary consideration in the design of computer hardware and operating systems. The operating system must be protected from the problem program(s); in addition, each problem program in a multiprogramming system must be protected from the deprivations of other programs. As we observed in Section 5, parts of the supervisor are extensions of the hardware, and therefore a "clobbered" supervisor may create the illusion of a hardware failure. Failures of this kind are easily "repaired," once they are correctly diagnosed; it is only necessary to reload the operating system. However, the resulting interruption of service may be intolerable.

Storage protection is particularly important on a large-scale multiprogramming system, and is essential when the computer workload includes many programs under development. Such a program is likely to attempt to trespass outside its own region(s) of storage and such a trespass, if allowed, is likely to induce an apparent failure in another program, complicating enormously the difficulty of debugging. On the other hand, storage protection between jobs may be required to guard sensitive or confidential information [35].

For efficiency of execution, protection of HSM must be basically a hardware function. The details of the protection hardware have a strong impact on the design and capabilities of the operating system as a whole. There are two common forms of HSM protection: *storage keys* [30], which place the protection mechanism within HSM itself, and address mapping hardware (see Section 5.5).

Storage protection is a valuable facility within a job as well as between jobs. It is small comfort to a programmer debugging a large and complex application program that he can "only" clobber his own code or data. For example, overrunning an array is a frequent programming error that may lead to obscure and therefore costly program bugs. There is, fortunately, some promise that future hardware will include more adequate provision for protection within, as well as between, jobs. In a machine with memory segmentation hardware (see Section 5.5), each natural arraylike data aggregate of the program can be made a separate segment. The memory-mapping hardware will then force an interrupt if the program attempts to access memory beyond the end of a particular segment. Some machines [2, 12] use a more general form of memory accessing, essentially *iterated segment* mapping, which allows the hardware to verify that each individual subscript in a multidimensional array falls within acceptable bounds. The urgent need for comprehensive memory protection to reduce the cost of debugging programs is one of the most compelling arguments for segmentation hardware.

9.3. Spheres of Protection

The storage protection problem is considerably complicated by the desire to share common code and data segments. Different processes may need different types of access (for example, read-only, execute-only, or read/write) to a shared data object.

There are many problem programs, particularly in time-sharing environments, which act as subsupervisors; that is, they appear like a problem program to the supervisor, but like a supervisor to problem programs which they control. The storage access privileges of the problem programs should be a subset of the access allowed to the subsupervisor; that is, storage protection domains should be nestable. These considerations have led to the important concept of nested *"spheres of protection"* for the processes in a multiprogramming mix [5].

Furthermore, it is desirable to protect problem programs and the supervisor itself from (parts of) the supervisor. Some computer hardware removes all memory protection in supervisor mode, allowing the supervisor to access any memory without checking; however, this is neither logically necessary nor desirable. Supervisor mode allows the supervisor to execute privileged instructions and grant itself access to any particular area of storage as necessary. On the other hand, multiprogramming supervisors are large and complex programs which are never perfectly debugged, so they ought not to have access to all HSM at once.

9.4. Interlocks

The requirement for communication and synchronization among distinct execution threads is fundamental to the design of multiprogramming systems. Different threads are generally asynchronous; one may interrupt another at any point, or they may run concurrently on different CP's of a multiprocessor. Each thread will include certain *critical sections* during which it must not be interrupted by a cooperating thread. Two threads communicate or are synchronized by testing and setting common data values, usually switches or pointers; the critical sections are the points in the code at which the common data is manipulated. Therefore, it is necessary to protect critical sections with interlocks which allow only one thread at a time to traverse them; this is called the *mutual exclusion* problem. Synchronization and mutual exclusion are distinct but closely related problems of interlocking threads [6].

Figure 5 shows a simple example of a program that will (occasionally) fail if mutual exclusion is not enforced. Two processes, A and B, execute the same code segment which increments a common counter X. Suppose that (as indicated by the dashed arrows in Figure 5), B happens to interrupt A and increment X in the instant when A itself is in the midst of incrementing X. When A resumes after the interruption and stores its incremented value in X, it will obliterate the result of B; thus, the result in this case will be to increment X by only 1. Normally, however, B will interrupt A outside the critical section, and X will be incremented by 2 (once each by A and B). Thus, mutual exclusion of A and B from the critical section is required to get a predictable result in X.

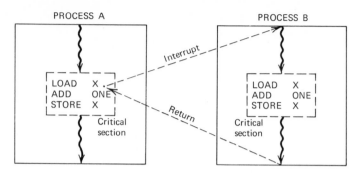

Figure 5.   Example of two critical sections interfering.

More interesting examples of threads that require interlocking are:

1. Two interrupt handlers that manipulate common switches and are triggered by preemptive priority interrupt levels so the higher-priority level may interrupt the other level.

2. Simultaneous execution of the Dispatcher code by two or more CP's of a multiprocessor.

3. A process that is buffering an input file and the process that is consuming the input from the buffers.

Each of these interlock problems is generally handled in a different manner.

In the first example, the usual technique for mutual exclusion is for the lower-priority IH to disable the higher-priority interrupt for the duration of the critical section. A typical supervisor is sprinkled with interrupt enable-disable sequences, surrounding every critical section which needs protection. Usually a few unexpected critical sections are discovered six months after a new system is placed in production.

We turn now to the second example, mutual exclusion of different CP's of a multiprocessor. This interlock problem can be solved by a single indivisible machine operation, which we call "fetch-and-set-bit" (FASB).

> FASB: Load a specified bit from memory into a CP register and simultaneously set the bit in memory to one; no other CP is allowed to access this bit between the fetch and the store.

An interlock bit is assigned for every critical section, and each CP is programmed to enter a critical section only after it has performed a FASB on the corresponding interlock bit, tested the result, and found the bit zero. When the CP leaves the critical section, the program clears the interlock bit to zero, allowing another CP to enter.

The third example is a particular case of interlocking two problem processors (processes that run in problem mode). An I/O buffering package is often treated as a special case, since it is a problem process that is part of the operating system and that can protect its critical sections by disabling I/O interrupts (on a single CP machine). Since a problem process cannot issue the privileged instruction to disable interrupts, the critical sections of the buffering package are simply incorporated in the supervisor to be invoked via Supervisor Calls.

However, a normal problem process cannot be allowed to incorporate its critical sections within the supervisor. Therefore, a multiprogramming supervisor must provide, via Supervisor Call routines, interlock service(s) for synchronization and mutual exclusion of problem processes. A prototypical interlock service would consist of two Supervisor Call operations, *lock(f)* and *unlock(f)*. The parameter f is a word in HSM to be used as a flag or *semaphore*.

> *lock(f)*: If $f = 0$, set f to 1 and allow the process to proceed. Otherwise, place process in wait state until another process executes *unlock (f)*.

> *unlock(f)*: If any other processes are waiting on f, allow one of them to proceed and set f to 1; otherwise, set f to 0.

See Figure 6 for flow charts of *lock* and *unlock*; Figure 7 illustrates their use to provide mutual exclusion from the critical section of Figure 5.

On a multiprocessor, the implementation of *lock* within the supervisor may use the FASB instruction to test f and set it in a single indivisible operation, ensuring mutual exclusion of different CP's.

10. CONCLUSIONS

The operating system is fundamentally concerned with creating an environment—a fancy word for the *machine*, real or apparent—within which application programs may run. The direction of future evolution of operating system design will be determined by changes in computer architecture (see Chapter 4) as well as by changes in the environment presented to application programs. Thus, a significant decrease in cost of any major hardware component (for example, high speed memory or secondary storage) will profoundly affect the organization of the operating system.

For example, as CPU hardware becomes increasingly less expensive, there is a trend toward use of powerful "mini-computers" for scientific applications. Extrapolating this trend, one might conclude that every user

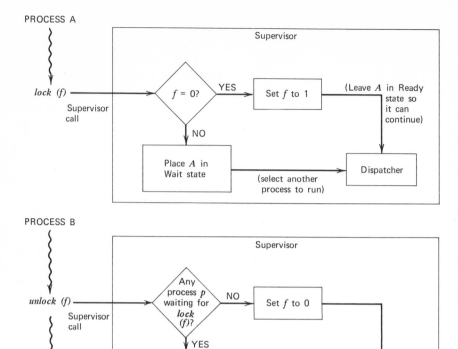

Figure 6. Flowcharts of *lock* and *unlock* operations.

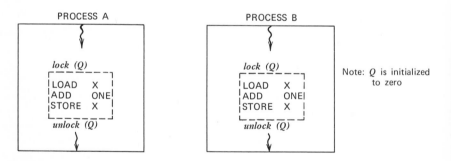

Figure 7. The application of *lock, unlock* to mutual exclusion from a critical section (see Figure 5).

will eventually have his own personal CPU instead of sharing a centralized ultrapowerful machine. It would seem to follow that an elaborate multiprogramming system which allows batch and time-sharing users to share a single large machine may be likened to a *dinosaur* in the metaphor of evolution of computer software. However, for a number of reasons complex operating systems are unlikely to become extinct. Large machines with complex multiprogramming operating systems will continue to be required by many large commercial and real-time service centers because of their need for large on-line data files in conjunction with considerable computing power.

In the future, scientific computing power in laboratories and engineering firms will probably be partially decentralized, distributed among CPU's which are intermediate in power and shared by groups or departments. Such a CPU might drive a dozen time-sharing consoles, and do some local batch-processing. In addition, it will serve as a terminal for entry into a network (Chapter 8) of larger machines for solving problems that have outgrown its capacity, and to utilize programs available only remotely.

As hardware cost decreases and many new applications are undertaken, the cost of application program development and debugging becomes increasingly significant. Many of the basic operating system facilities discussed earlier—for example, multiprogramming, dynamic storage allocation, deferred binding, memory protection, virtual memory, and segmentation—were introduced with the ultimate aim of lowering the cost of application programming and of making possible programming tasks which were once too difficult or expensive. Therefore, many users who do have personal mini-computers will be using sophisticated operating systems, including a supervisor to handle interrupts, to create a virtual memory, and to control a hierarchy of memory protection facilities. These users will need a programming system and a variety of on-line terminal languages for calculation and program development.

On the other hand, faster and cheaper CPU hardware will affect operating systems in another way: increasingly the basic supervisor functions will be realized through microprograms called *firmware*, since they are intermediate between hardware and software.

At the present time there is much research in progress to understand the fundamental structural principles and basic algorithms underlying operating systems. This work undoubtedly will lead to new insights and models and will give operating system designers a quantitative understanding of the tradeoffs among alternative algorithms. The surface has only been scratched in many areas; for example, there has been little investigation of the most basic memory allocation algorithms discussed in Section 8.3 (except in the special case of equal-sized chunks).

Although this formal understanding of the subject will be valuable, the actual creation of a large-scale operating system will continue to be a difficult and expensive task requiring many systems programmers. We expect that significant advances will be made in lowering this cost, by several means:

(a) Higher-level system-programming languages will be used almost universally for writing operating systems.

(b) System designers will learn how to create software which can recover from many of the bugs that must inevitably lurk in a program as large and complex as an operating system.

11. REFERENCES

1. Boehm, E. M., and Steel, T. B., Jr., "The SHARE 709 System: Machine Implementation of Symbolic Programming," *J. ACM*, **6** (2), 134–140 (April, 1959).

2. Burroughs Corp., *The Descriptor—A Definition of the B5000 Information Processing System*, Detroit, Mich., 1961.

3. Clark, W. A., Mealy, G. H., and Witt, B. I., "The Functional Structure of OS 360, *IBM System J.*, **5** (1), 3–51 (1966).

4. Coffman, E. C., and Kleinrock, L., "Computer Scheduling Methods and Their Countermeasures," *Proc. AFIPS 1968 SJCC*, **32**, Thompson Book Co., Washington, D. C., 1968, 11–21.

5. Dennis, J. B., and Van Horn, E. C., "Programming Semantics for Multiprogrammed Computations," *CACM*, **9** (3), 143–155 (March, 1966).

6. Dijkstra, E. W., *Cooperating Sequential Processes*, EWD 123, Math Dept., Technical U. Eindhoven, Netherlands, 1965.

7. Dijkstra, E. W., "Structure of 'THE' Multiprogramming System," *CACM*, **11** (5), 341–346 (May, 1968).

8. Evans, T. G., and Darley, D. L., "On-Line Debugging Techniques: A Survey," *Proc. AFIPS 1966 FJCC*, Spartan Books, Washington, D. C., 37–50.

9. Ferguson, D. E., "Evolution of the Meta-Assembly Program," *CACM*, **9** (2), 190–196 (March, 1966).

10. Freeman, D. N., "A Storage Hierarchy System for Batch Processing," *Proc. AFIPS 1968 SJCC*, **32**, Thompson Book Co., Washington, D. C., 229–243.

11. Havender, J. W., "Avoiding Deadlock in Multitasking Systems," *IBM Sys. J.*, **7** (2), 74–84 (1968).

12. Jodeit, J. G., "Storage Organization in Programming Systems," *CACM*, **11** (11), 741–746 (November, 1968).

13. Kleinrock, L., "Time-Shared Systems: A Theoretical Treatment," *JACM*, **14** (2), 242–261 (April, 1967).

14. Knuth, Donald E., *The Art of Computer Programming*, Vol. 1, Addison-Wesley, 1968.

15. Lett, A. S., and Konigsford, W. L., "TSS/360: A Time-Shared Operating System," *Proc. AFIPS 1968 FJCC*, **33** (1), Thompson Book Co., Washington, D. C., 15–28.

16. McCarthy, J., Boilen, S., Fredkin, E., and Licklider, J. C. R., "A Time-Sharing Debugging System for a Small Computer," *Proc. AFIPS 1963 SJCC*, **23**, Spartan Books, Baltimore, Md., 51–58.

17. McCarthy, J., Corbato, F. J., and Daggett, M. M., "The Linking Segment Subprogram Language and Linking Loader," *CACM*, **6** (7), 391–395 (July, 1963).

18. Marcotty, M. J., Longstaff, F. M., and Williams, A. P. M., "Time-Sharing on the Ferranti-Packard FP6000 Computer System," *Proc. AFIPS 1963 SJCC*, **23**, Spartan Books, Baltimore, Md., 29–40.

19. Martin, J., *Design of Real-Time Computer Systems*, Prentice Hall, Englewood Cliffs, N. J., 1967.

20. Mealy, G. H., Operating Systems, Rand Corporation paper, P-2584, May, 1962.

21. Randell, B., and Kuehner, C. J., "Dynamic Storage Allocation Systems," *CACM*, **11** (5), 297–306 (May, 1968).

22. Rosin, Robert F., "Supervisory and Monitor Systems," *Comp. Surveys*, **1** (1), 37–54 (March, 1969).

23. Ross, D. T., "AED Free Storage Package," *CACM*, **10** (8), 481–492 (August, 1967).

24. Rosin, R. F., "Contemporary Concepts of Microprogramming and Emulation," *Comp. Surveys*, **1** (4), 197–212 (December, 1969).

25. Thompson, R. N., and Wilkinson, J. A., "The D825 Automatic Operating and Scheduling Program," *Proc. AFIPS 1963 SJCC*, **23**, Spartan Books, Baltimore, Md., 41–50.

26. Vyssotsky, V. A., Corbato, F. J., and Graham, R. M., "Structure of the Multics Supervisor," *Proc. AFIPS 1965 FJCC*, **27** (1), Spartan Books, New York, 203–212.

27. Wegner, P., *Programming Languages, Information Structures, and Machine Organization*, McGraw-Hill Book Company, 1968, esp. pp. 15–19.

28. Wegner, P., "Intermediate Languages and Programming Systems," pp. 73–85 in *Introduction to System Programming*, (P. Wegner, Ed.), Academic Press, London and New York, 1964.

29. Wolontis, V. M., *A Complete Floating-Decimal Interpretive System for the IBM 650 Magnetic Drum Calculator*, IBM Corp., Applied Science Division Tech. Newsletter No. 11, 1956.

30. Blaauw, G. A., and Brooks, F. P., Jr., "The Structure of System/360, Part I—Outline of the Logical Structure," *IBM Systems J.*, **3** (2 and 3), 119–135 (1964).

31. Bock, R. V., "An Interrupt Control for the B5000 Data Processor System," *Proc. AFIPS 1963 FJCC*, **24**, Spartan Books, Baltimore, Md., 229–241.

32. Corbato, F. J., and Vyssototsky, V. A., "Introduction and Overview of the Multics System," *Proc. AFIPS 1965 FJCC*, **27** (1), Spartan Books, Washington, D. C., 185–196.

33. Crisman, P. A. (Ed.), *The Compatible Time-Sharing System: A Programmer's Guide*, MIT Press, Cambridge, Mass., 1965.

34. Dennis, Jack B., "Segmentation and the Design of Multiprogrammed Computer Systems," *JACM*, **12** (4), 589–602 (October, 1965).

35. Hoffman, L. J., "Computers and Privacy: A Survey," *Comp. Surveys*, **1** (2), 85–103, (June 1969).

36. Kent, W., "Assembler-Language Macro Programming," *Comp. Surveys*, **1** (4), 183–196 (December, 1969).

37. Lampson, B. W., "Interactive Machine Language Programming," *Proc. AFIPS 1965 FJCC*, **27** (1), Spartan Books, Washington, D. C., 473–481

38. Leonard, G. F., and Goodroe, J. R., "More on Extensible Machines," *CACM*, **9** (3), 183–188 (March, 1966).

39. Randall, B., "A Note on Storage Fragmentation and Program Segmentation," *CACM*, **12** (7), 365–369 (July, 1969).

40. Coffman, E. G., Jr., Elphick, M. J., and Shoshani, A., "System Deadlocks," *Comp. Surveys*, **3** (2), 67–78 (June 1971).

41. Smith, E. C., Jr., "A Directly Coupled Multiprocessing System," *IBM Sys. J.*, **2**, 218–229 (September–December, 1963).

42. Princeton University, *Proceedings, Second Symposium on Operating Systems Principles*, October 20–22, 1969.

43. Denning, P. D., "Virtual Memory," *Comp. Surveys*, **2** (3), 153–189 (September, 1970).

Chapter 7

On-Line Computing
and Graphic Display

Walter J. Karplus

University of California
Los Angeles

1. INTRODUCTORY REMARKS

The recent development and widespread acceptance of on-line computing systems represents the closing of a circle in the evolution of digital
computers. When modern electronic digital computers were first introduced
in the late 1940s and the early 1950s, computing speeds were relatively low
and the cost of computer systems was relatively modest. Under these conditions it was feasible and practical for the engineer or scientist with a
problem to be solved, to be present in the computing facility and perhaps
even to operate the computer himself while his problem was being run. By
observing the output of the computer, he could readily spot errors in programming or malfunctions of the computer and could make important on-
the-spot decisions such as when to stop the computer run and when to
switch over to another program. The man was therefore directly on-line
with the computer, and the computer solution represented a joint effort of
man and machine. As digital computers became faster and more costly,
such computer operation proved execessively inefficient. In large facilities
every millisecond of computer time had to be used efficiently and it became
impossible to permit the scientist or engineer to interrupt a carefully
scheduled computing procedure to make on-line decisions. Eventually it
proved necessary to bar all but the professional computer operators from
the computing facility. Thus, computer operation changed from on-line to
batch processing. The man with a problem had to prepare a comprehensive,
complete program, including all decisions that he would have preferred to
make on-line, and to submit this program to the computing center to be
processed as time became available. Usually, the results of the calculation
came back to him with a delay (turn-around time) of at least eight hours.
This proved to be a relatively inconvenient method of operation, since the
detection and correction of each programming error required a separate
eight-hour period, and since vast quantities of useless data were generated
and printed out, data which the engineer on-the-spot could easily have
suppressed. Yet, so compelling were the economic arguments for total and
efficient utilization of the computation facility, that these weaknesses of
the batch-programming approach gradually became part of an accepted
way of life.

By the mid-1960s there began a trend to put the computer user back
on-line with the computer, but in a manner quite different from that in the
early days of digital computing. Recognizing that it is economically unfeasible to permit a single customer to "tie up" or monopolize the computing facility even for a very limited period of time, modern computer systems
are being equipped with a large number of control consoles each connected
directly to the central computer and each capable of instructing the com-

puter to process a specific program. In essence, this approach represents an effort to alleviate the "impedance matching" problem which exists when only one user is attempting to operate and utilize the digital computer. The computer makes decisions and performs mathematical operations in a matter of nanoseconds while the man employing the computer requires seconds or even minutes to reach a decision as to what to do next. Therefore, if only one operator is making use of the computer, the computer will necessarily be idle much of the time. By permitting a large number of users to employ the computer simultaneously in a time-shared fashion, with the aid of a large number of remote consoles, each user obtains the impression that he alone is in communication with the computer, while the computer itself is utilized virtually at full capacity.

The advent of time-shared on-line computing had to await the development of sophisticated electronic circuity, the development of suitable computer architecture (both hardware and software), and the retraining of computer users to take full advantage of the on-line computing approach. This chapter presents a general and brief qualitative discussion of the basic concepts involved in on-line operation from an external device point of view. The final sections are devoted to a discussion of graphic display terminals. Leonard Kleinrock, in Section 4 of Chapter 8 in this book, models and analyzes quantitatively time-shared systems. Alfonso F. Cárdenas, in Section 7 of Chapter 10, illustrates the utilization of time-shared interactive facilities with the programming language BASIC. More detailed discussions of the topics mentioned in this chapter are to be found in the references listed at the end of this chapter.

2. BASIC CONCEPTS

In order to make a meaningful analysis of on-line computing, it is necessary to establish the precise definitions of the basic terms involved. Unfortunately, even in as young a field as on-line computing, these terms have assumed different significances in different applications and have been defined differently by various authors and manufacturers. The definitions presented below may, therefore, be considered as representing an "average" of the meanings assigned to these terms in current usage.

The term *computer*, unless qualified by such terms as analog or hybrid, refers to a digital computer capable of storing information consisting of data and instructions and capable of performing sequential logical operations upon these data. Such a computer employs a binary number system and is programmed most efficiently in a machine language characteristic of the specific machine. Computers generally have available a variety of assemblers, interpretive subroutines, and compilers to facilitate the programming effort (see Chapter 10). The operator initiates and controls the data-processing operations within the computer by means of an assemblage of switches provided on the operator *console*.

A computer is considered to be *on-line* if a device external to the computer system, possibly operated by a man, and the computer itself alternately take action, such that the external device affects the data processing operation and such that the computer affects in some way the external device. If a man or a number of men are "in-the-loop," a *man-computer* system exists.

If the exchange of information between the external device and the computer is sufficiently rapid so that the computational results have an immediate and desired effect upon the external system (of which the device is a part), the system is said to be operating in *real-time*. Of key importance in determining whether real-time operation is possible is the system *response* time, defined as the time required by the system to react to and to respond to an external input.

If a number of devices are connected to a single computer and if each of these devices is capable of communicating with this computer, a *multiple-access* system is formed. If each of these devices can be serviced either sequentially or simultaneously by the computer and the user is given the impression that the whole processing system is servicing him only, the on-line system is termed a *time-shared* system. Time-sharing techniques were introduced long before modern on-line computing systems became popular.

Early time-sharing activities centered around the more efficient use of a single-console digital computer system. In particular, input-output of information usually requires considerably more time than does the performance of a long-sequence of arithmetic operations. For example, the input or output of a few characters may require milliseconds, whereas an addition or subtraction may be performed in a few microseconds or even less. Consequently, if only a single program is processed on a digital computer, the arithmetic unit must stand idle for a considerable percentage of time while input-output is taking place. To overcome this shortcoming, multiprogramming concepts were introduced. In this mode of operation several programs are stored in the computer memory and are processed "simultaneously" in an interleaved fashion, such that while one program employs the input-output equipment, another program makes use of the arithmetic unit. This approach to improving the efficiency of computing systems has been extensively applied in modern computers.

The term *multiprogramming* refers to the concurrent operation of two or more programs within a computer, whether output equipment is involved or not, such that one program need not be completed before another program is started. A *multiprocessing* system is one in which several programs or program portions are executed simultaneously within a system consisting of two or more processing units.

Of key importance in a multiple-access on-line system is the capability of the external devices to stop temporarily the program being processed by the computer so that data required by the device may be generated at once. Usually, whenever the external device desires access to the computer, it transmits a signal in the form of a changed logic level to a special input channel of the computer. The term *interrupt* is used to designate the capability of the computer to react to this signal by interrupting the normal data flow within the computer. Under these conditions the external devices may be processed by the central computer either in the order in which interrupt signals are received from them or in an order determined by a priority schedule. In either case, if there is an appreciable volume of work, these external channels must "wait on line" until the computer is ready for them. The term *queue* is used to designate these "lines" which are formed by incoming messages. The mathematical discipline of queuing theory deals with the prediction of the probability of the length of queues under various conditions. The queuing problem becomes particularly complex, if it is decided in advance that certain devices and certain messages have greater importance than others and should therefore be handled first. Under these conditions a *priority interrupt* system is used, and messages with higher priority are processed before messages with lower priority are handled. The interested reader may now refer to Section 4 on "Time-shared System Modeling and Analysis" in Chapter 8 for a discussion of the operation and performance of time-shared systems based on mathematical queuing models. Also, the first part of Chapter 5 presents, from a different point of view, many of the concepts discussed so far in this chapter.

3. CLASSIFICATION OF ON-LINE SYSTEMS

In order to obtain a perspective of the on-line computing field it is useful to attempt to categorize the various ways in which on-line concepts have been realized. This task is complicated by the fact that the variety and application areas of on-line systems are constantly expanding, and that the structure and characteristics of any on-line system can be radically changed by the addition of special hardware devices. Nonetheless, it appears practical to classify on-line systems into two broad categories: on-line systems involving man-computer interaction and on-line systems operating essentially automatically with no "conversation" between man and computer.

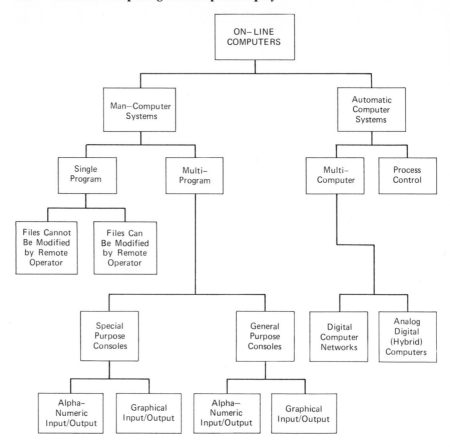

Figure 1.   Classification of on-line computers.

A number of subcategories may be recognized in each of these two broad divisions of the on-line field. This is illustrated in Figure 1.

One major division of on-line computing systems which do not involve direct intervention by human operators is constituted by systems in which a number of computers are interconnected. Extensive networks of digital computers are already in operation, and considerably more ambitious interconnections are currently on the drawing board (see Chapter 8). Such multidigital computer systems have computing capabilities (particularly as far as memory is concerned), far exceeding those of a single digital computer installation. Furthermore, it becomes possible in this way to share the use of files and other data and to make use of special peripheral equipment available in one facility but not in another. The efficient management of such a digital computer network involves highly complex monitor programs as well as challenging administrative problems.

Another variety of automatic multicomputer systems involves interconnection of digital and analog computers to form a hybrid computer system, as described in V. Vemuri's Chapter 9 in this textbook. Analog computers operate in a parallel mode, all arithmetic and mathematic computations necessary to treat the problem being performed simultaneously. Consequently, as the complexity of a problem increases, the analog computing time required to solve this problem is not increased; instead, a greater amount of equipment is needed. Analog computers are therefore well suited for real-time operation, but are limited in accuracy by the quality of the components (solution accuracies in excess of 0.1% are usually difficult to attain). Furthermore, certain computational operations such as logical decisions and function generation are more effectively performed digitally. By linking an analog and a digital computer in a closed loop, some of the advantages of the analog and of the digital approaches can be blended so as to produce a faster and more powerful computing system. Hybrid computer systems are particularly useful if it is desired to include actual hardware (for example, an autopilot from a space vehicle) or analog instrument data in a simulation.

In another important class of automatic on-line systems, the digital computer is connected directly to an industrial plant or process. Typically in such process control systems, a large number of process variables, such as temperature, pressure, and chemical compositions, are measured by electrical instruments. These data are converted to digital form and processed sequentially in a digital computer. The computer is employed to monitor the process so as to assure that all variables remain within specified limits, and to initiate remedial actions by means of signals to actuators such as valves, switches, and the like. In more sophisticated process control systems, the digital computer also performs an optimization function by controlling the process parameters so as to minimize a specified cost function.

Man-computer systems can be categorized as being either single-program or multiprogram systems. In a single-program system each of a large number of operators has access to the same program within the machine. Usually the purpose of this program is to facilitate access to extensive files kept in the computer memory. For example, in an airline reservations system, each reservation counter is equipped with a small console which can be employed to interrogate the central memory system as to the availability of space on any specific flight, and to reserve seats if space is available. Similarly in a system now in wide use in stock brokerage houses throughout the United States, a client may obtain the latest prices of all stocks on the New York and American stock exchanges. A subtle distinction exists between these two systems cited as examples. In the airline reservation system, the remote user is capable of reading and modifying the information in the central files; in the stock system, on the other hand, the files are updated at the central computer facility and the remote user can only inquire as to the file contents. The latter type of approach is employed in most so-called information retrieval systems.

In multiprogram, man-computer systems the user can select one of a variety of programs within the computer memory. These systems make extensive use of relatively complex remote consoles which have provisions for specifying programs as well as for entering data. In some on-line systems these consoles are highly specialized for a specific application while in other systems the consoles are relatively general in purpose. A special-purpose console may include keys labeled with terms and symbols characteristic of a special application (for example, military commands), while a general-purpose console often resembles a typewriter or a number of typewriters. Special-purpose multiprogram systems usually employ highly specialized computer languages while general-purpose systems tend to employ languages similar to FORTRAN or PL/I (see Chapter 10). The interested reader may now refer to Section 7 of Chapter 10, which illustrates the utilization of time-shared interactive facilities with the programming language BASIC. Some multiprogram systems make provision for the readout to the remote user only of numbers and letters (alpha-numeric output). This output may either be printed copy or it may take the form of numbers and letters flashed on an oscilloscope screen. Other output systems make provision for graphic display including lines, drawings and symbols, as well as numerical data. In some highly sophisticated systems there is provision for entering graphic data on the oscilloscope screen with the aid of a so-called light-pencil, as described in Section 5.

Within each of the above categories, it is possible to differentiate between systems in terms of their response time, their capacity, and their complexity. Some systems, which may be termed high-speed on-line systems, make provision for the processing of specific messages from remote stations in fractions of a second. In other systems a number of seconds or even minutes may elapse before a response is received by a remote station. In terms of capacity, on-line systems range all the way from systems with one remote console capable of employing only one program stored in the computer to systems with thousands of remote consoles capable of drawing upon an enormous amount of file data and programs.

4. ON-LINE SYSTEMS WITH GRAPHIC INPUT/OUTPUT

The most widely used forms of communication with a digital computer are via keypunches, typewriters, printers, and other devices utilizing characters and numbers. It has long been recognized that such an alphanumeric method for representing input and output data is far from ideal in many applications. Very often a graph, an isometric or perspective drawing, or some other form of pictoral representation would be far more effective and efficient than tables of numbers and letters. The need for pictoral or graphic data representation becomes even more pronounced in an on-line environment in which a man is in direct communication with a digital computer. Here, it is particularly important to convey to the operator as rapidly and compactly as possible the result of a series of computations, in order that the operator may make the decisions and judgments required of him. Graphical input/output devices have been developed to this end.

So-called digital plotters and other electromechanical graphical output devices have been in use since the late 1950s. These devices generally involve the displacement of a pen or printing head in both the x and the y directions, as specified by the digital computer, either as increments (Δx and Δy) or as positions (x and y). By the early 1970s these devices had reached a high state of development and were offered in a wide variety of sizes and formats. One manufacturer (Spatial Data Systems Inc.) even had a three-dimensional electromechanical display available. Here, pins were positioned at appropriate points in the x-y plane and caused to protrude from a horizontal surface to a height determined by the z coordinate. Electromechanical displays have the advantage of furnishing permanent, hard-copy records, and of providing a static accuracy and precision as yet unobtainable with all-electronic devices. On the other hand, electromechanical plotters are relatively slow and cumbersome. Moreover, while they constitute excellent output media, the rapid introduction of information into the digital computer by means of such devices is relatively difficult. For these reasons, all-electronic input/output devices utilizing cathode-ray tubes have come to play a dominant role as graphical displays for on-line computations.

Cathode-ray tube (CRT) displays are useful in the alphanumeric mode as well as in the graphical mode. The former application is less demanding of auxiliary hardware and of the communication links connecting the console to the computer. They are, therefore considerably less expensive. A survey article [20] published in mid-1968 listed thirty commercially available CRT consoles selling for under $20,000. These units display numbers and letters as read out of a computer or as applied by means of a typewriter.

Although, viewed externally, a CRT display resembles a commercial television receiver, the internal functioning is markedly different. As described in more detail below, the objective of the internal organization of graphic display consoles is to minimize the data transfer that is required between the CPU and the consoles.

By 1970 graphic display techniques had found applications in a wide range of areas. Some of these are described by Orr [3], by Parslow et al.[9], and by Smith [21], and range all the way from detailed engineering design to computer-aided instruction to management information systems. In all applications, graphic display terminals facilitate a degree of man-computer interaction impossible by other means.

5. HARDWARE FOR GRAPHIC DISPLAY

Graphic display systems are on-line, time-shared systems, organized to facilitate the use of cathode ray tubes as the input and output medium. As such, they include, in addition to the CPU, one or more auxiliary display processors, display generators, line adapters, the CRT units, and the various input devices. One possible configuration of these major units is shown in Figure 2. The operation and function of these units is described briefly below.

More extensive discussions of display hardware and software have been published by Davis [6], Desmonde [7], and Lewin [13].

5.1. Display Processor

The major computing function of large-scale graphic display systems is performed by a large digital computer—the CPU. This computer services in a time-shared fashion numerous other on-line terminals as well as batch jobs. Figure 3a is a block diagram showing a CPU serving several graphic display terminals directly connected to it. Although such a configuration is technically feasible and has occasionally been implemented, it is usually not practical if reasonably demanding and complex tasks are to be performed at the display terminal. Under these conditions the large amount of data transfer necessary between the CRT and the CPU places an excessive burden upon the CPU, saturating its input channels and interfering with its other computing tasks. This is particularly true if the CRTs are not of the storage type, so that the displays must be refreshed 10 to 30 times per second, as described below. If the display terminal or terminals are to be located at some distance from the CPU (a remote system) the required data flow rate usually exceeds the bandwidth capability of low-cost trans-

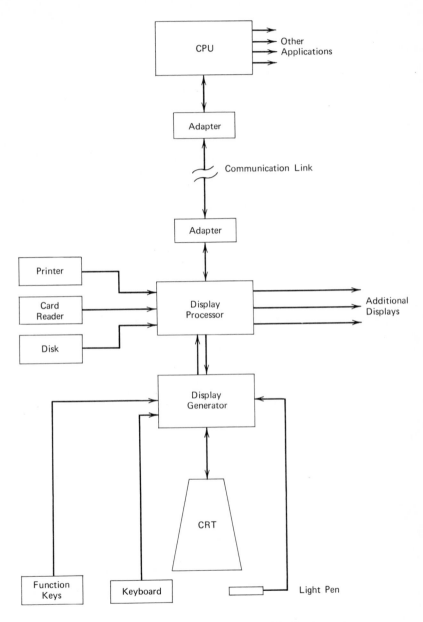

Figure 2. Major units comprising a graphic display system.

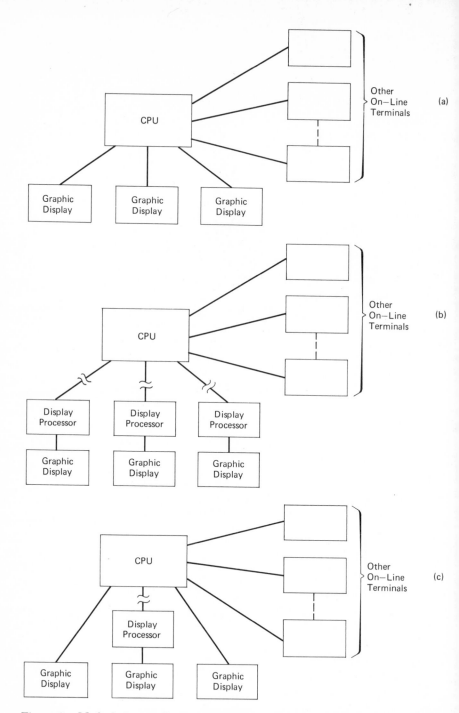

Figure 3. Methods for coupling several display consoles to a single central processor unit.

234

mission lines. For these reasons it has become the practice to equip the display terminals with small digital computers of their own—the display processors. These computers act as buffers between the CPU and the terminals, provide the refresh data, and perform a variety of other computing functions which would otherwise have to be performed by the CPU. A separate display processor may be provided for each display terminal (Figure 3*b*). If numerous terminals are located near each other, a single display processor may be time-shared by these terminals (Figure 3*c*). In any event, the display processor may represent a major portion of the cost of the facility, both from the point of view of hardware and from the point of view of software. Frequently, the processor is a small digital computer also marketed commercially for applications other than graphic display.

5.2.   Cathode Ray Tube

A variety of CRTs have been successfully applied to graphic display consoles. These are usually similar to the tubes employed in conventional oscilloscopes and television receivers, having phosphor coatings with decay times smaller than 0.5 second so that to assure flicker-free displays it is necessary to "refresh" or repeat projecting the image many times per second. This implies that the digital processor must store in its memory all instructions necessary to form the picture and to output these instructions to the display generator at frequent intervals. Alternatively, a so-called storage CRT can be utilized. In such a tube the image is stored with the aid of a metal mesh at the tube face and requires no external refreshing signals. On the other hand, graphic input is relatively more difficult using a storage CRT rather than a conventional tube. Some commercial display terminals have provisions for projecting a photographic slide onto the CRT screen or for projecting a slide as well as the CRT image onto a separate screen. This permits the superposition of CRT and photographic pictures.

5.3.   Display Generator

Deflection of the CRT beam is accomplished either by electrostatic deflection plates inside the tube envelope, by electromagnetic deflection coils outside the tube, or by combinations of both. In any event, the deflection of the beam demands that analog voltages (d-c voltages having magnitudes proportional to the coordinates to which the beam is to be moved) be applied to the CRT deflection circuitry. It is the purpose of the display generator to accept instructions in digital code from the display processor (or the CPU) and to translate these instructions into suitable analog voltages. It should be recognized that a television-type raster-scan is generally unsuitable for graphic displays. In a television receiver the beam methodically sweeps across the tube face, line-by-line, periodically contacting every point on the tube face; at the same time the intensity of the beam is adjusted to the light level required by each "dot" of the picture. The generation and refreshing of such a display would place an excessive load upon the digital processor, since some information would have to be provided to the display generator for each "dot" for each refresh frame. Instead, in graphic display terminals the beam is deflected directly only to those points on the tube face which need to be illuminated for each specific display. The deflection circuitry must therefore be able to deflect the beam randomly—that is, to direct it to any specified x and y coordinates. Blanking circuitry is provided to darken the beam while traveling from one point to be illuminated to another.

While all displays make it possible to direct the beam to illuminate one or a number of dots at specified locations, most displays also permit the generation of lines (vectors), circles, and alphanumeric characters in response to brief commands by the display processor. To this end, the display generator is equipped with special analog function generators. For example, the display processor may issue a command to draw a circle of specified radius, centered at specified coordinates. An analog circuit in the display generator is then called into action to provide the x and the y deflection plates with those time-varying d-c voltages required to cause the beam to illuminate the desired circle. Similarly, alphanumeric characters can be formed by utilizing combinations of straight lines and curves (often formed by Lissajous figures) generated by suitable analog hardware. Special techniques are available for character generation. Often letters and numbers are formed by selectively illuminating dots chosen from a 5×7 array of closely spaced points. Occasionally a special CRT, containing a template with the character set imprinted on it, is employed.

5.4. Input Devices

Graphic input devices permit the operator to introduce information into the display processor and perhaps the CPU. They include function keys, keyboards, light-pens and tablets. The function keys are merely switches which cause interrupts in the digital processor, so as to initiate desired subprograms. These permit the operator to call for various displays, to enable or disable the light-pen, and to cause a number of other commands to be executed. The typewriterlike keyboard is used to "write" characters on the face of the CRT as well as to input data into the digital processor and the CPU. Graphic input is accomplished mostly with the aid of a light-pen. This device is a hand-held stylus capable to detecting the light generated by the CRT beam. When the stylus is held against the tube face, the passage of the beam causes a photocell within the light-pen to emit an electrical pulse which, in turn, causes the x and the y deflection voltages at that instant to be detected and stored. The coordinates in the x-y plane to which the pen is pointed are thus recorded and may be employed immediately or at a later time to cause that point on the CRT face to be illuminated. If the pen is moved across the tube face, the trajectory of the pen can be detected and stored as a series of points or as lines and curves. The pen can therefore be used to "write" on the CRT face, and the resulting pictorial information can be stored for later use. Storage may be either in the digital processor or the CPU. The light-pen is also used in conjunction with alphanumeric displays. For example, by pushing a function key the operator can cause a "menu," a list of alternative instruction, to be displayed on the CRT. By bringing the pen close to one of the display lines, the operator can then select one of the instruction for execution. Tablet input devices, such as the RAND tablet, permit the user to "write" by moving a stylus across a plane surface and to have the trajectory of the stylus motion displayed on the CRT screen [12]. This requires more complex circuitry than does the light-pen.

5.5.   Line Adapters

Information transmitted between the CPU and the remote digital processor is usually sent one bit or one character at a time—that is, serially. Both the CPU and the digital processor are parallel-word devices, requiring that all bits corresponding to a word be available simultaneously. The line adapter performs the necessary parallel-to-serial and serial-to-parallel conversion. In addition, the adapter may change voltage levels, word format, and the like, as required to link the two digital computers.

6.   SOFTWARE FOR GRAPHIC DISPLAY

The preparation of programs is particularly challenging in the case of graphic display systems. Here, in addition to the usual software to support on-line operation, separate program packages must be prepared to facilitate user-machine interaction. The most important of these fall into the following classifications: display commands, data sets, data manipulation, and special applications.

6.1.   Display Commands

These are the basic programmed commands causing the CRT beam to assume a specified position and to draw or erase characters, lines, or curves;

they are used to enable the light-pen, function keys, and keyboard; and they command all the other operations that are basic to the functioning of the graphic display.

6.2. Data Sets

The picture to be displayed is described digitally by a set of words. These may represent, for example, the coordinates of various displayed characters or the beginning and terminal points of lines and curves. This information must be transmitted from the display processor to the display generator many times per second to permit the display to be refreshed. These data sets must therefore be as compact as possible and must be organized in such a way as to facilitate manipulation as demanded by the input devices or by the CPU. Data sets may be fragmented or organized into hierarchies, so that portions of a picture may be manipulated without affecting other portions. Some data sets may be provided by the manufacturer as permanent subroutines, for example character generation programs, while other sets may be user designed.

6.3. Data Manipulation

The operator of the display console must be given the facility of manipulating data sets in a variety of ways. Portions of the displayed picture may have to be expanded or "blown up," rotated about axes normal or parallel to the CRT face, or moved in more complex ways; hidden lines may have to be illuminated; animation may have to be provided to permit the viewing of dynamic as well as static events. All of these operations demand special software permitting the manipulation of the x and y coordinates locating each element of the display on the screen, thus permitting the mapping of each point of an image to a different point. Such manipulation may be performed entirely by programming or use may be made of analog function generators provided in the display generator.

6.4. Application Programs

In addition to the above-mentioned software packages, each application demands special programs. It is the development of this application software that makes the utilization of graphic displays feasible and practical, and which over the years represents a bigger and bigger portion of the user's investment. To facilitate the preparation of these programs, it is desirable to permit the use of familiar problem-oriented languages such as FORTRAN, ALGOL, and PL/I. The vocabulary and syntax of these languages must of course be modified and adapted to on-line, graphic display needs.

The IBM GPS and PL/I PL/OT programs represent such extensions of existing languages. In some application-areas special languages, such as APT for geometric work, have been introduced.

7. FINAL REMARKS

The original motivation for on-line computation was to increase the efficiency of digital computer use, by permitting simultaneous access to the central processor unit by means of a number of remote control consoles and other hardware units. The success of the initial attempts of on-line operation and of time-sharing has resulted in a vast proliferation of on-line computing systems. By 1971, batch programming was still the predominant mode of computer usage; however, more and more large computer systems especially designed for time-shared operation were being marketed and acquired by industrial and institutional users. It appears clear that the use of on-line techniques will continue to grow larger and larger every year, until it may finally overshadow batch programming.

The higher-level programming languages, described by Alfonso F. Cárdenas in Chapter 10, had an almost revolutionary effect upon computer usage, by taking computer programming out of the preserve of highly trained specialists; they thereby made it possible for a wide range of users to construct their own programs. On-line computing systems promise to constitute a similar breakthrough from the point of view of hardware, in facilitating the use of digital computers by a large number of potential users who heretofore were discouraged by the economic and practical impediments of batch operation. As a result, many disciplines, including those within the social sciences, life sciences, and humanities, can be expected to become oriented more and more toward quantitative techniques —leading, in turn, to profound changes in the fundamental approaches to many basic subjects. Further conceptual changes in approach are sure to be stimulated by the increased availability of graphic display devices, which make it possible to communicate with the computer via pictures rather than by using words and numbers. Thus, on-line and time-shared computing is assuming an importance and significance far greater than was ever imagined by the early designers of on-line systems.

8. REFERENCES

General Texts

1. Karplus, W. J. (editor), *On-Line Computing*, McGraw-Hill Book Company, Inc., New York, 1967.

2. Martin, J., *Programming Real-Time Computer Systems*, Prentice-Hall, New Jersey, 1965.

3. Orr, W. D. (editor), *Conversational Computers*, John Wiley and Sons, New York, 1963.

4. Watson, R. W., *Time Sharing System Design Concepts*, McGraw-Hill Book Co., New York, 1970.

5. Martin, J., *Telecommunications and the Computer*, Prentice-Hall, New Jersey, 1969.

Texts on Graphic Display

6. Davis, S., *Computer Data Display*, Prentice-Hall, New Jersey, 1969.

7. Desmonde, W. H., *A Conversational Graphic Data Processing System*, Prentice-Hall, New Jersey, 1969.

8. Fetter, W. A., *Computer Graphics in Communication*, McGraw-Hill Book Company, Inc., New York, 1967.

9. Parslow, R. E., R. W. Prowse, and R. E. Green, *Computer Graphics*, Plenum Press, New York, 1969.

Articles on Graphic Displays

10. Chasen, S. H., and R. N. Sietz, "On-Line Systems and Man-Computer Graphics," *Astronautics and Aeronautics*, pages 48–55, April 1967.

11. Corbin, H. S., "A Survey of CRT Display Consoles," *Control Engineering*, Vol. 12, pp. 77–83, December 1965.

12. Gallenson, L., "A Graphic Tablet Display Console for Use in Time-Sharing," *Proceedings, Fall Joint Computer Conference*, pp. 689–695, 1967.

13. Lewin, M. H., "An Introduction to Computer Graphic Terminals," *Proceedings of the IEEE*, Vol. 55, pp. 1544–1552, September 1967.

14. Machover, C., "Family of Computer Controlled CRT Graphic Displays," *Information Display*, pp. 43–46, July/August 1966.

15. Machover, C., "Graphic CRT Terminals—Characteristics of Commercially Available Equipment," *Proceedings, Fall Joint Computer Conference*, pp. 149–159, 1967.

16. Rapkin, M. D., and O. M. Abu-Gheida, "Stand-Along/Remote Graphic System," *Proceedings, Fall Joint Computer Conference*, pp. 731–746, 1968.

17. Rosenbloom, M., "Computer-Control Displays," *Computer Design*, pp. 20–22, July 1966.

18. *Scientific American*, Issue on Computers and Information, Volume 215, No. 3, September 1966.

19. Sutherland, W. R., and J. W. Forgie, "Graphics in Time-Sharing: A Summary of the TX-2 Experience," *Proceedings, Spring Joint Computer Conference,*, pp. 629–636, 1969.

20. Theis, D. J., and L. C. Hobbs, "Low-Cost Remote CRT Terminals," *Datamation*, Vol. 14, pp. 22–29, June 1968.

21. Smith, L. B., "A Survey of Interactive Graphical Systems for Mathematics," *Computing Surveys*, Vol. 2, No. 4, December 1970, pp. 261–301.

Computer Networks

Leonard Kleinrock

University of California
Los Angeles

1. HISTORICAL DEVELOPMENT

First came the vacuum-tube computers in the early 1950s [1]. They were of moderate speed (tens of thousands of instructions per second) and of small memory (a few thousand words). Those machines were used mainly by scientists for mathematical and scientific calculations in an on-line fashion whereby one man had exclusive use of the full machine for hours at a time. This procedure was highly efficient from the user's point of view, but sadly wasteful of the machine's capability for work.

Next came the organizers in the mid-to-late 1950s who introduced batch-processing (see Chapter 6) in order to use the faster, larger machines (hundreds of thousands of instructions per second with 32 to 65 thousand

241

word memories) in a more efficient fashion [2]. Thus the user was thrown out of the computer room and his punched cards or tape were his sole input, yielding reams of paper output. This succeeded in efficient use of machine time, but was accomplished at the expense of the highly inefficient use of the user, resulting in many hours for turn-around from when a job was submitted until it was returned complete. This procedure was frustrating when it came to debugging programs.

In the early 1960s a major breakthrough was made with the advent of time-sharing. One of the first demonstrated time-sharing systems was developed at M.I.T. with more than one flexowriter (a computer-connected electric typewriter) simultaneously using the computer [3]. The principle behind time-sharing is that no single user typically requires all the resources of a computer facility at one time, and therefore many simultaneous users can share these resources. It will be shown later that a measure of the number of simultaneous and noninterfering users is approximately the ratio of the user's average "thinking" time plus his average required computer time divided by his average computing time. For example, if each user spends 19 seconds generating a request that requires one second of computing time, then approximately 20 such users can be scheduled on a continuous, simultaneous basis without significant interference. These time-shared systems clearly are efficient in the user's time and are also rather efficient in the use of the computer.

Time-shared facilities have grown up across the United States during the past decade and a variety of different kinds of services are available at relatively low cost to the user [4]. These facilities effectively allow the user access to the computer room, except now he is coupled to the machine through a remote terminal. These remote terminals may be as simple as a teletype console or as sophisticated as a terminal which includes graphical input and output devices for the display of characters, curves, diagrams, and the like. Novel input devices have been invented, such as light-pens, wands (three-dimensional input devices), mice (two-wheeled devices which detect X-Y motion), and eyes (in the form of television cameras or head-mounted displays). This strongly interactive relationship between man and machine has naturally led people to consider what should be the proper interface between a human and a computer and what limitations each places upon the other. This question is discussed by Walter J. Karplus in Chapter 7 and is further discussed below.

Under time-sharing, facilities and systems have grown and developed into sophisticated and rather unique sites. Across the country, we have seen rather specialized capabilities developing at universities and research laboratories [5]. These special features take the form of exceptional computer programs, data files, hardware devices, and other resources. These capabilities are available only at the computer center where they have been developed and are, in general, not easily transferable. It is clear, however, that these special resources should be available for use by others than those at the site. This desire naturally leads to the concept of *computer networks* and represents the next major breakthrough in the use of computers.

One of the earliest computer networks was the SAGE defense network in the 1950s [6]. This highly specialized military net demonstrated for the first time that software requirements of large computer systems could be as costly and difficult as the hardware equipment. The American Airlines SABRE Reservation System came shortly thereafter [7]; this too was a collection of rather uniform equipment for a highly specialized application. The electronically switched telephone system has, for a time, been the world's largest computer network, which again is highly specialized and single-purposed [8]. Recently, Control Data Corporation announced its nation-wide network [9].

It is our intention in this chapter to demonstrate techniques for analyzing and synthesizing computer networks. In doing this, we shall describe the structure, operation, and user environment for some such networks. The tools we develop are, of necessity, at this stage of development (early 1970), rather crude and approximate; however, they are effective for understanding the important behavior of computer networks and for conducting a first-cut analysis of these systems.

In carrying out the steps necessary to achieve this goal, it is necessary to describe, in some detail, the results already obtained from the analysis of both time-shared systems and communication networks. As will be seen shortly, a computer network may be viewed as a communication net which feeds a collection of time-shared computer systems. Thus, in order to understand the behavior of computer nets, we must first gain some understanding of the operation and analysis of the other two systems.

Therefore, this chapter is organized in the following way. We begin, in Section 2, with a general description of a computer network, using as our example, the ARPA network. In Section 3 we briefly discuss the importance of the user interface. Section 4 presents the results of modeling and analyzing time-shared systems. A discussion of network flow theory is contained in Section 5, followed by analytical models and results for a class of communication nets. In Section 7 we pull together all the previous material in a discussion of computer networks; we consider both operational questions as well as analytical models. The result of simulation experiments are also reported here. Finally, in Section 8, we conjecture on the future use and form of computer networks.

2. GENERAL DESCRIPTION OF COMPUTER NETWORKS— AN EXAMPLE

A computer network is a collection of nodes (computers) connected together by a set of links (communication channels). Messages, in the form of commands, inquiries, transmissions, and the like, travel through this network over data transmission lines. At the nodes, the tasks of relaying messages (with all appropriate routing, acknowledging, error control, queueing, and so on) and inserting and removing messages, which originate and terminate at that node, must be carried out. Often these tasks are separated from the main computing functions required of the node, as will be seen in the example below.

It is convenient to describe the structure and operation of computer networks through the use of an example.* The system from which this example is drawn is the United States Defense Department's Advanced Research Projects Agency (ARPA) Experimental Computer Network [11]. The concepts basic to this network were clearly stated in Reference 12 by L. Roberts of the Advanced Research Projects Agency who originally conceived this system. By mid-1971 this network will provide store-and-forward communication paths between a set of approximately 15 nodes in the continental United States. The computers located at each of the nodes are highly incompatible (e.g., X.D.S. 940, DEC PDP-10, IBM 360/67, GE 635, ILLIAC 4, and TX-2), and one of the major challenges is to design a network in which this assortment of varied hardware and software systems can communicate and cooperate with each other.

The principal motivation for creating this network is to provide to each of the computer research centers the special resources that have been created at the other centers. For example, Stanford Research Institute will provide the role of network librarian and will offer its sophisticated text editing capability for massaging this vast data base; access will be permitted to the extremely high parallel processing speeds of the ILLIAC 4; the University of Utah will serve as a major graphics center for picture processing; and the University of California at Los Angeles will process network measurement data and compare these to simulation and analytically predicted results.

The topology and identity of the various nodes in this net have undergone considerable change since the early design stages. Nevertheless, for purpose of our example, we shall choose a given set of 19 nodes (an original network design); again we emphasize that the details below regarding

---

* Material for this description and for the results in Section 7 has been drawn partly from Reference 10.

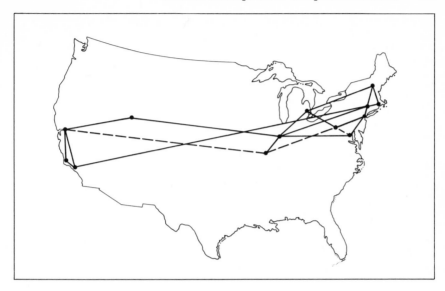

Figure 1. Two configurations of the ARPA network and a list of participating centers. Advanced Research Projects Agency, Washington, D.C. (ARPA); Bell Telephone Laboratories, Murray Hill, N.J. (BTL); Bolt, Beranek & Newman, Cambridge, Mass. (BBN); Carnegie-Mellon University, Pittsburgh, Pa. (CMU); Dartmouth College, Hanover, N.H. (DC); Harvard University, Cambridge, Mass. (HU); Lincoln Laboratories (MIT), Lexington, Mass. (LL); Massachusetts Institute of Technology, Cambridge, Mass. (MIT); Rand Corp., Santa Monica, Calif. (RAND); Stanford Research Institute, Palo Alto, Calif. (SRI); Stanford University, Palo Alto, California (SU); Systems Development Corp., Santa Monica, Calif. (SDC); University of California, Berkeley, Calif. (UCB); University of California at Los Angeles, (UCLA); University of California, Santa Barbara, Calif. (UCSB); University of Illinois, Urbana, Ill. (UI); University of Michigan, Ann Arbor, Mich. (UM); University of Utah, Salt Lake City, Utah (UU); Washington University, St. Louis, Mo. (WU).

topology and identification of nodes have been and still are being changed. This last also applies to some of the operating procedures.

The example set of 19 nodes (mostly ARPA research contractors at universities) to be used in this chapter is listed in Figure 1 and connections between these geographical centers is shown; two configurations are considered for the purposes of this chapter. Figure 2 shows these two configurations in a more readable topological form. Notice that net 2 has three cross-country links, whereas net 1 has only two.

In order to interfere least with the existing operation of these various facilities, the message handling tasks (relay, acknowledgment, routing, and buffering) will be carried out in a special purpose Interface Message

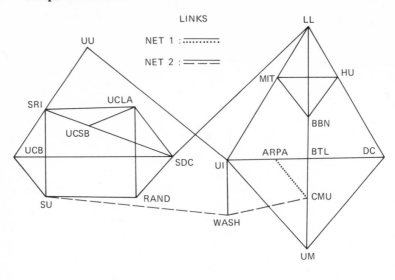

LINKS

NET 1 : ··········
NET 2 : ═ ══

NET CONFIGURATIONS

Figure 2.   Topological network diagram for the two configurations.

Processor (IMP) collocated with the principal computer (denoted HOST computer) at each of the computer research centers. The communication channels will (in most cases) be 50 kilobit/sec fully duplex telephone lines, and only the IMPS (not the HOSTS) will be connected to these lines. This communication net, consisting of these lines, IMPS and data sets, serves as the store-and-forward system for the HOST computer net. Thus, for transmission between UCLA and UU, the direct path of store-and-forward transmission would pass through the UCLA HOST to the UCLA IMP to the SRI IMP to the UU IMP and then finally to the UU HOST (Figure 3).

When the HOST has a message ready for transmission, it will be broken into a set of smaller packets (each of size approximately 1024 bits or less) with appropriate header information. The IMP will accept up to eight of these (an assembly set) at a time. The packets will then individually make their way through the IMP network where the appropriate routing procedure will direct the traffic flow. For each IMP to IMP packet transmission, a positive acknowledgment is expected within a given time; absence of an acknowledgment (caused perhaps by channel noise detected by a cyclic error detecting code, by lack of buffer space, and the like) will force the transmitting IMP to try the same or some different channel for retransmission. An initial network of four nodes (SRI, UCLA, UCSB, and UU) became operational late in 1969 and has since grown and will continue

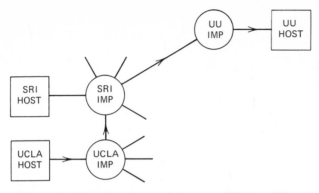

Figure 3.   Example of transmission from UCLA to UU.

to grow. One of the design goals is to achieve a response time less than 1/2 sec (round-trip) for short messages.

The traffic matrix (Figure 4) gives the current (gross) estimate of traffic requirements between nodes (these numbers do not include the effect of acknowledgment traffic). We assume that the messages fall into two broad categories: one-packet short messages, typically averaging approximately 350 bits due to short commands and acknowledgments; and long, or multi-packet, messages due to larger data transfers. In the subsequent results of Section 7, we vary the mix of short and long (multipacket) messages (while maintaining an average input data rate to the entire net of 225 kilobits/sec —see Figure 4—so as to study the effect of mix variation independent of load).

The estimated cost for all communication equipment (IMPS, modems, and channels) is somewhat less than $1 million. However, a more meaning-ful statement regarding network cost is that the average cost for trans-mitting 6000 characters (roughly one page of single-spaced typewritten text) between 2 nodes is only .01 dollar! This is equivalent to a rate of approximately 0.20 dollars/megabit. Notice that such costs compete very well with current airmail postage charges!

This example should provide the reader with a fair understanding of the operation and structure of computer networks. We shall return to this particular example later in Section 7 where we undertake to analyze such nets.

3. THE USER INTERFACE

In studying computer networks, we begin from outside the net and pro-ceed inward; thus, we begin as the user encounters the machine (this

ARPA NETWORK

From \ To	1	2	3	4	5	6	7	8	9	10	11	12	13	14	15	16	17	18	19	Node Output Total	Node Input Total	I/O Rate Total
1. Dartmouth (DC)		2		1		2	1	1	1					1		1	1			8	4	12
2. M.I.T.	1		1	2	2	1	1	1	1	1	1		2	1	2	1	1	1	1	21	15	36
3. B.B.N.	1	1		1			1						2	1						7	12	19
4. Harvard (HU)	1	1	1		1		1	1												6	11	17
5. Lincoln Lab. (LL)	1	1				1	1		1	1		2		1			1	1		10	18	28
6. B.T.L.	2	1												1						4	8	12
7. Pentagon (ARPA)					1										1		1			3	10	13
8. Carnegie (CMU)	1	1				2			2	1		1		2	1		1	1		10	9	19
9. U. of Michigan (UM)	1	1			1	1	1	1	1	1	1			1		1			1	9	8	17
10. U. Illinois (UI)	2	2		1	5	1	1	1	1			20	1	2	2	10	1	1	1	50	13	63
11. Washing. U. (WU)	1			1	1	1								1						3	5	8
12. U. Utah (UU)	1	1			5	1	1	2	1	8				1	1	5	1	1		26	29	55
13. U.C. Berkeley (UCB)	1	1	6	3	1	1	1	1	1		1	1		3	1	1	1	1		20	6	26
14. S.R.I.	1	1	2	1	1	1	1	1	1		1	1	2		2	1	1	1	1	21	19	40
15. Stanford U. (SU)	1	1								1	1	1		1						3	8	11
15. Santa Barbara (UCSB)				1	1	1			1		1					1	1			5	22	27
17. U.C.L.A.				1	1											1	1	1	1	4	10	14
18. RAND Corp.						2	2					1					1	1	1	8	10	18
19. S.D.C.	1	1												1			1	1		7	8	15
Total																				225	225	

Figure 4. Assumed traffic matrix for ARPA network (entries in kilobits/sec.).

current section), followed by the time-shared system with which he inter-
acts (next section), and finally we consider the network itself. The user
interface is adequately discussed by Walter J. Karplus in Chapter 7; here
we shall only discuss certain of the salient features associated with the
characteristics and limitations of the man-machine boundary.

Men are logically deep; they represent things in patterns, compute in
parallel at a relatively slow rate, and are imprecise and redundant in many
of their representations. On the other hand, computers are logically shallow;
they work with bit streams and strings of characters, process serially at
fantastic speeds, and are quite precise and unambiguous in their representations and instructions. These differences require clever and careful
design in the creation of any interface between men and machines.

Let us demonstrate some of the redundancies apparent in humans and in
their language. TH VWLS HV BN RMVD FRM THS SNTNC ND
STLL MST PPL HV LTTL DFFCLTY NDRDSTNDNG THS NGLSH
WRDS. Also try,

ARE YOU KIDDING YOURSELF

ABOUT YOUR BUSINESS FUTURE

This redundancy in printed English can be taken advantage of in a number
of ways and can also be modeled rather well by using discrete state Markov
processes [13].

Regarding human responses, it has been determined by experiments that
the following kinds of limitations exist. A man cannot respond any faster
than approximately 1/10 of a second if he is required to indicate yes or
no; his response time is approximately 1/7 of a second if he is required to
push a button in response. If his own speech is fed back to him with about
a half-second delay, he cannot continue to speak because of the confusion.
One can identify seven plus or minus two stimuli in a single dimension (this
has the venerated label of "Rule of 7 ± 2"); this, however, can be applied
to numerous hierarchal levels simultaneously. Defining an information bit
as the logarithm to the base two of the number of equally like choices, we
find that the rule of 7 ± 2 is equivalent to 2.8 ($+.4, -.5$) bits per stimulus.
The maximum rate at which humans can accept information (under
favorable conditions of using a large and familiar alphabet of samples or
sounds) is approximately 40 bits per second [14].

These observations about human behavior are useful and important in
coupling man with machine. The creation of an efficient, comfortable, and
responsive terminal is one of the most important goals in the area of computer research.

4. TIME-SHARED SYSTEM MODELING AND ANALYSIS

As the supply and demand for readily accessible, inexpensive computing power grows, so grows the need for quantitative analysis of the performance of time-shared systems. This need is beginning to be met, as is evidenced by a survey of the literature [15–21]. In this section we review some recent results and interpretations that we feel are significant in predicting the performance of these systems.

Time-shared systems are often designed with the intent of appearing to a user as his personal processor (where, ideally, he is unaware of the presence of any other users). Of course, no such ideal systems can guarantee a full-capacity full-time machine to any user (in the time-shared mode), but rather they offer a fractional-capacity "full-time" machine to each user. In the ideal case, at any time, the fraction of the total capacity offered to any user will be inversely proportional to the number of users currently requesting service. Moreover, it is the usual case that these time-shared systems seek to provide preferential treatment to shorter computational jobs as opposed to (and also at the expense of) longer jobs.

The usual approach taken in preparing a mathematical model for existing or proposed time-shared service (processing) facilities is to treat them as queueing systems. Since the time to generate a new request and the required processing time are both unpredictable, we treat both as random variables. The theoretical results divide into two classes: *infinite* input population and *finite* input population. The first class is illustrated in Figure 5 in which we see the basic structure wherein a new arrival (from an infinite population of possible customers) enters a system of queues, is treated according to the imposed queueing discipline, finally reaching the head of the queue, is allowed entry into the service facility for a given number of seconds (a quantum) and then either (a) departs if the quantum was enough to satisfy his requirement or (b) cycles back to the system of queues to wait for another turn in service. Once we specify the structure of the system of queues and the nature of the quanta, we have then specified the

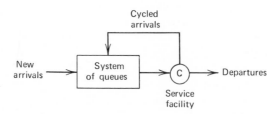

Figure 5.   Feedback queueing systems.

scheduling algorithm. We recognize that whenever a customer is moved out of service and another is taken into service, a period of time (called the "swap-time") is required for the transfer. In many of the following models, we assume for the sake of mathematical tractability that this cost (the swap-time) is zero. In models involving a finite quantum, we may think of a portion of that time as being used for swapping; this alters the service time distribution in a predictable way. Similarly, in the case where the quantum shrinks to zero (called processor-sharing models [18]), the notion of swapping may be accounted for by assigning a given fraction of the shrinking quantum to swapping. The quantity typically solved for is $T(t)$, which is the average response time for jobs that require t seconds of processing; *response time* is the interval from when a request is made of the system until that request is satisfied.

Most time-sharing systems make use of a *quantum* (or *time slice*) Q which is the interval of time given to a customer once he obtains the attention of the service facility. In this chapter we consider only the case in which $Q \rightarrow 0$. The reason for going to this limit is that the mathematical analysis and results become much simpler as opposed to the finite quantum case; the results so obtained contain the fundamental behavior of the finite quantum systems as well and eliminate undue complications due to the finite nature of the quantum. These zero quantum systems correspond to time-shared systems in which each customer cycles through the system of queues infinitely fast for an infinite number of cycles and spends an infinitesimally small amount of time in the service facility each time he visits it. In a real sense, then, all customers present in the system are using a fraction of the service facility's capacity on a full time basis. This operating procedure is called a "processor-shared" system and a discussion of its behavior is given in Reference 18.

We begin with the *round-robin* processor-shared system (the first time-shared system studied was that of the discrete time round-robin system [15]). The structure of this system is shown in Figure 6. New arrivals join the tail of a single queue and work their way forward in a first-come first-served fashion until they reach the service facility. After they receive their quantum of service they then cycle back and join the tail of that same queue and repeat the procedure. In the zero quantum case our customers are cycling around infinitely fast and give rise to a processor-shared system. We assume that the service requirement of customers is expresssed in terms of the number of operations l required by a customer and we assume that this number of operations is a random variable which is distributed exponentially,

$$p(l) = \mu e^{-\mu l} \qquad (1)$$

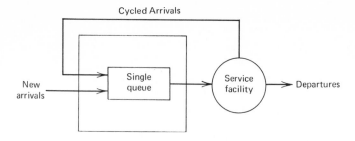

Figure 6.   The round-robin system.

where $p(l)$ is the probability density function for the number of operations l. We further assume that we have a Poisson arrival mechanism with an average of λ units arriving per second; that is, the time between arrivals is exponentially distributed. Thus we have an average of λ customers arriving per second where each customer requires on the average $1/\mu$ operations. We further assume that the service facility is a computer whose capacity is C operations (say additions) per second. It is then clear that a customer requiring l operations thus requires l/C seconds of service in that facility.

For such a system it has been shown in [18] that the average value $T(l/C)$ of the response time in the round-robin processor-shared system for a customer requiring l operations is

$$T\left(\frac{l}{C}\right) = \frac{l/C}{1 - \rho} \tag{2}$$

where

$$\rho = \lambda/\mu C = \text{system load } (= \text{ average arrival rate}$$
$$\text{times average service time}) \tag{3}$$

The quantity ρ is referred to as the utilization factor and is merely the ratio of the rate at which work arrives to the system to the maximum processing rate of the system; clearly, it must never exceed 1 if the system is to remain stable. Notice the extremely simple dependence of the response time on the job length l; namely, response time is linear with job length! The dependence upon ρ is also rather simple, giving sensitive behavior as ρ approaches 1.

The expected value $T_{\text{FCFS}}(l/C)$ of the response time in the strict first come first served system* for a unit whose required number of operations is l is

$$T_{\text{FCFS}}\left(\frac{l}{C}\right) = \frac{l/C}{1-\rho} + \left(\frac{\rho/C}{1-\rho}\right)\left(\frac{1}{\mu} - l\right) \tag{4}$$

We note that the first term of Equation 4 is equal to the response time given in Equation 2; the second term in Equation 4 may be positive or negative, depending on the size of l as compared to $1/\mu$. Recall that the average number of operations l among service requirements is, in fact $1/\mu$. We thus conclude that customers requiring less (greater) than an average number of operations spend less (more) time on the average in the round-robin system than in the first-come first-served system. It is interesting that the crossover point for jobs occurs exactly at the average job length. We thus see the way in which the round-robin time-sharing system discriminates among short and long jobs, clearly giving preferential treatment to the shorter jobs, as was the intention. Observe also that the average number of customers present in the system, both in the round-robin and first-come first-served cases, is given by

$$\text{Average number in system} = \frac{\rho}{1-\rho} \tag{5}$$

and exhibits the same sensitivity to ρ as does the average response time.

It is possible to define a continuum of time-shared scheduling algorithms which allow us to range from the first-come first-served algorithm all the way to the round-robin algorithm in the processor-sharing case [37]. We do this by defining a notion of priority for a customer and agree that an entering customer arrives with 0 priority and gains priority at a rate of α units per second so long as he is not being served. When a customer is taken into the service facility his priority increases at a rate β. The service facility will always take into service that customer or customers with the highest priority among those in the system. Thus, while a customer is being served he gains priority at a rate β and while he is waiting he gains priority at a rate α. We consider the case $0 \leq \beta \leq \alpha$. In this range it is clear that once a customer is allowed into service he will never leave until his service requirement is complete; when N customers are in the service facility, then each customer receives $1/N$ of the capacity C available from the service facility. We call this kind of system a selfish round-robin (SRR) processor-shared system, and it yields the following result for the average response time.

---

* This is a reference (batch) system and corresponds to the more usual case where a customer receives his complete processing requirement the first time he enters service.

$$T_{SRR}\left(\frac{l}{C}\right) = \frac{1/\mu}{1 - \rho} - \frac{(l/C) - (1/\mu)}{1 - \rho[1 - (\beta/\alpha)]} \tag{6}$$

It is interesting to compare the behavior of the various SRR systems and in Figure 7 where we plot the quantity $W(l/C) = T(l/C) - l/C$, which represents the wasted time in system.

Now consider a processor-shared system in which there are P priority groups with Poisson arrivals at an average rate of λ_p per second and an exponentially distributed service requirement with a mean of $1/\mu_p$ operations ($p = 1, 2, \ldots, P$). Assign a customer from the pth priority group a capacity f_pC when there are n_i type i customers in the system; f_p is given by

$$f_p = \frac{g_p}{\sum\limits_{i=1}^{P} g_i n_i} \tag{7}$$

For such a system, the expected value $T_p(l/C)$ of the response time spent in the priority processor-shared system for a customer from priority group p who requires l operations is

$$T_p\left(\frac{l}{C}\right) = \frac{l}{C}\left[1 + \sum_{i=1}^{P} \frac{g_i \rho_i}{g_p(1 - \rho)}\right] \tag{8}$$

where $\rho_p = \lambda_p/\mu_p$

The expected number, E_p, of type p customers in the system is

$$E_p = \frac{\rho_p}{1 - \rho}\left[1 + \sum_{i=1}^{P}\left(\frac{g_i}{g_p} - 1\right)\rho_i\right] \tag{9}$$

For completeness, consider a strict first-come first-served system with the same input and service requirements as in our priority model. The first-come first-served system with a priority input yields, for customers with l required operations, an expected response time as follows:

$$T\left(\frac{l}{C}\right) = \frac{l}{C} + \frac{\rho/\mu C}{1 - \rho} \tag{10}$$

where $\qquad \dfrac{1}{\mu C} = \dfrac{\rho}{\sum\limits_{p=1}^{P} \lambda_p} \qquad$ and $\qquad \rho = \sum\limits_{P=1}^{P} \rho_p$

Notice that $P = 1$ yields the (nonpriority) processor-shared system.

We see in all of the processor-shared systems studied that the average response time is directly proportional to the job length l. This is an espe-

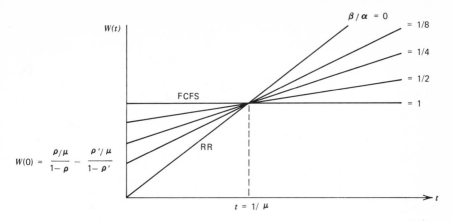

Figure 7. Performance of the SRR system.

cially nice property in that it discourages users from partitioning their jobs into smaller tasks (which would be their tendency if it were true that the sum of the response times for many smaller jobs turned out to be less than that for one equivalent long job) or into "collected" longer jobs.

Other infinite-population models have been studied and are reported in the literature [16–18]. Let us now consider models for the *finite* input population where we assume that M consoles generate requests for use of the service facility. These requests impinge on the system (whose internal structure is identical to that of the infinite population models shown in Figure 5); upon departure, these customers "return" to their original console to generate new requests as shown in Figure 8. We refer to the time required for a console to generate a new request as the *think time*. The

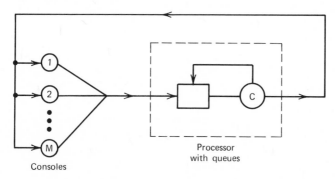

Figure 8. Finite population model.

system response time is the elapsed time from when a request is made to when that request is satisfied completely; during this interval, the console, from which this request was made, is idle (nonthinking). The request is for a given number of "operations" in the service facility which can process at a rate of C operations/second.

Below, we assume both that the think time for each console and that the size of each request are exponentially distributed with an average value of $1/\gamma$ sec for thinking and $1/\mu$ operations for each request, respectively; this assumption is an approximation to measured data (see Reference 21 and its references). All quanta are assumed to be infinitesimal, and swap-time (the time lost in changing jobs) is assumed to be zero, thus leading to a processor-shared model. In this case, then, when we find m consoles actively competing for use of the computer, we see that each console is being processed at a rate of C/m operations per second. The exponential assumptions along with the infinitesimal quanta produce a model for our time-shared system which is a continuous-time Markov process [22]. As before, we let T be the average response time and take this as our performance measure.

The simple model has been carefully studied by queueing theorists [23] and corresponds to the finite-population single-server exponential queueing system. Below we give the (easily obtained) results for the steady-state probability (denoted p_m) of finding $m(\leq M)$ consoles actively competing for use of the computer facility (these consoles are said to be in the "system"). From any standard reference (such as page 121 of Reference 23) we observe that

$$p_m = p_0 \frac{M!}{(M-m)!} \left(\frac{\gamma}{\mu C}\right)^m \qquad m = 0, 1, 2, \ldots, M \qquad (11)$$

where

$$p_0 = \left[\sum_{m=0}^{M} \frac{M!}{(M-m)!} \left(\frac{\gamma}{\mu C}\right)^m\right]^{-1} \qquad (12)$$

From simple considerations, it follows that

$$T = \frac{M}{\mu C(1-p_0)} - \frac{1}{\gamma} \qquad (13)$$

This result was first used by Scherr [19] for time-shared systems. Scherr also tested the value of this model in the MIT time-sharing system. His principal finding is shown in Figure 9 where he has compared the results of measurement (shown as dotted data points and the least-squares fit, B-B, to the points) with the results of model analysis given by Equation 13

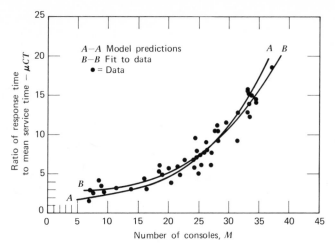

Figure 9. Comparison of measured and predicated performance.

(curve A-A). As can be seen, the normalized* response time, μCT, is accurately predicted by our model, in spite of the fact that the MIT time-sharing system does not operate according to the assumptions of the model.

Because of the finite value of M, one questions whether it is possible to *saturate* the system. Indeed, if we define saturation as that point where the system goes unstable in some sense, such as average response time growing to infinity, then we see immediately that our system is never saturated (for $\gamma/\mu C < \infty$). (Such unstable behavior is possible in the infinite population case.) Nevertheless there does exist an appropriate definition of saturation here as follows. If we replace each service time by its average $(1/\mu C)$, and if we schedule the arrivals to occur uniformly in time, each spending exactly $1/\gamma$ sec thinking, then we see that the system can handle at most a number of consoles, M^* given by

$$M^* = \frac{1/\mu C + 1/\gamma}{1/\mu C} = \frac{\mu C + \gamma}{\gamma} \tag{14}$$

without any mutual interference. For example, if each customer requires 19 sec for thinking and 1 sec for computation, then 20 such customers can be handled. This provides the basis on which we define M^* as the

---

* If provided the full capacity, a customer will spend an average of $1/\mu C$ seconds in the system. We choose to normalize T with respect to this giving μCT which represents the factor by which a customer is delayed (due to his sharing the system) in relation to his time in the system without sharing.

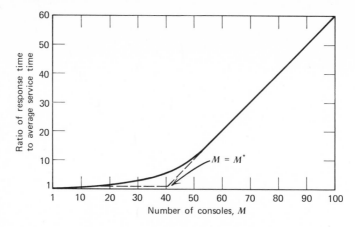

Figure 10. Performance and saturation.

saturation point for our M-console system.† We plot Equation 13 again in Figure 10 where $M^* = 41$ $(1/\mu C = .88, 1/\gamma = 35.2)$. We see that μCT begins to increase sharply in the vicinity $M \approx M^*$. For $M \ll M^*$, we see that μCT grows very slowly, since customers tend to request computation during other customers' think-time; indeed, it can be shown that in this region, the results from infinite population queueing theory hold true, giving

$$\mu CT \simeq \frac{1}{1 - [(M - 1)\gamma/\mu C]} \qquad \text{for} \qquad M \ll M^* \qquad (15)$$

For $M \gg M^*$, we see from Equations 12 and 13 that

$$\mu CT \simeq M - (\mu C/\gamma) = M - M^* + 1 \qquad (16)$$

since $p_0 \to 0$. This asymptote is shown dashed in Figure 10, and we observe that in intersects the line $\mu CT = 1$ at $M = M^*$, since

$$M^* - \frac{\mu C}{\gamma} = 1$$

Since the slope of this asymptote is 1, it shows that each additional user "completely" interferes with all other users, adding one more unit of normalized delay to μCT. The fact that the asymptote crosses $\mu CT = 1$ at precisely M^* shows, for $M \gg M^*$, that the system has "absorbed" M^*

† This is similar to a definition given by Scherr [19].

users and converted them into one user, and is now experiencing complete interference among the other $M - M^*$ users (i.e., the additional delay added to the response time for each user is $M - M^*$, since from Equation 16, $\mu CT \simeq 1 + M - M^*$).

Further studies have been conducted for the finite population case and are available in the literature [20, 24]. Much remains to be done in the modeling and analysis of time-shared systems; however, it is clear that considerable progress has been made recently.

5. NETWORK FLOWS

In studying networks, we immediately encounter questions of feasibility of flow within the network. Recall that a network is a collection of nodes connected together in some fashion by a set of directed links. These links are each capable of a maximum flow (of some appropriate commodity such as bits, water, freight cars). Some natural questions arise about the capability of these networks to support various flow patterns.

The answer to such questions of maximal traffic flow in a variety of networks is nicely settled in a well-known result in Network Flow Theory referred to as the Max-Flow-Min-Cut Theorem [25]. This result is demonstrated in Figure 11a.

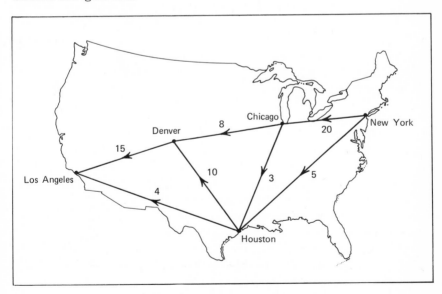

Figure 11a.   Diaper transport problem.

For example, assume that we are attempting to transport diapers across the United States from New York to Los Angeles and we are to use the network shown in the figure with the labels on the branches indicating the maximum number of tons of diapers which may be transported over that branch per week. We inquire as to the maximum flow which may pass from New York to Los Angeles per week. We define a *cut* as a set of branches which, once removed from the network, will separate the origin (New York) and the destination (Los Angeles). We define the *capacity* of such a cut to be the total flow which can travel across that cut in the direction from origin to destination. For instance, one cut consists of the branches from Chicago to Denver, Houston to Denver, and Houston to Los Angeles; the capacity of this cut is clearly 22 tons of diapers per week. The Max-Flow-Min-Cut theorem states that the maximum flow which can pass between two nodes is the minimum capacity of all cuts. In our example, it can be seen that the maximum flow is therefore 16 tons of diapers per week.

In general, then, we must consider *all* cuts which separate a given origin and destination. This computation can be extremely time consuming. Fortunately, there exists an extremely powerful method for finding not only what is the maximum flow but also gives a flow pattern which achieves this maximum flow. This procedure is known as the Labeling Algorithm* and is computationally efficient in that the computational requirement grows linearly with the number of nodes. The algorithm is described as follows.

Let the maximum flow capacity of the branch (link) connecting node x and node y be $c(x,y)$ and let the flow actually assigned to this branch be $f(x,y)$. Let Γ be the set of branches in the network where (i,j) is a branch directed from node i to node j. Let s be the source (origin) node and t be the termination (destination) node. The algorithm breaks into two parts:

Labeling Routine
1. Label vertex s by $[s, +, \epsilon(s) = \infty]$. s is now labeled and unscanned and all other vertices are unlabeled and unscanned.
2. Select any labeled and unscanned vertix x.
   (a) For all y if $(y,x) \, \epsilon\Gamma$, y is unlabeled and $f(y,x) > 0$ then label vertex y by $[x, -, \epsilon(y)]$ where $\epsilon(y) = \min[\epsilon(x), f(y,x)]$. Change the label on x by encircling the plus or minus entry. x is now labeled and scanned. y is labeled and unscanned.
   (b) For all y if $(x,y) \, \epsilon\Gamma$, y is unlabeled and $c(x,y) > f(x,y)$ then label y by $[x, +, \epsilon(y)]$ where $\epsilon(y) = \min[\epsilon(x), c(x,y) - f(x,y)]$. Change

---

* This algorithm is attributable to Ford and Fulkerson [25].

the label on x by encircling the plus or minus entry. x is now labeled and scanned. y is labeled and unscanned.

3. Repeat step 2 until t is labeled or until no more labels can be assigned. In the latter case the algorithm terminates. In the former case proceed to the augmentation routine.

Augmentation Routine

1. Let $z = t$ and go to step 2.
2. If the label on vertex z is $[q, +, \epsilon(t)]$ then increase $f(q,z)$ by $\epsilon(t)$. If the label on vertex z is $[q, -, \epsilon(t)]$ then decrease $f(z,q)$ by $\epsilon(t)$.
3. If $q = s$, erase all labels and return to step 1 of the labeling routine. Otherwise, let $z = q$ and return to step 2.

The application of the above procedure is highly effective. For the example given, we find that a maximal flow is as shown in Figure 11b. This solution may be obtained in five passes through the algorithm as follows. We label the nodes (for convenience) by: $s =$ New York; $c =$ Chicago; $h =$ Houston; $d =$ Denver; and $t =$ Los Angeles. Table 1 shows the results of labels and flows for the five passes, which lead to the solution given in Figure 11b.

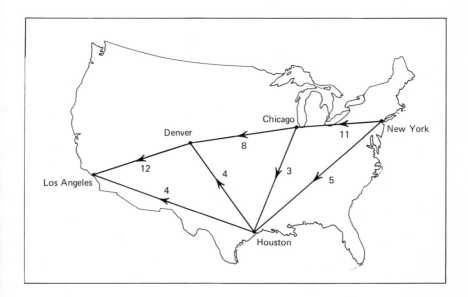

Figure 11b.   Diaper-transport problem, showing a maximal-flow solution.

Table 1   Results of Labels and Flows for Five Passes

		Pass 1	Pass 2	Pass 3	Pass 4	Pass 5
Node	s	$(s, +, \infty)$	$(s, +, \infty)$	$(s, +, \infty)$	$(s, +, \infty)$	$(s, +, \infty)$
	c	$(s, +, 20)$	$(s, +, 12)$	$(s, +, 9)$	$(s, +, 9)$	$(s, +, 9)$
	h	$(s, +, 5)$	$(c, +, 3)$	$(s, +, 5)$	$(s, +, 4)$	Terminate
	d	$(c, +, 8)$	$(h, +, 3)$	$(h, +, 5)$	$(h, +, 4)$	Algorithm
	t	$(d, +, 8)$	$(h, +, 3)$	$(h, +, 1)$	$(d, +, 4)$	
$f(s, c)$		8	11	11	11	
$f(s, h)$		0	0	1	5	
$f(c, d)$		8	8	8	8	
$f(c, h)$		0	3	3	3	
$f(h, d)$		0	0	0	4	
$f(d, t)$		8	8	8	12	
$f(h, t)$		0	3	4	4	

6. DELAYS IN COMMUNICATION NETS

In the previous discussion, we considered questions regarding feasibility and optimality of steady flow in a network. We now discuss the *delay* experienced by messages that travel in a communication net. We give the results that will be pertinent to the study of computer networks in Section 7.

The efficient design of a communcation net is an extremely complex problem. The number of design parameters and operating modes is considerable, and the definition of efficiency is by no means unique. Furthermore, the environment in which the net must operate strongly influences its construction. As a consequence, many discussions of communication network design tend to be either shallow qualitative treatments of rather general situations or detailed treatments of highly specialized and simplified nets. Here we give quantitative results for an interesting class of networks and then discuss the implications of these results as certain of the other design parameters are varied. My philosophy of communication network design draws on material presented in my book [27] where there is a more detailed explanation.

As described in Section 2, a communication net (much like a computer net) is made up of a collection of communcation centers (nodes) which are connected by a set of communication channels (ordered links). Messages (which are described by their origin, destination, origination time, length, and priority class) flow through the network in a store-and-forward fashion (as opposed to direct-wire or telephone traffic). A set of operating rules for handling the message traffic must also be given in describing a communication net.

The primary function of the network is to provide rapid and reliable communication between many of its communication centers simultaneously. The design of such networks involves a number of operational aspects of the stochastic flow of message traffic: message routing procedures; priority queueing disciplines; channel capacity assignments; and topological configurations. Furthermore, the environment in which the net must operate may be highly variable and even hostile. In the following discussion, we describe these operational procedures and give an indication of the form they should take in a variety of environments.

A *message routing procedure* is a decision rule which determines, according to some algorithm (possibly random), the next node which a message will visit. The specification of the algorithm specifies the routing procedure. The parameters involved in the algorithm may include such things as: origin and destination of the message; priority of the message; availability of certain channels; and congestion (or annihilation) of certain nodes.

We define a *fixed routing procedure* as one in which a message's path through the net is uniquely determined once its origin and destination are given. If more than one path is allowed, then we consider this to be an alternate routing procedure. An alternate routing procedure may choose its alternate paths either deterministically or at random (from some appropriate distribution) from among the operating links based on the parameter values mentioned above; the former may be referred to as *deterministic alternate routing* and the latter as random alternate routing (or more simply as *random routing procedures*) [27–29].

In passing through the net, messages are often required to form a queue while awaiting transmission between nodes, and very often a priority discipline describes the structure of the queue. *Priority queueing* refers to the disciplines in which an entering message is assigned a set of parameters (either at random or based on some property of the message) which determine its relative position in the queue. This position may vary as a function of time because of the appearance of higher priority messages in the queue. In attempting to meet the user's demands in regard to a priority structure, these demands, in their most useful form, must stipulate:

1. The number of priority classes.

2. The relative performance each class expects from the network (expressed in terms of average delay time).

3. The average number of messages arriving per second and the average message length for each priority class.

In addition, it would be helpful (but not necessary) if the *cost* as a function of message delay for the various priority classes were supplied by the user; this information would allow a careful determination of the necessary service given each class (item 2 above). It should be emphasized that even partial information here is useful; for example, if an extremely high relative cost is associated with the highest priority class, then some form of preemptive queue discipline [30] is almost surely called for. If the distribution of message arrival times and message lengths were available, this too would permit the development of a more realistic model for analysis.

With such a set of user demands, it is possible to design priority queueing disciplines with enough adjustable parameters so as to be able to comply with these demands (see, for example, [31]).

In many communication systems, each channel may naturally be broken into a number of subchannels. The conditions under which this may be desirable must be carefully considered; such considerations include the cost (in terms of delay) of preemption, the particular priority class structure, and so on. In a nonpriority case, it can be shown that one should never subdivide a channel if delay is the only criterion where message length is assumed to be exponentially distributed (see [27], Theorem 4.2).

The *topological* configuration of the communication net strongly affects its behavior as regards reliability, message delay, routing, and the like [27–29]. It is clear that complete freedom is not generally available in the design of the topology for most nets. In fact, not only may the topology be constrained, but also it may be that the structure of the network will be changing during the period of its operation. However, proper advantage must be taken of the freedom which does remain in the restructuring during configuration changes so that "optimal" performance is achieved.

Once the topological constraints have been met, there remains the crucial problem of selecting the capacity of each channel in the net (the *channel capacity assignment*). Let us discuss this problem.

Consider the general case of an interconnected net with N channels subject to a fixed routing procedure. We assume the interarrival times and message lengths are independent random variables throughout the net (see the Independence Assumption [27]). Furthermore, the externally applied traffic is Poisson in nature and the message length is exponential. Consequently, we find that the interarrival times for messages arrivals throughout the net are also Poisson [32].

The average message delay T now must be carefully defined as

$$T = \sum_{j,k} \frac{\gamma_{jk}}{\gamma} Z_{jk} \tag{17}$$

where

γ_{jk} = average number of messages entering network, per second, with origin node j and destination node k

$$\gamma = \sum_{j,k} \gamma_{jk}$$

Z_{jk} = average message delay for messages with origin j and destination k

That is, T is appropriately defined as the overall average message delay, where the weighting factor for Z_{jk} is taken to be proportional to the number of messages which must suffer the delay Z_{jk}. For any pair jk, the quantity Z_{jk} is composed of the sum of the average delays encountered in passing through each channel on the fixed route from node j to node k. If we break Z_{jk} into such components, and if we also form T by summing over the individual delays suffered at each channel in the net (instead of summing the delays for origin-destination pairs), we immediately see that

$$T = \sum_{i=1}^{N} \frac{\lambda_i}{\gamma} T_i \tag{18}$$

where

λ_i = average number of messages per second traveling on the ith channel,

T_i = average time a message spends in waiting for and passing through the ith channel

and where clearly λ_i is calculated as the sum of all γ_{jk} for which the (fixed) jk route includes channel i.

We also define

$1/\mu$ = average length of messages (bits/message)

C_i = capacity of ith channel (bits/sec)

$$C = \sum_{i=1}^{N} C_i \tag{19}$$

$$\lambda = \sum_{i=1}^{N} \lambda_i \tag{20}$$

$$\bar{n} = \frac{\lambda}{\gamma} \tag{21}$$

$$\rho = \frac{\gamma}{\mu C} = \text{network load} \tag{22}$$

In addition, we assume infinite nodal storage capacity, noiseless communication channels, and a fixed routing procedure.

A fundamental result for such communication nets is given in Reference 27. This result gives the optimal channel capacity assignment (i.e., the assignment which minimizes T) under the "cost" constraint expressed in Equation 19 as

$$C_i = \frac{\lambda_i}{\mu} + C(1 - \bar{n}\rho) \frac{\sqrt{\lambda_i}}{\sum\limits_{j=1}^{N} \sqrt{\lambda_j}} \tag{23}$$

provided that

$$C > \sum_{i=1}^{N} \lambda_i/\mu \tag{24}$$

Notice that the optimum assignment operates in the following way. Each channel is first apportioned just enough capacity to satisfy its average required flow of λ_i/μ bits/sec. After this apportionment, there remains an excess capacity $C - \sum\limits_{i=1}^{N} \lambda_i/\mu = C(1 - \bar{n}\rho)$ which is then distributed among the channels in proportion to the square root of their average message flow λ_i. Equation 24 expresses the obvious condition that there be enough capacity initially to satisfy the minimum requirements of the average flow in each node. This equation is equivalent to requiring $\bar{n}\rho < 1$.

With this optimum assignment,

$$T_i = \frac{\sum\limits_{j=1}^{N} \sqrt{\lambda_j}}{\mu C(1 - \bar{n}\rho)\sqrt{\lambda_i}} \tag{25}$$

and the average message delay T is

$$T = \frac{\bar{n}\left(\sum\limits_{i=1}^{N} \sqrt{\lambda_i/\lambda}\right)^2}{\mu C(1 - \bar{n}\rho)} \tag{26}$$

where $\bar{n}(=\lambda/\gamma)$ is properly interpreted as the *average path length* for messages.

The single most significant performance measure of a communication net (operating in a relatively stable, peaceful environment) is the average time, T, that a message spends in the net. Indeed, the assignment given by Equation 23 is that which minimizes T, and the value it takes on is given by Equation 26. This last equation reveals the trade-off between two crucial properties of the net, namely, the average path length, $\bar{n}$, and the degree to which the traffic is concentrated (see below). We consider that the network designer is given values of μ, C, and γ (and, therefore, also the network load ρ). He has available, as design parameters, the routing procedure, the channel capacity assignment, the topology and the priority discipline. Equation 26 assumes that the C_i have been optimally chosen according to Equation 23 and that a given topology and fixed routing procedure are in effect. However, since any fixed routing procedure and any topology applies, the designer may choose these in a way which minimizes T.

The numerator sum in Equation 26 is a convex function of λ_i/λ and thus attains its minimum value when $\lambda_i = \lambda$ for some $i = i_0$ and $\lambda_i = 0$ for $i \neq i_0$ subject to the condition $\sum_{i=1}^{N} \lambda_i/\lambda = 1$. Since the λ_i depend on the input traffic (not a design variable) and the topology and routing procedure (clearly design variables), we should attempt to concentrate the λ_i as much as possible in order to minimize the numerator sum in Equation 26. Complete concentration is not possible, since each node may be required to serve as both an origin and destination for some message traffic; subject to this, however, a net which achieves a high degree of concentration of traffic is the star net, shown in Figure 12. We observe that this configuration groups all traffic leaving a node into a single channel (and likewise for the traffic entering a node) with the exception of the central node. Notice that $\bar{n} \approx 2$ for the star net.

On the other hand, the denominator in Equation 26 contains the term $(1 - \bar{n}\rho)$. As $\rho \to 1/\bar{n}$ we see that this term dominates the behavior of T,

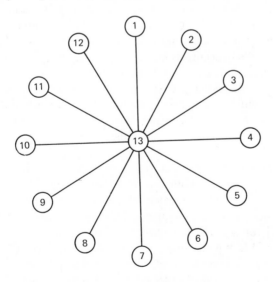

Figure 12. The star net.

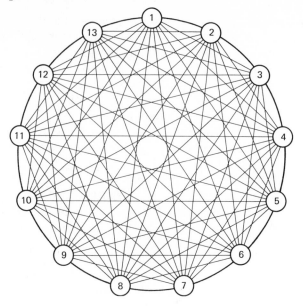

Figure 13.   The fully connected net.

and so we must take care to minimize $\bar{n}$ in such a circumstance. The net which minimizes $\bar{n}$ is the fully connected net shown in Figure 13. For this net, all paths are of length unity and so $\bar{n} = 1$ (its minimum value).

It is clear that these two factors (i.e., the numerator sum which reflects the degree of traffic concentration, and the average path length $\bar{n}$) cannot be minimized independently. The trade-off between these two is apparent: a highly *concentrated* traffic pattern (star net) yields an $\bar{n} \approx 2$; the (fully connected) net which minimizes $\bar{n}$ results in a maximally *dispersed* traffic pattern. The choice as to which net to use is determined by that factor which dominates the behavior, and this is a function of ρ. Indeed, an optimal sequence of network topologies can be found [27] which varies from nets similar to the star net (for $\rho \ll 1$) to the fully connected net (as $\rho \to 1$). The sequence is obtained by adding, to the star net, some direct connections between nodes, eventually obtaining the fully connected net. The performance of such a sequence has been obtained from a digital simulation [27] for a particular class of 13-node nets and the results are given in Figure 14. We see that the minimum envelope of the family of message delay curves gives the performance of the sequence of optimal nets.

Having discussed the effect of topology and channel capacity assignment on message delay, we now examine the effect of alternate routing proce-

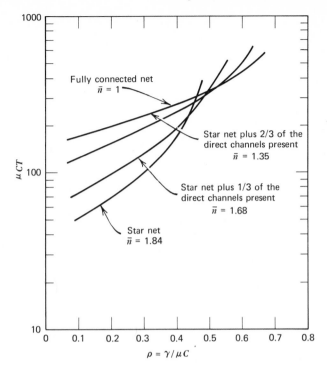

Figure 14. Message delay for the sequence of optimal nets as obtained by simulation of 13-node nets.

dures. Equation 23 assumes that the message traffic is stationary in time and also that a fixed routing procedure is used. It is clear that the communications requirement for many communication networks may change during their period of operation (especially if the environment is fluid and/or hostile). Conseqeuntly, the network must be capable of dynamically altering its characteristics during such changes. In that case, one cannot hope to maintain a fixed channel capacity assignment such as that given in Equation 23 and a fixed routing procedure. Indeed, if the input traffic requirements are changing, then the numbers λ_i cannot be calculated and C_i cannot be chosen according to Equation 23. In such a circumstance, a judicious alternate routing procedure serves a major role. Indeed, such a routing procedure automatically matches the traffic pattern to the network topology. Furthermore, it tends to distribute the traffic so that the channel capacity assignment which happens to exist at any time appears as one in which the traffic and capacity are proportional [27]. This resultant proportional channel capacity assignment is clearly *not* the optimum (indeed, that given by Equation 23 is the optimum); however, it is nearly optimum, and is therefore desirable. Moreover, as the environment becomes more hostile and/or mobile, directory-type routing procedures require more and more of the communication capability to update the rapidly changing directory [28, 29, 33]; in such cases, it is important to rely less upon exact and complete directories and to depend more upon *local* network information making use of alternate routing. A degree of caution must be exercised, however, since uncontrolled alternate routing in a congested net can lead to chaos. Indeed, the telephone company tends to limit (and even prohibit completely) alternate routing on unusually busy days (Mother's Day, for example).

The emphasis in this section has been on the minimization of the average message delay in a capacity-constrained communication network. The approach taken was to concentrate on the optimal assignment of channel capacity to the various links in a network with a given fixed routing procedure. From this assignment, it was possible to expose the critical design trade-offs in the network design, namely, the average path length and the degree of concentration of the traffic. From these observations, it was then possible to derive an optimal sequence of topologies as a function of the network load. Indeed, as shown in Reference 27, in a communications environment for which the terminal traffic conditions are known and time-invariant, the most efficient network design incorporates a topology chosen from the optimal sequence (dependent upon ρ), uses the channel capacity assignment given by Equation 23, and follows a fixed routing procedure. However, if the required traffic between nodes is either unknown or time-varying, then some form of alternate routing is essential. This statement follows from the observation that alternate routing procedures dynamically assign the traffic in a way which matches the message flow to the *current* network capabilities.

In the previous discussion, a fixed "cost" constraint (equal to the total channel capacity C) was assumed. Other cost functions that depend on the channel capacity in a linear fashion have also been handled [27]. We use such a function where cost is proportional to capacity as well as line length in Section 7 (see Equation 29). Cost functions which are nonlinear with the capacity suggest the use of iterative solution methods (e.g., steepest descent) for optimization. It is clear that many other factors enter into the performance of a communications net, for example, the network vulnerability to attack or failure. Considerations such as these require a new problem formulation; however, it appears that the results reported here give an indication of the general form and operation of networks optimized for a variety of situations.

7. COMPUTER NETWORK PERFORMANCE

We described a typical computer network in Section 2. Here we relate the operational requirements of nets with the mathematical results from Sections 4 to 6 in order to create a useful model of computer networks.

We will discuss some rather elementary mathematical models for computer networks along with some preliminary results. We construct our model so as to account for many of the salient features of the ARPA network, described above, although they clearly apply to more general systems as well.

We have studied communication nets by using methods from queueing theory which provide an effective approach to these problems. We shall use similar methods here for computer networks. The characteristics that distinguish computer networks from the communication nets studied in Reference 27 include:

(a) Nodal storage cpaacity is finite and may be expected to fill occasionally.

(b) Channel and modem errors occur and cause repeated transmission.

(c) Acknowledgment messages increase the message traffic rates.

(d) Messages from HOST A to HOST B typically create return traffic (after some delay) from B to A.

(e) Nodal delays become important and comparable to channel transmission delays.

Our elementary models will account for only a few of these, and as our models gain sophistication, more features will be included.

As in the study of communication nets, we assume that the message arrivals form a Poisson process with the average rates given in Figure 4 and also that message lengths are exponentially distributed with mean of 350 bits (notice that we are, in some sense, only accounting for short messages and neglecting the multipacket traffic in this model). As justified in Reference 27, we again make the independence assumption which allows a node-by-node analysis. We shall also include features (c) and (e) above, but we shall neglect the others for the moment. We assume a fixed routing procedure (unique allowable path from origin to destination).

Considering line costs and termination costs (exclusive of IMPS and of course HOSTS), net 1 costs roughly $818,200 and net 2 costs $929,800 (see Figure 2). These costs assume a fixed channel capacity of 50 kilobit/sec on each line shown. In this case (as in Reference 27), we may calculate the average delay due to waiting for and transmitting over the ith channel (say) as T_i where

$$T_i = \frac{1}{\mu C_i - \lambda_i} \tag{27}$$

where $1/\mu = 350$ bits, $C_i = 50$ kilobits and λ_i = average message rate on channel i (as determined from the traffic matrix, the routing procedure and accounting for the effect of acknowledgment traffic). We may then calculate the delay T averaged over the entire network as

$$T = \sum_i \frac{\lambda_i}{\gamma} (T_i + 10^{-3}) \tag{28}$$

where γ = total input data rate, and the term $10^{-3} = 1$ millisec is included to account for the assumed (fixed) nodal processing time. Equation 28 is the same as the expression given for T in Equation 18 except that the term 10^{-3} has been added.

Carrying out this computation for nets 1 and 2 we get the average delay as a function of data rate shown as *fixed* delays 1 and 2, respectively, in Figure 15. The data rate is adjusted by multiplying all entries in the traffic matrix by a constant between zero and one, where $\gamma = 225$ kilobits/sec at full data rate. The net, and therefore its cost, is held fixed in these computations. We see that net 2 is considerably more stable near full data rate as compared to net 1; this, of course, is because of the additional cross-country link.

For theoretical purposes, we may allow ourselves the freedom of optimally assigning the channel capacity subject to the fixed cost constraint (as in Section 6). The cost per channel is now assumed to be a constant (termination charges) plus a linear function of capacity where the slope depends on the length of the channel. From this calculation we obtain an assignment (where we temporarily use a double subscript to indicate the channel from node i to node j):

$$C_{ij} = \frac{\lambda_{ij}}{\mu} + \frac{\left(D - \frac{1}{2}\sum_{m,n} \frac{\lambda_{mn}}{\mu} d_{mn}\right)}{d_{ij}/2} \left[\frac{\sqrt{\lambda_{ij}d_{ij}}}{\sum_{m,n} \sqrt{\lambda_{mn}d_{mn}}}\right] \tag{29}$$

where $D = \$477,300$ for net 1 and $\$579,600$ for net 2 (the line termination costs are subtracted from the total net costs to yield D), $d_{ij} = .048\ L_{ij}$ $K\$$ = cost per unit of capacity on the channel from node i to node j and where L_{ij} is the length (in miles) of this channel. This is a more general cost

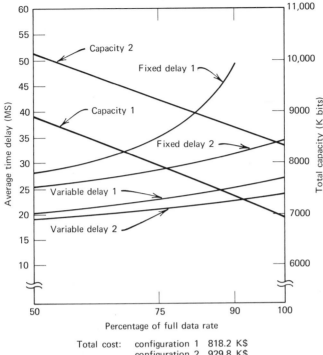

Figure 15.   Capacity and average delay computed from model at fixed cost.

function than that given in Equation 19 where the fixed cost constraint is now given as

$$D = \sum d_{ij} C_{ij} \qquad (30)$$

where D is constant for a given net. The delay for channel i (we now revert to a single subscript again) is given by Equation 25. From this we may calculate T from Equation 28 for nets 1 and 2. These results are given in Figure 15 and are labeled *variable* delay. We note that the improvement obtained for net 1 is significant near full data rate; this is not as dramatic for net 2, since the offered load did not especially tax this net's capability even with fixed capacities of 50 kilobit/sec. In this figure, we also show the fashion in which the total net capacity varies with data rate in the optimal assignment case; notice that the capacity decreases linearly with increasing load. Figure 16 shows the percentage comparison between nets 1 and 2 for these variables. We see the importance of providing sufficient excess capacity for the high usage paths; for example, at only 90% of full data rate, an increase

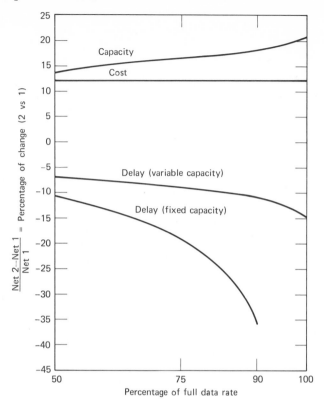

Figure 16. Percentage variation between nets 1 and 2.

of approximately 12% in cost can reduce the average delay by roughly three times the cost increase (in percentage) for the 50 kilobit/sec nets.

In computing the optimal channel capacity assignment, we observe that certain of the channels require capacity greatly in excess of 50 kilobit/sec. Since the true physical net cannot support a continuum of capacities, we take the results of optimization and strongly quantize the capacities as follows. Beginning with 50 kilobit/sec channels in net 2, we identify the channel which would like the largest capacity (from the optimization); this is the SDC-RAND link. We then replace this with a 250 kilobit/sec channel and compute the average delay. Of course, this increases the cost of the network; we therefore also calculate the average delay for a new optimized net with this new cost constraint. We then replace the next largest requirement with 250 kilobit/sec, and so on. The results of this operation for the eleven most "needy" channels are shown in Figure 17.

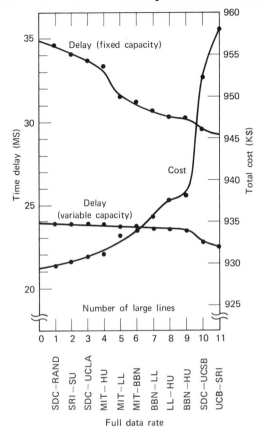

Figure 17.   Effect of adding large lines of 250 kilobits/sec.

We observe that the optimized net improves slowly, whereas the fixed net improves in a more significant fashion. The cost increases rather slowly until the tenth large line is added; this is because the SDC-UCSB distance is larger than the others. The trade-offs are clear.

To generalize this simple model, we must account for item (d) at the beginning of this section: the response from HOST B because of a request from HOST A. We suggest that an appropriate model is to recognize that HOST B is a time-shared computer system and model it as such. Numerous results are available which describe the behavior of the response time for time-shared systems as given in Section 4. *The model we suggest therefore is that of a communication net whose destinations are time-shared systems; both the nets and time-shared systems have been modeled separately and we propose that the output of one feed the input of the other.*

Further generalizations allow one to consider more general message length distributions by using the famous Pollaczek-Khinchin formula for the delay T_i of a channel with capacity C_i where the message length has mean $1/\mu$ bits and variance σ^2, where λ_i is the average message rate and $\rho_i = \lambda_i/\mu C_i$ as [23]

$$T_i = \frac{2 - \rho_i(1 - \mu^2\sigma^2)}{2(\mu C_i - \lambda_i)} \tag{31}$$

Notice that for the exponential distribution, $\sigma^2 = 1/\mu^2$ and then Equation 31 reduces to Equation 27. We propose that this be used for T_i in Equation 28 for the average net delay T. We recognize, by relaxing the assumption of an exponential distribution, that we are destroying the beautiful Markovian property of the traffic flow and thus our node-by-node analysis is incorrect; however, we offer this as a first approximation to the true behavior.

Regarding the buffer storage capacity in item (a), a most important consideration, we propose only a zeroth order approximation at this time. Specifically, one can create an infinite nodal storage model and then calculate the probability that more than a particular finite capacity was exceeded. What this fails to describe is the back-up effect of such buffer-induced blocking throughout the network. Models such as those constructed for sequential processing machines [34] may be helpful in this regard.

More elaborate models might include: general distributions for nodal delays; priority disciplines for message types at the nodes; recognition of the fact that response traffic is usually much greater in volume than request traffic; more detailed structure of delays and buffers within the nodes; and alternate routing considerations.

Since many of the mathematical models developed do not lend themselves to analysis, it is expedient to take advantage of the results obtainable from *digital simulation* methods (see, for example, [35]). We have done this for the model described in Section 2 and have included the five characteristics (*a* through *e*) listed in the third paragraph of this section.

The network simulation program was written in GPSS (General Purpose Simulation System language) and was run on an IBM 360/91. It provides for the following variables: number of nodes; topology; channel capacity; traffic matrix and distribution of interarrival times; total data rate; nodal buffer size; modem and channel propagation delays; channel error rate; HOST ↔ IMP transfer delays; short/long message mix with appropriate distributions at each node; IMP buffer level control; and IMP message management. The routing procedure is variable (e.g. fixed, adaptive alternate, random); however, only fixed routing algorithms are reported here.*

---

* Additional studies for adaptive routing techniques are reported in [39].

Delays for various message types and nodes, queue sizes, counts of non-acknowledged messages, channel utilizations, and the like are output variables whose statistics are measured by this program.*

As in the mathematical analysis, the most singificant overall performance measure is the average time T for a message to pass through the computer network from its origin to its destination. In Figure 18 we plot the simulation results for nets 1 and 2 with 15% of the total data rate in the form of multipacket messages; we show the average message delay as a function of data rate. In Figure 15 we plotted similar curves for the case of *no* multipacket traffic; in both cases, we see the significant improvement of net 2 over net 1 at high data rates.

The most critical path in net 2 is from UI to UU; this is clearly seen from the traffic matrix in Figure 4 where the largest entry (by a factor of 2) is the UI to UU requirement. Since a channel exists between these two, the routing is direct. Figure 19 shows the channel utilization (fraction of time in use) for the two links UI to UU and UU to UI for both nets 1 and 2. We see that the utilization drops nicely for the UU to UI channel when the third cross-country link is added to net 1 to form net 2; however, we find at full data rate that the UI to UU channel is still running at an excessively high utilization for both nets. The effect of this high usage is to cause the large message delay times at full load shown in Figure 18.

* I take great pleasure in acknowledging the assistance of G. Fultz and K. Chen in generating the numbers shown for the simulations and calculations in these figures.

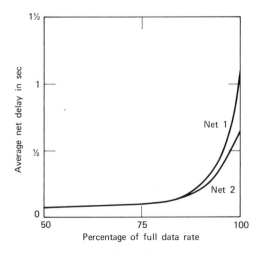

Figure 18. Average message delay as a function of data rate from simulation.

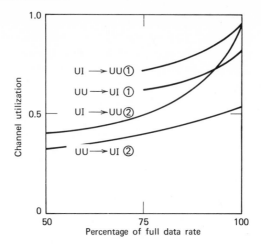

Figure 19.   Channel utilization for two critical channels.

One may observe the queue behavior as a function of time by studying Figure 20. We identify two packet storage locations: those waiting in the HOST for transmission to the IMP which are held up because of lack of storage room in the IMP (*note*: only a fraction of the IMP storage is assumed to be available for this HOST to IMP traffic—the rest is for IMP to IMP relay traffic); and those currently in the network in the process of making their way to their destination—these are said to be in "system."

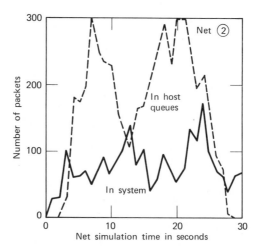

Figure 20.   Queueing behavior of net.

We observe a certain oscillatory behavior for these two curves which are out-of-phase with respect to each other. Figure 21 gives the cross-plot with time as the parameter; this more clearly shows the "seesaw" queueing effect. This behavior results from HOSTS depositing many packets at once (from multipacket messages) into the net when the IMP provides sufficient space; this shifts the queueing load from the HOST to the IMP. The IMP then blocks further transmission from the HOST until it discharges some of these packets. As a consequence, when the IMP is emptying, the HOST tends to be filling, and vice versa.

Whereas all curves shown in this section were for a mix of 85% short and 15% long (multipacket) messages, we now wish to examine the effect of changing this mix. The change in the average message delay is shown in Figure 22. The average data rate into the net was held constant at 225 kilobit/sec for this plot. The effect is rather dramatic: multipackets increase the net delay significantly. The reason behind this is clear from a number of observations. First, we know that the increased variance inherent in the large range of multipacket messages will increase queueing delays—see Equation 31. Also, increasing message lengths while reducing input message rates (i.e., keeping λ_i/μ constant to maintain constant data rates) will increase message delays in proportion to $1/\mu$—see Equation 27. Moreover, the buffer blocking effect due to many packets entering simultaneously will inhibit IMP to IMP transmission until these buffers reduce their load. Other of our simulations indicate that these effects can be reduced for the

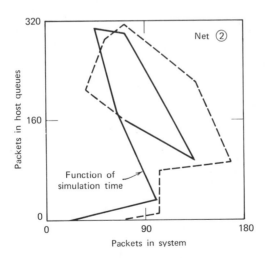

Figure 21.   Cross-plot of host queues versus system queues.

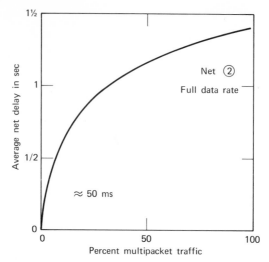

Figure 22.   Effect of changing the mix of messages.

short messages by giving them priority over the multipacket traffic when the conflict arises in an IMP.

The finite nodal storage capacity appears to be one of the major causes of delay due to the blocking effect of full buffers. A preliminary investigation of this behavior has recently been carried out. Analytic and simulation approaches to this problem have proven useful [40].

It is important in any investigation of this sort to compare the results obtained analytically with those obtained through simulation. One comparison of this sort is given in Figure 23 where we plot the average message delay as a function of data rate both for the mathematical model analyzed and for simulation. This theoretical curve is for an average message length $1/\mu = 350$ bits; however, this length has averaged the traffic due to acknowledgment messages. Since these acknowledgments should not be included in those messages whose average system delay is being calculated, we must increase the average length to be $1/\mu' = 560$ bits, but must continue to include the loading effects of such traffic; we do this by calculating

$$T'_i = \frac{\lambda_i/\mu C_i}{\mu C_i - \lambda_i} + \frac{1}{\mu' C_i} \tag{32}$$

to use in Equation 28 where the first term in Equation 32 is the average queueing delay (which includes interfering acknowledgment traffic) and the second term is the average message transmission time (whose value is for messages alone, excluding acknowledgments). This theoretical curve with adjustments for acknowledgments is also shown in Figure 23. Considering the simplicity of the analytical model, it is most reassuring that the results agree as well as they do. Two other acknowledgment correction procedures may be used: first, the nonexponential distribution of message lengths may be accounted for by using the Pollaczek-Khinchin formula for queueing delay in Equation 32 (as was suggested in Reference 10, Equation 4); second, one may include the effect whereby acknowledgments are given priority in the queue over regular messages (as included in the ARPA net and the simulation) by using fixed priority queueing theory with two priority classes (see Reference 27, pp. 74–75). Incorporation of these last two refinements produces an excellent match to the simulation curve and is also shown in Figure 23.

Recently, generalizations to the cost function as given in Equation 30 have been considered [38]. Recall that the originally posed problem gave

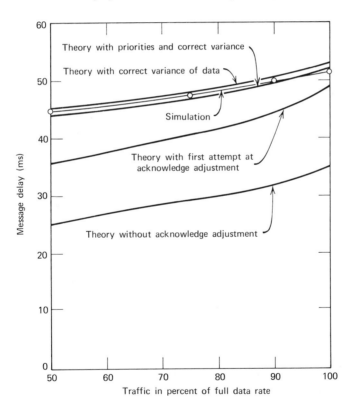

Figure 23.   Comparison of theoretical and simulation results for the 50 kilobit/sec. system—net 2.

rise to a square root channel capacity assignment as given in Equation 29, and this came from a cost constraint which was linear in capacity as in Equation 30. If one considers a cost function where cost is proportional to the logarithm of the capacity as well as proportional, say, to the length of the channel, then an extremely simple channel capacity assignment results, namely, an assignment wherein capacity is directly proportional to the traffic carried by that channel. The reason for considering other than linear cost functions is that published channel rates for high speed data lines tend to grow more slowly than does our linear model. In fact, it appears that an appropriate fit to the cost function is one in which cost grows in proportion to a fractional power of the capacity of the channel on a per mile basis. The logarithmic cost function is an approximation to this growth. In Reference 38 a procedure is outlined whereby one can optimize the assignment of channel capacity for an arbitrary power law (see this reference for additional details).

8. PROJECTED APPLICATIONS

As we have seen, computer networks are in the embryonic stages at present and hold much promise as a means for efficient and viable use of computer resources which are widely separated geographically.

A number of short-term lessons are being learned with regard to the use of time-shared systems and networks. For example, as always, the software cost easily equals and often exceeds that of the equipment cost in terms of time and effort. Moreover, the demands placed on communication channels, which connect data processing machines, is enormous. New methods of data transmission, new tariffs, and new views of communication must be developed rapidly to meet the needs of these computer networks.

Such notions as computer networks naturally develop into the concept of a computer utility, which lately has been much discussed [36]. Systems of this kind will provide computational power to the community, much the same as electric power and telephone service is currently provided. At first, of course, this will be provided to the scientific and research community through such efforts as the ARPA network. Shortly following this, commercial services will probably become available. Central data files, specialized equipment, and special-purpose programs will typically be the class of service available. At some later stage, consumer services should appear in the form of encyclopedic inquiry-response systems, teaching aids, scheduling and appointment recording, and straightforward computational capability. A number of significant problems must be solved before this mode of operation will appear, however; the principal item here is that of a "comfortable" language for man-machine communication. The physical device which should be capable of bringing this service to the consumer is already in his home—the telephone system. Eventually, we expect to see the picturephone emerge as a possible graphical terminal for such purposes.

9. REFERENCES

1. Rosen, S., "Electronic Computers: A Historical Survey," *Computing Surveys*, Vol. 1, No. 1, March 1969, pp. 7–36.

2. Rosin, R. F., "Supervisory and Monitor Systems," *Computing Surveys*, Vol. 1, No. 1, March 1969, pp. 37–54.

3. Corbató, F. J., M. Merwin-Daggett, and R. C. Daley, "An Experimental Time-Sharing System," *Proceedings of Spring Joint Computer Conference*, May 1962. pp. 335–344.

4. Hammerton, J. C., "Business Time-Sharing: User Economics," *Datamation*, Vol. 15, No. 6, June 1969, pp. 70–81.

5. Corbató, F. J., and V. A. Vyssotsky, "Introduction and Overview of the Multics System," *Proc. AFIPS 1965 Fall Joint Computer Conference*, Vol. 27, Part 1, Spartan Books, Washington, D.C., pp. 185–196.

6. Everett, R. R., C. A. Zraket, and H. D. Benington, "SAGE: A Data Processing System for Air Defense," *EJCC*, pp. 148–155, 1957.

7. Evans, J., "Experience Gained from the American Airlines SABRE System Control Program," *Proc. ACM National Meeting*, August 1967, pp. 77–83.

8. Keister, W., R. W. Ketchledge, and H. E. Vaughan, "No. 1 ESS: System Organization and Objectives," *Bell System Tech. Journal*, September 1964.

9. *Business Week*, February 8, 1969, p. 38.

10. Kleinrock, L., "Models for Computer Networks," *Proc. of the International Communications Conference*, University of Colorado, Boulder, Colorado, June 1969, pp. 21–9—21–16.

11. Dickson, P. A., "ARPA Network will Represent Integration on a Large Scale," *Electronics*, September 30, 1968, pp. 131–134.

12. Roberts, L. G., "Multiple Computer Networks and Intercomputer Communications," ACM Symposium on Operating Systems Principles, Gatlinburg, Tenn., October 1967.

13. Shannon, C. E., "Prediction and Entropy of Printed English," *Bell System Tech. Journal*, Vol. 30, No. 1, pp. 50–64, January 1951.

14. David, E. E., Jr., "Physiological and Psychological Considerations," pp. 107–128 in W. J. Karplus (ed.), *On-Line Computing*, McGraw-Hill, New York, 1967.

15. Kleinrock, L., "Analysis of a Time-Shared Processor," *Naval Research Logistics Quarterly*, Vol. 11 (1964), pp. 59–73.

16. Coffman, E. G., and L. Kleinrock, "Feedback Queueing Models for Time-Shared Systems," *JACM*, Vol. 15, No. 4, October 1968, pp. 549–576.

17. Schrage, L. E., "The Queue M/G/1 with Feedback to Lower Priority Queues," *Management Science*, Vol. 13 (1967), pp. 466–474.

18. Kleinrock, L., "Time-Shared Systems: A Theoretical Treatment," *JACM*, Vol. 14 (1967), pp. 242–261.

19. Scherr, A. L., "An Analysis of Time-Shared Computer Systems," MIT Research Monograph No. 36, 1967.

20. Adiri, I., and B. Air-Itzhak, "A Time-Sharing Queue with a Finite Number of Customers," *Journal of the A.C.M.*, Vol. 16, No. 2, pp. 315–323, April 1969.

21. Estrin, G., and L. Kleinrock, "Measures, Models and Measurements for Time-Shared Computer Utilities," *Proc. of 22nd Nat'l. Conf. of the ACM*, August 1967, pp. 85–96.

22. Howard, R. A., *Dynamic Programming and Markov Processes*, MIT Press (1960).

23. Saaty, T. L., *Elements of Queueing Theory with Applications*, McGraw-Hill, New York (1961).

24. Greenberger, M., "The Priority Problem and Computer Time-Sharing," *Management Science*, Vol. 12 (1966), pp. 888–906.

25. Ford, L. R., Jr., and D. R. Fulkerson, *Flows in Networks*, Princeton University Press, Princeton, N.J., 1962.

26. Frank, H., and I. T. Frisch, "Communication, Transmission and Transportation Networks," Addison Wesley, 1971.

27. Kleinrock, L., *Communication Nets: Stochastic Message Flow and Delay*, McGraw-Hill, New York, 1964.

28. Prosser, R. T., "Routing Procedures in Communication Networks, Part I: Ransom Procedures," *IRE Trans. on Communication Systems*, CS-10(4), pp. 322–329 (1962).

29. Prosser, R. T., "Routing Procedures in Communication Networks, Part II: Directory Procedures," *IRE Trans. on Communication Systems*, CS-10(4), pp. 329–335 (1962).

30. White, H., and L. S. Christie, "Queueing with Pre-emptive Priorities or with Breakdown," *Operations Research*, Vol. 6 (1958), pp. 79–95.

31. Kleinrock, L., and R. P. Finkelstein, "Time Dependent Priority Queues," *Operations Research*, Vol. 15, No. 1 (1967), pp. 104–116.

32. Burke, P. J., "The Output of a Queueing System," *Operation Research*, Vol. 4 (1956), pp. 699–704.

33. Baran, P., "On Distributed Communication Networks," *IEEE Trans. on Communications Systems*, pp. 1–9, March 1964.

34. Kleinrock, L., "Sequential Processing Machines (SPM) Analyzed with a Queueing Theory Model," *JACM*, Vol. 113, No. 2 (April 1966), pp. 179–183.

35. Gordon, G., *System Simulation*, Prentice-Hall, Englewood Cliffs, N. J., 1969.

36. Gruenberger, F. (ed.), *Computers and Communications—Toward a Computer Utility*, Prentice-Hall, Englewood Cliffs, N.J., 1968.

37. Kleinrock, L., "A Continuum of Time-Sharing Scheduling Algorithms," *Proceedings of the Spring Joint Computer Conference, 1970*, AFIPS Press, pp. 453–458.

38. Kleinrock, L., "Analytic and Simulation Methods in Computer Network Design," *Proceedings of the Spring Joint Computer Conference, 1970*, AFIPS Press, pp. 569–580.

39. Fultz, G., and L. Kleinrock, "Adaptive Routing Techniques for Store-and-Forward Computer-Communication Networks," *Proceedings of the International Communication Conference*, Montreal, Canada, June 1971, pp. 39–1—39–8.

40. Zeigler, J. and L. Kleinrock, "Nodal Blocking in Large Networks," *Proceedings of the International Communications Conference*, Montreal, Canada, June 1971, pp. 39–9—39–15.

Analog and Hybrid Computation

Venkateswararao Vemuri

Purdue University

1. INTRODUCTION

This chapter deals with analog and hybrid computation—a concept totally different from digital computation. We begin with a narrative description of the history of analog computation; then the hybrid computer is introduced as an evolutionary trend in the development of the modern analog computer.

An analog computing device is simply any computing device or apparatus designed specifically to exploit an analogy in such a way that visual or

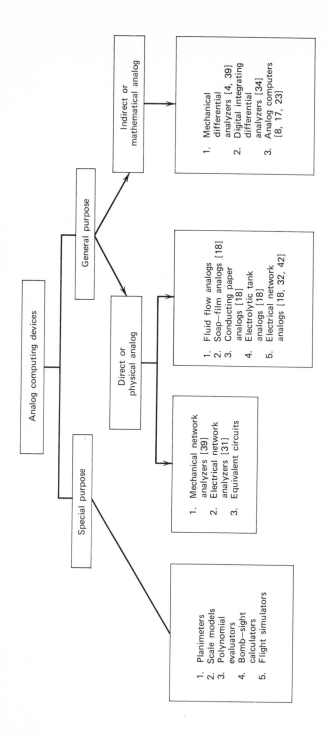

Figure 1. Spectrum of analog computing devices.

quantitative solutions to problems in the field of interest can be obtained. This broad definition embraces a wide variety of calculating devices (Figure 1). At the root of this computing technique lies the concept of an analogy: an analogy between two things is said to exist whenever there is a resemblance not necessarily of the two things themselves but of two or more attributes, circumstances, or effects. For instance, concepts of continuity and conservation of energy are relevant to several fields of study and leads one to suspect the existence of some kind of analogy among the various fields. Specifically, analogies allow the possibility of drawing quantitative and experimental conclusions concerning phenomena in better-known fields. For example, conduction of heat can be studied by the conduction of electricity. Transonic and supersonic gas and vapor flows can be studied by using a suitably designed fluid-flow analog.

2. HISTORY OF ANALOG COMPUTATION

One of the earliest attempts at analog computation was perhaps made by the Babylonians. Around 3800 B.C., they invented surveying and map-making techniques for the purpose of taxation. In 1620, Edmund Gunter utilized Napier's logarithms to create a slide rule with no moving parts, and in 1632 William Oughtred improved this by introducing a sliding scale. In 1814, the planimeter was introduced by J. A. Hermann. Lord Kelvin and his brother James Thompson invented the all important integrating mechanism, and in 1816 they conceived the idea of connecting these devices together to solve differential equations. Later in 1900 and onward, a variety of analogs such as the soap-film and fluid-flow analogs, conducting paper and electrolytic tank analogs, came into popular use.

The direct current (dc) network analyzer consisting of resistors only first appeared in 1925 and its use was limited to the study of steady-state problems. The more versatile alternating current (ac) network analyzer appeared in 1929, introduced an element of flexibility, and was the forerunner of the "transient-network analyzer."

During World War I mechanical integrating devices, such as the ball and disk integrators, were greatly improved upon and were successfully·used in the construction of naval gun-fire computers. Work done at M.I.T. by Vannevar Bush and others during 1920–1931 resulted in the first large-scale mechanical differential analyzer. Subsequently many devices, both mechanical and electrical, such as simultaneous equation solvers and harmonic analyzers, appeared on the scene.

With improved sophistication in the field of electronics, dc electronic differential analyzers quickly outpaced the mechanical equipment. Originally, the term "differential analyzer" was meant to imply any device, electrical or otherwise, that is a differential equation solver, and an "analog computer" is any computing device operating on the principle of analogy. However, nowadays, the term "analog computer" stands for the dc electronic differential analyzer with the modern operational amplifier as its basic building block. Most of the terminology and symbology in the field of analog computation has been standardized by the Institute of Radio Engineers [16].

Analog devices—whether computers, simulators, or analyzers—share a common characteristic: numbers in the problem to be solved are represented by corresponding physical quantities in the machine. This chapter is concerned with the evolution of such devices in general and the analog computer in particular.

3. ANALOG VERSUS DIGITAL TECHNIQUES

Even though there are many structural and technological differences in the construction and operation, the discerning eye can find many similarities in the processes of analog and digital computation (Figure 2). Just as digital computer programming consists of numerical analysis and coding, so does analog computer programming. "Numerical analysis" in analog computing consists of rearranging a given equation so that the solution is obtained by a finite number of certain predefined operations realized through an interconnection of functional operator blocks such as integrators, summers, multipliers, potentiometers, function generators, comparators, and so forth. The flow chart of digital programming corresponds to the well known analog block diagram, which shows the mode of interconnection of the various functional blocks. Coding in the context of analog programming is the actual interconnection of these operational blocks by means of wires called patch cords on a removable programming board called *patch panel*. The patch cords and panel can be seen on the right-hand side of photograph 1 of the EAI 580 computer. This block diagram is mathematically equivalent to the given (differential) equation. After the required initial conditions (IC) are applied, the computer can be placed in COMPUTE mode and the solution can be recorded by connecting the outputs of integrators and other computing elements to a recorder—whether it is an $x - y$ plotter, channel recorder, or an oscilloscope.

ANALOG	DIGITAL
1. Variables are represented in continuous form.	1. Variables represented in discrete form.
2. Parallel operation—all computational elements operate simultaneously.	2. Sequential operation involving time-sharing of all operational and memory units.
3. High-speed and real-time operations possible. Computing speeds are limited primarily by the bandwidth of the computing elements and not by the complexity of the problem.	3. Slower operation speed. Computing speeds are determined by (a) size and complexity of the problem, (b) numerical techniques used, and (c) the memory cycle time of the computer.
4. Solution progresses at a rate proportional to the rate of progression of the system studies.	4. In general, no correspondence between solution speed and system's progression in time.
5. Component accuracy is rarely better than 0.01% of full scale. As problem size increases, the problem is hardware-expandable.	5. By trading off solution time, any desired precision can be obtained. As problem size increases, the computer is time-expandable.
6. Efficient in the performance of addition, multiplication, and integration of quantities which are functions of time.	6. All mathematical operations must be performed via discrete approximation techniques.
7. Easy to include parts of actual system in the computer simulation.	7. To include parts of a system in simulation, it is necessary to use conversion equipment and real-time computing speeds.
8. Direct and powerful simulation techniques are available.	8. Simulation is of an indirect form.
9. Programming is by hardware patching, and scaling is a tedius job.	9. No scaling problems due to the ability to perform floating point arithmetic.
10. No memory in the digital sense.	10. Memory permits logical operations on stored

Figure 2. A comparison of analog and digital devices.

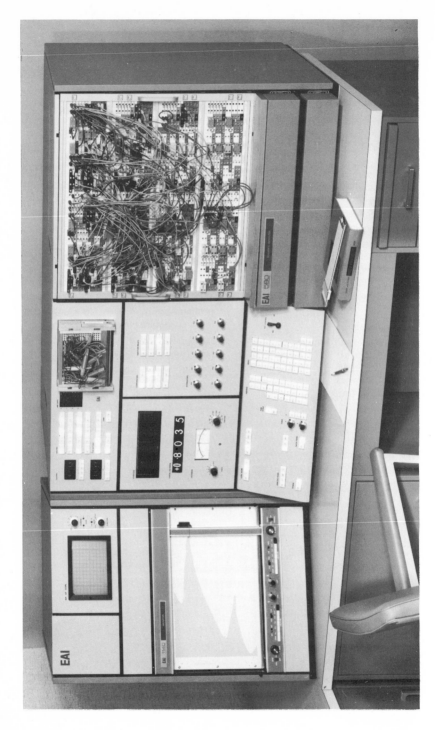

Electronic Associates Computer model EAI 580 (Courtesy of Electronic Associates).

Example. To illustrate the technique of programming an analog computer, consider the method of solving the differential equation

$$\frac{d^2x}{dt^2} - t\frac{dx}{dt} + x = 1; \qquad t \geq 0 \tag{1}$$

with the two initial conditions

$$x(t = 0) = x(0) = 1$$

$$\frac{dx(t = 0)}{dt} = \frac{dx(0)}{dt} = -1 \tag{2}$$

Solution.   Equation 1 is first rearranged so that only the highest derivative term appears on the left-hand side.

$$\frac{d^2x}{dt^2} = 1 - x + t\frac{dx}{dt} \tag{3}$$

The solution $x(t)$ can be obtained by integrating both sides of (3) two times. Assuming that the right-hand side of (3) is a known quantity, it can be treated as an input to an *integrator* whose output will be $-(dx/dt)$ as shown in Figure 3a. The negative sign in front of (dx/dt) is a consequence of the way the electronic circuit inside the operational block operates and hence has to be accounted for during programming. Integrating this quantity, that is, $-dx/dt$ again (Figure 3b) the value of $x(t)$ is obtained. The unfinished job is now to find out a way of generating the unknown quantity on the right-hand side of (3), which was assumed to be known while drawing Figure 3a.

The quantity 1 (the first input to Figure 3a) can be easily obtained by connecting that input terminal to a voltage source of 1 volt. The second input, that is, the quantity $-x$ can be obtained by changing the sign of the output of the integrator I2 (Figure 3c). To generate $t(dx/dt)$, the third input, the quantity t is first obtained by integrating unity (Figure 3d). The product $t(dx/dt)$ can now be generated by multiplying $-(dx/dt)$ (available at the output of I1) and $+t$ (generated above) using a *multiplier* (Figure 3e).

Now, the solution of (1) can be obtained by interconnecting the blocks in Figures 3a to 3e as shown in Figure 3f. Notice that the schematic in Figure 3f allows the recording of only $x(t)$ and $-[dx(t)/dt]$. If one wants to record $[d^2x(t)]/dt^2$ also, it is necessary to modify this figure slightly as shown in Figure 3g. The solution corresponding to this arrangement is shown in

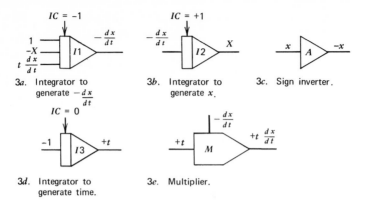

3a. Integrator to generate $-\dfrac{dx}{dt}$

3b. Integrator to generate x.

3c. Sign inverter.

3d. Integrator to generate time.

3e. Multiplier.

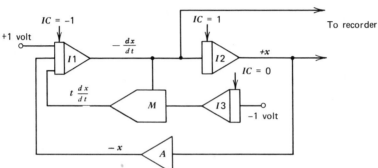

3f. Interconnection of Figs. a–e to solve Eq. 1.

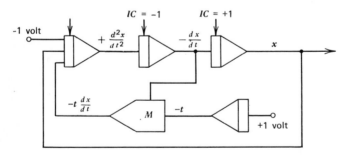

3g. Modified version of Fig. f.

Figure 3. A pictorial description of the method of solving Equation 1.

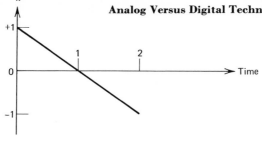

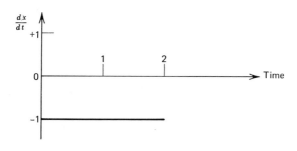

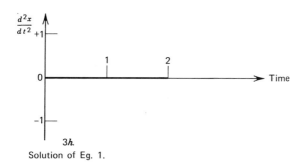

3*h.*
Solution of Eg. 1.

Figure 3.   A pictorial description of the method of solving Equation 1 (continued)

Figure 3*h*. The recorded answer can be verified by solving (1) exactly for its true solution, which is

$$x(t) = 1 - t$$

$$\frac{dx(t)}{dt} = -1$$

$$\frac{d^2x(t)}{dt^2} = 0$$

From Equation 4 and Figure 3g, it is evident that $(d^2x/dt^2) = 0$ for $0 \le t \le 2$ seconds and the novice may wonder why one would want to record (d^2x/dt^2) in the first place. It is important to remember that the above solution corresponds to the initial conditions (IC) specified in (2). For any other IC the answer would be different.

4. METAMORPHOSIS OF THE ANALOG COMPUTER

Since the early 1950s two kinds of pressures started to develop that substantially contributed to the state of the present-day analog computers. From one side, digital computers, with high versatility and armed with a whole spectrum of problem oriented languages, started to make inroads into an area that traditionally has been a monopoly of the analog computer. From the other side, the complex nature of problems, stimulated perhaps by the space-age research, prompted the analog-computer user to search for ways to widen the utility of his analog computers. These efforts (Figure 4) resulted not only in an improvement of the hardware in quality and concept but also spurred the development of new computational techniques for analog computer use.

Analog computers first found their widest field of application in the simulation of systems that can be characterized by ordinary differential equations [8]. When an analog computer, programmed to simulate a system, is required to play the role of a "live model" of the system, then it is necessary that it respond to inputs and produce outputs in the same way and at the same speed as would the actual system. Such *real-time* solution speeds permit the coupling of the model to the actual system and allows the possibility for *on-line* monitoring of the system behavior. Typical real-time simulations do not place heavy demands on the dynamic characteristics of the computing elements.

The early 1950s saw the emergence of repetitive operation (*rep-op*) machines to meet the demands of those problems where faster than real-time (*high-speed*) solution rates are desirable [40]. These produced solutions at a 30- or 60-per-second rate so that a cathode ray tube could be used to produce a flicker-free solution. Rapid operation of such machines permits immediate observation of the effects of parameter changes on the solution.

Rep-op analog computer techniques led naturally to the development of means for automating the variation of parameters from run-to-run to influence the parameter values in the subsequent run from a knowledge of the solution in the present run. The introduction of such automated features as clock-controlled RESET or TRACK mode to follow an initial condition (IC) input, COMPUTE mode to integrate an input, HOLD mode to hold

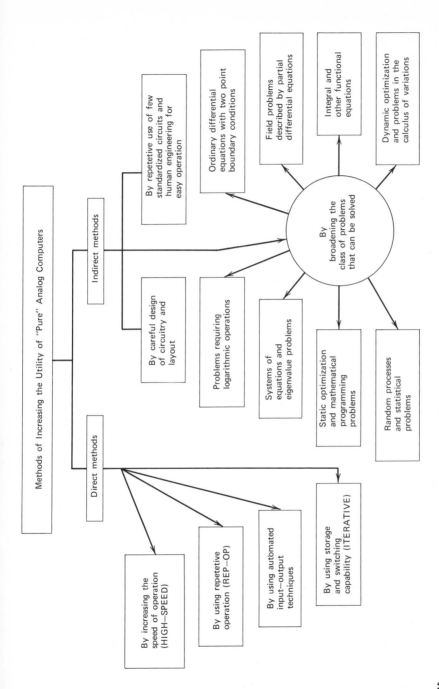

Figure 4. Trends in broadening the utility of analog computers.

295

the output from a previous computational cycle and use of high speed relays, decision-making comparators and digital logic to switch analog circuits permits repetitive operations at thousands of runs per second. Order-of-magnitude improvements in the speed and off-set characteristics of electronic integrator switches have not only improved repetitive computation but also established the electronically switched integrator as a novel analog computing element which can serve as an *analog memory cell* as well as an integrator or summer. In the TRACK mode this integrator can sample values of a variable applied to the IC terminal and make possible the *sequential* and *iterative analog computation*.

Iterative analog computers not only permit a variety of iterative problem-solving strategies but also allow sequential operations resulting in a substantial hardware economy. A fast iterative analog computer can produce a complete solution to a fairly complex set of differential equations in less than a millisecond. This feature renders this computer highly suitable to conduct statistical studies or parameter searches that may require several thousands of solutions. In spite of all this processing power, the potential of the iterative analog remains limited because the form of the equation(s) being solved can be changed only slightly in the course of successive iterations. A chronological account of this progress is summarized in Figure 5 and many reviews stressing various viewpoints have been published [15, 22, 33, 41].

As the analog computer demonstrated commendable progress in its hardware development, the situation did not remain static. The speed advantage of real-time analog computers was being crowded not only by the increasing speeds of digital computers but also by their versatility. New compiler routines permitted the digital computer user to write programs directly from analog type block diagrams [2, 5, 12, 13, 26]. In the face of these developments in digital technology, analog computers survived mainly because of their speed derived from their parallel processing capability and the flexibility afforded by the analog computer through its removable patch-board concept. Analog computers are losing this edge in the face of challenging developments in digital technology such as parallel processing, on-line and time-shared (see Chapter 7) data processing systems. The spectrum of new ideas in digital technology represent not only new innovations in hardware but also new methods of arranging various computer building blocks, programming techniques, and so forth. One class of examples in this spectrum includes multiprocessing (in which several conventional digital machines are tied together) high speed functional units such as the CDC 6600 and associative memory in which logic is incorporated into the memory to allow a parallel data search. At the other end of the spectrum is an approach to investigate the advantages of linking high speed parallel processing analog hardware as an extension to the conventional

Year	Model	Manufacturer	Major Features Introduced
1951	C100	Reeves Instruments	20-Amplifier computer; servo amplifiers; removable patch board first introduced.
1954	31-R	Electronic Associates	Integrated slaving system introduced.
1956	131R C400	Electronic Associates Reeves Instruments	Human engineered for faster and easier programmer use; electronic time-division multipliers, vacuum tube diode function generators and mechanical digital voltmeters were introduced.
1959 1960 1961	231R RAT-700 RA-800 TAC	Electronic Associates Telefunken Telefunken Nippon	Modular concept in parch-board construction; fast response and switching times by significant improvements in amplifier bandwidths; solid-state function generators; electronic digital voltmeters and rep-op capability became available.
1962 1964	231R 231RV EASE	Electronic Associates Electronic Associates Beckman	Quarter square multipliers, point-storage capability, card-set function generators.
1964	EAI8900	Electronic Associates	A complete hybrid computer with an 8400 scientific digital computer and an 8800 analog computer with 338 amplifiers of 100-volt reference.
1969	CI-5000	Comcor-Astrodata	100-volt solid-state fully integrated analog/hybrid system with a separate logic patch board and analog patch board.

Figure 5. Progress of analog computing devices. (Copyright, 1967, by Simulation Councils, Inc., P.O. Box 2228, La Jolla, Cal. 92037, reprinted by permission.)

digital arithmetic unit. Essentially the analog hardware, either special purpose or general purpose, is conceived to act as a subroutine in an otherwise digital oriented computer program [20].

5. THE CONCEPT OF ANALOG SUBROUTINES

Once conceived, the idea of using analog hardware as subroutines can be viewed from many profitable angles. It is conceivable to use a "fast" analog circuit as a subroutine in a "slower" analog computer. The repetitive-iterative differential analyzer with memory permits the introduction of fast repetitive analog subroutines in a slow analog computer setup. Examples of such applications include, among other things, repetitive computation of the inner integral of a double integral, approximate solution of partial differential equations by difference-differential equation approximations, and the sequential solution of heat- and mass-balance equations at different points of a chemical distillation process.

Making one step forward, it is conceivable to assign the principal computing function as well as all control to a general purpose digital computer with the analog computer or analog circuitry acting only as auxiliary equipment. In this technique, analog devices are primarily employed to accelerate what would otherwise be an exessively time-consuming digital operation. One example of this category is a hybrid simulator, developed at Massachusetts Institute of Technology, wherein an assemblage of high-speed analog integrators is used to supplement a high-speed digital computer so as to facilitate the real-time solution of the set of ordinary differential equations governing the flight of an aircraft [6]. The simulator therefore contains a hybrid arithmetic unit.

A second example belonging to this category is the discrete-space and discrete-time (DSDT) hybrid computer developed at the University of California at Los Angeles [19, 20]. In this system analog devices connected in a closed loop with a digital computer act as a major subroutine and carry out all the mathematical steps required for the performance of a specific computational task. One specific subroutine of this kind is a passive resistance network used to invert matrices associated with the finite-difference approximations of partial differential equations. Because a network of passive resistors relaxes instantaneously to its steady state, a solution to the matrix inversion operation can be obtained almost instantaneously by using this method.

When solving large-scale problems, the concept of an analog subroutine can be further extended to what may be called "time-shared" analog subroutines. One of the major drawbacks of the conventional subroutine concept is that the size of the problem that can be solved is hardware limited. For instance, while studying neurological phenomena it is often necessary to simulate the interaction of tens of thousands of individual neurons. Similarly, while solving partial differential equations over extended domains it is necessary to use tens of thousands of finite difference grid points. In order to handle such large-scale problems it is necessary to introduce methods of solving the equations piecewise, the size of each piece being governed by the capacity of the analog and interface equipment available.

The use of analog hardware as a subroutine is just one of many ways of utilizing the better features of both analog and digital computers. In contrast to these digital computer-oriented methods of hybridization, there exists a variety of other tasks where an analog computer plays the central role and digital equipment provides auxiliary support such as control of the analog modes, generating multivariable functions, providing variable time delay, and so on. Indeed, many computing machines now in use are neither pure analog machines nor pure digital machines (Figure 6). Strictly speaking, any of the machines that lie in between the two extremities can be termed a *hybrid computer*.

6. THE HYBRID COMPUTER

Classification of hybrid computers based on their configuration is one of several accepted ways. Based on this, four distinct classes of hybrid computers can be recognized.

1. An analog computer with digital logic added to it.
2. A digital computer with analog elements added to it.
3. A digital computer linked to an analog computer.
4. Balanced linkage or "true-hybrid" systems.

The term "all-parallel hybrid" has often been used by some authors to describe the first type, and the iterative analog computers discussed earlier actually belong to this class. The MIT system and the DSDT system of UCLA belong to the second class and are often referred to also as sequential hybrid computers. However, a majority of hybrid computers in current commercial use belong to the third category. Many hybrid systems of the third type also contain patchable logic elements and hence are also capable of solving problems within the province of the hybrids of the first type. Hybrid computers of the fourth class, the "true-hybrids," contain neither an analog nor a digital computer intended for independent use. Considerable development work in this area has been done at the University of Arizona primarily for differential equation solving and statistical system studies. Figure 7 shows the general block diagram of a typical hybrid computer system of the third and fourth categories.

Referring to Figure 6, it is obvious that there are some computer configurations that fail to satisfy any of the requirements of any of the four above mentioned classifications. The digital-analog simulator programs and the digital differential analyzers are a case in point.

6.1. Digital-Analog Simulators

Digital analog simulators are special routines [26] by means of which a digital computer is programmed to appear like an analog computer to the

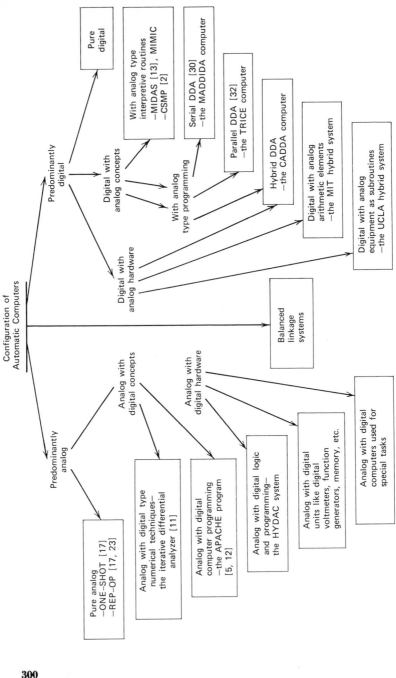

Figure 6. Spectrum of hybrid computer mechanizations (courtesy of G. A. Bekey and W. J. Karplus, *Hybrid Computation*, Wiley, New York, 1968).

300

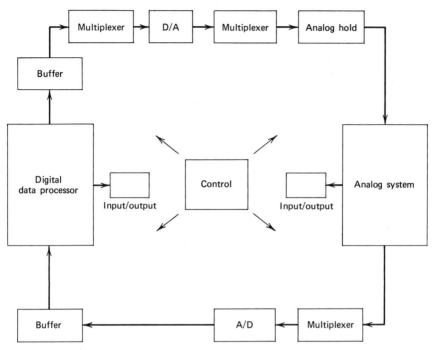

Figure 7.   General block diagram of a hybrid computer system (courtesy of G. A. Bekey and W. J. Karplus, *Hybrid Computation*, Wiley, New York, 1968).

user. In other words, instead of using a procedure-oriented language such as FORTRAN or ALGOL, the user starts with a set of predefined functional blocks from which he can build the system under study. These blocks perform the same functional operations as standard analog computer components such as potentiometers, integrators, summers, function generators, relays, comparators, and so forth. Just as in analog computation, the user interconnects these blocks to define his system. However, the interconnection is not by means of patch cords but by means of a sequence of *configuration statements*.

Generally, a digital-analog simulator language consists of three distinct sections. The configuration or structural section defines how the various functional blocks are to be interconnected. The IC/parameter section defines the initial conditions and parameters to be associated with each block. Finally, the control section determines how the run will be made, what type of numerical integration scheme to use, the total time the computer remains in COMPUTE mode, what outputs are to be printed, the format of printing, and so forth.

One of the earliest digital-simulator programs was the SELFRIDGE developed by Selfridge himself in 1955 [26]. Afterwards a number of improved versions mushroomed on the scene, the most popular ones being the MIDAS (an acronym for Modified Integration Digital Analog Simulator), the MIMIC (not an acronym for anything), and the CSMP (the Continuous System Modeling Program) [2]. Unfortunately, many of these languages suffer from the lack of a sufficient number of computational and control functions. For instance, the popular MIDAS language is not interactive, while MIMIC, DSL 90, and IBM's 360 CSMP are very much FORTRAN-oriented. Efforts to develop and improve on-line interactive, problem-oriented digital-analog simulation languages are still going on actively.

6.2. Digital Differential Analyzers

The DDA belongs to a family of computational devices called incremental digital computers. The DDA was first introduced in the early 1950s in an effort to combine the advantages of the use of operational blocks reminiscent with analog programming with the high accuracy of digital computers. In the so-called *serial* DDA, the operational blocks time-share a single magnetic drum for storage purposes; it is therefore slow in its operation. In the *parallel* DDA, each operational unit has its own memory which permits the simultaneous operation of all operational blocks as in analog computers [32]. In the *hybrid* DDA, the integration units are made up of a combination of analog and digital hardware thus permitting the realization of better accuracy than by the use of serial or parallel DDAs alone.

In spite of several spirited attempts by many individuals and manufacturing concerns, the DDA never gained much popularity.

7. ERRORS IN HYBRID COMPUTATION [28]

If a problem is solved on a digital computer the solution obtained is only an approximate one. The errors involved are essentially a result of the nature of the solution process and hence can be termed *solution errors*. The so-called *truncation errors* are the errors introduced by taking only a finite number of terms from an infinite series representation of a function. The *round-off errors* are the errors that enter during the solution process because of finite size of registers used in the arithmetic units of digital computers [1].

Component errors, on the other hand, are errors resulting from component tolerances and are nonexistent in digital calculations but play a dominant role in analog computations [23]. Errors due to drift, phase-shift, and offset characteristics of operational amplifiers, errors in the setting of potentiometers, and the like belong to this class.

In a hybrid computer, both solution and component errors are of equal importance and any meaningful discussion of hybrid computation should include an analysis of errors. In addition to the errors in analog and digital portions, a hybrid computer solution suffers from errors occurring in the interface equipment (for example, samplers, A/D converters, D/A converters, and multiplexers) and those due to time-delays [29].

In the operation of actual hybrid computer systems [29], errors are committed by each component during each computational subcycle. These *per-step errors* tend to accumulate; this causes the solution to deviate more and more from the true solution. If a hybrid system is to be operated over a specified length of time, it is of great interest to know the result of the accumulation of these errors. This is by no means a trivial problem and has not yet been solved completely.

8. APPLICATIONS OF HYBRID COMPUTATION

The class of problems that have the potential to derive maximum benefit from the use of hybrid computers can be broadly divided into two categories: problems requiring simulation and problems requiring signal processing.

Strictly from a mathematical point of view, a major "bottleneck" situation in simulation is a necessity to solve, in general, nonlinear partial differential equation, or integral equations or some such higher functional equations. Therefore it is not an exaggeration to say that a good deal of effort is being spent in developing hybrid computer methods of solving these equations. In a wide variety of problems such as optimization and parameter search, spacecraft flight simulations, simulation of random processes, and a variety of other applications in biomedical sciences, econometrics, and the like, the necessity to solve complex differential equations inevitably arises and the possibility for hybrid computation arises naturally.

The fact that analog computers excel in doing certain operations and digital computers excel precisely where analog computers are inefficient can be used profitably in hybrid computation. Of course, the way these computational methods are combined depends a great deal on the particular application as discussed below.

Simulation of distributed parameter systems [19, 20, 66].   Diffusion, vibration, and wave propagation are processes of fundamental importance in applied physics and dynamical equations of these processes are partial differential equations containing more than one—and as many as seven—independent variables. Analog computers are generally limited to one independent variable—time; all other variables must be discretized. In nonlinear cases, the equipment requirements in analog methods and time requirements in digital methods become uneconomically large. In such cases, considerable advantage can be gained by formulating a closed loop of analog and digital hardware so that the analog circuits serve as subroutines in a digital computation.

Random process simulation [24, 25].   Hybrid computing techniques provide a convenient way to evaluate probability density and distribution functions. They also lend themselves very well to the application of random walk techniques to the solution of partial differential equations.

Simulation of biomedical processes [48, 56].   The process of information flow in living organisms is essentially hybrid; dynamics of a biochemical reaction are essentially continuous in nature, whereas pulse trains created as a consequence of these reactions are discrete. Hybrid computers are ideal in solving problems of this nature.

Simulation of man-machine systems [1], [68].   Problems such as the simulation of piloted aircraft and manned spacecraft fall into this class. Indeed, any situation where a human operator forms a part of a control loop leads to a man-machine system. Hybrid computers played a prominent role in simulating the response of human dynamics in such an environment.

Simulation of behavioral systems.   Problems of economics [50, 63] and business management are characterized by difference-differential equations. Interaction of legal, political, and social factors with economic matters results both in immediate as well as delayed reactions. Hybrid computation—for that matter, the technique of simulation in general—is still in its infancy in the study of behavioral systems.

Other applications [1].   There are a variety of other fields where hybrid computation can play an important role. Simulation of sampled data systems [9], problems of dynamic optimization, studies in guidance and control of space vehicles, and problems of environmental dynamics are just few instances where hybrid computation has been profitably employed in the past.

A second basic scientific problem of modern society involves the efficient storing and retrieving of data in task oriented projects. For instance, the operation and efficiency of a general practitioner or a specialist can be vastly improved by providing him with more information concerning a patient more quickly and in a way that can be easily absorbed. Computer analysis of cardiograms is a case in point. In physiological research, analysis of EKGs and EEGs is essentially an analysis of complex waveforms, and hybrid computers are being employed profitably as research tools in these areas. In its wider context, hybrid computation is attractive for signal processing problems in conjunction with storage, retrieval, and analysis of data in such diverse fields as aircraft flights tests, seismology, and so forth.

Some unusual applications of simulation. In addition to the various applications of the hybrid computer mentioned above, there exists a variety of unusual problems that one can solve by using simulation techniques. To give an idea about the range of applications, some unusual and unexpected areas of research where simulation plays a role are cited in the references.

9. HARDWARE AND SOFTWARE FOR HYBRID COMPUTERS

Some of the more important factors that influence the choice of analog and digital components, peripheral and interface equipment that go into a hybrid facility are listed below.

Digital speed.   Problems requiring hybrid computation are characterized by their requirement for on-line communication between the machine and its environment. In such cases, the speed of execution becomes an important factor. This speed is predominantly a function of memory access time and multiplier speed. The use of random access magnetic core memory of reasonable size (say, 16 K or more) and more than one index register often contributes to the overall program speed.

Word structure.   A binary word of 24-bits length seems to be the prevalent choice. Because round-off errors affect the last several bits, smaller word size would result in a dynamic range limitation of less than 10^6, thus limiting the dynamic range of the entire system. Decimal format and character oriented machines are usually slower than binary computers of equivalent size and do not offer any speed advantage.

Peripheral equipment.   Hybrid computer applications, in general, require only a minimum of peripheral equipment. A paper tape reader, card reader, and a typewriter are usually sufficient and a graphic display equipment would be desirable. In addition, a means of communicating control signals to and from the analog section is a necessity. *Interrupt* signals, from outside the computer, permit the transfer of command to another sequence of instructions and *sense lines* indicate to the digital program the current state of devices outside the computer.

Interface equipment.   In providing data communication between the digital and analog portions, three kinds of devices are commonly used: the multiplexer, the analog to digital converter (ADC), and the digital-to-analog converter (DAC). The output of commonly used ADCs is a binary number of 10 to 14 bits. A 13-bit binary output represents a resolution of 1 in 8000 which is compatible with analog computer resolutions of the order of 1 in 10,000. A typical conversion time of 100 allow the converter to be shared by 16 analog signals. DACs should, in general, have the same word size as ADCs. More about the design and selection of interface equipment can be found in the literature cited at the end of the chapter [14, 36, 37].

Special features. Depending on the nature of the jobs to be handled, special features, such as external timing of ADCs and multiplexers, real-time clock to establish sampling frequency, the use of sense lines to reduce conversions, and the use of multiple sampling frequencies and asynchronous sampling, will be useful additions to a hybrid computer facility.

Software. It is software that turns a computer into a usable unit and hybrid simulation software requirements are different from those of general-purpose data processing [7]. One of the basic requirements of software in hybrid computation is that it operates in a real time environment. The use of special instructions for subroutine entry, and the use of interrupts for accurate time synchronization to initiate data conversions and other events can help increase computing speeds. The operating system, both hardware and software, must therefore be capable of processing both synchronous and asychronous priority interrupt requests initiated by an arbitrary number of external sources.

Floating point computations are easier for the programmer but are time consuming during execution. Dependence on floating point arithmetic at the expense of speed is not desirable because an equivalent of fixed point scaling is a necessary part of analog programming.

In a hybrid facility, the normal manner of operating an analog computer involves a fair amount of noncomputing time when the analog part remains in HOLD or RESET mode. By incorporating appropriate interrupt and memory lockout features in the software, it is possible to time-share a digital computer for both hybrid and pure digital applications.

Finally, for pure hybrid use the language must be natural and must be efficiently implemented. That is, the language must be compiled into an efficient machine language program. Compiling time is relatively unimportant, since it is usually done "off-line," but the running time of the object program is of vital consideration. Furthermore, to simulate a truly "live model" the compiler must be able to accept ADD and DELETE statements on-line in order to implement major modifications.

Standard diagnostic routines are a necessary part of any hybrid software. These routines conduct not only standard dynamic and static checks of the analog subsystem but also of the hybrid interface.

10. FUTURE OF ANALOG AND HYBRID COMPUTATION

Before the "computer revolution," one of the dominant themes of applied mathematical research can be seen in the series of attempts to circumvent, avoid, or overcome arithmetic. With the aid of digital computers it is relatively routine now to get numerical solution of hundreds of simultaneous differential equations with amazing accuracy. Paradoxically, the digital computer is probably one of the most inefficient machines ever devised; a roomful of equipment can do only one arithmetic operation at a time. Essentially, modern high-speed digital computers are slow calculating machines. "Parallelization"—that is, design of computers of the hybrid type that will contain different components or subcomputers carrying out different operations simultaneously—is the new trend in computer design. This new trend is a direct consequence of the engineer's determination to meet the challenge from a new genre of mathematical problem of contemporary interest—the study of large-scale physical systems such as weather forcasting, air-pollution control, water resource management, nuclear reactor design, and so forth.

In dealing with such complex processes, a new type of mathematical problem arises—that of partitioning the computational process into subcomputations. Some of these computations will be carried out solely by digital techniques; some by analog techniques; and some by using the resources of the human operator. Thus, in many applications, the mere blending of analog and digital hardware is not sufficient; it is also necessary to blend both algorithmic and heuristic methods resulting in truly hybrid computation.

In addition to being a tool of science, analog computation is an art; no art can afford to remain static without becoming sterile, and analog computation is not exception to this rule. Just as arts and sciences react, the art of analog computation reacted strongly to the period of turmoil in culture and technology. Indeed, the explosive growth of digital technology did not pronounce an epitaph to analog computation; instead, it created a new zeal in the analog school and heralded the development of hybrid computation. Similarly, the "transistor revolution" substantially contributed to several new trends in the design of analog and hybrid computers. Microelectronic operational chips containing integrated operational amplifiers as basic building blocks may soon become standard parts of arithmetic units. If the present trend is any indication, passive circuit models containing resistors, capacitors, inductors, and transformers will gain more excellence and expand in application—not in their present form, but in a miniaturized form that is compatible with future technology. A plane passive resistance network, with or without "feed-in" capacitors, can easily be miniaturized on a small chip of dielectric material and soon may become a matrix inversion hardware subroutine. Similarly, miniaturized digital-analog circuits simulating thousands of neurons may become available as optional features in future generation computers.

Another field where analog and hybrid techniques will play a basic role is in on-line instrumentation and data processing. The operational amplifier is already playing a basic role in instrumentation technology. The advantages of continuous analog apparatus make the use of feedback concepts and operational amplifiers irresistible.

Models and analogs are extremely powerful tools. Indeed, the entire edifice of quantum mechanics was built on model concepts. The concept of a model is very primitive and will continue to play a basic role as a tool in teaching both physical and behavioral sciences. If history is any guide, one cannot help but wonder at the durability of the method of analogs.

11. REFERENCES

The entries marked with an asterisk contain extensive bibliographies, and interested readers may refer to them.

Theory

1. *Bekey, G. A., and W. J. Karplus, *Hybrid Computation*, Wiley, New York, 1968.
2. Brennan, R. D., and M. Y. Silberg, "The System/360 Continuous System Modelling Program," *Simulation*, Vol. 11, No. 6, pp. 301–308, December, 1968.
3. Brunner, W., "Philosophy of Managing a Hybrid Computer Laboratory," *Simulation*, Vol. 9, No. 3, pp. 116, September, 1967.
4. Bush, V., and A. H. Caldwell, "A New Type of Differential Analyzer," *J. Franklin Institute*, Vol. 240, No. 4, pp. 255–326, October, 1945.
5. Clamey, J. J., and M. S. Fineburg, "Digital Simulation Languages: A Critique and a Guide," Proceedings, *AFIPS Fall Joint Computer Conference*, Part I, pp. 23–36, November, 1965.
6. Connelly, M. E., "Real-Time Analog Digital Computation," *IRE Transactions on Electronic Computers*, Vol. 11, pp. 31–41, February, 1962.
7. Dames, R. T., "Simulation Software—the SDS Approach," *Datamation*, Vol. 11, No. 10, pp. 29–34, October, 1965.
8. Fifer, S., *Analogue Computation: Theory, Techniques and Applications*, 4 Vols., McGraw-Hill, New York, 1961.
9. Freeman, D. E., "Discrete Systems Simulation: A Survey and Introduction," *Simulation*, Vol. 7, No. 3, pp. 142–148, September, 1966.
10. Gelman, R., "Corrected Inputs—Method for Improved Hybrid Simulation," Proc. *Fall Joint Computer Conference*, Las Vegas, pp. 267–276, 1963.

11. Gilliland, M. C., "The Iterative Differential Analyzer," *Instruments and Control Systems*, Vol. 34, No. 4, pp. 675–680, April, 1961.

12. Green, C., H. D. Hoop, and A. Debroux, "APACHE—A Breakthrough in Analog Computation," *IRE Trans. Electronic Computers*, Vol. 11, No. 5, pp. 699–706, October, 1962.

13. Harnett, R. T., F. J. Sansom, and L. M. Warshawsky, "MIDAS—An Analog Approach to Digital Computation," *Simulation*, Vol. 3, No. 3, pp. 17–43, September, 1964.

14. Hoeschele, D. G., *Analog-to-Digital/Digital-to-Analog Conversion Techniques*, Wiley, New York, 1968.

15. Hogan, T. G., "Hybrid Computation," *Datamation*, Vol. 11, No. 10, pp. 24–28, October, 1965.

16. Institute of Radio Engineers, "Proposed IRE Standards for Analog Computers," *Simulation*, Vol. 2, No. 1, pp. S1-S12, January, 1964.

17. Jackson, A. S., *Analog Computation*, McGraw-Hill, New York, 1960.

18. Karplus, W. J., *Analog Simulation: Solution of Field Problems*, McGraw-Hill, New York, 1958.

19. Karplus, W. J., "A Hybrid Computer Technique for Treating Nonlonear Partial Differential Equations," *IEEE Trans. Electronic Computers*, Vol. 13, No. 5, pp. 597–605, October, 1964.

20. Karplus, W. J., "Analog Subroutines for Digital Computer Programs," *Simulation*, Vol. 4, No. 3, pp. 145–150, March, 1965.

21. Karplus, W. J., and J. Vidal, "Characterization and Evaluation of Hybrid Systems," *IFAC Proc. Symposium on System Engineering*, Tokyo, Japan, August, 1965.

22. Korn, G. A. "The Impact of Hybrid Analog-Digital Techniques on the Analog Computer Art," *Proc. IRE*, Vol. 50, No. 5, pp. 1077–1086, May, 1962.

23. *Korn, G. A., and T. Korn, *Electronic Analog and Hybrid Computers*, McGraw-Hill, New York, 1964.

24. Korn, G. A., "Hybrid Computer Monte-Carlo Techniques," *Simulation*, Vol. 5, No. 4, pp. 234–245, October, 1965.

25. *Korn, G. A., *Random-Process Simulation and Measurements*, McGraw-Hill, New York, 1966.

26. *Linebarger, R. N., and R. D. Brennan, "A Survey of Digital Simulation: Digital Analog Simulator Programs," *Simulation*, Vol. 3, No. 6, pp. 22–36, December, 1964.

27. McLeod, J. (ed.), *Simulation*, McGraw-Hill, New York, 1968.

28. Miller, K. S., and F. J. Murray, "A Mathematical Basis for an Error Analysis of Differential Analyzers," *J. Math. and Physics*, Nos. 2 and 3, pp. 136–163, 1953.

29. Miura, T., and J. Iwata, "Effects of Digital Execution Time in a Hybrid Computer," *Proc. Fall Joint Computer Conference*, Las Vegas, pp. 251–266, 1963.

30. Palevsky, M., "The Digital Differential Analyzer," *Computer Handbook*, ed., Huskey and Korn, McGraw-Hill, New York, 1962.

31. Paschkis, V., and F. L. Ryder, *Direct Analog Computers*, Wiley-Interscience, New York, 1968.

32. Reichardt, O. A., M. W. Hoyt, and W. T. Lee, "The Parallel Digital Differential Analyzer and Its Application as a Hybrid Computer System Element," *Simulation*, Vol. 9, No. 2, pp. 109–113, February, 1965.

33. Skramstad, H. K., "Combined Analog-Digital Techniques in Simulation," *Advances In Computers*, Vol. 3, edited by F. L. Act and M. Rubinoff, Academic Press, New York, 1963.

34. Sprague, R. E., "Fundamental Concepts of the Digital Differential Analyzer Method of Computation," *Math. Tables and Other Aids to Computation*, Vol. 6, No. 3, pp. 61–69, January, 1952.

35. Starr, D. A., and J. J. Johnson, "The Design of an Automatic Patching System," *Simulation*, Vol. 10, No. 6, pp. 281–288, June, 1968.

36. Stephenson, B. W., *Analog-Digital Conversion Handbook*, Digital Equipment Corporation, Maynard, Mass.

37. Susskind, A. K., *Notes on Analog-Digital Conversion Techniques*, Technology Press, M.I.T.; Cambridge, Mass., 1957.

38. Sutherland, I. E., "Sketchpad: A Man-Machine Graphical Communication System," *Simulation*, Vol. 2, No. 5, pp. R.3–R.19, May, 1964.

39. Svoboda, A., *Computing Machines and Linkages*, McGraw-Hill, New York, 1948.

40. Tomovic, R., and W. J. Karplus, *High-Speed Analog Computers*, Wiley, New York, 1962.

41. Truitt, T. D., "Hybrid Computation—What Is it? Who Needs IT?," *IEEE Spectrum*, Vol. 1, Nol 6, pp. 132–146, June, 1964.

42. Volyanskii, B. A., and V. Ya. Buchman, *Analogues for the Solution of Boundary Value Problems*, Pergamon Press, New York, 1965.

43. Weiss, E., "Application of CRC105 Digital Differential Analyzer," *IRE Trans. Electronic Computers*, Vol. 1, No. 4, pp. 19–24, December, 1952.

Applications

44. Bekey, G. A., "Optimization of Multiparameter Systems by Hybrid Computer Techniques, Parts I, II, " *Simulation*, Vol. 2, pp. 19–32, pp. 21–29, February and March, 1964.

45. Bellman, J. A., "Railroad Network Model," *Simulation*, Vol. 12, No. 1, pp. 5–13, January, 1969.

46. Bridgman, A. D., "Analog Techniques for Filter Simulation," *Simulation*, Vol. 8, No. 4, pp. 191–199, April, 1967.

47. Butler, B. R., and P. E. Stanley, "Stuttering Problem Considered from an Automatic Control Point of View," *Simulation*, Vol. 8, No. 1, pp. 331–336, June, 1967.

48. *Clymer, A. B., and C. F. Graber, "Trends in the Development and Applications of Analog Simulations in Biomedical Systems," *Simulation*, Vol. 2, No. 4, pp. 41–60, April, 1964.

49. Crow, W. J., "A Study of Strategic Doctrines Using the Internation Simulation," *Simulation*, Vol. 5, No. 1, pp. 47–53, July, 1965.

50. Engel, A., and J. J. Kennedy, "Modeling Dynamic Economic Systems on the Analog Computer," *Intl. J. of Computer Mathematics*, Vol. 1, No. 4, pp. 289–311, December, 1965.

51. Garfinkel, D., "A Simulation Study of the Effect on Simple Ecological Systems of Making Rate of Increase of Population Density-Dependent," *Simulation*, Vol. 8, No. 5, pp. 275–281, May, 1967.

52. Gilbert, E. G., "Selected Bibliography on Parameter Optimization Methods Suitable for Hybrid Computation," *Simulation*, Vol. 8, No. 6, pp. 350–352, June, 1967.

53. Gullahorn, J. E., and J. T. Gullahorn, "Computer Simulation of Human Interaction in Small Groups," *Simulation*, Vol. 4, No. 1, pp. 50–61, January, 1965.

54. Howard, R. A., E. M. Grould, and W. G. O'Regan, "Simulation for Forest Planning," *Simulation*, Vol. 7, No. 1, pp. 44–52, July, 1966.

55. McHenry, R. R., "Computer Simulation of Automobile Accidents . . . a New Research Tool," *Simulation*, Vol. 11, No. 1, pp. 27–34, July, 1968.

56. *McLeod, J., "Computer Simulation of the Hydrodynamics of the Cardiovascular System," *Simulation*, Vol. 2, No. 3, pp. 33–41, March, 1964.

57. Meissinger, H. F., "Simulation of Infrared Systems," *Simulation*, Vol. 2, No. 3, pp. R.23–R.32, March, 1964.

58. Otoba, K., K. Shibatani, and H. Kuwata, "Flood Simulator for the River Kitakami," *Simulation*, Vol. 4, No. 2, pp. 86–98, February, 1965.

59. Parente, R. J., and D. F. Boyd, "A Description of Steamship Cargo Operations," *Simulation*, Vol. 11, No. 4, pp. 195–202, October, 1968.

60. Rastogi, P. N., "Protracted Military Conflict, and Politico-Economic Stability," *Simulation*, Vol. 12, No. 1, pp. 23–36, January, 1969.

61. Reitman, J., "Simulation of a Manufacturing System," *Simulation*, Vol. 8, No. 1, pp. 311–317, June, 1967.

62. Sage, A. P., and J. Melsa, "Electronic Simulation of Daily Rhythm in Nocturnal Animals," *Simulation*, Vol. 5, No. 1, pp. 54–60, July 1965.

63. Sasser, W. E., and T. H. Naylor, "Computer Simulation of Economic Systems—an Example Model," *Simulation*, Vol. 8, No. 1, pp. 21–32, January, 1967.

64. Taylor, J. G., and J. A. Navarro, "Simulation of a Court System for the Processing of Criminal Cases," *Simulation*, Vol. 10, No. 5, pp. 235–240, May, 1968.

65. Thompson, D. G., and J. L. Conossen, "Simulation Model of a Computer Controlled Automatic Warehouse," *Simulation*, Vol. 10, No. 6, pp. 297–304, June, 1968.

66. Vemuri, V., and W. J. Karplus, "Identification of the Non-linear Parameters of a Ground Water Basin via Hybrid Computation," *Water Resources Research*, Vol. 5, No. 1, pp. 172–185, February, 1969.

67. Ahmed, S. S. F., "Use of Modelling and Simulation to Solve Cash Management Problems," *Proceedings, 1971 Summer Computer Simulation Conference*, Boston, Mass. pp. 1317–1323.

68. Fancher, P. S., and P. Grote, "Development of a Hybrid Simulation for Extreme Automobile Maneuvers," Proceedings, 1971 Summer Computer Simulation Conference, Boston, Mass., pp. 566–575.

Some of the more important publications where new material is continually appearing are *Simulation, Proceedings of the International Association for analog Computation, AFIPS Proceedings, Proceedings of the IFIP Congress, Datamation, IEEE Transactions on Computers, Computer Journal, ICC Bulletin* and, particularly, *Proceedings of the Summer Computer Simulation Conference* (annual).

PART II

Languages, Translators, and Applications

Programming Languages

Alfonso F. Cárdenas

University of California
Los Angeles

1. BASIC CONCEPTS

During the early days of the computer in the late 1940s, all programs had to be written in machine language, the only language that any computer can understand directly. *Machine language* consists of combinations of zeros and ones. Thus, all users had to write programs made up of long strings of zeros and ones to specify numerically the addresses of information and of operation codes to be performed. A few years later, so-called translators were developed that would accept as input some sort of mnemonic or symbolic language which would then be converted by the machine itself into machine language. These translators came to be known as assemblers. Assembly systems, although relieving the coder of much of the drudge work, still were not attractive for most users. It was considerably annoying to have to specify, although symbolically, addresses and operation codes. Problems still had to be programmed in a cumbersome language similar to machine language.

The next step in the automation of coding was the one-to-many translation. Unlike the assembly system, where the translation was one to one, the one-to-many translator allowed the coder to write his instructions in a more convenient source or programming language; each instruction would be automatically translated into several corresponding assembly or machine language instructions. These one-to-many translators were the early FORTRAN and ALGOL compilers.

It is convenient to refer to machine language as *0 level language*; to assembly language as *1st level language*; and to programming languages, such as FORTRAN and ALGOL, as *2nd level languages*. In recent years an even higher level language has been produced: the *special purpose* or *problem oriented language* which can be conveniently called a *3rd level language*. Such languages make it possible to use the power of the computer more easily and quickly, often reducing even more total problem-solving times in the special areas for which the languages have been designed. So-called 3rd level translators translate such languages into lower level languages, often translating into a 2nd level language first. Figure 1 illustrates the typical translation process. Second and 3rd level languages are normally referred to as *higher level languages* or *programming languages*. It should be

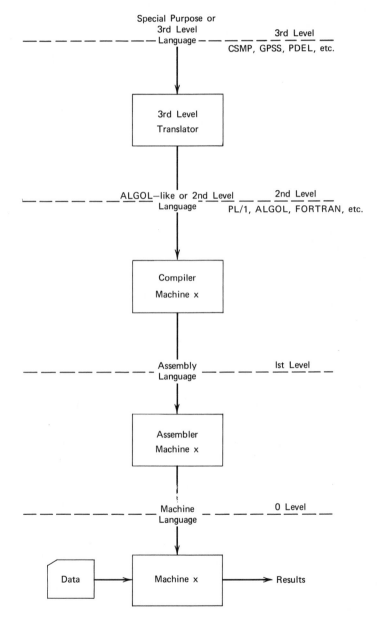

Figure 1. The typical translation process.

stressed that a processing system must always eventually translate the user's program into an equivalent program in the language of the machine so that the machine may process it. See Chapter 11 by Leon Presser on "Translation of Programming Languages" in this book for an in-depth treatment of this subject.

There is no universally accepted definition of a programming language. Recent formalisms have been developed in an attempt to formalize the definition of a language [1–4]. In general, it is taken for granted that a *language* is the finite set of allowed basic symbols combined according to certain rules of the language. These rules are called rules of syntax. Various forms of rules of syntax are in use to describe current programming languages [5–7]. The *Backus-Naur form*, first used to define the ALGOL language [6], was the first publicized formalism for defining the syntax of a language, and is the most widely used notation.

It is usually pointed out that a programming language is the set of characters and the rules for combining them, which has the following characteristics [8].

1. The language requires no knowledge of machine code or of equipment features.

2. The language is significantly independent of a particular computer, that is, it can be used in various types of computers.

3. There is a one-to-many translation of instructions from source code to object code.

One of the most important breakthroughs in the art of computing, and very likely the most important one, was the development and implementation of higher level languages. Programming languages have brought the power of the computer to practically every profession. The general and overall advantage of such languages is the reduction of total problem solving time.

The purpose of this chapter is to present the history, development, and state of the art of higher level languages; to outline the basic features and capabilities of the most widely used languages—FORTRAN IV, ALGOL 60, COBOL, PL/I, and BASIC; and to point out future developments in higher level languages.

2. HISTORY OF HIGHER LEVEL LANGUAGES

The first generation of computers was based on vacuum tubes. During its span from about 1947 to 1959 many established companies, as well as new companies, entered the computer field. The second generation was a line of transistorized computers that began to appear in 1959. In 1964 the third generation characterized by integrated circuitry and new computer organizational concepts began to appear. The early 1970s are bringing on a more powerful fourth generation.

The early first generation computers had to be coded directly in machine language. A short time later, assembly codes began to appear. Many of the early computer systems came out of university research projects sponsored by government military and research organizations; for example, ENIAC at the University of Pennsylvania [9], EDSAC at the University of Cambridge in England [10], IAS at Princeton University [11], Whirlwind at MIT [12], and others. EDSAC was probably the first computer in which programs were stored in a large memory.

Many of the university pioneers then went into industry, the most well-known being the group that founded what is now UNIVAC and which produced in 1951 the first commercially available large scale electronic computer, the UNIVAC I. A short time later, IBM produced its 700 series of computers (701, 702, and then 705). RCA, Burroughs, Raytheon, and Honeywell were among the companies that soon afterward entered the commercial race.

In the early 1950s a tremendous amount of effort went into the production of the first second level languages. The early programming languages FLOWMATIC of UNIVAC and Speedcode for the IBM 701 pointed out the way. In 1954 IBM started out a project that resulted in the FORTRAN (FORmula TRANslation) I language and the first FORTRAN compiler (for the IBM 704) in 1957 [13]. This breakthrough is probably the most impressive development in the early history of automatic programming. FORTRAN II followed shortly thereafter, and IBM went far ahead of all competitors. It has been in that position ever since. FORTRAN IV was then marketed and it has become the most popular programming language in the world.

At about the time that FORTRAN was finished, both the European organization GAMM (association for applied mathematics and mechanics) and the Association for Computing Machinery in the United States, supported by many groups, formed an international group to produce a worldwide, computer-independent, scientific oriented language. After a preliminary report in 1958, the group issued in 1960 the famous report on the language ALGOL (ALGOrithmic Language) 60, which was then revised in 1962 [6]. The revised ALGOL 60 was the second major programming language and the efforts of the designers resulted in much needed formalisms in programming languages. At the end of 1968, a new ALGOL called ALGOL 68 was proposed [14]. It is significantly different from previous ALGOL's; it includes additional facilities and new concepts in programming languages. However, it is not generally available commercially and its future cannot be distinguished yet. In spite of the many advantages of ALGOL over FORTRAN IV, FORTRAN IV is still the most widely used computer language.

With the backing of the Department of Defense of the United States, in 1959 representatives of users, manufacturers, and government began work on a much needed common business oriented language. The result was the COBOL (COmmon Business Oriented Language) language, first presented in 1961 [7]. There was some initial resistance of some manufacturers to construct COBOL compilers, but now COBOL is widely available and is the most popular business oriented language.

In 1964, IBM and the organization of users of IBM equipment (SHARE) began work on the design of a new language, more powerful than FORTRAN IV, and capable of doing essentially everything that ALGOL and COBOL can do, and more. In 1965 IBM specified its new language PL/I (Programming Language One) [5], and a year later introduced PL/I compilers with its new 360 family of computers. PL/I has had a great impact, but it is too early to distinguish its long-run effects. As of 1971, IBM was the only computer manufacturer that marketed it. However, some manufacturers have indicated that they will provide PL/I with some new machines.

There are a few other ALGOL-like languages that have been developed, but they are mostly outgrowths of the early ALGOL (e.g., NELIAC [15] and JOVIAL [16]) or the result of university projects. They are of lesser commercial importance.

Soon after the early 2nd level languages were publicized, the first 3rd level languages started to appear, mostly the result of research groups and university projects. Probably the earliest ones were the digital simulation languages of the late 1950s whose main aim was to simulate analog computer operation or solve systems of ordinary differential equations. In the early 1960s, 3rd level languages began to be marketed commercially. Users in various special areas found them to be quite useful; such languages take computing one step closer to the user than the ALGOL-like languages. Some of the most widely used special languages are pointed out in Section 4. There are more 3rd level languages in use than 2nd level languages, but they are less extensively used.

With the advent of the new generation computers, higher level languages that operate in an *on-line* mode (also called *interactive* mode, *conversational* mode or *time-sharing* mode) are now available. The distinguishing characteristic of such systems to get computing results on the spot (instead of having to wait for them several hours or days as in batch operation) is of major significance. Many of the on-line languages are essentially subsets of some traditional batch programming language, but with powerful additions for interactive use. This is illustrated in Section 7.

More recently, some on-line systems with *graphic facilities* have been developed. These systems, mostly still in an experimental stage, typically permit communication of graphs, figures, etc. on television-like consoles. This is a very new area in which the most significant software developments are in the making. See W. J. Karplus' Chapter 7 on "On-Line Computing and Graphic Display" in this book for a further treatment of this subject.

3.   HIGHER LEVEL LANGUAGES VERSUS LOWER LEVEL LANGUAGES

From a user's point of view, the main advantages of higher level languages over assembly and machine languages are the following:

1. They are easier to learn because they are more human-like than machine-like. They are not molded by the idioscyncracies of the hardware of the computer as all assembly and machine languages are, and are more oriented to problem solving.

2. Programs are much easier to code in programming languages. Furthermore, it is much easier to read, to understand, to modify, and to correct (debug) a program when it is written in a programming language. Because of the one-to-many instruction correspondence, less statements have to be written in a programming language than in a lower level language to accomplish a given computation.

3. Programs written in higher level languages are usually machine independent and hence are not restricted to any one particular machine. Such programs can be processed by any machine for which there is an appropriate compiler. This is a most important feature. It implies that such programs can be utilized in different computer centers independent of the brand of machinery, thus avoiding unnecessary and costly duplication effort.

Unfortunately, advantages are not gained without sacrifice. Some disadvantages are incurred when programs are written in higher level languages:

1. They have to be translated or compiled into machine language by a translator, and thus a price in computer time is paid.

2. The object code generated by a compiler might be inefficient compared to an equivalent assembly program written by an expert programmer, or the 2nd level code (e.g., FORTRAN) generated by a translator might be inefficient compared to an equivalent 2nd level program written by an expert programmer. However, translators (particularly compilers) in today's competitive market are usually quite efficient.

3. If the translator does not provide proper debugging aids and tools, the user might have to spend an unreasonable amount of time trying to debug the program at assembly language level. It has been often complained that 3rd level translators lack adequate diagnostics.

In spite of the disadvantages, higher level languages have proved their worth. The advantages outweight the disadvantages by far. The result is a reduction of total problem solving time.

Since the development of FORTRAN in the mid-1950s, the number of people coding in the various programming languages available has increased so steadily and sharply that now only a minority of people code in assembly or machine language. The development of better translators and operating systems, faster computers and time-shared, on-line systems has made this possible. The recent development of conversational or interactive systems which allow the user to type in source statements on-line to the computer and to execute them immediately, the addition of graphic facilities in these systems, and the future availability of voice communication with a computer indicate the trend of placing man away from the low level of the machine and of taking the power of the machine up to the level of man.

4. HIGHER LEVEL LANGUAGES AVAILABLE

Since the development of FORTRAN, many programming languages have been designed and developed in industry, research institutions, and universities. Sammet reported in 1970 one hundred thirty-eight higher level languages (2nd and 3rd level) available in the United States [17]. One must add to this a number of other languages usually of a special purpose nature, whose availability is restricted by company and institutional policies. Furthermore, a few other languages have been developed in European and Soviet countries [18, 19]. The work by Sammet [20] is one of the best references on the history and fundamentals of the higher level languages available in the United States by early 1968.

As of 1970, of the 82,000 computer installations in the whole world, about 70,000 of them used machinery made by United States manufacturers [21]. Since most computers are seldom installed without some higher level translators or compilers, higher level languages produced by United States institutions make up a large majority of all available languages in the world. As a result, most higher level languages involve English language forms.

There are many general purpose programming languages. Some countries and some institutions have preference for certain languages. However,

FORTRAN IV, ALGOL, and COBOL are still by far the most widely used languages, with FORTRAN IV a solid first. These languages are outlined in Section 6. Because of the power of PL/I and because of IBM's tremendous share of the world computer market (IBM equipment accounted for about 39,000 of the estimated 82,000 worldwide installations in 1970 [21]), the impact of PL/I has been growing steadily in spite of the natural opposition of IBM's competitors. It is the fourth language outlined in Section 6.

There is a large number of powerful 3rd level languages available. Many of them are pointed out in References [17] and [22]. As has been stated, in many situations they would be preferred over 2nd level languages. More than half of the higher level languages available are for special areas. However, their actual commercial utilization is still below that of ALGOL-like languages and, therefore, no representative language is outlined in this chapter.

Some areas for which special purpose languages have been specifically designed are:

1. Continuous systems characterized by ordinary differential equations: MIMIC [23], CSMP [24], and CSSL [25].

2. Continuous systems characterized by partial differential equations: PDEL [26].

3. Discrete systems: GPSS [27], SIMSCRIPT [28], and SIMULA [29].

4. Machine tool control: APT [30, 31].

5. Formula manipulation: FORMAC [32].

6. String manipulation: SNOBOL [33].

7. Civil engineering: STRESS [34] and COGO [35].

8. List processing: IPL-V [36] and LISP 1.5 [37].

9. Information retrieval: DATAPLUS [38], EASY ENGLISH [39], and DIALOG [40].

10. Circuit analysis and design: ECAP [41] and NASAP [42].

11. Writing of compilers: META5 [43] and FSL [44].

At the programming language level, usually two broad application areas are distinguished: scientific applications and business or data processing applications. FORTRAN and ALGOL are designed for scientific applications, COBOL for business applications, while PL/I encompasses both areas. However, languages have been used sometimes in areas for which they were not originally intended.

In the last few years, with the advent of time sharing systems and on-line consoles, an unusually large number of interactive languages has emerged. Computer users are no longer limited to the traditional batch utilization of computers that FORTRAN IV, ALGOL, COBOL and their various offsprings usually entail.

Some of the newer systems now provide on-line versions of ALGOL, COBOL, and FORTRAN IV [45]. Many of the new interactive languages are essentially a subset of some traditional batch programming language, with some additions for on-line and interactive use. The time-sharing language BASIC is one of the most popular; it is essentially a subset of ALGOL with some powerful facilities for interaction [46]. In Section 7, some of the most important features of BASIC are illustrated with an example. Other languages that operate in a time-sharing environment are JOSS's [47] (one of the earliest ones, first used in the mid 1960s), DIALOG [40], and APL/360 [48].

Practically all medium- and large-scale general purpose computers have a FORTRAN, an ALGOL, and a COBOL compiler. Most minicomputers (computers priced below $25,000 including the basic hardware and software) have a FORTRAN compiler, while a few have ALGOL and COBOL compilers [49]. The newer medium- and large scale computers also provide many of the new 3rd level and on-line languages. Even many of the small computers provide a conversational language [49], typically the time sharing BASIC language, and a few even on-line versions of FORTRAN.

Time sharing services in the United States, since their commercial availability in 1965, have grown tremendously. At present, most of the higher level language usage is done on a batch mode, particularly outside the United States. However, there is every indication that time sharing languages will probably take over in the 1970s a large portion of the market, although not all of it, particularly if needed time-sharing technology advances prove successful to reduce the relatively high cost of time-sharing operations.

5. FACTORS IN THE CHOICE OF A HIGHER LEVEL LANGUAGE

With the costs of software now approximating those of hardware [50], designation of the best language for specific applications has become a critical matter of dollars and cents. The key question is then: What is the best 2nd level, or perhaps 3rd level language for a particular application? This is indeed a very difficult question. There is no scientific nor logical way of reaching an answer. However, several important factors should be considered in arriving at a proper choice:

1. The *functional* or *nontechnical characteristics* of a language and its implementation—mainly economic aad political aspects and of managerial concern.

2. The *technical characteristics* of a language—aspects concerned with the specifications and details of a language; for example, the syntax or grammar of executable statements, the punched card format to be observed for an input program, and the like.

5.1. Functional Characteristics

The most important questions of a functional nature that must be answered in order to pick the proper language are:

1. Was the language designed to apply to the general area of interest? For scientific problems, one must usually select languages such as ALGOL, FORTRAN IV, and PL/I, rather than list processing languages such as LISP 1.5 or business languages such as COBOL. If the problem area is narrower, special purpose languages may apply, perhaps.

2. Can the language be used in the available computers? In other words, is there a translator or compiler for the machines that are available?

3. Is the language easy to learn and code? Learning a language and coding are a considerable portion of the total problem solving effort on digital computers.

4. Is documentation and system support adequate? A language that is badly documented and supported will lose most prospective users no matter how good it is; few users will be able to learn it and use it. A language is as good as its documentation. Two types of documentation are essential: (a) a reference manual with the exact specifications, and (b) a tutorial or introductory manual.

5. Are sufficient debugging aids provided? In other words, are the diagnostics or hints printed out by the particular compiler being considered adequate to help a nonprofessional programmer locate and correct programming errors? Very often the major portion of the total problem solving time is spent in debugging the computer program.

6. How usable or compatible with other machines is the language? How dependent is it on a particular computer or class or brand of computers? Machine independency is often very important in order to be able to run a program in various installations having different machinery.

7. How efficient is the translator in generating object code? It should be pointed out that usually it is the user who writes an inefficient source program and, as a result, the object code generated is inefficient. However, it is true that the first compilers and 3rd level translators for a new language tend to be inefficient; for example, the new PL/I compilers [51]: They remain that way until better translation techniques are found and money, time, and interest permit the improvement.

5.2. Technical Characteristics

There is an even larger list of technical characteristics that demand attention. The amount of technical detail that a user might need to know usually increases with the complexity of the application. A convenient classification of the technical characteristics of a 2nd level language is proposed and illustrated in Section 6 as the main characteristics of FORTRAN IV, ALGOL, COBOL, and PL/I are exposed. The main components in such a classification are not too different from those proposed by Sammet [20] and are:

1. Basic elements.
2. Data types.
3. Expressions and statements.
4. Nonexecutable statements.
5. Program structure.
6. Others.

This classification is not unique. Various authors use various ways of dividing a language into its elements when presenting it.

The goal of comparing technical characteristics of several languages is to expose the language with the best features for the particular application. For example, if within the area of numeric applications one is interested in problems involving considerable array handling, such as in solving partial differential equations, then the type and amount of subscripting and array manipulation must be a significant factor. However, there is a special purpose language for partial differential equations [26], and it should be seriously considered.

It must be stressed that functional factors have had, and will continue to have, a very strong weight when choosing the language for a given task. For example, the efficiency of the object code generated by a translator is particularly important for repetitive problems which often occur in routine business data processing (e.g., payroll processing).

6. OUTLINE OF PROGRAMMING LANGUAGES:
FORTRAN IV, ALGOL 60, COBOL, AND PL/I

FORTRAN IV, ALGOL 60, and COBOL are the programming languages that have had the greatest impact, and are still the most widely used. Because of their importance, their general characteristics are outlined, and compared when possible, in this section. The impact of PL/I has been growing and is therefore also outlined. It is practically impossible to present in a few pages all the features of the four languages, or even only most of them. What is presented here, instead, is a concise outline of an "average" of their most important widely used characteristics. These characteristics are organized into basic elements, data types, expressions and statements, nonexecutable statements and others, and are tabulated in tables 1 to 6, respectively.

The various facilities presented in Tables 1 to 6 and discussed in Sections 6.1 to 6.6 are normally available in other 2nd level languages, whether used in a batch mode or in an on-line mode. However, they usually vary from language to language in format, limitations, and so on. The facilities of 2nd level languages are, of course, usually different to those of 3rd level languages. Third level languages provide special tools for a particular application area, whereas ALGOL-like languages usually provide the general capabilities illustrated here.

In Sections 6.7 to 6.10, four complete programs, one in each of the four languages, are used in conjunction with Tables 1 to 6 to illustrate the facilities of the languages. Readers who pursue more details and a further knowledge of other facilities of the languages should refer to the various publications available on FORTRAN IV [13, 20, 45, 52, 53], ALGOL [6, 20, 54–56], COBOL [7, 20, 57–59], and PL/I [5, 20, 60).

The circled numbers in Tables 1 to 6 indicate the statements in the appropriate program (program 1, 2, 3, or 4) exemplifying the facilities of the language being outlined.

6.1. Comments on the Basic Elements (Table 1)

Computer input and output equipment (e.g., keypunches and teletypewriters) has not been completely standardized and, as a result, there are variations in the character set of the equipment. However, there is usually a 48 character set and a 60 character set, either of which may be used for actual input/output of programs in any of the languages. As an illustration, the FORTRAN operator less than is .LT. in the 48 character set and < in the 60 character set.

There is no commercially available input/output equipment that can handle all of ALGOL's character set. In all cases, small case letters are not handled. Some symbols are often replaced by other commercially available keys (e.g., [and] by (/ and /), respectively).

Reserved words are series of symbols which have a special meaning in the language and which may not be used as identifiers by the programmer. Most FORTRAN and ALGOL implementations do not carry reserved words, but some of the smaller compilers do reserve some words.

The operators indicate some kind of manipulation on such data items as identifiers and constants.

Ease in physical input format of a program is of great importance. Many inconveniences and also programming errors arise because the user cannot always keep in mind unreasonable numbers of rules specifying where the program statements must be placed and where blanks must be placed. PL/I and then ALGOL are the best in this respect, next follows FORTRAN IV, while COBOL ranks low in comparison.

6.2. Comments on Data Types and Variables (Table 2)

The types of information that may be handled vary from language to language. The following types of data can be usually manipulated.

1. Numeric or arithmetic (allowed in every language), which is used in arithmetic computations; for example: 40.80.

2. String (allowed in many languages), which is not used in arithmetic computations; for example: **'COMPUMEX CORPORATION'**.

3. Logical or Boolean (allowed in every language), which is used in Boolean computations or in logical operations; it always take the value TRUE or FALSE, or their equivalent.

4. Complex (allowed in scientific languages), which is used in complex number computations.

An identifier which represents or holds a single data item is called a *simple variable*. An *array* is a subscripted identifier which represents a collection of items of the same type; for example, the one dimensional array **QUANT (1), QUANT (2), . . ., QUANT (10)** may be used to store -0.10, **0.40, ... 20.6**, respectively. Quite often in business applications, interrelated conglomerations of different types of data arise. Such information is represented by so called *data structures* or *hierarchies*. For example, the simplified structure format **01 EMPLOYEE 02 NAME 02 NUMBER 02 ADDRESS**, may be used to represent **'A. F. CARDENAS' 1020 'COMPUTER SCIENCE DEPT., UCLA.'**

While the type of information that FORTRAN and ALGOL allows is of a scientific nature (e.g., complex numbers, very large and very small numbers) and that of COBOL is mainly of a business nature (e.g., hierarchies), PL/I is capable of dealing with all such types of information.

The array handling facilities are often very important in various scientific applications. In this respect, PL/I would rank the best (e.g., operations on whole arrays or rows and columns of arrays allowed), ALGOL second, and last FORTRAN and COBOL.

Character string manipulation is important in nonnumeric applications (e.g., language translation). PL/I is capable of handling and performing various important operations on character strings. COBOL has just some minor capability, and FORTRAN and ALGOL essentially none.

6.3. Comments on Expressions and Executable Statements (Table 3)

The main motivation for using a programming language is to facilitate the manipulation and transformation of various types of information. When the series of executable statements that make up the heart of every program is executed by the processing system in the sequence and manner specified, the transformation of information is accomplished.

An *expression* is a combination of various data items (called operands), operators (e.g., $+$, $-$, $<$, $=$) and perhaps function calls [e.g., SIN(A)] and parentheses, which can be evaluated to give a single value. The expression may be of an arithmetic, logical or character string nature. For example, the arithmetic expression (A * 30.1 + 60)/(B ** 2) will have a value of 7.51 if A = 2.0 and B = 4.0; the logical expression (X > 100) AND (Y ≠ 20) will have a value of TRUE if both X is greater than 100 and Y is not equal to 20, otherwise the value is FALSE.

There are usually two main classes of statements: the *assignment statement* and the *control statement*. The assignment statement is used to assign the value of an expression to a variable, or to various variables (multiple assignment). For example, execution of AA = (X ** 2) + 10 stores the value of (X ** 2) + 10 in AA.

The control statements are used to control the sequence of execution of the various statements in a program. ALGOL-like languages invariably provide three main types of statements:

1. Transfer of control statements, which may be: (a) unconditional, which transfers control to a labeled statement. Usually the general form is GO TO label; and (b) conditional, which transfers control to one of several alternative labeled statements, depending on the value of a certain variable or expression. Its form varies from language to language. It is not described in Table 3.

2. IF or conditional statement, in which a logical expression is evaluated to determine whether or not a given statement is executed. If the value is TRUE a certain statement is executed; if it is FALSE, the next statement in sequence is executed (e.g., FORTRAN). Another form is the two-way IF statements allowed in most languages (e.g., ALGOL, PL/I) in which either of two statements is executed depending on whether the value of the logical expression is TRUE or FALSE. In Table 3 only the two most important types of IF statements of ALGOL, COBOL, and PL/I are summarized.

Table 1 Basic Elements

	FORTRAN IV	ALGOL 60	COBOL	PL/I
Character set	48 symbols: A, B, C...Z 0, 1,...9 b = + − * / ( ) , . $ '	Undefined number, but usually: A, B, C...Z a, b, c,...z 0, 1, 2,...9 b + − × / ÷ ↑ < ≦ = ≧ > ≠ ≡ ⊃ ∧ ∨ ⌐ , . 10 : ; := ( ) [ ] ' '	51 symbols: A, B,...Z 0, 1, 2...9 b = + − * / $ < > , . ; " ( )	60 symbols: A, B, C...Z 0, 1, 2...9 b = + − * / ( ) , . ' % ; : ⌐ & | > < − ? $ @ #
Identifiers	Up to six letters and/or digits long; first must be alphabetic. e.g., AMAX, STOCK3	Series of letters and/or digits, first of which must be a letter; length undefined, but usually up to six characters in most implementations	Series of not more than 30 letters and/or digits and/or hyphens, first and last of which cannot be a hyphen. e.g., STOCK-NO3	Series of not more than 31 letters and/or digits and/ or break character; first character must be a letter
Arithmetic operators	** Exponentiation * Multiplication / Division − Subtraction + Addition	↑ Exponentiation × Multiplication / Division ÷ Integer division − Subtraction + Addition	** EXPONENTIATED BY * MULTIPLIED BY OR TIMES / DIVIDED BY − MINUS + PLUS	** Exponentiation * Multiplication / Division − Subtraction + Addition

Other operators	Relational: .LT. Less than .LE. Less than or equal .EQ. Equal to .NE. Not equal to .GT. Greater than .GE. Greater than or equal to	Relational: < Less than ≦ Less than or equal = Equal ≠ Not equal to > Greater than ≧ Greater than or = Equal to	Relational: > IS GREATER THAN < IS LESS THAN = IS EQUAL TO EXCEEDS IS UNEQUAL TO EQUALS	Relational: > Greater than > = Greater than or equal >¬ Not greater than = Equal to ¬= Not equal to < Less than < = Less than or equal
	Logical: .AND. logical and .OR. logical or .NOT. negation	Logical: ≡ Equivalence ⊃ Implication ∨ Disjunction (OR) ∧ Conjunction (AND) ¬ Negation	Logical: AND OR NOT	Logical: & Logical and | Logical or ¬ Negation string: || Concatenation
Reserved words	None	None	Noise words, all verbs, about 250 reserved words	None
Comments	A series of characters in a card is considered a comment when a c is placed in column 1 ⓒ	Usual form: ; COMMENT any sequence not containing ; ; ⓒ	All strings following the verb NOTE.	All strings enclosed in / * and * / ; may be placed wherever a blank is permitted.

(Continued)

Table 1 (continued)

	FORTRAN IV	ALGOL 60	COBOL	PL/I
Physical format	Very card oriented: all statements start in column 7; a character in column 6 indicates a continuation card; indentation usually not allowed; one statement per card.	Not card oriented: continuous string; statements may start in any column and are separated by ; ; no continuation marks; indentation allowed; several statements allowed in a card.	Very card oriented; considerable card column restrictions: certain sub-units of a program must start in columns 8–11, others in columns 12–72; hyphen in column 7 indicates continuation; considerable indentation allowed; many rules on where to place blanks; more than one statement per card.	Not card oriented: continuous string; statements may start on any column and are separated by ; ; no continuation marks; indentation allowed; several statements allowed in a card.

3. Iterative statement, through which a series of statements is executed repeatedly, with the value of a variable changing automatically by certain increments from iteration to iteration. Table 3 illustrates and summarizes the general form of the FORTRAN and COBOL iterative statements, while only the most important ALGOL and PL/I iteration statements are exposed.

ALGOL and PL/I provide more flexible and more powerful control statements than COBOL and FORTRAN. FORTRAN ranks lowest in this respect. The iterative statements of ALGOL and PL/I pointed out in Table 3 are superior, and they are not the only forms available.

6.4. Comments on Declarations or Nonexecutable Statements (Table 4)

Every language includes *declaration statements*. These declarations are usually needed by the translation system; quite often they are of critical importance. The types and formats of declarations varies of course from language to language.

Data structures and the size of any arrays to be used must be usually declared by the programmer for memory allocation purposes. For example, the declaration of an array **A** with 40 entries and array **B** with 20 × 20 entries: **DIMENSION A(40), B(20,20)** in FORTRAN. The type of data associated with each data name (identifier) is usually either assumed by default by the compiling system or explicitly declared by the user. In some languages, like ALGOL and COBOL, they have to be explicitly declared. For example, the ALGOL declaration of variables **JM** and **AB** to be of integer type: **INTEGER JM, AB**. See Table 4.

In some of the newer languages, like ALGOL and PL/I, the declarations do not have to appear at the beginning of a program like they do in FORTRAN. In such cases declarations may appear in the middle of a program, as long as they are at the head of a group of statements making up a block or a procedure (see Table 5 for a definition of block and procedure). However, variables thus declared can be used only within the block or procedure in which they are declared (this refers to the principle of "scope of variables"), since storage is allocated for them at execution upon entry to the block or procedure and released upon exit from it (this refers to the principle of "dynamic storage allocation" as opposed to "static storage allocation" in FORTRAN and COBOL in which storage for a variable is allocated throughout the whole program, or the whole FORTRAN subprogram in which it is declared).

Table 2   Data Types and Variables

	FORTRAN IV	ALGOL 60	COBOL	PL/I
Integer data	A signed or unsigned integer number. e.g., 40, −5	A signed or unsigned integer number. e.g., 801, −37	A signed or unsigned integer number. e.g., −40, +11	A signed or unsigned integer number. e.g., 60, −73
Real data	A signed or unsigned number with a decimal point and an optional indication of multiplication by a power of ten. e.g., 20.1, −0.1E+04	A signed or unsigned number with a decimal point and an optional indication of multiplication by a power of ten. e.g., −0.1, −4.1	A signed or unsigned number with a decimal point. e.g., −0.010, 12.35	A signed or unsigned number with a decimal point and an optional indication of multiplication by a power of ten. e.g., −0.13E3
Complex data	An ordered pair of real numbers representing a complex number. e.g., (35, 2.5E−01) represents .35 + .25i	Not available	Not available	An ordered pair of numbers representing a complex number
Logical or Boolean Data	Takes the values .TRUE. or .FALSE.	Takes the values TRUE or FALSE	Not available	Takes the Boolean values 0 or 1
String data	Essentially unavailable; no operations can be performed on it.	Essentially unavailable; it is defined but no operations can be performed on it.	Some available	Character string: any set of characters enclosed in quotes e.g., 'STOCK LEVEL', 'XMAS'. Bit string: any series of Boolean 0's and 1's enclosed in quotes.

	Simple or scalar variable	Array	Data structure or hierarchy
	An identifier representing one data item of a given type	An identifier followed by subscripts which represent a collection of data items of the same type. Each combination of subscripts represents one data item. e.g., AM(10,1), V(10) Usually up to three subscripts allowed	Not available
	An identifier representing one data item of a given type	An identifier followed by subscripts which represent a collection of data items of the same type. Each combination of subscripts represents one data item. e.g., AM [10,4], L [100] A large number of subscripts allowed	Not available
	An identifier representing one data item of a given type	An identifier followed by subscripts which represent a collection of data items of the same type. Each set of subscripts represents one data item. e.g., STOCK (100,11) Usually up to three subscripts allowed	An organized, level by level conglomeration of different types of data items. e.g., 01 EMPLOYEE 02 NAME 02 NUMBER 02 PAY-RATE 03 REGULAR 03 OVER-TIME
	An identifier representing one data item of a given type	An identifier followed by subscripts which represents a collection of data items of the same type. Each set of subscripts represents one data item. e.g., DIN (10,100,4,1) A large number of subscripts allowed	An organized, level by level conglomeration of different types of data items. e.g., 1 PART 2 PRICE 2 STOCK-NUMBER 2 QUANTITY

Table 3 Expressions and Executable Statements

	FORTRAN IV	ALGOL 60	COBOL	PL/I
Arithmetic expression	A combination of arithmetic operands, arithmetic operators and perhaps function calls and parentheses, which can be evaluated to give a single arithmetic value e.g., VOLT/(3.1*(A+B)) Usually all operands must be of same data type	A combination of arithmetic operands, arithmetic operators and perhaps function calls and parentheses, which can be evaluated to give a single arithmetic value e.g., N/SQRT (20 × F)	←Same→ e.g., STOCK-LEVEL TIMES 4.8	A combination of arithmetic operands, arithmetic operators and perhaps function calls and parentheses, which can be evaluated to give a single arithmetic value e.g., A**2 + I*(40.1−A)
Logical expression, or condition (COBOL terminology)	A combination of logical operands, logical operators and/or relational operators, and perhaps arithmetic expressions which can be evaluated to give a single logical value e.g., (V.LT.A) .OR. 6000.GT.NIVEL	←Same→ e.g., (x<y) & (x>3) ∣ (60.1/A) < x	←Same→ e.g., A = B AND D GREATER THAN (X**2)	←Same→ e.g., M<SQRT (20) ∣ (A = B & M>SQRT (20))

String expression	Not available	Not available	A combination of string operands, string operators and parentheses which when evaluated gives a character string	A combination of string operands, string operators and parentheses which when evaluated gives a character string.
Assignment statement	Assigns the value of an expression to a variable, and is of the form: variable = expression e.g, TAX = 0.08 * AMT (7), (8), (10), (11), (12), (14), (15)	Assigns the value of an expression to one or more variables, and is of the form: variable := expression or variable := variable := ... variable := expression. e.g., F: = 60/SIN (A) (16), (17), (18), (20)	Assigns the value of an expression to variable v, and takes a variety of English-like forms: (1) COMPUTE v = arithmetic expression (2) MOVE v_1 TO v_2 e.g., MOVE A IN C TO D IN C2 (90)	Assigns the value of an expression to one or more variables, and is of the form: variable = expression or variable, variable, . . . variable = expression e.g., COMPANYNAME = 'AABB CORP' (67), (68), (70), (73), (74), (75), (76)
Unconditional transfer of control	Transfers control of execution of the program to another statement, and is of the form: GO TO label e.g., GO TO 101 (13), (19)	←Same→ e.g., GO TO LAB2	Transfers control of execution of the program to another paragraph (segment of the Procedure Division) and is of the form: GOTO paragraph name e.g., GOTO PAR-2 (78), (82)	Transfers control of execution of the program to another statement, and is of the form: GO TO label e.g., GO TO LL10

(Continued)

Table 3 (continued)

	FORTRAN IV	ALGOL 60	COBOL	PL/I
IF or conditional statement	General form of logical **IF**: **IF** (l) s where l ≡ logical expression s ≡ any executable statement except IF or DO statement If l is .TRUE. then s is executed, otherwise it is not. e.g., **IF (A.GT.B) C = 1** ⑬, ⑲	General form: IF l.e. **THEN** u.s. or IF l.s. **THEN** u.s. **ELSE** s. l.e. ≡ logical expression u.s. ≡ unconditional statement s. ≡ any executable statement If l.e. is true then u.s. is executed otherwise s. is executed. e.g., **IF A < 1 THEN GOTO L** **ELSE SW: = 100;** ⑤ & ⑦, ⑫ & ⑭, ㉓	General form: IF logical expression THEN statement 1 or IF logical expression THEN statement 1 ELSE statement 2 where statement 1 and statement 2 are any kind of executable statements. If logical expression is TRUE then statement 1 is executed otherwise statement 2 is executed. e.g., **IF A = B THEN GO TO READIN** ㊄	General form: Same as for COBOL e.g., **IF VOLUME ≦ BREAKEVEN AND SEASON = 'W' THEN GO TO MESSAGE** ㉑, ㊆, ⑧⓪, ⑧②

Iterative or DO or *for* statement	General form:	Most important form:	Most important form:	Most important form:
	DO n i=m_1, m_2 or DO n i=m_1, m_2, m_3 where n $\equiv$ statement label i $\equiv$ an integer scalar variable m $\equiv$ unsigned integer constant or unsigned nonsubscripted variable Action of this statement is to execute the statements following it up to and including the statement labeled n, first with i = m_1, then with i = $m_1 + m_3$, with i = $m_1 + 2m_3$, etc. up to the largest value that does not exceed m_2 e.g., to sum the odd elements of an array: SUM=0.0 DO 50 K=1,21,2 50 SUM = SUM + DATA(K) ⑨	FOR v: = a.e. STEP a.e. UNTIL l.e. DO statement where v $\equiv$ single variable a.e. $\equiv$ arithmetic expression l.e. $\equiv$ logical expression explicitly controls a sequence of values for v for which the statement is to be executed e.g., FOR I: = −10 STEP 2 UNTIL M > N DO S: = S + A (I); ⑤, ⑫, ⑰, ㉓	PERFORM procedure name VARYING integer scalar variable FROM i_1 BY i_2 UNTIL logical expression where both i_1 and i_2 are integer numbers or integer variables. Action of this statement is to execute all the statements in the indicated procedure (procedure is a group of statements), first with v = i_1, then with v = $i_1 + i_2$, then with v = $i_1 + 2i_2$, etc. until the logical expression is true. e.g., PERFORM PROC1 VARYING J FROM 1 BY 1 UNTIL J > 200	DO v = $a.e._1$. TO $a.e._2$. BY $a.e._3$. where v is a single variable and a.e. is any arithmetic expression. Action of this statement is to execute all the statements following it up to the END statement that closes the DO loop, first with v = $a.e._1$. then with v = $a.e._1$ + $a.e._3$., then with v = $a.e._1$. + $2a.e._3$., etc., until v $\geq$ $a.e._2$. e.g., DO II = 20 TO MAX BY 3 ㊹

Table 4 Declarations/or Nonexecutable Statements

	FORTRAN IV	ALGOL 60	COBOL	PL/I
Data type declarations	Implicit: all variables starting with I, J, K, L, M, or N are of integer type; all others are real (with a decimal point). Explicit declarations of type and precision made with type statement: REAL var_1, var_2, . . . INTEGER var_1, var_2, . . . COMPLEX var_1, var_2, . . . LOGICAL var_1, var_2, . . . DOUBLE PRECISION var_1, var_2, . . .	All simple and array variables must be explicitly declared to be of type real, integer or Boolean as follows: REAL var_1, var_2, . . . REAL ARRAY ar_1, ar_2, . . . INTEGER var_1, var_2, . . . INTEGER ARRAY ar_1, ar_2, . . . BOOLEAN var_1, var_2, . . . BOOLEAN ARRAY ar_1, ar_2, . . .	All simple and array variables, and all structures (records) must be explicitly declared in the Data Division with a PICTURE or equivalent form e.g., ⑮ through ㉗, ㊳ through ⑥⓪	Implicit: all variables starting with I, J, K, L, M, or N may be integers or may carry decimal points, but no exponential; all others have an exponential part (inside the machine). Explicit: declarations of type and precision of variable made with a DECLARE statement: (1) DECLARE (v_1, v_2, . . .) arithmetic type (precision)

	var_n ≡ a variable name or array name e.g., REAL I(10), JM ①	where var_n ≡ a variable name ar_n ≡ an array name with the bounds of the subscripts e.g., ①, ②	(2) DECLARE v_1, v_2, . . .) CHARACTER (length) (3) DECLARE (v_1, v_2, . . .) BOOLEAN e.g., ⑥₁, ⑥₂
Dimension or array declarations	Array storage must be allocated for array variables by: (1) Type statement or (2) DIMENSION ar_1, ar_2, . . . where ar_n ≡ array name with subscript bounds e.g., DIMENSION A (10), K (5,15)	Array storage must be allocated for array variables with a type statement as shown above e.g., REAL ARRAY A[−1:10], CANT [0:100, 0:10] Array storage must be allocated for array variables with a special declaration statement in the Data Division	Array storage must be allocated for array variables with a special declaration statement which may also include a data type declaration e.g., DECLARE (A,D (−10:10)) CHARACTER ⑥₁

6.5.   Comments on Program Structures and Subprograms (Tables 5 and 6)

A complete *program* is made up of a series of statements. In 2nd level languages the programmer specifies the sequence in which they are to be executed by appropriately ordering and grouping them and by means of control statements (e.g., **GOTO** . . ., **IF** statement). Statements may be grouped or organized into identifiable units or *program structures*. The main program structures usually found in programming languages are (1) *blocks*, and (2) *subprograms* or *procedures*.

A block is usually a set of statements typically separated from the rest of the program by BEGIN and END. Refer to the description of ALGOL and PL/I blocks in Table 5.

A subprogram (FORTRAN terminology) or procedure (ALGOL and PL/I terminology) is usually a set of statements separated from the rest of the program by a declaration indicating the name of the subprogram and its arguments. These arguments are variable names used in computations inside the subprogram. When the subprogram is "invoked," that is, when execution is sent from the point of invocation to the head of the subprogram, the "input" arguments are given an initial value. These arguments are used inside of the subprogram to compute the values of one or more "output" arguments which are sent back to that part of the program in which the subprogram was invoked. When the end of the subprogram is reached, control goes to the statement following the statement which invoked the subprogram.

The subprogram that is invoked in an expression (or at the right hand side of an assignment statement) and that places the value of the output argument at the point of invocation is called a function subprogram or function procedure. The type of subprogram that is not invoked in an expression and that returns one or more values, but does not place a particular value at the point of invocation, is called a subroutine subprogram (FORTRAN terminology) or a procedure (ALGOL and PL/I terminology). Most language implementations provide various standard function subprograms to perform often needed tasks (e. g., in the FORTRAN statement **A** = **SQRT(C*D)** the function **SQRT** is used to compute the square root of **C*D**). See program 4 and Section 6.10 for an example in PL/I of the use of procedures.

The main differences between blocks and procedures are: (1) blocks are executed when execution scan reaches them, whereas procedures have to be explicitly invoked or called in order to be executed, and (2) procedures are separately compiled. One of the main uses of procedures is to perform computations for various sets of parameters (the arguments) sent from various parts of a program.

Table 5 presents the various program structures in FORTRAN, ALGOL, COBOL, and PL/I. Table 6 shows a pictorial outline of the structure of FORTRAN, ALGOL, COBOL, and PL/I programs. Notice that a FORTRAN program is a main program optionally followed by subprograms that may be called from the main program or from other subprograms. ALGOL and PL/I have the same program structure: a main program with perhaps blocks and procedures inside of it; blocks and procedures may in turn contain other inner blocks and/or procedures. This program structuring is associated with the principles of dynamic storage allocation and scope of variables mentioned in the discussion on declaration statements. COBOL has the unique and rigid program structure discussed in Section 6.9. The structure of the procedure division is not like that of ALGOL or PL/I, and is more like FORTRAN's [e.g., all storage is allocated throughout the program, all variables used are known throughout the whole program, blocks are not defined, procedures (called paragraphs in COBOL) may not be nested].

6.6. Comments on Input/Output Statements

The facilities of a language to input and output information from a program are invariably among the most difficult to master and one of the main causes of programming errors. Input/output (I/O) is typically rigid and cumbersome, particularly in FORTRAN and COBOL. However, recent languages, such as PL/I, provide more convenient facilities.

The official ALGOL specifications do not define explicitly I/O, and as a result, such an important part of ALGOL varies from compiler to compiler. The I/O statements in program 3 (e.g., statements 3, 9, 10, 21) are for an IBM/360 compiler; they are difficult to use and will not be discussed any further. However, the I/O of some ALGOL compilers is better than that of some FORTRAN compilers. FORTRAN, COBOL, and PL/I have well defined and standardized I/O.

The I/O conventions in most scientific oriented languages are: (1) variables to receive new inputs or to have their values sent to an output device are specified in a list of variables in an input or output statement; (2) the order in which values are to be transmitted is governed by the order in which the variables are named in the list; and (3) the format in which the data appears for input, or is to be printed out, is specified usually by the user (e.g., in the FORMAT statement in FORTRAN). For example, in program 1 the FORTRAN statements 2 and 4 read into X(1), X(2), . . ., X(10)

Table 5 Program Structures and Subprograms

	FORTRAN IV	ALGOL 60	COBOL	PL/I
Structure of complete program	A main program with optional subprograms; main program and subprograms made up of statements	A block of the form: **BEGIN** S_1; S_2; . . . . . . S_n **END;** where the S's are Algol statements, other blocks, procedures, etc.	A COBOL program is made up of four divisions. See the description under *COBOL* in this Section 6.	A main program or main block of the form **PROCEDURE** S_1; S_2; . . . . . . S_n; **END;** where S's are PL/I statements, other blocks, procedures, etc.
Compound statement	Not defined	A set of statements S_1, S_2, . . . grouped into a unit, separated by **BEGIN** and **END; BEGIN** S_1; S_2; . . . **END;** [17], [18]	Not defined	Not defined as such, but a PL/I block (see below) without declaration is the equivalent
Block	Not defined	A compound statement in which one or more declarations follow **BEGIN**: e.g., **BEGIN REAL J, TAX; TAX:** = **B * I; . . . END;**	Not defined	A set of statements S_1, S_2, . . . grouped into a unit and separated from the rest of the program by **BEGIN** and **END: BEGIN;** S_1; S_2; . . .; **END;**

Built-in or supplied function subprograms	Subprograms supplied by the manufacturer so that user may automatically invoke them to return one value are usually numerous	Subprograms (procedures) supplied by the manufacturer so that user may automatically invoke them to return one value; usually include at least the trigonometric functions	Not available	Procedures supplied by the manufacturer so that user may automatically invoke them to return one value; PL/I includes a large variety of them, including some that operate on whole arrays ⑥⑧, ⑥④
Function subprograms or function procedures	A group of statements not contained in the main program and which can be compiled independently of it. It is invoked from an expression in the main program and parameters are passed to the subprogram so as to compute a single value which is placed right at the point of invocation. General form: t FUNCTION n $(a_1, a_2 \ldots)$ S_1 S_2 . . . END	Same function and principle found in ALGOL procedures as in FORTRAN function subprograms; the format is not exactly the same	Not available	Same function and principle found in PL/I function procedures as in FORTRAN function subprograms, but format is: n_1: PROCEDURE $(a_1, a_2 \ldots)$ . . . RETURN (a_x); . . . END n_1; where $n_1 \equiv$ name of procedure $a_x \equiv$ value that is placed at point where n_1 is invoked. a's $\equiv$ arguments passed to procedure n_1 *(Continued)*

345

Table 5 (continued)

	FORTRAN IV	ALGOL 60	COBOL	PL/I
	where t ≡ optional type declaration n ≡ name of subprogram a's ≡ arguments passed to subprogram			e.g., TAX = AVERAGE (G, C) . . . . AVERAGE: PROCEDURE (A1, A2); . . . RETURN (AG); END;
Subroutine subprograms or procedures	See Section 6.5	See Section 6.5	Not available	See Section 6.5. Format is the same as that of function procedure, except that a_x is not used. e.g., ⑥⑩ through ⑧⑧

Table 6   Pictorial Structure of FORTRAN, ALGOL, COBOL, and PL/I Programs

FORTRAN	ALGOL and PL/I	COBOL
Main program	Main program	Identification Division
	Block or procedure	Enviroment Division
Subprogram		Data Division
⋮		
Subprogram	[⋯ ⋯]	Procedure Division
		Procedure (paragraph)
		⋮
		Procedure (paragraph)

ten data fields, each field being one integer occupying one column of the punched card. If the X array were of type REAL and if the data fields were to be a maximum of five digits long with two decimal digits, then the FORMAT statement would have to specify 10F5.2 instead.

In COBOL, the format of each variable is specified in the Data Division. For example, in program 3, statement 22 indicates that IDNUMBER contains a string of letters and/or digits, up to 6 characters in length. Statement 81 copies everything in REKORD-1 into REKORD-3 (the name of the record in the output file UPDATED-FILE) and then writes out the contents of it, which have the format indicated in statements 45-51. When reading or writing in COBOL, information must appear exactly in the form specified in the Data Division.

PL/I has two types of I/O: (1) stream-oriented, which is similar to but much more convenient than the I/O of FORTRAN, ALGOL and other scientific oriented languages; and (2) record-oriented, which is similar to and more convenient than the I/O of COBOL. Record-oriented I/O is used to handle records and subrecords. Stream-oriented I/O normally handles simple variables and arrays. For example, in program 4, statement 66 says to skip to the fifth line from the last line printed out **(SKIP(5))** and to then print out **DISTANCE   MINIMUM POTENTIAL** = , followed by the value of **PNMIN** in exponential format with six decimal digits **(E(13,6))**, followed by fifty spaces **(X(50))**, followed by **MAXIMUM POTENTIAL** = , followed by the value of **PNMAX** in the same exponential format as **PNMIN**. Practically all other languages provide facilities to do this, that is, to: (1) print out (a) values (numeric or non-numeric) of variables, and (b) comments or strings or characters (e.g., in program 1 the FORTRAN statements 20 and 22 print out **CONDITION—OVERFLOW**), and (2) to control the column and line position of print out (usually referred to as "carriage control"). The syntax of I/O statements varies considerably from language to language.

6.7. FORTRAN IV

The facilities presented in Tables 1 to 6 form most of the ASA (American Standards Association) FORTRAN [61], which is handled by most small and medium sized FORTRAN IV compilers. Many of the more complex compilers for the larger machines go beyond it and provide additional facilities [52]. Practically all general purpose computers have a FORTRAN IV compiler.

A FORTRAN program consists of a main program, followed perhaps by a series of subprograms, made up of a series of statements. The statements are written, sequenced, and organized into a program (plus perhaps subprograms) by the programmer in order to manipulate and transform information according to his specifications.

Program 1 illustrates some of the main facilities of FORTRAN IV. The program simulates a 10 bit binary adder, that is, it takes as input two binary numbers of ten digits each, and produces their binary sum. The reader should go through the FORTRAN IV part in Tables 1 to 6, cross-referencing to this program to gain an understanding of the lauguage's main features.

6.8. ALGOL 60

The facilities presented in Tables 1 to 6 make up most of the ALGOL defined in the revised ALGOL 60 report [6], usually accepted as the inter-

```
      C    SIMULATION OF A 10 BIT ADDER. THE TWO BINARY NUMBERS ARE
      C    ENTERED WITH LEAST SIGNIFICANT DIGIT FIRST AND THEIR SUM
      C    IS THEN PRINTED.
 1         INTEGER C(11),X(10),Y(10),D(10)
 2         READ(5,1CO) (X(I),I=1,10)
 3         READ(5,1CO) (Y(I),I=1,10)
 4     100 FORMAT (10I1)
 5         WRITE (6,101) X(10),X(9),X(8),X(7),X(6),X(5),X(4),X(3),X(2),X(1),
          1Y(10),Y(9),Y(8),Y(7),Y(6),Y(5),Y(4),Y(3),Y(2),Y(1)
 6     101 FORMAT (2X,10I2/1H,'PLUS'/1H,2X,10I2/1H,'EQUALS'/1H0)
 7         C(1)=0
 8         C(11)=0
 9         DO 10 I=1,10
10         J=I+1
11         D(I)=X(I)+Y(I)+C(I)
12         C(J)=0
13         IF(D(I).LT.2) GO TO 10
14         D(I)=D(I)-2
15         C(J)=1
16      10 CONTINUE
17         WRITE (6,1C2) C(11),D(10),D(9),D(8),D(7),D(6),D(5),D(4),D(3),D(2)
          1,D(1)
18     102 FORMAT (1H0,11I2)
19         IF (C(11).EC.0) GO TO 11
20         WRITE (6,103)
21      11 CONTINUE
22     103 FORMAT ('CONDITION--OVERFLOW')
23         STOP
24         END
```

```
    1 0 0 0 1 1 0 1 0 1
 PLUS
    1 0 0 1 1 1 0 1 1 0
 EQUALS


    1 0 0 1 0 1 0 1 0 1 1
 CONDITION--OVERFLOW
```

Program 1.   (FORTRAN IV).

national standard. ALGOL is a more concise and more powerful language than FORTRAN. Most ALGOL compilers have been implemented for various subsets of full ALGOL. It is unfortunate that these subsets have had various differences. This, plus the fact that input/output differs greatly from implementation to implementation because it has not been defined in the ALGOL reports, has caused a problem; the input/output statements of ALGOL programs usually have to be modified in order to run on a different machine.

ALGOL has been used a great deal to describe algorithms and computational processes, but not as much as actual input to computers. Various companies market it as their main language, particularly Burroughs Corp. Europe is the best ALGOL market.

Program 2 in this section is the ALGOL program that simulates the same 10 bit binary adder simulated in FORTRAN IV in program 1. The reader

```
LEVEL 1JUL67                    OS ALGOL F                         DATE JAN 24
                               SOURCE PROGRAM
     SC      SOURCE STATEMENT

     C0000   'BEGIN'
     C0000   'COMMENT' SIMULATION OF A 10 BIT ADDER;
     C0000   'INTEGER''ARRAY'T(/2:11/);'BOOLEAN''ARRAY'X,Y(/2:11/),S,C(/1:11/);
     C0002   'INTEGER' I;
     C0003   'COMMENT' INPUT X THRU T AND OUTPUT X;
     C0003        INTARRAY(0,T);OUTSTRING(1,'('  INPUT X IS    ')');
     C0005        'FOR' I:=2 'STEP' 1 'UNTIL' 11 'DO'
     C0005        'IF'T(/I/)=1'THEN''BEGIN'X(/I/):='TRUE';OUTSTRING(1,'('1 ')');
     C0007                'END'
     00007        'ELSE''BEGIN'X(/I/):='FALSE';OUTSTRING(1,'('0 ')')'END';
     C0009            'COMMENT' SKIP A LINE;
     C0009            SYSACT(1,14,1);
     00010            'COMMENT' I/O Y;
     00010        INTARRAY(0,T);OUTSTRING(1,'('  INPUT Y IS    ')');
     00012        'FOR' I:=2 'STEP' 1 'UNTIL' 11 'DO'
     00012        'IF'T(/I/)=1'THEN''BEGIN'Y(/I/):='TRUE';OUTSTRING(1,'('1 ')');
     C0014                'END'
     00014        'ELSE''BEGIN'Y(/I/):='FALSE';OUTSTRING(1,'('0 ')')'END';
     00016   C(/11/):='FALSE';
     00017        'FOR' I:=11 'STEP' -1 'UNTIL' 2 'DO'
     00017        'BEGIN' S(/I/):=¬X(/I/)&¬Y(/I/)&C(/I/)|¬X(/I/)&Y(/I/)&¬C(/I/)
     00017            |X(/I/)&¬Y(/I/)&¬C(/I/)|X(/I/)&Y(/I/)&C(/I/);
     00018            C(/I-1/):=C(/I/)&X(/I/)|C(/I/)&Y(/I/)|X(/I/)&Y(/I/); 'END';
     C0020        S(/I/):=C(/I/);
     00021        'COMMENT' SKIP A LINE AND OUTPUT S;
     C0021            SYSACT(1,14,1);OUTSTRING(1,'(' OUTPUT S IS ')');
     00023        'FOR' I:=1 'STEP' 1 'UNTIL' 11 'DO'
     00023            'IF' S(/I/) 'THEN' OUTSTRING(1,'('1 ')')
     00023                        'ELSE' OUTSTRING(1,'('0 ')');
     C0024        'END'
```

```
   INPUT X IS     1 0 0 1 1 0 1 0 1 0
   INPUT Y IS     1 1 0 1 1 0 1 1 0 0        THE IBM ALGOL PROGRAM ABOVE RESULTS IN
   OUTPUT S IS  1 0 1 1 1 0 1 0 1 1 0        THIS PRINT OUT
```

Program 2.   (ALGOL 60).

should go through the ALGOL part in Tables 1 to 6, cross-referencing to this program to gain an understanding of the language's main features.

6.9.   COBOL

Tables 1 to 6 cover only the most popular facilites of the basic COBOL [7] usually implemented. Virtually every major computer manufacturer has implemented COBOL. Because of COBOL's size and verbosity, various subsets of it have been implemented. However, the larger COBOL compilers go beyond and provide additional facilities such as sorting and report generation.

COBOL is particularly designed to easily define files and record items, to input/output and to manipulate such items, and to do various tasks typical of the business environment.

The structure of COBOL differs from that of the scientific oriented languages. The reader should go through the COBOL part in Tables 1 to 6, cross-referencing to program 3 to gain an understanding of the language's main characteristics.

A COBOL program is divided into four divisions corresponding to the four different categories of information (statements referred to below are those in program 3):

1. Identification Division, in which the program is identified, and the name of the author, date, etc. are specified. See statements 1–3.

2. Environment Division, in which the computer hardware being used is specified; the computer(s) used and the memory size are indicated; user defined names of files (file: an organized collection of related information) are assigned to hardware files (hardware file: a storage device, such as a magnetic tape or a disk, in which the information is stored); etc. See statements 4–12.

3. Data Division, in which the data that the object program will manipulate is described and organized into the logical records and subrecords that will be contained in the files.* For example, statements 15–27 describe a PERMANENT-FILE made up of a series of records. Each record (REKORD-1) is 80 characters long as follows: the first four characters are to be ignored (FILLER indicates so), the next six are alphanumeric (PICTURE X(6)) and make up the subrecord IDNUMBER, the next four are ignored, the next eight are numeric with two decimals (999999V99) and make up COUNT. The next two are ignored, the next twenty-one are alphanumeric and make up IDFIELD and the last thirty-five are ignored.

The storage space needed in main memory to temporarily hold and manipulate records and its subunits is also specified in this division. See statements 52–66.

4. Procedure Division, in which only the executable statements specifying the manipulations to be performed on the data are placed. This is often called the "program"; it is the heart of a complete COBOL program. Refer to statements 67–85 and note that the English-like nature of COBOL assists in understanding the various statements.

The function of program 3 is to update the information stored in a permanent file PERMANENT-FILE and to print out the updated information. This is one of the most common tasks in business data processing [58]. Program 3 reads in a record REKORD-2 which contains a given

---

* Logical record: any consecutive set of related information, organized into a hierarchy. The logical record may be smaller, equal, or even greater than the physical record (e.g., the eighty column IBM punch card).

```
00001    CCC010 IDENTIFICATION DIVISION.
00002    C0C020 PROGRAM-ID. 'UPDATEPM'.
00003    C00030 AUTHOR. A.F.CARDENAS
C00C4    CCC040 ENVIRONMENT DIVISION.
C0005    C00050 CONFIGURATION SECTION.
C0006    C00060 SCURCE-COMPUTER. IBM-360.
00007    C00070 OBJECT-COMPUTER. IBM-360.
C0008    CCC08C INPUT-OUTPUT SECTION.
00009    C00090 FILE-CONTROL.
00010    C00100    SELECT PHILS-INPUT ASSIGN TO 'DATAIN' UTILITY.
00011    CCC110    SELECT PERMANENT-FILE ASSIGN TO 'PERCELL' UTILITY.
00012    C00120    SELECT UPDATED-FILE  ASSIGN TO 'PRINT' UTILITY.
00013    C00130 DATA DIVISION.
C0014    C00140 FILE SECTION.
00015    C00150 FD  PERMANENT-FILE
C0016    C00160    LABEL RECORDS OMITTED RECORDING MODE IS F
C0017    C00170    BLOCK CONTAINS 10 RECORDS
C0018    C00180    RECORD CONTAINS 80 CHARACTERS
00019    C00190    DATA RECORD IS REKORD-1.
C0020    000200 01 REKORD-1.
C0021    C00210    C2 FILLER    PICTURE A(4).
00022    C00220    02  IDNUMBER PICTURE X(6).
C0023    C00230    02  FILLER PICTURE A(4).
00024    C00240    C2  COUNT PICTURE 999999V99.
00025    C00250    C2  FILLER PICTURE A(2).
00026    C00260    C2  IDFIELD PICTURE X(21).
00027    C00270    C2  FILLER PICTURE A(35).
00028    000280 FD  PHILS-INPUT.
00029    000282    LABEL RECORDS OMITTED RECORDING MODE IS F
00030    C00284    BLOCK CONTAINS 10 RECORDS
00031    C00286    RECORD CONTAINS 80 CHARACTERS
00032    C00288    DATA RECORD IS REKORD-2.
00033    000289 01 REKORD-2.
C0034    000290    C2 FILLER PICTURE A(4).
00035    C00300    C2 IDNUMBER PICTURE X(6).
00036    C00310    C2 FILLER PICTURE A(4).
00037    C00320    02 COUNT PICTURE 999999V99.
00038    CCC330    C2 FILLER PICTURE A(58).
00039    C00340 FD  UPDATED-FILE
C0040    000342    LABEL RECORDS OMITTED RECORDING MODE IS F
00041    CCC344    BLOCK CONTAINS 30 RECORDS
00042    C00346    RECORD CONTAINS 80 CHARACTERS
C0043    C00348    DATA RECORD IS REKORD-3.
C0044    C00349 01 REKORD-3.
```

Program 3. (COBOL).

account number (**IDNUMBER**) and some numeric information (**COUNT**) about the account, adds this numeric information to the corresponding information of the record having the same account number stored in the permanent file, and prints out the updated record (**REKORD-3**). For example, if the permanent file contains the 80-character-long records (**b** stands for blank):

bbbbA0000bbbbb00001230bbITEM 1, BREAD LOAVES bbb....bb
bbbbA00002bbbb00150000bbITEM 2, MILK CARTONS bbb....bb
bbbbA00003bbbb00001000bbITEM 3, DOZEN EGGS bbb....bb

and the records read in (**REKORD-2** in file **PHILS-INPUT**) are:

bbbbA00001bbbb00005000bbbbb.........................bb
bbbbA00003bbbb00010000bbbbb.........................bb

```
00045    C00350    02 FILLER PICTURE A(4).
00046    C00360    02 IDNUMBER PICTURE X(6).
00047    C00370    02 FILLER PICTURE A(4).
C0048    C00380    C2 COUNT PICTURE 999999V99.
00049    C00390    02 FILLER PICTURE A(2).
00050    000400    02 IDFIELD PICTURE X(21).
00051    C00410    02 FILLER PICTURE A(35).
00052    C00420 WORKING-STORAGE SECTION
00053    C00430 01  REKORD-1A.
00054    000510    02 FILLER PICTURE A(4).
C0055    C00520    02 IDNUMBER PICTURE X(6).
00056    C00530    02 FILLER PICTURE A(4).
00057    000540    02 COUNT PICTURE 999999V99.
00058    C00550    C2 FILLER PICTURE A(2).
C0059    000560    02 IDFIELD PICTURE X(21).
00060    000570    02 FILLER PICTURE A(35).
00061    000580 01  REKORD-2A.

00062    C00590    02 FILLER PICTURE A(4).
00063    C00600    02 IDNUMBER PICTURE X(6).
00064    000610    02 EILLER PICTURE A(4).
00065    C00620    02 COUNT PICTURE 999999V99.
C0066    C00630    02 FILLER PICTURE A(58).
00067    000670 PROCEDURE DIVISION.
00068    C00680    OPEN INPUT PHILS-INPUT,PERMANENT-FILE,OUTPUT UPDATED-FILE.
00069    C00785 READ-IN-INPUT.
00070    C00790    READ PHILS-INPUT RECORD INTO REKORD-2A AT END GO TO
00071    000791        READ-IN-PERM.
C0072    000800 READ-IN-PERM.
C0073    000810    READ PERMANENT-FILE RECORD INTO REKORD-1A AT END GO TO
00074    000811        LAST-ONE.
00075    C00821    IF IDNUMBER IN REKORD-2A = IDNUMBER IN REKORD-1A GO TO
00076    000821        UPDATE.
C0077    000830    WRITE REKORD-3 FROM REKORD-1A.
00078    C00840    GO TO READ-IN-PERM.
00079    C00850 UPDATE.
00080    000860    ADD COUNT IN REKORD-2A TO COUNT IN REKORD-1A.
00081    000870    WRITE REKORD-3 FROM REKORD-1A.
00082    000880    GO TO READ-IN-INPUT.
00083    000890 LAST-ONE.
00084    000900    CLOSE PHILS-INPUT,PERMANENT-FILE,UPDATED-FILE.
00085    000910    STOP RUN.
```

Program 3. (continued).

the printout is

```
bbbbA00001bbbb00006230bbITEM 1, BREAD LOAVES bbb.....bb
bbbbA00002bbbb00150000bbITEM 2, MILK CARTONS bbb.....bb
bbbbA00003bbbb00011000bbITEM 3, DOZEN EGGS bbb.....bb
```

6.10. PL/I

Tables 1 to 6 cover only the major portion of the full PL/I language [5]. The form and structure of PL/I is very similar to ALGOL's. For example, the block and procedure structuring, the scope of variables, dynamic storage allocation, etc. PL/I's business oriented facilities are rather different to COBOL's, but they permit to do everything that COBOL allows, plus some more, in a more convenient way.

```
1   FIRST: PROCEDURE OPTIONS (MAIN);
                    .
                    .
40          CALL PLOTOUT(PLOTOUTXINT) ;
                    .
                    .
                    .
60          PLOTOUT: PROCEDURE(PLOTOUTXINT) ;
61              DECLARE  LINE(132)            CHARACTER(1);
62              DECLARE K FLOAT DECIMAL (7);
63              PNMAX=MAX(PN);
64              PNMIN=MIN(PN);
65              PUT EDIT ( 'PLOT OF THE FIELD POTENTIAL');(X(55),A) PAGE;
66          PUT EDIT (  ' DISTANCE    MINIMUM POTENTIAL = ',PNMIN,
            'MAXIMUM POTENTIAL = ',PNMAX) (A,E(13,6),X(50),A,E(13,6))
                    SKIP(5);
67              LINE(*)= ' ';
68              IP=0;
69          LOOP2:  DO I=0 TO IMAX BY PLOTOUTXINT;
70              X= I*DX;
71,72           IF MOD(IP,10) = 0 THEN LINE(*) = '-' ;
73              IP= IP + 1;
74,75           LINE(1) = 'I' ;    LINE(118) = 'I' ;
76              K=-(PNMIN*118)/(PNMAX-PNMIN);
77,78           IF K>=1& K<=118 THEN LINE(K) ='+' ;
79              K = (PN(I) - PNMIN*118)/(PNMAX - PNMIN) ;
80,81           IF K <= 1 THEN K=1 ;
82,83           IF K >= 118 THEN K=118 ;
84              LINE(K) = '*' ;
85              PUT EDIT ( X        , ' ',(LINE(K) DO K=1 TO 118))
                    (E(13,6),A(1),(118)A(1)) SKIP(1) ;
86              LINE(*) = ' ' ;
87          END LOOP2 ;
88          END PLOTOUT ;
                    .
                    .
            END FIRST ;
```

Program 4. (PL/I).

Program 4 illustrates the use of procedures and of string (nonmuneric) manipulation capabilities. Although written in PL/I, it still illustrates the concept of procedures (outlined in Section 6.5) and of string manipulation generally available in programming languages. It is assumed that the main part of the program (its statements not shown) stores in a one-dimensional array PN(O), PN(1), ... PN(IMAX) values of a function $y = f(x)$ at x_i, $x_{i+1}, \ldots x_{i+IMAX}$. When the procedure PLOTOUT (statements 60–88) is invoked (statement 40), it produces a discrete plot of the value PN(O), PN(PLOTOUTXINT), PN(2*PLOTOUTXINT), . . ., PN(IMAX) vs. I., where I=0, PLOTOUTXINT, 2*PLOTOUTXINT, . . ., IMAX; that is, a discrete plot of $y = f(x)$ is printed out for a range of x's.

Statements 1 and 89 must always delimit a PL/I program. It is assumed that array PN, and perhaps IMAX, is declared at the beginning of the main program so that it may be known to procedure PLOTOUT and thus used within it (a variable declared in a block or procedure is known throughout the block or procedure, as well as within all other blocks or procedures within it). In the first part of **PLOTOUT**, the maximum and minimum values in **PN** are located (statements 63, 64). In **LOOP2**, a value **K**, where $1 \leq K \leq 118$ since the number of columns to be used for printout is 118, is found for **PN(I)** so that the value of **K** is directly proportional to the value of **PN**. A single blank is stored in each entry of character array **LINE** (statements 67, 86), except the Kth entry which is set to '*'. Then the array **LINE** is printed out. **LOOP2** is executed for **PN(PLOTOUTXINT)**, **PN(2*PLOTOUTXINT)**, . . ., **PN(IMAX)**. The result is a discrete plot, such as the one shown in Figure 2.

The organization of a large program into various modules or procedures is of great utility in actual practice. Not only can each section of the program be executed repeatedly with various parameters if it is organized as a procedure, but it can be actually developed, tested, and debugged separately from the main program. Modularity is important in large programs such as translators.

7. INTERACTIVE PROGRAMMING LANGUAGES: BASIC

The general structure of interactive languages (also called conversational, on-line, or time-sharing languages) and batch-oriented languages is basically the same. The great difference is in the manner in which the language is used: in interactive systems the user is in direct and immediate question and answer operation with the computer, whereas in batch and remote batch systems he is not in such direct communication. Conversational programming languages usually provide facilities similar to those of batch-oriented languages presented in Tables 1 to 6. However, conversational languages provide various additional features for the interactive environment. The interactive characteristics of the language BASIC outlined below are typical of all interactive languages. BASIC is the most popular time-sharing language.

The part of a language that tends to differ the most in the two modes of operation is the I/O. Interactive systems provide the basic batch I/O in more convenient form, as well as new conversational I/O features. This is shown below.

7.1. The Time Sharing Language BASIC

In 1963 a project was started at Dartmouth College in the United States, which by 1966 resulted in the development and implementation of the BASIC language [62]. Soon afterward, industry took the language and be-

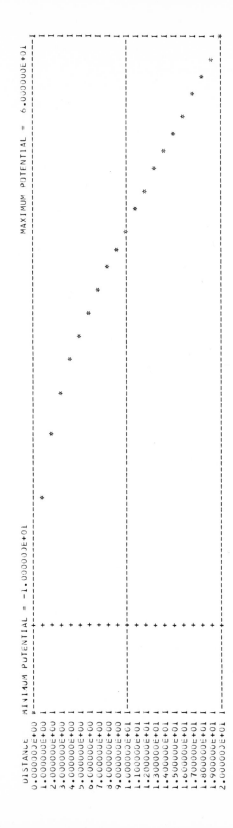

Figure 2. Plot produced by the PL/I Program (Program 4).

gan to market it commercially with the new third generation machines capable of providing immediate on-line response. BASIC is implemented for a wide variety of computers. It is essentially a subset of ALGOL with some powerful extensions for conversational operation [46]. It can be easily learned in a few hours.

The computer and the BASIC user normally talk to each other via a teletypewriter, or a console. The user types in some instructions telling the computer what to do; the system then provides the results immediately. The computer may also display on the teletypewriter some special messages to the user (e.g., programming errors, completion of execution) so that he may take immediate action. All statements are labeled with a number, so that when the program is executed the statements will be executed in the order of ascending statement numbers. The statement number is always followed by an English word that identifies the type of statement that it is.

Table 7 illustrates the manner in which a user could use BASIC to find out how much he would have to get back per year (A) for a given number of years (Y) so as to obtain a required rate of return (R) for an initial investment (I). On top of the listing of Table 7, the indicated statements play the following role:

Statements 10, 25: print out the message enclosed in quotes in the order shown

Statement 20:   a command to input I and R

Statements 30–35: executable statements, which compute the annuity to be received according to the standard formula [63]: $A = I/[1/(1 + R) + 1/(1 + R)^2 + \ldots + 1/(1 + R)^Y]$

Statement 40:   print out the variables indicated

When the user types the **RUN** command, the program is executed. The teletypewriter will type a question mark, indicating that the input is to be typed. After the two numbers are typed, the rest of the program is executed and the solution is printed. The system types **READY** to continue processing.

Suppose now the user wants to obtain the annuity required to earn 12% on an investment of 100,000 for 5, 6, 7, 8, 9, and 10 years. He can do this by writing statements 30, 45, and 50 and then saying **LIST** if it is desired to get the complete new program with the new statements inserted in their proper places. The system says it is **READY** and the user says **RUN**. The system asks for the new input parameters (investment and rate of return) and, once they are typed in the rest of the program is executed and produces the desired results.

Table 7   Interactive Use of BASIC

```
10   PRINT "INPUT INVESTMENT I AND RATE OF RETURN R"
20   INPUT I, R
25   PRINT "INVESTMENT," "RATE," "YEARS," "ANNUITY"
30   LET Y = 5
31   LET F = 0.0
32   FOR K = 1 TO Y STEP 1
33   LET F = F + (1/(1+R)**K)
34   NEXT K
35   LET A = I/F
40   PRINT I, R, Y, A
RUN

INPUT INVESTMENT I AND RATE OF RETURN R
?50000, 0.12
INVESTMENT      RATE      YEARS       ANNUITY
   50000        0.12        5         13869.62
READY

30   FOR Y = 5 TO 10 STEP 1
45   NEXT Y
50   PRINT "THESE CALCULATIONS RELATE TO PROJECT A-11; A. CARDENAS."
LIST

10   PRINT "INPUT INVESTMENT I AND RATE OF RETURN R"
20   INPUT I, R
```

This example illustrates only part of the main features of BASIC. It also provides many other facilities such as IF statements, GO TO statements, array data handling, etc., enough so that it may be used for many significant applications.

8.   COMMENTS TO MANAGEMENT AND USERS ON ACQUISITION AND USE OF HIGHER LEVEL LANGUAGES

With the costs of software now approximating those of hardware [50], and with the rather recent policies of IBM and other manufacturers to separate pricing of hardware and software, the acquisition and use of higher level languages, or any software for the matter, is a critical matter of dollars and cents and of both managerial and user concern.

8.1.   Comments on Acquisition

There are cases in which costs-benefits considerations would advise the availability of certain higher level languages or special programs, but no

Table 7   Interactive Use of BASIC—(continued)

```
25   PRINT "INVESTMENT," "RATE," "YEARS," "ANNUITY"
30   FOR Y = 5 TO 10 STEP 1
31   LET F = 0.0
32   FOR K = 1 TO Y STEP 1
33   LET F = F + (1/(1 + R)**K)
34   NEXT K
35   LET A = I/F
40   PRINT I, R, Y, A
45   NEXT Y
50   PRINT "THESE CALCULATIONS RELATE TO PROJECT A-11; A. CARDENAS."
READY
```

RUN

```
INPUT INVESTMENT I AND RATE OF RETURN R
?100000, 0.12
```

INVESTMENT	RATE	YEARS	ANNUITY
100000	0.12	5	27739.26
100000	0.12	6	24324.98
100000	0.12	7	21910.60
100000	0.12	8	21028.82
100000	0.12	9	18768.76
100000	0.12	10	17699.11

THESE CALCULATIONS RELATE TO PROJECT A-11; A. CARDENAS.

READY

one in the computer installation knows about them or is adequately aware of them. This is perhaps because the supplier of the electronic data processing (EDP) equipment being used, or the favorite salesman, does not point them out because they are a competitor's product. As a result, available software is improperly used or the better software is not acquired for potential users.

Computer systems differ in the type of software provided. Sometimes the system with the proper software is not acquired. Sometimes a computer system is acquired, only to find out a few months later that it is inadequate for the desired new software. Some computers place an inherent limit on the type of software that may be produced for them. Sometimes special application packages are bought at a very high price while not knowing that other suppliers provide them with less facilities but at a much lower cost.

These and many other typical costly situations are usually caused by both the EDP supplier and the EDP user. The EDP salesman naturally tends to be more interested in selling his product. The EDP user usually does not consider seriously other alternatives and their economic implications because he does not know about them or, as is often the case, because he really does not know how to evaluate them properly. As a result, he may end up making a bad decision. Many of these costly errors can be avoided with the aid of independent outside consultants.

8.2. Comments on Use

The typical EDP user has usually faced annoying experiences from the time that the use of computing power is considered to the time that he actually uses it and obtains its benefits. Some of these annoyances must be pointed out so that a user may be on the lookout, and so that the management of computer installations may try to avoid such deterrents of computer utilization.

Sometimes the best software for a given application is available but it is not properly supported by the manufacturer and/or by the computer installation. Proper documentation such as introductory manuals and reference manuals are a "must." The proper atmosphere in the installation toward languages is important. In some places, most of the computer users remain only in the assembly language world, or in the FORTRAN world, for example, and lure other users from the possibility of using other languages that may prove better. Too often the lack of adequate support and environment prevents the use of the proper language. This is one of the functional aspects of a language discussed in Section 5, which a user will consider heavily (consciously or unconsciously) in accepting or rejecting a language.

Most users make frequent programming errors. The total time spent in debugging is usually a considerable portion of total problem solving time. Quite often commercial translators do not provide adequate diagnostics, and the user must then resort to a professional programmer. But to his surprise, programming help may be inadequate or there may even be no professional programmer with good knowledge of the language and computing system; as a result, he will spend an undue amount of time and effort in debugging, and maybe end up with an undebugged program. This costly situation happens too often.

Independent of the languages available, there are always some procedures to be followed in the use of a computer facility. Furthermore, certain special commands coded in the so-called job control language must be properly attached to every program in order to tell the operating system of the computer what to do with the program (e.g., compile it only, compile and execute it, and the like) [64]. Sometimes the procedures for using the computing facility are changed or the required job control language commands are varied for many reasons, and too often the casual user finds out about it only after he submits a program and gets it back rejected. It is imperative that even casual users be notified in writing of all changes that might be of concern; such notifications are a heavy administrative burden.

9. OVERVIEW AND FUTURE OUTLOOK

Without question, one of the main reasons for the tremendous success of computers is the development of higher level languages. With the availability of FORTRAN, ALGOL, COBOL, PL/I, and various other general purpose languages, the communication gap between man and machine has been shortened enough to enable nonspecialists to use the computer in a broad range of disciplines, and to prove its economic benefit. The special purpose languages that also have been developed have, in many instances, taken computing power one step closer to man in the special applications for which they are designed. However, general purpose languages are and will continue to be the most widely used because of their general applicability and because of the support of computer manufacturers.

The batch mode of accessing computers in higher level or more human-like languages, although a very important first step, is still not very convenient in most cases. With the advent of the newer technology and the new generation of computers, on-line languages and systems have been and are being developed to interact more like humans like to interact: quickly and in a conversational mode. Such systems have been very successful. The emphasis of future developments will be in providing better and more economical interaction between the user and the machine. Interactive systems with graphical facilities and systems with more orientation towards natural languages are a step in the right direction. The possibility of practical voice communication with a machine is still too far in the future.

The popularity and use of FORTRAN IV, ALGOL, and COBOL will continue well into the 1970s. PL/I will continue picking up more and more support. Conversational languages such as BASIC, APL, and larger interactive languages such as the interactive versions of FORTRAN and PL/I will continue rising to prominence.

10. REFERENCES

1. Chomsky, N., "Formal Properties of Grammars," *Handbook of Mathematical Psychology*, Luce, Bush, and Galanter (Eds.), Wiley, 1963.
2. Ginsburg, S., *The Mathematical Theory of Context Free Languages*, McGraw-Hill, 1966.

3. DiForino, A. C., "Some Remarks on the Syntax of Symbolic Programming Languages," *Communications of the ACM*, August 1963, pp. 456–460.

4. Gilbert, P., "On the Syntax of Algorithmic Languages," *Journal of the ACM*, January 1966, pp. 90–107.

5. *IBM Systems Reference Library*, "System/360; PL/I Language Specifications," Form C28-8201.

6. Naur, P. (Ed.), "Revised Report on the Algorithmic Language Algol 60," *Computer Journal*, April 1963, pp. 349–367.

7. *U.S. Government Printing Office*, "COBOL-1961: Revised Specifications for a Common Business Oriented Language," D-598941, 1961.

8. Sammet, J., "Fundamental Concepts of Programming Languages," *Computers and Automation*, February 1967.

9. Goldstine, H. H., and A. Goldstine, "The Electronic Numerical Integrator and Computer (ENIAC)," *Math. Tables Aids Comp.*, July 1946, pp. 97–110.

10. Wilkes, M. V., and W. Renwick, "The EDSAC, an Electronic Calculating Machine," *Journal of Scientific Instruments*, December 1949, pp. 385–391.

11. Burks, A. W., H. H. Goldstine, and J. Von Neumann, "Planning and Coding of Problems for an Electronic Computing Instrument," Part I (1946), Part II (1947–48), Institute for Advanced Study, Princeton, N. J.

12. Everett, R. R., "The Whirlwind I Computer," *Electronic Engineering*, August 1952, pp. 681–686.

13. Backus, J., et al., "The Fortran Automatic Coding System," *Proceedings of the Western Joint Computer Conference*, Los Angeles, 1957, pp. 188–198.

14. Van Wijngaarden, A. (Ed.), "Draft Report on the Algorithmic Language ALGOL 68 (Supplement to ALGOL Bulletin 26)," *Mathematisch Centrum* MR93, Amsterdam, Holland, January 1968.

15. Huskey, H. D., R. Love, and N. Wirth, "A Syntactic Description of BC NELIAC," *Communications of the ACM*, July 1963, pp. 367–75.

16. Perstein, M. H., "The Jovial (J3) Grammar and Lexicon," TM-555-002-04, *System Development Corp.*, Santa Monica, Calif., 1966

17. Sammet, J., "Roster of Programming Languages," Computer Directory and Buyers' Guide Issue in *Computers and Automation*, Vol. 19, No. 6B, Nov. 30, 1970, pp. 6–11, 21.

18. Yershov, A. P., et al., "Input Language for an Automatic Programming System," *APIC Studies in Data Processing*, No. 3, Academic Press, 1963.

19. Holland, W. B. (translator), "Report on the Algorithmic Language ALGEC," Memorandum RM-5136, The Rand Co., Santa Monica, December 1966.

20. Sammet, J., *Programming Languages: History and Fundamentals*, Prentice-Hall 1969.

21. McDonald, N., "World Computer Census," Computer Directory and Buyers' Guide Issue in *Computers and Automation*, Vol. 19, No. 6B, November 30, 1970, pp. 53–56.

22. Tiechroew, D., and J. F. Lubin, "Computer Simulation—Discussion of the Technique and Comparison of Languages," *Communications of the ACM*, October 1966, pp. 723–741.

23. Sansom, F. J., and H. E. Petersen, "MIMIC Programming Manual," Technical

Report SEG-TR-67-31, *Systems Engineering Group*, Wright Patterson Air Force Base, Ohio, July 1967.

24. *IBM Systems Reference Library*, "System/360; Continuous System Modeling Program, User's Manual," Form H20-0367-2.

25. Strauss, J. C., et al., "The Sci Continuous System Simulation Language," *Simulation*, December 1967, pp. 281–303.

26. Cárdenas, A. F., and W. J. Karplus, "PDEL—A Language for Partial Differential Equations," *Communications of the ACM*, March 1970.

27. *IBM Systems Reference Library*, "General Purpose Simulation System/360; User's Manual," Form H20-0326.

28. Markowitz, H., et al., SIMSCRIPT: *A Simulation Programming Language*, Prentice-Hall, 1966.

29. Dahl, D., and K. Nygaard, "SIMULA: An Algol-based Simulation Language," *Communications of the ACM*, September 1966, pp. 671–678.

30. Brown, S. A., C. E. Drayton, and B. Mittman, "A Description of the APT Language," *Communications of the ACM*, Vol. 6, No. 11, November 1963.

31. Feldmann, C. G., "Subsets and Modular Features of Standard APT," *Fall Joint Computer Conference*, 1968, pp. 67–73.

32. Sammet, J., and E. Bond, "Introduction to FORMAC," *IEEE Transactions on Electronic Computers*, Vol. EC-13, No. 4, August 1964.

33. Farber, D., et al., "SNOBOL, A String Manipulation Language," *Journal of the ACM*, Vol. 11, No. 1, January 1964.

34. Fenves, S. J., et al., "STRESS: A User's Manual; A Problem Oriented Computer Language for Structural Engineering," MIT Press, Cambridge, Mass., 1964.

35. *Massachusetts Institute of Technology*, "Engineer's Guide to ICES COGO," Dept. of Civil Engineering, R 67-46, Cambridge, Mass., August 1967.

36. Newell, A., et al. (Eds.) *Information Processing Language V Manual*, Prentice-Hall 1965.

37. Weissman, C., *LISP 1.5 Primer*, Dickenson Publishing Co., Belmont, Calif., 1967.

38. Sinowitz, N. R., "DATAPLUS: A Language for Real Time Information Retrieval from Hierarchical Data Bases," *Proceedings, 1968 Spring Joint Computer Conferecne*, pp. 395–401.

39. Rubinoff, M., S. Bergman, H. Cautin, and F. Rapp, "EASY ENGLISH, A Language for Information Retrieval Through a Remote Typewriter Console," *Communications of the ACM*, October 1968, pp. 693–696.

40. Cameron, S. H., D. Ewing, and M. Liveright, "DIALOG: A Conversational Programming System with a Graphical Orientation," *Communications of the ACM*, June 1967, pp. 349–57.

41. *S/360 General Program Library*, "ECAP/360-E, Electronic Circuit Analysis Program," IBM Corporation, 360D-16.4-001.

42. McNamee, L. P., and H. Potash, *A User's Guide and Programmer's Manual for NASAP*, Report No. 68-38, Department of Engineering, University of California, Los Angeles, August 1968.

43. Oppenheim, D. K., and D. P. Haggerty, "META5, A Tool to Manipulate Strings of Data," *Proc. of the ACM 21st National Conference*, 1966, pp. 465–68.

44. Iturriaga, R., et al., "Techniques and Advantages of Using the Formal Compiler

Writing System FSL to Implement a Formula ALGOL Compiler," *Proceedings, 1966 Spring Joint Computer Conference*, pp. 241–52.

45. *Tymshare, Inc. Reference Series*, "Fortran IV," September 1968, 141 pp.

46. Kemeney, J. G., and T. E. Kurtz, *BASIC Programming*, Wiley, 1967.

47. Shaw, J. C., "JOSS: A Designer's View of an Experimental On-Line Computing System," *Proceedings, 1964 Fall Joint Computer Conference*, Vol. 26, Part 1, 1964, pp. 455–64.

48. *IBM Student Text*, "APL/360 Primer," 1969.

49. Theis, D. J., and L. C. Hobbs, "Mini-Computers for Real Time Applications," *Datamation*, March 1969, pp. 39–61.

50. Conway, M. E., "On the Economics of the Software Market," *Datamation*, October 1968, pp. 28–31.

51. Rubey, R. J., "A Comparative Evaluation of PL/I," *Datamation*, November 1968, pp. 20–25.

52. *IBM Systems Reference Library*, "IBM System/360, FORTRAN IV Language," Form C28-6515.

53. McCraken, D., *A Guide to FORTRAN Programming*, Wiley, 1965.

54. Bauman, R. M., et al., *Introduction to ALGOL*, Prentice-Hall, 1964.

55. *IBM System Reference Library*, "IBM System/360, ALGOL Language," Form C28-6615.

56. McCracken, D., *A Guide to ALGOL Programming*, Wiley, 1962.

57. IBM Systems Reference Library, "IBM System/360, COBOL Language," Form C28-6516.

58. McCracken, D., and U. Garbassi, *A Guide to COBOL Programming*, Wiley, 1970.

59. Melichar, Paul R., *COBOL/360, Program Fundamentals*, International Business Machines, 1968.

60. Weinberg, G. S., *PL/I Programming:* A Manual of Style, McGraw-Hill, 1970.

61. Heising, W. P., "FORTRAN IV vs. Basic FORTRAN," *Communications of the ACM*, Vol. 7, October 1964, pp. 590–625.

62. Kemeney, J. G., and T. E. Kurtz, *BASIC, User's Manual*, Dartmouth College Computation Center, Hanover, N. H., January 1966.

63. Weston, F. J., and E. F. Brigham, *Managerial Finance*, Chapter 7, "Capital Budgeting," Holt, Reinhart and Winston, 1966.

64. Brown, G. D., *System/360 Job Control Language*, Wiley, 1970.

The Translation of
Programming Languages

Leon Presser

University of California
Santa Barbara

1. INTRODUCTION

During the system design phase (Chapter 4) of a computer, decisions are made concerning which facilities are to be cast into hardware and which are to be added later to the system by means of software. Thus, when the hardware is completed the computer is capable of obeying a number of wired-in instructions that represent its *machine language*. Since in almost all cases computer hardware is constructed with binary (two-state) devices, a most appropriate machine language program would consist of a string of ones and zeros (e.g., 1011100 . . .); this is indeed the typical situation.

Machine language programs are natural to direct the operations of a computer; but it is a very unnatural and an error-prone process for a human to create such strings of ones and zeros. To alleviate this extremely important man-machine communication problem, a number of programming languages (Chapter 10) have been developed which are more English-like and/or more appropriate to the treatment of problems in certain application areas. Examples of such programming languages are FORTRAN [1] and ALGOL [2, 3], which were designed for scientific applications; COBOL [4] which was directed to business applications; and more recently PL/I [5] which is intended to be a general purpose programming language. These languages are referred to as *high-level languages*.

When a user writes a program in a high-level language this program must be translated into an equivalent machine language program before it can be executed on a computer, which only understands its machine language. Since we want the computer to carry out as much of the work as possible, a *translator* program is written that accepts as input a high-level language program and when executed produces as output an equivalent machine language program which is then executed.

Of course, there are at present a large number of different high-level languages and computers, and a translator is needed for each high-level language-computer combination. Translators are important and expensive components of the software provided with a computer system.

We shall give a brief description of different language levels available for man-computer communication, and then we shall discuss the structure of the various types of translators in existence, generalized systems for the writing of translators, and a number of considerations in the implementation of translators.

2. LANGUAGE LEVELS AND TRANSLATION

2.1. A Microcomputer

For the purposes of our discussion we shall introduce a very simple computer which, we shall assume, will execute our programs. The basic unit of information on this computer is a word consisting of sixteen *binary* digi*ts* (*bits*). Computer words used for instructions have the following format:

Operation code	Register	Reference address

Operation code is a field containing a code that indicates which operation is to be performed. (See Table 1 for the operations allowed.) Since there are twelve different operations, this field need be only four bits long ($2^4 = 16 > 12$). *Register* is a field containing the address of a working register. If we assume that there are two working registers, R0 and R1, this field need be only one bit long ($2^1 = 2$). *Reference address* is a field containing a memory address. If we assume that the memory area consists of 2048 words, this field need be only eleven bits long ($2^{11} = 2048$).

Table 1   Microcomputer Instructions

Operation Name	Operation Mnemonic	Operation Code	Meaning
Load Word	LW	0001	Load the contents of the memory cell designated by the reference address into the register designated by the register field.
Store Word	STW	0010	Store the contents of the register designated by the register field into the memory cell designated by the reference address.
Add Word	AW	0011	Add the contents of the memory cell designated by the reference address and the contents of the register designated by the register field, and store the sum into the register designated by the register field.
Compare Word	CW	0100	Compare the contents of the register designated by the register field with the contents of the memory cell designated by the reference address and set the condition register [a] appropriately.

(*Continued*)

Table 1 (continued)

Operation Name	Operation Mnemonic	Operation Code	Meaning
Branch Greater	BG	0101	If the condition register [a] is set to 10, next execute the instruction located at the memory cell designated by the reference address. If the condition register is not set to 10, proceed to execute the instruction following the BG instruction in the program sequence.
Branch Less	BL	0110	If the condition register [a] is set to 01, next execute the instruction located at the memory cell designated by the reference address. If the condition register is not set to 01, proceed to execute the instruction following the BL instruction in the program sequence.
Branch Equal	BE	0111	If the condition register [a] is set to 00, next execute the instruction located at the memory cell designated by the reference address. If the condition register is not set to 00, proceed to execute the instruction following the BE instruction in the program sequence.
Branch	B	1000	Executed next is the instruction located at the memory cell designated by the reference address.
Input	IN	1001	Transfer information from the input unit into sequential memory cells starting at the cell designated by the reference address. The number of locations transferred depends on the input record size; that is, on the manner in which data is grouped in the input unit. For simplicity, we assume a card reader with a record size of 40 words.

(Continued)

Table 1   (continued)

Operation Name	Operation Mnemonic	Operation Code	Meaning
Output	OUT	1010	Transfer information from sequential memory cells starting at the cell designated by the reference address to the output device. The number of locations transferred depends on the output record size. For simplicity, we assume a typewriter with a record size of 35 words.
Jump Ready	JR	1011	If the input or output (I/O) unit is not carrying out an I/O operation, execute next the instruction located at the memory cell designated by the reference address. If the I/O unit is carrying out an I/O operation, proceed to execute the instruction following the JR instruction in the program sequence. If the register field is set to 0, test the input unit; otherwise, test the output unit.
Stop	S	1100	Stop execution.

[a] We shall assume the existence of a special 2-bit register called the *condition register* (different from the working registers R0 and R1). At the completion of the Compare Word instruction, the condition register is set by the hardware as follows:

Result of Comparison	Condition Register
Contents of working register equal to contents of memory cell	00
Contents of working register less than contents of memory cell	01
Contents of working register greater than contents of memory cell	10

2.2.   Machine Level Language

Suppose that we want to carry out the following procedure on our microcomputer:

1. Input three positive integer numbers now in the input device and go to Step 2.

2. If the first number read is larger than the second number read, output the second number and go to Step 5; otherwise, go to Step 3.

3. If the first number read is smaller than the third number read, output the third number and go to Step 5; otherwise, go to Step 4.

4. Output the first number read and to to step 5.

5. Stop.

Given that the third integer read is smaller than the second integer, the above procedure determines whether the first integer read is above the upper limit set by the second integer, below the lower limit set by the third integer, or between the limits. Assuming that memory locations (i.e., cells, words) are numbered sequentially from 0 to 2047 the machine language program shown in Table 2, which commences at memory location 0, would carry out the above procedure.

In Table 2 the "—" represents "don't care" entries. Furthermore, we assume that the input consists of a card containing only six digits (two digits per number) in its first six columns. Therefore, cells 2003 through 2039 will contain blanks after the input operation is completed.

2.3.   Assembly Level Language and Assemblers

The first step taken to ameliorate the man-computer communication problem was the creation of *assembly language* and assemblers. The main difference between assembly and machine language is that mnemonics (i.e., memory aids) are substituted in assembly language programs for each instruction code, and symbols provided by the programmer are substituted for the other fields of an instruction. Utilizing the mnemonics in Table 1 we can write the above procedure in assembly language form as shown in Table 3.

The translator program that transforms an assembly language program into an equivalent machine language program is referred to as an *assembler*.

Instructions to the assembler are called *pseudoinstructions*. When the assembler encounters a pseudoinstruction it performs a bookkeeping or control operation instead of a translation.

In the above assembly language program **LABEL RES n** is an instruction to the assembler to reserve n cells (and to refer to the first cell with the symbol appearing in the label field) in a data area where data will be stored when the corresponding machine language program is executed. ENTRY is an instruction to the assembler to make the symbol present in the address field accessible to other programs. END notifies the assembler that there are no more instructions to assemble; its address field specifies the location at which program execution is to commence. Notice that, with the exception of pseudoinstructions, there is a one-to-one correspondence be-

Table 2

Memory Location	Machine Language			Comments
0	1001	—	11111010000	Input a record. As a result, the three integer numbers will be stored in cells 2000 through 2002.
1	1011	0	00000000011	Test the input device. If it is idling, go to instruction at cell 3.
2	1000	—	00000000001	Go to the instruction at cell 1.
3	0001	1	11111010000	Load the contents of cell 2000 (first integer read) into working register **R1**.
4	0100	1	11111010001	Compare the first two integers read.
5	0110	—	00000001010	If the first integer read is smaller than the second integer read, go to the instruction at cell 10.
6	0111	—	00000001010	If the first integer read is equal to the second integer read, go to the the instruction at cell 10.
7	0001	1	11111010001	Load the contents of cell 2001 (second integer read) with working register **R1**.
8	0010	1	11111010010	Store the contents of working register **R1** into cell 2002.
9	1000	—	00000001111	Go to the instruction at cell 15.
10	0001	1	11111010000	Load the contents of cell 2000 into working register **R1**.
11	0100	1	11111010010	Compare the first to the third integer read.
12	0110	—	00000001111	If the first integer read is smaller than the third integer read, go to the instruction at cell 15.
13	0001	1	11111010000	Load the contents of cell 2000 into working register **R1**.
14	0010	1	11111010010	Store the contents of working register **R1** into cell 2002.
15	1010	—	11111010010	Output a record. As a result, an integer number representation is typed out.
16	1011	1	00000010010	Test the output device. If it is idling, go to the instruction at cell 18.
17	1000	—	00000010000	Go to the instruction at cell 16.
18	1100	—	-----------	Stop.

Table 3

Assembly Language			
Label	**Operation**	**Address**	**Comments**
J	RES	1	Reserve the next available cell in the data area and name it **J**.
K	RES	1	Reserve the next available cell in the data area and name it **K**.
L	RES	1	Reserve the next available cell in the data area and name it **L**.
START	IN	J	Input a record starting at a cell named **J**. As a result, the three integers will be stored in three consecutive cells starting at **J**.
	ENTRY	START	Make the instruction labeled **START** accessible to other programs.
L1	JR,O	L2	Test the input device. If it is idling go to the instruction labeled **L2**.
	B	L1	Go to the instruction labeled **L1**.
L2	LW,R1	J	Load the contents of **J** into working register **R1**.
	CW,R1	K	Compare the contents of **R1** to contents of **K**.
	BL	L3	If the contents of **R1** are less than the contents of **K**, go to the instruction labeled **L3**.
	BE	L3	If the contents of **R1** are equal to the contents of **K**, go to the instruction labeled **L3**.

tween assembly and machine language programs. See References 6 and 7 and the user's manual of any reasonable assembly language for many other possible pseudoinstructions.

Figure 1 depicts a simple assembler. Figure 2 shows the tables used by the assembler and the information that these tables would contain when our sample program is assembled. Tables are important data structures in the translation process. For an introductory discussion of table design techniques, see Reference 8.

Binary operation codes corresponding to mnemonic operation codes are stored in an op-code table such as Table 1. Similarly, if the register field may contain mnemonics designating any of a number of working registers, a table containing the correspondence between mnemonics and binary register numbers would exist. We assume that the machine language in-

Table 3   (continued)

Assembly Language

Label	Operation	Address	Comments
	LW,R1	K	Load the contents of K into working register R1.
	STW,R1	L	Store the contents of R1 into the cell named L.
	B	L4	Go to the instruction labeled L4.
L3	LW,R1	J	Load the contents of J into working register R1.
	CW,R1	L	Compare the contents of R1 to the contents of L.
	BL	L4	If the contents of R1 are less than the contents of L, go to the instruction labeled L4.
	LW,R1	J	Load the contents of J into working register R1.
	STW,R1	L	Store the contents of R1 into the cell named L.
L4	OUT	L	Output a record starting from the cell named L. As a result, an integer number is typed.
L5	JR,1	L6	Test the output device. If it is idling, go to the instruction labeled L6.
	B	L5	Go to the instruction labeled L5.
L6	S		Stop execution.
	END	START	End of the assembly language program. Begin execution at the instruction labeled START.

structions produced by the assembler are placed in a block of contiguous cells which we call the *machine code memory block*.

The assembler of Figure 1 utilizes two counters. The Instruction Counter (IC) is employed as an index to the machine code memory block; the values of the instruction counter correspond to relative instruction addresses—relative to the beginning of the machine code memory block. Similarly, the Data Counter (DC) is employed as an index to the data area.

The column headed Instruction Counter in the Defined Symbol Table is used to keep track of the location of labeled instructions. The Undefined Symbol Table is employed, during assembly, to keep track of those addresses where the use of a symbol has been encountered before its definition (e.g., when BL L3 is encountered during assembly of the above program, the symbol L3 has not yet been defined). The Undefined Symbol Table is utilized to fill in the undefined addresses when the END pseudoinstruction

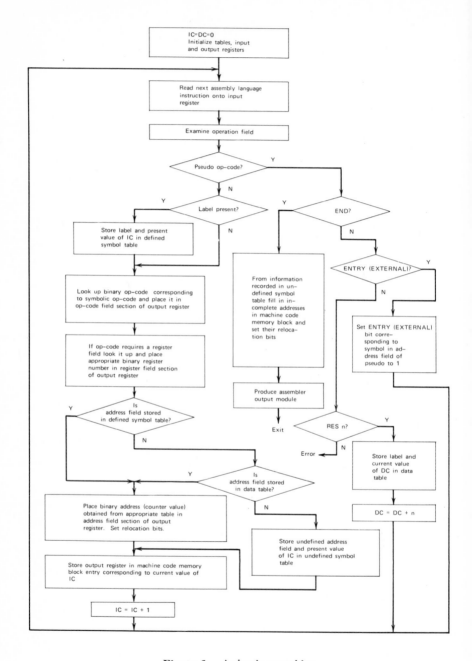

Figure 1. A simple assembler.

Symbol	Data Counter
J	0
K	1
L	2

Data Table

Symbol	Instruction Counter (Symbol Definition)	External (Defined in Other Program)	Entry (Accessible to Other Programs)
START	0	0	1
L1	1	0	0
L2	3	0	0
L3	10	0	0
L4	15	0	0
L5	16	0	0
L6	18	0	0

Defined Symbol Table

Symbol	Instruction Counter (Symbol Usage)
L2	1
L3	5
L3	6
L4	9
L4	12
L6	16

Undefined Symbol Table

Figure 2. Assembler tables.

is encountered. Alternative solutions to the undefined-symbol problem are described in Reference 3. The Data Table relates to the data area.

The simple assembler of Figure 1 requires that assembly language programs have all **RES** pseudoinstructions occurring prior to any reference to the cells they define. It also requires that all **ENTRY** pseudoinstructions appear after the definitions of the symbols in their address fields. Furthermore, the flowchart of Figure 1 assumes the existence of an input register, onto which the next assembly language instruction is read, and the existence of an output register, onto which a machine language instruction is assembled.

Addresses in the assembly language instructions may be classified as follows.

1. Relative instruction addresses corresponding to IC values (e.g., the address field of the instruction **B L1**).

2. Relative data addresses corresponding to DC values (e.g., the address field of the instruction **LW,R1 J**).

3. Nonrelative, or absolute, addresses (e.g., the address field of instruction **J RES 1**).

The output of the assembler is eventually the input to a program called a *loader* (Chapter 6), which is responsible for loading the machine language version of the assembly language program into memory for execution. The loader should be able to locate a given program into whatever memory area is available at loading time. This need arises since other programs (e.g., the loader) are usually present in memory during loading and execution of the program to be loaded, and we wish to make efficient use of memory by loading this program into the smallest contiguous block of cells that satisfies its storage requirements.

The loader must receive information from the assembler specifying for each address produced which ones are relative to the beginning (base) of the machine code memory block, which are relative to the beginning (base) of the data area, and which are not relative (i.e., are absolute). The assembler can obtain this information from its tables and convey it to the loader by associating two bits with the address field of every instruction and setting these bits as follows.

1 0   If address is relative to machine code memory block.

1 1   If address is relative to data area.

0 –   If address is absolute.

Typically [9], the storage for variables (i.e., data area) is embedded within the machine code memory block and thus a single relocation bit suffices. However, for the sake of clarity we have separated the data area from the machine code memory block.

All the addresses produced by the simple assembler of Figure 1 are relative. However, full-size assemblers may produce absolute address fields such as a count [7]. In general, the assembler determines that the address field of an instruction is absolute by examining the operation field or by the fact that it is not symbolic.

It should be emphasized that *relocatable* (i.e., relative) code can be loaded into any section of memory for execution but *absolute* code, which is associated with specific locations in memory, must be loaded into those locations if it is to be executed properly.

In essence, in order to load a program the loader adds the base address at which it is to load the first instruction of the machine code memory block to every relative address in this block referring to an instruction address, and it adds the data area base address to every relative address referring to a data address.

The assembler is responsible for detecting *external symbols*. These are symbols defined in one program and referred to in another program. The user may indicate external symbols to the assembler by means of pseudo-instructions. **ENTRY** designates the symbol names that are defined in this program and may be used by other programs. The pseudocode **EXTERNAL** designates the symbol names that are used in this program and are defined in another program. In order to record information pertaining to external symbols, two one-bit wide columns (**EXTERNAL** and **ENTRY**, respectively) are added to the symbol table.

The output from the assembler to the *operating system*—the supervisory program responsible for overall control of the computer system (Chapter 6) —is a *file*, *module*, or *data set* (i.e., collection of related information) consisting of:

1. *Machine code memory block and associated data*, which contains the machine language instructions and any associated data.

2. *Relocation information*, which designates those addresses in the machine code memory block that are relative to the machine code memory block itself, those that are relative to the data area, and those addresses that are absolute.

3. *External symbol information*, which contains two lists indicating the location within this assembler output module of: symbols that are referred to in this program but defined in other programs, and symbols defined in this program which may be used by other programs.

4. The beginning and length of assembler output module and the address at which execution is to start.

The reader should be able to translate the previous assembly language program into its corresponding machine language program by using Figure 1 and Table 1. The base address for the machine code memory block should be set to 0 and the base address of the data area should be set to 2000. We are assuming that the rectangle labeled *Produce assembler output module* in Fig. 1 is responsbile for formatting the output module as previously described. The assembler tables appearing in Figure 2 show the information they should contain on completion of this translation.

The output of the assembler is the input to a program called a *linker* (Chapter 6) which is responsible for resolving all external references between separately assembled programs. The output of the linker is the input to the loader (see Figure 3). Notice that the overall strategy of translation displayed in Figure 3 permits the very important *modular approach* to programming. That is, a program may be subdivided into subprograms

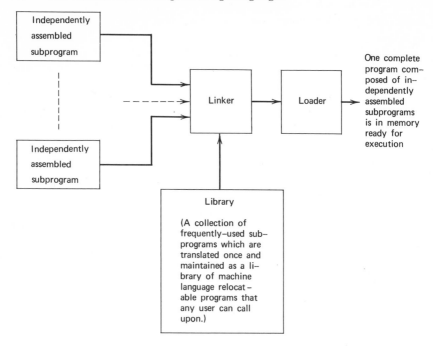

Figure 3. Overview of part of the software of a computer system.

which may be coded, tested, and assembled independently by various programmers maintaining some agreed-upon conventions for communication between their programs.

In summary, the main advantages of assembly over machine language programming are that the writing of programs becomes a little more natural to the human, and the programmer is relieved of some of the bookkeeping tasks. For example, if a new instruction were to be inserted somewhere at the beginning of the machine language program, it would be the responsibility of the machine language programmer to appropriately change the reference address fields of many subsequent instructions. The assembly language programmer need not be concerned with such clerical tasks; the assembler would take care of such chores.

2.4. Higher Level Languages and Compilers

The next step in the process of bringing the level of programming languages closer to that of the human was the development of languages that were not only more natural to the user but also more appropriate to the application areas for which they were intended. The most widely adopted high-level language has been COBOL [4], which is intended for business applications. High-level languages are treated in detail by Alfonso F. Cárdenas in Chapter 10.

We can now write the previous procedure in a high-level language form as follows:

```
INTEGER   J,K,L;
GETDATA;
IF   J>K   THEN   L:= K   ELSE   IF   J≥L   THEN   L:= J;
PUTDATA   L;
STOP
```

Note that the above program consists of four main sections. The first part (**INTEGER J,K,L**) is a declaration which states that **J**, **K**, **L** are integer variables as opposed to floating point variables, for instance. The second section of the program (**GETDATA**) is concerned with the input of data. The third section is a computation part. The fourth section (**PUTDATA L**) is concerned with the output of results. The **STOP** command is interpreted directly by the operating system. The ";" denotes the end of a statement. The input data is present at the input device in the form: (called *data directed*)

$$J = \text{----}, \quad K = \text{----}, \quad L = \text{----};$$

where the ";" indicates end of input. The command **GETDATA** will input such data and store it in the cells previously reserved by the declaration statement for these data items. Similarly, the command **PUTDATA L** will output (print out) results in the form: $L = \text{----}$.

A *compiler* is a translator program that either transforms a high-level language program into an assembly language form for subsequent assembly to machine language or which directly transforms the high-level language program into an equivalent machine language program. Both definitions are employed in the literature. In the remainder of this chapter we shall assume that a compiler outputs assembly code, unless otherwise stated. Notice that in general each high-level language statement will produce a number of assembly (machine) level instructions.

It is now evident that it is a much more natural process to state the above procedure in the high-level language form that in assembly language. Actually, it is even more appropriate than English, which is a very high-level language (albeit full of ambiguities) but is not tailored for expressing the above type of operations.

3. A COMPILER MODEL

In order to convey the flavor of what is involved in the writing of compiler programs, a conceptual model [9–11] of a compiler is displayed in Figure 4.

A translator (e.g., compiler) is activated by the operating system under which it functions. Upon activation, the operating system supplies to the translator two data sets:

1. A data set which contains the program to be translated (i.e., the *source program*).

2. A data set which contains control information (e.g., what kinds of listings are to be produced).

In Figure 4, a rectangle with a missing side represents a data set input to or output from the compiler. We shall next discuss the conceptual model of Figure 4 in some detail.

3.1. Determination of Syntactic Structure

A program in some language is simply a string of symbols where the symbols are elements of some basic vocabulary. When forming strings of symbols over a given vocabulary, we may form "legal" strings (e.g., in conventional infix notation: $A = B + C/D$), and we may also form "illegal" strings (e.g., in infix notation: $A = A + /$). The set of rules that specify the legal symbol combinations of a language is called the *syntax* of the language. Various formalisms exist [2, 12, 13, Chapter 12] for defining the syntax of programming languages. These formalisms are normally referred to as *syntactic metalanguages*, since they are concerned with the syntax of languages. We shall next discuss a possible formalism for syntactic description.

The formalism is best explained by example [2]:

$$\langle DIGIT \rangle \; ::= \; 0|1|2|3|4|5|6|7|8|9$$

Sequences of characters enclosed in the brackets $\langle \; \rangle$ represent metalinguistic variables whose values are sequences of symbols. The metalinguistic mark | has the meaning "OR." The metalinguistic mark $::=$ defines the metalinguistic variable on its left with what appears on its right. Juxtaposition of marks and/or variables signifies juxtaposition of the sequences denoted. Thus, the above example states that a DIGIT is either a 0, or a 1, or a 2, or a 3, . . ., or a 9. We may similarly define LETTER to consist of any of the letters of the alphabet. As another example, consider:

$$\langle IDENTIFIER \rangle \; ::= \; \langle IDENTIFIER \rangle \; \langle LETTER \rangle$$
$$| \; \langle IDENTIFIER \rangle \; \langle DIGIT \rangle$$
$$| \; \langle LETTER \rangle$$

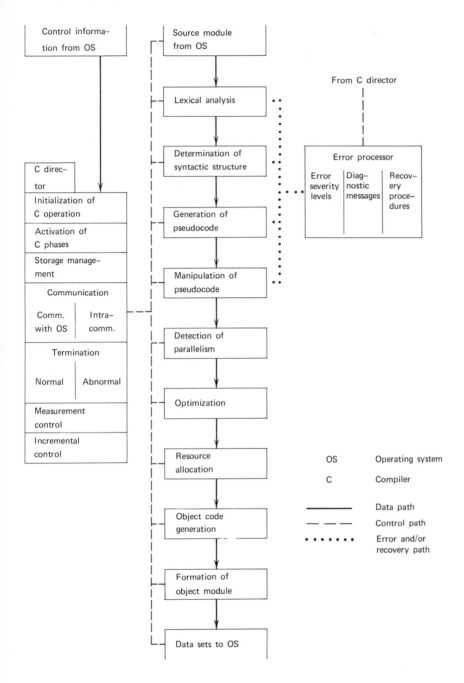

Figure 4. Model of a compiler.

which states that an **IDENTIFIER** is a sequence of letters or digits, the first of which is a letter. This last example illustrates the important concept of *recursion* (what is being defined is referred to in the definition) in syntactic formalisms. For an excellent tutorial discussion of recursion, see Reference 14.

Figure 5 shows the syntactic description of a very simple high-level language. The high-level language program previously discussed is a legal program as far as the syntax displayed in Figure 5 is concerned. The type of formalism presented in Figure 5 is basic to a sound understanding of language definition and translator writing. If one views the ":: =" as a "generator," all possible legal strings in the defined language can be generated from such a syntax definition!

Figure 6 displays in tree form the syntactic structure of the high-level language program previously presented. That is, it shows precisely which syntactic definitions, and in what order, are required to map the syntactic variable PROGRAM (the only variable in Figure 5 that does not appear in the right side of an :: =) into the given string of input symbols (the input program), or vice versa. It is the responsibility of the compiler phase referred to as *determination of syntactic structure* to produce such a syntactic tree structure.

A syntax definition is said to be *unambiguous* if for each possible legal string one and only one syntactic tree structure can be drawn between the string and the metalinguistic variable (called the *distinguished variable*) that does not appear on the right of any :: =. The syntax of Figure 5 is unambiguous. There may exist different syntax definitions that generate exactly the same set of input programs, some may be ambiguous and some unambiguous. If all possible syntax definitions generating the language employed to write the programs are ambiguous, the language is said to be *inherently ambiguous*. In the sequel, we shall see that there is a correspondence between a syntactic tree structure and the meaning of the associated program. Therefore, it is important that programming languages be defined through unambiguous syntax definitions. Otherwise, different syntactic trees could be produced on different translations of a given input program and different results obtained when the translated programs are executed.

The most general technique available to determine the syntactic structure (also referred to as *recognizing* or *parsing*) of a string (e.g., a program) with respect to a defined syntax is to thread through the syntax definition in some organized fashion while attempting to match the syntax definition with the symbols of the string. A syntax definition may contain a number of alternative subdefinitions; thus, when threading through the syntax definition it is possible to reach points from where one could proceed along

```
            ⟨PROGRAM⟩  :: =  ⟨STATEMENT BLOCK⟩
    ⟨STATEMENT BLOCK⟩  :: =  ⟨STATEMENT BLOCK⟩  ⟨STATEMENT⟩  ;
                            | ⟨STATEMENT⟩  ;
           ⟨STATEMENT⟩  :: =  ⟨LABEL⟩  :  ⟨BASIC STATEMENT⟩
                            | ⟨BASIC STATEMENT⟩
               ⟨LABEL⟩  :: =  ⟨IDENTIFIER'⟩
                            | ⟨DIGIT⟩
     ⟨BASIC STATEMENT⟩  :: =  ⟨CONDITIONAL STATEMENT⟩
                            | ⟨UNCONDITIONAL STATEMENT⟩
                            | ⟨DECLARATIVE STATEMENT⟩
                            | ⟨INPUT STATEMENT⟩
                            | ⟨OUTPUT STATEMENT⟩
⟨CONDITIONAL STATEMENT⟩  :: =  ⟨IF STATEMENT⟩  ELSE  ⟨BASIC STATEMENT⟩
                            | ⟨IF STATEMENT⟩
        ⟨IF STATEMENT⟩  :: =  ⟨IF CLAUSE⟩  THEN  ⟨UNCONDITIONAL STATEMENT⟩
           ⟨IF CLAUSE⟩  :: =  IF  ⟨BOOLEAN EXPRESSION⟩
  ⟨BOOLEAN EXPRESSION⟩  :: =  ⟨IDENTIFIER⟩  ⟨RELATIONAL OPERATOR⟩  ⟨IDENTIFIER'⟩
  ⟨RELATIONAL OPERATOR⟩  :: =  <
                            | >
                            | =
                            | ≤
                            | ≥
          ⟨IDENTIFIER'⟩  :: =  ⟨IDENTIFIER⟩
⟨UNCONDITIONAL STATEMENT⟩  :: =  ⟨ASSIGNMENT STATEMENT⟩
                            | ⟨GO TO STATEMENT⟩
 ⟨ASSIGNMENT STATEMENT⟩  :: =  ⟨IDENTIFIER⟩  : =  ⟨IDENTIFIER'⟩
      ⟨GO TO STATEMENT⟩  :: =  GOTO  ⟨LABEL⟩
⟨DECLARATIVE STATEMENT⟩  :: =  ⟨TYPE⟩  ⟨LIST⟩
                ⟨TYPE⟩  :: =  INTEGER
                            | FLOATING
                ⟨LIST⟩  :: =  ⟨IDENTIFIER⟩      ⟨LIST⟩
                            | ⟨IDENTIFIER⟩
          ⟨IDENTIFIER⟩  :: =  ⟨IDENTIFIER⟩  ⟨LETTER⟩
                            | ⟨IDENTIFIER⟩  ⟨DIGIT⟩
                            | ⟨LETTER⟩
      ⟨INPUT STATEMENT⟩  :: =  GETDATA
    ⟨OUTPUT STATEMENT⟩  :: =  PUTDATA  ⟨LIST⟩
              ⟨LETTER⟩  :: =  A
                            | B
                            ⋮
                            | Z
               ⟨DIGIT⟩  :: =  0
                            | 1
                            ⋮
                            | 9
```

Figure 5. Syntax.

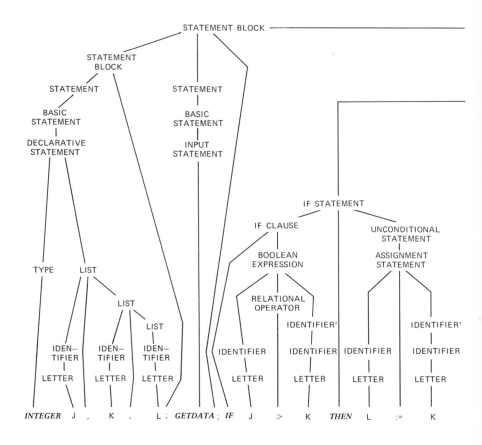

Figure 6. Syntactic tree of sample program.

a number of different paths—only one of which should lead to successful recognition of a string generated by an unambiguous syntax definition. A convenient way to solve this problem is with the mechanism of *backtrack*: when a point of alternative paths is reached the status of the recognizer is recorded, then a single path is selected and pursued until the process is found to be inconsistent with the symbols present in the string or successful determination of the syntactic structure of the complete string is achieved. In the event an inconsistency is found, the recognizer is backtracked to the

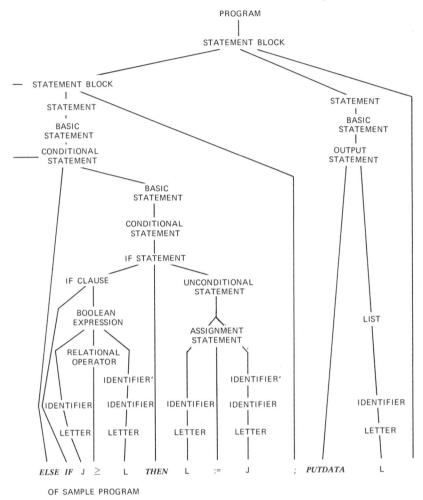

Figure 6. (continued)

last encountered point of alternative paths (last recorded recognizer status) and an alternative path is pursued. This plan of action is continued until successful determination of the syntactic structure of the complete string or exhaustion of possible paths; the latter implies an illegal string.

Two extreme strategies can be followed in determining the syntactic structure of a string. One strategy "grows" the syntactic tree from the distinguished variable downward to the input symbols; this is called a *top-down* strategy [15, 16]. The other "grows" the syntactic tree from the input symbols upward to the distinguished variable; this is called a *bottom-up* strategy [13, 17]. In practice, existent systems employ varying mixtures of these extreme strategies.

A recognizer with the ability to backtrack is powerful but slow since the backtrack mechanism is very time consuming [18]. Several workers [19–27] in the field have succeeded in defining languages amenable to recognition, and thus translation, with specialized techniques that do not require the backtrack mechanism. A subset of such languages is referred to as *precedence languages* and their defining syntax as *precedence syntax*. Precedence languages are unambiguous [22].

The basic idea in the simplest type of precedence languages, called *simple precedence languages*, is that its definition is such that during the recognition process it is possible to determine precisely which alternative syntactic sub-definition to use next by comparing the last syntactic constituent within the recognizer with the incoming symbol in the input string. For a discussion of this topic, see Reference 22. The syntax of Figure 5 defines a simple precedence language.

Another approach to syntax definition (i.e., language design) and to the determination of the syntactic structure of programs is to incorporate unique *key symbols* as a part of possible syntactic subunits (e.g., statements) in the syntax definition. Using these *key words* as a guide, the translator can determine syntactic subunits. For example, IF, THEN, GOTO are key words in the syntax of Figure 5. The BASIC and COBOL languages [28, 29] possess such a syntax definition. The FORTRAN language contains many key words. Existent FORTRAN translators usually employ some form of key word analysis [30].

It should be emphasized that either a backtracking or a precedence approach to the determination of syntactic structure may be implemented with the syntax definition as a parameter. This is not the case when the determination of the syntactic structure is based on key words characteristic of a particular language definition. The precedence approach is superior to the other two; however, in most cases it is only applicable if taken into consideration at the time the programming language is designed.

3.2.   Lexical Analysis

The intial effort in the determination of syntactic structure is concerned with the recognition of relatively simple syntactic entities (*tokens, atoms*) such as identifiers and constants. It turns out that this intial effort is not only very time consuming [18] but also dependent on such practical considerations as character sets and peculiarities of the input facilities of a given computer [10, 31]. Because of these reasons it has been found convenient not only to separate this part from the rest of the process of determination of syntactic structure, but also to define a *lexical analysis* phase with the following responsibilities:

1. To obtain, decode, and buffer source module elements.

2. To recognize and store away in appropriate tables the internal representation of the lexical atoms and members of the language vocabulary that it recognizes and to output information as to where these entities were stored. The output information [10] is a stream of pairs of the form (T,L), where T identifies a table and L identifies the entry within the table T where the atom and/or facts relevant to it reside. Such (T,L) pairs have been referred to as *descriptors*.

Thus, as shown in Figure 4, the lexical analysis operates on the source data set, generating a number of information tables and producing as output a stream of symbol descriptors. It is this stream of descriptors that is input to the section that determines the syntactic structure of the source program. By *information tables* [9] is meant the aggregate of tables which a translator forms and/or uses during the translation process. Notice that the lexical phase not only effects a compression of the input string, but also produces a uniform string of descriptors which facilitates the more complex phase of syntactic structure determination that follows.

Lexical analysis lends itself to an elegant treatment by results in the theory of automata [32, Chap. 12].

3.3. Generation of Pseudocode

It is the responsibility of this phase (see Figure 4) to produce from the syntactic tree structure a linear (i.e., one-dimensional) representation of the tree structure. Since such a linear representation could be interpreted as the machine language of some imaginary computer, it is often referred to as a *pseudocode* representation.

There are a number of ways of representing a tree structure by some linear arrangement of the nodes of the tree. Postfix, or reverse Polish, notation (e.g., A + B becomes AB+ in postfix notation) is an example. For an excellent treatment of techniques for producing linear representation of trees, see Reference 33. For the purposes of our discussion, let us assume that the output of this phase will be in some pseudocode form.

3.4. Manipulation of Pseudocode [34]

In this phase of the compilation process certain manipulations are carried out on the previously generated pseudocode representation of the sequence of operations prescribed in the source program. The main goal of this phase is to simplify the tasks of the remaining compiler stages. Possible manipulations are:

1. *Compilation time computations.* As an example, suppose the source program of some programming language contained the statement

$$I = J + 3*2*5.$$

During this phase the pseudocode representation of this statement may be changed to

$$I = J + 30.$$

2. *Incorporation of compiler-generated calling sequences for contacting external data sets subsequent to translation.* Examples of this type of manipulation are calling sequences for the future incorporation of routines from the library. An important case is the incorporation of I/O routines calling sequences so that the I/O routines are brought into action through these calling sequences at execution time. Interestingly, earlier systems [e.g., Autocoder on IBM 1401] incorporated, during this phase, the actual I/O routines rather than an appropriate calling sequence. However, modern systems [9] employ the calling sequence approach. This permits the operating system to postpone work until the last possible time, that is, execution time.

There are a number of other manipulations that may be carried out during this phase, but the above two are sufficient to convey the flavor.

3.5. Detection of Parallelism

This phase is responsible for extracting the necessary information and transforming the present pseudocode representation of the sequence of operations prescribed in the source module into a pseudocode representation that appropriately displays the inherent parallelism. Based on this pseudocode representation, computations will be sequenced, resources allocated, and object code generated for parallel execution in subsequent phases.

This phase is optional and of main importance to compilers for computer systems with parallel operation capabilities (e.g., Control Data Corp. 6600). For example, if the appropriate hardware units (and supporting software !) exist, the arithmetic expression

$$(A+B) * (C+D) * (E+F) * (G+H)$$

could be computed by evaluating $(A+B)$, $(C+D)$ $(E+F)$, and $(G+H)$ in parallel with four different adders. The results of addition are paired and multiplied in parallel with two different multipliers, and then the final multiplication is performed. This topic is dealt with in References 9, 35, and 38.

Notice that, in essence, as far as the implementation of the parallelizer and optimizer (discussed in the sequel) are concerned, there exists a common kernel, namely the extraction of source module structure. Thus, if these two functional units are to coexist as part of a compiler, they definitely should be designed jointly.

3.6. Optimization

This phase is responsible for extracting the necessary information and transforming the present pseudocode representation of the sequence of operations prescribed in the source module into a pseudocode representation based upon which an "optimum" *object code* (the code finally output by a translator) will be generated.

A compiler may be able to carry the optimization process to various degrees [9]. Hence, the control information supplied by the operating system to the compiler may include an indication of the amount of effort to be dedicated to optimization.

There are many manipulations that can be carried out in order to optimize a program. Possible ones are given below.

1. Elimination of redundant store and/or load instructions. For instance, in the assembly (machine) language version of the sample program which we have been considering, the third and fourth Load Word instructions are redundant and can be eliminated.

2. Detection of computations that are invariant in some larger computations. For example, some computations can be moved from the interior to the exterior of loops [9, 39].

3. Detection of computations that need not be carried to completion. For example, in a programming language which allows logical expressions $A \wedge B \wedge C \wedge D \wedge E$ (where "$\wedge$" represents the logical "AND") will be zero if any component is zero.

4. Detection of statements that will never be executed and thus need not be translated. By examining the possible paths of program flow the translator can detect sections of the program, if any, that will never be executed.

3.7. Resource Allocation and Object Code Generation

It is the responsibility of these phases to allocate available resources and to generate the required object code from both the present pseudocode representation of the sequence of operations prescribed in the source module and the information gathered in the information tables.

In our simple example the allocation of resources by the compiler is limited to assignment to one of two possible working registers; however, the resource allocation problem can be a very complex one [8, 36].

We have already discussed formalisms for syntax definition and methods for forming syntactic structures. The meaning associated with a syntactic structure is often referred to as the *semantics* of the syntactic structure. We may relate semantics to syntax by associating semantic actions (e.g., search a table, generate code) with : (1) each possible right part of a syntax definition, or (2) each possible syntactic subtree, or (3) the complete syntactic tree.

The syntactic definition of a language must be such that it allows the association of the desired semantics with the possible syntactic structures. In order to illustrate this important point consider the following definition:

⟨CONDITIONAL STATEMENT⟩ :: =

If we use the approach of associating semantics with the right parts of syntax definitions, we must define **CONDITIONAL STATEMENT** as in Figure 5, that is:

```
⟨CONDITIONAL STATEMENT⟩  :: =  ⟨IF STATEMENT⟩  ELSE  ⟨BASIC STATEMENT⟩
        ⟨IF STATEMENT⟩  :: =  ⟨IF CLAUSE⟩  THEN  ⟨UNCONDITIONAL STATEMENT⟩
          ⟨IF CLAUSE⟩  :: =  IF  ⟨BOOLEAN EXPRESSION⟩
```

This is necessary in order to be able to insert test and branch instructions at the required places in the code being generated. Notice that both of the above definitions of **CONDITIONAL STATEMENT** recognize the same strings.

Some, or all, of these type of considerations may have been taken care of at the time a pseudocode representation is produced in an earlier phase of compilation. Thus, all that may be needed at this point is to generate assembly code directly from the present pseudocode representation.

Utilizing a very simple approach which associates semantics with possible syntactic subtrees we generate assembly code directly from the syntactic representation in the case of programs in our sample high-level language. Figure 7 displays the semantics to be associated with the syntax of Figure 5. Allocating working register R1 throughout, the reader should be able to compile the program of Figure 6 into its corresponding assembly language version. For further discussion of code-generation techniques, see References 8, 16, 22, and 40.

3.8.   Formation of Object Module

It is the responsibility of this section of the compiler to prepare the assembly language module for transmittal to the operating system. For example, it may be responsible for incorporating the END pseudoinstruction into the assembly language module.

3.9.   Data Sets to Operating System

Based on the control information (e.g., assemble, list) supplied to the compiler by the operating system all data sets required are prepared, if not ready, and made available to the operating system through mediation of the translator director discussed in the sequel. Consider, for example, the formation of the data sets required to implement the following two options:

1. *Assembly.* If necessary, causes the module to be recorded on the expected location, if it does not reside there already, and makes the data set available to the operating system, which eventually supplies it as input to the assembler.

2. *Source module listing.* Normally, during lexical analysis a *record* (a collection of records constitutes a data set) is obtained from the source module and is recorded on the appropriate location; thus, conceptually, it is at this time that the complete data set is made available to the operating system for eventual listing.

3.10.   Compiler Director [9]

It is the function of the *compiler director* to control the overall operation of the compiler and to communicate with the operating system.

The compiler director receives control from the operating system, and when the compilation process terminates (normally or abnormally) it returns control to the operating system. The functional composition of the compiler director is discussed next.

3.10.1.   Initialization of Compiler Director

It is the responsibility of this unit to initialize the compiler before a compilation commences. This involves such tasks as obtaining control information (e.g., programmer-specified options) from the operating system and initializing the communication area and any other unit of the compiler which requires initialization.

3.10.2.   Activation of Compiler Phases

If the compiler is brought into main memory by phases as in [9], it is the responsibility of this unit to request, through the compiler director com-

SYNTACTIC SUBTREES   SEMANTICS

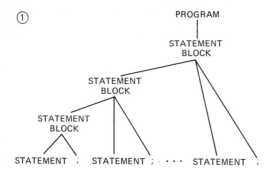

①   Null

② STATEMENT
    |
  BASIC STATEMENT   Null

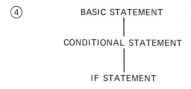

③   If label is present
                                    associate it with the
                                    first instruction of
                                    the basic statement,
                                    otherwise null.

④ BASIC STATEMENT
        |
  CONDITIONAL STATEMENT   Null
        |
  IF STATEMENT

The assembly code associated
with the if statement should
be in the following format:

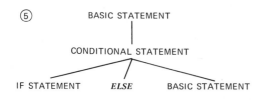

⑤   LW,R— I_1

                                    CW,R— I_2

                                    $\bar{R}$ A,

Figure 7. Semantics.

392

SYNTACTIC SUBTREES	SEMANTICS

assembly code corresponding
to unconditional statement

$$B \qquad A_2$$

$A_1 - -$ assembly code corresponding
to basic statement

$A_2 - -$ $\bar{R}$, I_1 and I_2 are defined in
the associated if statement.
A_1 represents the address
of the first instruction of
the basic statement.
A_2 represents the address
of the instruction immediately following the basic
statement.

$$LW,R- \quad I_1$$
$$CW,R- \quad I_2$$
$$\bar{R} \qquad A_1$$

assembly code corresponding
to unconditional statement.

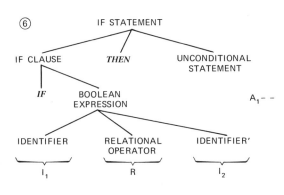

⑥ IF STATEMENT

IF CLAUSE   THEN   UNCONDITIONAL
STATEMENT

IF   BOOLEAN
EXPRESSION $A_1 - -$

IDENTIFIER   RELATIONAL   IDENTIFIER'
OPERATOR

I_1 R I_2

$\bar{R}$ stands for the opcodes
representing the complement
of the relation R (E.g., if
R is BG then $\bar{R}$ is a BL instruction followed by a BE
instruction.)
A_1 represents the address
of the first instruction following the unconditional
statement.

⑦
BASIC STATEMENT

UNCONDITIONAL STATEMENT

Null

⑧
UNCONDITIONAL STATEMENT

ASSIGNMENT STATEMENT

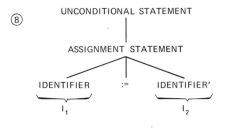

IDENTIFIER   :=   IDENTIFIER'

I_1 I_2

$$LW,R- \quad I_2$$
$$STW,R- \quad I_1$$

Figure 7. (continued)

SYNTACTIC SUBTREES   SEMANTICS

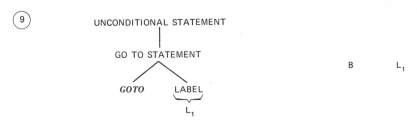

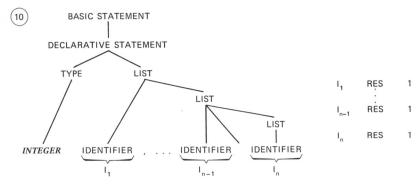

(If the type is *FLOATING*, assume it requires two cells per structure
and thus produce instructions of the form: I RES 2)

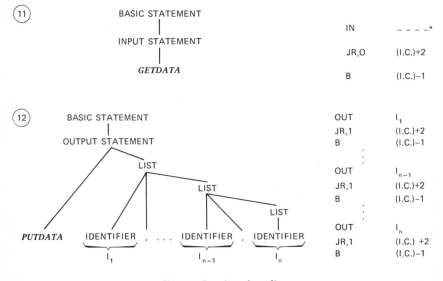

Figure 7. (continued)

SYNTACTIC SUBTREES   SEMANTICS

(13)   IDENTIFIER'
                             | Null
                             |
                         IDENTIFIER

I. C. = Instruction Counter

Note: An address field of the form (I.C.)+2 implies the creation of a unique label to
        refer to the cell corresponding to the present contents of the Instruction Counter
        plus two.

*   The address field is obtained from the input information.

Figure 7. (continued)

munication section, the loading of the required phase and to appropriately
activate it once it is loaded. If all compiler phases reside in main memory,
this unit may only be responsible for the appropriate phase activation.

3.10.3. *Storage Management*

The storage management unit is responsible for requesting storage from
the operating system through the compiler director communication section, for distributing and keeping track of storage assigned to the compiler,
and for releasing storage that the compiler no longer needs to the operating
system.

To understand how this unit may be implemented, assume that the
operating system, upon request, assigns a large storage area to the compiler.
The reserving and freeing of blocks of consecutive memory cells from this
area during compiler execution is referred to as *dynamic storage allocation*
[33]. A good and simple solution to the problem of maintaining a large area
of available storage space is to include within each available block two
additional fields: *Size* field to contain the length (say in bytes or words)
of the block, and a *Pointer* field to point to the beginning address of the
next available block. Assume that the address of the first available block is
contained in a cell called AVAIL. Then the AVAIL list appears as shown
in Figure 8.

When a translator phase submits a storage request, say of n consecutive
words, to the translator director, the director carries out the following steps:

1. Traces through the AVAIL list and according to some strategy selects
a block with at least n contiguous cells.

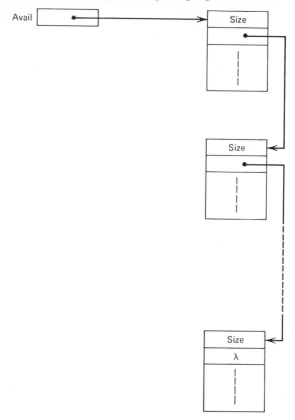

λ is a special symbol which indicates the null pointer
or last block in a list

Figure 8.   The AVAIL list.

2. Makes available the address of the selected block to the requesting phase.

3. Makes the pointer of the block which precedes the one selected in the AVAIL list point to the one which follows the selected block; that is, the selected block is by-passed.

When a request cannot be satisfied, the director can emit a message and give up, or it can request more storage from the operating system, or it can attempt to recover blocks of storage that are no longer in use and place them back in the AVAIL list. For a detailed discussion of possible storage recovery techniques, see References 33 and 41. The important point in a recovery technique is that the director must detect when a block of storage is no longer being used and return it to the AVAIL list. In order to return a block to the AVAIL list, the director sets the pointer of the block being returned to point to the block that AVAIL is pointing to, and sets AVAIL to point to the block being returned.

When the compilation process is complete, the storage area assigned to the compiler is returned to the operating system. Note that the operating system itself may employ the above strategy to manage main storage.

3.10.4. Communication

The responsibilities of the communication unit may be discussed in two parts:

1. *Communication with operating system.* This section is responsible for performing such tasks as:

    (a) Requesting I/O.

    (b) Notifying the operating system (calling program) of whether a compilation came to a normal or abnormal termination; in the latter case it supplies the operating system with error information.

    (c) Communicating with a user through operating system mediation.

2. *Intracommunication.* This section is a central gathering area employed for communication among the various compiler phases. It may contain such information as:

    (a) Programmer-specified options.

    (b) An indication of the starting points of the information tables (e.g., through pointers).

    (c) An indication of the phase currently in control.

3.10.5. Termination

This unit is responsible for performing and/or overseeing whatever tasks (e.g., formation of object module) are necessary when the compilation process terminates. There exist two cases:

1. *Normal termination,* which occurs when an indication (e.g., end-of-file) of end of source program is encountered.

2. *Abnormal termination,* which occurs when the error level (discussed below) exceeds a predefined threshold during the compilation process.

3.10.6. Measurement Control

It is the responsibility of this unit to direct the collection of data (i.e., measurements) about the compilation process and the compiler performance. Measurements may be gathered through software probes strategically located throughout the compiler.

The measurement process can be carried to varying degrees. Hence, as part of the control information supplied by the operating system to the compiler there may be an indication of the amount of effort to be dedicated to the collection of measurement data. With the aid of this unit the compiler designers (and the users) can isolate bottlenecks and thus are able to focus compiler improvement efforts. For a detailed discussion of this unit, its utilization and cost, see Reference 18.

3.10.7. Incremental Control

The incremental control unit is responsible for the additional control functions that an incremental compiler must carry out. Incremental compilers are discussed in Section 4.

3.11. Error Processor

Conceptually, it is the responsibility of the error processor of a translator to perform the following tasks for each error detected in the process of translation.

1. Record its location, if possible.

2. Assign an error severity level.

3. Select, prepare, and record on the appropriate data set a diagnostic message.

4. Pass the error severity level to the translator director.

5. If so instructed by the translator director, to attempt an appropriate recovery procedure and inform the translator director of the outcome.

The fact that in Figure 4 the error processor is only connected to the earlier sections of the compilation process should be interpreted as implying that the bulk of the error analysis takes place in these early stages.

I must emphasize that the structural description of a compiler introduced here represents a very general conceptual model. In practice, for reasons of efficiency, some of the functional units discussed, if present, may be diffused throughout the translator. Moreover, some of the units described here as part of the compiler director are often considered the domain of the operaring system. This is justifiable since the tasks carried out by these units are common to complex programs such as compilers.

4. INCREMENTAL COMPILERS

Compilers, as discussed thus far, do not allow a programmer to modify or execute program statements during compilation. These compilers suffice

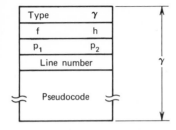

Figure 9. Data structure used by incremental compiler for representation of program elements.

if the computer installation operates in a *batch* mode. That is, the programmer submits his program to the computer operator who collects a number of programs, inputs the batch to the computer system, and eventually returns computer outputs to the programmers.

In the modern *on-line* (Chapter 7) mode of operation of computer systems, the user inputs information to the computer and receives information from the computer through a console. In such an interactive environment it is desirable to provide the user with the ability to modify and/or execute program statements during compilation. Compilers that allow these features have been referred to as *on-line*, *interactive*, and *conversational* compilers. In particular, such compilers have been called *incremental* if it is possible to modify, delete, or insert a program statement without recompiling the complete program.

An incremental compiler must maintain the structure of the program being translated as a set of self-contained linked elements (e.g., statements) in order to localize the effect of program modifications. For example, following the work of Lock [42], we may employ the data structure shown in Figure 9 to represent the syntactic elements of Figure 5.

Referring to Figure 9 we have:

TYPE   contains an indication of element type: statement block, declarative statement, input statement, etc.

γ is an integer that specifies the number of words in the element.

f is a pointer to the element representing the next logical statement in the program.

h is a pointer to the element representing the structure of which this element is a component.

p_1, p_2 are pointers depending on element type and are only used in the following element types.

TYPE	p_1 POINTS TO	p_2 POINTS TO
Statement Block	list of declarative statements	list of statements other than declarative statements
If Statement	statement following **THEN**	Statement following **ELSE**

line number	is a unique number for each element which may be used for reference by the programmer for editing and execution.
pseudocode	is the pseudocode version of high-level language element. It is assumed here that it is possible to generate the corresponding high-level language element from its pseudocode representation.

Figure 10 displays our sample high-level language program utilizing the data structure discussed above. Notice that it is possible to modify, delete, or insert a program statement without recompiling the complete program. Moreover, the data structure shown in Figure 9 is powerful enough to support the implementation of an incremental ALGOL compiler [42].

Incremental compilers require additional facilities in order to control the execution of incrementally compiled code. The incremental control section previously mentioned, as part of the compiler director, is responsible for structuring the program being compiled and controlling the execution of such incrementally compiled code [42–45].

5. INTERPRETERS

In compilation, a pseudocode representation of the complete source program is generated when the phase that determines syntactic structure is completed. As the compilation process proceeds, this pseudocode is manipulated and transformed until eventually machine code is generated.

A pseudocode representation could be interpreted as the machine language of some pseudocomputer. A computer and associated routines that behave as such a pseudocomputer are referred to as an *interpreter* of the corresponding pseudocode.

The main difference between an interpreter and a compiler is that an interpreter determines the syntactic structure of source language statements one at a time, and as the pseudocode of each statement is produced, it is immediately executed on the associated pseudocomputer.

Interpreters are popular translators which possess the following advantages over compilers.

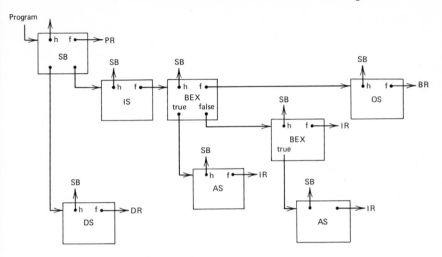

SB	=	<STATEMENT BLOCK>
DS	=	<DECLARATIVE STATEMENT>
IS	=	<INPUT STATEMENT>
OS	=	<OUTPUT STATEMENT>
AS	=	<ASSIGNMENT STATEMENT>
BEX	=	<BOOLEAN EXPRESSION>
PR	=	PROGRAM RETURN
BR	=	BLOCK RETURN
DR	=	DECLARATION RETURN
IR	=	IF-STATEMENT RETURN

Figure 10. Incremental compiler representation of sample program.

1. They are easier to implement.

2. Errors (*bugs*) are easier to trace, since statements are translated and executed one at a time.

They also possess the following disadvantages.

1. They do not allow tasks, during translation, that require examination of program being translated as a whole. (Examples of such tasks are detection of parallelism and optimization.)

2. They have slower execution times.

The model of Figure 4 corresponds to a compiler; however, all that is required to accommodate the process of interpretation is to assume that source language statements are analyzed one at a time and that the generated pseudocode is input to the appropriate pseudomachine for interpretation.

6. EMULATORS

A machine language instruction may be envisioned as a series of *micro-instructions* of a lower level (e.g., register-to-register). Consequently, each machine language instruction may be thought of as a *microprogram*. As a result of technological advances, many modern computer systems (e.g., various IBM System/360 models), making explicit use of this fact, include a fast-read control store which contains the microprograms corresponding to the "machine language" instructions [60]. Thus, the "machine language" of these computers may be modified by appropriate microprogram alterations.

Following Rosin [46], we may use the term emulator to describe the complete set of microprograms which, when embeded in a control store, define a "machine language." We may call the computer associated with this "machine language" the *guest computer* and the computer that supports the microprograms the *host computer* [46]. The difference between an interpreter and an emulator is that the former produces a (pseudo) computer by traditional programming methods while the latter produces a (guest) computer through microprogramming techniques.

The point here is the fact [47] that it is possible to think of languages, such as FORTRAN, ALGOL, PL/I, or some lower-level language, as the machine language of some imaginary computer and to produce an emulator for such a computer. As indicated in Reference 46, more information is needed on the implications of such an approach to language implementation. Notice that in order to simplify the preparation of emulators a language for writing microprograms is required, which in turn necessitates a translator.

7. TRANSLATOR WRITING SYSTEMS

Translator writing systems (TWS) have been described by several names such as Syntax Directed Compilers, Metacompilers, and Compiler-Compilers (C^2). By a translator writing system we mean the approach and/or aggregate of tools that facilitates the writing of translators for various languages and different computers.

A TWS may be defined parametrically as a device that accepts as input four different sets of specifications:

1. A source language syntax specification (L_S).
2. A specification of a translation algorithm (TA).
3. A specification of the computer (C_T) on which the translator (T) to be produced is to translate.

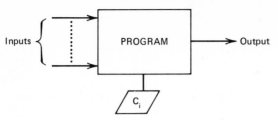

Figure 11.   Program, with a single or multiple number of inputs, operating on computer C_i.

4. A specification of the computer (C_E) which will execute programs translated by the C_T–T combine.

The TSW outputs a T which operates on C_T. The generated T accepts as input a program, P_S, written in the specified source language L_S and outputs a machine language program, P_M, for the specified computer C_E. Finally, data is input to P_M and results are obtained from P_M. This general definition or conceptual model of a TWS as a function of time is presented as Figure 12; the notation explained in Figure 11 is used. The TWS functions as, or on, another computer designated C_M.

Existing TWS satisfy this definition to varying degrees. No present system contains all of the defined facilities. Typically, we encounter systems where $C_M = C_T$ and a partial specification of C_E is embedded in TA. Techniques for syntax specification are well known (e.g., Figure 5), while

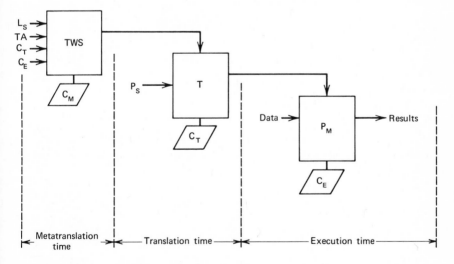

Figure 12.   Model of a translator writing system.

the ability to completely specify a computer to a translator is an open problem. For a detailed treatment of TWS, and an extensive list of pertinent references, see References 11 and 48.

8. MODULARITY, SYSTEM INTEGRATION, AND DOCUMENTATION

The successful and efficient development and subsequent maintenance of a large programming effort requires careful consideration and planning. Translators are usually relatively large and important programs; therefore, their implementation should be well planned. An excellent approach to translator implementation is to redefine the task as the programming of a set of modules [18]—each module with well-defined inputs and outputs.

The modular architecture of a translator is of importance because of the following reasons:

1. In some cases, the operating system might not require parts (modules) of the translator. For instance, optimization may be an optional feature, as in the case of Reference 9.

2. Modularity permits future growth (or reduction) of a translator with minimal effort.

3. Modularity permits replacement of modules for more (or less) efficient versions.

4. Modularity facilitates translator maintenance, and, in particular, it facilitates the writing of programs which exercise the various parts (modules) of a translator.

5. Modularity facilitates system integration, since modules may be checked out independently.

6. Modules can be programmed by programmers who need not be familiar with the details of the entire project.

Adequate documentation is of importance to the proper maintenance and use of translators. Three types of documentation should exist:

1. *Structural-functional.* Delineates the structural or functional composition of the translator and its interfaces with the rest of the software.

2. *Detailed.* Well-commented code.

3. *Maintenance.* Describes maintenance procedures.

9. SUMMARY

This chapter has discussed a number of topics relating to the problem of programming language translation. For more detailed information, the reference list contains extensive bibliographies. Particularly, References 3, 6–8, 10, 13, 23, 30, 31, 40, and 49–59 are pointed out as possible concurrent or subsequent reading material.

With respect to the future, we may expect translator writing to be influenced by:

1. Newer computer generations having a higher level machine language than previous generations, thus simplifying the writing of translators.

2. The combination of technological advances and a better understanding of the man-computer communication problem, which will allow a more complete integration of hardware and software considerations in programming language and translator design.

3. The development of powerful translator writing systems.

10. REFERENCES

1. McCracken, D. D., *A Guide to FORTRAN IV Programming*, John Wiley and Sons, Inc. New York, 1965.

2. Dijkstra, E. W., *A Primer of ALGOL 60 Programming*, Academic Press, Inc., New York, 1962.

3. Wegner, P., *Programming Languages Information Structures and Machine Organization*, McGraw-Hill, Inc., New York, 1968.

4. McCracken, D. D., *A Guide to COBOL Programming*, John Wiley and Sons, Inc., New York, 1963.

5. Bates, F., and Douglas, M. L., *Programming Language One*, Prentice-Hall, Inc., Englewood Cliffs, New Jersey, 1967.

6. Flores, I., *Computer Software*, Prentice-Hall, Inc., Englewood Cliffs, New Jersey, 1965.

7. Gear, C. W., *Computer Organization and Programming*, McGraw-Hill, Inc., New York, 1969.

8. Hopgood, F. R. A., *Compiling Techniques*, American Elsevier Publishing Company, Inc., New York, 1969.

9. IBM System/360 Operating System FORTRAN IV (H) Program Logic Manual, Form Y20-0012-0.

10. Cheatham, T. E., Jr., The Theory and Construction of Compilers CA-6606-0111, Computer Associates, Inc., Wakefield, Massachusetts, 1966.

11. Presser, L., The Structure, Specification, and Evaluation of Translators and Translator Writing Systems, Report No. 68-51, Department of Engineering, University of California, Los Angeles, California, 1968.

12. Chomsky, N., "Formal Properties of Grammars," in *Handbook of Mathematical Psychology, Vol. 2*, Luce, Bush and Galanter (Eds.), John Wiley and Sons, Inc., New York, 1963, pp. 323–418.

13. Evans, A., "An ALGOL 60 Compiler," in *Annual Review in Automatic Programming, Vol. 4*, Pergamon Press Limited, England, 1964, pp. 87–124.

14. Minsky, M., *Computation: Finite and Infinite Machines*, Prentice-Hall, Inc., Englewood Cliffs, New Jersey, 1967.

15. Metcalfe, H. H., "A Parametrized Compiler Based on Mechanical Linguistics," in *Annual Review in Automatic Programming, Vol. 4*, Pergamon Press Limited, England, 1964, pp. 125–165.

16. Cheatham, T. E., and Sattley, K., Syntax Directed Compiling, Proceedings AFIPS 1964 SJCC, Vol. 25, pp. 31–57.

17. Feldman, J. A., "A Formal Semantics for Computer Languages and Its Application in a Compiler-Compiler," *Comm. ACM*, Vol. 9, January 1966, pp. 3–9.

18. Presser, L., and Melkanoff, M. A., "Software Measurements and Their Influence Upon Machine Language Design," *Proceedings AFIPS 1969 SJCC*, Vol. 34, pp. 733–737.

19. Floyd, R. W., "Syntactic Analysis and Operator Precedence," *Journal ACM*, Vol. 10, July 1963, pp. 316–333.

20. Floyd, R. W., "Bounded Context Syntactic Analysis," *Comm. ACM*, Vol. 7, February 1964, pp. 62–67.

21. Knuth, D. E., "On the Translation of Languages from Left to Right," *Information and Control*, Vol. 8, Oct. 1965, pp. 607–639.

22. Wirth, N., and Weber, H., "EULER—A Generalization of ALGOL, and Its Formal Definition: Part I," *Comm. ACM*, Vol. 9, January 1966, pp. 13–25.

23. McKeeman, W. M., et al., *A Compiler Generator*, Prentice-Hall, Inc., Englewood Cliffs, New Jersey, 1970.

24. Presser, L., and Melkanoff, M. A., Transformation to Simple-Precedence, Dept. of Engineering, University of California, Los Angeles, California, 1968.

25. Crespi-Reghizzi, S., and Presser, L., "Extensions to Precedence Techniques for Syntactic Analysis," *Proceedings Purdue Centennial Year Symposium on Information Processing*, April 1969, Vol. 1, pp. 161–172.

26. Haynes, H. R., Extended Simple Precedence Syntactic Analysis, Report TSN-8, Computation Center, The University of Texas, Austin, Texas, 1969.

27. Colmerauer, A., "Total Precedence Relations," *Journal ACM*, Vol. 17, January 1970, pp. 14–30.

28. Kemeny, J. G., and Kurtz, T. E., *Basic Programming*, John Wiley and Sons, Inc., New York, 1968.

29. Conway, M. E., "Design of a Separable Transition-Diagram Compiler," *Comm. ACM*, Vol. 6, July 1963, pp. 396–408.

30. Lee, J. A. N., *The Anatomy of a Compiler*, Reinhold Publishing Corp., New York, 1967.

31. Cocke, J., and Schwartz, J. T., Programming Languages and Their Compilers, Courant Institute of Mathematical Sciences, New York University, New York, 1969.

32. Johnson, L. W., et al., "Automatic Generation of Efficient Lexical Processors using Finite State Techniques, *Comm. ACM*, Vol. 11, December 1968, pp. 805–813.

33. Knuth, D. E., *The Art of Computer Programming: Vol. 1, Fundamental Algorithms*, Chapter 2, Addison-Wesley Publishing Co., Reading, Massachusetts, 1968.

34. Cheatham, T. E., Jr., The Architecture of Compilers, CAD-64-2-R, Computer Associates, Inc., Wakefield, Massachusetts, 1964.

35. Baer, J. L., and Bovet, D. P., "Compilation of Arithmetic Expressions for Parallel Computation," *Proceedings IFIPS 1968, Software 1*, Booklet B, pp. 4–10.

36. Martin, D., The Automatic Assignment and Sequencing of Computations on Parallel Processor Systems, Report No. 66-4, Dept. of Engineering, University of California, Los Angeles, Calif, 1966.

37. Baer, J. L., Graph Models of Computations for Computer Systems, Report No. 68–46, Department of Engineering, University of California, Los Angeles, Calif., 1968.

38. Russell, E. C., Jr., Automatic Program Analysis, Report No. 69–12, Dept. of Engineering, University of California, Los Angeles, Calif., 1969.

39. Lowry, E. S., and Medlock, C. W., "Object Code Optimization," *Comm. ACM*, Vol. 12, January 1969, pp. 13–22.

40. Forsythe, A. I., et al., *Computer Science: A First Course*, John Wiley and Sons, Inc., New York, 1969.

41. Weizenbaum, J., "Symmetric List Processor," *Comm. ACM*, Vol. 6, September 1963, pp. 524–544.

42. Lock, K., "Structuring Programs for Multiprogram Time-Sharing On-Line Applications," *Proceedings AFIPS 1965 FJCC*, Vol. 27, Part 1, pp. 457–472.

43. Ryan, J. L., et al., "A Conversational System for Incremental Compilation and Execution in a Time-Sharing Environment, *Proceedings AFIPS 1966 FJCC*, Vol. 29, pp. 1–21.

44. Katzan, H., Jr., "Batch, Conversational, and Incremental Compilers," *Proceedings AFIPS 1969 SJCC*, Vol. 34, pp. 47–56.

45. Rishel, J. R., "Incremental Compilers," *Datamation*, Vol. 16, January 1970, pp. 129–136.

46. Rosin, F. R., "Contemporary Concepts of Microprogramming and Emulation," *Computing Surveys*, Vol. 1, December 1969, pp. 199–212.

47. Weber, H., "A Microprogrammed Implementation of EULER on IBM System/360 Model 30, *Comm. ACM*, Vol. 10, September 1967, pp. 549–558.

48. Feldman, J., and Gries, D., "Translator-Writing Systems," *Comm. ACM*, Vol. 11, February 1968, pp. 77–113.

49. Davis, R. M., "Programming Language Processors," in *Advances in Computers*, Vol. 7, Academic Press, Inc., New York, 1966, pp. 117–180.

50. Glass, R. L., "An Elementary Discussion of Compiler/Interpreter Writing," *Computing Surveys*, Vol. 1, March 1969, pp. 55–77.

51. Halstead, M. H., *Machine-Independent Computer Programming*, Spartan Books, Washington, D. C., 1962.

52. Grau, A. A., et al., "Translation of ALGOL 60," in *Handbook for Automatic Computation*, Vol. I, Part b, Bauer, et al. (Eds.), Springer-Verlag New York, Inc., 1967.

53. Ingerman, P. Z., *A Syntax Oriented Translator*, Academic Press, Inc., New York, 1966.

54. Randell, B., and Russell, L. J., *ALGOL 60 Implementation*, Academic Press, Inc., London, 1964.

55. Brooks, F. P., and Iverson, K. E., *Automatic Data Processing System/360 Edition*, John Wiley and Sons, Inc., New York, 1969.

56. Bolliet, L., "Compiler Writing Techniques," in *Programming Languages*, Genuys (Ed.), Academic Press, Inc., New York, 1968, pp. 113–288.

57. Freiburghouse, R. A., "The Multics PL/I Compiler," *Proceedings AFIPS 1969 FJCC*, Vol. 35, pp. 187–199.

58. Rosen, S. (Ed.), *Programming Systems and Languages*, McGraw-Hill, Inc., New York, 1967.

59. Gauthier, R., and Ponto, S., *Designing Systems Programs*, Prentice-Hall, Inc., Englewood Cliffs, New Jersey, 1970.

60. Husson, S. S., *Microprogramming: Principles and Practices*, Prentice-Hall, Inc., Englewood Cliffs, New Jersey, 1970.

Formal Languages and
Their Related Automata

David F. Martin

University of California
Los Angeles

1. INTRODUCTION

In most sciences the study of physical, or "real world," objects has motivated the development of abstract mathematical formalisms to be used as models of their real-life counterparts. The intended use of such theoretical models is to provide a general framework whose study hopefully yields greater understanding, intuition, and insight concerning the physical systems that they represent.

Computer science is no different in this respect. Formal languages and automata are mathematical systems used as theoretical models of computation. The motivation for the development of these models arose from the study of "natural" (i.e., biological) and man-made computers, as well as natural (e.g., English) and "artificial" (e.g., computer programming) languages.

In this chapter a hierarchy of formal languages and a related hierarchy of automata will be introduced. These hierarchies grew out of formal methods developed by Chomsky [8] for the description and classification of languages by grammars. This material is part of a "core" of subject matter with which everyone seriously interested in computer science should be familiar.

1.1. Principal Results

The principal results presented here relate classes of formal languages to classes of automata by demonstrating that formal grammars and automata are equivalent chracterizations of classes of languages. In reality, only very special kinds of automata, *acceptors*, will be considered here. An acceptor is an automaton that processes its input and delivers essentially one bit of output information: *input accepted* or *input not accepted*. In addition to the previously mentioned equivalence, formal languages and automata (acceptors) will be placed in hierarchies that indicate their relative generality.

All of these results are summarized in the ladderlike structure of Figure 1. The horizontal "rungs" indicate the equivalence of certain classes of formal languages and automata, for example, context-free languages and push-down store automata. The vertical "sides" represent the parallel hierarchies of formal languages and automata.

1.2. Overall Plan

Because of space limitations, it is not possible to cover completely the entire subject of formal languages and their related automata. The primary

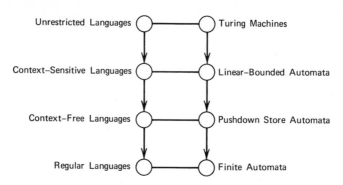

Formal Languages   *Automata (Acceptors)*

Figure 1.   The related hierarchies of the formal languages and automata.

focus here will be on the *characterization theorems* relating classes of formal languages and automata.

A section on mathematical preliminaries (Section 2) is included for completeness. Next, in Section 3, a brief introduction to the hierarchy of phrase-structure languages is provided. Various classes of formal languages are discussed in more detail in Sections 4, 7, and 12; classes of automata are presented in Sections 5, 8, 10, and 13. The characterization theorems relating formal languages and automata are given in Sections 6, 9, 11, and 14. Elementary decision problems are discussed in Section 15, and references to related topics for further study are given in Section 16.

Almost no proofs of theorems are given, but many examples are provided. The reader who is interested in proofs should consult the cited references.

I hope that this brief presentation will encourage a further study of formal languages and automata. There are many books and research papers on this fascinating and challenging subject.

2.   MATHEMATICAL PRELIMINARIES

In order that this tutorial chapter be self-contained, certain mathematical notions will be introduced in this section.

2.1.   Sets

A *set* is a collection of objects, called the *elements* or *members* of that set. The members of a set A can be specified explicitly, for example,

$$A = \{a, b, c, \ldots\},$$

or as a collection of objects all of which possess a common attribute, for example,

$$A = \{x \mid x \text{ has a given attribute}\}.$$

The notation $x \in A$ means that x is an element (or member) of set A, and $x \notin A$ means the contrary.

A set that has a finite number of elements is called a *finite set*; otherwise it is an *infinite set*. A set whose elements can be placed in one-to-one correspondence with the natural numbers $\{0, 1, 2, \ldots\}$ is called a *countable* set; otherwise, it is *uncountable*. For example, $A = \{a_0, a_1, a_2, \ldots\}$ is countable, whereas $B = \{t \mid t > 0\}$ is not. Only countable sets will be used in the remainder of this chapter. A finite set is always countable. The number of elements in a finite set A is called the *order* or *cardinality* of A, written $|A|$, for example,

$$A = \{a_1, a_2, \ldots, a_k\}; \qquad |A| = k.$$

Two sets A and B are *equal* if and only if they contain exactly the same elements, that is, every element of A is an element of B and vice versa. Let A and B be sets. B is a *subset* of A, written $B \subseteq A$, if every element of B is also an element of A. Thus A is a subset of itself, that is, $A \subseteq A$. The notion of subset can be used to define set equality, namely, $A = B$ if and only if $A \subseteq B$ *and* $B \subseteq A$. Any subset B of A which is *not* equal to A is called a *proper subset* of A, written $B \subset A$ or sometimes $B \subsetneq A$.

2.2. Operations on Sets

There are several elementary operations that can be performed on sets:

(*a*) *Intersection.* The *intersection* of two sets A and B, written $A \cap B$, is the set of elements common to A and B, defined as

$$A \cap B = \{x \mid x \in A \wedge x \in B\}.$$

The symbol $\wedge$ is read "and." Obviously $A \cap A = A$. If A and B have *no* elements in common, they are said to be *disjoint*, and their intersection contains no elements. It is convenient to define a set that contains no elements, the *empty set* Φ. Then if A and B are disjoint, $A \cap B = \Phi$. Note that

(i) Φ is finite; $|\Phi| = 0$.

(ii) $A \cap \Phi = \Phi$, where A is any set.

(iii) Φ is a subset of *every* set, that is, $\Phi \subseteq A$.

(*b*) *Union.* The *union* of two sets A and B, written $A \cup B$, is the aggregate set of elements in A and B, defined as

$$A \cup B = \{x \mid x \in A \vee x \in B\}.$$

The symbol $\lor$ is read "or." Note that

(i) $A \cup A = A; \; A \cup \Phi = A.$
(ii) $A \cap B \subseteq A \cup B.$

(c) *Difference.* The *difference* of two sets A and B, written $A - B$, is the set of elements in A but *not* in B, defined as

$$A - B = \{x \mid x \in A \land x \in B\}.$$

Note that

(i) $A - A = \Phi; \; A - \Phi = A.$
(ii) if $A \subseteq B$, then $A - B = \Phi.$

(d) *Complement.* If $B \subseteq A$, the difference $A - B$ is called the *relative complement of B with respect to A*. It is sometimes convenient to define an absolute complement by introducing the "universal" set of "all" objects W. Care must be taken to not make this set too all-encompassing, or anomalies such as Russell's paradox [45] result. For our purposes, it will be assumed that W is such that no such difficulties arise. Under this assumption, the *absolute* complement of a set A, written $\bar{A}$, is defined as $W - A$. Note that

(i) $\bar{\Phi} = W - \Phi = W.$
(ii) $\bar{W} = W - W = \Phi.$
(iii) if A is a set, $A \subseteq W.$

2.3. Algebra of Sets

Let A, B, and C be sets. The intersection, union, and absolute complement operations obey the

(a) Commutative laws:
$$A \cap B = B \cap A$$
$$A \cup B = B \cup A$$

(b) Associative laws:
$$A \cap (B \cap C) = (A \cap B) \cap C$$
$$A \cup (B \cup C) = (A \cup B) \cup C$$

(c) Distributive laws:
$$A \cup (B \cap C) = (A \cup B) \cap (A \cup C)$$
$$A \cap (B \cup C) = (A \cap B) \cup (A \cap C)$$

(d) DeMorgan's Laws:
$$\overline{(A \cap B)} = \bar{A} \cup \bar{B}$$
$$\overline{(A \cup B)} = \bar{A} \cap \bar{B}$$

2.4. Sets of Sets

The objects of which sets are composed can of course, themselves be sets. If S is a set of sets, for example, $S = \{A, B, C, \ldots\}$ where $A, B, C, \ldots$ are sets, care must be exercised in the use of notation, namely, if $A \in S$ and $x \in A$, it is *not* meaningful to write $x \in S$. A very important set of sets is the *set of all subsets* or *power set* of a set A, written 2^A and $P(A)$, respectively. It is defined as

$$2^A = \{B \mid B \subseteq A\}.$$

If A is finite, then so is 2^A, and

$$|2^A| = 2^{|A|}.$$

For example, if $A = \{a,b\}$, then

$$2^A = \{\Phi, \{a\}, \{b\}, \{a,b\}\}.$$

2.5. Cartesian Product

Let A and B be sets. The *Cartesian product* of A and B, written $A \times B$, is the set of *ordered* pairs defined as

$$A \times B = \{(a,b) \mid a \in A \wedge b \in B\}.$$

The cartesian product of more than two sets is analogously defined, that is, $A_1 \times \ldots \times A_k = \{(a_1, \ldots, a_k) \mid a_1 \in A_1 \wedge \ldots \wedge a_k \in A_k\}$. Note that in general $A \times B \neq B \times A$, and that $(A \times B) \times C \neq A \times (B \times C)$.

2.6. Binary Relations on Sets

A *binary relation* R between (members of) two sets A and B is defined as any subset of $A \times B$, that is, $R \subseteq A \times B$. For example, let $A = \{a,b\}$ and $B = \{1,2,3\}$. The relation $R = \{(a,1), (b,2), (b,3)\}$ can be represented by the Boolean matrix (matrix of zeros and ones)

$$\begin{array}{c} \\ a \\ b \end{array} \begin{array}{ccc} 1 & 2 & 3 \\ \left[\begin{array}{ccc} 1 & 0 & 0 \\ 0 & 1 & 1 \end{array}\right]. \end{array}$$

If $A = B$, then $R \subseteq A \times A$ is called a relation *on* A. The *composition* of two relations $R_1 \subseteq A \times B$ and $R_2 \subseteq B \times C$, written $R_1 R_2$, is defined as

$$R_1 R_2 = \{(a,c) \mid (a,b) \in R_1 \wedge (b,c) \in R_2\}.$$

It is readily verified that the Boolean matrix representation of the composition of two relations is the (Boolean) product of their individual Boolean matrix representations. Composition, like matrix product, is associative but *not* commutative.

Let R be a relation on a set A. The *transitive closure* of R, written R^+, is defined as

$$R^+ = \bigcup_{k=1}^{\infty} R^k,$$

where R^k is the k-fold composition of R with itself. The *reflexive transitive closure* of R, written R^*, is defined as

$$R^* = \bigcup_{k=0}^{\infty} R^k = R^0 \cup R^+,$$

where R^0 is the *identity relation* $\{(a,a) \mid a \in A\}$ on A, represented by the unit Boolean matrix.

The transitive closure of a relation R is the least transitive relation containing R. The concept of transitive closure is most easily understood in terms of connectivity and paths on directed graphs. A directed graph consists of a set of *nodes* $N = \{n_1, n_2, \ldots, n_k\}$ and a set of directed *arcs* (arrows) connecting nodes to one another. A directed graph is shown in Figure 2a.

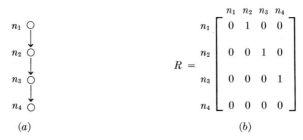

(a)   (b)

Figure 2.   An example directed graph and its corresponding direct connectivity relation. (a) A directed graph. (b) Corresponding direct connectivity relation.

Let the direct connectivity relation R on N be defined as

$$R = \{(n_i, n_j) \mid \text{there is an } arc \text{ from } n_i \text{ to } n_j\}.$$

The Boolean matrix representation of R is given in Figure 2b. The transitive closure of R is

$$R^+ = \{(n_i, n_j) \mid \text{there is a } path \text{ from } n_i \text{ to } n_j\},$$

where a *path* is a sequence of one or more arcs connected in a head-to-tail fashion. For example, in Figure 2a, there is a path from n_1 to n_4. The reader can verify that

$$R^k = \{(n_i,n_j) \mid \text{there is a path of exactly } k \text{ arcs from } n_i \text{ to } n_j\}.$$

The relation R^+ consists of all pairs of nodes between which there exists a non-null path. A node n_j is *reachable* from a node n_i if (1) there exists a non-null path from n_i to n_j, or (2) $n_i = n_j$, that is, n_j is reachable from itself. Thus the reflexive transitive closure of R is

$$R^* = \{(n_i,n_j) \mid n_j \text{ is } reachable \text{ from } n_i\}.$$

The Boolean matrix representations of R^+ and R^* are

$$R^+ = \begin{bmatrix} 0 & 1 & 1 & 1 \\ 0 & 0 & 1 & 1 \\ 0 & 0 & 0 & 1 \\ 0 & 0 & 0 & 0 \end{bmatrix}; \qquad R^* = \begin{bmatrix} 1 & 1 & 1 & 1 \\ 0 & 1 & 1 & 1 \\ 0 & 0 & 1 & 1 \\ 0 & 0 & 0 & 1 \end{bmatrix}$$

2.7. Mappings (Functions)

Let A and B be sets. A *mapping* (or *function*) f of A *into* B, written $f\colon A{\to}B$, is a binary relation between A and B such that every $a \in A$ is related to exactly one $b \in B$. The set A is called the *domain*, and B the *range*, of f. If $b = f(a)$, then $b \in B$ is called the *image of $a \in A$ under f*, and $a \in A$ the *preimage of $b \in B$ under f*. Notice that the domain and/or range of a function may be sets of sets. We shall often encounter in the sequel functions whose ranges are sets of sets.

2.8. Strings

Let $V = \{b_1, b_2, \ldots, b_n\}$ be a finite, nonempty set of *symbols* called an *alphabet* or *vocabulary*. A *string* is a finite number of juxtaposed symbols from a vocabulary, including the null string. An example is $x = a_1a_2...a_k$, where $a_i \in V$ for all i. If $k = 0$, x is the *empty* or *null string*, written λ, that is, $x = \lambda$. The *length* of a string x, written $\lg(x)$, is equal to the number of symbols in x, for example,

$$\lg(a_1a_2...a_k) = k,$$

$$\lg(\lambda) = 0.$$

Let $x = a_1a_2...a_k$ and $y = b_1b_2...b_m$ be two strings. These strings are equal $(x = y)$ if and only if

$\qquad$ (a) $\lg(x) = \lg(y)$, that is, $m = k$;

and

$\qquad$ (b) $a_i = b_i, \qquad i = 1,2,...,k.$

2.9.   Operations on Strings

1. *Reversal (Reflection, Transposition).*   If $x = a_1a_2...a_k$, the *reversal* of x, written x^R, is $x^R = a_ka_{k-1}...a_1$.

2. *Concatenation.*   Let x and y be the strings defined above. the *concatenation* of x and y, written $x \cdot y$ (the dot is often omitted), is

$$x \cdot y = a_1a_2...a_kb_1b_2...b_m.$$

Concatenation is

(i)   associative: $x \cdot (y \cdot z) = (x \cdot y) \cdot z$;
(ii)   *not* commutative: $x \cdot y \neq y \cdot x$.

The null string λ functions as an identity element under concatenation, that is, $x \cdot \lambda = \lambda \cdot x = x$.

3. *Powers.*   If x is a string, the (nonnegative, integral) powers of x are defined as

$$x^0 = \lambda$$
$$x^1 = x$$
$$x^k = x \cdot x^{k-1}, \qquad k = 2,3,...$$

2.10.   Substrings

A string y is a *substring* of a string x if there exist strings u,v such that $x = uyv$. If $uv \neq \lambda$, then y is a *proper substring* of x.

2.11.   Languages

Any (countable) of L of strings over a vocabulary V is called a *language*. If L is a lnaguage, any string $x \in L$ is called a *sentence* (or *word*) of L. If L is finite, then L is called a *finite language*; Otherwise L is an *infinite language*. For example, let $V = \{a,b\}$. The language $L_1 = \{\lambda, aa, aba, abba\}$ is finite, whereas $L_2 = \{a^kb^k \mid k = 0, 1, 2, ...\}$ is infinite.

2.12.   Operations on Languages

Since languages are sets, the operations of union and intersection can be applied to them. Also important are the following operations on languages.

1. *Reversal.*   If L is a language, its *reversal* L^R is the language $L^R = \{x^R \mid x \in L\}$.

2. *Concatenation (Product).*   Let L_1 and L_2 be languages. Their *concatenation* (or *product*), written $L_1 \cdot L_2$ (or simply L_1L_2), is defined as

$$L_1 \cdot L_2 = \{x_1x_2 \mid x_1 \in L_1 \wedge x_2 \in L_2\}.$$

Concatenation is (as before):

(i) associative: $L_1 \cdot (L_2 \cdot L_3) = (L_1 \cdot L_2) \cdot L_3$

(ii) *not* commutative: $L_1 \cdot L_2 \neq L_2 \cdot L_1$

Define a set Λ containing only the null string, that is, $\Lambda = \{\lambda\} \neq \Phi$. Then Λ functions as the identity when concatenating languages, that is, $L \cdot \Lambda = \Lambda \cdot L = L$. Note that since Φ has no elements, $L \cdot \Phi = \Phi \cdot L = \Phi$.

(a) *Concatenation distributive over union*

$$L_1 \cdot (L_2 \cup L_3) = (L_1 \cdot L_2) \cup (L_1 \cdot L_3)$$

(b) *Union not distributive over concatenation*

$$L_1 \cup (L_2 \cdot L_3) \neq (L_1 \cup L_2) \cdot (L_1 \cup L_3)$$

(c) *Concatenation not distributive over intersection*

$$L_1 \cdot (L_2 \cap L_3) \neq (L_1 \cdot L_2) \cap (L_1 \cdot L_3)$$

(d) *Intersection not distributive over concatenation*

$$L_1 \cap (L_2 \cdot L_3) \neq (L_1 \cap L_2) \cdot (L_1 \cap L_3)$$

3. *Powers*

$$L^0 = \Lambda$$
$$L^1 = L$$
$$L^k = L \cdot L^{k-1}, \quad k = 2,3...$$

4. *Closure.* The *closure* of a language L, written L^*, is the set of all *finite* strings constructed from the elements of L, including the null string. L^* is defined as

$$L^* = \bigcup_{k=0}^{\infty} L^k.$$

Note that $\Lambda^* = \Lambda$ and $\Phi^* = \Lambda$ ($\Phi^0 = \Lambda$). It is often convenient to consider a closure that specifically does *not* contain the null string. For this purpose $L^+ = L^* - \Lambda$ is defined.

5. *Complementation.* If L is a language over vocabulary V, then $L \subseteq V^*$. Hence the *complement* of L, written $\bar{L}$, is defined as

$$\bar{L} = V^* - L = \{x \epsilon V^* \mid x \notin L\}.$$

3. PHRASE-STRUCTURE LANGUAGES

The most interesting languages are nearly always infinite. A deep study of the properties of these language is made much more convenient by defining a class of finitely describable systems for generating them, called *phrase-structure grammars* (PSG's). Unfortunately, phase-structure grammars cannot generate *all* languages, but they do generate a sufficiently large and interesting class of languages, giving rise to a large and important body of knowledge within computer science. This class of languages, called *phrase-structure languages* (PSL's) has provided useful models for many disciplines of computer science, notably the automatic translation of programming languages and the modelling of computation itself.

The classic hierarchy of phrase-structure grammars and languages studied by Chomsky [8] is the subject of this section.

3.1. Phrase-Structure Grammars

A *phrase-structure grammar* is a system $G = (V_N, V_T, P, S)$ where:

1. V_N is a vocabulary called the *nonterminal vocabulary*.
2. V_T is a vocabulary called the *terminal vocabulary*.
3. $V_N \cap V_T = \Phi$; $V = V_N \cup V_T$ is called the *total vocabulary*.
4. $S \in V_N$ is a special member of V_N called the *distinguished symbol* or *head of the language*.
5. P is a finite subset of $V^+ \times V^*$, called the set of *productions* or *rewriting rules*. Normally pairs from $V^+ \times V^*$ would be written (x, y), but a special notation will be used, namely, $x \rightarrow y$. The notation $x \rightarrow y$ is read: "the string x is rewritten as the string y," where $x \in V^+$, $y \in V^*$.

A grammar generates a language in the following way:

(a) Start with a string (called the *string in hand*) consisting only of the distinguished symbol.

(b) Apply productions from P to the string in hand until it consists only of terminal symbols (members of V_T). Such a string of terminal symbols is said to be *a member of the language generated by G*.

Example 3-1. Consider $G = (\{A, B\}, \{a, b\}, P, A)$, where P consists of

$$
\begin{array}{ll}
A \rightarrow Ba & B \rightarrow BB \\
Aa \rightarrow Bb & B \rightarrow b \\
B \rightarrow bA & A \rightarrow a \\
Ab \rightarrow \lambda &
\end{array}
$$

The generation of *bbab* in G is

$$A \Rightarrow Ba \Rightarrow bAa \Rightarrow bBb \Rightarrow bbAb \Rightarrow bbab.$$

The above derivation was obtained via

Production Applied	String in Hand Obtained
	A
$A \to Ba$	Ba
$B \to bA$	bAa
$Aa \to Bb$	bBb
$B \to bA$	$bbAb$
$A \to a$	$bbab$

Example 3-2. Consider the pseudo-English grammar $G = (V_N, V_T, P, \langle \text{sentence} \rangle)$, where

$$V_N = \{ \langle \text{sentence} \rangle, \langle \text{noun phrase} \rangle, \langle \text{verb phrase} \rangle,$$
$$\langle \text{prepositional phrase} \rangle \},$$

$V_T = \{A, B, \ldots, Z, a, b, \ldots, z, \_, .\}$, and P consists of

$\langle \text{sentence} \rangle \to \langle \text{noun phrase} \rangle \langle \text{verb phrase} \rangle$
$\langle \text{noun phrase} \rangle \to \langle \text{noun phrase} \rangle \langle \text{prepositional phrase} \rangle$
$\langle \text{noun phrase} \rangle \to$ A_friend_
$\langle \text{prepositional phrase} \rangle \to$ of_a_friend_
$\langle \text{verb phrase} \rangle \to$ is_a_friend_indeed.

The language generated by G consists of sentences of the form
A_friend_{of_a_friend_}$_0^\infty$ is_a_friend_indeed. The operator $\{ \ \}_0^\infty$ indicates that the phrase "of_a_friend_" may appear zero or more times, e.g., A_friend_of_a_friend_of_a_ friend_of_a_friend_is_a_friend_indeed.

3.2. Derivations

The process of using a grammar to generate strings is sometimes called *derivation*. A string v is *immediately derived from* a string u in a phrase-structure grammar $G = (V_N, V_T, P, S)$, written $u \underset{G}{\Rightarrow} v$, if there exist strings $z_1, z_2 \in V^*$, $x \in V^+$, $y \in V^*$, such that

$$u = z_1 x z_2$$
$$v = z_1 y z_2$$
$$x \to y \in P$$

A string v is *derived from* a string u in a phrase-structure grammar G, written $u \underset{G}{\overset{*}{\Rightarrow}} v$, if there exist, for $r \geq 0$, strings $w_0, w_1, \ldots, w_r$ such that

$$u = w_0$$
$$w_i \underset{G}{\Rightarrow} w_{i+1}, \qquad 0 \leq i < r$$
$$w_r = v$$

The case $r = 0$ implies that $u = v$, that is, no immediate derivations are involved. The relation $\overset{*}{\underset{G}{\Rightarrow}}$ is the reflexive transitive closure of $\underset{G}{\Rightarrow}$. If it is desired to exlude the case $r = 0$ $(u = v)$, the transitive closure $\overset{+}{\underset{G}{\Rightarrow}}$ of $\underset{G}{\Rightarrow}$ can be defined. When no confusion results, $\underset{G}{\Rightarrow}$, $\overset{*}{\underset{G}{\Rightarrow}}$ and $\overset{+}{\underset{G}{\Rightarrow}}$ will be written simply $\Rightarrow$, $\overset{+}{\Rightarrow}$, and $\overset{*}{\Rightarrow}$. The concept of derivation can be used to formalize the notion of a language generated by a phrase-structure grammar.

The language $L(G)$ generated by a phrase-structure grammar $G = (V_N, V_T, P, S)$, called a *phrase-structure language*, is defined as

$$L(G) = \{x \in V_T^* \mid S \overset{*}{\underset{G}{\Rightarrow}} x\}$$

Two PSG's G_1 and G_2 are called *weakly equivalent* if they generate the same language, that is, $L(G_1) = L(G_2)$.

3.3.   The Empty Language

The *empty language* is the language containing no strings at all, that is, the *empty set*. The empty language is generated by any grammar that does not generate any strings consisting entirely of terminal symbols. For example, the grammar $G = (\{S\}, \{a\}, \{S \rightarrow aS\}, S)$ generates sentential forms $a^k S$, $k = 1, 2, 3, \ldots$, but since none of them consists entirely of terminal symbols, $L(G) = \Phi$.

3.4.   Types of Phrase-Structure Grammars and Languages

The most general form of production allowed in phrase-structure grammars is $(x,y) \in V^+ \times V^*$. Chomsky [8] has, by placing certain restrictions on the elements of P, defined a hierarchy of phrase-structure grammars and languages.

3.4.1.   Unrestricted (Type 0) Phrase-Structure Grammars

An *unrestricted* (type 0) PSG is one in which no restrictions are placed on the productions in P, that is, P is a finite subset of $V^+ \times V^*$. No loss of generality results from specifying that P be a finite subset of $V_N^+ \times V^*$, because each terminal symbol in $x \rightarrow y$ can be replaced by its own nonterminal "stand-in." Productions of the form $x \rightarrow \lambda$, $x \epsilon V^+$, are called *erasing rules*.

Example 3-3. Consider the grammar $G' = (\{A,B,C,D\},\ \{a,b\},\ P',\ A)$ where P' consists of

<table>
<tr><td>1. $A \to BC$</td><td>6. $B \to D$</td></tr>
<tr><td>2. $AC \to BD$</td><td>7. $A \to C$</td></tr>
<tr><td>3. $B \to DA$</td><td>8. $C \to a$</td></tr>
<tr><td>4. $AD \to \lambda$</td><td>9. $D \to b$</td></tr>
<tr><td>5. $B \to BB$</td><td></td></tr>
</table>

It should be clear that $L(G') = L(G)$, where G is the grammar of Example 3-1. The nonterminals C and D are "stand-ins" for the terminal symbols a and b. The languages generated by type 0 PSG's are known as the *recursively enumerable sets*. Informally, a recursively enumerable set is one whose elements can be generated by a procedure, that is, by a sequence of steps that can be carried out "mechanically" by, say, a computer.

3.4.2. Context-Sensitive (Type 1) Phrase-Structure Grammars

A *context-sensitive* (Type 1) PSG is one in which all productions are of the form

$$z_1 A z_2 \to z_1 x z_2,$$

where $z_1, z_2 \in V^*$, $A \in V_N$, and $x \in V^+$. In the above production, the nonterminal symbol A is rewritten as the (non-null) string x only in the "context" $z_1\_\_\_z_2$. The strings z_1 and z_2 are called the *left* and *right contexts* of A, respectively. It should be noted that under the above restrictions, no context-sensitive grammar can generate the null string. In order to circumvent this "difficulty," the special production $S \to \lambda$ is sometimes allowed, provided that the rest of the productions satisfy the above restrictions, and that the distinguished symbol S does not appear on the right hand side of any production. The latter condition is easily arranged.

Example 3-4. The context-sensitive grammar $G = (\{S,T,B,C,D\}, \{a,b,c\}, P, S)$, where P consists of

<table>
<tr><td>$S \to \lambda$</td><td>$CB \to CD$</td></tr>
<tr><td>$S \to T$</td><td>$CD \to BD$</td></tr>
<tr><td>$T \to aTBD$</td><td>$bB \to bb$</td></tr>
<tr><td>$T \to abD$</td><td>$D \to c$</td></tr>
<tr><td>$DB \to CB$</td><td></td></tr>
</table>

generates $L(G) = \{a^k b^k c^k \mid k \geq 0\}$. For example, the derivation of $a^2 b^2 c^2$ is

$$S \Rightarrow T$$
$$\Rightarrow aTBD$$
$$\Rightarrow aabDBD$$
$$\Rightarrow aabCBD$$
$$\Rightarrow aabCDD$$
$$\Rightarrow aabBDD$$
$$\Rightarrow aabbDD$$
$$\Rightarrow aabbcD$$
$$\Rightarrow aabbcc.$$

3.4.3. Context-Free (Type 2) Phrase-Structure Grammars

A *context-free* (Type 2) PSG is one in which all productions are of the form

$$A \rightarrow x,$$

where $A \in V_N$ and $x \in V^*$. The nonterminal symbol A is rewritten as the (possibly null) string x regardless (or *free*) of the context surrounding A. Context-free grammars can generate the null string.

Example 3-5. The context-free grammar $G = (\{S\}, \{a,b\}, P, S)$ where P consists of

$$S \rightarrow \lambda$$
$$S \rightarrow aSb,$$

generates $L(G) = \{a^k b^k \mid k \geq 0\}$.

3.4.4. Regular (Type 3) Phrase-Structure Grammars

A *regular* (Type 3, sometimes called *finite-state*) PSG is one in which all productions are of the forms

(i) $A \rightarrow aB;$ $A, B \in V_N, a \in V_T$
(ii) $A \rightarrow b:$ $A \in V_N, b \in V_T \cup \Lambda.$

Such grammars are called *right-linear regular* grammars. Alternatively, *left-linear regular* grammars can be defined containing productions of the forms

(iii) $A \rightarrow Ba;$ $A, b \in V_N, a \in V_T$
(iv) $A \rightarrow b;$ $A \in V_N, b \in V_T \cup \Lambda.$

Example 3-6. The right-linear regular grammar $G_1 = (\{S,A\}, \{a, b\}, P_1, S\})$ where P_1 consists of

$$S \rightarrow \lambda \qquad\qquad A \rightarrow bA$$
$$S \rightarrow aS \qquad\qquad A \rightarrow \lambda$$
$$S \rightarrow bA$$

generates $L(G_1) = \{a^i b^j \mid i \geq 0, j \geq 0\}$. The left-linear regular grammar $G_2 = (\{S,A\}, \{a,b\}, P_2, S)$, where P_2 consists of

$$S \to \lambda \qquad\qquad A \to Aa$$
$$S \to Sb \qquad\qquad A \to \lambda$$
$$S \to Aa$$

generates $L(G_2) = \{a^i b^j \mid i \geq 0, j \geq 0\}$; thus $L(G_2) = L(G_1)$.

3.5. The Hierarchy of Phrase-Structure Languages and Grammars

A phrase-structure language is called *Type k* ($k = 0,1,2,3$) if there exists a Type k PSG that generates it.

Let $\mathcal{L}_k$ be the set of type k phrase-structure languages. Then

$$\mathcal{L}_3 \subset \mathcal{L}_2 \subset \mathcal{L}_1 \subset \mathcal{L}_0,$$

that is, every regular language is context-free (but not vice versa), every context-free language is context-sensitive (but not vice versa), and so on.

It is clear that $\mathcal{L}_3 \subseteq \mathcal{L}_2$ since all $\mathcal{L}_3$-productions are of $\mathcal{L}_2$-format. The inclusion is proper, that is, $\mathcal{L}_3 \subset \mathcal{L}_2$, because there exists at least one context-free language that is not regular, namely, $\{a^k b^k \mid k \geq 0\}$ (Example 3-5). It is also clear that $\mathcal{L}_1 \subseteq \mathcal{L}_0$, because all $\mathcal{L}_1$-productions are of $\mathcal{L}_0$-format. The inclusion is proper, that is, $\mathcal{L}_1 \subset \mathcal{L}_0$, because there exists at least one unrestricted language that is not context-sensitive (for an example, see Reference 36).

The erasing rules allowed in Type 2 grammars raise a slight difficulty in demonstrating that $\mathcal{L}_2 \subseteq \mathcal{L}_1$. If erasing rules were not allowed in Type 2 grammers, then clearly all $\mathcal{L}_2$-productions would have $\mathcal{L}_1$-format. However, it can be shown (Theorem 7-1) that every type 2 PSG is weakly equivalent to a type 2 PSG in which there are no erasing rules except possibly $S \to \lambda$. Under these conditions it is clear that $\mathcal{L}_2 \subseteq \mathcal{L}_1$. The inclusion is proper because there exists at least one context-sensitive language that is not context free: $\{a^k b^k c^k \mid k \geq 0\}$ (Example 3-4).

In the sequel, the classes of sets accepted by Turing machines, linear-bounded automata, pushdown store automata, and finite automata will be denoted by $\mathcal{C}_0$, $\mathcal{C}_1$, $\mathcal{C}_2$, and $\mathcal{C}_3$, respectively.

4. REGULAR LANGUAGES

In this section two very elementary results concerning regular languages are given. Unlike the sequel, however, detailed proofs are supplied in order to give the reader the flavor of proofs typical to the field of formal languages and automata.

Theorem 4-1. To any given right-(left-) linear regular grammar G, there exists a corresponding left-(right-) linear regular grammar G' such that $L(G') = L(G)$. That is, a language is generated by a right-linear regular grammar if and only if it is generated by some left-linear regular grammar.

Proof (right-linear to left-linear). Let $G = (V_N, V_T, P, S)$ be a right-linear regular grammar. Construct $G' = (V_N \cup \{S'\}, V_T, P', S')$, where S' is a *new* symbol not in V_N, and P' is constructed as follows.

(a) Include $S' \rightarrow \lambda \in P'$ if $S \rightarrow \lambda \in P$.
(b) Include $B \rightarrow Aa \in P'$ if $A \rightarrow aB \in P$.
(c) Include $S' \rightarrow Aa \in P'$ if $A \rightarrow a \in P \vee A \rightarrow aB \in P \wedge B \rightarrow \lambda \in P$.
(d) Include $S \rightarrow \lambda \in P'$ if $S \rightarrow aA \in P \vee S \rightarrow a \in P$.

The proof that $L(G') = L(G)$ proceeds in two stages, by demonstrating that $L(G) \subseteq L(G')$ *and* $L(G') \subseteq L(G)$.

1. $L(G) \subseteq L(G')$

Let $x = a_1a_2...a_k \in L(G)$. If $k = 0$, then $x = \lambda$ and hence $S \rightarrow \lambda \in P$, thus $S' \rightarrow \lambda \in P'$. Thus $x = \lambda \in L(G')$.

If $k > 0$, $S \underset{G}{\overset{*}{\Rightarrow}} x$, that is, either

(a) $S \Rightarrow a_1A_1 \Rightarrow a_1a_2A_2 \Rightarrow \ldots \Rightarrow a_1 \ldots a_{k-1}A_{k-1} \Rightarrow a_1 \ldots a_k = x.$

This implies that

$$
\begin{array}{lll}
S \rightarrow a_1A_1 \in P, & \text{which implies} & S \rightarrow \lambda \in P' \wedge A_1 \rightarrow Sa_1 \in P'; \\
A_1 \rightarrow a_2A_2 \in P, & \text{which implies} & A_2 \rightarrow A_1a_2 \in P'; \\
& \vdots & \\
A_{k-2} \rightarrow a_{k-1}A_{k-1} \in P, & \text{which implies} & A_{k-1} \rightarrow A_{k-2}a_{k-1} \in P'; \\
A_{k-1} \rightarrow a_k \in P, & \text{which implies} & S' \rightarrow A_{k-1}a_k \in P'.
\end{array}
$$

Thus $S' \underset{G'}{\Rightarrow} A_{k-1}a_k \underset{G'}{\Rightarrow} \ldots \underset{G'}{\Rightarrow} A_1a_2 \ldots a_k \underset{G}{\Rightarrow} Sa_1 \ldots a_k \underset{G}{\Rightarrow} a_1 \ldots a_k = x,$ and hence $S' \underset{G'}{\overset{*}{\Rightarrow}} x$, $x \in L(G')$.

or   (b) $S \underset{G}{\Rightarrow} a_1A_1 \underset{G}{\Rightarrow} \ldots \underset{G}{\Rightarrow} a_1 \ldots a_kA_k \underset{G}{\Rightarrow} a_1 \ldots a_k = x.$

this implies that

$$
\begin{array}{lll}
S \rightarrow a_1A_1 \in P, & \text{which implies} & S \rightarrow \lambda \in P' \wedge A_1 \rightarrow Sa_1 \in P'; \\
\left.\begin{array}{l} A_{k-1} \rightarrow a_kA_k \in P \\ A_k \rightarrow \lambda \in P \end{array}\right\} & \text{which imply} & \left\{\begin{array}{l} A_k \rightarrow A_{k-1}a_k \in P'; \\ S' \rightarrow A_{k-1}a_k \in P'; \end{array}\right.
\end{array}
$$

Thus $S' \underset{G'}{\Rightarrow} A_{k-1}a_k \underset{G'}{\Rightarrow} \ldots \underset{G'}{\Rightarrow} Sa_1 \ldots a_k \underset{G'}{\Rightarrow} a_1 \ldots a_k = x$, and hence $x \in L(G')$.

2. $L(G') \subseteq L(G)$

Let $x = a_1 a_2 \ldots a_k \in L(G')$. If $k = 0$, then $x = \lambda$ and hence $S' \to \lambda \in P'$ which implies $S \to \lambda \in P$ and thus $x = \lambda \in L(G)$.

If $k > 0$, $S' \underset{G'}{\overset{*}{\Rightarrow}} x$, i.e.,

$$S' \underset{G'}{\Rightarrow} A_{k-1} a_k \underset{G'}{\Rightarrow} A_{k-2} a_{k-1} a_k \underset{G'}{\Rightarrow} \ldots \underset{G'}{\Rightarrow} S a_1 \ldots a_k \underset{G'}{\Rightarrow} a_1 \ldots a_k = x.$$

This implies that

$S' \to A_{k-1} a_k \in P'$ which implies $A_{k-1} \to a_k \in P \lor$
$$\vdots \qquad\qquad A_{k-1} \to a_k A_k \in P \land A_k \to \lambda \in P$$

$\left. \begin{array}{l} A_1 \to S a_1 \in P' \\ S \to \lambda \in P' \end{array} \right\}$ which imply $S \to a_1 A_1 \in P.$

Thus either

(a) $S \underset{G}{\Rightarrow} a_1 A_1 \underset{G}{\Rightarrow} \ldots \underset{G}{\Rightarrow} a_1 \ldots a_{k-1} A_{k-1} \underset{G}{\Rightarrow} a_1 \ldots a_k = x$

or

(b) $S \underset{G}{\Rightarrow} a_1 A_1 \underset{G}{\Rightarrow} \ldots \underset{G}{\Rightarrow} a_1 \ldots a_k A_k \underset{G}{\Rightarrow} a_1 \ldots a_k = x.$

Therefore $S \underset{G}{\overset{*}{\Rightarrow}} x$, and $x \in L(G)$. The proof for conversion of left-linear grammars to right-linear is similar.

It should be apparent to the reader that the above proof is distinguished not by its essential difficulty, but by its length. Nevertheless, it is "typical" in consisting of (1). a construction and (2). a proof (often using double inclusion) that the construction accomplishes its stated objective.

Example 4-1. Let G_1 be the right-linear regular grammar of Example 3-6. Applying the construction of Theorem 4-1 yields $G_1' = (\{S', S, A\}, \{a, b\}, P_1', S')$, where P_1' consists of

$S' \to \lambda$	$A \to Sb$
$S' \to Sa$	$A \to Ab$
$S' \to Sb$	$S \to Sa$
$S' \to Ab$	$S \to \lambda$

The tree representations of the derivations of $a^2 b^3$ in G_1 and G_1' are shown in Figure 3. Compare G_1' to G_2 of Example 3-6.

Theorem 4-2. The class of finite languages is properly included in the class of regular languages.

Proof. It will be sufficient to demonstrate that every finite language can be generated by a regular grammar (and hence is regular), and further that there exists at least one regular language that is not finite.

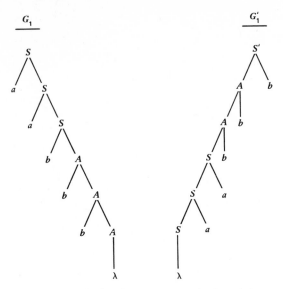

Figure 3.   Derivation trees of a^2b^3 in G_1 and G_1'.

Let $L_1 = \{x_1, x_2, \ldots, x_n\}$ be a finite language on an alphabet Σ. Let the ith member of L_1 be

$$x_i = a_{i1}a_{i2} \ldots a_{ik_i},$$

where $a_{ij} \in \Sigma$, $j = 1, 2, \ldots, k_i$. This string can be generated by the Type 3 productions

$$S \to a_{i1}[i,1]$$
$$[i,1] \to a_{i2}[i,2]$$
$$\vdots$$
$$[i,k_i-1] \to a_{ik_i},$$

where the symbols $[i,j]$ are nonterminals. If $x_i = \lambda$, then $k_i = 0$, and the only production included above is $S \to \lambda$. Construct the (right-linear) regular grammar $G_1 = (V_N, \Sigma, P, S)$, where

$$V_N = \{S\} \cup \{[i,j] \mid j = 1, 2, \ldots, k_i - 1; \quad i = 1, 2, \ldots, n\}$$

$$P = \{S \to a_{i1}[i,1] \mid i = 1, 2, \ldots, n\}$$
$$\cup \{[i,j-1] \to a_{ij}[i,j] \mid j = 1, 2, \ldots, k_i - 1; \quad i = 1, 2, \ldots, n\}$$
$$\cup \{[i,k_i-1] \to a_{ik_i} \mid i = 1, 2, \ldots, n\}.$$

Clearly $L(G_1) = L_1$, and hence every finite language is regular. The language $L_2 = \{a\}^*$ is not finite and is regular, since $L_2 = L(G_2)$, where $G_2 = (\{S\}, \{a\}, \{S \to aS, S \to \lambda\}, S)$.

Example 4-2.   The finite language $L = \{\lambda, ab, baab\}$ is generated by the regular grammar $G = (V_N, \{a,b\}, P, S)$, where

$$V_N = \{S, [2,1], [3,1], [3,2], [3,3]\}$$

and P consists of

$$S \rightarrow \lambda$$
$$S \rightarrow a[2,1]$$
$$[2,1] \rightarrow b$$
$$S \rightarrow b[3,1]$$

$$[3,1] \rightarrow a[3,2]$$
$$[3,2] \rightarrow a[3,3]$$
$$[3,3] \rightarrow b$$

5.   FINITE AUTOMATA [31]

The finite automaton, or finite-state machine, is the simplest kind of acceptor studied in this chapter.

Informally, a finite automaton (FA) is an abstract device consisting of a *control unit* which possesses a finite number of internal states, and an *input* which is a string of symbols read from left to right. The FA is "in" only one of its states at a given time. This device makes atomic moves (i.e., "operates") in the following manner:

(a) The FA starts in some designated initial state.

(b) In making an atomic move, the FA notes its present state and input symbol presently read, and if possible, makes a transition to another state and advances to the next input symbol.

(c) The FA *halts* if no more input is present. If it halts is a designated final state, the input is accepted; otherwise, the input is rejected.

Example 5-1.   A convenient method of illustrating finite automata is via a *flow table* [31]. Consider the flow table of Figure 4. In this example, the states are q_0 and q_1. The designated initial state is q_0 and the final states are q_0 and q_1, although this information is not displayed in the flow table. A

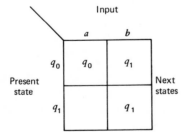

Figure 4.   Flow table of an example FA.

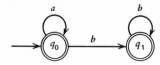

Figure 5.   Transition diagram of the example FA.

more pictorial way of representing a FA is via a *transition diagram* such as that in Figure 5. The state transitions are arrows labeled with input symbols, the intial state q_0 is pointed to by an arrow coming from no state, and the final states are enclosed in double circles.

Consider the "processing" of the input string a^2b^3. Starting in state q_0, the FA reads the first a and goes into state q_0 (in this case it remains in q_0). Next, being in state q_0, the FA reads the second a and remains in q_0. It then reads the first b and goes into state q_1, and so on, until it finally runs out of input, halting in state q_1. The sequence of states through which the FA moves while reading a^2b^3 is (q_0,q_0,q_1,q_1,q_1). Since the FA halts in a final state (q_1), a^2b^3 is accepted. It is clear that this FA accepts any string consisting of zero or more a's followed by zero or more b's, that is, members of $\{a^ib^j \mid i \geq 0, j \geq 0\}$.

5.1.   Unspecified Transitions

In the above example FA, it was unspecified what happens if the FA were in state q_1 and an a were read as input. Clearly this situation results from reading a "rejected" string, that is, one not in $\{a^ib^j \mid i \geq 0, j \geq 0\}$. It is a good, but not too common, practice to eliminate unspecified transitions by providing a special (nonfinal) "trap" state to which all formerly unspecified transitions are made. The "trap" state is never left once entered. The transition diagram of Figure 6 shows the addition of an appropriate trap state to the example FA.

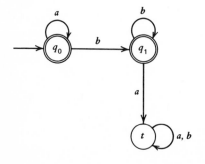

Figure 6.   The example FA with trap state added.

5.2. Formal Definition of Finite Automata

A *finite automaton* is a system $A = (Q, \Sigma, \delta, q_0, F)$, where (1) Q is a finite, nonempty *set of states*; (2) Σ is the *input alphabet*; (3) δ, the *direct transition function*, is a mapping $\delta : Q \times \Sigma \to Q$; (4) $q_0 \in Q$ is a designated *initial state*; and (5) $F \subseteq Q$ is the *set of final states*.

Example 5-1.   The previously discussed example FA (without trap state), defined formally, is

$$A = (\{q_0, q_1\}, \{a, b\}, \delta, q_0, \{q_0, q_1\}),$$

where δ consists of

$$\delta(q_0, a) = q_0$$
$$\delta(q_0, b) = q_1$$
$$\delta(q_1, b) = q_1$$

5.3. Extended Transition Function

It is sometimes convenient to extend the definition of the direct transition function, which defines state transitions due to the processing of a *single* input symbol, to a transition function that defines (multiple) state transitions due to the processing of a *string* of input symbols. For each $(q, a, x) \in Q \times \Sigma \times \Sigma^*$, define

$$\delta_e(q, \lambda) = q$$
$$\delta_e(q, xa) = \delta[\delta_e(q, x), a].$$

The transition function δ_e is a mapping $\delta_e : Q \times \Sigma^* \to Q$.

5.4. Set of Strings Accepted by a FA

An FA $A = (Q, \Sigma, q_0, F)$ *accepts* a string $x \in \Sigma^*$ if A, starting in state q_0 and reading the *leftmost* symbol of x, reads *all* of x and halts in some final state. Using the extended transition function δ_e, the set $T(A)$ of all strings accepted by a FA A is formally defined as

$$T(A) = \{x \in \Sigma^* \mid \delta_e(q_0, x) \in F\}$$

5.5. Nondeterministic Finite Automata

It is convenient to introduce a slightly different (but no more general) kind of FA. A *nondeterministic finite automaton* is a system $A = (Q, \Sigma, \delta, q_0, F)$, where Q, Σ, q_0, and F are as in the FA, and the direct transition function δ is a mapping

$$\delta : Q \times \Sigma \to 2^Q,$$

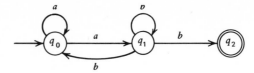

Figure 7.   An example nondeterministic FA.

that is, a mapping of (state, input symbol) pairs into *subsets* of Q rather than individual elements of Q.

Example 5-2.   Consider the nondeterministic FA $A = (\{q_0, q_1, q_2\}, \{a, b\},$ $\delta, q_0, \{q_2\})$, where δ is implicity defined via the transition diagram in Figure 7. The mapping δ consists of

$$\delta(q_0, a) = \{q_0, q_1\}$$
$$\delta(q_1, b) = \{q_0, q_1, q_2\}$$
$$\delta(q_0, b) = \delta(q_1, a) = \delta(q_2, a) = \delta(q_2, b) = \Phi.$$

The mappings into Φ represent unspecified transitions.

A nondeterministic FA is somewhat abstract, since it may be impossible to implement a device that is in two or more states "simultaneously." Some workers like to think of a nondeterministic FA making "copies" of itself, each copy executing different possible sequences of transitions. For example, in executing $\delta(q_0, a) = \{q_0, q_1\}$, the nondeterministic FA splits into two "copies," the first executing $\delta(q_0, a) = q_0$ and the second $\delta(q_0, a) = q_1$.

5.6.   Instantaneous Description

An *instantaneous description* (ID) of a nondeterministic FA $A = (Q, \Sigma,$ $\delta, q_0, F)$ is any element of $Q \times \Sigma^*$. An ID $(q, y) \in Q \times \Sigma^*$ means that A is in state q reading the leftmost symbol of y, where y is the *unprocessed* portion of the input.

5.7.   Atomic Move

A nondeterministic FA makes an *atomic move* in executing a single state transition, moving from one ID to another. Let $A = (Q, \Sigma, \delta, q_0, F)$ be a nondeterministic FA. Define a relation $\vert_{\overline{A}}$ between ID's of A as follows. For $p, q \in Q$, $a \in \Sigma$, $x \in \Sigma^*$,

$$(q, ax) \vert_{\overline{A}} (p, x) \text{ iff } p \in \delta(q, a).$$

In making the atomic move from (q, ax) to (p, x) input symbol a is processed (expended, read) and A changes from state q to state p. Sequences (possibly null) of atomic moves are represented by the reflexive transitive closure $\left|\frac{*}{A}\right.$ of $\left|\frac{}{A}\right.$.

5.8. Set of Accepted Strings

The set of strings $T(A)$ accepted by a nondeterministic FA A can be defined using ID's and atomic moves:

$$T(A) = \{x \in \Sigma^* \mid (q_0,x) \left|\frac{*}{A}\right. (q,\lambda),\ q \in F\}$$

From the transition diagram viewpoint, $x \in T(A)$ if and only if there exists *some* path from q_0 to $q \in F$ labeled (in order) with the symbols of x.

5.9. Deterministic Finite Automata

A nondeterministic FA is called *deterministic* if for all $(q,a) \in Q \times \Sigma$, $\mid \delta(q,a) \mid\ \leq 1$. Satisfying this condition insures that there will never be a choice of transitions out of any state, which might occur in a nondeterministic FA. Thus a deterministic FA as defined above is equivalent to the kind of FA first discussed at the beginning of this section.

A fundamental result of automata theory is the equivalence of nondeterministic and deterministic FA's. This is stated in Theorem 5-1.

Theorem 5-1.   Given any nondeterministic FA A, a deterministic FA B can be constructed such that $T(B) = T(A)$.

Example 5-3.   Let A be the FA of Example 5-2. Its deterministic equivalent is shown in Figure 8. Both deterministic and nondeterministic finite automata will be simply called finite automata in the sequel.

Example 5-4.   Consider the acceptance of the string *aaabb* by the nondeterministic FA of Example 5-2. The various state sequences through which the "copies" of the FA could move during acceptance of this string can be represented as paths in a tree, as shown in Figure 9. Since there exists a path from q_0 to $q_0 \in F$, namely, $(q_0,q_0,q_0,q_1,q_1,q_2)$, the string *aaabb* is accepted.

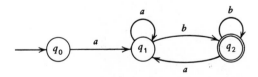

Figure 8.   Deterministic equivalent of the FA of Example 5-2.

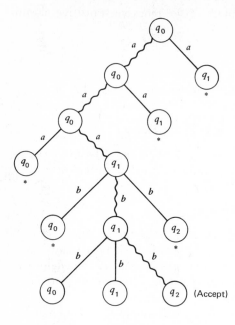

Figure 9. State sequence tree of FA of Example 5–2 when accepting *aaabb*. (The asterisk indicates a "blocked" configuration.)

6. FINITE AUTOMATA AND REGULAR LANGUAGES

The equivalence of regular (Type 3) PSL's and the sets accepted by FA's is expressed in the following characterization theorem.

Theorem 6-1. A PSL is regular (Type 3) if and only if it is accepted by some FA, that is, $\mathcal{L}_3 = \mathcal{C}_3$.

The proof of this theorem consists of proving, via appropriate constructions both $\mathcal{L}_3 \subseteq \mathcal{C}_3$ and $\mathcal{C}_3 \subseteq \mathcal{L}_3$. These proofs are found in References 10 and 36.

Example 6-1. Let $L(G_1)$ be the regular language of Example 3-6. This language is accepted by the FA of Example 5-1.

Example 6-2. The (nondeterministic) FA of Figure 10 accepts the language L of all strings in $\{0,1\}^*$ containing either two consecutive zeros or two consecutive ones. A regular grammar G such that $L(G) = L$ is $G = (\{S,A,B,C,D\}, \{0,1\}, P, S)$, where P consists of

$$S \to 0S \qquad\qquad B \to 1B$$
$$S \to 1S \qquad\qquad B \to \lambda$$
$$S \to 0A \qquad\qquad C \to 1D$$
$$S \to 1C \qquad\qquad D \to 0D$$
$$A \to 0B \qquad\qquad D \to 1D$$
$$B \to 0B \qquad\qquad D \to \lambda$$

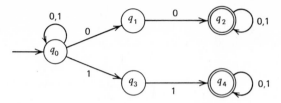

Figure 10. An FA that accepts all strings in $\{0,1\}^*$ containing either two consecutive zeros or two consecutive ones.

7. CONTEXT-FREE LANGUAGES

The study of context-free languages has been both intense and rewarding. The motivation for this study has come from the use of context-free grammars as a syntactic model of natural languages and of computer programming languages [47]. It has been demonstrated that context-free grammars are not adequate [17] for either of these purposes, but since these grammars are "almost" good models for the syntax of programming languages, they continue to be used for this purpose [14, 18].

To illustrate this latter point, the following (context-free) productions represent the essential syntactic structure of ALGOL 60 type declarations [47] (also see Chapter 10):

$\langle$type declaration$\rangle \rightarrow \langle$type$\rangle \langle$type list$\rangle$

$\langle$type$\rangle \rightarrow$ **real**

$\langle$type$\rangle \rightarrow$ **integer**

$\langle$type$\rangle \rightarrow$ **Boolean**

$\langle$type list$\rangle \rightarrow \langle$identifier$\rangle$, $\langle$type list$\rangle$

$\langle$type list$\rangle \rightarrow \langle$identifier$\rangle$

$\langle$identifier$\rangle \rightarrow \langle$letter$\rangle$

$\langle$identifier$\rangle \rightarrow \langle$identifier$\rangle \langle$letter$\rangle$

$\langle$identifier$\rangle \rightarrow \langle$identifier$\rangle \langle$digit$\rangle$

$\langle$letter$\rangle \rightarrow a$

$\vdots$

$\langle$letter$\rangle \rightarrow z$

$\langle$digit$\rangle \rightarrow 0$

$\vdots$

$\langle$digit$\rangle \rightarrow 9$

It is readily verified that the nonterminal $\langle$type declaration$\rangle$ could generate the following string:

$$\textbf{real } q2765, q2765$$

The variable "$q2765$" is declared twice, which might be interpreted as an "error" by some ALGOL compilers. Worse yet, suppose the following productions were added to those already given:

$$\langle \text{block head} \rangle \rightarrow \textbf{begin} \ \langle \text{declaration} \rangle$$
$$\langle \text{block head} \rangle \rightarrow \langle \text{block head} \rangle \ ; \ \langle \text{declaration} \rangle$$
$$\langle \text{declaration} \rangle \rightarrow \langle \text{type declaration} \rangle$$

A $\langle$block head$\rangle$ could be

$$\textbf{begin real } q2765; \textbf{ integer } q2765.$$

The point is, of course, that *context-free* productions could permit such illegal declarations; each declaration is generated independent of its "context": previous declarations. Thus the set of legal ALGOL 60 programs is not a context-free language, but rather is a subset of the language generated by the associated context-free grammar.

The structure and generative power of context-free grammars are richer than those of regular grammars, yet simple enough to allow a deep investigation of their properties. In this section several properties of context-free grammars and languages will be discussed.

7.1. Elementary Questions

Lemma 7-1.   There exists an algorithm to determine whether the language generated by a given context-free grammar is empty.

Proof.   Let $G = (V_N, V_T, P, S)$ be context-free. Define

$$W_1 = \{A \mid A \rightarrow x \in P \ \wedge \ x \in V_T{}^*\};$$
$$W_{k+1} = W_k \cup \{A \mid A \rightarrow x \in P \ \wedge \ x \in (W_k \cup V_T)^+\};$$
$$W = W_n, n = |V_N|.$$

It is clear that

$$W = \{A \in V_N \mid A \overset{*}{\underset{G}{\Rightarrow}} x, x \in V_T{}^*\},$$

and that $L(G) = \Phi$ if and only if $S \notin W$.

Lemma 7-2.   Let $G = V_N, V_T, P, S)$ be a context-free grammar. There exists an algorithm to determine whether $\lambda \in L(G)$.

Proof.   If the set $W = \{A \mid A \overset{*}{\underset{G}{\Rightarrow}} \lambda\}$ could be found, then $S \in W$ implies $\lambda \in L(G)$. Define

$$W_1 = \{A \mid A \rightarrow \lambda \in P\}$$
$$W_{k+1} = W_k \cup \{A \mid A \rightarrow x \in P \ \wedge \ x \in W_k{}^+\}, k \geq 1.$$

It can easily be verified that $W = W_n$, where $n = |V_N|$.

Example 7-1.   Let $G = (\{S,A,B\}, \{a,b\}, P, S)$, where P consists of

$$S \to AB \qquad\qquad A \to \lambda$$
$$A \to aAb \qquad\qquad B \to \lambda$$
$$B \to Bb$$

Using first the construction of Lemma 7-1,

$$W_1 = \{A,B\}; (W_1 \cup \{a,b\})^+ = \{\ldots, AB, aAb, Bb, \ldots\}$$
$$W_2 = \{A,B\} \cup \{D \mid D \to x \in P \wedge x \in (W_1 \cup \{a,b\})^+\}$$
$$= \{A,B,S\} = W.$$

Since $S \in W$, $L(G) \neq \Phi$, for example, $S \Rightarrow AB \Rightarrow B \Rightarrow \lambda$. Now using the construction of Lemma 7-2,

$$W_1 = \{A,B\}; W_1^+ = \{A, B, AA, AB, BA, \ldots\}$$
$$W_2 = \{A,B\} \cup \{D \mid D \to x \in P \wedge x \in W_1^+\}$$
$$= \{A,B,S\} = W$$

Since $S \in W$, $\lambda \in L(G)$.

7.2.   Context-Free Grammars of Simplified Form

Productions of the form $A \to \lambda$ are called *erasing rules*, and those of the form $A \to B$, $B \in V_N$, are called *renaming rules*. Given a context-free grammar, a weakly equivalent context-free grammar can be found containing no renaming rules and no erasing rules except possibly $S \to \lambda$.

Theorem 7-1.   For every context-free grammar G, there exists a context-free grammar G' containing no productions of the form $A \to \lambda$ except possibly $S \to \lambda$ if and only if $\lambda \in L(G)$, such that $L(G') = L(G)$.

Theorem 7-2.   For every context-free grammar G, there exists a context-free grammar G' containing no productions of the form $A \to B$, $B \in V_N$, such that $L(G') = L(G)$.

Basically, both Theorems 7-1 and 7-2 are proved by "absorbing" erasing and renaming rules into the right hand sides of appropriate productions such that $L(G') = L(G)$. See Reference 36 for details.

Example 7-2.   Let G be the context-free grammar of Example 7-1. A context-free grammar G' containing no erasing rules except $S \to \lambda$, such that $L(G') = L(G)$, is $G' = (\{S,A,B\}, \{a,b\}, P', S)$, where P' consists of

$$S \to AB \qquad\qquad A \to aAb$$
$$S \to A \qquad\qquad\quad A \to ab$$
$$S \to B \qquad\qquad\quad B \to Bb$$
$$S \to \lambda \qquad\qquad\quad B \to b.$$

Notice that G' contains renaming rules. A context-free grammar G'' containing no renaming rules, such that $L(G'') = L(G') = L(G)$, is $G'' = (\{S,A,B\}, \{a,b\}, P'', S)$, where P'' consists of

$$
\begin{array}{ll}
S \to \lambda & S \to b \\
S \to AB & A \to aAb \\
S \to aAb & A \to ab \\
S \to ab & B \to Bb \\
S \to Bb & B \to b.
\end{array}
$$

7.3.   Reduced Form Context-Free Grammars

Although renaming and almost all erasing rules can be removed from context-free grammars, these kinds of productions are not necessarily "useless," since they may participate in the derivation of sentences in the language generated by the grammar. On the other hand, it may turn out that some productions and nonterminal symbols in a context-free grammar are indeed "useless" in the above sense.

A context-free grammar $G = (V_N, V_T, P, S)$ is in *reduced form* if, for every $A \in V_N$,

$$(1) \ \ S \overset{*}{\underset{G}{\Rightarrow}} u_1 A u_2, \qquad u_1, u_2 \in V^*$$

and

$$(2) \ \ A \overset{*}{\underset{G}{\Rightarrow}} x, \qquad x \in V_T^*.$$

In other words, there are no "useless" nonterminals in a reduced-form grammar, that is, every nonterminal participates in the derivation of at least one member of $L(G)$. Every context-free language can be generated by a reduced form grammar.

Theorem 7-3.   There exists an algorithm to determine whether a given context-free grammar is in reduced form, and if not, to find a reduced form context-free grammar G' such that $L(G') = L(G)$.

This theorem is proved by first finding all the useless nonterminals, and then deleting from the grammar all productions containing any instance of these nonterminals; see Reference 36. It is easily verified that all of the example context-free grammars considered thus far are in reduced form.

Example 7-3.   Let $G = (\{S,A\}, \{a,b\}, P, S)$, where P consists of

$$
\begin{array}{ll}
S \to SS & S \to ab \\
S \to aSb & A \to aA \\
S \to A &
\end{array}
$$

Since the nonteriminal A does not generate any terminal strings, A does not satisfy condition (2) of the reduced form definition. Removing $S \rightarrow A$ and $A \rightarrow aA$ from P and A from V_N puts G into reduced form.

7.4. Two Important Properties of Context-Free Grammars and Languages

7.4.1. The Self-Embedding Property [8]

A context-free grammar $G = (V_N, V_T, P, S)$ is called *self-embedding* if this exists some $A \in V_N$ such that $A \overset{*}{\underset{G}{\Rightarrow}} z_1 A z_2, z_1, z_2 \in V^+$. The nonterminal A is also called self-embedding. The self-embedding property distinguishes context-free languages from regular languages, but even though G is self-embedding, $L(G)$ could still be regular. For example,

$$G = (\{S\}, \{a,b\}, \{S \rightarrow aS, S \rightarrow Sb, S \rightarrow \lambda\}, S)$$

is self-embedding ($S \Rightarrow aS \Rightarrow aSb$), but $L(G) = \{a^i b^j \mid i \geq 0, j \geq 0\}$ is a regular language. The precise result is stated in Theorem 7-4.

Theorem 7-4. A context-free language L is not regular if and only if *all* context-free grammars generating L are self-embedding.

7.4.2. The p-q Theorem [4]

A necessary, but not sufficient, condition that a language be context-free is given by Theorem 7-5.

Theorem 7-5. Let L be a context-free language. There exist positive integers p and q such that if $z \in L$, with $\lg(z) > p$, then

      (1) $z = xuwvy, \qquad uv \neq \lambda$
      (2) $\lg(uwv) \leq q$
      (3) $z_k = xu^k wv^k y \in L, \qquad k = 0, 1, 2, \ldots$

Notice that the p–q theorem is only a "one-way" statement, that is, it says that all context-free languages have the "p–q property," but not that all languages having the p–q property are context-free. The p–q theorem is effectively used in the contrapositive sense: if a language does *not* have the p–q property, it is *not* a context-free language. The classic example of this is the proof that $\{a^k b^k c^k \mid k \geq 0\}$ is not context-free [19].

The p–q theorem also provides a test of whether a given context-free grammar generates a finite or infinite number of strings. If G is context-free, then $L(G)$ is infinite if and only if there exists some $z \in L(G)$ such that $p < \lg(z) \leq p + q$, where p and q are the integers of the p–q theorem [36].

Example 7-4. Let $L = \{a^k b^k \mid k \geq 0\}$. L is context-free, and is generated by $G = (\{S\}, \{a,b\}, P, S)$, where P consists of

$$S \rightarrow aSb$$
$$S \rightarrow \lambda$$

For $p = 1$, $q = 2$, $x = y = \lambda$, $u = a$, $v = b$, $w = \lambda$,

$$z = xuwvy = ab \in L$$
$$z_k = xu^k wv^k y = a^k b^k \in L, \; k = 0, 1, 2, \ldots$$
$$\lg(z) = \lg(ab) > 1 = p, \; \lg(uwv) = \lg(ab) \leq 2 = q$$

Since $ab \in L(G)$ and $1 < \lg(ab) \leq 3$, $L(G)$ is infinite.

7.5. Normal Forms of Context-Free Grammars

Two well-known "normal" forms into which all context-free grammars can be transformed are the Chomsky and Greibach Normal Forms.

Theorem 7-6 (Chomsky Normal Form [8]. For every context-free grammar G there exists a context-free grammar G' such that $L(G') = L(G)$, containing only productions of the forms

$$(1) \; A \rightarrow BC, \qquad A, B, C \in V_N$$
$$(2) \; A \rightarrow a, \qquad a \in V_T$$
$$(3) \; S \rightarrow \lambda, \qquad \text{iff } \lambda \in L(G).$$

Theorem 7-7 (Greibach Normal Form) [28]. For every context-free grammar G there exists a context-free grammar G', such that $L(G') = L(G)$, containing only productions of the forms

$$(1) \; A \rightarrow ay, \qquad a \in V_T, \, y \in V_N{}^*$$
$$(2) \; S \rightarrow \lambda, \qquad \text{iff } \lambda \in L(G).$$

Example 7-5. Let G be the grammar of Example 7-1. An equivalent Chomsky normal form grammar has the productions

$$
\begin{array}{ll}
S \rightarrow \lambda & A \rightarrow B_1 C_1 \\
S \rightarrow AB & A \rightarrow B_1 B_2 \\
S \rightarrow B_1 C_1 & B \rightarrow BB_2 \\
C_1 \rightarrow AB_2 & B \rightarrow b \\
S \rightarrow B_1 B_2 & B_1 \rightarrow a \\
S \rightarrow BB_2 & B_2 \rightarrow b \\
S \rightarrow b &
\end{array}
$$

An equivalent Greibach normal form grammar has the productions

$$S \to \lambda \qquad\qquad B \to bC_3$$
$$S \to aAC_4C_1 \qquad B \to b$$
$$S \to aC_4C_1 \qquad\quad C_1 \to bC_2$$
$$S \to bC_2 \qquad\qquad C_2 \to bC_2$$
$$S \to aAC_4 \qquad\quad C_2 \to b$$
$$S \to aC_4 \qquad\qquad C_3 \to bC_3$$
$$S \to b \qquad\qquad\quad C_3 \to b$$
$$A \to aAC_4 \qquad\quad C_4 \to b$$
$$A \to aC_4$$

8. PUSHDOWN AUTOMATA

Pushdown automata are abstract devices related to context-free languages. A *pushdown automaton* (PDA) is a device consisting of (1) a *control unit* and *input*, and (2) an *auxiliary memory*, which is a *semi-infinite tape* with a particular kind of restricted access. The PDA's infinite memory makes it more powerful than a FA. The restricted access to the auxiliary memory is of the *last-in, first-out* kind, that is, only the element *last* inserted into this memory is *first* accessible for reading or writing. Such a memory behaves like a stack of trays in a cafeteria, and is called a *pushdown* store. A PDA is shown in Figure 11.

Formally, a PDA is a system $A = (Q, \Sigma, \Gamma, \delta, q_0, Z_0, F)$ where:

1. Q is a finite, nonempty set of *control unit states*.
2. Σ is the *input alphabet*.
3. Γ is the *pushdown store alphabet*.
4. δ, the direct transition function, is a mapping $\delta : Q \times (\Sigma \cup \Lambda) \times \Gamma \to$ *finite subsets* of $Q \times \Gamma^*$.
5. $q_0 \in Q$ is the *initial state*.
6. $Z_0 \in \Gamma$ is the *initial pushdown store symbol*.
7. $F \subseteq Q$ is a *set of final states*.

As shown in Figure 11, the PDA's control unit is in present state q, and the PDA is reading the *leftmost* symbol of the unprocessed input and the *leftmost* symbol of the string representing the contents of the pushdown store.

8.1. How the PDA Operates

There are basically two kinds of atomic move that a PDA makes:

1. $(p,w) \in \delta(q,a,Z), \qquad (p,w) \in Q \times \Gamma^*, \qquad (q,a,Z) \in Q \times \Sigma \times \Gamma$

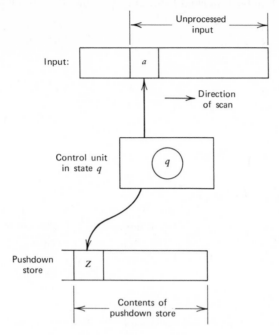

Figure 11.   A pushdown automation.

In its present configuration, the PDA is in state q, reading input symbol a at the left end of the unprocessed input, and reading pushdown symbol Z at the "top" of the pushdown store. In making the atomic move, the PDA's control unit transfers into state p, the input symbol a is *processed* (the input head moves one symbol to the right), and the topmost pushdown symbol Z is *rewritten* (replaced) as the string $w \in \Gamma^*$. If $w = \lambda$, Z is *erased*, that is, the pushdown store loses its topmost symbol. If $\lg(w) = 1$, Z is replaced by another symbol, possibly itself. If $\lg(w) > 1$, symbols are added to the pushdown store.

$$2. \ (p,w) \in \delta(q,\lambda,Z), \qquad (p,w) \in Q \times \Gamma^*, \qquad (q,\lambda,Z) \in Q \times \Lambda \times \Gamma$$

This notation means that in making the atomic move, the PDA does *not* process any input symbol (the input head does not move). In fact, the PDA *ignores* the input; such moves are called λ-*moves*. In this case the PDA may still change state and modify the contents of its pushdown store.

8.2.   Instantaneous Description

An *instantaneous description* (ID) of a PDA $A = (Q, \Sigma, \Gamma, \delta, q_0, Z_0, F)$ is any element $(q,x,w) \in Q \times \Sigma^* \times \Gamma^*$, where

$$q = \text{present state of control unit}$$
$$x = \text{unprocessed input}$$
$$w = \text{contents of pushdown store.}$$

8.3.   Atomic Move

An atomic move of a PDA A is represented by a relation $\vert_{\overline{A}}$ between ID's of A as follows. For each $(q,a,Z) \in Q \times (\Sigma \cup \Lambda) \times \Gamma$, $(p,w) \in Q \times \Gamma^*$, $x \in \Sigma^*$, $y \in \Gamma^*$, let

$$(q,ax,Zw) \vert_{\overline{A}} (p,x,yw) \qquad \text{if} \qquad (p,y) \in \delta(q,a,Z).$$

The reflexive-transitive closure $\vert_{\overline{A}}^{*}$ of $\vert_{\overline{A}}$ is defined in the usual manner. Note that $Zw \neq \lambda$, that is, the PDA may *not* move (it halts) if its pushdown store is empty.

8.4.   Sets of Strings Accepted by PDA's

There are two distinct kinds of sets of strings accepted by PDA's distinguished by the final configuration of the PDA upon acceptance.

1. *Acceptance upon entering final state*

$$T(A) = \{x \in \Sigma^* \mid (q_0,x,Z_0) \vert_{\overline{A}}^{*} (q,\lambda,w), (q,w) \in F \times \Gamma^*\}$$

2. *Acceptance upon empty pushdown store*

$$N(A) = \{x \in \Sigma^* \mid (q_0,x,Z_0) \vert_{\overline{A}}^{*} (q,\lambda,\lambda), q \in Q\}$$

It turns out that T-acceptance and N-acceptance are equivalent (Theorem 8-1).

Theorem 8-1 [36].   (a) if $L = N(A)$ is the set of strings N-accepted by some PDA A, then there exists a (T-accepting) PDA B such that $T(B) = N(A)$. (b) If $L = T(A)$ is the set of strings T-accepted by some PDA A, then there exists a (N-accepting) PDA B such that $N(B) = T(A)$.

8.5.   Deterministic Pushdown Automata

In general PDA's are nondeterministic, that is, for some $(q,a,Z) \in Q \times (\Sigma \cup \Lambda) \times \Gamma, \vert \delta(q,a,Z) \vert > 1$. A PDA is *deterministic* if (1) for all $(q,a,Z) \in Q \times (\Sigma \cup \Lambda) \times \Gamma, \vert \delta(q,a,Z) \vert \leq 1$, and (2) if $\delta(q,\lambda,Z) \neq \Phi$, then $\delta(q,b,Z) = \Phi$ for all $b \in \Sigma$.

Example 8-1.   Let $L_1 = \{xcx^R \mid x \in \{a,b\}^*\}$ be a set of palindromes (i.e., strings equal to their own reversals) with center marker "c." L_1 is generated by the context-free grammar $G_1 = (\{S\}, \{a,b,c\}, P_1, S)$, where P_1 consists of

$$S \rightarrow aSa$$
$$S \rightarrow bSb$$
$$S \rightarrow c$$

A deterministic PDA that T-accepts L_1 is

$$A = (Q, \Sigma, \Gamma, \delta, q_0, Z_0, F),$$

where

$$Q = \{q_0, q_1, q_2\}$$
$$\Sigma = \{a, b, c\}$$
$$\Gamma = \{a, b, Z_0\}$$
$$F = \{q_2\},$$

and δ consists of, for each $a_1, a_2 \in \{a,b\}$,

$$\delta(q_0,c,Z_0) = \{(q_1,Z_0)\}$$
$$\delta(q_0,a_1,Z_0) = \{(q_0,a_1Z_0)\}$$
$$\delta(q_0,a_1,a_2) = \{(q_0,a_1a_2)\}$$
$$\delta(q_0,c,a_1) = \{(q_1,a_1)\}$$
$$\delta(q_1,a_1,a_1) = \{(q_1,\lambda)\}$$
$$\delta(q_1,\lambda,Z_0) = \{(q_2,Z_0)\}$$

A transition diagram representing a PDA can be constructed using the following notation:

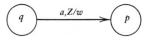

The above represents $(p,w) \in \delta(q,a,Z)$.

The PDA A (Figure 12) copies its input into the pushdown store until it encounters "c," and then the contents of the pushdown store are compared with the remaining input for agreement. It is readily seen that $T(A) = L(G_1)$.

Example 8-2.   Let $L_2 = \{xx^R \mid x \in \{a,b\}^*\}$ be a set of palindromes without center marker. L_2 is generated by the context-free grammar $G_2 = (\{S\}, \{a,b\}, P_2, S)$, where P_2 consists of

$$S \rightarrow aSa$$
$$S \rightarrow bSb$$
$$S \rightarrow \lambda$$

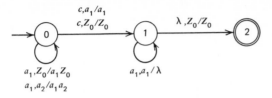

Figure 12.   Transition diagram of A.

A nondeterministic PDA B that N-accepts L_2 is

$$B = (\{q_0,q_1\}, \{a,b\}, \{a,b,Z_0\}, \delta, q_0, Z_0, \Phi),$$

where δ is given by the transition diagram shown in Figure 13. The PDA B is nondeterministic because of:

1. $\delta(q_0,a_1,a_1) = \{(q_0, a_1a_1), (q_1,\lambda)\}$
2. $\delta(q_0,\lambda,Z_0) = \{(q_1,\lambda)\}$ and $\delta(q_0,a_1,Z_0) = \{(q_0,a_1Z_0)\}$

Not being blessed with a center marker in its input, B is forced to *guess* whether it has reached the center of the input—(1) above— and whether its input was the null string—(2) above. B copies some of its input into the pushdown store, *guesses* that it has reached the center, and then compares the remainder of the input with the contents of the pushdown store. Since one of the guesses made by B will be correct (assuming acceptable input), $N(B) = L(G_2)$.

It is not always possible, given a nondeterministic PDA, to find a deterministic PDA that accepts the same set of strings. For example, there exists no deterministic PDA that accepts L_2 above.

9.   PUSHDOWN AUTOMATA AND CONTEXT-FREE LANGUAGES

The equivalence of context-free (Type 2) PSL's and the sets accepted by PDA's is expressed in the characterization theorem.

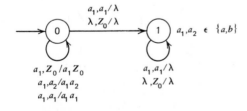

Figure 13.   Transition diagram of B.

Figure 14.   A PDA that accepts $L(G)$ of Example 7-1.

Figure 15.   A PDA that accepts L_1 of Example 8-1.

Theorem 9-1.   A PSL is context-free (Type 2) if and only if it is accepted by some PDA, that is, $\mathcal{L}_2 = \mathcal{C}_2$.

The proof that $\mathcal{L}_2 \subseteq \mathcal{C}_2$ consists of constructing a one-state, nondeterministic PDA that N-accepts the given context-free language [9, 13]. $\mathcal{C}_2 \subseteq \mathcal{L}_2$ is proved similarly [9, 13].

Example 9-1.   Let G be the context-free grammar of Example 7-1. A one-state, nondeterministic PDA that N-accepts $L(G)$ is given in Figure 14.

Example 9-2.   Let L_1 be the context-free language of Example 8-1. A one-state, nondeterministic PDA that N-accepts L_1 is given in Figure 15.

10.   TURING MACHINES

The Turing machine is an abstract device introduced by the mathematician A. M. Turing in 1936 [55]. Its operation is strikingly like that of modern electronic computers, although the structure of the Turing machine is certainly not a faithful representation of modern computer structure. Turing was interested primarily in modeling the fundamental processes involved in carrying out computation. The Turing machine has been generally accepted as a mathematical model for describing sequences of operations (or instructions) that can be mechanically performed. Such sequences of instructions are called *procedures*. We shall accept the working hypothesis that the Turing machine model can be used to represent procedures or any computation that can be done on a modern digital computer. This hypothesis, while not mathematically provable or disprovable, has withstood the test of time, for no one else has yet advanced a more general theoretical model of computation.

10.1.   Informal Description of Turing Machine

A *Turing machine* (TM) is an automaton that consists of (1) a *control unit*, and (2) an *auxiliary memory*, which is an infinite tape with relatively unrestricted access. A Turing machine is shown in Figure 16.

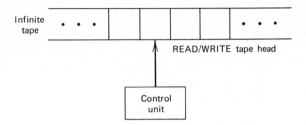

Infinite tape

READ/WRITE tape head

Control unit

Figure 16. A Turing machine.

The infinite tape is viewed as being divided into squares, each one containing one symbol (including a symbol which functions as a blank). A read/write tape head is able to move along the tape in either direction, reading and/or writing the contents of one square at a time. The tape initially stores the input to the Turing machine, and subsequently the Turing machine uses its tape as working storage.

10.2. Formal Description of Turing Machine

Formally, a *Turing machine* (TM) is a system $A = (Q, \Sigma, \Gamma, \delta, q_0, F)$, where:

1. Q is a finite, nonempty set of *control unit states*.
2. Σ is an *input alphabet*.
3. Γ is a *tape alphabet*, where $\Sigma \subset \Gamma$.
4. δ, the *direct transition function*, is a mapping $\delta : Q \times \Gamma \to$ subsets of $Q \times \Gamma \times \{L,N,R\}$.
5. $q_0 \in Q$ is the *initial state*.
6. $F \subseteq Q$ is the *set of final states*.

10.3. How the Turing Machine Operates

The operation of a TM is inherent in its direct transition function:

$$(p,A_2,d) \in \delta(q,A_1)$$

means that

1. The TM's control unit is presently in state $q \in Q$ and the symbol $A_1 \in \Gamma$ is read under the tape head.
2. In making an atomic move, the TM's control unit changes to state $p \in Q$, the symbol $A_1 \in \Gamma$ is *replaced* by $A_2 \in \Gamma$, and the tape head moves one square in direction $d \in \{L,N,R\}$. If

$$d = L, \quad \text{the tape head moves one square } \textit{left}.$$
$$d = N, \quad \text{the tape head does } \textit{not} \text{ move}.$$
$$d = R, \quad \text{the tape head moves one square } \textit{right}.$$

It should be noted that the *tape head* moves, while the tape remains stationary. Some authors write $\{L,N,R\}$ as $\{-1,0,1\}$.

10.4. Instantaneous Description

An *instantaneous description* (ID) of a TM is any element of $\Gamma^*Q\Gamma^+$. The three substrings u,q,v of an ID $uqv \in \Gamma^*Q\Gamma^+$ represent the following.

1. $u \in \Gamma^*$ represents the symbols on the tape located to the *left* of the tape head.
2. $q \in Q$ is the state of the control unit.
3. $v \in \Gamma^+$ represent the symbols on the tape located *beneath and to the right* of the tape head.

A somewhat strange, but notationally convenient, way of interpreting the ID will be used. At any given time, only a finite (but unbounded), contiguous region of the tape has been used, namely, those squares that either contained the input string or were visited by the tape head, or both. Only the squares thus used will be included in the ID; the unused remainder of the tape does not appear in the ID. Let $B \in \Gamma$ be a special tape symbol known as the *blank*. If the tape head is required to move off either end of the "used" region of the tape, a fresh square containing B materializes under the tape head.

10.5. Atomic Moves

Atomic moves of a TM are represented via a relation $\vdash_A$ between ID's. Let $A = (Q, \Sigma, \Gamma, \delta, q_0, F)$ be a TM, and let $A_1, A_2, A_3 \in \Gamma, u, v \in \Gamma^*$, $w \in \Gamma^+, q \in Q$. Typical atomic moves are:

1. $uqA_1w \vdash_A uA_2pw$ if $(p,A_2,R) \in \delta(q,A_1)$.
2. $uqA_1v \vdash_A upA_2v$ if $(p,A_2,N) \in \delta(q,A_1)$.
3. $uA_3qA_1v \vdash_A upA_3A_2v$ if $(p,A_2,L) \in \delta(q,A_1)$.
4. $qA_1v \vdash_A pBA_2v$ if $(p,A_2,L) \in \delta(q,A_1)$.
5. $uqA_1 \vdash_A uA_2pB$ if $(p,A_2,R) \in \delta(q,A_1)$.

Cases 4 and 5 represent tape head movement off the left and right ends of the tape, respectively. As usual, a sequence of atomic moves is represented by $\vdash_A^*$.

10.6. Set of Strings Accepted by a TM

The set of strings $T(A)$ accepted by a TM $A = (Q, \Sigma, \Gamma, \delta, q_0, F)$ is defined as

$$T(A) = \{x \in \Sigma^+ \cup \{B\} \mid q_0 x \mathbin{\vert\!\overset{*}{}_A} uqA_1v \wedge \delta(q,A_1) = \Phi,$$
$$u, v \in \Gamma^*, A_1 \in \Gamma, q \in F\},$$

that is, the input x is accepted if and only if the TM *halts* in a *final* state. The case $x = B$ represents null input.

10.7. Deterministic Turing Machines

A TM $A = (Q, \Sigma, \Gamma, \delta, q_0, F)$ is *deterministic* if, for all $(q,Z) \in Q \times \Gamma$, $|\delta(q,Z)| \leq 1$. Otherwise the TM is *nondeterministic*. Deterministic and nondeterministic TM's are equivalent, as expressed in

Theorem 10-1. For each nondeterministic TM A, there exists a deterministic TM D such that $T(D) = T(A)$.

The TM D is constructed such that it systematically (and deterministically) makes all the possible moves made by A, until A would have halted. See Reference 36 for details.

10.8. Transition Diagram Notation

The transition diagram

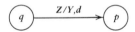

represents $(p,Y,d) \in \delta(q,Z)$.

Example 10-1. Consider a deterministic TM that adds unity to a binary integer placed between two endmarkers "$\#$." The tape head is initially placed on the left endmarker and returns there when the computation is finished. The least significant digit appears at the right of the binary integer. The transition diagram of this TM is given in Figure 17.

The reader can readily verify that the TM performs its indicated task. Viewed as a computer, the TM calculates the function $f(N) = N + 1$, where N is the binary integer processed. Viewed as an acceptor of strings,

$$T(A) = \{\#, \lambda\}\{0,1\}^+\{\#\},$$

where the TM bears the name "A."

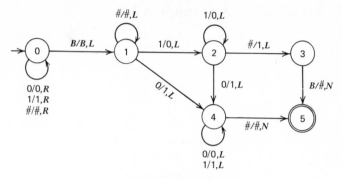

Figure 17. Transition diagram of TM of Example 10–1.

Example 10-2. Consider a deterministic TM that copies a non-null string of 1's. The copy is made to the right of the original, and the two copies are separated by a single "0." The tape head begins on the left edge of the original input, and ends up on the separating "0." The transition diagram of this TM is shown in Figure 18. The work symbol "*" aids in the copying process.

Many more examples of Turing machines and techniques used for their construction are found in References 6, 11, and 45.

10.9. Universal Turing Machines

The direct transition function of a TM in a very real sense constitutes the fixed "program" that the TM executes. A modern stored-program computer, on the other hand, is able to execute a whole *class* of programs,

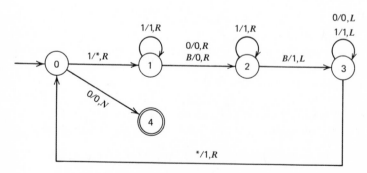

Figure 18. Transition diagram of TM of Example 10–2.

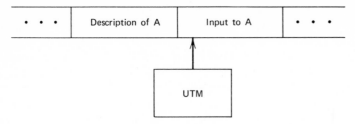

Figure 19. A universal TM simulating a TM A.

a member of this class being input to the computer's memory and then appropriately interpreted. A *universal Turing machine* (UTM) operates very much like a stored-program computer. A UTM has on its tape both the *description* (i.e., direct transition function) of some TM and the input to that TM. The UTM then *simulates* the operation of the TM whose description it has upon the TM's input. There are many possible UTM's, examples of which are found in References 45 and 54. A typical UTM is shown in Figure 19.

10.10. Variations of the Basic Turing Machine

Certain variations of the basic Turing machine presented in this section are often found in the literature. Some of these appear more general, and some less general, than our basic model. However, all these variations are equivalent to the basic model. The more common variations, which occur singly or in combination, are Turing machines which have:

(a) Only a two-symbol tape alphabet.
(b) A control unit having only two states.
(c) k infinite tapes, where k is finite.
(d) A tape with k "tracks," or "channels."
(e) A semi-infinite tape.

For the proofs of the above, see for (a): [36, 54]; for (b): [54]; for (c): [54]; for (d): [36]; and for (e): [36, 45].

11. TURING MACHINES AND UNRESTRICTED LANGUAGES

The characterization theorem stating the equivalence of Turing machines and type 0 languages is given below.

Theorem 11-1. A PSL is unrestricted (Type 0) if and only if it is accepted by some TM, that is, $\mathcal{L}_0 = \mathcal{A}_0$.

The proof that $\mathcal{L}_0 \subseteq \mathcal{Q}_0$ is obtained by constructing a TM which, when provided with a type 0 PSG, performs the derivation of a terminal string and compares this string with the input [candidate member of $L(G)$]. If the strings are equal, the TM accepts. Otherwise, the TM tries another derivation. See References 8 and 36 for details. The proof that $\mathcal{Q}_0 \subseteq \mathcal{L}_0$ uses the construction of a type 0 grammar from the given TM. This grammar generates a representation of a terminal string and then simulates the action of the given TM on that string. If and only if the string is accepted by the TM is it in the language generated by the constructed type 0 grammar; see References 8 and 36.

12.   CONTEXT-SENSITIVE LANGUAGES

In Section 3 context-sensitive (Type 1) grammars were defined to have productions only of the form

$$z_1 A z_2 \rightarrow z_1 x z_2,$$

where

$$A \in V_N, x \in V^+ \quad \text{and} \quad z_1, z_2 \in V^*.$$

In this section a related class of grammars is introduced.

A grammar is *monotonic* if it contains productions only of the form

$$x \rightarrow y; \quad \lg(x) \leq \lg(y); \quad x, y \in V^+.$$
$$S \rightarrow \lambda \text{ can be included if and only if } \lambda \in L(G).$$

Theorem 12-1.   A phrase-structure grammar G is context-sensitive if and only if there exists a monotonic phrase-structure grammar G' such that $L(G) = L(G')$.

All context-sensitive grammars are trivially monotonic. The converse is, as usual, proved by a suitable construction.

Example 12-1.   Consider the context-sensitive grammar of Example 3-4. An equivalent monotonic grammar is $G = (\{S,T,B\}, \{a,b,c\}, P, S)$, where P consists of

$S \rightarrow \lambda$	$T \rightarrow abc$
$S \rightarrow T$	$cB \rightarrow Bc$
$T \rightarrow aTBc$	$bB \rightarrow bb$

The production $S \rightarrow \lambda$ is not strictly monotonic, but is an *ad hoc* addition to generate the null string, as previously discussed. The derivation of $a^2b^2c^2$ is

$$S \Rightarrow T$$
$$\Rightarrow aTBc$$
$$\Rightarrow aabcBc$$
$$\Rightarrow aabBcc$$
$$\Rightarrow aabbcc.$$

Compare the above derivation with its counterpart in Example 3-4.

13. LINEAR-BOUNDED AUTOMATA

A *linear-bounded automaton* (LBA) is a single-tape Turing machine which is restricted to use only those squares on its tape upon which the input string originally appeared. In other words, an LBA is a Turing machine which works on a finite tape.

13.1. Formal Definition

An LBA is a system $A = (Q, \Sigma, \Gamma, \delta, q_0, F)$, where Q, Σ, Γ, δ, q_0, and F are as in Turing machines. There exist, as usual, both deterministic and nondeterministic LBA's, depending on the nature of the direct transition function δ. However, it is not known whether for each nondeterministic LBA there exists a corresponding deterministic LBA.

The instantaneous description and atomic move of an LBA are like those of a Turing machine, except that (unlike the TM) attempts to move off either end of the finite tape are not defined, and hence the LBA halts when such attempts are made.

13.2. Set of Strings Accepted by an LBA

The set of strings $T(A)$ accepted by an LBA $A = (Q, \Sigma, \Gamma, \delta, q_0, F)$ is defined as $T(A) = \{x \in \Sigma^* \mid q_0 x \vdash_{A}^{*} y, y \in \Gamma^* F \Gamma^*\}$.

13.3. Endmarkers

In order to formally deal with attempted moves off the ends of the finite tape, some authors find it convenient to provide *endmarkers* ¢ and $ at the ends of the tape of an LBA. In this case an ID becomes an element (of appropriate length) of $\{¢\}\Gamma^* Q \Gamma^* \{\$\}$. Such endmarkers are not really needed, because:

Theorem 13-1. For each LBA A equipped with endmarkers, there exists an LBA B without endmarkers such that $T(B) = T(A)$.

See References 24 and 27 for the proof of this result.

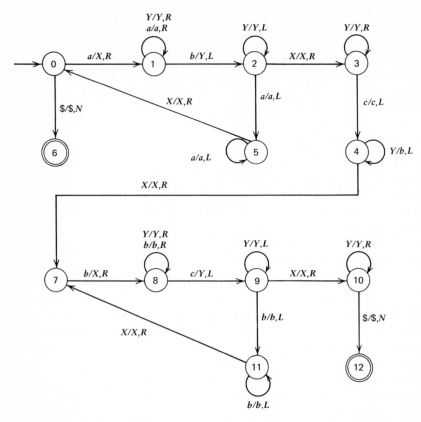

Figure 20. A deterministic LBA with endmarkers that accepts $L = \{a^n b^n c^n \mid n \geq 0\}$.

Example 13-1. A deterministic LBA with endmarkers that accepts $L = \{a^n b^n c^n \mid n \geq 0\}$ is shown in Figure 20. First the prefix $a^n b^n c$ is detected, converting the contents of the tape to $\text{¢}X^n Y^n c^n\$$. Then the tape is changed to $\text{¢}X^n b^n c^n\$$, with the tape head reading the leftmost b, and the control in state q_7. Then the suffix $b^n c^n$ is accepted, and thus $a^n b^n c^n$ is accepted, and the LBA halts in state q_{12}. The transition to state q_6 accepts the empty string.

14. LINEAR-BOUNDED AUTOMATA AND CONTEXT-SENSITIVE LANGUAGES

The characterization theorem relating context-sensitive languages and the sets accepted by linear-bounded automata is given below.

Theorem 14-1. A phrase-structure is context-sensitive (Type 1) if and only if it is accepted by some linear-bounded automaton, that is $\mathcal{L}_1 = \mathcal{Q}_1$.

The proof that $\mathcal{L}_1 \subseteq \mathcal{Q}_1$ is similar to that of $\mathcal{L}_0 \subseteq \mathcal{Q}_0$, with the additional observation that since context-sensitive grammars are monotonic, the length of a sentential form in the derivation of the input string need never exceed the length of the input. See Reference 40. The proof of $\mathcal{Q}_1 \subseteq \mathcal{L}_1$ is accomplished via a suitable construction; see References 30 or 39 for details.

A deterministic LBA with endmarkers that accepts the context-sensitive language $L = \{a^n b^n c^n \mid n \geq 0\}$ is given in Example 13-1.

In Section 8, it was pointed out that all context-free languages could not be accepted by deterministic pushdown store automata, for example, $L = \{ww^R \mid w \in \{a,b\}^*\}$. However, Kuroda [39] has shown that:

Theorem 14-2. Each context-free language is accepted by some *deterministic* LBA.

15. DECISION PROBLEMS

In the foregoing sections there have appeared theorems stated as: "There exists an algorithm to determine whether . . .." The proofs of these theorems always involved a construction and procedure that could be mechanically carried out by, in particular, a Turing machine. Moreover, a Turing machine that performs any of these procedures can do so in a *finite* number of moves just prior to halting. In Section 10 the hypothesis equating mechanical procedures and Turing machines was accepted. At that time, however, nothing was said about whether the procedure in question could be performed in a finite number of steps, that is, whether the corresponding Turing machine ever halted. As far as we are concerned, nonterminating procedures and hence nonhalting Turing machines cannot furnish any general answers to questions because, in fact, we simply cannot wait an infinite time for answers to be given or calculations to be performed. Accordingly, the term *algorithm* will be used for a procedure consisting of a finite number of steps, that is, a procedure performed by a Turing machine *guaranteed to halt for all inputs*.

For example, suppose we were given some Turing machine and its input and asked the question "Does this Turing machine ever eventually halt when started on this input tape?" One approach to answering this is experimental: start the Turing machine and observe whether it ever halts. But suppose one waits patiently for one million years, and the machine is still running. Can it be concluded that the machine will never stop running? Of course not; it might halt after running two million, or even two billion, years. The experimental approach requires infinite patience and an avoidance of "hasty" decisions.

A better approach would be to have some Turing machine compute, when presented as input with the description and input of some other Turing machine, whether the latter Turing machine will ever halt. The former Turing machine must, of course, halt if we are to receive an answer. This question is called the *Turing Machine Halting Problem* (TMHP). If A and x are, espectively, the Turing machine and input in question, the pair (A,x) is called an *instance* of the TMHP. The TMHP therefore consists of *all* its possible instances. Does a halting Turing machine that solves the TMHP exist? The answer is given by Theorem 15-1.

Theorem 15-1. There exists no algorithm to determine whether an arbitrarily chosen Turing machine started on an arbitrary input will ever halt or not.

Proofs based on the theory of recursive functions are found in many standard works on automata theory; see Reference 11. A more elementary proof based on a logical contradiction similar to that inherent in Russell's Paradox is found in Reference 45.

Table 1   Summary of Some Decision Problems of Phrase-Structure Languages

| | If | | |
| | G, G_1, G_2 Are All Type | | |
Question	3	2	1	0
Is $L(G)$ empty? Finite? Infinite?	D	D	U	U
$L(G_1) \subseteq L(G_2)$? $L(G_1) = L(G_2)$?	D	U	U	U
$L(G) = R$, R a given regular language?	D	U	U	U
$L(G) = V_T{}^*$?	D	U	U	U
Is $L(G)$ regular?	T	U	U	U
$L(G_1) \cap L(G_2) = \Phi$?	D	U	U	U
If G type k, is $\overline{L(G)}$ type k?	T	U	?	U
If G_1, G_2 type k, is $L(G_1) \cap L(G_2)$ type k?	T	U	T	T
If G_1, G_2 type k, is $L(G_1) \cdot L(G_2)$ type k?	T	T	T	T
For $x, y \in V^* : x \underset{G}{\overset{*}{\Rightarrow}} y$?	D	D	D	U
For $y \in V^*: S \underset{G}{\overset{*}{\Rightarrow}} y$?	D	D	D	U

Key.   D = decidable; U = undecidable; T = true for all languages of that type; and ? = unknown.

The TMHP is said to be *unsolvable* or *undecidable*. More particularly, Theorem 15-1 says that there is a least one instance of the TMHP for which the halting question cannot be answered.

15.1.   Other Undecidable Questions

There are many other questions that can be shown to be decidable if and only if the TMHP is decidable, which of course is not the case. One such problem is *Post's Correspondence Problem* [48]. A summary of some decision problems of phrase-structure languages is given in Table 1 [41].

16.   REFERENCES TO OTHER RELATED TOPICS AND FUTURE DIRECTIONS

As stated in the beginning of this chapter, this survey was somewhat narrow in scope in order that some depth could be achieved. Some topics were not mentioned, but will certainly be of interest to the reader that desires to pursue this subject further. Some of these topics are:

1. Operations on and closure properties of languages [19, 27, 29, 36, and 40].
2. Complexity of computation [5, 31, 35, 36, and 50].
3. Deterministic context-free languages and deterministic pushdown automata [36, 38].
4. Stack automata [22, 23, 34, and 36].
5. Unified theories of formal languages and automata [21, 25, 33, and 53].
6. Other types of phrase-structure grammars such as programmed grammars [51], indexed grammars [1], macro grammars [15], and transformational grammars [26].
7. Formal models of compilation such as syntax-directed transduction [3, 14, 42], and tree automata [52].
8. Formal models of computer programs [43, 44].
9. More realistic models of computers [12, 45].
10. Other related surveys [2, 18, 19, 32, and 36].

16.1.   Future Directions

The immediate future directions of the study of formal languages and automata are *applications* and *unification*. Many of these are included in the previously mentioned related topics.

As is the case with almost all theoretical studies, their application is not far behind. Interest is increasing in the study of models of the symbolic manipulation processes of compilation [3, 14, 42], modeling and proving the correctness of computer programs [43, 44], and a more powerful syntactic definition of computer programming languages such as ALGOL 68 [56].

The proliferation of formal languages and automata has led to unified theories such as abstract families of languages (AFL's) and acceptors (AFA's) [21, 25, 29], and balloon automata [33]. Since strings are not the only kind of data structure in which symbols can be stored, interest has turned to automata accepting other data structures, notably trees [52].

The development of these future directions will see the study of formal languages and automata become more widespread and vital in computer science.

17. REFERENCES

1. Aho, A. V., "Indexed Grammars—An Extension of Context-Free Grammars," *J. ACM*, **15**, 647–671, 1968.
2. Aho, A., and J. Ullman, "Theory of Languages," *Math Syst. Theory*, **2**, 97–125, 1968.
3. Aho, A., and J. Ullman, "Transaltions on a Context Free Grammar," Conf. Record ACM Symp. on Theory of Computing, Marina Del Ray, Calif., 1969, pp. 93–112.
4. Bar-Hillel, Y., M. Perles, and E. Shamir, "On Formal Properties of Simple Phrase-Structure Grammars," *Z. Phonetik, Sphrachwiss. Kommunikationsforsch.*, **14**, 143–172, 1961.
5. Blum, M., "A Machine-Independent Theory of Recursive Functions," *J. ACM*, **14**, 322–336, 1967.
6. Booth, T., *Sequential Machines and Automata Theory*, Wiley, New York, 1967.
7. Brzozowski, J., "A Survey of Regular Expressions and Their Applications," *Trans. IEEE*, **EC-11**, 324–335, 1962.
8. Chomsky, N., "On Certain Formal Properties of Grammars," *Info. and Contr.*, **2**, 137–167, 1959.
9. Chomsky N., "Context-Free Grammars and Pushdown Storage," *Quart. Prog. Rept. No.* **65**, MIT RLE, pp. 187–194, 1962.
10. Chromsky, N., and G. Miller, "Finite State Languages," *Info. and Contr.*, **1**, 91–112, 1958.
11. Davis, M., *Computability and Unsolvability*, McGraw-Hill, New York, 1958.
12. Elgot, C. C., and A. Robinson, "Random-Access, Stored-Program Machines—An Approach to Programming Languages," *J. ACM*, **11**, 365–399, 1964.
13. Evey, J., "The Theory and Application of Pushdown Store Machines," Ph.D. Thesis, Harvard Univ., 1963.
14. Feldman, J., and D. Gries, "Translator Writing Systems," *Comm. ACM*, **11**, 77–113, 1968.
15. Fischer, M., "Grammars with Macro-Like Productions," Conf. Record of IEEE Ninth Ann. Symp. on Switching and Automata Theory, 1968, pp. 131–142.

16. Fischer, P., "Multitape and Infinite State Automata—A Survey," *Comm. ACM*, **8**, 799–805.

17. Floyd, R., "On the Nonexistence of a Phrase-Structure Grammar for ALGOL 60," *Comm. ACM*, **5**, 483–484, 1962.

18. Floyd, R., "The Syntax of Programming Languages—A Survey," *Trans. IEEE*, **EC-13**, 346–353.

19. Ginsburg, S., *The Mathematical Theory of Context-Free Languages*, McGraw-Hill, New York, 1966.

20. Ginsburg, S., and S. Greibach, "Deterministic Context-Free Languages," *Info. and Contr.*, **9**, 620–648, 1966.

21. Ginsburg, S., and S. Greibach, "Abstract Families of Languages," *Memoirs of the AMS*, No. 87, pp. 1–32, 1969.

22. Ginsburg, S., S. Greibach, and M. Harrison, "Stack Automata and Compiling," *J. ACM*, **14**, 172–210, 1967.

23. Ginsburg, S., S. Greibach, and M. Harrison, "One-Way Stack Automata," *J. ACM*, **14**, 389–418, 1967.

24. Ginsburg, S., and M. A. Harrison, "On the Elimination of Endmarkers," *Info. and Control*, **12**, 103–115, 1968.

25. Ginsburg, A., and J. Hopcroft, "Two-Way Balloon Automata and AFL's," *J. ACM*, **17**, 3–13, 1970.

26. Ginsburg, S., and B. Partee, "A Mathematical Model of Transformational Grammars," *Info. and Control*, **15**, 297–334, 1969.

27. Ginsburg, S., and G. Rose, "Preservation of Languages by Transducers," *Info. and Contr.*, **9**, 153–176, 1966.

28. Greibach, S., "A New Normal Form Theorem for Context-Free Phrase-Structure Grammars," *J. ACM*, **12**, 42–52, 1965.

29. Greibach, S., and J. Hopcroft, "Independence of AFL Operations," *Memoirs of the AMS*, No. 87, pp. 1–32, 1969.

30. Haines, L., "Generation and Recognition of Formal Languages," Sc.D. Thesis, MIT, 1965.

31. Hartmanis, J., and R. Stearns, "On the Computational Complexity of Algorithms," *Trans. AMS*, **117**, 285–306, 1965.

32. Hopcroft, J., and J. Ullman, "A Survey of Formal Language Theory," Proc. First Ann. Princeton Conf. on Info. Sci. and Syst., 1967, pp. 68–75.

33. Hopcroft, J., and J. Ullman, "An Approach to a Unified Theory of Automata," *Bell Syst. Tech. J.*, **46**, 1763–1829, 1967.

34. Hopcroft, J., and J. Ullman, "Nonerasing Stack Automata," *J. Comp. Syst. Sci.*, **1**, 166–186, 1967.

35. Hopcroft, J., and J. Ullman, "Relations Between Time and Tape Complexities," *J. ACM*, **15**, 414–427, 1968.

36. Hopcroft, J., and J. Ullman, *Formal Languages and Their Relation to Automata* Addison-Wesley, Reading, Mass., 1969.

37. Kleene, S. C., "Representation of Events in Nerve Nets and Finite Automata," *Automata Studies*, (J. McCarthy, Ed.), Princeton Univ. Press, pp. 3–42, 1956.

38. Knuth, D., "On the Translation of Languages From Left to Right," *Info. and Contr.*, **8**, 607–639, 1965.

39. Kuroda, S., "Classes of Languages and Linear-Bounded Automata," *Info. and Contr.*, **7**, 207–223, 1964.

40. Landweber, P. S., "Three Theorems on Phrase Structure Grammars of Type 1," *Info. and Control.* **6**, 131–136, 1963.

41. Landweber, P. S., "Decision Problems of Phrase-Structure Grammars," *Trans. IEEE*, **EC-13**, 354–362, 1964.

42. Lewis, P., and R. Stearns, "Syntax Directed Transduction," *J. ACM*, **15**, 464–488, 1968.

43. Manna, Z., "Properties of Programs and the First-Order Predicate Calculus," *J. ACM*, **16**, 244–255, 1969.

44. Manna, Z., "The Correctness of Programs," *J. Comp. Syst. Sci.*, **3**, 119–127, 1969.

45. Minsky, M. L., *Computation: Finite and Infinite Machines*, Prentice-Hall, Englewood Cliffs, N. J., 1967.

46. Myhill, J., *"Finite Automata and The Representation of Events,"* WADC Tech. Rept. 57-624, 1957.

47. Naur, P. (Ed.), et al., "Revised Report on the Algorithmic Language ALGOL 60," *Comm. ACM*, **6**, 1–17, 1963.

48. Post, E. L., "A Variant of a Recursively Unsolvable Problem," *Bull. AMS*, **52**, 264–268, 1946.

49. Rabin, M. O., and D. Scott, "Finite Automata and Their Decision Problem," *IBM J. Res. and Devel.*, **3**, 115–125, 1959.

50. Rogers, H., *The Theory of Recursive Functions and Effective Computability*, McGraw-Hill, New York, 1967.

51. Rosenkrantz, D. J., "Programmed Grammars and Classes of Computation," *J. ACM*, **16**, 107–131, 1969.

52. Doner, J., "Tree Acceptors and Some of Their Applications," *J. Comp. Syst. Sci.*, **4**, 406–451, 1970.

53. Scott, D. N., "Some Definitional Suggestions for Automata Theory," *J. Comp. Syst. Sci.*, **1**, 187–212, 1967.

54. Shannon, C. E., "A Universal Turing Machine With Two Internal States," *Automata Studies* (J. McCarthy, Ed.), Princeton Univ. Press, 1956, pp. 129–153.

55. Turing, A. M., "On Computable Numbers With an Application to the Enstcheidungsproblem," *Proc. London Math. Soc.*, **42**, 230–265, 1936. A correction in this paper appears in *ibid.*, **43**, 544–546.

56. van Wijngaarden, A. (Ed.), et al., "Report on the Algorithmic Language ALGOL 68," *Report No. MR 101*, Mathematisch Centrum, Amsterdam, October 1969.

Business Applications

R. Clay Sprowls

*University of California
Los Angeles*

This chapter is a qualitative summary of the complex and extensive field of business data processing. It consists of three main sections, preceded by a description (Section 1) of the various functions of the business firm on which the computer may be brought to bear. The first main section (Section 2) is a survey of applications, which classifies them by type of computing, processing mode, and time period since the computer was introduced into business operations. Next, there is a review (Section 3) of the various programming languages and programming packages that are used in business applications. And, finally, Section 4 focuses on the impact of the computer, on the way in which businesses conduct their operations, on the organizational structure of business, and on management itself.

1. FUNCTIONS OF A BUSINESS

Business applications of computers are best understood in the context of the functions that a business enterprise is called upon to perform. Although these functions may differ in specific details from one enterprise to another (for example, some businesses manufacture a product, while others deal only in services), their description is broad enough to provide a general framework for those who have not studied business as a form of organized activity. Relating this overview to other readings and contacts with business enterprises should provide a sufficient background for this survey of computer applications.

Figure 1 is one diagram of a "typical" business system. It could have been drawn differently. In this simplified form it shows vendors supplying certain inputs to the production operations. These operations produce products for sale to customers. Inventories of both the raw material inputs and product outputs are kept. Resources of the firm are applied to operations from the financial, accounting, personnel, and facilities functions.

The activities that surround each of the several functions shown involve flows of different kinds: information flows, physical flows, and money flows. For example, physical raw materials come from vendors into inventory and physical products are shipped to customers. Information flows about these physical flows are in the form of shipping documents and invoices. Money flows are initiated because the vendor is paid for the raw materials and the customer pays for the products.

Information and money flows also originate in the personnel activities. Employees are paid for their services. Information about employees circulates not only within the firm itself but also to outside agencies such as local, state, and federal governments, to insurance companies and to medical facilities. Information flows tend to generate considerable paper work.

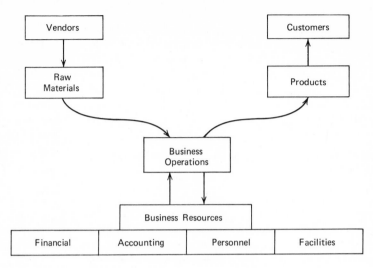

Figure 1.   Diagram of a business firm.

To the extent to which payments are represented by checks, even money flows generate paper work. Some of this paper work is absolutely necessary because legal requirements demand a signed document or contract. Much of it is records, summaries, and reports that are embodied in trade practices to enable management to account for its past activities and, to a lesser extent, plan and control the future.

The information flows connected with these major business activities create data on a daily, weekly, and monthly basis. Data inputs of previous periods have resulted in records and files relating to customers, employees, inventories, and all other phases of the business. Current data are processed against these master files for updating them and also preparing various reports and documents. Examples of the data that major business activities can create are shown in Figure 2 in the form of major files, each of which contains many items. For example, the sales data file may contain such items as orders received, stockouts, back orders, invoices, special orders, customer claims and salesmen reports. The files are shown around a central computer facility in keeping with the perspective of this book and the future trend that is already discernible with respect to the computer's position in the business firm.

The electronic computer made its debut within this business activity framework in approximately 1953, only a few short years after its initial introduction into scientific activities. Some types of business have been

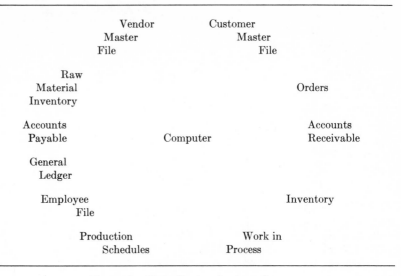

Figure 2.   Data files in a business firm.

more affected than others; some activities are more pervasive than others. One would be hard pressed, however, not to find a computer somewhere in any type of business or business activity he would wish to name.

2. SURVEY OF APPLICATIONS

A survey of business applications is presented by classifying the various applications in three different ways: (1) by type of computing; (2) by processing mode; and (3) by time period since the computer became available. These classifications are not mutually exclusive, but organized in this manner, the survey will give a complete perspective on the whole field of business computing.

2.1. Type of Computing

Business applications may be separated by type of computation into "data processing" and "scientific" categories. This has been a traditional classification that led to the design and production of two different kinds of computers in the early 1950s. One emphasized input/output facilities with lesser computational ability for the processing of business data. The other emphasized very large and fast computational abilities with more limited input/output for scientific work. This classification has very much less validity with respect to the design and use of computers today. Many data processing applications also involve large amounts of computation and scientific applications very often involve large amounts of data. Moreover, both types of computing can now be done on the same computer systems, especially the larger ones that are commonly found in the business environment. The separation is made here to enhance the clarity of an applications summary.

2.1.1. Data Processing

Data processing applications may be further subdivided into record keeping, control systems, and the currently in-vogue management information system (MIS), discussed in Chapter 14. Examples of record keeping processing are payroll, accounts receivable and payable, insurance, order entry and billing, and ledger accounting. These applications are clerical functions in which the computer is introduced as a substitute for clerks, sometimes in an effort to control clerical costs and sometimes as the only means to deal with the volume of work.

Examples of control systems are inventory control and production scheduling. These applications include a certain amount of information feedback with which they are controlled. In inventory control this may mean that economic order quantity computations are made and reordering is triggered automatically by the computer. In production scheduling, it may mean applications of queueing theory, network analysis, and simulation for which data from the production process are used to plan and control the scheduling. This is different from the mere routine processing of clerical transactions.

Finally, MIS as a concept embraces the system that provides the information that management requires for decision making. It cannot provide all of the information for management decision making, because even if not unfeasible with a computer based MIS, it is uneconomical. MIS is to be differentiated from the "traditional" data processing activities that support record keeping and operational functions. It implies overall management goals and criteria for measuring performance as well as a knowledge of the basic methods of decision making and the information needed to apply those methods.

2.1.2. Scientific Computing

Scientific computing within business may also be further subdivided according to the areas or techniques to which the computing process applies. Statistical analysis of data is a very large business application. Mathematical techniques are used in budgeting and funds analysis. Operations research and management science (here used as two different names for the same discipline) contribute to business applications through linear programming, queueing theory, various other optimization techniques and simulation.

Simulation is the development and use of models for the study of various situations. The computer is one of the best tools for the study of business applications through simulation. The activity is represented by a model in a form amenable to computer solution. The simulation model is then exercised on the computer to obtain information about the activity that the model represents. Applications include very specific parts of the firm as well as more ambitious attempts to model and simulate the entire enterprise.

2.2.   Processing Modes

Classification by processing mode is according to the way in which the computer is used. Key methods include batch processing, on-line operation, and time-sharing.

2.2.1.   Batch Processing

The traditional mode of business computer operations is batch processing. Data are batched and then submitted for computer processing in one run. Examples are the batching of time cards for employees. These are then processed against the personnel file for updating, perhaps daily or in the once-a-week batch run against the master file to write payroll checks. Another is the daily batching of transactions in an insurance company with a once-a-day batch run against the master files to produce all of the reports necessary to operate an insurance company. Batch processing is the only economical way of processing sequential files, especially when the files reside on magnetic tape or on punch cards.

These applications are from data processing, but scientific applications may also be processed in a batch mode. Here "batch" refers not so much to the batching of data for processing as to the batching of different computer jobs: a statistical analysis, followed by a linear programming problem, followed by a budget simulation.

2.2.2.   On-line Updating and Retrieval

A computer is said to be on-line if an external device may be operated by an individual so that his action affects the computer operation and the computer affects him in some way. (See Chapter 7.) On-line computing activities are of growing importance in the business environment, for both retrieval of information and for updating the contents of business files.

Inquiries may be made against a file so that a manager may control some business function. An inventory control system might be operated in this mode. A batch system accomplishes the basic file processing but a manager inquires about the inventory file status on-line to the computer. Customer and employee files are candidates for this type of processing. Basic changes in customer or employee data are made to files in a batch system. Sales personnel may inquire about customer data and the personnel office about employee data on-line in order to manage and control their operations.

Commercial applications of this mode are growing. One is the computerized credit bureau. Data are maintained centrally at a computer service center. Authorized users inquire about credit status in an on-line mode for such purposes as cashing checks, issuing new credit, and selling on previously established credit standards which may have significant updated information about the individual. Another is in the real estate field where data on basic real estate activities (for example, a listing of properties for sale) are available to many real estate agents. Again, the data files are updated and maintained centrally and inquiries are made on-line.

On-line computer operations are being extended to include file updating activities in addition to the retrieval of information. Batch processing may be taking place in the computer system to utilize it more efficiently, but file support activities for some applications are taken out of the batch mode and placed on-line to the computer.

An inventory control system is an obvious candidate for on-line updating. As transactions occur that affect the file, they are immediately processed against it from an external device. File status is always current for those who wish to access it for data. An airline reservation system is a prime example. A stock market quotation system is another. The need for timely and up-to-the-minute data to control operations in both systems is the motivation for on-line processing.

2.2.3. Time Sharing

A multiple access system is formed when a number of external devices, each capable of communicating with the computer, are connected to a single computer. If, in addition, each of these devices can be served sequentially or simultaneously by that computer and the user is given the impression that the computing system is servicing him only, the on-line system is said to the time-shared. (See also Chapter 7.)

Whereas time sharing is usually associated with scientific and engineering computing, it is now becoming well entrenched in many management applications. The remote access and quick response characteristics of time sharing are appealing for a variety of users. Some examples are rate of return computations in capital investment, cash budgeting, sales forcasting models, bond bidding and pricing models, lease or buy analysis, and job shop scheduling. The applications tend to have small amounts of data, to require only a modest amount of computing, and to involve a significant degree of user interaction that requires a fast response.

2.3. Chronological Classification

Since 1953, computer applications to business problems have evolved in stages that may be identified with time periods: from 1953 to 1965 is one period and from 1965 to date is a second. Although there are exceptions to the general characteristics ascribed to these periods below, they are approximately correct and suffice to give a flavor of the changing business application world.

2.3.1. 1953 to 1965

Applications in this time period were characterized primarily as unrelated and elementary uses of the computer to do essentially what clerks had done before. The operations were carried out electronically rather than by the clerks. Thus, one saw computers involved in the elementary processes of business functions. They kept the general ledger for accounting, wrote the payroll checks for personnel, processed orders and wrote customer bills for marketing, kept track of inventory levels, and printed production reports for operations. Each of these activities is a necessary business function. Each is characterized by large volumes of transactions that are represented by masses of paper documents and traditionally processed by large clerical staffs who are in short supply at ever increasing cost. Little wonder, then, that the computer made its first impact on business as a clerk substitute in the best data processing needs of the firm.

2.3.2. 1965 to the Present

The second time frame is roughly the present. The scope of applications for some business firms has widened to effect changes in how the business operates and what it does. Some examples will show the directions that applications have taken.

From the simple order entry and billing, the computer is providing customer service in a more general sense. The accounting ledger application is expanded to cash and budget control. Inventory stock-keeping now includes as well forecasts with statistical smoothing and economic order quantity computations. Personnel applications include skills inventories. Just beginning is the introduction of external data for analysis in decision making. Initial steps are being taken to develop applications that relate to each other through their common uses of data. The emphasis is shifting from routine data processing to planning and control. Management activity is able to focus on reduction in inventory levels rather than mere reporting of existing levels; on customer relations rather than orders and bills; on projecting and reducing balances rather than counting cash.

2.3.3. Summary

This summary of business computing activity by type of computing, processing mode, and chronology is intended to provide an overview of business applications by examining them from different points of view in order to get a sense of the change and evolution that is taking place. For example, inventory processing started in the early years of 1954 and 1955 as a straightforward data processing application run in a batch processing mode as a replacement for clerks. In some instances it has now evolved into an on-line and even a time-shared activity with scientific computations for economic order quantity imbedded in the data processing.

Some firms are today still in the "1953–1965" mode of application. A key factor that determines the position of any individual firm in this development gradient is economic justification which for it remains to be shown.

3. PROGRAMMING LANGUAGES AND PACKAGES

Assembly language is used in business applications and a knowledge of assembly language is needed by at least some of the business computing staff to maintain and modify operating systems and compilers. No emphasis is given to assembly language here. Instead, the focus is on higher level languages and complete programming packages that place considerable emphasis on commercial data processing applications. Therefore, FORTRAN, ALGOL, and programs developed for scientific use are passed over even though they might be used in a business application. These languages, as well as COBOL and PL/I mentioned below, are described and illustrated by Alfonso F. Cardenas in Chapter 10 in this text.

3.1. COBOL

An acronym for common business oriented language, COBOL, was proposed in 1959 by a group of government users and computer manufacturer representatives as a language for business. The first version appeared as COBOL 60.

COBOL is specifically designed to process data organized into records that are part of files. Sequential file processing that is so common to business data processing applications receives primary attention. Moreover, the organization of data records is in a structure that permits data items to be imbedded within others so that data levels are explicitly defined. Only at a level at which it is no longer subdivided is the data item described. The level structure of COBOL data records is an important aspect of the language capability.

All data in COBOL are described in a separate DATA DIVISION of the source program. Mere use in a COBOL sentence is not enough to define it. The advantage of such an approach is that the DATA DIVISION becomes a blueprint to all of the data in a program. Each file is named and described; each record is systematically defined by its level structure. The documentation inherent in this language feature enhances its usefulness in business applications.

Some other notable features are considerable editing facilities for dollar signs, commas, and accounting symbols which are necessary to produce final business reports. Longer variable names (up to 31 characters) simplify the task of naming by mnemonics. Operators in English (ADD, SUBTRACT, MULTIPLY, DIVIDE) are not necessarily an advantage to one who is accustomed to program writing. They are an advantage to the functional business specialist because the near-Englishlike sentence structure of the statements is understandable to one not well versed in programming arts.

COBOL is the most widely used general purpose language for business applications. Its most recent version (USA COBOL-1968) is updated to direct access input and output suitable for on-line computing as a supplement to the long standing sequential processing.

The interested reader may now refer to Section 6.9 in Chapter 10 in this text, which describes and illustrates COBOL by means of an example of updating of a sequential file.

3.2. PL/I

A recent addition to higher level languages, PL/I is becoming more used in business applications. The commercial part of PL/I supports the organization of data into structures with levels similar to COBOL. It provides also extensive editing facilities. The organization of the source program into procedures is useful in segmenting large data processing applications into manageable programming tasks.

Character and bit string operations and functions extend the language in a way that is useful to many business applications. For example, bit strings will support information retrieval applications from business files. Character strings are useful in "personal" letter writing which has become important not only in direct mail advertising but also in political campaigns. Finally, PL/I supports data files on direct access storage devices for on-line access.

Although PL/I may well be used merely as a substitute to FORTRAN and ALGOL for various kinds of scientific applications, these features extend its usefulness to business.

3.3.   Report Generators

Printed reports abound in data processing applications. Both recurring and special reports are prepared from basic file processing operations as well as special computer runs. COBOL has recently incorporated a report section in the source language to facilitate report design and programming. Special report generation languages are also available. RPG (for Report Program Generation) is one example.

The basic functions contained in RPG are retrieval of data records, calculations on the data, table lookup, branching, sequence checking, and report writing. These functions are specified in detail by filling in specification sheets which are the "high-level language" of RPG. Thus, there are input specification, calculation specification, report design, and file description sheets. These become the input to the RPG program.

The general functions described above are broken down into things like record and field descriptions; addition and subtraction operators; control fields for record to record comparisons; total calculations; detail, total and group printing; summary punching; testing for zero, negative and positive balances; high, low and equal comparisons; multiplication and division operations; sequence checking and table lookup. The intent in RPG is to provide a simple way to retrieve and report data from files by providing standard worksheets on which the details of the report request are filled in or checked off.

3.4.   SORT

The organization of data files into records sequenced according to a key makes sorting an important business computer task. Large files maintained on magnetic tape dictate sequential files. Transactions that are to be processed for file maintenance, insertion of new records, record deletion, and updating are first sorted into file sequence and then processed for the maintenance operation.

Files may be maintained in one order and then sorted into another order for a special purpose. For example, more and more files with records that represent data on people (employees, students, and the like) are organized according to social security number. Transactions are sorted into this order for file maintenance. However, if a listing of the employees is desired alphabetically, the file must be sorted from social security number sequence into alphabetical sequence. Moreover, the listing may be needed by department code and possibly even job classification within a department. The file must be sorted by department order, by job classification within the department, and finally into alphabetic sequence to print the desired listing.

A similar file might be used to mail literature to employees. For this purpose, the post office desires (and increasingly demands) mail sorted by Zip Code. In fact, mail sorted this way commands a lower postal rate in bulk mailings. The original social security number sequence is not much use and the file must be sorted by Zip Codes before printing address labels.

Sorting is so important that some higher level languages have a sort verb as a part of their specifications. Sort programs are also available as special programs for which one describes file and record descriptions and the sort keys to be used as parameters. The sort processor then generates a program or executes a program to accomplish the sorting.

3.5. Decision Tables

Decision tables are a form of tabular logic for describing actions that follow certain conditions. They are an alternative to a flow chart for complicated decision-logic specifications. Although used as a system design technique from which a programmer may write source language statements in one of a number of languages, attempts have also been made to imbed decision table forms in another language. DETAB-X in COBOL, and FORTAB and DETRAN in FORTRAN are examples. The inclusion here is possibly more as a systems analysis technique which has application to the decision logic of business applications than as a language.

3.6. Simulation

Business modeling and simulation are important applications outside the realm of the data processing. A variety of mathematical, statistical, and logical methods are applied in designing the models. Simulations can be programmed in general purpose higher level languages, but the description of the attributes of various entities in the model and particularly the timing mechanism that is necessary to the simulation are tedious programming tasks. As a result, special simulation languages are available. Two of these languages in rather widespread use are GPSS and SIMSCRIPT.

Both languages use standard forms on which the simulator describes the various attributes, relations, and operations of the model. These are then converted to machine processible form for input to the simulation processor which produces computer code. The emphasis in each is on the logic and intent of the simulation model rather than upon computer programming.

3.7. Time-Sharing

The growing importance of time sharing is attested to by the increasing number of commercial time sharing services being marketed. With this increase also comes a larger number of languages with which to program in a time shared environment. BASIC is the language described in Section 7 in Chapter 10 and is most likely the leading language specifically designed for terminal use with time sharing systems. APL is another candidate. Time sharing versions of FORTRAN, COBOL, and PL/I also exist. Each of these languages is adaptable to programming business applications.

Some (like BASIC) are simple enough in an elemental form to be learned by practicing business managers who have little desire to become deeply involved either with the computer or a sophisticated programming language. They do wish to solve problems, perhaps as simple as an interest rate computation. With such a programming language and a terminal connected to a time-shared system, they are able to use the computer as a tool. This easy access to the computer, combined with a manager's ability to program and use it himself, has been a large force in the growth and acceptance of time sharing in the business community.

3.8. Generalized File Processors

Under the heading of generalized file processors are an increasing number of programming packages that are of such growing importance they must be included in any discussion of the business computing environment. Some of them are complete systems, some are enhancements to an existing language, and some are special programs for a business application.

The motivation for generalized file processors is quite simple. Scientific computing has had generalized programs almost from the beginning. Programs for special computations like matrix inversion, linear programming, and statistical analyses have long existed so that a new program need not be written each time an application arises. Mathematicians, engineers, and statisticians have recognized the wisdom of using programs already developed by others with the same need and have not felt obligated to rewrite them for their own application.

This has not been the case in business for the file processing that is the heart of the data processing application. Each business has tended to write its own application programs in order to tailor-make them to its own needs. This has even happened among different divisions of a single firm and, yet, all file processing tends to follow the same general operations for maintenance, search, and summarization. The files and data records change from one application to another, but the basic file processing remains the same.

The development of generalized file processors is an attempt to provide a system and/or language in which the details of the file and record data are specified; somewhat general operations are permitted; simplified report forms are supplied; and a program is then generated to reflect the specific details of the application. The emphasis is thus placed on the process or the application and not on the programming. Computer implementation is accomplished by specifying the detailed characteristics of the system needs to the generalized processor. Some evidence exists that the whole character of implementing a business application may change as a result because programming an application no longer means what it used to mean. Not all advertised systems are this general or this complete. The list discussed here is not exhaustive but is representative of approaches.

3.8.1. IMS

An acronym for information management system, IMS is a terminal-oriented, on-line system designed to support large direct-access data bases in the aerospace industry. Data files are defined, created, maintained, and reorganized by using a special language named DL-2, version 2 of the Data Language. Users may then program computations and reports in conventional high-level languages like COBOL or PL/I. IMS provides all of the data organization and management support services as well as routines for communication control and message processing from terminals and telephones, but users have the responsibility for application programming.

IMS supports batch processing and scientific application programs as well. Engineering groups, for example, may use the same computer system for FORTRAN programs.

Although designed for aerospace files of basic engineering drawings and spare parts inventory, the IMS system has a potential for other types of data as well. Employee files of a personnel office and student files of a college or university are likely candidates for IMS implementation.

3.8.2. IDS

IDS (for integrated data store) augments a host language like COBOL. The user defines a file structure in IDS but all manipulations and reporting of data are programmed in the host language which uses IDS to manage the storage, retrieval, and updating of the data files on direct access devices. IDS users are professional programmers.

The basis file structure is defined as a chain in which a master record points to a detail record, which in turn points to another detail record, and so on, to the limit necessary to describe the data relationships. Since the last detail record points back to the master record, the data relationship is in the form of a ring. The programmer may create new records within the data set, insert data records on established rings, and search rings to find data values. Statements exist for removing records from rings and for deleting records from files. Ring structures are an extension of a list data organization such that the last record points back to the first record in the ring. This structure permits nesting to any level required by the logical relationships in the data, that is, a hierarchial storage organization.

From the practical standpoint of business file processing applications, IDS economizes the use of direct access storage by a reduction of redundant information in a file via this form of data structuring. A data value that is a part of several records or files may be recorded in the data storage just once. It is known to the different files and records of which it is a part by their pointers. Changing this one data value with a file maintenance or updating program automatically changes it in all records and files within which it is logically located, thus ensuring the identical value in all uses.

Data organization into lists, inverted lists, rings, and other forms is beyond the scope of this chapter. IDS is mentioned only as an example of one type of data management system that has useful business application.

3.8.3. COGENT

As a preprocessor, COGENT generates a standard COBOL program. This makes it machine independent. Including a capability for file creation, maintenance, arithmetic and logical operations, data extraction and data presentation, COGENT is intended to simplify the generation of new file maintenance systems, reduce program checkout time, and reduce both the time to document and the documentation requirements as compared with programming in COBOL. The compatibility with COBOL enables a programmer to drop down to that source language if necessary. COGENT includes a simplified procedure for satisfying management requests for data in special reports.

The system's attractiveness to management stems from the provision for both data management and data presentation processing. This contrasts with other systems that manage data but put the burden of report writing on application programs and still others that provide selection and report writing but not general file maintenance. The machine independency, by virtue of a standard COBOL data set, is in contrast with those systems that produce machine language.

3.8.4.   MARK IV

This generalized file management system provides facilities for file definition, file creation, file updating, and interrogation. The "programming language" is a set of tabular forms that are provided to perform these processes. The output of Mark IV processing is in machine language.

. MARK IV can be used for file conversion as well as the reconstruction of an existing file. It will sort on multiple files and fields. The output language supports sorting, editing, and statistical computations like averages, ratios, maximum and minimum values, for multiple reports in one computer run. Input to MARK IV is from standardized coding sheets and the output is in machine code. Its chief goal is to facilitate batch commercial data processing. The use of tabular forms makes information retrieval and maintenance easier for commercial systems users by focusing their attention on the basic processes and needs of their commercial system rather than on programming.

3.8.5.   QWICK QWERY

This system is designed to simplify requests for tailor-made analyses and reports from existing data files. The data file is described in a dictionary where names and their attributes are recorded. Request forms are filled out for each request. These describe basic definitions, computations, synonyms, selections, sorts, analysis, and display requirements. A report may be in a standard form or customized. The request forms are the input to the program; the output is in machine language.

3.9.   Summary

The programming activities that support business applications include a variety of programming languages and packages. COBOL is important as is the commercial subset of some other langauge like PL/I. Report generators and sort routines may be imbedded in another language or operate as independent programs. Decision tables and simulation languages are a part of the business computing environment. Of growing importance are time sharing and generalized file processors. The latter include systems that provide both file maintenance and reports as well as more specialized systems for maintenance, or reports. Some systems produce a higher level language data set like COBOL; others produce machine language programs. Some operate on existing files, others reorganize a file to their requirements. The examples given here are representative of approaches rather than exhaustive. Other acronyms that appear in the computing literature are: GIS, GIM, MANAGE, INFOL, UL/I, CDMS, ASA*ST, DM-1, MULTI-

LIST, ISL-1, SC-1, FORMAT-1, RAPS, AEGIS, SCORE, CULPRIT, and INFORMS. Many more proprietary systems are available from the myriad of programming sources that have developed in the past few years.

4. IMPACT ON BUSINESS OPERATIONS

As with any new and developing technology, the computer has had widely differing effects on business. It has affected some industries more than others and has had more effect on some firms than others within the same industry. The impact appears to be less related to size, product, or service than to a knowledgeable and approving management that realizes the potential inherent in computer applications and insists upon positive results.

The elementary and unrelated uses of the computer as a replacement for clerical operations have already been discussed. An expansion from basic clerical functions to a larger set of activities and new applications more related to each other and to management planning and control is now occurring. Even these limited activities have had an effect on the way business operates, and sometimes the effect is not what was planned. For example, while replacing clerical help and reducing the problem of securing employees of the clerical category, the computer has substituted sizeable staffs of a different kind. Management now faces problems with respect to acquiring and managing computer specialists, ranging from operators and programmers to systems and management personnel. This change has had a sizeable impact on management, for here is a whole new group dedicated to business applications with a technology that some managements do not understand and others have no desire to understand. Perhaps this impact is more significant than any change in the way of doing business.

Examples of how traditional ways of doing business have changed are not difficult to find. Some of them also affect every citizen in his everyday life. Only a brief list is given.

4.1. Application Examples

Income tax processing as a business application is different by computer than by clerk. The inherent ability to retain data over several years' time for subsequent analysis and comparison has an effect on some taxpayers. The federal government's present steps to coordinate with state governments for cross-checking certain items of income and expenses add a whole new dimension to tax collecting.

The speed with which banks can and do process machine readable checks by computer has drastically shortened the lag between the time a check is written and an account is posted with the amount of the check. The "float" inherent in previous systems for both the individual and business has been significantly reduced.

Utility bills are now often printed by computer in the form of a turn-around document that is machine readable. The key information is printed in a character font that can be optically scanned or read upon its return with a payment.

Department stores print customer bills with a brief description of the item and no longer return a copy of the original sales slip to the customer. The traditional way of dealing with charge account customers is drastically changed.

The speed of processing and forecasting inventory levels by computer has significantly reduced inventory levels and thus inventory carrying costs. In some instances, manufacturers supply their larger customers with inventory control programs free of charge. Their payoff is through the faster acquisition of sales data with which to plan production schedules. A next step is to tie the customer inventory and sales processing into the manufacturer's system for automatic reordering according to jointly agreed upon rules. This changes the whole relationship between customer and manufacturer, especially the traditional role of the "buyer" and his order book.

The computerized credit system gives the credit grantor of the check casher more immediate information with which to control his credit system.

The centralized real estate file gives a local realtor a broader base of marketing knowledge than he might otherwise have. This should be of some benefit to the would-be purchaser also; for example, an executive relocating to a new city.

Computerized ticket sales through a nationwide network of sales offices to a centralized ticket data base have an immediate effect on the individual's ability to procure seats to local and distant events, as well as the previous structure of the marketing system.

The availability of data on the nation's business firms through a nationwide data service adds a whole new dimension to market research. Not only are more data accumulated in one place, but they are immediately available to more interested persons without the necessity to process volumes of annual statements and other reports.

Investment appraisal is now more sophisticated with respect to valuing alternative investment opportunities and their terms, present values, and rates of return, all because of the computer's ability to evaluate rather complicated formulas quickly.

Stock market analysis can now embrace more stocks and more factors about each stock than ever before for the security analysts of investment firms and brokerage houses. Even the operation of the major stock exchanges themselves are changing over to computerized systems as the volume of paper work swells beyond the limit of clerical processing capability.

The list of such applications and the changes in the way of doing business is very large. No more need be given here. One who is interested need only read the daily newspaper or peruse journals and magazines devoted to the business scene to add to the list. *Business Week*, for example, established a whole department for Computers and Communications beginning in June, 1969. Of more interest to students and practitioners of management theory and organization is the impact of the computer on organization structure and management itself.

4.2. Management Impact

The success with computer tasks in the mid-1950s and early 1960s generated great enthusiasm for meshing the computer more directly into managerial activities. The role of the middle manager is questioned and some "authorities" claim that the whole concept of the middle manager will disappear as the computer takes over the routine decision-making function now almost exclusively the province of the middle manager. Others make the opposite claim.

Some authorities view the computer as the means to centralize all data processing activities of previously decentralized large firms. Others continue to believe that, even with the computer's ability to handle large communication systems that in principle can serve centrally the data needs of decentralized units, this will not happen.

Management scientists have an implicit faith in the quantitative approach to business decision making and this faith leads them to the belief that there is no management decision of any importance that does not land itself to computerization in one way or another.

Computers have inspired hopes for a "total system" or a "management information and control system" and these hopes have led to large development investments. All of the vital statistics of a corporation are to be stored in the computer system and immediately available to the chief executive. He is pictured as sitting at a display console in his office requesting data and reducing his problem solving to the computerized output of neat mathematical models.

There is some evidence that the traditional bookkeeping department has been completely removed by the computer as accountants have broadened their scope into company-wide activities for cost and financial control. Similarly, credit management, warehousing, and sales departments have been integrated into one function that embraces a larger total activity hant the three formerly independent activities. Other examples will show that such realignments are not taking place and that whole sections of middle management have not been eliminated.

General Motors has computerized its world-wide communications system to process orders for automobiles and spare parts and to control inventories and production. It insists that it will maintain decentralized operations and that only the information processing is centralized.

Westinghouse Electric has centralized its communications around a computer but maintained decentralized operations. Whereas it was in the vanguard of developments to aid executives and its enthusiasts talked about equipping vice presidents with desk top computer consoles, its new headquarters appears to lack such consoles in the new executive offices.

United States Steel has recentralized its classic structure of a large decentralized firm and left division presidents to seek new jobs.

Pillsbury centralized all of its information systems and then, ten years later, formally decentralized them. Managers learned how to use the computer during the centralization period with time sharing terminals readily available to them. With the decentralization, each division has its own computer center, but each will also have a remote access to a centralized information system.

Dupont simulates the entire dye industry and the company's stake in it with a management science model. Risk analysis is used to assess the odds that a new product will produce profits, and how large they are likely to be.

Owens-Illinois has a corporation model to let executives test ideas and strategies.

Pillsbury tried to formulate a model of the entire company's operations but now is satisfied with a number of simplified submodels for such things as pricing and introducing new grocery products.

Ingalls keeps track of their own and competitors' shipbuilding orders in relation to yard capacity in order to predict competitive bids on new ships and, therefore, its own bid.

Sun Oil has a model of operations and sales to predict net income for the entire company one year in advance.

Anheuser-Busch models its advertising decisions with respect to budgets in regional markets with a reported reduction in budget with no loss of sales.

Enthusiasts point to such applications as these for evidence of success and things to come. Detractors, however, argue that these applications are far short of earlier claims. They argue that the bulk of the evidence is that management is becoming less and less quantifiable, rather than more so.

Business has gone through a stage of regarding itself as a science and is now increasingly regarding itself as an art. The most vocal critics even claim that the management scientist is likely to warp the problem so that he can find a solution, or to omit relevant variables so that the solution is to something that is not the problem. Their view is that the best that can be hoped for is contributory information to improve a design: the possibility to evaluate alternatives; to discern what variables are the most important, to test decisions in a what-if-questioning mode.

Suffice it to say that the impact on organizational structure and management activities is in such a state of flux that not all of the evidence is yet accumulated and the final results are still in the future.

4.3. Impact from Communications

Another approach to studying the impact of the computer on business activities is by examining the methods that have been and are being developed to use the computer in the business environment. Here the computer is intimately linked with communications. The prediction by some is that such linkages will lead to worldwide information networks using satellite communications. The keys to such systems are remote access to the computer, communication links for data transmission, and large data bases stored in machine processible form. Examples of such developing systems have already been mentioned—ticket sales, credit data, real estate data, and the GM and Westinghouse examples. These already combine the three features listed above into successful systems.

Coincidental with these developing systems is a growing acceptance of time sharing by the business community. It also embraces remote access, communications and often centralized data files but on a lesser scale in many applications. The applications presently using time sharing computer systems cover a wide variety of business problems, both small and large users, and firms with and without their own computer centers. A partial list of such current applications is given to acquaint the reader with the current level of activity. This list is shown in Figure 3.

These applications vary considerably in size and complexity and cut across different functional areas of the firm. Represented in the list are applications from such functions as finance, marketing, sales, production, accounting, personnel, and general management. Although diverse in nature, the applications do have some common underlying characteristics, some of which are imposed by the nature of time-sharing computing.

The volume of data is typically small as compared with the very large files used in other types of data processing. The volume of computation is modest in relation to other computer processes. The demand for user

Accounts receivable analysis	Long range planning model
Aircraft scheduling	Merger analysis
Branch site locations	New product costing
Cash flow projections	New product pricing
Corporate earnings projection	Pension fund performance
Credit screening	Population projections
Direct labor analysis	Portfolio analysis
Enrollment projections	Production scheduling
Financial lease analysis	Project budgeting
Financial statements	Rate of return calculator
Flight crew manning	Real estate financing
Job shop simulation	Sales analysis
Lead time analysis	Savings and demand deposit model
Lease or buy analysis	Tax projections

Figure 3.   Partial list of time sharing applications.

interaction and a quick response is very high. Moreover, with few exceptions (possibly accounts receivable analysis, financial statements, production scheduling and the like), the applications are and can be independent of the normal data processing activities of the firm. This independence makes them prime candidates for time sharing which may not be an integral part of the computing activities serviced by the computation center.

The growing acceptance of time sharing as a mode of computing for business applications and of communications-oriented data base systems together support the argument that world-wide computer and communication information networks will materialize.

4.4. Interesting Problems

The current and future development of business applications is fraught with interesting problems. Some of these are highly technical design problems for the organization of computer and communications systems. Some involve the relationships of human beings in the use of these systems. Still others are software developments to support the activities that business firms wish to pursue. A few areas are briefly discussed below.

As remote computing usage grows and terminals develop into graphic and display devices, the whole man-machine relationship becomes an area for research. To the extent that the engineer ignores this in his equipment and systems design, he ignores an important part of the application process. It may be too much to ask that all computer designers engage in a serious pursuit of knowledge about how users interact with these systems, but some must be so involved or the systems will fail to satisfy the basic needs as management defines them for the business.

Examples of generalized file processors have already been given in an earlier section. This concept is growing in importance and its impact may well change how business systems are programmed in the future. The impact on computer specialists is twofold. On the one hand, he may become intimately involved in the implementation of such a file system for which a technical knowledge is necessary. On the other hand, his current and salable knowledge about detailed computer programming and operations may become less valuable as business computing grows to rely more on a general system which emphasizes system needs than on programming in a more detailed computer language.

Related to generalized file processing and to the development of large scale computer-communications systems that are predicted in the previous section is the whole subject of data structures. The basic organization of data into records and files is a fruitful area for research. Examples were given in the earlier discussion of generalized file processing (IDS, for instance) and of sorting, a large activity in data processing applications. These developments must continue to contribute to studies of how data should be organized for the future systems.

Standardized application programs have not been as abundant for business applications as for scientific computing. More and more effort is being expended to develop programming packages that will be general enough to adapt to business needs. In the past, even the development of such a program as a payroll processor was difficult because each individual firm has or thinks it has unique requirements, different enough from anyone else that a standard program will not work. One answer has, of course, been the generalized file processor. Another is a revision of the approach to developing standard programs so that they will fit the special needs of each firm or at least the cost of revision will be so small as to make it economically attractive. Hopefully, program designers will have learned enough about business problems that the design specifications more generally meet the needs of a user, a requirement for acceptance and success.

Computerized control of data transmission and communication is at the heart of many presently developing and future systems. Aside from the technical problems of equipment design and operation are the problems of what and how much data to transmit. In this area, management must deal with the problem of valuing information.

Finally, here at least, the whole area of input-output comes up for serious study. Dealing with remote terminals has already been mentioned. Optical character recognition is a growing field of importance. Voice input and output from computers are still in their infancy. Graphics are just beginning to make an impact. Even such a mundane thing as replacing a punch card with a direct keyboard to magnetic tape instrument impacts on the business application.

A wide variety of researchers from many disciplines can easily find interesting and important problems to work on in the business world.

4.5.   Exhortation to the Computer Scientist

Since 1953 management has been exhorted to learn about computers. During this time their dealings with computer scientists has not always been to the scientist's credit. Engulfed in jargon, held at arm's length, and often misled with advice, managements have sometimes been frustrated and disenchanted with this new technology that they must now embrace to keep pace in the competitive business world. The result is too often an overextension of computer facilities, a change to new and more sophisticated equipment, and more and more costly computer systems with less and less evidence of profitable operations and applications.

The changing emphasis noted throughout the previous sections is also bringing a change in management attitude toward computers. From criteria such as what can be computerized at a cost reduction or what can be duplicated electronically, a new criteria of effectiveness is emerging. The deliberate purpose for which computer applications are sought and approved is to improve profits by helping management. The real effectiveness in this sphere is the management capacity to plan and control. Therefore, evaluation will, more and more, be in terms of management control processes.

One immediate path to this end is the active searching out of specific men with specific responsibilities in the firm, identifying them and what they do and how they can use the computer to change what they do in a meaningful and profitable way. The emphasis is upon the value of information in the hands of the manager, not the reduced clerical cost of processing that information.

In this changing environment, the computer specialist is exhorted to learn about management and managerial problems. With new criteria, management will manage rather than delegate, for in the change from emphasis upon cost cutting to profit making, only the manager knows best the places where profits will accrue.

The computer scientist should be aware that business now stands at the threshhold not only of using the advances in technology but at the threshhold also of a new attitude toward and treatment of the computer's role in business. The decade of the 1970s will bring to fruition some of the trends already discernible in the present. These are:

1. Changes in management structure.

2. New concepts of how to use the computer in large networks with large data bases and communication systems.

3. New criteria for effectiveness in measuring the usefulness of the system.

No longer can a computer specialist argue for more core memory to run a sophisticated multiprogramming operating system when the computer is loaded only one shift. No longer will equipment be ordered and applications undertaken to satisfy the egos of the computer center managers. Management will apply similar criteria and standards to the computer functions as to other functions for which standards have long been worked out and applied.

The computer scientist will be forced to learn how to live in this new environment and he should find the learning an exciting and rewarding activity. For the computer (his specialty) will be at the center of this information processing activity for management planning and control.

5. REFERENCES

1. Burck, Gilbert, *The Computer Age*, Harper and Row, 1965.
2. Solomon, Irving, and Laurence Weingart, *Management Uses of the Computer*, New American Library, 1968.
3. Halacy, D. S., *Computers: The Machines We Think With*, Harper and Row, 1962.
4. Hugo, I. St. J., *Marketing and the Computer*, Pergamon Press, 1967.
5. Boore, William, and Jerry Murphy, *The Computer Sampler: Management Perspectives on the Computer*, McGraw-Hill, 1968.
6. Sisson, Roger, and Richard Canning, *A Manager's Guide to Computer Processing*, Wiley, 1967.
7. Parkhill, D. F., *The Challenge of the Computer Utility*, Addison-Wesley, 1966.
8. Canning, Richard, and Roger Sisson, *The Management of Data Processing*, Wiley, 1967.
9. Mulvihill, Donald, *Guide to the Quantitative Age*, Holt, Rinehart and Winston, 1966.
10. Malcolm, Robert, and Malcolm Gotterer, *Computer in Business: a FORTRAN Introduction*, International Textbook, 1968.
11. Carter, Norman, *Introduction to Business Data Processing*, Dickenson, 1968.
12. Kemeny, John, and Thomas Kurtz, *Basic Programming*, Wiley, 1967.
13. Reichenback, Robert, and Charles Tasso, *Organizing for Data Processing*, American Management Association, 1968.
14. Sprowls, R. Clay, *Introduction to PL/I Programming*, Harper and Row, 1969.
15. Li, David, *Accounting, Computers, Management Information Systems*, McGraw-Hill, 1968.
16. Naylor, Thomas, Joseph Balintfy, Donald Burdick, and Kong Chu, *Computer Simulation Techniques*, Wiley, 1966.

17. Boutell, W., *Computer-Oriented Business Systems*, Prentice-Hall, 1968.
18. Meadow, C. T., *The Analysis of Information Systems, A Programmer's Introduction to Information Retrieval*, Wiley, 1967.
19. Blumenthal, S. C., *Management Information Systems: A Framework for Planning and Developing*, Prentice-Hall, 1969.
20. Spencer, Donald, *A Guide to Basic Programming: A Time-Sharing Language*, Addison-Wesley, 1970.
21. Spencer, Donald, *Computer Application Packages*, Science Associates/International, 1969.
22. Lefkowitz, David, *File Structures for On-Line Systems*, Spartan Books, 1969.
23. Gordon, Geoffrey, *System Simulation*, Prentice-Hall, 1969.
24. Pritsker, A., and Philip Kiviat, *Simulation with GASP II*, Prentice-Hall, 1969.
25. Lande, Henry, *How to Use the Computer in Business Planning*, Prentice-Hall, 1969.
26. Lande, Henry, *A Survey of Generalized Data Base Management Systems*, The Association for Computing Machinery, 1969.
27. McLaughlin, John, *Information Technology and Survival of the Firm*, Irwin, 1969.
28. Saxon, James, *System 360/20 Programming*, Dickenson, 1968.
29. Martin, James, *Telecommunications and the Computer*, Prentice-Hall, 1969.
30. Schmidt, J., and R. E. Taylor, *Simulation and Analysis of Industrial Systems*, Irwin, 1970.
31. O'Brien, J., *Management Information Systems*, Van Nostrand Reinhold, New York, 1970.

Management Information Systems

Arnold E. Amstutz

Massachusetts Institute of Technology
Cambridge, Massachusetts

The words "management information system" refer to the conceptual structure, data, programs, procedures, personnel, and equipment required to provide management with computer-aided decision and planning support. Since a management's approach to planning and decision making is determined by their perceptions, priorities, objectives, goals, and resources, information systems necessarily differ in their structure, functions, data content, size, and complexity.

The initial objective of management system development is, therefore, to determine how management perceives the environment in which it operates—which elements and processes are essential to an explicit definition of that operating sphere. Once defined, management insights can be structured in a conceptual framework which provides an organized layout of major elements, thereby facilitating the identification of important interactions among those elements. The processes encompassed by the structure are then examined and points at which management wishes to assess the nature or extent of selected interactions are identified. Procedures are established to obtain measures relating management action to environmental response. These measures become the input to the computer data files.

Designing and developing a management information system to meet the requirements of a particular management's decision and planning style makes significant demands on management time and thought. If the resulting product is to be compatible with management's perspective, priorities, and measures, management must make explicit its models of the decision environment and provide the basis for system design. In addition, management must evaluate alternative system structures on criteria that only they can supply. Intelligent choice between alternatives depends on management's understanding of the implications of available structures. To achieve understanding, the manager must take the time to become familiar with the management implication of basic system design concepts.

1. CHARACTERISTICS OF SUCCESSFUL SYSTEMS

Although the specific functions information systems perform are as varied as the managements for which they perform them, four characteristics of successful system design and development can be identified.

1. The system is based on management's perception of the decision environment.

2. Management understands system structure.

3. The system is based on disaggregated data files.

4. The system is designed to permit expansion—to increase in sophistication through a process of gradual evolution.

1.1. Management Perception of the Environment

If a system is to provide meaningful information to a particular management, it must reflect that management's priorities. It must incorporate and provide information pertinent to the management decision and planning process. Generally, this requires that relevant information be generated in a form that assists management in monitoring and controlling its environment.

It also requires that an information system be based on management's perception of the decision environment. In most instances, management's initial definition is stated in vague and ambiguous "business terms." Before meaningful insights are produced, this initial statement must be redefined in explicit terms to delineate relevant factors from those less relevant.

1.2. Management Understanding

Management must be involved in the quantitative specification of system boundaries. It must understand and accept the conceptual structuring of system requirements and be able to explicitly define the measures and analytic procedures that the system is to encompass. If this level of communication is not achieved, it will be impossible to develop a system that effectively serves management.

As with any specialized tool, the information system must be carefully designed to meet the specific requirements of those who will use it, and the user must understand its functions and capabilities.

1.3. The Disaggregated Data File

A key element in all successful information systems is a disaggregated data file in which relevant information is maintained in the time sequence in which it is generated. As new data are received they are maintained along with existing information. They are not combined with old data to form sums, averages, or aggregate distributions. As a result, structural biasing that destroys much information value is avoided.

Exhibit 1 illustrates the concept of a disaggregated data file. A disaggregated customer file, for example, contains a customer's name, address,

Customer File

Name	Address	Region	Demographic	Financial Experience

Transaction Record

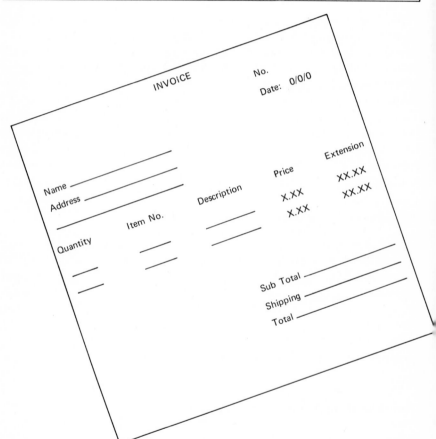

Exhibit 1. Disaggregated data file

demographic, and financial experience records. Each transaction between customer and company is recorded in chronological order so that at any point in time the company can recreate its interactions with each consumer. Similarly, a product file is organized to reference a detailed chronological sales record. Given access to detailed chronological data, the manager can test new concepts and ideas against historical data, asking "what would have happened if we had used these criteria in our monitor system—performed this analysis to isolate actionable situations?"

The importance of a disaggregated file rests partially on the evolutionary process through which successful informations systems develop. In the first stages of system development, it is impossible to anticipate the direction of later advancement. Although initially an information system may perform limited functions, these functions will change as management gains experience. If data are structured to meet first stage requirements, later modification of system functions involves costly file reorganization.

A disaggregated file facilitates system evolution. It provides the flexibility that is a prerequisite of system expansion.

1.4. Design for Evolution

In addition to flexibility, data files must be designed to permit expansion. Variable rather than fixed record length file structures and self-expanding file constructs are basic to the well-planned system.

As managements gain experience in working with well-organized and accessible data, they become increasingly interested in and prepared to use more advanced analytic procedures. The system's analytic structure must not preclude this advancement. Programs must be organized to permit the experimental use of new techniques as well as the permanent incorporation of newly developed capabilities.

2. DIMENSIONS OF SYSTEM EVOLUTION

Although no two managements have the same information needs, it is possible to identify five dimensions along which the evolution of various management information systems may be traced. These dimensions are used to evaluate particular systems and to isolate similarities and differences among alternative systems or stages of system development.

2.1. Information Recency

The first dimension, information recency, refers to the time lapse between occurrence of an event in the environment and inclusion of data describing that event in the system. This may range from several weeks for certain market developments to a few hours or minutes for automated inventory control.

2.2. Information Aggregation

The second dimension, information aggregation, describes the detail with which information is maintained in the data files. Inventory control systems, maintaining information on product components or subassemblies at the item level, represent relatively disaggregate data files. Industry market share statistics, developed through trade associations, represent highly aggregate data maintenance.

As Figure 1 illustrates, there is generally a positive relationship between aggregation level and the time delay required to incorporate the data in the system.

2.3. Analytic Sophistication

The third dimension, analytic sophistication, refers to the sophistication of the system's models or structure. In Figure 2 the lowest level of analytic sophistication is that required to identify a particular file and record. At

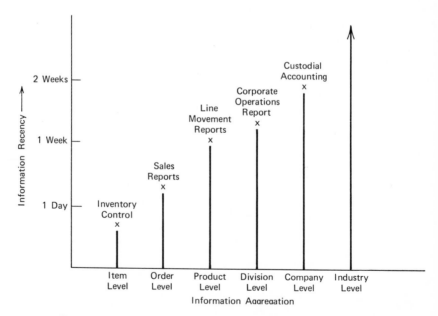

Figure 1. Dimensions of system evolutions dimensions 1 and 2.

this level the computer retrieves the specified record and displays the information it contains. The second level of analytic sophistication involves the aggregation of one or more records to produce a total or subtotal. At the third level, the system may perform arithmetic averaging or compute differences. Logical analysis, the fourth level, introduces classification schemes which aggregate data within subsets or conditionally segment data.

At the next level of analytic sophistication, statistical techniques may be used to develop extrapolations from historic data, statistical best estimates, analyses of variance, or trend estimates.

Macro process models may be used at the sixth level to relate multiple factors in the decision environment to current or expected future conditions. At this level of analytic sophistication, process flow models are used to examine dynamic relationships over time [1]. Management receives information based on analyses of a process rather than on the values of selected variables.

At the seventh level of analytic sophistication, micro analytic behavioral models are met. These behavioral simulations are used to create an artificial environment duplicating the real world environment that the information system monitors [2]. Before such systems are productively employed, management must be convinced that simulated circumstances duplicate relevant, real world response patterns. Inputs to the information system are directly related to process variables in the simulation models. At this level of sophistication, the system permits management to test proposed policies and strategies in the simulated environment, to choose between alternatives on the basis of resulting outputs, to implement the policies in the real world environment, and to evaluate the effectiveness of implemented plans through the information system. The manager references the simulated environment to ask "What if?" and the information system monitoring the real world environment to determine "What is?"

Some highly sophisticated information systems are designed to evaluate alternative parameter settings or model structures against data from the monitored environment. The words "adaptive heuristics" in Figure 2 refer to these evaluative systems that are programmed to "learn from experience" as they accumulate validating information over time [3].

2.4. System Authority

The fourth dimension, system authority, is closely associated with analytic sophistication. Management more willingly delegates authority to sophisticated systems, and as management places greater demands on an information system, a higher level of analytic sophistication is required.

At the lowest level, management may delegate authority to retrieve and

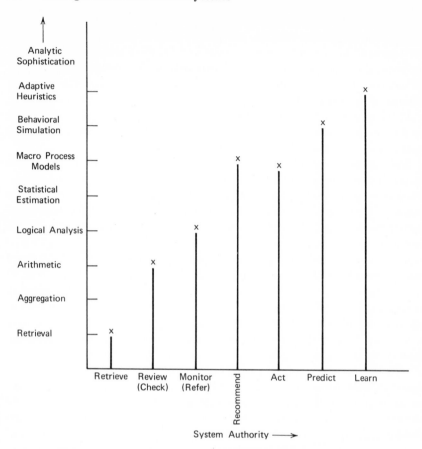

Figure 2. Dimensions of system evolutions dimensions 3 and 4.

identify information from specified records and files. Once a retrieval and identification capability has been established, management may conclude that while the computer is "looking at" each record's content, it should also check for gross clerical errors. Hence, the system assumes a supervisory function and checks on human personnel responsible for input.

When management accepts system review for error detection, it is quite natural to suggest that the computer perform additional analyses on records being reviewed and refer for further examination and action those situations meeting management-established criteria. Thus, the system performs a monitor function.

Management often finds that certain kinds of monitor output are consistently subject to additional analyses to determine whether action is warranted. In these situations, the computer can be programmed to execute additional calculations and to add to the monitor report a recommendation for action.

As management gains experience with computer-based recommendations, it may find that the system's recommendations can be implemented without further investigation. Management may modify criteria to isolate only nontypical cases for additional review. The system then has authority to act on the remaining cases in which its recommendations have proved a valid basis for action.

The hierarchy in Figure 2 suggests that delegating authority to predict requires a greater degree of management dependence on the computer than delegating authority to act [4]. Although the models on which the system bases its action generally involve prediction, the potential impact of computer-based prediction is often greater than computer action. Actions relate to the operating sphere while predictions are the basis for planning. Thus, inaccurate prediction can damage a firm's activities for months or years while erroneous actions can be corrected in days or weeks.

The chance for successful computer-based prediction is ironically reduced by the nature of management/computer interaction. Since predictions are often based on relatively sophisticated models, management may hesitate to accept the computer's prognostication until it has gained experience with the system and has "seen how well it does." It is likely that management's satisfaction will increase as the computer's predictions are verified by experience. However, as time passes, the modeled environment may change—the original models becoming less applicable. Finally when management may be ready to act on the basis of computer predictions, the models may be outdated and inaccurately represent the decision environment. It is such considerations that argue strongly for management involvement in the system design process, for its familiarity with system structure, and for its understanding of models on which system decisions and predictions are based.

When management has sufficient confidence in particular heuristics that adapt system models to changing environmental conditions, it may permit the system to modify selected parameters without prior management approval. Using such adaptive procedures magnifies the problems noted for prediction. Management must understand the implications of not only the operating decision models but also of the adaptive procedures that modify the operating system.

2.5. Management Access

The final dimension of system evolution—management access—refers to the time lapse between management's request for specific information and receipt of the desired report or display. Access time may range from several months for manual compilation of extensive statistics to fractions of a second for on-line computer access to information in primary storage.

3. COMPUTER-BASED SYSTEM DESIGN CONSIDERATIONS

The decision to develop a system having characteristics defined by the five dimensions must be made by management. In addition, management must define objectives, priorities, and performance criteria for the system. These management-oriented system specifications provide an explicit description of:

1. Planning and decision procedures to be supported by the system.
2. The environment to be monitored.
3. The models and measures to be used.
4. Functions to be performed by the system.
5. Criteria for evaluating system performance.

Working with management-oriented system specifications, systems analysts produce detailed computer-oriented specifications, which provide an explicit master plan controlling all programming, testing and implementation activities, and which determine:

1. System organization.
2. Hardware and software requirements.
3. Program structures.
4. Measurement and data processing procedures.
5. Management/system interfaces.

The system designer must determine which storage devices, organization schemes, file maintenance procedures, and language structures will provide management with a system meeting its specifications. Basically the system designer must consider the following technical aspects [5]:

1. Hardware requirements—storage devices and computer capability.
2. Data organization and associated indexing techniques relating to the structure of the disaggregated file.
3. Software requirements—the programming language, file maintenance procedures, data retrieval, and display requirements.

3.1. Storage Devices

The two most common storage devices are magnetic tape units and disk drives, for example, IBM 2314. Each has its advantages and disadvantages.

Magnetic tapes, for instance, can be accessed only in sequential mode, while disk drives can access records either sequentially or randomly.

Since most management systems do not involve vast amounts of computation, data access speed can be an extremely important design consideration. In rare instances, when computation in the central processing unit takes longer than the time required to read a data record, the cheapest available storage device should be used.

3.2. Data Organization

There are three major methods of data file organization: sequential, random, and list [16].

3.2.1. Sequential

If files are organized sequentially, records are stored in ascending or descending order. For example, a customer file may be sequenced alphabetically by the customer's surname. To access a particular record on a sequential file, all preceding records must be read.

3.2.2. Random

When data are stored in random mode, a direct relationship is established between the records and their corresponding locations on the storage device. For example, customer X's record may start in location 724 and consist of 300 characters. With this kind of file organization, the storage device will go directly to location 724 and read into the computer all 300 characters of the record.

Random mode is generally slower than sequential mode when there are many records to be accessed. However, when there is low activity, random organization is more advantageous. Regardless of storage device, the majority of today's large management information systems has sequential file organization.

3.2.3. List

List file organization is intended to facilitate rapid access to all records within a predefined sequence. Each record in the sequence contains a pointer to the next record in that particular sequence. For example, a file may be accessed first in NAME sequence and second in CITY sequence. The initial record in the NAME sequence will contain a pointer to the second record in the NAME sequence. In the latter case, the procedure is the same. Although the records are on the storage device in the same order, they are being accessed in the CITY sequence and a pointer will appear on the first CITY sequence record that locates the second record in that same sequence. The second then locates the third, and so on, for as many records as the sequence includes.

3.3. Software Considerations

Problems associated with the design of file maintenance routines for large management information systems are complex and beyond the scope of this chapter. The tendency today is to move from specialized machine-oriented computer language procedures, which are efficient but difficult to understand and manipulate, toward user-oriented language.

4. AN EXAMPLE OF SYSTEM EVOLUTION

The remainder of this chapter examines representative management information system development processes along the five dimensions of system evolution.

4.1. A Batch Processed Retrieval System

The first system is a market-oriented information retrieval system developed by a small United States company in 1960 [6]. The firm was entering a new and undefined market with a product that was completely new in concept and function. Management's most pressing problem was to learn as much as possible about its new market. Because of financial limitations, they could not engage in extensive test marketing. It was necessary to promote and sell the product while learning about the market's structure and composition and while discovering how to effectively reach and develop it.

The company hoped to introduce a new product line to diverse market segments. Initial sales were to be generated through media advertising. The promotion was designed to generate orders and requests for further information. Inquiries sent directly to the company or forwarded by its distributors were answered with brochures describing the product line. Products were sold directly and through distributor-retail channels.

The primary justification for the system was the computer's ability to perform order and inquiry processing more efficiently, accurately, and inexpensively than clerical personnel. Additional contributions made by the computer were gained from designing it to organize and maintain information met while performing routine clerical operations.

Since operating requirements did not justify leasing or purchasing electronic data processing equipment, the only computer-related equipment on company premises was two card punches. Computer time was rented on a small computer during off-hours at a local service bureau [6]. Substantial cost savings were realized by using "nonprime" weekend time at the computing center. Input data were prepared during the regular working day at the company office and batched for processing. Computer runs were made each weekend.

4.1.1. Example of System Use

Four reports generated by this system illustrate its use as a source of management information.

A standard array of financial reports were produced during order processing. Management could vary their format and content to obtain information for particular analysis. Figure 3 illustrates a quarterly sales summary that was structured to distinguish between direct and distributor sales for five elements of a new product line.

ALL CHANNELS SUMMARY – QUARTER 1   YEAR 1962

	JANUARY	FEBRUARY	MARCH	FIRST QUARTER
DIRECT SALES				
−MIN*	39,168.00	16,419.50	17,296.81	72,884.31
−MIN/1	0.0	0.0	1,666.25	1,666.25
−C/R	25.00	48.50	2,705.23	2,778.73
−MAN	370.00	196.00	665.62	1,231.62
−PARTS	49.00	64.31	39.80	153.11
DISTRIBUTOR SALES				
−MIN	3,376.00	5,856.75	18,278.00	27,510.75
−MIN/1	0.0	0.0	1,007.50	1,007.50
−C/R	0.0	0.0	31.86	31.86
−MAN	7.0	6.0	13.00	26.00
−PARTS	0.0	0.0	0.0	0.0
	− − − −	− − − −	− − − −	− − − −
	3,383.00	5,862.75	19,330.36	28.576.11
	− − − −	− − − −	− − − −	− − − −
TOTAL SALES—ALL CHANNELS				
	42,995.00	22,591.06	41,704.07	107,290.13

Figure 3.   Quarterly Sales summary.

* Five coded elements of a product line.

Figure 4 illustrates a channel analysis report providing the sales manager with an outlet's product sales summary during the first six months of 1962. Since the system records prevailing trade margins, it can estimate the outlet's dollar gross margin as well as unit and dollar sales by product during the specified period. The third column illustrates the value of a centralized data file. The system processes orders through all channels and additionally handles all warranty cards returned by purchasers. It can estimate product movement through each distributor and approximate each outlet's existing inventory.

CHANNEL CLASS – ELECTRONIC SUPPLY

DATES COVERED – 01/01/62 THROUGH 06/31/62

			EST.
TOTAL SALES FOR PERIOD	UNITS	DOLLARS	INVENTORY UNITS
–MIN*	158	9,756.50	32.
–MIN/1	26	2,619.50	8.
–MAN	12	72.00	0.0
–C/R	19	304.00	25.
TOTAL SALES TO THIS CHANNEL		12,752.00	
ESTIMATED CHANNEL GROSS MARGIN		6,883.00	

Figure 4.   Channel analysis report.

* Coded elements of a product line.

Some information relevant to management's interest in evaluating alternative market segments could be obtained from invoices prepared by the system. As an example, the analysis of direct sales presented in Figure 5 provides a rough percentage breakdown of sales to consumers, secondary schools, colleges, business, government, and foreign purchasers in May 1962 for four of the company's products, based on a simple category selection rule.

More detailed information on market composition was obtained from warranty cards purchasers returned to the company. Figure 6 provides a sample warranty analysis for a single product based on warranties received in the first five months of 1962. The report summarizes the number and percentage of units sold to each of five age groups. In examining Figure 6, it is important to remember that the data on which this analysis is based were included in the customer file as characteristics of consumers who had purchased the product. Thus, when the company was ready to market a new product believed to appeal to 15- to 18-year-olds, these data were used for a selective mailing to consumers of the appropriate age.

SALES DISTRIBUTION ANALYSIS — DIRECT SALES — PERCENTAGE BREAKDOWN

PERIOD COVERED — 05/01/62 THROUGH 05/31/62

	CONSUMER	SECONDARY	COLLEGES	BUSINESS	GOVERNMENT	FOREIGN
–MIN*	48.0	18.0	8.0	9.0	7.0	10.0
–MIN/1	14.0	30.0	22.0	24.0	9.0	1.0
–C/R	51.0	6.0	10.0	18.0	3.0	12.0
–MAN	12.0	0.0	9.0	3.0	3.0	73.0

Figure 5.   Analysis of direct sales.

* Coded elements of a product line.

WARRANTY ANALYSIS — UNIT/PERCENTAGE BREAKDOWN

PERIOD COVERED — 01/01/62 THROUGH 05/31/62

PRODUCT

AGE	UNITS	PERCENT
15 – 18	129	16.9
19 – 25	72	9.4
26 – 35	78	10.2
36 – 45	246	32.3
46 –	239	31.2

Figure 6.   Warranty analysis.

4.1.2.   *Evaluation Using Four Dimensions*

This relatively simple batch processed retrieval system falls between one and two weeks time lag on the information recency dimension. Information received by mail is manually transferred to cards and entered into the computer system weekly.

Disaggregated data files are maintained at the order level with product items identified. The system could aggregate data to the company level. Since competitive information is not available, industry level aggregation is not possible.

On the analytic sophistication dimension, the system has capabilities through the level of basic logical analysis. System authority is limited to retrieval and error checking functions.

Management access time ranges from two days for a request made on Friday to one week for an inquiry submitted on Monday. Since the computer is run only on weekends, requests accumulate during the week and are processed on Saturday. Management receives system produced reports on Monday.

4.2. An On-Line Retrieval System

As a first example of system evolution, consider the impact of change along the management access dimension from the batch processing system's one week response time to ten second response time using an "on-line" system. The system remains unchanged on the other four dimensions of evolution.

The term "on-line" [7] refers to systems in which direct man/machine communication is possible. By using remote access consoles, management may interrogate or, given appropriate programs, interact with the computer. The point of origin device is generally a teletype or comparable typewriterlike machine. In more recent systems, video display consoles using a televisionlike display unit in lieu of paper output have been employed. Television displays facilitate rapid presentation of extensive information. In most instances the manager using a display unit can also obtain hard copy through ancillary printers.

The on-line system directly parallels the off-line or batch process system. The remote access console serves the same function as the card reader or input tape unit in the batch system, communicating the desired report format and source references to the computer. With the introduction of direct access capability the problem of communication language must be considered. The language problem is avoided in batch processing since clerical personnel code requests for card input. It is, of course, possible to continue using the card code structure with the on-line system. The manager requesting information must type onto his console the same information punched in the batch process request card. Since card codes are designed to be economically communicated and directly read by the machine, this coding procedure forces the manager to work with numeric code structures. Although not an impossible requirement, this kind of communication can be frustrating.

Simpler communication is frequently achieved through control words or function keys. The manager uses a function specifier, that is, CHART, DISPLAY, or CALCULATE, to indicate the action the machine is to take, or he presses a "function" key which generates the desired process code. The function specifier is then followed, usually in relatively strict format, by a series of nouns and adjectives that indicate the data source on which the desired report is to be based. The statement "DISPLAY BRAND X SALES, 6/1/61–12/31/61, DOLLARS, UNITS, MONTHLY" represents this kind of request.

From the executive's viewpoint, the easiest form of communication is achieved when the machine is programmed to accept "free form English language requests." The language is never totally free form, since the machine has a limited vocabulary. It is assumed that the person communicating with it will limit himself to a predetermined set of topics. Without strict formatting, there is a danger that ambiguity will lead to misunderstanding between manager and computer. Proper preparation of report formats insures that the manager is notified of that which the computer thought he wanted. If the report content indicates that the computer is "confused," the manager restates his request in a different word order or a more explicit statement. With experience, the manager avoids ambiguous expressions.

The output [8] illustrated in Figure 7 was obtained via an on-line console interrogating the retrieval system. The manager typed his request, "REPORT DISTRIBUTOR ACTIVITY FROM SEPTEMBER 1965 THROUGH OCTOBER 1965." The computer interpreted the word "ACTIVITY" to mean "sales and estimated profit"—a definition consistent with management's emphasis on providing profit computations whenever sales figures are given.

REPORT DISTRIBUTOR ACTIVITY FROM SEPTEMBER 1965 THROUGH OCTOBER 1965

SALES AND ESTIMATED PROFIT

SEP

ALLIED	1170.53	399.95
CENCO	649.63	238.77
HARVEY	755.08	284.51
LAFAYE	1066.97	348.56
RAD.SH	541.01	197.43

OCT

ALLIED	990.63	327.04
CENCO	567.18	186.53
HARVEY	707.95	218.86
LAFAYE	850.51	297.83
RAD.SH	520.11	189.10

Figure 7. Example of on-line output.

Figure 8 illustrates a second request and corresponding computer response which demonstrates another aspect of system design. Although not obvious to the reader, the request for "company" information provided data applicable to only one region of the firm's operations and a limited portion of the product line. Through a password convention, the system had established the identity of the inquiring individual. The information displayed in response to the word "COMPANY" was at the highest level of aggregation to which *this individual* had access on the basis of predetermined priorities.

READY

REPORT COMPANY QUARTERLY SALES, PROFIT FROM FIRST 1965 THROUGH THIRD 1965

	SALES	GROSS PROFIT
QUARTER 1	149600.55	34184.92
QUARTER 2	114589.05	28875.66
QUARTER 3	73799.81	21130.12

READY

Figure 8.   On-line output illustrating individual specific aggregation.

Similar rules of aggregation were imposed in the report illustrated in Figure 7. Security control insures that each individual using the system will only have access to data relevant to him. Through aggregation structures which interpret limiting words such as "company" in context of a need-to-know hierarchy, the system designer may insure that, once correctly identified by the computer, the president requesting "value of company inventory" will receive actual balance sheet figures, while the custodian making a similar inquiry will be given the value of janitorial supplies in stock.

4.3.   A Monitor System

Expanding the system's capability only along system authority dimensions, management may grant additional authority to the computer by developing programs which enable it to monitor the content of all accessed files. This step in the evolutionary process gives the system authority for review and referral. The information system is used to implement a policy of *management-by-exception* with the computer directed to review all relevant data and refer to management only those situations which meet previously established criteria.

Implementation of a monitor system introduces new management problems. Policies must be formulated and vague descriptions of the "sort of situation we are looking for" must be translated into explicit definitions of that which constitutes an exception appropriate for referral. These specifications must indicate the data to be reviewed, the frequency of review, and selection criteria.

Figure 9 illustrates one kind of monitor report obtained by adding such capabilities to the retrieval system. The report indicates that the computer has met a situation in which a statistically significant, adverse sales trend has been established in one outlet of a particular distribution channel class while other outlets in the same class show a favorable trend.

MONITOR REPORT

PRODUCT – 601–CONV.
BASIS – DOLLAR SALES TREND
DATES COVERED – 01/01/64 – 0/08/64
CHANNEL – ELECTRONIC SUPPLY
OUTLET – RAD.SH

AVG. CHANNEL SALES	800.	PROFIT 250.	TREND	+46
THIS OUTLET	210.	62		−34.

Figure 9. Sample monitor output.

4.4. The Advisor Function

Further evolution along the authority dimension requires that management specify criteria for referral and the procedures to be followed when specific situations are met, for example, write a letter, schedule a salesman call. Given such criteria and procedures, the computer may be programmed to recommend an appropriate course of action. Expanding the system to encompass this function generally requires movement along the sophistication dimension. System capabilities must be consistent with the level of authority delegated. More complex analytic programs must be developed and tested. Using historical data, the implications of alternative policies can be examined to establish which recommendations would have been made had each policy been implemented during a past time period.

4.5. The Decision Function—Direct Computer Action

Once management is satisfied with the quality of computer-based recommendations, it may extend computer authority, and permit it to take the recommended action, for example, write the letter or send the order, subject to intermittent review by supervisory personnel [9].

From a systems standpoint, differences between advisory and decision making functions are small. It is as easy to program the computer to write a letter as it is to program it to generate a report indicating a letter should be written. However, from management's viewpoint, the relative impact of the computer is greatly increased once it is permitted to act on the company's behalf.

Successful implementation of the decision function depends on management's understanding of the procedures controlling computer action and on management's careful specification of the level of authority granted the computer. In some instances management requires that supervisory personal approve computer-based actions which involve resource commitments above a certain level. In all instances, management sets orderly review procedures for a continuing assessment of computer-based actions. Just as policies implemented by human subordinates are reviewed to determine their continuing applicability, it is necessary to insure that models governing computer actions continue to be applicable in changing environmental conditions.

4.6. Learning through Simulated Experience

Given access to a detailed disaggregated data file and flexible program structure, management can test under historical conditions the effect of alternative analytical approaches. Management can determine through simulation what would have happened if a particular decision procedure had been used at a particular time in the past.

In simulating past conditions, the computer only has access to information that was available at that point in time. Therefore, the computer has no more information at a decision point than was, in fact, available at that time. The system must base its decision on analyses of then existing conditions and on historical records of conditions prevailing prior to that time. As the computer moves through simulated time, additional information becomes available to it but only when it enters the simulated time period in which that information was generated. After extensive testing of alternative criteria, the decision procedures yielding the highest performance are implemented in the operating system. Through this process, years of hypothetical operating experience may be simulated in a few months of research.

4.7. Real Time Data Acquisition

Today's computer hardware permits the manager to expand along the information-recency dimension and move toward shorter time lags between event occurrence and system notification of the event. Current operating systems provide instantaneous reports of changes in the status of production processes, distribution systems and rapidly changing market environments. Rapid data acquisition has improved the quality of airline reservation services, inventory control, and environmental surveillance systems. There is, however, an unfortunate tendency, aggravated by computer salesmen, to apply the real time capability when there is no need for real time data acquisition [11]. More rapid file updating is not necessarily harmful but the emphasis on recency created by the real time capability can cause management to give undue attention to recent events while ignoring more significant long-range trends.

4.8. Simulation-Based Information Systems

Systems discussed in the preceding sections have generally been based on relatively simple arithmetic or statistical models relating selected indicators to a single dependent performance measure. Since the planning and implementation of management programs involve coordination of various management activities, information systems have been designed to incorporate realistically complex representations of processes occurring in the decision environment. Market-oriented management information systems have, for example, been built around models which represent in detail the interactions among a firm's retailers, distributors, salesmen and consumer or industrial purchasers [12].

The data files maintained by these information systems encompass measures of the extent and nature of company and competitor inputs to the market environment. The objectives of simulation-based information system development are to create an artificial environment that accepts inputs from the information system, and to generate outputs which adequately duplicate those obtained from the real world environment.

Figure 10 illustrates the structure of a simulation-based marketing information system. A preprocessor system reviews inputs from the market environment and formats them for the master file. The data file becomes the reference source for the information system and provides the historical data base for simulation model initialization.

Management can directly interrogate the data file and obtain responses by using procedures comparable to the basic retrieval system. "A" in Figure 10 represents this kind of interaction. Management's use of the simulation model for testing proposed programs is illustrated by interaction set "B." Proposed plans which determine the hypothetical conditions are communicated to the information system which establishes specified conditions for simulation model runs. Results of plan performance in the simulated environment are received by the information system which formats them

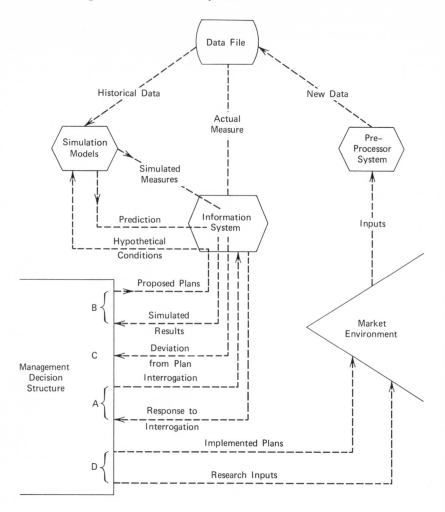

Figure 10.   Simulation-based system structure.

for presentation to management. Following this process, management can evaluate the conditional results of proposed programs via the same procedures and equipment it uses to assess the current state of the market.

Once a proposed plan is finalized, it is established as a reference, and simulated measures based on the plan are generated for use by the information system's monitor sector. As the plan, tested in the simulated environment, is implemented in the real world market environment, measures of its actual market performance are compared with its performance in the simulation. Significant deviation between simulated performance and real world performance becomes the criterion for monitor referral to management, which "C" in Figure 10 indicates. The information system may be used to evaluate the results of research activities and operating plans, as indicated by "D."

Development of a microanalytic simulation involves procedures similar to those used when developing less complex models. However, because of structural detail, the extent of management involvement is greatly increased. Model development begins with management's definition of system scope and the objectives to be achieved through system use. As the development process continues, increasingly detailed descriptions of behavior within key sectors of the environment and interactions between sectors are established. Models are designed to facilitate the simulated generation of measures referencing key backlogs, delays, and transfer points at which the rate of product, information, or value flow may be monitored. Key decision and response elements are identified and factors influencing these processes are delineated. Hypothesized relationships between actions and observable behavior are formulated in terms of measurements which permit model validation against real world data. Once validated at the function level, decision and response formulations are combined in a simulation structure that encompasses artificial populations which exhibit actions and responses determined by these formulations.

Population group behavior within each simulation sector is described by accumulating simulated individual behavior. Population behavior may be summarized by the proportion of purchases allotted to each brand, changes in population attitude distributions toward brands, or any other measures encompassed by the real world information system. Once the simulation models have been validated to management's satisfaction, the simulation structure may be used to reproduce conditions over time comparable to those existing in the real world market environment [13].

4.9. Adaptive System Structures

The complexity and subtlety of adaptive system constructs precludes full exposition of this level of system sophistication in this Chapter [14]. The simplest adaptive system structures are based on system comparison of actual and simulated (or predicted) measures. Deviations are recorded and used to determine the nature and extent of model modification. More advanced systems use processes similar to those illustrated by interaction "B" in Figure 10 to test alternative parameter values against historic as well as current conditions. The importance of management understanding of such procedures and cognizance of changes in model structure imposed by the system cannot be overemphasized.

5. FUTURE IMPLICATIONS OF CURRENT MANAGEMENT INFORMATION USE

A recent survey [15] of the 500 largest United States industrial corporations provides an interesting profile of current management information system use and development. Corporations responding to the survey questionnaire could be divided into two categories: users (those with operating systems) and planners (those developing systems). A comparison of user and planner systems along the five dimensions of evolution points to current patterns in system development and isolates trends in current or planned use.

On the first dimension—information recency—planners are tending toward data file update within an hourly to daily range. In contrast, the most significant number of users updates files within a two week to monthly range.

On the information aggregation dimension, companies developing systems plan to maintain more disaggregate data than users currently do. Similarly, on the management access dimension, planners are tending toward more rapid management access than user companies now have. The majority of planners expects to have access to data within a one to eight hour range, while the majority of users now has access within a one to five day range.

On the remaining two dimensions—analytic sophistication and system authority—the data show that users' systems incorporate more sophisticated models and are delegated more authority than planner systems. Although a comparable number of users and planners indicate that their systems perform and will perform relatively simple analytic functions, user companies show significantly greater use of advanced analytic techniques. Figure 11 illustrates the analytic capability of current systems and the expected range of analytic capability of planner systems.

On the system authority dimension, the data indicate that users delegate more authority to their systems than planners expect to. Both users and planners reflect a strong interest in a direct information retrieval function. Planners, however, indicate that they are reluctant to give an untried system the responsibility for monitoring, advising, or decision making. Figure 12 shows the amount of authority that users are delegating to their systems and the levels of system authority that planners expect to delegate.

It is not surprising to find that planners are establishing system development trends along the information recency, management access, and information aggregation dimensions. There are literally no technical barriers to such progress. Today's computer hardware permits the system designer to move toward shorter time lags between event occurrence and system

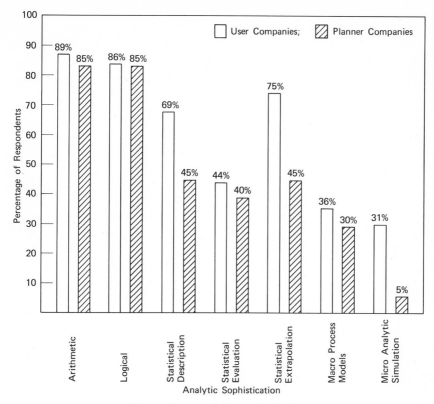

Figure 11.   Analytic sophistication.

notification of the event. The amount of recent discussion devoted to on-line and interactive systems and the computer manufacturers' descriptions of the advantages of direct manager/machine communication have likely encouraged the trend toward more rapid access time.

The fact that users incorporate more sophisticated analytic techniques and delegate more authority to their systems than planners expect to seems to substantiate the premise that system development is an evolutionary process. The data seem to reflect the importance that experience plays in a company's decision to invest its system with greater analytic capabilities or to delegate to it greater authority.

Having experimented with their systems over time, users are more likely than planners to be aware of the system's limitations and of the need to refine the system to fit the specific and, perhaps, more sophisticated needs of those it serves. Users have more confidence in a system's capa-

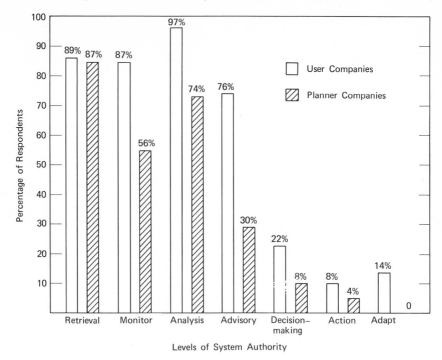

Figure 12. Levels of system authority.

bilities—confidence that is an outgrowth of experience proving the system's reliability.

As mentioned previously, progress along the system authority dimensions requires simultaneous advancement along the analytic sophistication dimension to develop a capability consistent with the delegated level of authority. More complex analytic programs must be developed and tested. Management must specify criteria for exception reporting and explicitly outline the procedures to be followed when exceptions are met. If the computer is to relieve management of routine decision making, then management must establish in precise terms the conditions that isolate nontypical cases to be referred to management for consideration.

In the initial stages of system development, management's inexperience with system performance and capability inhibits the level of early system contribution. As management gains confidence in system capability and experience with its performance, more authority is granted the computer and it begins to function in a more strategic way for the management it serves.

5.1.   Management Information Systems of the Future

The above analysis of management information system use and development in the United States has implications for management information systems of tomorrow. It is likely that future systems will not differ markedly in form or structure from today's more advanced systems. The process of evolution will continue and will be coupled with and propelled by both hardware and software developments and refinements. Accurate and detailed data will be more readily available, and more sophisticated models will be validated. As managements gain confidence in the validity of these models greater authority will be delegated to the systems incorporating them.

With continuing advancements in computer technology, it is to be expected that information systems will be more widely used in the future than they are today. Smaller computers and time shared facilities are now providing smaller companies with computer capability at a reasonable price. Improvements in point of origin devices, such as the teletype or typewriter-like machine and video display consoles, have made communication with the computer easier. Software refinements contribute improved language structures. Control words, "menu" entries, or function keys facilitate rapid and unambiguous manager/machine communication. Finally, as the more technically oriented graduates of today's business schools infiltrate the managerial ranks, they will provide a substantial impetus for future information system use.

6.   NOTES

1. This type of modeling is illustrated by R. S. Weinberg, "Multiple Factor Break-Even Analysis: The Application of Operations Research Techniques to a Basic Problem of Management Planning and Control," *Operations Research*, Vol. 4 (April 1956), 152–186.

2. Management applications of the micro analytic behavioral simulation technique are discussed in A. E. Amstutz, *Computer Simulation of Competitive Market Response*, M.I.T. Press, Cambridge, 1967.

3. An example of a relatively simple adaptive system structure is provided in P. R. Winters, "Forecasting Sales by Exponentially Weighted Moving Averages," *Management Science*, April 1960, 324–42.

4. For a description of authority delegation and analytic capabilities of today's management information systems, see Section 5 in this chapter on Future Implications of "Current Management Information System Use."

5. The information contained in this section was supplied by David Zeitlin of Decision Technology International, London, England.

6. A detailed discription of this system is provided in A. E. Amstutz, "A Basic Market-

ing System: A Case Study in the Use of Economical Computerized Management Information System," in (Es.), *The Marketing Concept in Action*, American Marketing Association, Chicago, 1964, 373–92.

7. See Chapter 7 by W. J. Karplus, "On Line Computing and Graphics" in this book.

8. The output shown in Figures 7 and 8 was generated by the system used by Scientific Development Corporation of Watertown, Massachusetts, in 1961.

9. The automatic reorder decision associated with computer-based inventory control provides a simple example of programmed decision procedures. More elaborate process models have been employed by some firms to achieve automated resource allocations.

10. For a description of one such system, see A. E. Amstutz, The Computer: "New Partner in Investment Management," *Management Science*, November 1968.

11. "Real time" refers to data acquisition procedures which permit significant transactions or events to be assimilated by the system as they occur. The term has no absolute meaning since real time access to significant events in one process may require sampling once each second while another process may be effectively monitored in "real time" at daily intervals.

12. A description of one such system developed for a pharmaceutical firm is provided in A. E. Amstutz and H. J. Claycamp, "Simulation Techniques in the Analysis of Marketing Strategy," in Frank M. Bass, Charles W. King and Edgar A. Pessemier (Eds.), *Applications of the Sciences in Marketing Management*, Wiley, New York, 1968.

13. This process is detailed in A. E. Amstutz, *Computer Simulation of Competitive Market Response*, M.I.T. Press, Cambridge, Mass., 1967

14. A discussion of adaptive management system structures is provided in J. D. C. Little, "A Model of Adaptive Control of Promotional Spending," *Operations Research*, Vol. 14, No. 6, November–December 1966.

15. An analysis of current management information system development and use is found in A. E. Amstutz, "Market-Oriented Management Systems: The Current Status," *Journal of Marketing Research*, November 1969, 481–496.

16. For a more detailed discussion and analysis of data organization methods, see G. G. Dodd, "Elements of Data Management Systems," *Computing Surveys*, June 1969, pp. 117–133.

17. F. Gruenberger (Ed.), *Critical Factors in Data Management*, Prentice-Hall, Englewood Cliffs, N. J., 1969.

18. C. J. Byrnes and D. B. Steig, "File Management Systems: A Current Summary," *Datamation*, November 1969, pp. 138–142.

19. J. D. Aron, "Information Systems in Perspective," *Computing Surveys*, December 1969, pp. 213–236.

20. C. T. Meadow, *The Analysis of Information Systems*, Wiley, New York, 1967.

21. D. Lefkovitz, *File Structures for On-Line Systems*, Spartan Books, New York, 1969.

22. J. J. O'Brien, *Management Information Systems*, Van Nostrand Reinhold, New York, 1970.

23. J. Ross, *Management by Information System*, Prentice-Hall, Englewood Cliffs, N.J., 1970.

Index